AF372071

EDITORIAL 4/5

Vincent Katz: Brasilian Concrete Poetry / Konkrete Poesie aus Brasilien 6/11
Elisabeth Bronfen: Body Malaise—Annette Messager's Anatomical Theater /
Körperunbehagen – Annette Messagers anatomisches Theater 16/22

COLLABORATIONS 31

MAURIZIO CATTELAN 32
Nicolas Bourriaud: A Grammar of Visual Delinquency /
Eine Grammatik des künstlerischen Schurkenstreichs 34/42
Alison Gingeras: A Sociology Without Truth / Eine Soziologie ohne Wahrheit 50/54
Francesco Bonami: Every Artist Can Be a Man / Jeder Künstler kann Mensch sein 60/66
EDITION FOR PARKETT: MAURIZIO CATTELAN 72

YAYOI KUSAMA 74
Ursula Panhans-Bühler: "Between Heaven and Earth: This Languid Weight of Life" 77/86
Midori Matsui: Beyond Oedipus: Desiring Production of Yayoi Kusama /
Jenseits von Ödipus: Yayoi Kusamas Wunschproduktion 92/100
Griselda Pollock: Three Thoughts on Femininity, Creativity and Elapsed Time /
Drei Gedanken über Weiblichkeit, Kreativität und verlorene Zeit 107/114
EDITION FOR PARKETT: YAYOI KUSAMA 124

KARA WALKER 126
Gwendolyn Dubois Shaw: Final Cut / Letzter Schnitt 129/133
Elizabeth Janus: As American as Apple Pie / So amerikanisch wie Apple Pie 139/141

DIE PARKETT-REIHE MIT GEGENWARTSKÜNSTLERN / THE PARKETT SERIES WITH CONTEMPORARY ARTISTS

Book Series with contemporary artists in English and German, published three times a year. Each volume is created in collaboration with artists, who contribute an original work specially made for the readers of Parkett. The works are reproduced in the regular edition and available in a limited and signed Special Edition.

Buchreihe mit Gegenwartskünstlern in deutscher und englischer Sprache, erscheint dreimal im Jahr. Jeder Band entsteht mit Künstlern oder Künstlerinnen, die eigens für die Leser von Parkett einen Originalbeitrag gestalten. Diese Werke sind in der gesamten Auflage abgebildet und zusätzlich in einer limitierten und signierten Vorzugsausgabe erhältlich.

PARKETT NR. 60 ENTSTEHT IN COLLABORATION MIT • **CHUCK CLOSE, DIANA THATER, LUC TUYMANS** • WILL BE COLLABORATING ON PARKETT NO. 60

JAHRESABONNEMENT (DREI NUMMERN) / ANNUAL SUBSCRIPTION (THREE ISSUES) SFR. 108.– (SCHWEIZ), DM 130,– (BRD), SFR. 118.– (ÜBRIGES EUROPA), US$ 80 (USA AND CANADA ONLY)

Zürichsee Druckereien AG (Stäfa) Satz, Litho, Druck/Copy, Printing, Color Separations

No parts of this magazine may be reproduced without publisher's permission. We appreciate seeing any mention of Parkett in critical reviews.
Nachdrucke jeder Art sind nur mit Genehmigung des Verlags erlaubt, bei Besprechungen bitten wir um Belege.

Parkett does not assume any responsibility for unsolicited texts and pictures.
Für unaufgefordert eingesandte Texte und Bilder übernimmt der Verlag keine Verantwortung.

Copyright Parkett & Pro Litteris

PARKETT-VERLAG AG, ZÜRICH, SEPTEMBER 2000   **PRINTED IN SWITZERLAND**   **ISBN 3-907582-09-8**   **ISSN 0256-0917**

Hamza Walker: Nigger Lover or Will There Be Any Black People in Utopia? /
Nigger Lover oder: Wird es in Utopia Schwarze geben? 152/160
EDITION FOR PARKETT: KARA WALKER 166

Jan Avgikos: Anna Gaskell's Girl Art / Girlie-Kunst 168/174

INSERT: ANDREAS ZÜST (folded poster, loosely inserted / gefaltetes Poster, lose eingesteckt)

Les Infos du Paradis: Ali Subotnick on / über Fischerspooner 177/182
Cumulus from America: Margit Rowell 187/191
Cumulus aus Europa: László Földényi 194/197
Balkon: Michelle Nicol 199/202
Back Issues / Bisher erschienene Parkettbände 206
Artist's Monographs & Editions / Künstlermonographien & Editionen 211
Editions for Parkett No. 59 (with prices / mit Preisen) 213

Special thanks to Galerie Marlene Frei sowie Mara und Markus Züst, Zürich.

HEFTRÜCKEN / SPINE 58–60: DAVE EGGERS

Cover, front page / Umschlag: KARA WALKER, UNTITLED (KNEALING WOMAN WITH MASK), 1998, cut paper on paper / Scherenschnitt auf Papier.
Cover flap / Umschlagklappe: YAYOI KUSAMA, MACARONI SWEATER, photo collage, ca. 1964 (slightly cropped / leicht beschnitten).
Inside cover page & flap / Innere Umschlagseite und Klappe: MAURIZIO CATTELAN, DON'T FORGET TO CALL YOUR MOTHER, 2000,
cibachrome, plexiglas, aluminum back. (PHOTO: MARIAN GOODMAN GALLERY, NEW YORK)
Page / Seite 1: YAYOI KUSAMA, SPROUT, 1992, detail, acrylic on canvas / Ausschnitt, Acryl auf Leinwand. (PHOTO: NORIHIRO UENO)
Back cover / Rückseite: MAURIZIO CATTELAN, LA RIVOLUZIONE SIAMO NOI, 2000, detail, Migros Museum für Gegenwartskunst.
(PHOTO: ATTILIO MARANZANO)

PARKETT   Zürich New York Frankfurt

Bice Curiger Chefredaktorin/Editor-in-Chief; **Jacqueline Burckhardt** Redaktorin/Senior Editor; **Cay Sophie Rabinowitz** Redaktorin USA/Associated Editor US; **Susanne Schmidt** Textredaktion und Produktion/Editing and Production; **Trix Wetter · Hanna Koller** Graphik/Design; **Catherine Schelbert** Englisches Lektorat/Editorial Assistant for English; **Claudia Meneghini Nevzadi** Korrektorat/Proof Reading

Beatrice Fässler Vorzugsausgaben, Inserate/Special Editions, Advertising; **Brigitte Grüninger** Buchvertrieb, Administration/Distribution, Administration; **Conradin Bernoulli** Abonnemente/Subscriptions; **Ali Subotnick** Redaktionsassistenz, Vorzugsausgaben und Marketing USA/Assistant Editor, Editions and Marketing US; **Monika Condrea** Abonnemente USA/Subscriptions US; **Adrian Koerfer** Deutsche Verlagsvertretung/German Representative

Jacqueline Burckhardt – Bice Curiger – Dieter von Graffenried Herausgeber/Parkett Board; **Jacqueline Burckhardt – Bice Curiger – Dieter von Graffenried – Walter Keller – Peter Blum** Gründer/Founders

Dieter von Graffenried Verleger/Publisher

www.parkettart.com

PARKETT-VERLAG AG, QUELLENSTRASSE 27, CH-8031 ZURICH, TEL. 41-1-271 81 40, FAX 41-1-272 43 01
PARKETT, NEW YORK, 155 AV. OF THE AMERICAS, N.Y. 10013, PHONE (212) 673-2660, FAX (212) 271-0704
PARKETT-VERLAG AG, TANNENWALDALLEE 17, D-61348 BAD HOMBURG, FAX 06172-937 444

Editorial — Von Kunst, Maskeraden und Seelenpein

Die kniende Figur auf dem kontrastreichen Titelblatt dieser Ausgabe führt nicht einen wilden afrikanischen Tanz auf; sie kniet ergeben nieder und auch ihre festgezurrte Schürze scheint nicht zur verrutschten exotischen Maske zu passen. Dennoch greifen die Federn dieser Maske wie machtvolle Antennen in die Höhe beziehungsweise in den PARKETT-Schriftzug hinein: ganz symbolisch unsere Absicht unterstreichend, hier drei Künstlerinnen und Künstler zu vereinen, die mit ihrer Arbeit die Institutionen unserer westlichen Kunst und Kultur zugleich als Outsider und Insider mit provozierenden und bildhaften Gesten herauszufordern wissen.

So mehrdeutig die Maske auf dem Scherenschnitt von Kara Walker erscheint, so verunsichernd ist die Tatsache, dass neben dem eigentlichen Titelblatt gleichsam noch ein zweites Cover die Rückseite ziert und um Aufmerksamkeit wirbt. Der Puppe mit Maurizio Cattelans Gesichtszügen, von dem dieses «Gegentitelblatt» stammt, fehlt aber das Usurpatorische. Wohl mag man im Augenausdruck etwas leicht Diabolisches ausmachen, doch die Gesamtaufnahme derselben Figur auf Seite 65 zeigt, wie der Künstler als Homunkulus in beuysschen Filz gehüllt hilflos an einem Garderobehaken baumelt.

Mit ausgedehnten Maskeraden hat die japanische Künstlerin Yayoi Kusama schon in den 60er Jahren in der New Yorker Kunstwelt für Aufsehen gesorgt. Dass sie nun ein erfreuliches Revival feiert, durch grosse Ausstellungen und Publikationen geehrt wird, ist dem komplexen Lebenswerk nur angemessen. In ihm sind ungeahnte, wilde, schöne Energieströme sichtbar gemacht. Zugleich setzen ihre Arbeiten Fragen in den Raum, die auf einen gesellschaftlichen Kern hinzielen und auf Konventionen, in die auch die Kunst verstrickt ist.

In dieser PARKETT-Ausgabe ist viel von Seelenpein die Rede - aber nicht von expressionistischer Kunst. Wenn Gwendolyn Dubois Shaw in ihrem Text zu Kara Walker die Pein beschreibt, eine Identität als afroamerikanische Frau und Künstlerin präsentieren zu müssen, beschwört sie auch das Problem, dass die Selbstdarstellung zur «Verdinglichung der Künstlerexistenz» bis zum «Status als Konsumobjekt» führt. Auch Griselda Pollock schreibt über Yayoi Kusamas «titanischen Kampf gegen Zwänge», die innere wie äussere Gründe haben.

Dagegen erscheint Maurizio Cattelan als schwereloser Spieler. Doch gerade hinter seinem Skeptizismus ist auch von Unmöglichkeit die Rede, so entsagt er, wie Alison Gingeras schreibt, «der Rolle des Künstlers als Hüter der Aufklärung und ihrer Ideale – ethische Rationalität, historisches Bewusstsein und Wahrheit» und verfolgt stattdessen mit seiner «Soziologie ohne Wahrheit ein viel brüchigeres Szenario».

  # On Art, Masquerades, and Anguish

The figure on the cover page of this issue is not performing a wild African dance; she is kneeling as if in silent deference and her primly tied apron seems at odds with the exotic mask pushed away from her face. But the feathers of this mask reach up like powerful antennae into the PARKETT logo, symbolically underscoring our intention of bringing together three artists who, as both outsiders and insiders, exploit provocative imagery to challenge the institutions of art and culture in the West.

The ambiguity of the mask in Kara Walker's silhouette is compounded by the unsettling realization that our issue actually has two covers vying for the reader's attention, one on the front, the other on the back. However, there is a difference, for the dummy with the features of Maurizio Cattelan on the second "front cover" is not usurpative. Despite the slightly diabolic gleam of the eyes, the figure, reproduced in full on page 65, shows the artist as a homunculus wrapped in Beuysian felt and dangling helplessly on a clothes hook.

As early as the sixties, Japanese artist Yayoi Kusama's elaborate masquerades already caused a stir in the New York art world. The recent revival of interest in this artist, as evidenced by a number of important exhibitions and publications, is but appropriate to an intricate oeuvre, energized by unsuspected, wild and beautiful currents. At the same time, her works raise questions aimed at basic social issues and conventions which also govern art.

In this edition of PARKETT, much is said about anguish—although not about that of expressionist art. In her essay on Kara Walker, Gwendolyn Dubois Shaw discusses the anguish of having to establish identity as an Afro-American woman and artist, and places this quest within the broader context of "the pain of self-performance and of artistic commodification." Griselda Pollock also speaks of the "titanic struggle with pressures" that assail Yayoi Kusama both from within and without.

By comparison Maurizio Cattelan would appear to be a buoyant player, were it not for the burden of impossibility that lurks behind his skepticism. As Alison Gingeras writes, he "disavows the role of the artist as guardian of the Enlightenment ideals of moral rationality, historical consciousness, and truth. Instead his sociology-sans-truth sets into motion a much more disruptive scenario."

Bice Curiger

VINCENT KATZ

Brazilian Concrete Poetry

There's a horizontal plaque in the subway station. It hangs in the air from two pins bolted to the ceiling. About 14 inches high and seven feet long, with a depth of one inch, it is a three-dimensional object hanging in space. The whole is painted, including the sides, giving the object a highly finished look. The majority of the surface is painted yellow, with a thin band of black running across the top. Over the yellow, starting at the left edge, the words "Waiting area" have been painted in a sans serif font in letters six to eight inches high. Who made the decision to capitalize the "W" of "Waiting" but not the initial "a" of "area"? Who made all the other careful decisions that went into the making of this object? We live surrounded by signage, so inundated by it that we are often blinded to its intricacy and createdness. It becomes part of the natural environment. This urban environment was the setting and catalyst for Concrete Poetry, an international movement in the fifties and sixties, which got much of its energy, along with its name, from three of its earliest practitioners—the Brazilians Augusto de Campos, his brother Haroldo de Campos, and Décio Pignatari. All three were from São Paulo, South America's most populous and industrialized city, and the direct appeal of advertisements has long affected their work. As attuned as they were to

the present, they also diligently scoured the past for signs of intelligent life. Their devotion to literary, musical, and visual Modernism—Brazilian and foreign—was matched by their reverence for certain historical figures. Augusto de Campos has translated Blake, Donne, Keats, Mayakovsky, Pound, and Valéry. Haroldo de Campos has translated Dante, Homer, and Mallarmé. In their *Pilot Plan For Concrete Poetry,* published in 1958, the three poets outlined the basis of their desire for a poetry in which form is equivalent to content. The visual element steps to the fore as an exemplification of the poem's subject matter. They plotted out a poetic lineage, beginning with an unlikely figure, Stéphane Mallarmé—unlikely, that is, if one thinks only of the Symbolist poet, longing for the beyond. If one remembers his "Un coup de dés jamais n'abolira le hasard" (A Throw of the Dice Will Never Abolish Chance), one may see the connection. In this unprecedented poem, published in 1897, Mallarmé not only used the two-page spread as his frame, setting words within vast stretches of white space; he also made use of different

sizes and styles of lettering to differentiate different strands of thought. He even made word-pictures, as did Apollinaire in his *Calligrammes* not long afterwards. The Brazilians were also influenced by Ezra Pound, taking for their group the name *Noigandres,* from Pound's "Canto XX." Pound's interest in the ideogram made him a role model, and Concrete Poetry grew out of a desire to fuse image and poetic content, so that the poem ideally refers to nothing outside of itself.

The Brazilians started early, both in their own lives, and in the movement toward Concrete Poetry. In 1952, the three poets, then in their early twenties, began publishing a magazine, also called *Noigandres,* and entered into correspondence with Pound. In 1953, Augusto de Campos wrote a series of poems entitled *Poetamenos,* in which words are color-coded to indicate their being spoken by different voices. The colored words are also set against a colored background. The poet imagined these words blinking on and off like neon signs, but that was beyond his means at the time, so he devised a system of color distinctions, which work

VINCENT KATZ is a poet, critic, and translator. He is the author of *Life is Paradise: The Portraits of Francesco Clemente* (New York: Powerhouse Books, 1999).

simply on the printed page. With the advent of the computer era, he has finally been able to put his original idea into effect, alternating the poem in Portuguese with an English translation (accessible on his Web site—http://uol.com.br/augustodecampos/home.htm—an excellent source for his poems and theoretical essays). Pignatari, who worked in commercial design, made visual poems that have been called kinetic or cinematic, in that they unfold sequentially. In 1964, feeling that even Concrete Poetry was limited by its reliance on the word, he developed a technique for Semiotic Poetry, in which simple symbols, like naval flags, have fixed meanings, which nevertheless have words attached to them. Haroldo de Campos did some poems with a visual element, but his interest has been more in the theoretical and also in concrete sound poetry, where words are chosen for their aural similarity, resulting in surprising semantic juxtapositions. He has done a translation of the first book of the *Iliad*, drawing as much on the sounds of the original Greek as on its meaning. Concrete Poetry in the United States was not a cohesive movement, and worse, it seemed strident and at odds with mainstream culture at a moment when the influence of popular culture on art was timely. The Brazilians, by contrast, were able not only to refer to popular culture but to emulate its succinctness. American Concrete Poetry was made not by poets but rather visual artists seeking non-traditional forms. It is an extreme challenge for a visual artist to use words in a compelling manner. One poet included in the Concrete group is the American Aram Saroyan. Two of his books, *Pages* and *Aram Saroyan*, are mini-classics from the mid-

sixties, all printed in the typewriter typeface on which he composed them. Saroyan achieves a Haiku-like compression with contemporary sensibility and references, making these poems signal achievements whose brilliance has not dimmed with time:

**night
again
again**

or, perhaps more relevantly:

eye̩ye

and:

morni,ng

As a poet, I was disenchanted by what I saw of Concrete Poetry, aside from Saroyan. I don't claim that my knowledge of Concrete Poetry in the seventies was exhaustive, but reviewing now the anthologies from the sixties—*Concrete Poetry: A World View* (Bloomington, Indiana University Press, ed. Mary Ellen Solt, 1968) and *An Anthology of Concrete Poetry* (New York, Something Else Press, ed. Emmett Williams, 1967)—I can't say my opinion has changed since then. It was an international trend, a genre-bending move that established a form between visual art and literature, but on the whole it lacked literary potency. I probably couldn't have appreciated the Brazilian Concrete Poets in the seventies, partially because of the language barrier, but more so because of my limited cultural experience. Once I started going to Brazil in 1988 and to speak Portuguese, I was ready. I'm not sure which book I picked up. It may have been Décio Pignatari's *Poesia Pois É Poesia*, a collection of his work from 1950 to 1975. First, there was the

epigraph, in English—"Ride the pink horse"—the title of the Robert Montgomery film of 1947. Okay, my interest was certainly piqued, but hipness does not a poet make. So I began the first poem, "O Carrossel," from 1950:

> Entre escolher
> Montanha-russa
> Roda-gigante
> Ou trem-fantasma,
> Eu escolhi
> Meu carrossel.
> Paguei com vida
> —Engenho e arte—
> Pelo meu árdego corcel.

which might be translated:

> Stuck between
> The Roller Coaster
> The Ferris Wheel
> And The House of Horrors,
> I chose
> My carousel.
> I paid with life
> —Genius and art—
> For my raring charger.

I liked the poetry immediately. The more I read of this poet and his two partners in crime, Augusto and Haroldo de Campos, the more I realized that their ability to form word-pictures derives from their basic ability in poetry itself, nurtured for many years in various poetic lineages. Each of the three has devoted a substantial part of his energies to translating poetry, strengthening ties to distant times and places and giving the poet-translator skills that are impossible to acquire any other way. Augusto has also been the most visually prolific of the three. His "Olho Por Olho" (Eye For Eye) (1964) has been called a concrete poem with-

I write on a typewriter, almost never in hand (I
can hardly handwrite, I tend to draw words), and
my machine--an obsolete red-top Royal Portable--
is the biggest influence on my work. This red hood
holds the mood, keeps my eye happy. The type-face
is a standard pica; if it were another style I'd
write (subtly) different poems. And when a ribbon
gets dull my poems I'm sure change. (A.S.)

Text from/aus
ARAM SAROYAN,
PAGES, 1964.

out words. Here is part of Augusto's text explaining some of the imagery of the piece, which is a collage of photographs of eyes and a mouth that transcends collage's usual self-referentiality:

EYE FOR EYE: up to the eye. or, again, "questo visibile parlare" (dante). or "to see with free eyes" (oswald de andrade). pop videogram. reviews re-viewed. stars, starlets, politicians, poets, birds, a black jaguar, pelé, sousândrade, car lights, the washing-machine's eye, traffic signs. eyes. metamorphosis. mouths. BB's (tooth for tooth) mouth. a babel of eyes. haroldo baptized: BABŒIL (1964).

These three poets were eager to introduce popular culture to learned poetry from the beginning of the fifties, and the equivalencies Augusto created in "Olho Por Olho" between historical figures, paragons of Brazilian modernism, politicians, sports stars, movie stars, and machines represented an opening of the mind that had important repercussions in Brazilian culture in the sixties. Pop musicians from the sixties Tropicalia movement were influenced by the Concrete Poets' dense wordplay, and at least one subsequent artist, Arnaldo Antunes, in addition to being a rock musician, is an accomplished visual poet and artist who has exhibited at the São Paulo Bienal. Augusto has collaborated with musicians, including his son, Cid Campos. Father and son have composed a poetry and sound piece entitled POESIA É RISCO. Today, fifty years after they first burst onto the scene, Augusto, Haroldo, and Décio are still going strong. Augusto has embraced technological developments, creating interactive versions of his work on large-scale computerized screens. Haroldo has his "soundlations" (a word I just made up, getting in the mood, because this work calls for it), and Décio has published an experimental novel with visual elements. With the increased presence of the São Paulo Bienal and the emergence of many Brazilian visual artists onto the world stage, the Brazilian Concrete Poets are poised once again to conquer new audiences with their accessible yet erudite poems. They are able to circumvent poetry's usual language-bound limitations by an ardent adherence to simplicity and concentrated resonance. Looking beyond Pound's quotations to the sources of ideogrammatic thought, they found a way to translate a Zen flash of insight into twenty-first century imagery.

DECIO PIGNATARI, MORTE.

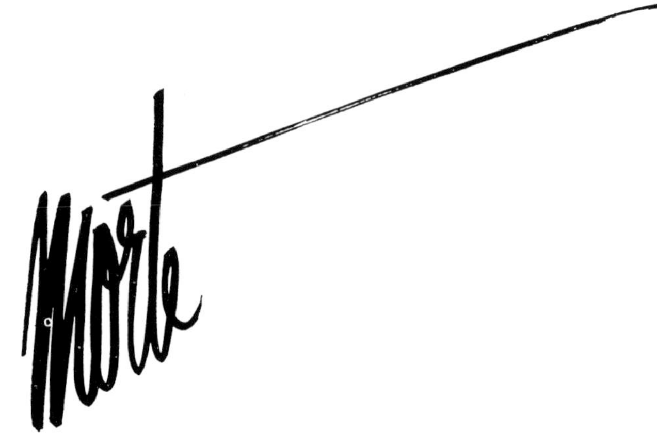

AUGUSTO DE CAMPOS, PSIU / SHHH, 1966,
collage of newspaper and magazine clippings,
23⅝" in diameter / Collage, Durchmesser 60 cm.

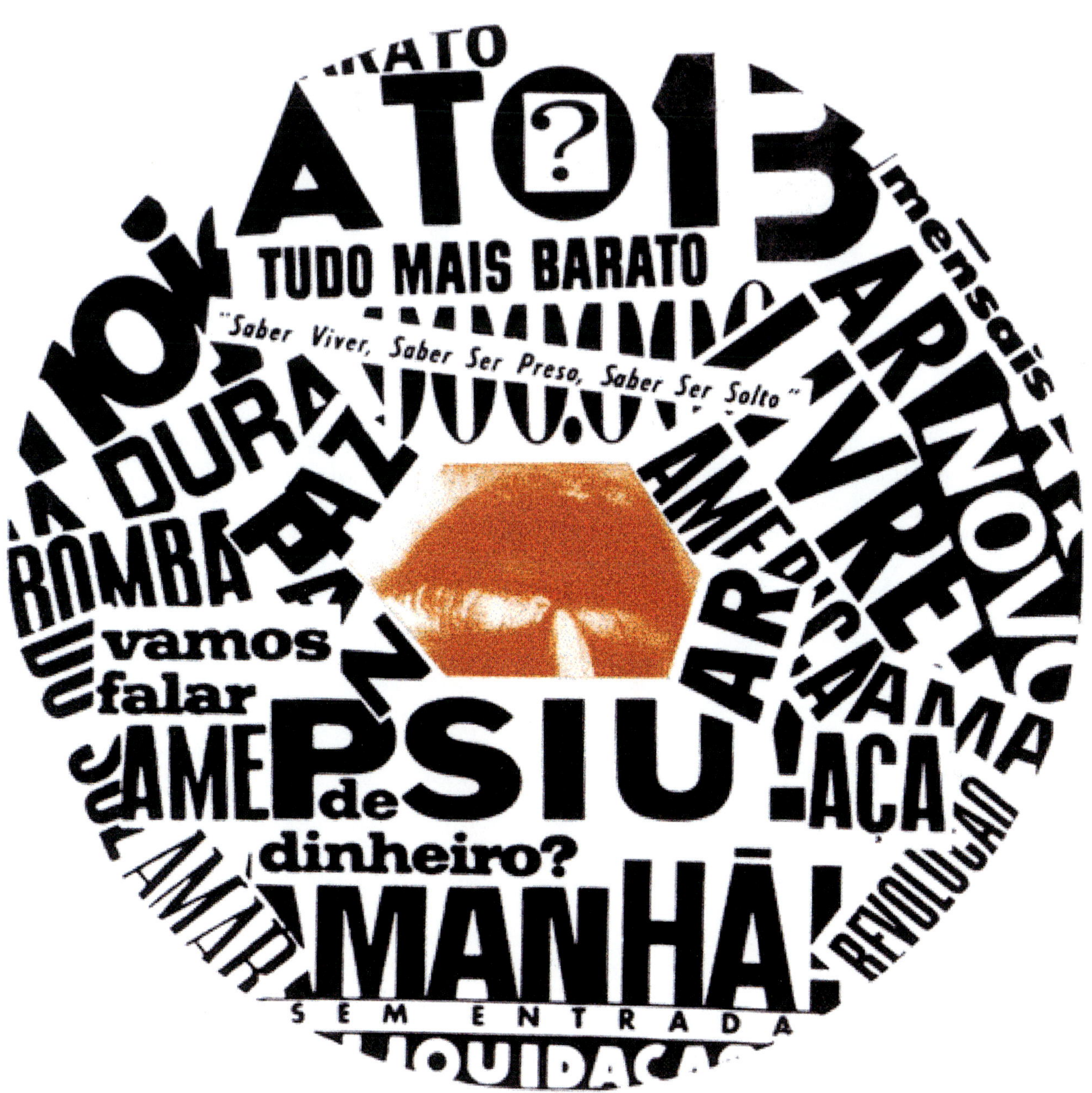

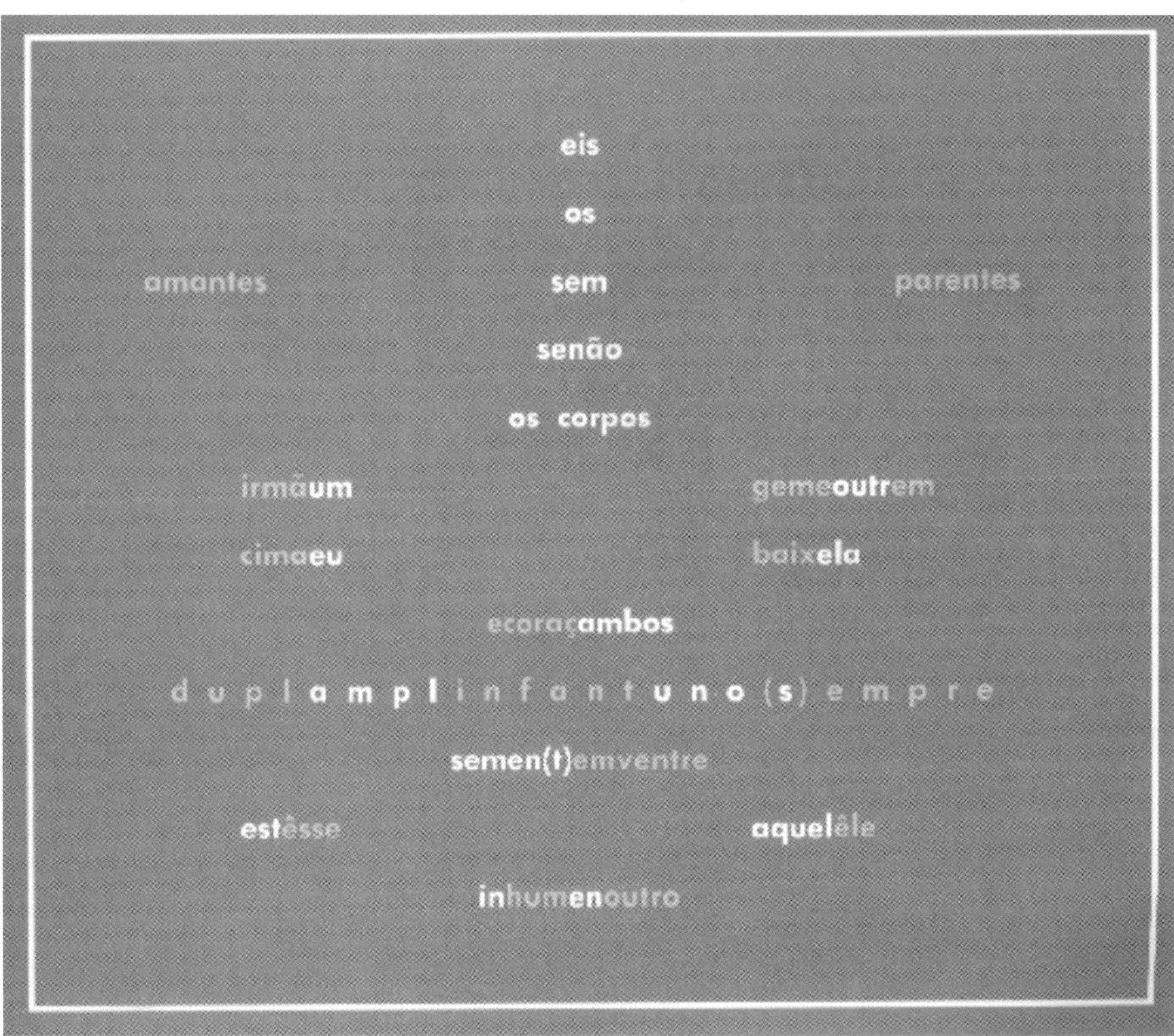

AUGUSTO DE CAMPOS, EIS OS AMANTES / HERE ARE THE LOVERS, 1953, from the series POETAMENOS, white and orange letters on light blue ground / DA SIND DIE LIEBENDEN, aus dem Zyklus POETAMENOS, weisse und orange Schrift auf hellblauem Grund.

Konkrete Poesie aus Brasilien

VINCENT KATZ

An der Haltestelle der Untergrundbahn hängt eine horizontale Tafel. Sie ist mit zwei Stiften an der Decke befestigt. Mit ihrer Höhe von 36 Zentimeter, einer Länge von gut zwei Meter und zweieinhalb Zentimeter Tiefe ist sie eigentlich ein dreidimensionales, im Raum schwebendes Objekt. Sie ist rundum bemalt, selbst an den schmalen Seitenflächen, was ihr den Anschein von Perfektion gibt. Der grösste Teil der Farbfläche ist gelb, ausser einem schmalen schwarzen Streifen am oberen Rand. Auf das Gelb wurden, ausgehend von der linken oberen Ecke, die Worte «Waiting area» gemalt, und zwar in einer serifenlosen, 15 bis 20 Zentimeter hohen Schrift. Wer hat wohl entschieden, dass das «W» von «Waiting» ein Grossbuchstabe sein sollte, aber das Anfangs-«a» von «area» nicht? Wer hat all die anderen wohl überlegten Entscheidungen im Zusammenhang mit der Herstellung dieses Objekts getroffen? Wir leben inmitten von Signalschildern und sind derart übersättigt, dass wir oft gar keine Augen haben für deren Komplexität und Machart. Sie sind ein Teil unserer natürlichen Umwelt geworden. Diese urbane Umwelt war auch der Hintergrund und Katalysator für die konkrete Poesie, eine internationale Bewegung der 50er und 60er Jahre, die einen grossen Teil ihrer Energie und auch ihren Namen drei ihrer frühesten Vertreter verdankt: den Brasilianern Augusto und Haroldo de Campos, zwei Brüder, und Décio Pignatari. Alle drei stammen aus São Paulo, Südamerikas bevölkerungsreichste und am stärksten in-

VINCENT KATZ ist Dichter, Kritiker und Übersetzer. Er ist der Autor von *Life is Paradise: The Portrait of Francesco Clemente* (Powerhouse Books, New York 1999).

dustrialisierte Stadt, deren schreiende Reklameschriften und Plakate denn auch ihr Werk früh beeinflusst haben. Mit beiden Beinen in der Gegenwart stehend durchforsteten sie jedoch auch die Vergangenheit gewissenhaft nach Zeichen intelligenten Lebens.

Ihrer Begeisterung für die literarische, musikalische und bildende Kunst der Moderne – in Brasilien und anderswo – entsprach eine nicht minder heftige Verehrung von Figuren der Vergangenheit. Augusto de Campos übersetzte Blake, Donne, Keats, Majakowski, Pound und Valéry. Haroldo de Campos übertrug Dante, Homer und Mallarmé. In ihrem 1958 (auch auf Englisch) erschienenen *Pilot Plan for Concrete Poetry (Leitbild der konkreten Poesie)* entwarfen die drei Dichter die Grundlage ihrer Forderung nach einer Poesie, in der Form und Inhalt gleichwertig sind. Danach soll das visuelle Element in den Vordergrund treten und den gegenständlichen, stofflichen Charakter des Gedichts vermitteln. Sie erstellten auch eine Liste ihrer poetischen Vorgänger, die mit einem überraschenden Stammvater beginnt, Stéphane Mallarmé – überraschend, sofern man an den Sym-

bolisten Mallarmé denkt mit seiner Sehnsucht nach Transzendenz. Wer sich dagegen an sein «Un coup de dés jamais n'abolira le hasard» erinnert, mag die Verbindung erkennen. In diesem 1897 veröffentlichten, unerhört innovativen Gedicht arbeitete Mallarmé nicht nur mit der Doppelseite als Gestaltungsmittel und setzte die Worte mitten auf ungeheure weisse Flächen; er verwendete auch verschiedene Schriftgrössen und -stile zur Unterscheidung verschiedener Gedankenstränge. Er machte sogar Wortbilder, wie das wenig später auch Apollinaire in seinen *Calligrammes* tat. Die Brasilianer standen auch unter dem Einfluss von Ezra Pound und gaben ihrer Gruppe den Namen *Noigandres* nach Pounds «Canto XX». Pounds Interesse für Ideogramme hatte Vorbildcharakter; die konkrete Poesie entstand ja aus dem Wunsch, Bild und poetischen Inhalt so miteinander zu verschmelzen, dass das Gedicht im Idealfall auf nichts ausserhalb seiner selbst mehr verwiese.

Die Brasilianer waren frühreif, in ihrem Leben ebenso wie in ihrer Entwicklung hin zur konkreten Poesie. 1952 brachten die drei Dichter, damals wenig über zwanzig, eine Zeitschrift heraus, die ebenfalls den Titel *Noigandres* trug, und traten in Briefwechsel mit Pound. 1953 veröffentlichte Augusto de Campos einen Gedichtband mit dem Titel *Poetamenos*, in denen die Wörter verschiedene Farben hatten zum Zeichen, dass sie von verschiedenen Stimmen gesprochen wurden. Die farbigen Wörter stehen auch noch vor einem farbigen Hintergrund. Der Dichter stellte sich vor, dass diese Wörter aufblinken und verlöschen sollten wie Lichtsignale, aber das war damals technisch noch nicht machbar, also entwarf er ein System von Farbunterscheidungen, das sich auf einer gedruckten Seite einfach umsetzen liess. Mit Beginn des Computerzeitalters konnte er dann endlich seine ursprüngliche Idee in die Tat umsetzen und das portugiesische Gedicht mit seiner englischen Übersetzung abwechselnd aufleuchten lassen. (Es ist auf seiner Website zugänglich: http://uol. com.br/augustodecampos/home.htm – ein ausgezeichneter Weg um an seine Gedichte und Aufsätze heranzukommen.) Pignatari, der als Werbegrafiker arbeitete, verfasste visuelle Gedichte, die man kinetisch oder kine-

matisch nannte, insofern sie erst nach und nach sichtbar werden. Da er fand, dass selbst die konkrete Poesie durch ihre Abhängigkeit vom Wort zu eingeschränkt sei, entwickelte er 1964 eine Technik für eine semiotische Poesie, in der einfache Symbole wie in der Flaggensprache der Seefahrt eine feste Bedeutung haben, zu der aber immer auch Worte gehören. Haroldo de Campos machte einige Gedichte mit visuellen Elementen, aber sein Interesse galt mehr der Theorie und dem konkreten Klanggedicht, wo die Wörter aufgrund akustischer Ähnlichkeiten ausgewählt werden, wobei sich erstaunliche semantische Kombinationen ergeben. Er hat eine Übersetzung des ersten Buches der *Ilias* gemacht, wobei er den Klang des griechischen Originals ebenso mit einbezog wie die Bedeutung. In den Vereinigten Staaten war die konkrete Poesie keine echte Bewegung, schlimmer noch, sie schien sich just in dem Moment quer zu stellen und gegen die Mainstream-Kultur zu richten, als der Einfluss der Populärkultur auf die Kunst wichtig wurde. Die Brasilianer dagegen waren nicht nur imstande diese Kultur zu integrieren, sondern nahmen es auch an Gradlinigkeit mit ihr auf. Die amerikanische konkrete Poesie wurde nicht von Dichtern gemacht, sondern von bildenden Künstlern, die nach neuen Formen suchten. Für einen bildenden Künstler stellt der überzeugende Umgang mit Wörtern eine extreme Herausforderung dar. Ein Dichter unter diesen Konkreten ist der Amerikaner Aram Saroyan. Zwei seiner Bücher, *Pages* und *Aram Saroyan*, sind kleine Klassiker der mittleren 60er Jahre, alle in der Schreibmaschinenschrift gedruckt, in der sie getippt waren. Saroyan erreicht eine haikuähnliche Verdichtung dank

einem feinen Gespür für seine Zeit, was diese Gedichte zu Glanzlichtern macht, deren Leuchtkraft unvermindert erhalten ist:

**night
again
again**

Oder vielleicht noch aussagekräftiger:

eye.ye

und:

morni,ng

Als Dichter war ich enttäuscht von dem, was ich neben Saroyan an konkreter Poesie zu Gesicht bekam. Ich behaupte nicht, dass meine Kenntnisse der konkreten Poesie in den 70er Jahren erschöpfend waren, aber wenn ich heute die Anthologien der 60er Jahre durchblättere – *Concrete Poetry: A World View*, Indiana University Press, Bloomington 1968, oder *An Anthology of Concrete Poetry*, Something Else Press, New York 1967 –, kann ich nicht behaupten, dass ich heute zu einem anderen Schluss käme. Es war ein internationaler Trend, eine genreübergreifende Bewegung, die irgendwo zwischen bildender Kunst und Literatur anzusiedeln war, aber insgesamt fehlte es ihr an literarischer Kraft. In den 70er Jahren hätte ich wohl die brasilianischen Vertreter der konkreten Poesie nicht zu schätzen gewusst, zum Teil wegen der Sprachbarriere, aber in erster Linie wegen meiner beschränkten kulturellen Erfahrung. Als ich 1988 begann nach Brasilien zu reisen und Portugiesisch zu lernen, war ich reif dafür. Ich bin mir nicht mehr sicher, mit welchem Buch ich begann. Es kann Décio Pignataris *Poesia Pois É Poesia* gewe-

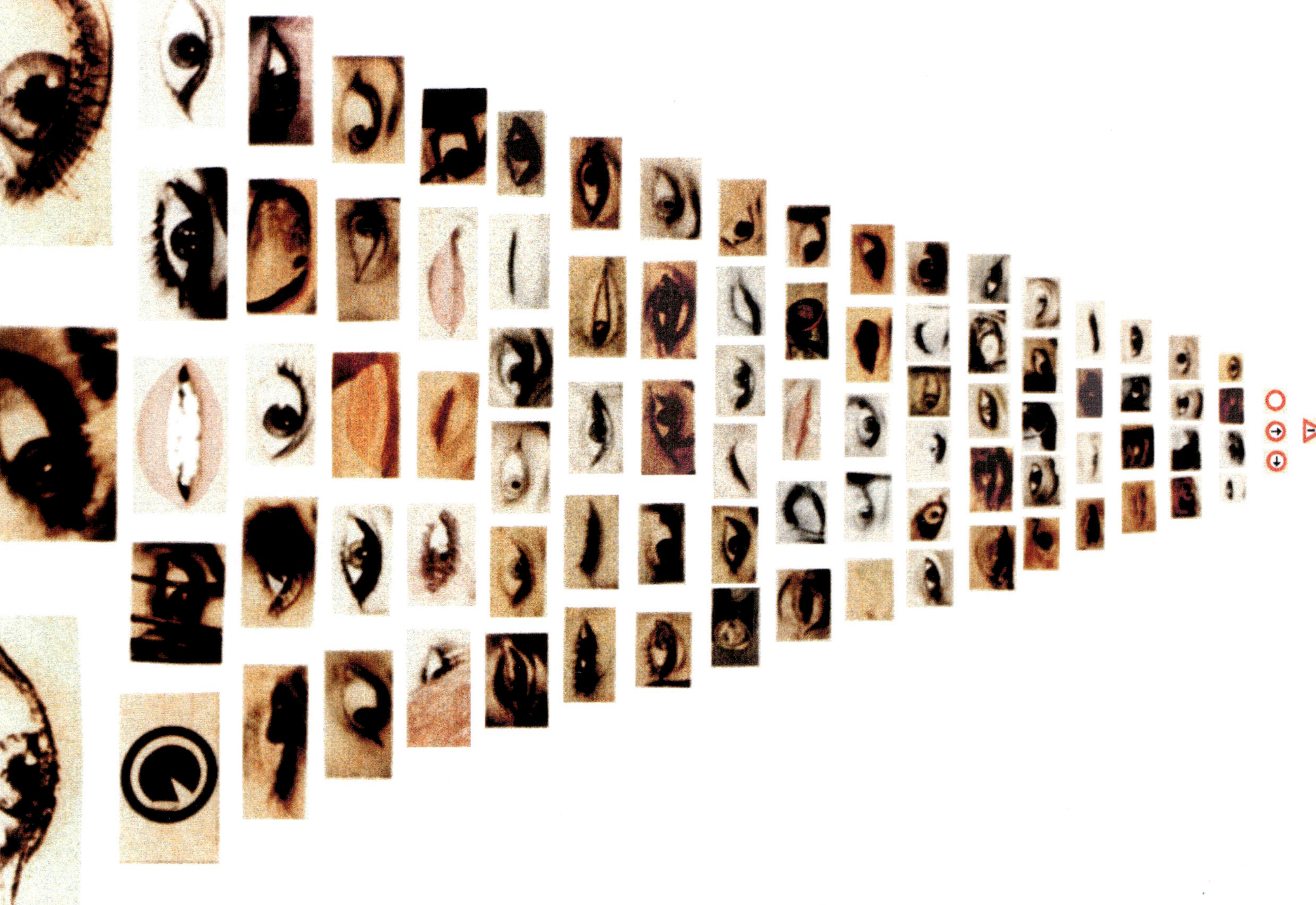

AUGUSTO DE CAMPOS, OLHO POR OLHO / EYE FOR EYE, 1964, collage of magazine clippings on cardboard, 27⅝ x 19¹¹/₁₆" / AUGE UM AUGE, Collage, 70 x 50 cm.

sen sein, eine Sammlung von Werken aus den Jahren 1950 bis 1975. Da war zunächst das englische Motto, «Ride the pink horse», Titel eines Robert-Montgomery-Films von 1947. Klar, dass damit mein Interesse geweckt war, aber wer hip ist, muss deswegen noch lange kein Dichter sein. Also begann ich das erste Gedicht zu lesen, «O Carrossel» aus dem Jahr 1950:

Entre escolher
Montanha-russa
Roda-gigante
Ou trem-fantasma,
Eu escolhi
Meu carrossel.
Paguei com vida
– Engenho e arte –
Pelo meu árdego corcel.

Das liesse sich etwa wie folgt übersetzen:

Unschlüssig zwischen
Der Achterbahn
Dem Riesenrad
Und der Geisterbahn
Wählte ich
Mein Karussell.
Ich bezahlte mit dem Leben
– Genie und Kunst –
für mein wackeres Streitross.

Die Gedichte gefielen mir auf Anhieb. Und je mehr ich von diesem Autor und seinen zwei Mitstreitern, Augusto und Haroldo de Campos, las, desto klarer erkannte ich, dass ihr Talent zur Schaffung gelungener Wortbilder mit einer dichterischen Grundbegabung zusammenhing, die sich während vieler Jahre aus unterschiedlichen poetischen Quellen genährt hatte. Alle drei haben einen grossen Teil ihrer Energie in Gedichtübersetzungen investiert und tragfähige Beziehungen zu fernen Zeiten und Orten geknüpft und sich so als Dichter und Übersetzer Fähigkeiten angeeignet, die man auf andere Weise gar nicht erlangen kann. Augusto war auch der in visueller Hinsicht Fruchtbarste der drei. Sein «Olho Por Olho» (Auge um Auge) (1964) wurde auch ein konkretes Gedicht ohne Worte genannt. Hier ist ein Ausschnitt eines Texts von Augusto, in dem er die Bildsprache dieses Werks erläutert, das eine Collage aus Photographien von Augen und einem Mund ist und über die übliche Selbstreferenzialität der Collage hinausgeht:

AUGE UM AUGE: hinauf bis zum auge. oder, wieder, «questo visibile parlare» (dante). oder «mit freien augen sehen» (oswald de andrade). pop-videogramm. re-visierte revuen. stars, sternchen, politiker, poeten, vögel, ein schwarzer jaguar, pelé, sousândrade, autoscheinwerfer, das auge der waschmaschine, verkehrsampeln. augen. metamorphose. münder. BBs (zahn um zahn) mund. ein babel der augen. haroldo getauft: BABŒIL (1964).

Seit Anfang der 50er Jahre versuchten diese drei Poeten die Populärkultur in ihre Dichtkunst zu integrieren, und die Art, wie Augusto in «Olho Por Olho» historische Figuren, Idole der brasilianischen Moderne, Politiker, Sportler, Filmstars und Maschinen gleichwertig auf eine Ebene stellte, ist ein Beispiel für die geistige Offenheit, die die brasilianische Kultur der 60er Jahre entscheidend prägte. Popmusiker des Tropik-Trends der 60er Jahre waren beeinflusst von den komplexen Wortspielen dieser konkreten Poesie und daraus ist auch mindestens ein Künstler hervorgegangen: Arnaldo Antunes, der nicht nur Rockmusiker ist, sondern auch ein grosser visueller Poet und bildender Künstler sowie Teilnehmer der Biennale von São Paulo. Augusto hat mit verschiedenen Musikern zusammengearbeitet, auch mit seinem Sohn, Cid Campos. Vater und Sohn haben zusammen ein Poesie- und Klangstück mit dem Titel POESIA É RISCO komponiert. Heute, fünfzig Jahre nach-

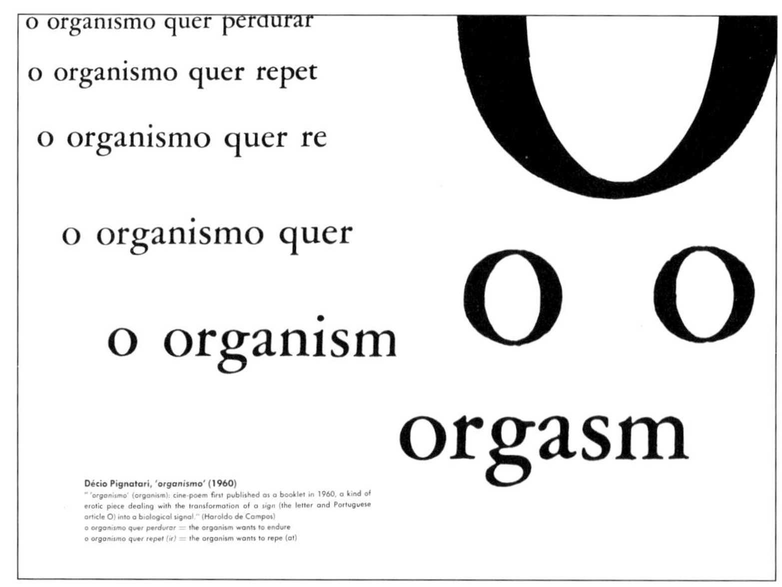

DECIO PIGNATARI, ORGANISMO, 1960.

Décio Pignatari, 'organismo' (1960)
"'organismo' (organism): cine-poem first published as a booklet in 1960, a kind of erotic piece dealing with the transformation of a *sign* (the letter and Portuguese article O) into a biological signal." (Haroldo de Campos)
o organismo quer perdurar = the organism wants to endure
o organismo quer repet (ir) = the organism wants to repe (at)

AUGUSTO DE CAMPOS,
LYGIA FINGERS, 1953, colored ink
on paper, dimensions variable / farbige
Tusche auf Papier.

HAROLDO DE CAMPOS,
CRISTAL CRISTAL FOME, white letters
on blue ground, from the series /
weisse Schrift auf blauem Grund,
aus der Serie
FOME DE FORMA / HUNGER
FOR FORM / FORMHUNGER, 1957–59.

dem sie die Bühne betreten haben, sind Augusto, Haroldo und Décio immer noch aktiv. Augusto freut sich über die neuen technischen Möglichkeiten und kreiert interaktive Versionen seiner Arbeiten auf grossformatigen elektronischen Bildschirmen. Haroldo macht seine «Klangübersetzungen» und Décio hat einen experimentellen Roman mit visuellen Elementen publiziert. Durch die wachsende Bedeutung der Biennale von São Paulo und dadurch, dass viele brasilianische Künstler den Schritt auf die Weltbühne geschafft haben, sind die brasilianischen Vertreter der konkreten Poesie einmal mehr auf dem Sprung, mit ihren leicht zugänglichen und doch raffinierten Gedichten ein neues Publikum zu erobern. Sie sind imstande die üblichen sprachgebundenen Grenzen der Poesie zu unterlaufen dank ihrer unverbrüchlichen Treue zum Einfachen, aber klanglich Ergiebigen. Über Pounds Zitate sind sie zu den Quellen des ideogrammatischen Denkens vorgedrungen und fanden einen Weg, die blitzartigen Einsichten des Zen in die Bildsprache des einundzwanzigsten Jahrhunderts zu übertragen.

(Übersetzung: Susanne Schmidt)

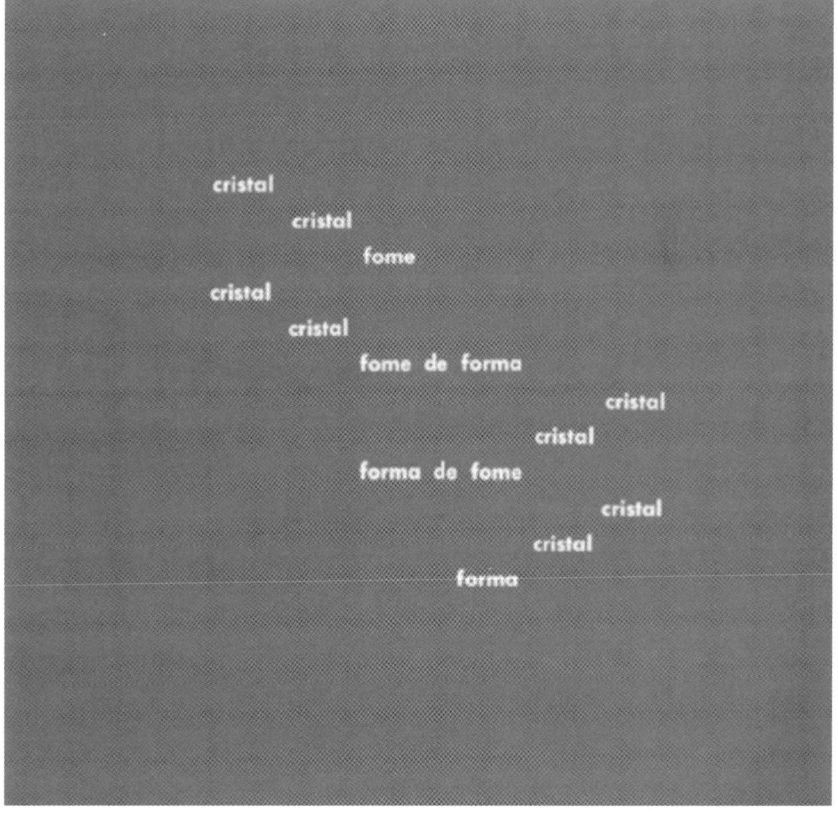

Body

ELISABETH BRONFEN

Malaise

For Annette Messager, museums figure as the churches of our world because of the theatricality upon which the force of their architectural design resides. Indeed, several series of works begun in the late eighties explore the strange proximity between secular art installations and traditional sacred spectacle. In MES VOEUX (My Vows, 1988–91) a multitude of gelatin-silver prints under glass, each depicting individual body parts, are attached to different lengths of strings and layered on top of each other. These personal "vows" commemorate a dual gesture of dissection and reassemblage. While on the one hand Messager has cut up the body of each of her models, with the represented body fragment severed from the whole, on the other hand these photographs, depicting fragments from a plethora of different bodies have been framed and compiled together so as to form new configurations. As abstract bodies, they nevertheless recall the very bodily materiality that, in the act of reassemblage, has been obliterated. Each geometric shape as a whole resonates with the individual parts contained in it; it recalls the triangular shape of pubic hair or nostrils, the circular form of nipples and navels, of a clenched hand, an opened mouth, or a protruding tongue, the vertical line of the sole of a foot, the line of a nose, the length of a penis.

ELISABETH BRONFEN teaches English Literature at the University of Zurich. Among her publications are *The Knotted Subject: Hysteria and its Discontents* (Princeton University Press, 1998), and *Over Her Dead Body: Death, Femininity and the Aesthetic* (New York: Routledge/Manchester University Press 1992).

The bodies that have come to be recreated in this installation are thus disturbingly hybrid because they perform the disquieting gesture of concealing as much as they reveal. The photographs that are assembled on top of each other, with the attached strings falling on top of individual images like a net, seem to offer an intimate view of particular body parts even as the technique of layering signifies that no unconstrained view is possible. In a similar vein, those photographs that are not layered nevertheless also stage an impaired vision. For here a second frame, containing a single word written over and over again, is superimposed on the photographic image. What is apparently an intimate view of the body becomes meaningful only in reference to the language we have to describe it. Even the most private parts of the body are textually constructed. What Messager appropriates from the Christian tradition of the exposed effigy is, thus, not only the recognition that precisely because the body is mutable it lends itself to the process of transformation. Rather, she also makes use of the fact that the meaning attached to any body fragments on display is also not stable, indeed as mutable as the body itself.

In her secular appropriation of the Christian display of the body Messager does not, however, limit herself to representations of the human body. In another series self-consciously entitled *Mes petites effigies* (My Little Effigies, 1988), one of the details consists in the assemblage of three different representational media: a framed photograph of a woman's pubic hair rests on the back of a dilapidated toy elephant, which in turn is placed on top of the first line of a textual

Annette Messager's Anatomical Theater

triangle consisting of the word "protection." This word is written over and over again such that its shape reiterates that of the photograph—the cluster of words comparable visually to the photographic representation. Ten years later Messager will once again use this word as part of an installation, only this time the letters are composed of diverse toy animals which she has cut up and reassembled, each letter an uncanny representation recalling the original toy shape, even while commemorating the dissection that has occurred. Seen as a whole the materially enacted word spells out a concept of solace yet each individual letter indicates that protection of the body's immutable integrity is precisely what has been violated.

With these macabre recompositions of representations of fractured bodies, Messager reiterates the iconography of Christian relics. Owing to the belief that the deceased continue to have an effect on the world they leave behind, miraculous powers were willingly ascribed to the remains of dead heroes, martyrs, and saints. Decked with rare jewels and rich fabrics their skulls and skeletons came to be staged as elaborate auto-icons. In Wil (St. Gall, Switzerland) the remains of St. Pancratius are shown standing upright, fully clothed in an ornate armor made of gold and silver. A knight fighting for the victory of Christian belief, he represents the valiant victory both over his aggressors and over death as such. And yet the metal clothes he wears are riddled with holes, so that the gaps in his armor render his skeleton visible. In a similar vein St. Prosper lies in a glass coffin as though he were on exhibition in Tavel, Switzerland. His skeleton is dressed in a red satin and brocade frock, elaborately lined with pearls and rubies. Leaning on his right arm in the posture of blissful repose, a gold tiara on his head, a golden feather in his left arm, he seems to be mirthfully enjoying his uncanny liminal state. The rich clothing and the bones supplement each other. Their sheer physicality emphasizes their worldliness, precisely because they are made of de-animated material. They are what remains or returns after death. Indeed, the rhetoric deployed by these relics is supremely duplicitous. Even while they are meant to warn the churchgoer of the inevitability of death and thus the futility of all earthly pleasures, they also forcefully celebrate the regeneration of life. These relics warn that death will come and at the same time emblematically perform a life produced out of inorganic body material. They are bodily materiality at its most crude, even while they are staged as embodied tropes.

Stuffed taxidermic specimens, decked with the heads of toy animals; a piece of fox fur studded with photographs of body parts; toy animals clothed in woolen masks and covered with nets; gloves to which pencils are attached as though to mimic artificial fingers, while the opening of each glove is covered up with photographic images of a body orifice such as the eye, the nose or the mouth—these are Messager's secular relics. Though her installations self-consciously transform the sacred into the profane, the hybrid bodies she creates by gutting, cutting up and reassembling representations of the body, also play with the duplicitous way in which the relic's auto-iconicity performs the murky interface between materiality and textuality. Messager uses her media to explicitly refer to the mortality of the body whose resurrection she also seeks to perform: As an agent of death the photograph transforms the body into a frozen image much as the word kills the thing it represents. For in both cases the medium of representation—the image, the word—severed from the body it stands in for, implicitly signifies a time when it will remain while its actual body referent will have died and decomposed. Her installations thus emphasize the sheer materiality of the bodies represented in precisely the double gesture of the relic. They are absent and present at the same time.

Using her secular relics to chart new geographies of the body, even while producing designs that can be read as pure embellishment, she recalls those interiors of religious sites, where bones and skulls as well as sculpted heads are brought together to decorate the walls. When she frames her photographs of individual body parts with strings and textual bodies made up of words, she self-consciously recalls the manner in which, in these churches, skeletons are placed in the center of an alcove, with intricate patterns made of bones adorning and framing them. When she deploys the re-assemblage of her framed photographs and text bodies, to configure simple shapes like a cross, a triangle or a circle, she recalls the manner in which skulls and bones came to be assembled as emblems of the deceased person, depicting his crown or coat of arms. Furthermore, even while she repeatedly invokes the display of sacred relics in museum sites, Messager also directly intervenes in church spaces. Part of her series *Mes ouvrages* (My Works, 1988), was installed in St. Martin du Méjean, Arles. The skulls of traditional relics were replaced with her personal effigies—images of the bodies she had fragmented in the act of photographing them, the remains of toy animals, decked not with rare jewels but with masks, images or nets.

In contrast to the traditional relics Messager replaces, her installations, of course, not only explicitly carry her signature. Their emblematic meaning is also not culturally fixed. The viewer must decipher what the refashioned shapes represent. Yet in so far as one of the meanings emerging from these macabre installations is the duplicitous presence of death in life, it is, nevertheless, useful to relate Messager's work to another privileged site for the display of bodily mutability—the stage. In his reflections on the origins of bourgeois tragedy Walter Benjamin argues that the cultural celebration of emblems prevalent in the Baroque period relies on the conviction that the organic must be shattered in order for its true meaning to emerge. Gutted human remains, fragmented body parts, become significant precisely because, in this state of decomposition, a second, allegorical meaning can be imposed onto the human shape, owing to which the body can experience an allegorical resurrection. According to Benjamin, the crucial figure of Baroque thought can be summarized as follows: The true meaning of human existence resides in an aesthetic staging of the human corpse—gutted, disemboweled, fragmented—which celebrates its translation into an emblem of mortality: "Seen from the perspective of death it is the production of the corpse which signifies life."[1]

In tandem with its celebration of revenge tragedies, the culture of the baroque significantly enjoyed another theatrical display of the human body's mutability—the anatomical theater. Dissected before an audience of learned and curious men, the opened human body, suspended between life and death, came to serve as a *memento mori* for the living. In a famous engraving of the Leiden Anatomy Theater, dated c. 1609, we see human and animal skeletons interspersed among the audience that has gathered around the stage where an anatomist is performing his art. They are holding banners with inscriptions, warning of the ephemerality of human existence and the punishment for their sins that awaits humankind on Judgment Day, while the anatomist compares the feminine body he has cut open to a text describing the shape and placement of the organs he is about to expose to his audience. To emphasize the uneasy alignment between a materialistic and an allegorical reading of the exposed dissected body, the top of the engraving not only shows the title naming the scene: *AMPHITEATRVM ANATOMICVM LVDVNO BATAVORVM*. Allegorical figurations of Adam and Eve float above the audience to remind us that the dissected body is to be read not only as a text meant to confirm preexisting writings on human anatomy. It also functions

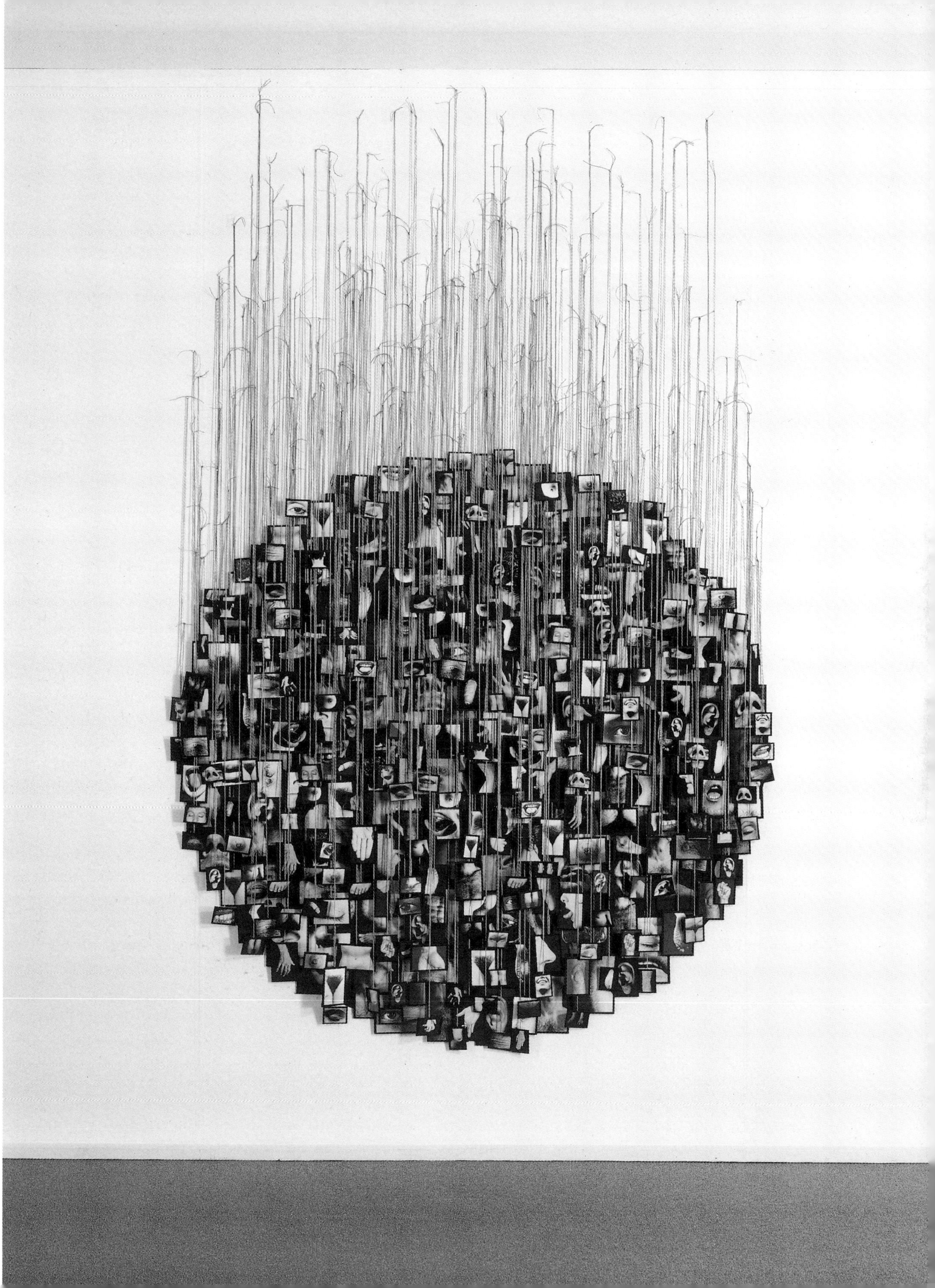

ANNETTE MESSAGER, MES VOEUX / MY VOWS, 1988–91, photos hanging on strings, collection MoMA, 157½ x 78¾" / MEINE GELÜBDE, an Fäden hängende Photos, 400 x 200 cm. (PHOTO: GALERIE CROUSEL-ROBELIN BAMA, PARIS)

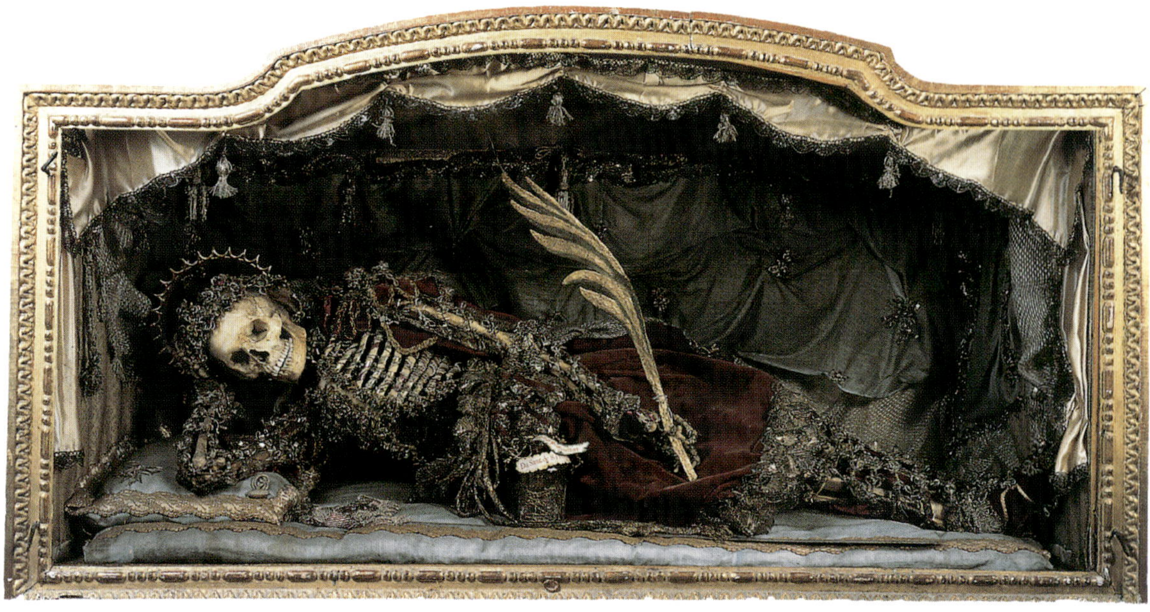

allegorically as an emblem of the true meaning of human existence. Putting death on display performs a reference to man's sinful fall from paradise and his concomitant mortality, for which the cultural celebration of relics is a small antidote.

Messager conceives of herself as an anatomist or vivisectionist of our times. In interviews she repeatedly insists that the element most central to her work is the body. She never shows it in its entirety but only as a fragment to indicate that, although we inhabit the world in and through our bodies, we hardly know what this body looks like. For this reason she seeks to explore the body's interiority, to incorporate its blood, its fluids into her aesthetic practice. One is tempted to see her project as an ironic feminine reiteration of such anatomist artists as Mary Shelley's Dr. Frankenstein. Rather than to the charnel houses and graves she goes to the taxidermy shops and department stores, to find the de-animated materials used to create a new species: monstrous and macabre hybrid bodies that, far from overcoming mortality, emblematically signify mutability. In so doing she plays with the masculine notion of romantic genius even while she parodically appropriates for herself the act of artificial regeneration normally attributed to male creation. For there is always also something playful written into her refiguration of the anatomic theater and the spectacle of the relic. When in a piece like ENSEMBLE (1998), she patches together a taxidermically prepared fox skin with several toy animals she has gutted and turned inside out, she uses explicitly quotidian objects to ironically engage with the iconography of baroque emblematics. She creates emblems, but they are comical rather than terrifying, silly rather than heroic. And yet precisely because her material is familiar, her macabre reassemblages have a disturbing effect. As the quotidian becomes monstrous we are jarred in the complacent self-assurance that we know the world of sensations and desires we inhabit.

In this disquieting gesture she implicitly recalls a postmodern appropriation of baroque theatricality—the slasher film. Exploring the murky interface between violence against the body, ritual display of body parts, and black comedy, Wes Craven offers his *Scream* trilogy to articulate the inescapable presence of death and mutability in the very site we believe protects us from it—the "hearth of the home." As his psychopathic killers gut their victims and display their corpses, they confirm Benjamin's hypothesis:

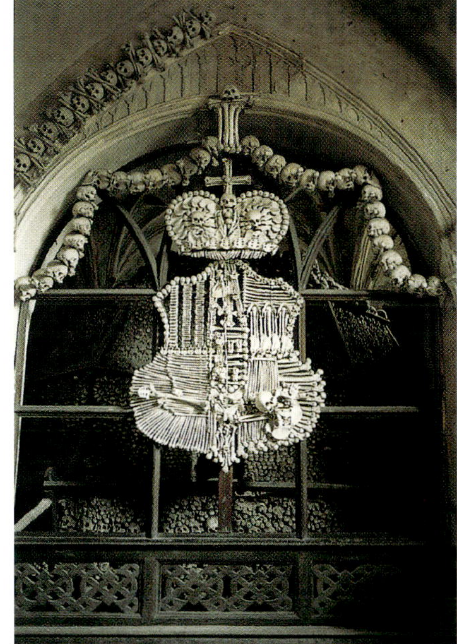

Two views of the chapel of Sedlec in Kutna-Hora, Czech Republic / Zwei Ansichten der Kapelle von Sedlec in Kutna-Hora, Tschechien.

Bottom / Ganz unten:
SAINT PANCRATIUS / SANKT PANKRAZ, 1777, from Augsburg, Germany, in the Catholic Church of Wil, St. Gall, Switzerland / katholische Kirche Wil, St. Gallen.

The production of the corpse transforms into the resurrection of the body as an emblem, notably for the return of repressed traumatic knowledge haunting the family. Like Messager's installations Craven's excessive cinematic renditions of sliced and slashed bodies, with the production of corpses and their textualization excessively and gleefully staged, pose as the anatomic theaters of today. Appropriating the rhetoric of baroque culture they lavishly broadcast a message about how death is always in our midst. And yet, as Messager taps into this celebration of the mutable and disfigured body she does so, like Craven, in the manner of black comedy so as to insist on the vexed alliance between playful creation and violence. The enjoyment of cutting open and reassembling favorite toys constitutes one of the most primary elements of children's games, much as the child in fantasy fragments the mother's body to fulfill its narcissistic demands. The disquieting message that comes to be broadcast on the stage of Messager's private anatomical theater is perhaps so poignant because it exposes a knowledge about our bodily existence that we seek to disavow. As familiar objects and conceptions of bodily integrity become uncanny, the intimate is shown to contain a kernel that is external, impenetrable, and ungraspable. And yet, as disconcerting as the recognition of the foreignness that haunts our fantasies of protection may be, it is also not really unfamiliar to us. We have always known that the acts of recomposition that satisfy us do so because they contain elements of shattering, dissecting, and decomposing. Indeed, the body we are most familiar with is our own—a body we see and experience only in fragments.

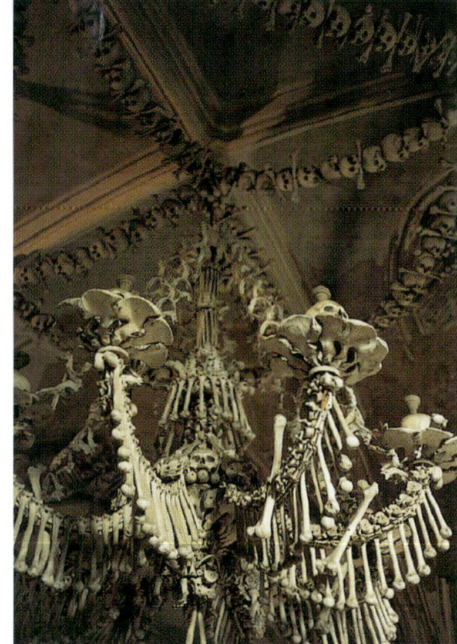

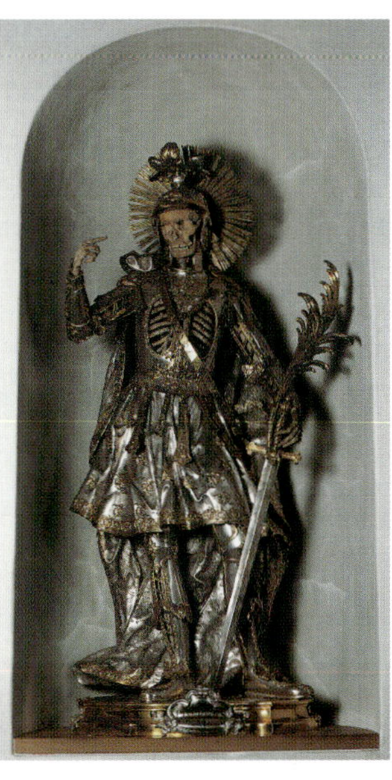

1) Walter Benjamin, *Ursprung des deutschen Trauerspiels* (Frankfurt am Main: Suhrkamp, 1972), pp. 245–46.

Körper Unbehagen

ELISABETH BRONFEN

Für Annette Messager haben die Museen dieser Welt, nicht zuletzt dank der theatralischen Wirkung ihrer Architektur, den Charakter von Kirchen angenommen. Und tatsächlich erkunden mehrere in den späten 80er Jahren begonnene Werkserien die merkwürdige Nähe säkularer Kunstinstallationen zum traditionellen sakralen Spektakel. MES VŒUX (Meine Gelübde, 1988–91) besteht aus zahlreichen Gelatine-Silber-Prints hinter Glas, die alle einzelne Körperpartien zeigen, an unterschiedlich langen Fäden hängen und übereinander angeordnet sind. Diese persönlichen «Votivtafeln» verweisen auf die zwiefache Gebärde des Sezierens und Neuzusammensetzens. Während Messager einerseits die Körper ihrer Modelle zerschnitten hat, wobei das jeweils abgebildete Körperfragment von den übrigen getrennt wurde, sind die Photographien, welche Fragmente einer Vielzahl verschiedener Körper darstellen, andrerseits so gerahmt und zusammengefügt, dass neue Figuren entstehen. Als abstrakte Körper erinnern sie dennoch an eben jene körperliche Materialität, die im Akt der Neukombination zum Verschwinden gebracht wurde. In jeder geometrischen Form als ganzer schwingen noch die in ihr enthaltenen individuellen Teile nach; sie erinnert an die Dreiecksform der Scham oder der Nasenflügel, die Kreisform der Brustwarzen und des Nabels, einer geballten

Faust, eines offenen Mundes oder einer gestreckten Zunge, an die vertikale Linie der Fusssohle, des Nasenrückens oder die Länge eines Penis.

Die Körper, die in dieser Installation neu geschaffen wurden, sind deshalb so verstörend hybrid, weil sie auf beunruhigende Weise ebenso viel verbergen wie enthüllen. Die Photographien, die derart hinter und übereinander angeordnet sind, dass sich die an ihnen befestigten Fäden wie ein Netz über die einzelnen Bilder legen, scheinen einen intimen Blick auf einzelne Körperteile freizugeben; zugleich macht die schichtweise Anordnung jedoch deutlich, dass ein direkter unverstellter Blick gar nicht möglich ist. Selbst in jenen Photographien, die einander nicht überlagern, wird eine verstellte Sicht inszeniert. Denn hier wird das photographische Bild von einem zweiten überblendet, das aus einem einzigen geschriebenen, mehrmals wiederholten Wort besteht. Was zunächst als intime Ansicht des Körpers erscheint, gewinnt seine Bedeutung erst im Zusammenhang mit der Sprache, die uns zu seiner Beschreibung zur Verfügung steht. Selbst die intimsten Teile des Körpers sind Textkonstrukte. Messager übernimmt also aus der christlichen Tradition der Darstellung des nackten Körpers nicht nur die Einsicht, dass gerade die Vergänglichkeit des Körpers den Prozess der Transformation nahe legt, sondern macht sich auch den Sachverhalt zunutze, dass die Bedeutung der zur Schau gestellten Körperfragmente ebenfalls nicht stabil, sondern genauso dem Wandel unterworfen ist wie der Körper selbst.

In ihrer säkularen Aneignung der christlichen Tradition der Körperdarstellung beschränkt sich

ELISABETH BRONFEN ist Professorin für Englische Literatur an der Universität Zürich. Zu ihren Publikationen gehören u. a. *Nur über ihre Leiche. Tod, Weiblichkeit und Ästhetik.* (Antje Kunstmann, München 1994) und *Heimweh. Illusionsspiele in Hollywood* (Volk & Welt, Berlin 1999).

Annette Messagers anatomisches Theater

Messager jedoch nicht auf den Körper des Menschen. In einer weiteren Serie mit dem selbstbewussten Titel *Mes petites effigies* (Meine kleinen Bildnisse) besteht eine der Besonderheiten in der Kombination von drei verschiedenen Medien. Eine gerahmte Photographie des Schamhaars einer Frau ruht auf dem Rücken eines lädierten Spielzeugelefanten, der seinerseits auf der Spitze einer aus dem Wort «protection» (Schutz) gebildeten Textpyramide steht. Auch dieses Wort wurde so viele Male niedergeschrieben, dass sein Erscheinungsbild – die Anhäufung von Worten – der Photographie ähnlich sieht. Zehn Jahre später wird Messager dieses Wort noch einmal als Teil einer Installation benutzen, doch diesmal bestehen die Buchstaben aus verschiedenen Spielzeugtieren, die sie auseinander geschnitten und neu zusammengesetzt hat, jeder Buchstabe ein unheimlicher Verweis auf die ursprüngliche Gestalt des Spielzeugs und auf die erfolgte Zerstückelung. Als Ganzes vermittelt das materiell inszenierte Wort eine beruhigende Vorstellung, zugleich aber zeugt jeder einzelne Buchstabe davon, dass das Recht auf körperliche Unversehrtheit eben nicht geschützt, sondern verletzt worden ist.

Mit dieser makabren Neukomposition von Darstellungen zerteilter Körper greift Messager die Ikonographie christlicher Reliquien auf. Aufgrund des Glaubens, dass Verstorbene auch nach ihrem Ableben eine Wirkung auf die von ihnen zurückgelassene Welt ausüben, schrieb man den Relikten toter Helden, Märtyrer und Heiliger gern übernatürliche Kräfte zu. Geschmückt mit seltenen Edelsteinen und wertvollen Gewändern wurden ihre Schädel und

Skelette als kunstvolle Ikonen ihrer selbst in Szene gesetzt. In Wil (St. Gallen) sind die Reliquien des vollständig in eine Schmuckrüstung aus Gold und Silber eingekleideten heiligen Pankraz' in aufrechter Haltung ausgestellt. Als kämpfender Ritter des christlichen Glaubens steht er ebenso für die heldenhafte Überwindung seiner Gegner wie des Todes schlechthin. Doch zugleich weist sein metallenes Gewand zahlreiche Löcher auf, hinter denen sein Skelett zu sehen ist. Ganz ähnlich liegt in Tavel (Tafers, Kanton Fribourg) der heilige Prosper in einem Glassarg, beinah wie in einer Ausstellungsvitrine. Sein Skelett ist in ein aufwendig mit Perlen und Rubinen verziertes Satin- und Brokatgewand gehüllt. In einer Haltung glückseliger Ruhe auf den rechten Arm gestützt, eine goldene Tiara auf dem Kopf, eine

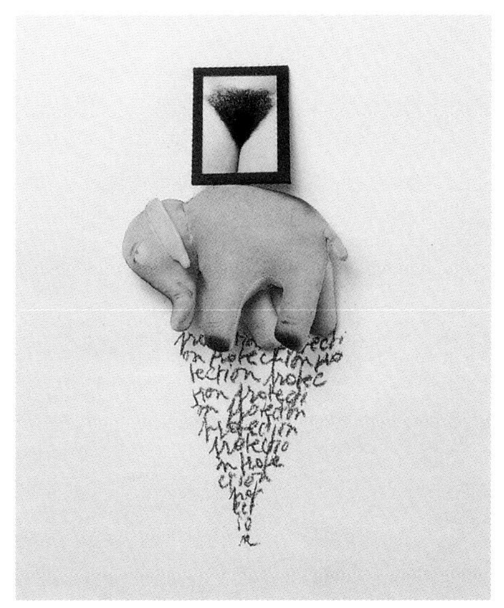

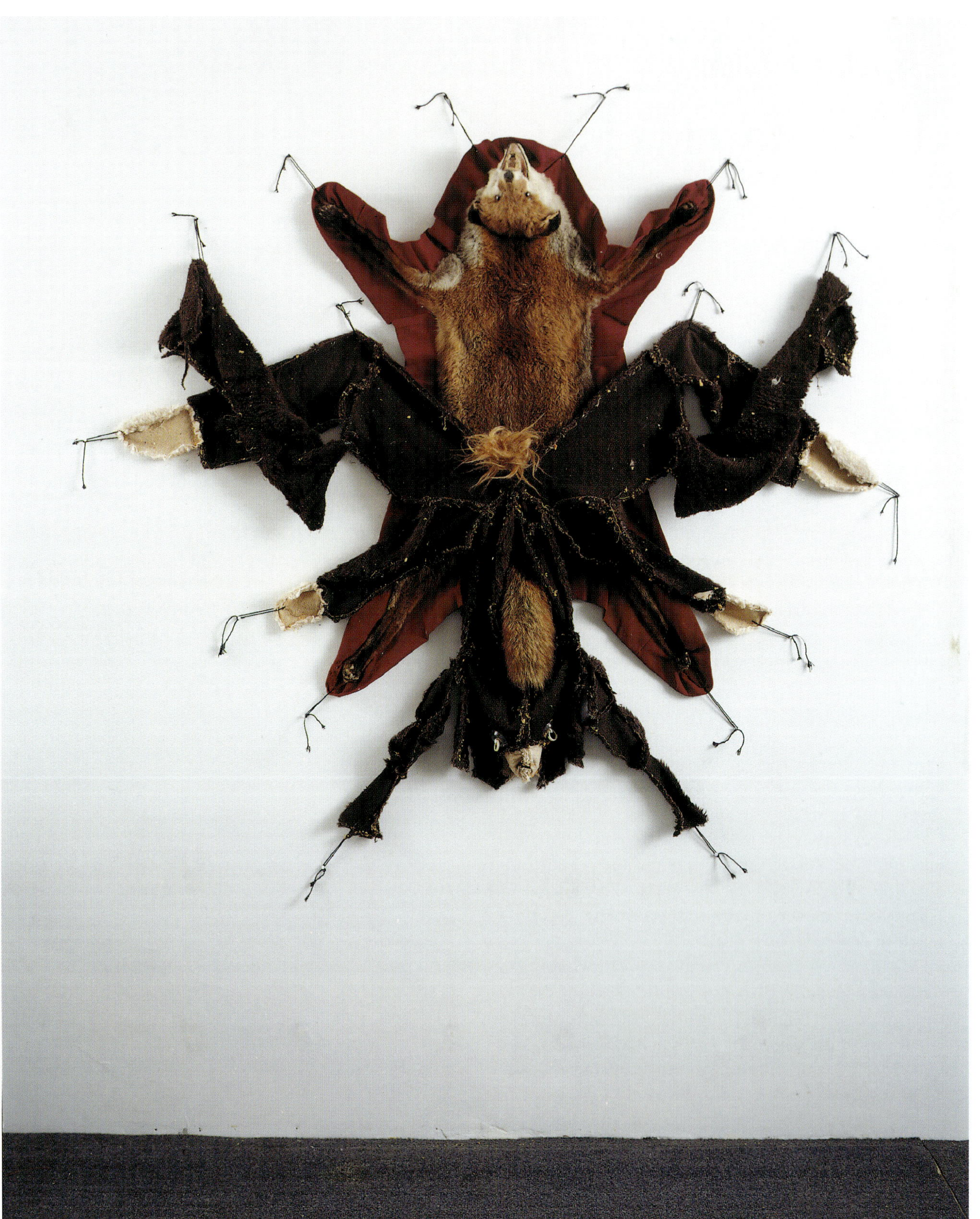

ANNETTE MESSAGER, ENSEMBLE, 1998, mixed-media, 59 x 61" / 150 x 155 cm.

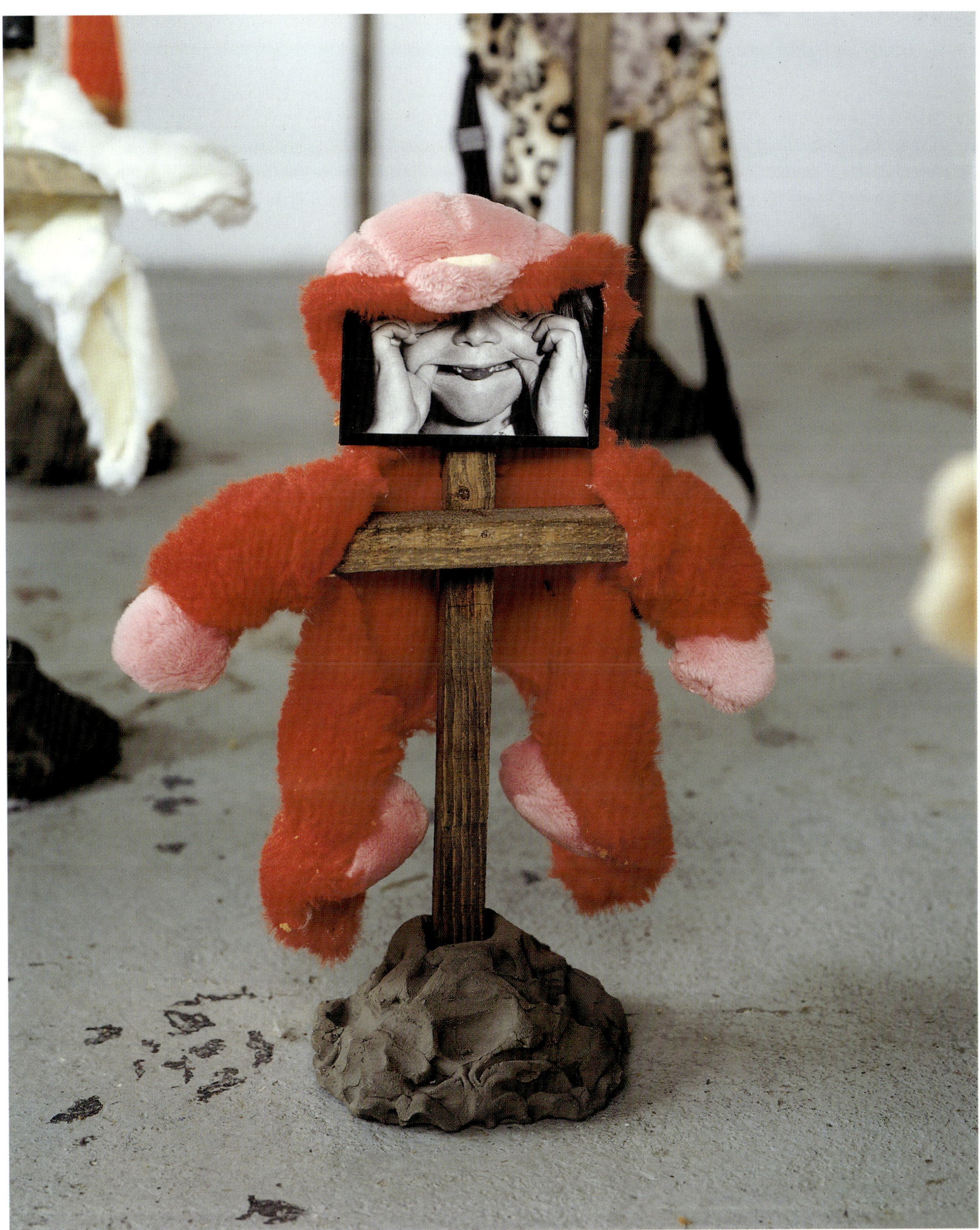

ANNETTE MESSAGER, 2 CLANS, 2 FAMILLES, 1997–98, detail, mixed media.

goldene Feder in der linken Hand, scheint er seinen unheimlichen Übergangszustand zu geniessen. Das wertvolle Gewand und die Knochen ergänzen einander bestens. Ihre blanke Körperlichkeit unterstreicht das Diesseitige, gerade weil sie aus unbelebtem Material bestehen. Sie sind das, was nach dem Tod übrig bleibt oder zurückkehrt. In der Tat sprechen diese Reliquien eine äusserst zwiespältige Sprache. Obwohl sie den Kirchgänger an die Unentrinnbarkeit des Todes und damit die Flüchtigkeit aller irdischen Freuden gemahnen sollen, feiern sie doch zugleich nachdrücklich die Erneuerung des Lebens. Diese Überreste mahnen uns, dass der Tod unweigerlich kommen wird, und führen zugleich symbolisch ein aus leblosem Körpermaterial inszeniertes Leben vor. Sie sind blanke Materie in ihrer rohesten Form und sollen doch das Geistige verkörpern.

Ausgestopfte Präparate, geschmückt mit den Köpfen von Spielzeugtieren; ein Stück Fuchspelz, dicht besetzt mit Photos von Körperteilen; mit Wollmasken bekleidete und mit Netzen bedeckte Spielzeugtiere; Handschuhe, an denen an künstliche Finger erinnernde Stifte befestigt sind und deren offene Stelle jeweils mit dem photographischen Bild einer

Körperöffnung (Auge, Nase oder Mund) verschlossen ist: Das sind die säkularen Reliquien Messagers. Obwohl ihre Installationen selbstbewusst Sakrales in Profanes verwandeln, spielen ihre hybriden Körperkompositionen mit derselben Zwiespältigkeit, die der Inszenierung der dunklen Schnittstelle zwischen Materialität und Textualität im Falle der Reliquien anhaftet. Messagers Arbeiten verweisen explizit auf die Sterblichkeit des Körpers, dessen Wiederauferstehung sie zugleich zu inszenieren suchen. Stellvertretend für den Tod verwandelt die Photographie den Körper in ein starres Bild, ähnlich wie das Wort die Sache, für die es steht, tötet. Denn in beiden Fällen verweist das Medium der Darstellung – das Bild, das Wort – losgelöst vom Körper, für den es steht, implizit auf eine Zeit, in der es weiter bestehen wird, während sein jetziger körperlicher Referent tot und verrottet sein wird. Messagers Installationen betonen also die reine Materialität der dargestellten Körper mit derselben Zwiespältigkeit wie die Reliquie. Sie sind abwesend und anwesend zugleich.

Die Künstlerin entwirft mit ihren säkularen Reliquien neue Geographien des Körpers und verweist dabei – auch wenn sie Gebilde herstellt, die sich als

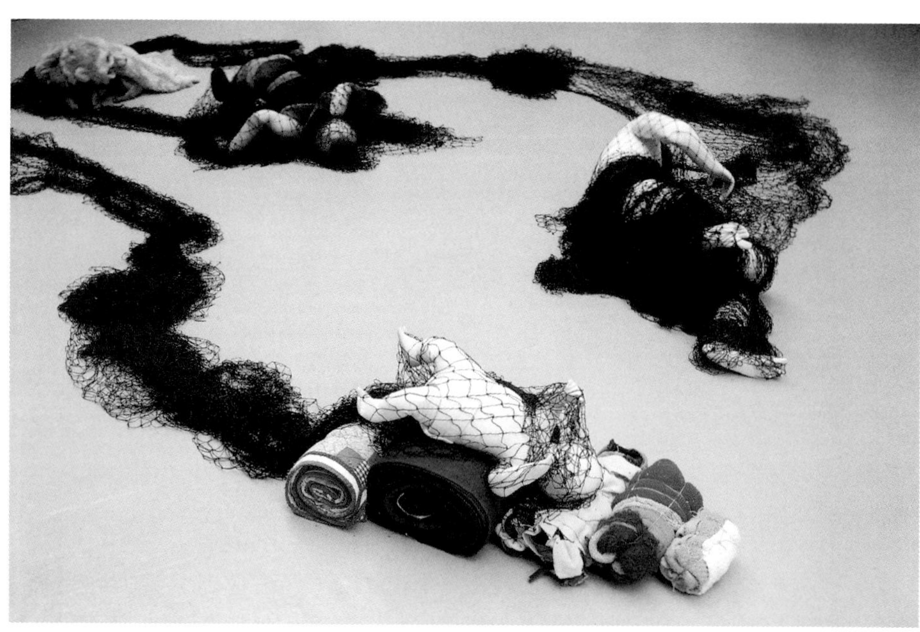

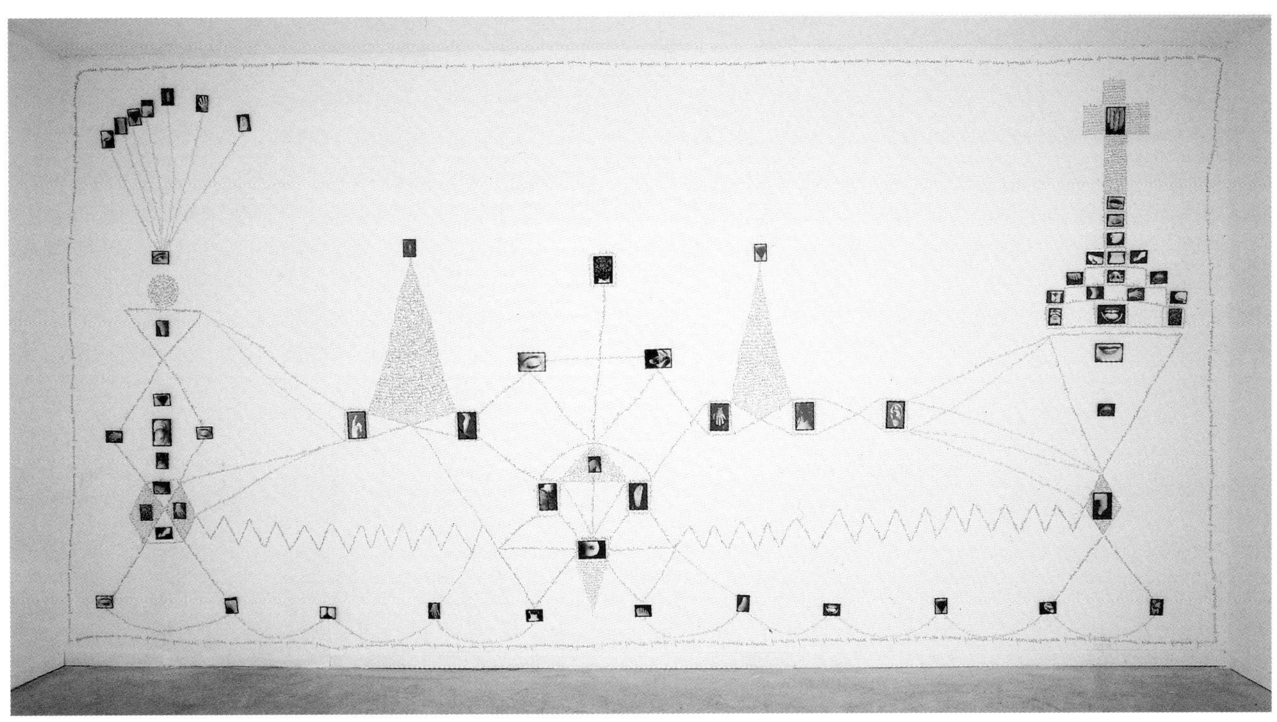

ANNETTE MESSAGER, MES OUVRAGES / MY WORKS, 1988,

mixed-media series, Le Consortium Dijon, 11 ½ x 19 ¾ ft / MEINE ARBEITEN, aus der gleichnamigen Serie, 350 cm x 600 cm.

reine Dekoration lesen lassen – auf die Innenräume sakraler Orte, wo Knochen, Schädel und modellierte Köpfe kombiniert als Wandschmuck dienen. Wenn sie ihre Photos von Körperteilen mit Bindfäden und aus Worten zusammengesetzten Textkörpern umgibt, evoziert sie bewusst die Art und Weise, wie in den Kirchen Skelette in der Mitte einer Nische platziert und mit aufwändigen Mustern aus Knochen verziert und umrahmt wurden. Und indem sie die Neuzusammensetzung ihrer gerahmten Photographien und Textkörper so gestaltet, dass einfache Formen, etwa ein Kreuz, ein Dreieck oder ein Kreis entstehen, ruft sie in Erinnerung, wie Schädel und Knochen als Symbole des Verstorbenen arrangiert wurden und seine Krone oder sein Wappen wiedergaben. Doch Messager evoziert nicht nur die Präsentation sakraler Reliquien in ihren Museumsinstallationen, sie interveniert auch in Kirchenräumen. Ein Teil ihrer Serie *Mes ouvrages* (Meine Arbeiten) wurde in der Kirche St-Martin du Méjean in Arles installiert. Sie ersetzte die Schädel echter Reliquien mit ihren eigenen Bildnissen: Bilder von Körpern, die durch das Photographieren fragmentiert worden waren, Relikte von Spielzeugtieren, nicht mit seltenen Juwelen, sondern mit Masken, Bildern oder Netzen geschmückt.

Im Gegensatz zu den traditionellen, von Messager ersetzten und ergänzten Reliquien tragen ihre eigenen Installationen nicht nur ausdrücklich die Signatur der Künstlerin, sondern ihr Symbolgehalt ist überdies nicht kulturell vorbestimmt. Hier müssen die Betrachter selbst herausfinden, was die umgestalteten Formen darstellen. Aber insofern, als eine der Bedeutungen, die in diesen makabren Installationen zum Vorschein kommt, die zwiespältige Präsenz des Todes im Leben ist, lohnt es sich doch, Messagers Werke mit einem anderen bevorzugten Schauplatz der körperlichen Verwandlungsfähigkeit in Verbindung zu bringen: nämlich der Bühne. In seinen Überlegungen zum Ursprung des bürgerlichen Trau-

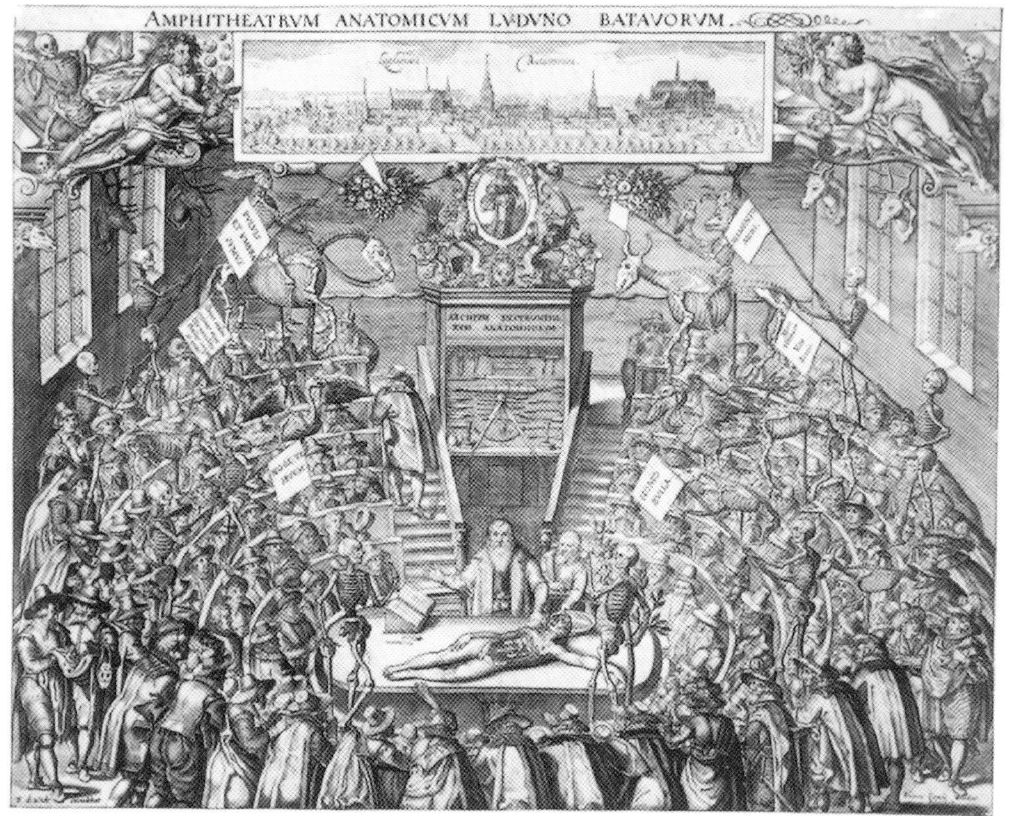

View of the Leiden anatomy theater, 1609 / Ansicht des Leidener Anatomiesaales von 1609. Beide Abbildungen stammen aus / Both images are taken from: Jonathan Sawday, "The Body Emblazoned" (London/New York: Routledge, 1995).

erspiels vertritt Walter Benjamin die These, dass der Hang zum Emblematischen im Zeitalter des Barock auf der Überzeugung beruhte, das Organische müsse zerschlagen werden, damit «in seinen Scherben» die wahre Bedeutung «aufgelesen» werden könne.[1] Ausgestopfte menschliche Relikte und fragmentierte Körperteile werden genau deswegen bedeutsam, weil sich der menschlichen Gestalt in diesem Zustand der Auflösung eine zweite allegorische Bedeutung zuschreiben lässt, durch die der Körper eine allegorische Wiederauferstehung erfahren kann. Benjamin zufolge lässt sich die entscheidende Denkfigur des Barock wie folgt zusammenfassen: Die wahre Bedeutung der menschlichen Existenz beruht auf einer ästhetischen Inszenierung des – ausgestopften, ausgeweideten, zerstückelten – menschlichen Leichnams, die seine Erhebung zum Emblem der Sterblichkeit feiert: «Produktion der Leiche ist, vom Tode her betrachtet, das Leben.»[2]

Neben der Vorliebe für «Rachedramen» ergötzte sich die Kultur des Barock bezeichnenderweise noch

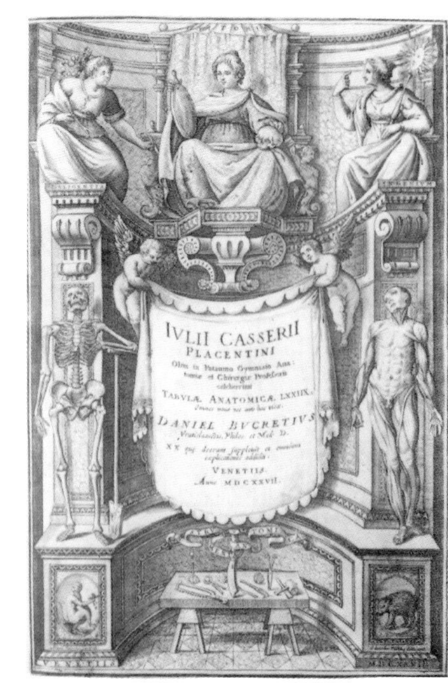

Title page from: Julius Casserius, "Tabulae Anatomicae," 1627 / Titelseite.

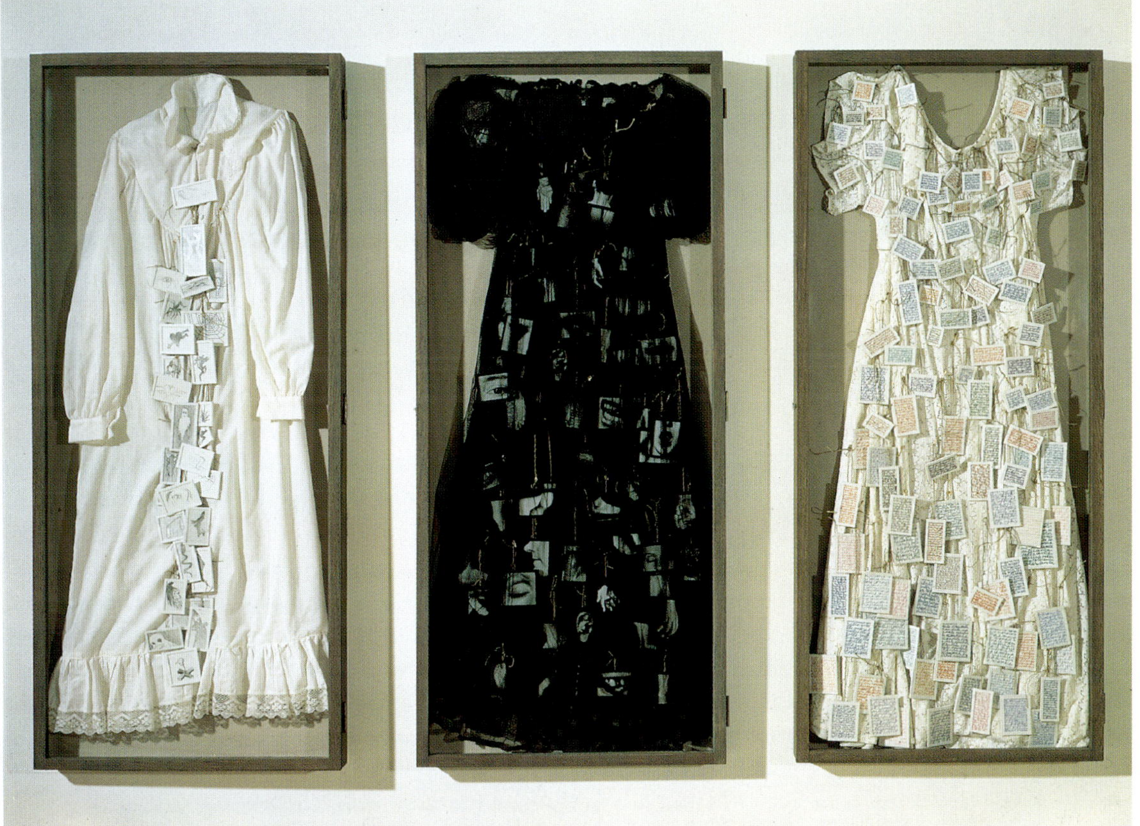

an einer weiteren theatralischen Präsentation der Vergänglichkeit des menschlichen Körpers: dem anatomischen Theater. Seziert vor einem Publikum gelehrter und wissbegieriger Männer, wurde der geöffnete, zwischen Tod und Leben «suspendierte» menschliche Leib zum Memento mori für die Lebenden. Auf einer berühmten Radierung des Leidener Anatomiesaals aus dem Jahr 1608 sehen wir im Publikum, das sich um die Bühne, auf der ein Anatom seine Kunst vorführt, versammelt hat, vereinzelt menschliche und tierische Skelette. Sie halten Bücher mit Inschriften, die vor der Vergänglichkeit der menschlichen Existenz und der Strafe warnen, welche die Menschheit am Tag des jüngsten Gerichts erwartet, während der Anatom den aufgeschnittenen weiblichen Körper mit einem Form und Anordnung der Organe beschreibenden Text vergleicht, den er dem Publikum sogleich erklären wird. Zur Unterstreichung der heiklen Verknüpfung von materialistischer und allegorischer Lesart des dargebotenen sezierten Körpers wird oben auf der Radierung nicht nur der Titel der Szene genannt, *AMPHITEATRVM ANATOMICVM LVDVNO BATAVORVM*, sondern überdies schweben darüber allegorische Darstellungen von Adam und Eva; ein Hinweis darauf, dass der sezierte Körper nicht nur als Text zu lesen ist, der bereits existierende Schriften über die menschliche Anatomie bestätigen soll, sondern auch allegorisch auf die wahre Bedeutung der menschlichen Existenz verweist. Die Zurschaustellung des Todes erinnert an den Sündenfall des Menschen im Paradies und die daraus resultierende Sterblichkeit, gegen die der feierliche Reliquienkult nur ein schwaches Heilmittel darstellt.

Messager begreift sich selbst als Anatomin oder «Vivisektionistin» unserer Zeit. In Interviews betont sie stets, dass der Körper im Mittelpunkt ihrer Arbeit steht. Sie zeigt ihn nie als Ganzes, sondern immer nur als Fragment, um anzudeuten, dass wir, obwohl wir in unserem Körper und durch ihn in der Welt weilen, kaum eine Vorstellung davon haben, wie dieser Körper aussieht. Aus diesem Grund versucht sie das Innere des Körpers zu erkunden und sein Blut, seine Säfte in ihrer Kunst zu veranschaulichen. Man ist versucht, ihre Arbeit als eine ironische und weibliche Wiederaufnahme des Treibens von Anatomiekünstlern wie Mary Shelleys Doktor Frankenstein zu begreifen. Statt Beinhäuser und Gräber besucht sie Tierpräparatoren und Kaufhäuser, aber auch sie verwendet die unbelebten Materialien, die sie dort findet, um eine neue Spezies zu erschaffen: monströse und makabre hybride Körper, die, weit davon entfernt, die Sterblichkeit zu überwinden, emblematisch auf die Vergänglichkeit verweisen. Dabei spielt sie mit dem männlich besetzten Begriff des romantischen Genies, während sie zugleich auf parodistische Weise den Akt der künstlichen Wiedererweckung für sich in Anspruch nimmt, der normalerweise einem männlichen Schöpfer vorbehalten ist. Denn ihre Nachinszenierung des anatomischen Theaters und des Reliquienkults hat immer auch etwas Spielerisches. Wenn sie etwa in ihrer Arbeit ENSEMBLE (1998) einen taxidermisch präparierten Fuchspelz mit mehreren ebenfalls «ausgeweideten» und umgestülpten Spielzeugtieren zusammenstückt, benutzt sie betont alltägliche Gegenstände, um sich ironisch mit der Ikonographie der barocken Emblematik auseinander zu setzen. Sie kreiert Embleme, die jedoch eher komisch als erschreckend und eher albern als heroisch sind. Doch eben weil das Material uns so vertraut ist, wirken ihre makabren Neukompositionen so verstörend. Das Alltägliche wird monströs und wir werden aus unserer selbstgefälligen Gewissheit, mit allen Empfindungen und Begierden unserer Lebenswelt vertraut zu sein, aufgeschreckt.

Mit dieser beunruhigenden Geste spielt sie implizit auf eine andere postmoderne Variante der barocken Theatralität an: den Schlitzerfilm. Wes Cravens Filmtrilogie *Scream* – eine Erforschung des dunklen Zusammenhangs zwischen gewaltsamer Körpermisshandlung, ritueller Zurschaustellung von Körperteilen und schwarzer Komödie – lokalisiert die unausweichliche Präsenz von Tod und Vergänglichkeit genau dort, wo wir meinen, davor am sichersten zu sein: am «heimischen Herd». Seine psycho-

pathischen Mörder, die ihre Opfer ausweiden und die Leichen zur Schau stellen, bestätigen Benjamins Hypothese: Die Produktion der Leiche verwandelt sich in eine Wiederauferstehung des Körpers als Emblem; in dieser Form kehrt denn auch das verdrängte traumatische Wissen zurück und sucht die Familie heim. Wie Messagers Installationen fungieren auch Wes Cravens exzessive filmische Darstellungen aufgeschlitzter und zerstückelter Leiber mit ihrem Übermass an Leichen und deren ausgiebig und freudig inszenierter Textualisierung als «anatomische Theater» von heute. Beide bedienen sich der Mittel der barocken Rhetorik um genüsslich die Botschaft zu verkünden, dass der Tod stets mitten unter uns weilt. Doch wenn Messager diesen Kult um den vergänglichen und verstümmelten Körper mitfeiert, so tut sie dies wie Craven im Stil der schwarzen Komödie und um die irritierende Nähe von spielerischer Kreativität und Zerstörung hervorzuheben. Die Freude daran, das eigene Lieblingsspielzeug aufzuschlitzen und wieder zusammenzusetzen, ist eines der Grundelemente kindlichen Spiels, so wie das Kind ja auch in seiner Phantasie den Körper der Mutter fragmentiert um seine narzisstischen Wünsche zu befriedigen. Die Botschaft, die auf der Bühne von Messagers privatem anatomischem Theater verkündet wird, ist vielleicht deshalb so beunruhigend, weil sie etwas über unsere körperliche Existenz verrät, was wir lieber nicht wahrhaben möchten. Wenn vertraute Gegenstände und die Vorstellung körperlicher Unversehrtheit unheimlich werden, müssen wir erkennen, dass das Intime einen Kern hat, der äusserlich, undurchdringlich und unfassbar ist. Und doch, so beunruhigend die Erkenntnis dieser Fremdheit, die unsere Geborgenheitsphantasien bedroht, sein mag: Ganz so fremd ist sie uns auch wieder nicht. Wir haben immer gewusst, dass das Neuzusammensetzen uns deshalb befriedigt, weil es Elemente des Zertrümmerns, Sezierens und Zerlegens beinhaltet. Der uns vertrauteste Körper ist der eigene, und gerade den sehen und erfahren wir immer nur bruchstückhaft.

(Übersetzung: N. G. Schneider/W. Parker)

1) Walter Benjamin, *Ursprung des deutschen Trauerspiels*, Suhrkamp, Frankfurt am Main 1972, S. 245.
2) Ebenda, S. 246.

MAURIZIO CATTELAN,
>BORN 1960 IN PADOVA, ITALY,
LIVES AND WORKS IN
NEW JERSEY.
>GEBOREN 1960 IN PADUA,
ITALIEN, LEBT UND ARBEITET
IN NEW JERSEY.

YAYOI KUSAMA,
>BORN 1929 IN MATSUMOTO-SHI,
NAGANO-KEN, JAPAN,
LIVES AND WORKS IN TOKYO.
>GEBOREN 1929 IN MATSUMOTO-SHI,
NAGANO-KEN, JAPAN,
LEBT UND ARBEITET IN TOKIO.

KARA WALKER,
>BORN 1969 IN STOCKTON,
CALIFORNIA, LIVES AND WORKS
IN PROVIDENCE, RHODE ISLAND.
>GEBOREN 1969 IN STOCKTON,
KALIFORNIEN, LEBT UND ARBEITET
IN PROVIDENCE, RHODE ISLAND.

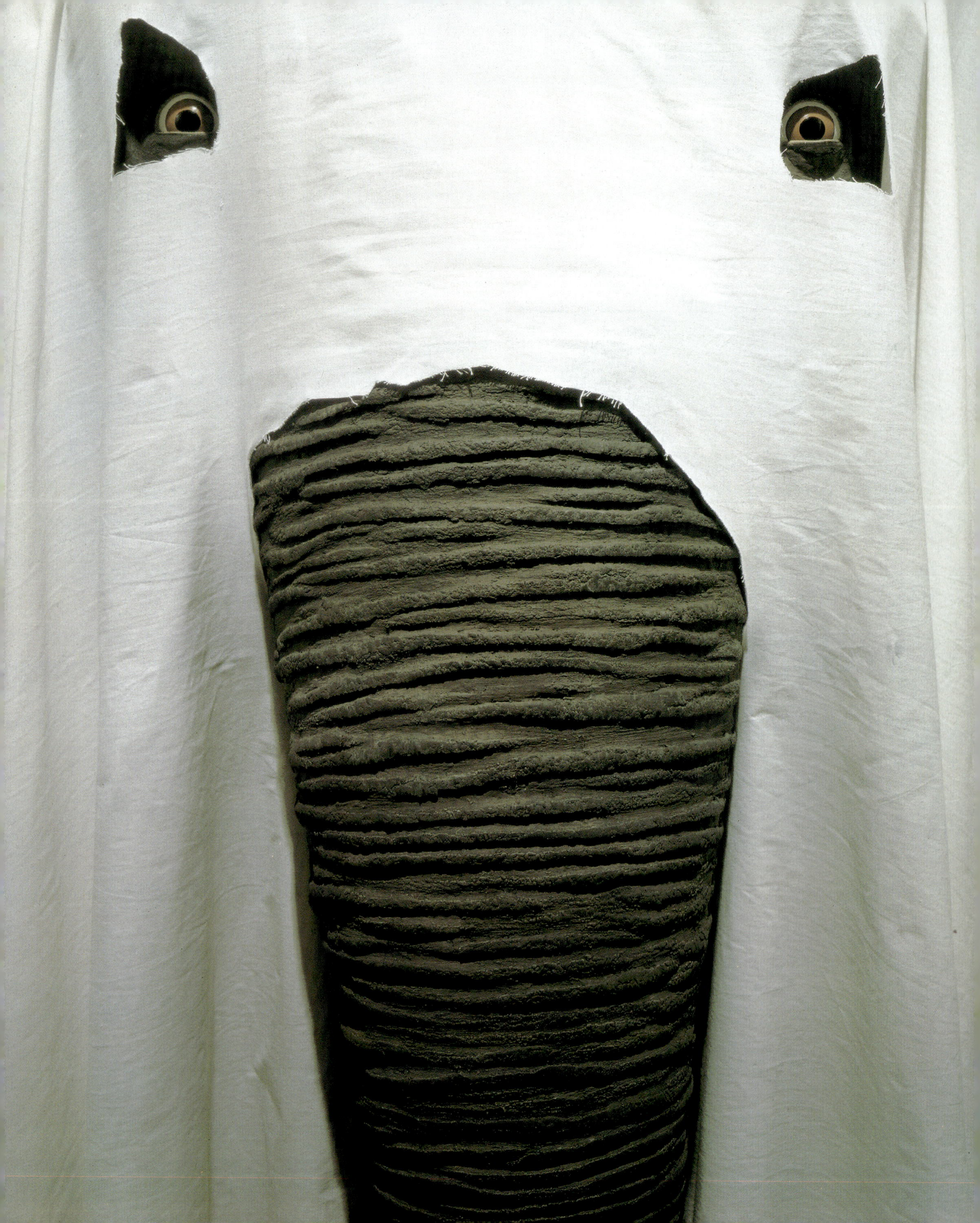

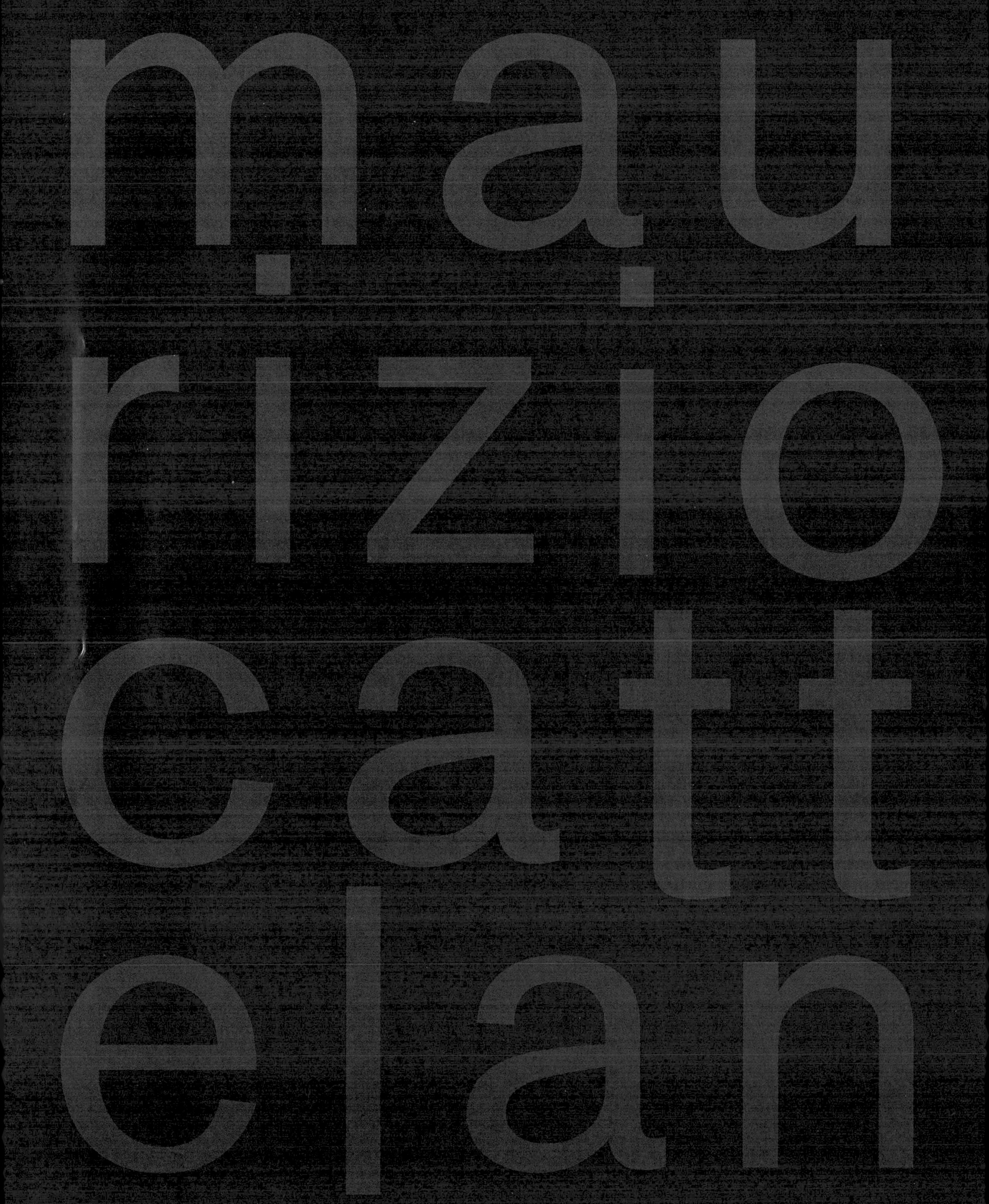

mau
rizio
catt
elan

NICOLAS BOURRIAUD

A Grammar of Visual Delinquency

It is quite a bit easier to situate the work of Maurizio Cattelan in his time than to articulate verbally the logic governing his figures in as much as this elusive artist proceeds by successive effects of captivation. Faced with each new apparition, one is always tempted to say: "No, it's not possible. He can't exhibit that, what audacity… ." Cattelan's laugh is vast, and the perpetual upping of the ante within his comic mechanism ends up creating a kind of screen around his work, discouraging analysis and leaving one flabbergasted. What audacity!

Zorro (on Sound Effects as Method)

UNTITLED (1993), acrylic on canvas, 80 x 100 cm. The canvas is slashed in three places, creating the Z of Zorro in the style of Lucio Fontana. In this way

Maurizio Cattelan establishes his character as the masked avenger who has sworn to shed light on the human comedy, through the filter of the art system. In this apparently very simple work, at once minimal and immediately accessible, one finds all the rhetorical figures that make up his work: the caricatured misappropriation of works of the past; the moralizing fable; and above all, that insolent manner of breaking and entering into our value system, which is the main feature of his style. But this unique work also features the moral position informing all of Cattelan's work: that of taking forms literally. What is initially striking about UNTITLED (1993) is of course its caricature of the series of *Concetti spaziali* made by Fontana in the fifties. The laceration of a canvas, for Fontana, was a symbolic gesture. Cattelan, on the other hand, shows us this act in its more current sense, as the use of a weapon and the gesture of a comic traitor. Going by the letter, not the spirit, each of his works reduces the spirit of art to the letter of social comedy, and tells a story of demystification punctuated with sardonic laughter and progressing by a succession of spoofs and gags.

NICOLAS BOURRIAUD is an art critic and curator based in Paris. He is the co-director of the Palais de Tokyo, a Parisian kunsthalle which will open in 2001. His essay "Relational Aesthetics" will be published in English this fall.

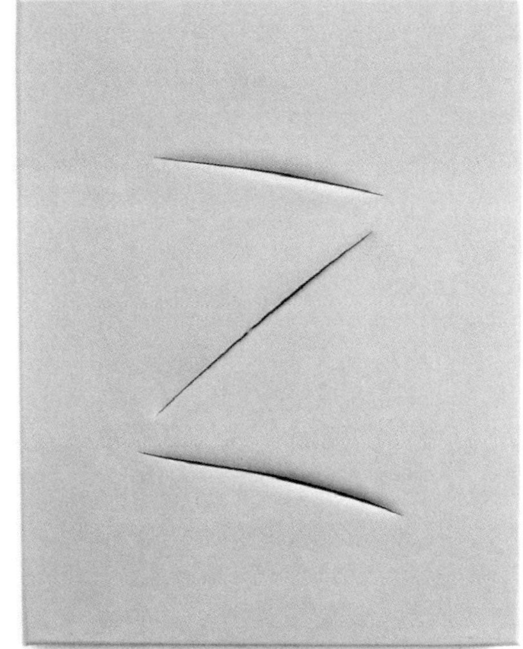

Page / Seite 32:
MAURIZIO CATTELAN, NOT AFRAID
OF LOVE, 2000, detail, polyester styrene resin,
paint, fabric, 81 x 123 x 54" /
KEINE ANGST VOR DER LIEBE, Polystyrol,
Farbe, Stoff, 205,7 x 312,4 x 137,3 cm.
(PHOTO: ATTILIO MARANZANO)

MAURIZIO CATTELAN, UNTITLED, 1986,
acrylic on canvas, 40 x 29½" / OHNE
TITEL, Acryl auf Leinwand, 101,5 x 75 cm.
(PHOTO: PEGGY LEBOUF)

Fontana's gesture, which is vertical, opens onto the infinity of space, onto that modernistic optimism that imagined a beyond behind the canvas, a sublime realm within our reach. Its re-enactment (in zigzags) by Cattelan takes Fontana to ridiculous extremes by identifying him with a more or less contemporary Walt Disney TV series. The zigzag is the movement most used in Cattelan's oeuvre: It is comical in essence, Chaplinesque, and corresponds to a wandering among things. The slalom-artist makes feints, his wavering motion provokes laughter, but he encircles forms and lightly brushes against them even while relegating them to the status of accessories and decor. UNTITLED (1993) is an entirely programmatic work, in terms of form as well method: The zigzag is Cattelan's trademark. If one considers the numerous "remakes" he has done, one notices that they all share a similar method: The formal structure seems familiar, but gradually and insidiously new layers of meaning radically upset our perceptions. Maurizio Cattelan's forms always present us with familiar elements accompanied, in an offstage voice, by cruel or sarcastic anecdotes.

In Jacques Tati's *Mon Oncle,* a man sees a concierge plucking a chicken. He then imitates the bird's clucking, startling the poor woman into thinking that the animal has come back to life. Most of Cattelan's works produce a similar effect, such as when he "sound-effects" the voice of Zorro onto a Fontana, or when one hears the Red Brigades while standing before a work that recalls Smithson or Kounellis, or when one thinks of a grave when looking at a hole in the style of the earthworks of the sixties. This is a THX version of conceptual art, remastered by a perverse sound engineer…[1]

The Bad Student

When he installed a living donkey in a New York gallery under a crystal chandelier, Cattelan was indirectly alluding to the twelve horses exhibited by Jannis Kounellis at the Attico gallery in Rome in 1969. But the work's title, WARNING! ENTER AT YOUR OWN RISK. DO NOT TOUCH, DO NOT FEED, NO SMOKING, NO PHOTOGRAPHS, NO DOGS, THANK YOU (1993), radically reversed the work's meaning, stripping it of

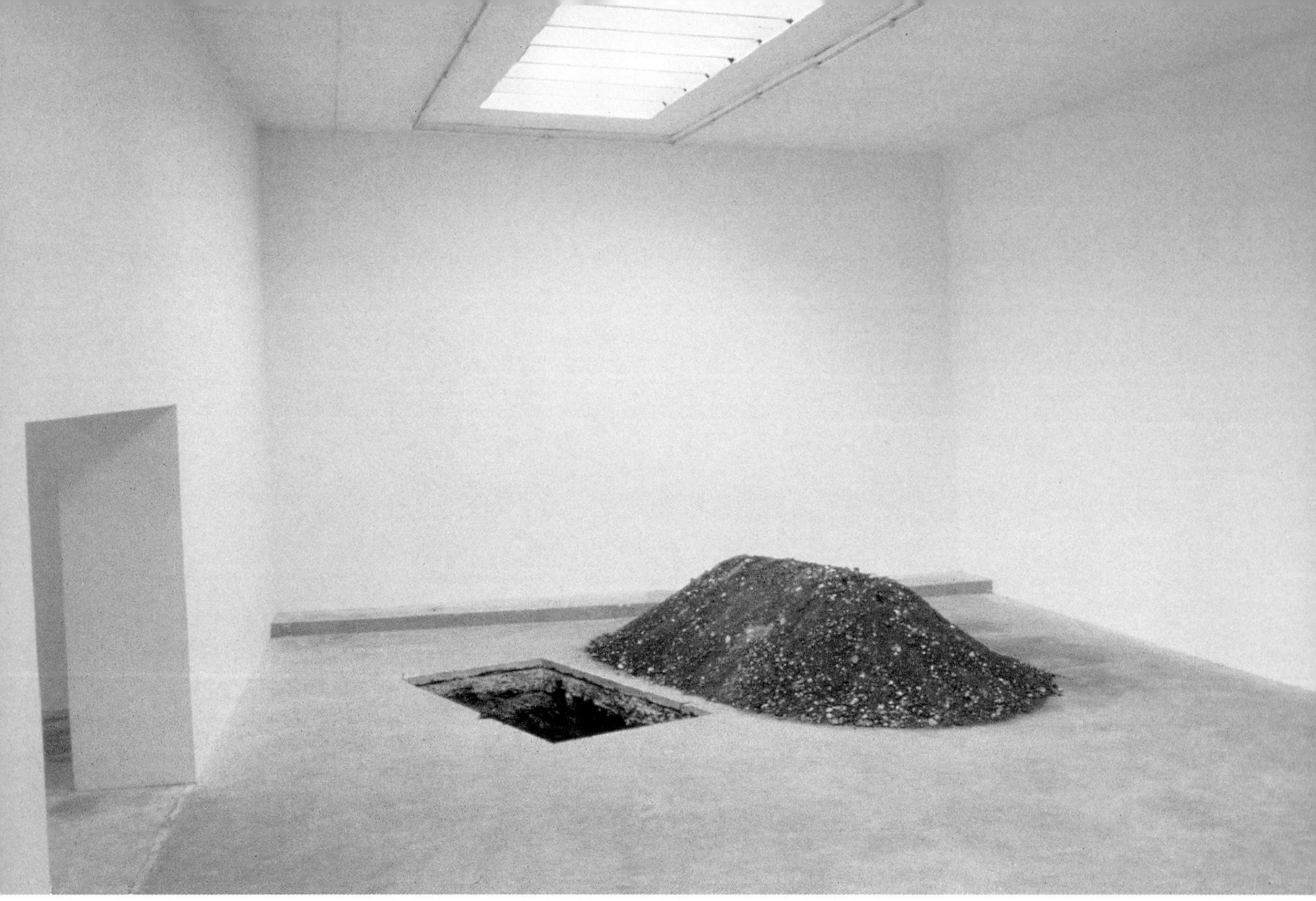

historicity and vitalist symbolism and directing it towards the system of representation, in the most spectacular sense of the term: that is, what we see is a burlesque spectacle under heavy surveillance, the outer boundaries of which are entirely judicial. The living animal is not presented as beautiful or new, but as a proposition at once dangerous to the public and prodigiously problematic for the gallerist. The reference to Kounellis is not gratuitous, since it is so clearly apparent that Arte Povera constitutes the principal formal matrix of Maurizio Cattelan's work, as far as concerns the composition of his images and the placement of ready-made elements in space. The fact is that he rarely uses mass-produced or high-tech objects, as his formal register involves more natural elements (Kounellis, Penone) and anthropomorphic elements (Paolini, Boetti). This is not, however, a question of influences, much less an homage to Arte Povera, but instead a kind of linguistic "hard drive," a rather discrete one in fact, which reflects his Italian visual education.

In 1968, Pier Paolo Calzolari mounted UNTITLED (MALINA), an installation in which he presented an albino dog chained to a wall in an environment that featured a pile of dirt and blocks of ice. Again one is reminded of Cattelan's menagerie, with its horses, donkeys, dogs, ostriches, pigeons and squirrels. Except that these animals symbolize nothing, referring to no transcendent meaning, but are content to embody types, characters and situations. The symbolic universe created by Arte Povera or Joseph Beuys disintegrates in Cattelan under the pressure of an "evil

MAURIZIO CATTELAN, UNTITLED, 1997, ditch, earth, installation at Le Consortium, Dijon, France, 79 x 39½ x 59" / OHNE TITEL, Grube, Erde, 200 x 100 x 150 cm.
(PHOTO: MORIN)

MAURIZIO CATTELAN, UNTITLED, 1996, black-and-white photograph, 19¹¹/₁₆ x 23⅝" / OHNE TITEL, Schwarzweissphoto, 50 x 60 cm.
(PHOTO: ARMIN LINKE)

spirit" unleashed and forever undermining forms through contradiction and violently resisting all positive meaning.

This manner of turning modernist forms against the ideology to which they were born (against the modernist ideologies of emancipation, against the sublime), and also against the art milieu and its beliefs, attests more to the ferocity of Cattelan's caricatures than to any supposed cynicism. Some of his exhibitions, at first glance, might call to mind a Michael Asher or a Jon Knight in as much as they lay bare the economic and social structures of the art system by focusing on the gallerist or the exhibition space. Quickly, however, the conceptual reference gives way to another more diffuse impression, that of

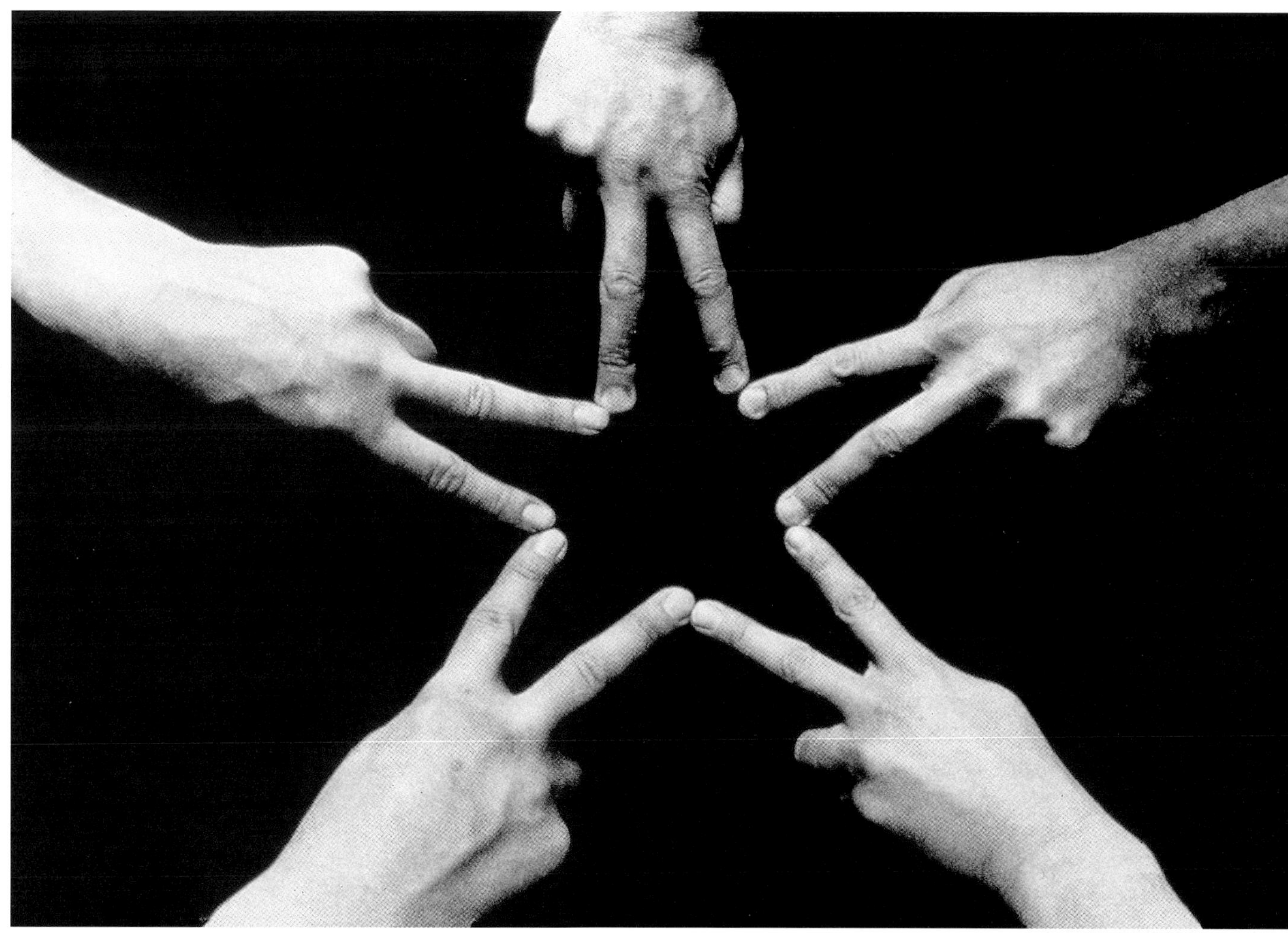

a real personalization of criticism, harking back to the form of the fable—as we shall later see—but also to a real will to undermine. Thus in 1993, Cattelan created a piece that took up the entire space of the Massimo De Carlo gallery in Milan and was only visible from the display window outside. Having explained his idea in an interview, the artist concluded by asserting: "I also wanted to see Massimo De Carlo outside the gallery for a month."

The wickedness of the eternal neer-do-well slouching at the back of the classroom.

One has the impression that Cattelan considers his formal repertoire to be an assortment of homework assignments and figures, in a kind of school program that the artist/class-clown takes great relish in turning into gags. One of his earliest important pieces, EDIZIONI DELL'OBBLIGO (Editions of Obligation, 1991) was made up of primary-school textbooks whose covers and titles had been modified by children in a kind of derisory revenge against all school programs. As for the cloth and fabric of Arte Povera and the anti-form of the sixties, these helped him... to flee the Castello di Rivara in 1992, when he was participating in his first important group show there: "I enjoyed watching what the other artists were doing, how they reacted to the situation. That work was not only metaphorical, it was also a tool: The night before the opening I let myself down from the window and ran away." The work presented was none other than a makeshift ladder made of sheets knotted together and hanging down the facade of the exhibition building.

Following the same principle, Cattelan, at "Manifesta II" in Luxembourg in 1998, exhibited an olive tree planted in a huge quadrilateral of earth. A hurried visitor might have taken it for a remake of Beuys or Penone; but in the end this vegetable element in no way participated in the meaning of the work, which was articulated around the offensive syntax developed by the artist, touching with his finger the physical and ideological boundaries of individuals and communities, testing the limits and patience of institutions.

Felix Gonzalez-Torres used an historicized formal repertory (minimal art, anti-form) to reveal ideological underpinnings and establish a new alphabet for combating sexual norms. Cattelan, for his part, directs the forms he manipulates towards conflict and comedy; through works of the most embarrassing, constraining and cumbersome sort he seeks conflicts with the administrators of the art system. The comedy he brings to light underscores the power relationships of this system, by means of narrative grids that divert the history of recent art in a burlesque direction. In a word, his conduct as an artist consists of orienting the forms he manipulates towards delinquency.

MAURIZIO CATTELAN, −76 400 000, 1992,

broken safe, detail / geknackter Safe.

(PHOTO: MAROSSI)

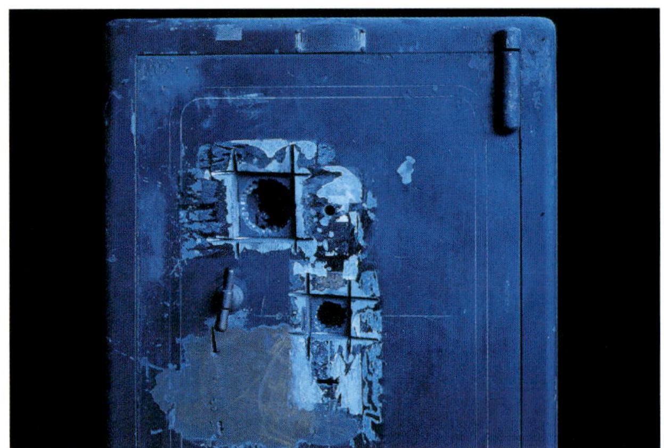

Appropriation as Burglary

−76 400 000 (1992): Cattelan combs the classifieds in search of safes belonging to burglarized institutions or individuals, then he exhibits these damaged safes such as he found them.

Thus, does the most emblematic of readymade objects in Cattelan's oeuvre make, once again, artistic gesture in the most literal sense possible? Appropriation, in Cattelan's work, becomes burglary. In other words, the Italian artist again translates the rhetori-

MAURIZIO CATTELAN, UNTITLED, 1998, olive tree, earth, water, wood, metal, plastic, installation, Casino de Luxemburg, "Manifesta 2," 26¼ x 16½ x 16½ ft / OHNE TITEL, Olivenbaum, Erde, Wasser, Holz, Metall, Plastikfolie, 800 x 500 x 500 cm. (PHOTO: ROMAN MENSING)

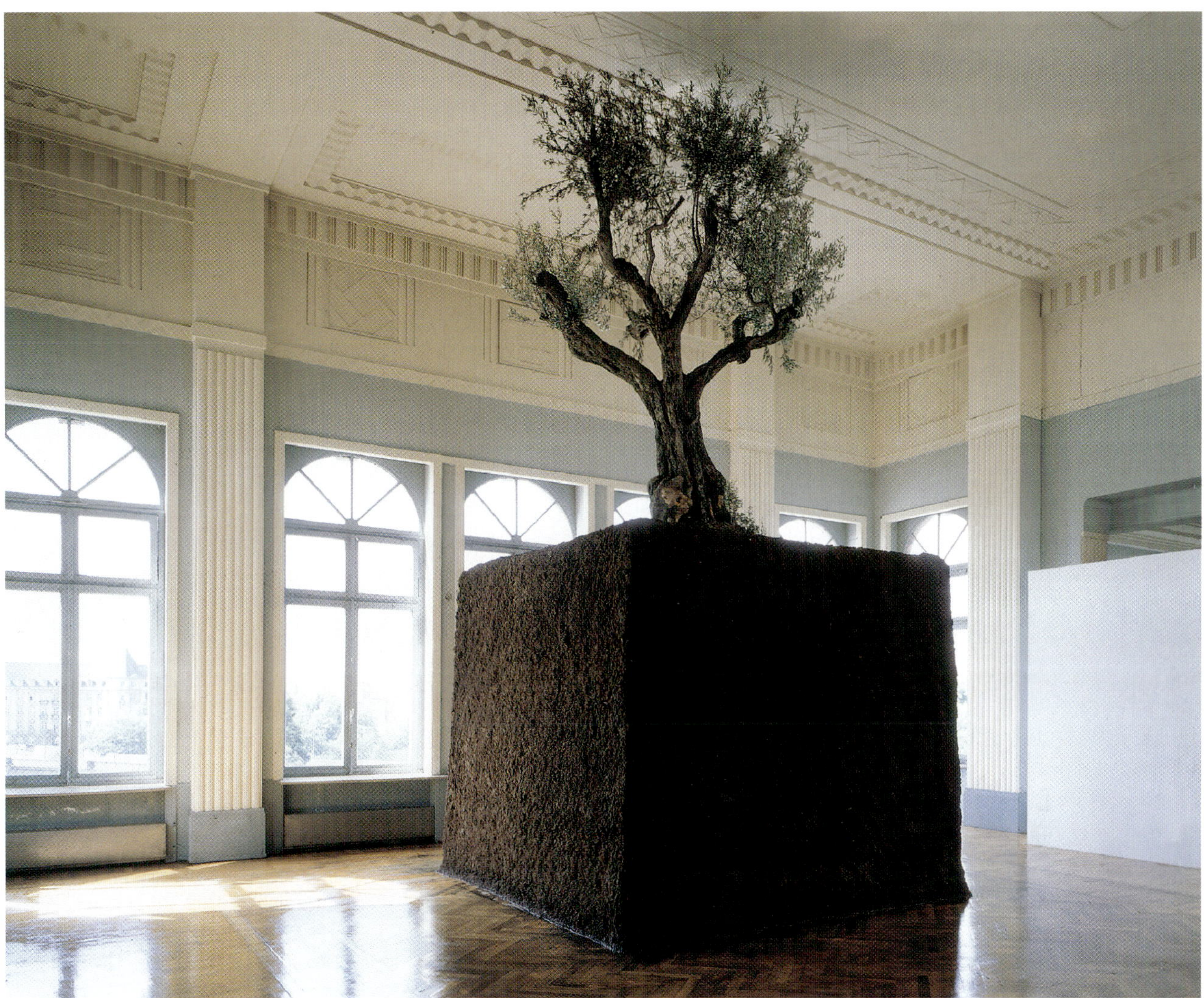

cal figures of modernity into the language of social violence. In fact, on the occasion of an exhibition in Amsterdam in 1996, Cattelan organized an actual break-in of the private gallery located opposite the Appel Foundation, exhibiting in the latter the products of his theft (ANOTHER FUCKING READYMADE, 1996)… To take another example, in LULLABY (1994), made up of two little piles, more or less rectangular in shape, of sacks of demolition rubble, wrapped in a sheet of transparent plastic, each of the two piles is set on top of a construction pallet. The material came from three edifices damaged by bomb attacks that bore the mark of the mafia: the Padiglione d'Arte Contemporanea in Milan, the Uffizi in Florence and a church in Rome. In a formal sense, LULLABY evokes Robert Smithson's "Nonsites," Kounellis's sacks of coal and the crude appearance of most Arte Povera, or, closer to us, Dan Peterman. But that all changes once we learn that this debris comes from the bombing of Italian institutions. Then one asks oneself other questions; one becomes a voyeur. The spectacle has won.

Pierre Joseph, in the catalogue to the "No Man's Time" exhibition (1991), enumerates the things one can do in an art institution today:

One can steal candies. Crush people with steel plates. (…) Spurt blood on the walls. Write graffiti, ride one's bicycle or skateboard in a public building without being arrested. Wear basketball shoes or come on horseback. One can make holes in the wall, or cracks or trenches in the floor. Burn tiles. Fire a machine gun. (…) Shoot at airplanes. Spy on the planet. Paint everything blue. Take up the whole space. Steal images and music. Work on Sunday. Keeping all of this in mind, one might think we are being offered places for simulating freedom and virtual experiences.

Maurizio Cattelan evolves in these border areas. Often drawing inspiration from past actions and classic works from the avant-garde repertoire, he strives to push them outside the law. For most of his shows, he tries the patience, the financial means and ethical mettle of his hosts. What could be more mischievous, for example, than to list the defeats of the British national soccer team on a kind of war memorial, for an exhibition in Great Britain?

Fables in THX Sound

This delinquent attitude does not, however, imply an absence of morals, quite the contrary. However much Cattelan may remove the bones from modernist forms and reconstitute them in the form of skeletons, as with the animals in LOVE LASTS FOREVER (1997), his formal universe is no less strongly marked by the classic form of the fable. This latter work, along with its counterpart, LOVE SAVES LIFE, indeed possesses all the technical characteristics of the fable: sharp opposition between two principles (love/flesh, love's end/skeleton); a clearly moralistic title; and an enactment of animal characters. Like Aesop or Jean de La Fontaine, Cattelan the fabulist uses animal imagery to denounce the failings of the human comedy and provoke laughter at people's expense. How does he explain the figure of the donkey at the New York show in 1994?

"My first idea was too expensive. My second idea was not possible to realize. So I felt like a donkey."

The work is recounted like a fable, with the clarity of a proverb and a punch line that justifies the meaning. The artist is the donkey who backpedals when asked to step forward, the stubborn, somewhat stupid animal that rejects authority, even if he must perform the thankless task of bearing the onus of art history. But he may also become a pet dog for group exhibitions (CHEAP TO FEED, 1998, stuffed animal) or a pigeon threatening the visitors at the Venice Biennale from its perch (TOURISTS, 1997, stuffed pigeons). Or the ostrich that refuses to look at the world around him, sticking his head in the ground (UNTITLED, 1997, stuffed ostrich).

This purified narrative mode, refined to its simplest expression, is fable itself, the preeminent tool of moralists. As in La Bruyère's *Caractères*, Cattelan classifies and caricatures his relationships as so many human types: thus two of his gallerists become a pair of lions (TARZAN & JANE, 1993) and a third had to carry on his shoulders the crushing image of his former patroness. Similarly, in 1993, he compelled his Parisian gallerist, Emmanuel Perrotin, to wear for the duration of the show a grotesque rabbit/pink phallus costume, which of course corresponded to a personal judgement of his lifestyle…

Cattelan takes aim at the system only through specific individuals: His field of intervention is relational, never abstract, and always disturbing to those who invite him and to the art establishment in general. It is this strategy of personalization, and the explosive charge detonated by his burlesque re-reading of the history of forms, that makes Cattelan's art, in the wake of Tati, one of the great comic works of our age.

(Übersetzung: Stephen Sartarelli)

1) THX: Cinema sound technique.

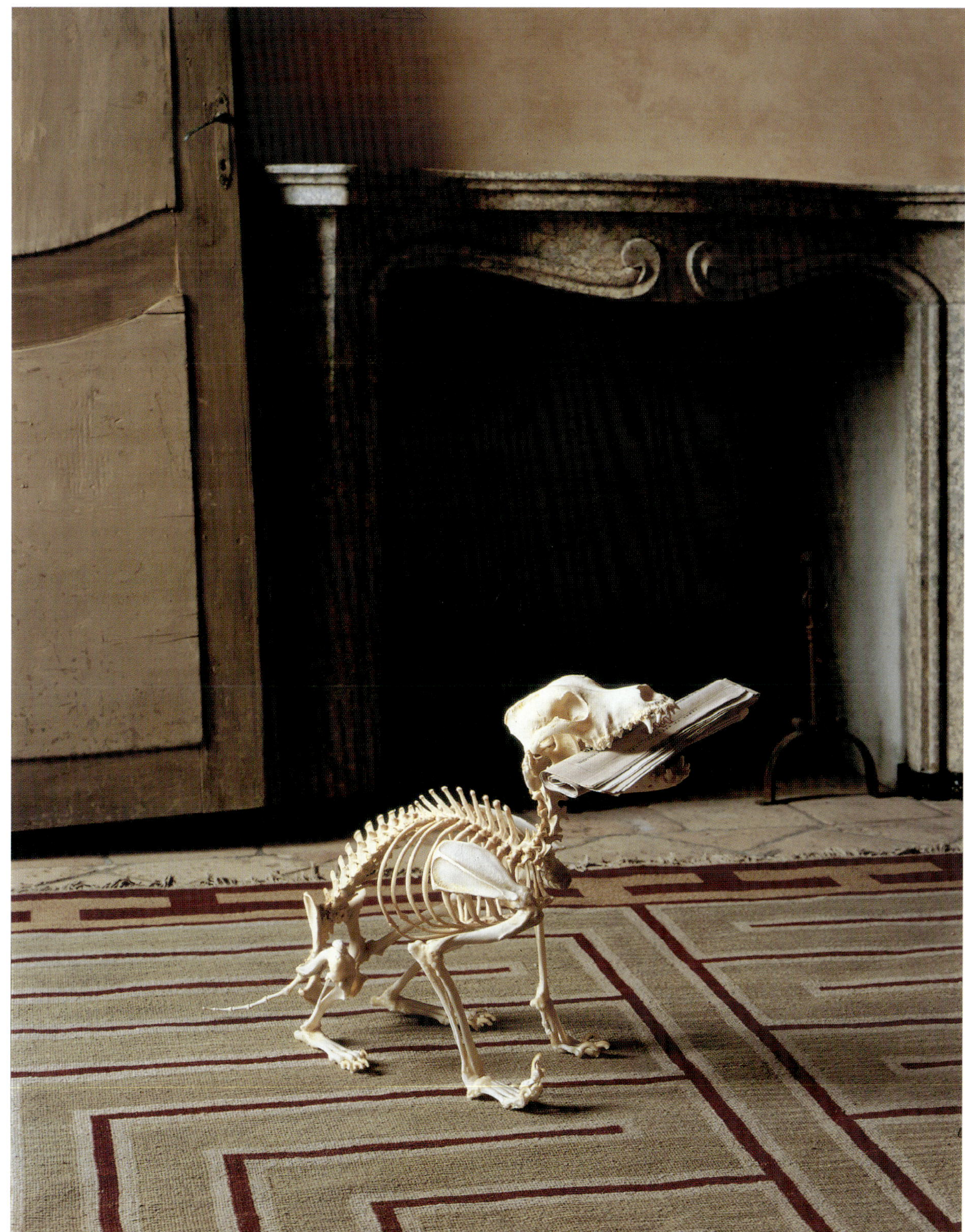

MAURIZIO CATTELAN, PLUTO, 1998, skeleton of a dog, newspaper, lifesize installation, Museum für Gegenwartskunst, Zürich / Hundeskelett, Zeitung. (PHOTO: MARANZANO)

NICOLAS BOURRIAUD

Eine Grammatik des künstlerischen Schurkenstreichs

Es ist weitaus einfacher, Maurizio Cattelans Schaffen zeitlich einzuordnen, als die Logik, der seine Figuren gehorchen, mit Worten zu erklären, setzt dieser schwer fassbare Künstler bei seiner Arbeit doch auf fortlaufende Überraschungseffekte. Bei jedem neuen Werk ist man versucht zu sagen: Nein, das ist nicht möglich, das kann er doch nicht ausstellen, er hat es tatsächlich gewagt… Cattelans Lachen ist unbändig und sein unentwegtes Sich-selbst-Überbieten

in der Produktion komischer Situationen lässt eine Art Schutzschild um seine Arbeit entstehen, der den Willen zur Analyse lähmt und einen verblüfft zurücklässt. Was für eine Frechheit!

Zorro (das Begleitgeräusch als Methode)

OHNE TITEL (1993), Acryl auf Leinwand, 80 x 100 cm. Die Leinwand weist drei Einschnitte im Stil von Lucio Fontana auf, die zusammen das Z von Zorro bilden. Maurizio Cattelan schlüpft also in die Rolle des maskierten Rächers, der sich geschworen hat, im Rahmen des Kunstbetriebs die menschliche Komödie unter die Lupe zu nehmen. In seinem scheinbar

NICOLAS BOURRIAUD ist Kunstkritiker und Kurator sowie Kodirektor des Palais de Tokyo, einer neuen Kunsthalle, die 2001 in Paris eröffnet wird. Zu seinen jüngsten Publikationen gehört der Essay *Formes de vie: l'art moderne et l'invention de soi*, Denoël, Paris 1999.

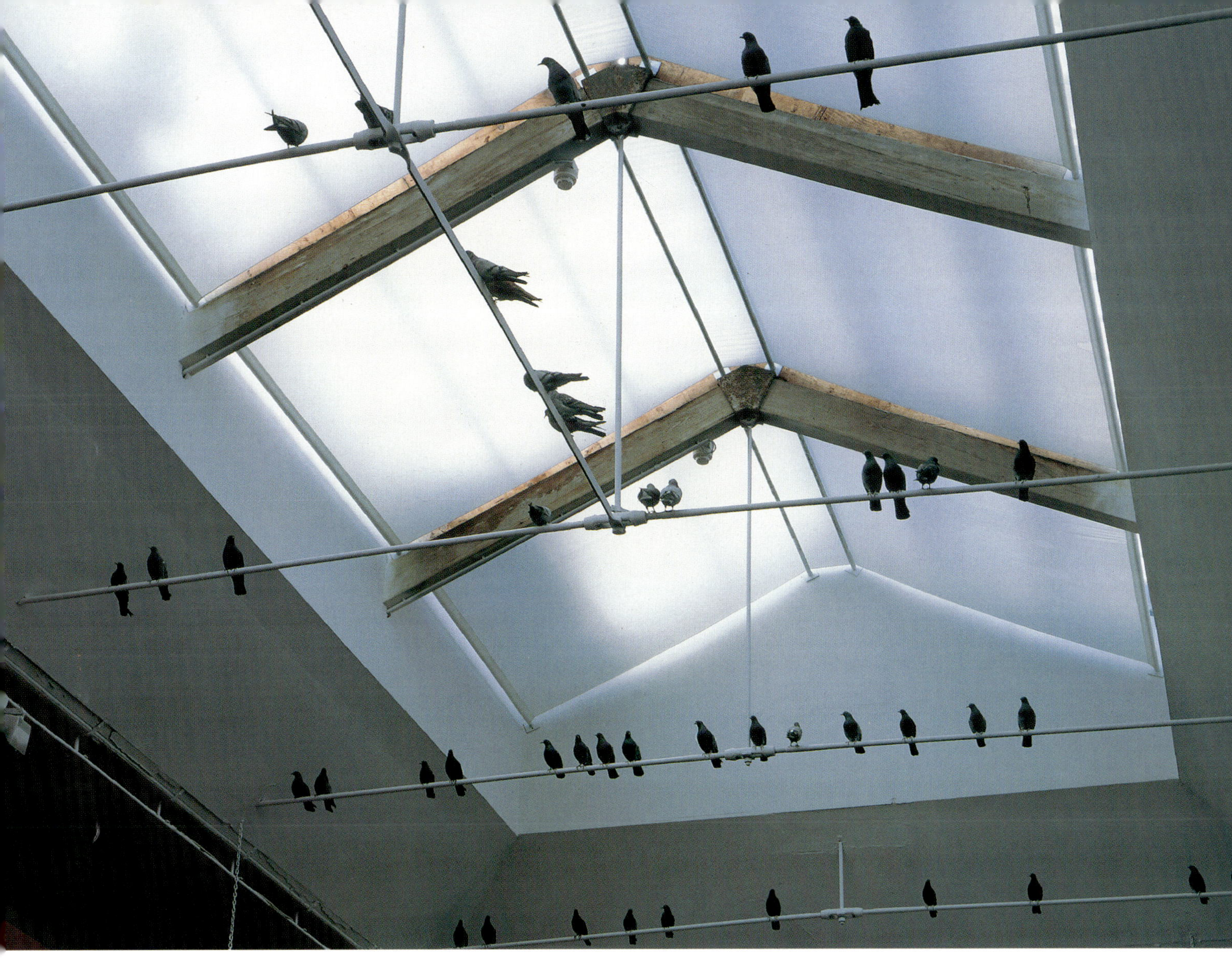

ganz einfachen, zugleich minimalen und unmittelbar zugänglichen Werk findet man alle rhetorischen Elemente, die sein Schaffen ausmachen: den karikierend verzerrenden Umgang mit Werken aus der Vergangenheit, die moralische Fabel, aber vor allem die unverschämte Art, unser Wertsystem aufzubrechen, die seinen Stil geradezu ausmacht. Aber dieses einzigartige Werk zeugt auch von der moralischen Haltung, die Cattelans Schaffen prägt: Formen wörtlich zu verstehen. Was bei OHNE TITEL (1993) auf den ersten Blick auffällt, ist natürlich das Karikieren von Fontanas Serie der *Concetti spaziali* aus den 50er Jahren. Für Fontana war das Aufschlitzen der Leinwand eine symbolische Geste. Cattelan dagegen führt uns diesen Akt in seinem geläufigeren Sinn

vor, als Verwendung einer Waffe und als Gebärde eines Filmschurken. Der Buchstabe kommt vor dem Geist: Jedes seiner Werke reduziert den Geist der modernen Kunst auf den Buchstaben der Gesellschaftskomödie, indem es eine demystifizierende Geschichte erzählt – eine Folge von Parodien und Gags, begleitet von höhnischem Gelächter.

Fontanas (vertikale) Geste war eine Öffnung hin zur Unendlichkeit des Raums, zum modernen Optimismus, in dessen Vorstellung eine Sphäre jenseits der Leinwand, ein erreichbares Erhabenes existierte. Deren Nachahmung (in Zickzackform) durch Cattelan gibt Fontana der Lächerlichkeit preis, indem sie ihn mit Walt Disneys TV-Serie *Zorro* in Verbindung bringt, die etwa zur selben Zeit entstand wie seine Werke. Zickzack ist die Bewegung, die in Cattelans Schaffen am häufigsten vorkommt: Es ist eine naturgemäss komische, chaplineske Bewegung, die für ein Hinundhergerissensein zwischen den Dingen steht. Der Slalom fahrende Künstler macht Täuschungsmanöver, seine unsichere Fahrt reizt zum Lachen, doch er kreist die Formen ein, die er dabei streift, und reduziert sie auf ihre Bedeutung als Beiwerk und Dekor. OHNE TITEL (1993) ist tatsächlich ein programmatisches Werk, sowohl was die Form als auch was die Methode betrifft: Der Zickzack ist Cattelans Markenzeichen.

Denkt man an seine zahlreichen «Reprisen», so erkennt man eine ähnliche Methode: Die formale Struktur erscheint vertraut, doch mit der Zeit tritt auf fast hinterhältige Weise eine neue Bedeutungsschicht zutage, die unsere Wahrnehmung radikal verändert. Maurizio Cattelans Formen zeigen uns immer vertraute Elemente, die von einer Off-Stimme mit grausamen oder sarkastischen Anekdoten begleitet werden.

In Jacques Tatis *Mon Oncle* sieht ein Mann, wie eine Concierge ein Huhn rupft. Er imitiert das Gackern des Tiers, worauf die arme Frau vor Schreck hochfährt, glaubt sie doch, das Huhn sei wieder lebendig geworden. Cattelans Werke haben meist eine ähnliche Wirkung – wenn er etwa einen Fontana mit dem Titelgesang der *Zorro*-Filme untermalt, wenn man vor einem Werk, das an Smithson oder Kounellis erinnert, die Roten Brigaden hört oder vor einem Loch im Stil der *Earthworks* der 60er Jahre an ein Grab denken muss. Eine THX-Version der Konzeptkunst, abgemischt von einem perversen Toningenieur...[1]

MAURIZIO CATTELAN, AC FORNITORE SUD VS. CESENA 12:47, 1991, black-and-white photograph of the players with STADIUM, 1991, soccer table of wood, glass, metal, plastic, 23 x 3¼ x 4 ft / Schwarzweissphoto der Spieler mit STADIUM, Fussballtisch aus Holz, Glas, Metall, Plastik, 700 x 100 x 120 cm. Galleria d'Arte Moderna, Bologna.

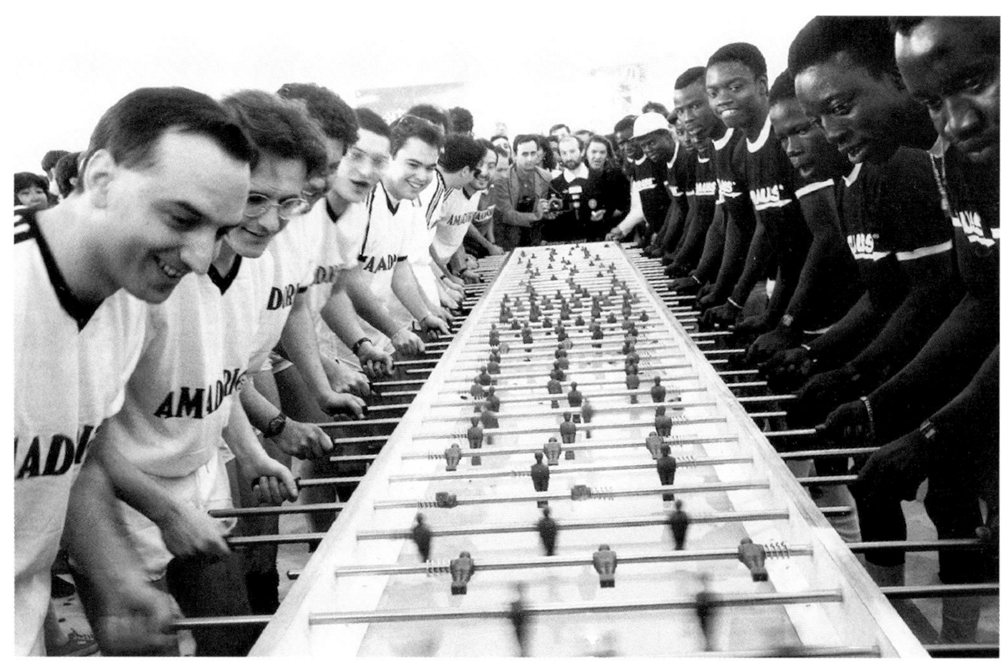

Der Tunichtgut

Wenn er in einer New Yorker Galerie unter einem Kristalllüster einen lebenden Esel ausstellt, spielt Cattelan indirekt auf die zwölf Pferde an, die Jannis Kounellis 1969 in der Galerie L'Attico in Rom zeigte. Doch der Werktitel – WARNING! ENTER AT YOUR OWN RISK. DO NOT TOUCH, DO NOT FEED, NO SMOKING, NO PHOTOGRAPHS, NO DOGS, THANK YOU (Warnung! Betreten auf eigenes Risiko. Bitte nicht berühren, bitte nicht füttern, Rauchen und Photographieren verboten, Hunde bleiben draussen. Danke. 1993) – ändert den Sinn des Werks radikal, beraubt es seiner Historizität und seiner vitalistischen Symbolik, um es im spektakulärsten Sinn des Wortes auf seine Darstellungsweise auszurichten: Was wir sehen, ist ein streng bewachtes, burleskes Spektakel, dessen Begrenzung rein rechtlicher Natur ist. Das lebende Tier wird weder als schön noch als neu dargestellt, sondern als ein Objekt, das für das Publikum gefährlich ist und für den Galeristen höchst problematisch. Auf Kounellis bezieht sich der Künstler nicht ohne Grund, wird doch klar erkennbar, dass die Arte Povera den wichtigsten Nährboden für Maurizio Cattelans Schaffen darstellt, vor allem was die Komposition seiner Bilder und die Anordnung der verwendeten Readymade-Elemente im Raum angeht. Tatsache ist, dass er kaum technische oder serienmässig hergestellte Gegenstände verwendet und sein formales Spektrum eher natürliche (Kounellis, Penone) oder anthropomorphe Elemente (Paolini, Boetti) beinhaltet. Es handelt sich dabei nicht um Einflüsse der Arte Povera und schon gar nicht um eine Hommage an diese, sondern um eine Art linguistischen, sehr diskreten «Festplattenspeicher», der das Italienische seiner künstlerischen Ausbildung widerspiegelt.

1968 zeigte Pier Paolo Calzolari OHNE TITEL (MALINA), eine Installation, in der nebst einem Erdhaufen und verschiedenen Eisblöcken ein an die Wand geketteter Albinohund zu sehen war. Führen wir uns nochmals die Menagerie von Cattelan vor Augen, die aus Pferden, Eseln, Hunden, Straussen, Tauben und Eichhörnchen besteht. Diese Tiere symbolisieren nichts, stehen für keinen transzendenten Wert, sondern begnügen sich damit, bestimmte Typen, Gestalten oder Situationen zu verkörpern: Die von der Arte Povera oder Joseph Beuys geschaffene symbolische Welt zerfällt in den Werken Cattelans unter dem Druck eines entfesselten «bösen Dämons», der die Formen ständig mit ihren Widersprüchen konfrontiert und sich allen positiven Werten strikt verweigert.

Diese Art, die modernistischen Formen gegen die Ideologie zu wenden, die sie hervorgebracht hat (moderne Emanzipationsideologien, die Idee des Erhabenen), aber auch gegen die Kunstwelt und ihre Überzeugungen, zeugt mehr von karikaturistischer Unbarmherzigkeit als für einen angeblichen Zynismus. Manche seiner Ausstellungen mögen auf den ersten Blick an einen Michael Asher oder Jon Knight erinnern, insofern, als sie den Galeristen oder den Ausstellungsraum zum Gegenstand haben und dadurch die wirtschaftlichen und sozialen Strukturen des Kunstbetriebs offen legen. Doch bald schon macht der Bezug auf die Konzeptkunst einem anderen, diffuseren Eindruck Platz, jenem einer echten Personalisierung der Kritik, die, wie wir später sehen werden, nicht nur auf die Form der Fabel zurückgeht, sondern auch auf das Bedürfnis Leute zu belästigen. So schuf Cattelan 1993 ein Werk, das den gesamten Raum der Galerie Massimo De Carlo in Mailand beanspruchte und nur durch das Schaufenster betrachtet werden konnte. Nachdem er in einem Gespräch seine Idee dargelegt hatte, bekannte der Künstler zum Schluss: «Ausserdem wollte ich Massimo de Carlo einen Monat lang aus der Galerie raushaben.»

Ein böser Schalk, wie der ewige Tunichtgut in der hintersten Schulbank, der nichts als Streiche ausheckt.

Man gewinnt den Eindruck, dass Cattelan sein formales Repertoire als Pflicht und zu erledigende Hausaufgaben betrachtet, im Rahmen eines Lehrplans, den der aufsässige Künstler und Klassenclown mit besonderem Vergnügen in Richtung Schabernack lenkt. Eine seiner ersten wichtigen Arbeiten, EDIZIONI DELL'OBBLIGO (Pflicht-Ausgaben, 1991) besteht aus Schulbüchern, deren Einbände und Titel von Schülern als eine Art höhnischer Rache gegen jeden Schulzwang verunstaltet wurden. Was die Tücher und Stoffe der Arte Povera und der Anti-

Form der 60er Jahre angeht, so schienen sie ihm tauglich… um aus dem Castello di Rivara zu entfliehen, wo er 1992 an seiner ersten wichtigen Gruppenausstellung teilnahm: «Es machte mir Spass zu beobachten, was die anderen Künstler machten, wie sie auf die Situation reagierten. Diese Arbeit war nicht bloss eine Metapher, sondern auch ein praktisches Hilfsmittel: In der Nacht vor der Eröffnung der Ausstellung seilte ich mich aus dem Fenster ab und ging.» Das gezeigte Werk war nichts anderes als eine behelfsmässige Leiter aus aneinander geknoteten Bettlaken, die an der Fassade des Ausstellungslokals herunterhing.

Nach demselben Prinzip stellt Cattelan 1998 an der «Manifesta II» in Luxemburg einen Olivenbaum aus, der auf ein riesiges, würfelförmiges Stück Erde gepflanzt ist. Ein Betrachter, der es eilig hat, könnte glauben, dass er es hier mit einem Remake von Beuys oder Penone zu tun hat; dabei trägt dieses pflanzliche Element nichts zur Bedeutung des Werks bei, die sich aus dem offensiven Vorgehen dieses Künstlers ergibt, der den Finger auf die physischen und ideologischen Grenzen des Einzelnen und der Gemeinschaft legt und dabei die Möglichkeiten und die Geduld der Institutionen auf die Probe stellt.

Felix Gonzalez-Torres verwendete ein historisch definiertes formales Repertoire (Minimal Art, Anti-Form), um ideologische Voraussetzungen zu enthüllen und ein neues Alphabet des Kampfes gegen sexuelle Normen zu entwickeln. Cattelan dagegen lenkt die Formen, mit denen er sich auseinander setzt, in Richtung Konflikt und Komödie. Er sucht durch immer unbequemer, einengender oder platzraubender werdende Arbeiten den Konflikt mit den Exponenten des Kunstbetriebs. Durch Inszenierungen, in denen er die Geschichte der neueren Kunst ins Burleske verzerrt, fördert er die Komik zutage, die den Kräfteverhältnissen im Kunstbetrieb zugrunde liegt. Mit einem Wort, sein künstlerisches Schaffen besteht darin, die Formen, mit denen er es zu tun hat, ins Schurkenhafte zu verkehren.

Appropriation als Einbruch

−76 400 000 (1992): Cattelan liest Meldungen über Einbrüche und setzt sich darauf mit den betroffenen Institutionen und Privatpersonen in Verbindung, um an die aufgebrochenen Geldschränke zu gelangen, die er dann so, wie er sie vorfindet, ausstellt.

So wird im symbolträchtigsten Readymade Cattelans die künstlerische Geste einmal mehr beim Wort genommen. Die Aneignung wird zum Einbruch, das heisst, der italienische Künstler übersetzt einmal mehr Stilfiguren der Moderne in die Sprache gesellschaftlicher Gewaltanwendung. 1996 organisiert Cattelan anlässlich einer Ausstellung in Amsterdam übrigens einen wirklichen Einbruch in eine private Galerie und stellt seine Beute unter dem Titel ANOTHER FUCKING READYMADE (Noch so ein verdammtes Readymade) in der gegenüberliegenden De Appel Foundation aus… Ein weiteres Beispiel ist LULLABY (Wiegenlied, 1994), das aus zwei beinah rechteckigen Haufen von Säcken mit Bauschutt besteht, die in eine transparente Plastikfolie gehüllt auf Transportpaletten liegen. Der Bauschutt stammt vom Padiglione d'Arte Contemporanea in Mailand, den Uffizien in Florenz und von einer Kirche in Rom, alles Gebäude, auf die damals Bombenanschläge verübt worden waren, die die Handschrift der Mafia trugen. Auf formaler Ebene erinnert LULLABY an Robert Smithsons *Nonsites*, Kounellis' Kohlensäcke und das karge Aussehen von Werken der Arte Povera oder – zeitlich etwas weniger weit zurückliegend – an Arbeiten Dan Petermans. Alles ändert sich, wenn man erfährt, dass dieser Schutt von Sprengstoffanschlägen auf italienische Institutionen stammt: Man stellt sich sofort andere Fragen und wird zum Voyeur. Die Sensationslust hat gesiegt.

Pierre Joseph zählt im Katalog zur Ausstellung «No Man's Time» (1991) auf, was man heutzutage in einer Kunstinstitution alles anstellen kann:

Man kann Bonbons aufspiessen, Leute mit Stahlplatten zermalmen. (…) Blut an die Wände spritzen. In einem öffentlichen Gebäude die Wände bekritzeln, Rad oder Skateboard fahren ohne verhaftet zu werden. Basketballschuhe tragen oder zu Pferd erscheinen. Man kann Löcher in die Wände bohren, am Boden Rinnen und Gräben ausheben. Leinwände verbrennen. Mit dem Maschinengewehr herumballern. (…) Auf Flugzeuge schiessen. Den Planeten ausspionieren. Alles blau anmalen. Den ganzen Raum in Anspruch nehmen. Bilder und Musik klauen. Am Sonntag arbeiten. Führt man sich all dies vor Augen, könnte man

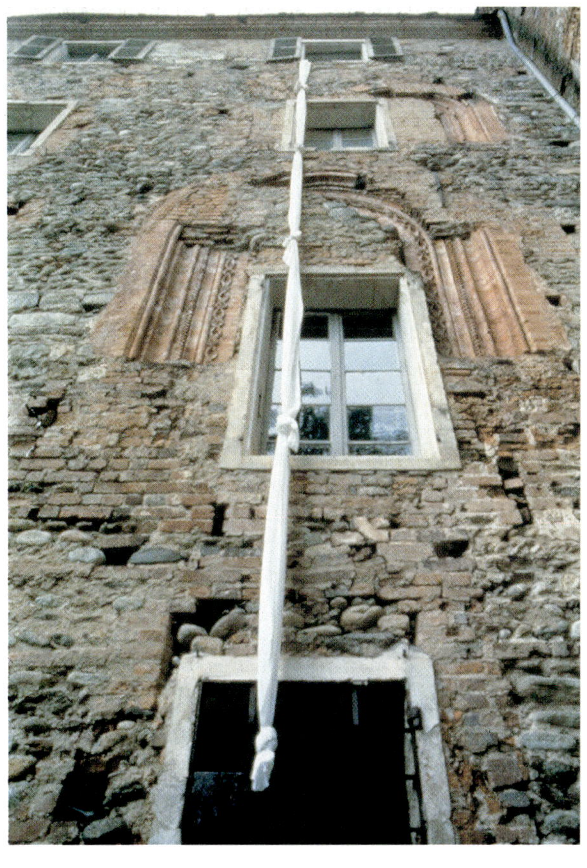

denken, dass man uns Orte zur Simulation von Freiheit und virtuellen Erfahrungen zur Verfügung stellt.

Maurizio Cattelan bewegt sich in diesen Grenzbereichen. Oftmals inspiriert von Aktionen der Vergangenheit und klassischen Werken des avantgardistischen Repertoires, bemüht er sich, diese ausserhalb der Schranken des Gesetzes weiterzuentwickeln; bei vielen seiner Ausstellungen stellt er die Geduld, die finanziellen Mittel und die ethische Haltung seiner Gastgeber auf eine harte Probe. Was könnte es beispielsweise Gemeineres geben, als anlässlich einer Ausstellung in Grossbritannien die Niederlagen der englischen Fussball-Nationalmannschaft auf einer Art Mahnmal aufzulisten?

Fabeln mit THX-Sound

Diese frevlerische Haltung deutet nicht auf eine fehlende Moral, ganz im Gegenteil. Cattelan kann noch so sehr die modernistischen Formen ausweiden und sie wie im Fall der Tiere in LOVE LASTS FOREVER (Liebe dauert ewig, 1997) als Skelette rekonstruieren, sein formales Universum ist deswegen nicht weniger stark von der klassischen Form der Fabel geprägt. Ja, dieses letztgenannte Werk und sein Pen-

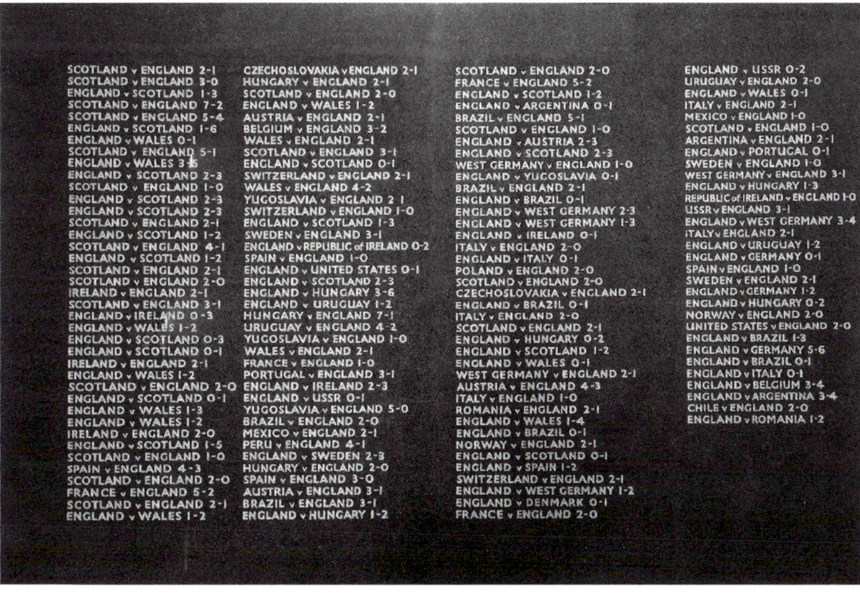

dant, LOVE SAVES LIFE (Liebe rettet Leben), besitzen alle typischen Merkmale der Fabel: Dualität der Begriffe (Liebe/Fleisch, Ende der Liebe/Skelett), ein offensichtlich moralischer Titel, Tierfiguren als Protagonisten. Wie Äsop oder Jean de La Fontaine verwendet der Fabeldichter Cattelan Tierfiguren, um die Widerwärtigkeiten der *Comédie humaine* anzuprangern und sich auf Kosten anderer Leute lustig zu machen. Wie erklärt er die Figur des Esels in seiner New Yorker Ausstellung von 1994?

«Meine erste Idee war zu teuer. Meine zweite war nicht realisierbar. Deshalb kam ich mir als Esel vor.»

Das Werk wird wie eine Fabel erzählt, mit der Klarheit des Sprichworts, mit einer Schlusspointe, die seine Aussage deutlich macht. Der Künstler ist der Esel, der zurückweicht, wenn man ihn auffordert, vorwärts zu gehen, das bockige und ziemlich dumme Tier, das sich der Autorität verweigert, selbst wenn es die undankbare Aufgabe erfüllen muss, die Last der Kunstgeschichte zu tragen. Aber er kann für eine Gruppenausstellung auch zum Begleithund werden – CHEAP TO FEED (Günstig im Unterhalt, 1998) – oder zur Taube, die von ihrer Stange aus die Besucher der Biennale von Venedig bedroht – TOURISTS (1997) –, oder aber zum Vogel Strauss, der den Kopf in den Sand steckt, um seine Umgebung nicht zur Kenntnis nehmen zu müssen – UNTITLED (1997).

Die Fabel, diese reine und auf den einfachsten Nenner gebrachte Erzählform, ist das Instrument par excellence des Moralisten. Wie La Bruyère in seinen *Caractères* karikiert Cattelan die Leute, mit denen er zu tun hat, und teilt sie in verschiedene Menschentypen ein: Zwei seiner Galeristen werden so zum Löwenpaar (TARZAN & JANE, 1993); ein Dritter muss das gigantische Bild seiner ehemaligen Chefin auf den Schultern tragen. 1993 nötigte er Emmanuel Perrotin, seinen Pariser Galeristen, während der ganzen Dauer der Ausstellung ein groteskes rosa Hasen-Phallus-Kostüm zu tragen, das wohlgemerkt Cattelans Meinung über dessen Lebensweise zum Ausdruck brachte…

Cattelan zielt nur auf dem Umweg über bestimmte Einzelpersonen auf das System: Sein Interventionsfeld ist beziehungsgebunden, niemals abstrakt, aber immer äusserst verstörend für jene, die ihn einladen, und für das Kunstestablishment als solches. Es ist diese Personalisierungsstrategie und die Sprengkraft seiner burlesken Lesart der Geschichte der Formen, die Cattelans Arbeiten zu einem der grossen komischen Œuvres unserer Zeit machen. Er wandelt auf den Spuren von Jacques Tati.

(Übersetzung: Irene Aeberli)

1) THX: Tontechnik für Kinofilme.

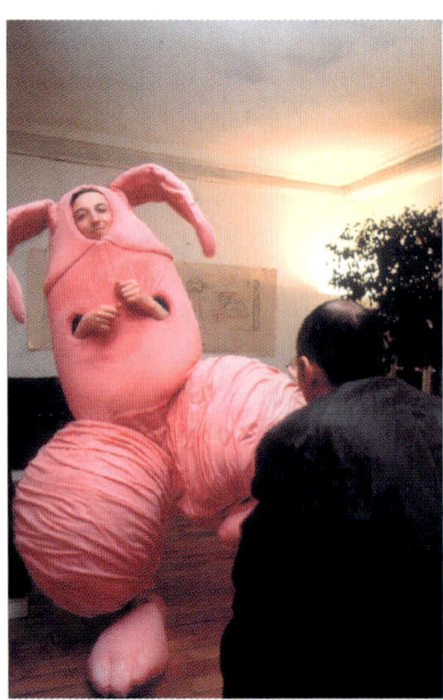 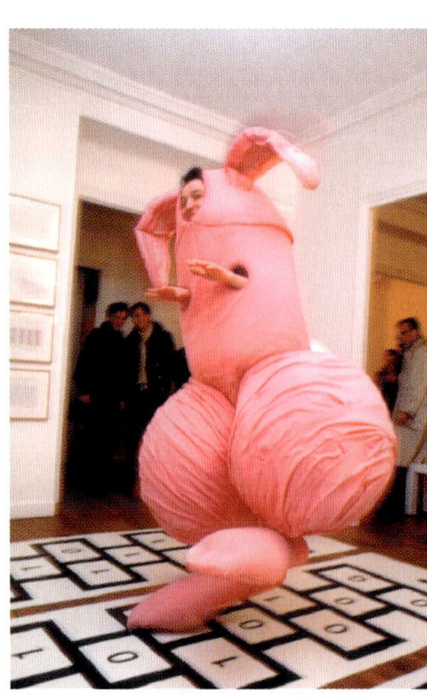 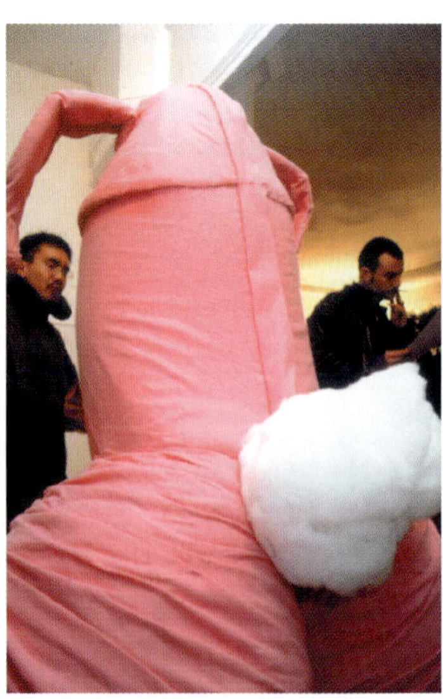

MAURIZIO CATTELAN, ERROTIN LE VRAI LAPIN / ERROTIN THE TRUE RABBIT, 1995, c-prints, Plexiglas, 72 x 48" (left) and 33½ x 23⅝" / ERROTIN, DAS WAHRE KARNICKEL, 183 x 122 cm (Bild links) bzw. 85 x 60 cm.
(PHOTOS: LIONEL FOURNEAUX)

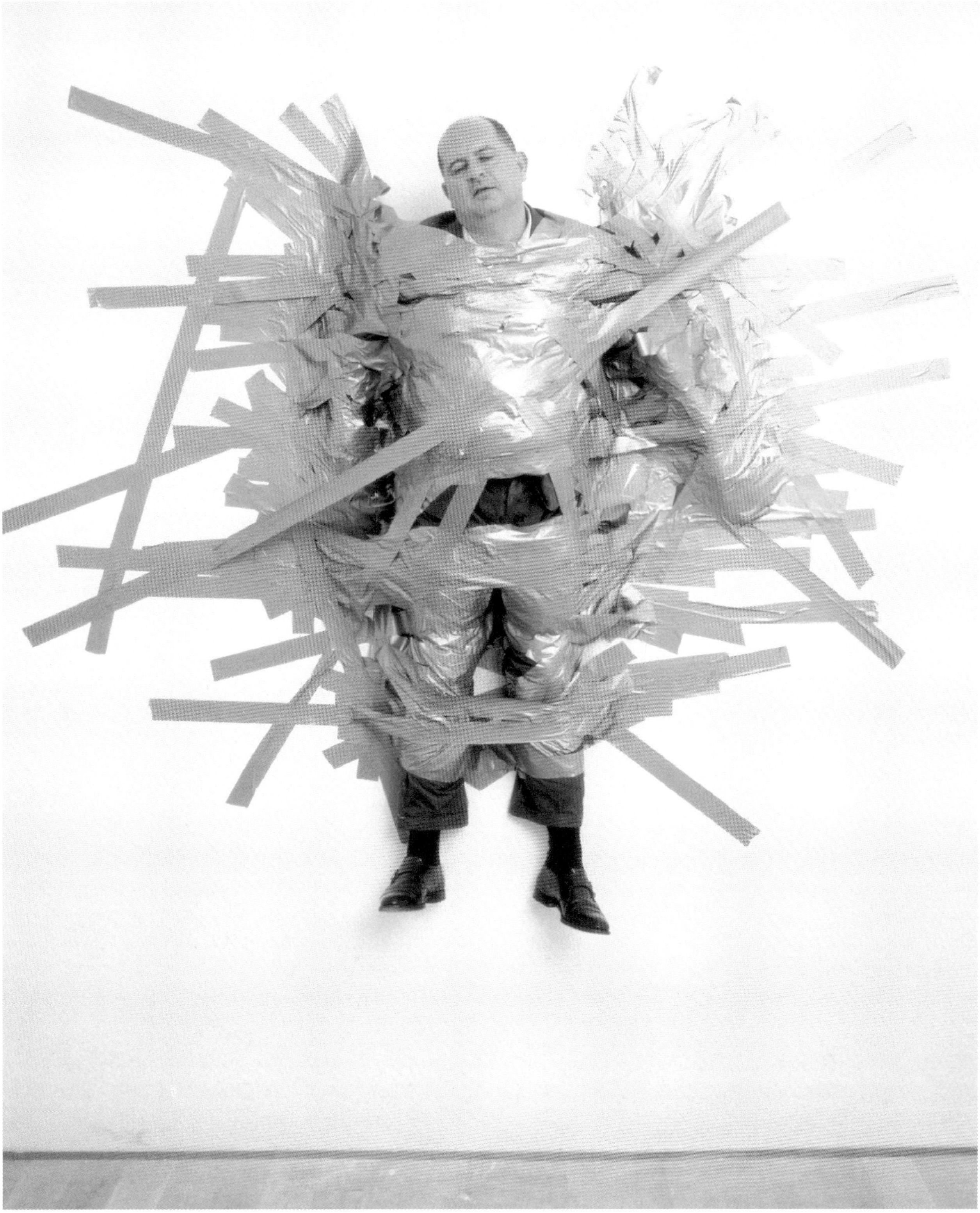

MAURIZIO CATTELAN, A PERFECT DAY, 1999, the artist's gallerist, Massimo de Carlo, adhesive tape, installation, Massimo de Carlo Gallery, Milan /

EIN VOLLKOMMENER TAG, Cattelans Galerist Massimo de Carlo, Klebeband. (PHOTO: ARMIN LINKE)

A Sociology Without Truth

ALISON M. GINGERAS

...the truth is not out there. It's just the moment that you claim something as your own. This is my truth; that is yours. Besides if we use other materials, you will still have the opportunity to observe how I work and I will have the opportunity to learn more about other people.

Comedians manipulate and make fun of reality, whereas I actually think that reality is far more provocative than my art.

– Maurizio Cattelan[1]

There are two positions that one can take when considering the reception of the slippery work (and equally hard to grasp persona) of Maurizio Cattelan. The first and most generous of these calls Cattelan a clown, whose carefully orchestrated self-effacement and oft-excessive humor offers a melancholic reflection on a sick society. Acutely narrativized both in terms of art-historical tradition and cultural specificity, this account sandwiches the artist between the neo-avant-garde pranks of Piero Manzoni and the tragicomic figures of Italian cinema, Federico Fellini and Roberto Benigni. In this reading, court-jester buffoonery is an excusable form of provocation because it can offer "an inverted and ironic mirror for contemporary culture."[2]

A second, less-forgiving account offers a portrait of Cattelan as a pure cynic whose opportunistic provocations cruelly transform the art world into the butt of his artistic gestures. This position also has a long tradition in postwar art criticism concerned with historical "legitimacy"—uniting under one lineage the fraudulence of Yves Klein's claim to have invented the monochrome, Martin Kippenberger's belligerent and drunken follies, and the art world's

ALISON M. GINGERAS is curator for contemporary art at the Musée National d'Art Moderne, Centre Georges Pompidou, Paris.

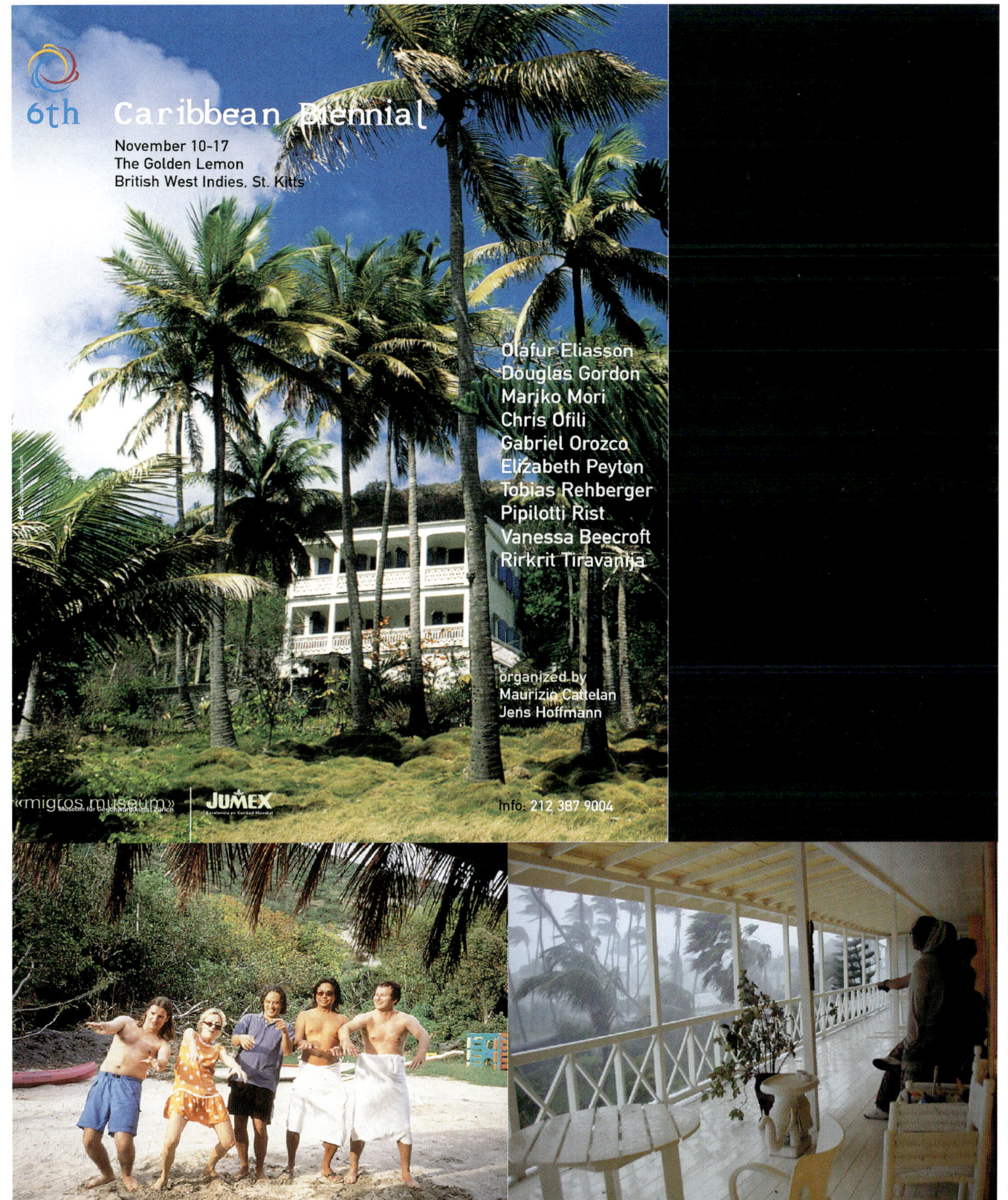
6th Caribbean Biennial
November 10-17
The Golden Lemon
British West Indies, St. Kitts
Olafur Eliasson
Douglas Gordon
Mariko Mori
Chris Ofili
Gabriel Orozco
Elizabeth Peyton
Tobias Rehberger
Pipilotti Rist
Vanessa Beecroft
Rirkrit Tiravanija
organized by
Maurizio Cattelan
Jens Hoffmann
«migros museum»
Museum für Gegenwartskunst Zürich
JUMEX
Excelencia en Calidad Mundial
info: 212 387 9004

favorite iceman, Jeff Koons. United by accusations of a-criticality, lack of political engagement, and anti-humanism, this cast of characters all too effectively disturbs claims to any notion of truth in artistic practice.

Chronicling an artist's reception can reveal more about his or her sensibility than a straight reading or interpretation of a given work. In the case of Cattelan, these two poles of reception have played themselves out in the literature about his recent project, the Sixth Caribbean Biennial. From November 10 through November 17, 1999, Cattelan, in collaboration with independent curator Jens Hoffmann, invited ten diverse and high profile artists from the international circuit to St. Kitts Island in the British West Indies for a free vacation.

All of the rules of the game were duly followed: Press releases were distributed; full-page color advertisements were placed in all the right periodicals; invitations were sent; reservations booked; limousines reserved; and rumors generated grist for the mill. Total status quo. The only unpredictable element was the weather. Hurricane Lenny kept this motley crew on the island several days longer than planned, adding an element of chance to the mix.

As must have been expected by the organizers, a delegation of critics arrived from *Artforum* and *Frieze* to cover the affair. Jenny Liu offered her scathing report in the pages of *Frieze*, weaving together the figures of clown and cynic in her account of Cattelan with pure rhetorical vitriol. The absence of exhibited art, or any public discourse from the artists, provoked Liu to attack. She writes,

There's something so sad about so cynical and ambivalent a gesture as the Caribbean Biennial: one would think that a critique of one's own practices would be ethical, even idealistic. Here the humor was both a performance of aggression and a weapon of despair, another cheerless rehearsal of irony and parody.[3]

Where is the institutional critique, they wondered? The main motivation for the Caribbean Biennial was to provide the artists with a paid vacation. Period. That fact was never hidden from the public, but openly promulgated.[4] The only possible "critical" statement was a purposefully obvious and thinly veiled pretext for the show. It pointed to the

banality of phenomena that have been thoroughly dissected: the over-saturation of international art calendars with biennial and triennial exhibitions (over forty at last count).

In one way, such accusations are an integral part of the Cattelan plan: They are frequently rendered and totally anticipated and could be easily dismissed by dwelling upon the naiveté and over-simplification behind them. Consider Cattelan's established track record of "escapism" from the traditional exhibition space. A few examples: UNA DOMENICA A RIVARA (1992), knotted bed sheets were hung out of a gallery window; OBLOMOV FOUNDATION (1992), Cattelan collected $10,000 from one hundred people to be given to an artist who would agree to abstain from exhibiting his/her work for one year, when the selected recipients refused to accept the grant, Cattelan took the money and ran—to New York; LAVORARE È UN BRUTTO MESTIERE (1993), selling his exhibition space at the Venice Biennale to an ad agency. How could anyone expect a "straightforward" biennial or some version of institutional critique? What values (criticality, legitimacy) underlie Liu's disappointment and disgust?

Despite the venom of Liu's words, her review might accidentally offer another way into breaking down this dismissive dichotomy of clown/cynic that runs through Cattelan's reception. Instead of a "hostile takeover of the art world within" as Liu suggests a few lines earlier, her review concedes that Cattelan sets up his biennial as a "f r a m i n g   d e v i c e." Creating a semi-private mise-en-scène of the art world's players and structures, the organization of this event might be considered a form of f i e l d w o r k. Following the logic of a sociologist, Cattelan creates and applies such institutional or situational frames (in this case, a biennial) to observe and subsequently display the microcosm of the art world.

From the Caribbean Biennial to his giant headed Picasso-as-theme-park-mascot at the entrance of the MoMA and his unrealized, fake neo-Nazi rally in Sonsbeek, Germany, Cattelan's many provocative art-as-event works may be seen as the artistic inheritors of the pioneering sociologist Erving Goffman. In *The Presentation of Self in Everyday Life* (1959), Goffman developed an extended metaphor, likening theatrical performance to the playing out of social roles in quotidian structures and activities. In conversation, the artist has esteemed one of the most salient sociological points of the Caribbean Biennial: each artist never "broke character," even if they were thousands of miles from any gallery. This fascination for behavior as dictated by social structure and context supplies the primary source for Cattelan's enterprise. Everyday life itself becomes the real *agent provocateur.*

Yet there is one main difference between what motivates Goffman's and Cattelan's "sociological" fieldwork. Cattelan has stated, "I'm always borrowing pieces—crumbs really—of everyday reality." Critics can not locate critique in Cattelan's practice because there is no search for truth or claims for legitimacy that underlie his actions. If Cattelan's work is understood as a framing of the "crumbs" of everyday reality—the relentless reinforcement of the theatrical roles assigned to him and the actors who surround him—any type of judgment is absent from his sociological set-ups. Like Kippenberger, Klein, and Koons before him, Cattelan disavows the role of the artist as guardian of the Enlightenment ideals of moral rationality, historical consciousness, and truth. Instead, his s o c i o l o g y - s a n s - t r u t h sets into motion a much more disruptive scenario. In lieu of a superficial rehearsal of institutional critique, where prescriptive and ultimately stable interpretations of the world are given, Cattelan points towards the flux of values that motivate the everyday performance of the self.

1) Interview with Nancy Spector, in: Francesco Bonami, Nancy Spector, Barbara Vanderlinden, *Maurizio Cattelan* (London: Phaidon Press Limited, 2000), pp. 9, 17.
2) Ibid., p. 17.
3) Jenny Liu, "Trouble in Paradise" in: *Frieze* (London), No. 51 (March/April 2000), pp. 52–53.
4) Cattelan readily admits that the biennial was conceived as a paid vacation in interviews with Nancy Spector (op. cit.), and Massimiliano Gioni with Jens Hoffmann, "Blown Away—Blown to Pieces" in: *Material*, No. 2 (Zurich: Migros Museum, 1999). Yet in a recent e-mail to the author in regard to Liu's statements, he admits that it was "everything and nothing, in a way. Jenny Liu was right, too (and she wasn't right at all!), it was non-ethical, not idealistic; it was aggression and irony and despair and parody. And it was a paid vacation."

MAURIZIO CATTELAN, SPERMINI / LITTLE SPERMS, 1997, *latex, paint, 500 parts, 4 x 5⅞ x 4" each; installation at Massimo Minini Gallery, Brescia, Italy / KLEINE SPERMIEN, Latex, Farbe, 500 Elemente zu 10 x 15 x 10 cm.*
(PHOTO: ATTILIO MARANZANO)

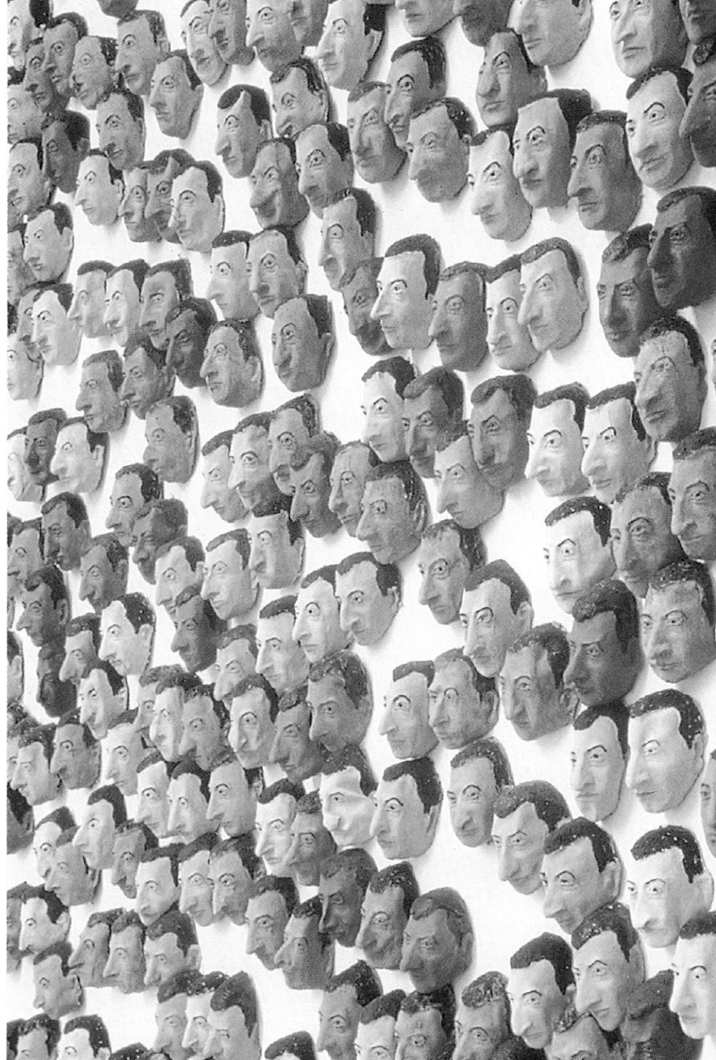

Eine Soziologie ohne Wahrheit

ALISON M. GINGERAS

... die Wahrheit ist nicht irgendwo ausserhalb. Sie ist genau der Augenblick, wo man etwas als sein Eigenes einfordert. Dies ist meine Wahrheit; das ist deine. Und wenn wir andere Materialien verwenden, so wirst du immer noch Gelegenheit haben zu beobachten, wie ich arbeite, und ich werde Gelegenheit haben mehr über andere Menschen zu erfahren.

Komödianten verzerren die Realität und machen sich über sie lustig, ich dagegen halte die Realität für weitaus provokativer als meine Kunst.

– Maurizio Cattelan[1]

Wenn es um die Rezeption des sich unserem Zugriff gern entziehenden Werks von Maurizio Cattelan (und seine nicht minder schwer fassbare Persönlichkeit) geht, gibt es zwei mögliche Haltungen. Die erste, grosszügigere nennt Cattelan einen Clown, dessen sorgfältig inszenierte Bescheidenheit und oft ausgelassener Humor uns das melancholische Spiegelbild einer kranken Gesellschaft vorhalte. Diese Auffassung presst den Künstler kunsthistorisch und kulturell in ein traditionelles Handlungsschema und klemmt ihn quasi ein zwischen den neo-avantgardistischen Klauen eines Piero Manzoni auf der einen und den tragikomischen Gestalten des italienischen Films eines Federico Fellini oder Roberto Benigni auf der andern Seite. In dieser Interpretation sind die Spässe des Hofnarren eine erlaubte Form der Provokation, weil sie «der zeitgenössischen Kultur einen ironischen Zerrspiegel vorzuhalten vermögen».[2]

Eine zweite, weniger freundliche Auffassung zeichnet von Cattelan das Porträt eines reinen Zynikers, der durch die opportunistische Provokation seiner künstlerischen Aktionen die Kunstszene erbarmungslos verspottet. Auch dieser Standpunkt hat eine lange Tradition in der Nachkriegs-Kunstkritik, die sich am liebsten mit historischer «Legitimität» beschäftigte und dabei Yves Kleins Behauptung, die Monochromie erfunden zu haben, Martin Kippenbergers aggressive und besoffene Verrücktheiten

ALISON M. GINGERAS ist Kuratorin für zeitgenössische Kunst am Musée National d'Art Moderne, Centre Georges Pompidou, Paris.

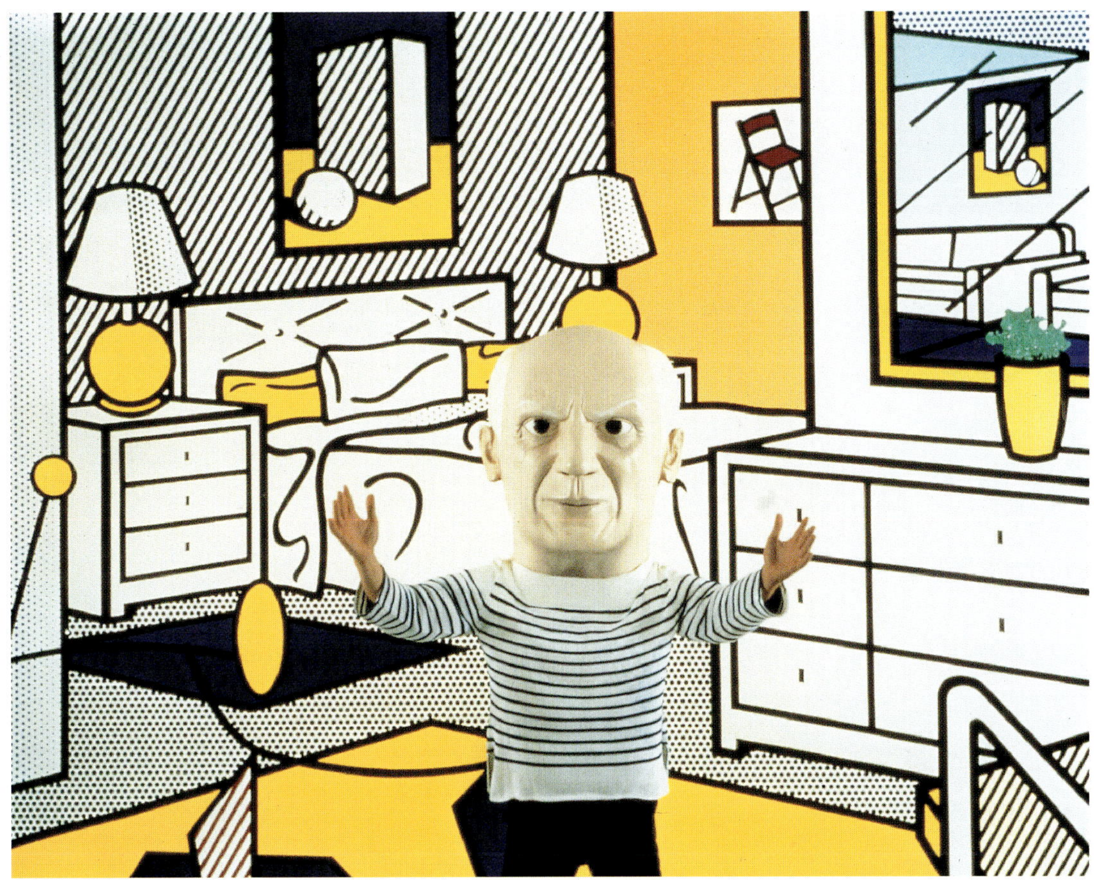

MAURIZIO CATTELAN, UNTITLED, 1998, project no. 65 (including ROY LICHTENSTEIN's INTERIOR WITH MOBILE, 1992),
The Museum of Modern Art, New York / OHNE TITEL. (PHOTO WITH PERMISSION OF THE ESTATE OF ROY LICHTENSTEIN: M. GUILLEN)

und Jeff Koons, den beliebtesten Eisverkäufer der Welt, gleichermassen tadelte. Allesamt wurden sie ihrer unkritischen Haltung, ihres fehlenden politischen Engagements und ihrer antihumanistischen Einstellung wegen angeprangert und enttäuschten nur allzu wirksam jede Forderung nach einem Wahrheitsbegriff in der künstlerischen Praxis.

Verfolgt man die Rezeption eines Künstlers, kann dies unter Umständen mehr über seine spezifische Sensibilität zutage fördern als die direkte Betrachtung und Interpretation eines seiner Werke. In der Literatur zu einem seiner jüngsten Projekte, der «6. Karibischen Biennale», werden die beiden genannten Extreme der Rezeption deutlich. Vom 10. bis 17. November 1999 lud Cattelan in Zusammenarbeit mit dem freien Kurator Jens Hoffmann zehn

bekannte und erfolgreiche Künstler aus der internationalen Szene zu Gratisferien auf die Insel St. Kitts in Britisch-Westindien ein.

Alle Regeln des Spiels wurden peinlich eingehalten: Pressetexte wurden in Umlauf gebracht; in allen wichtigen Zeitschriften ganzseitige Farbinserate geschaltet; Einladungen verschickt; Limousinen gebucht; ein paar Gerüchte trugen das ihrige bei. Alles wie gehabt. Nur das Wetter war nicht berechenbar. Der Hurrikan Lenny brachte den Zufall ins Spiel, indem er die bunt zusammengewürfelte Gruppe ein paar Tage länger als geplant auf der Insel festhielt.

Wie von den Organisatoren vorgesehen, traf auch eine Delegation von Kritikern von *Artforum* und *Frieze* ein um über das Ereignis zu berichten. Jenny Liu gab in *Frieze* einen vernichtenden Kommentar ab, in wel-

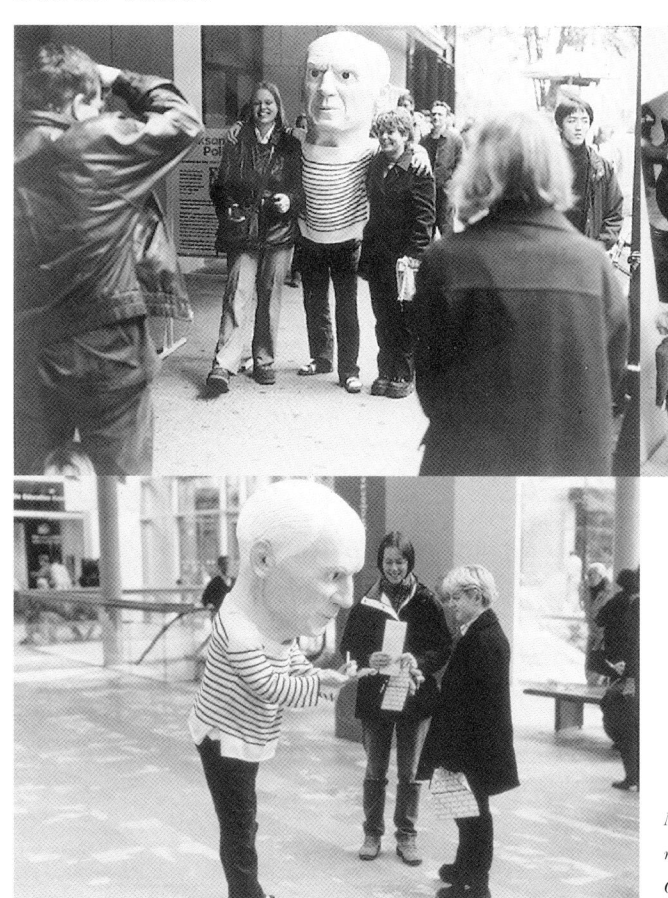

MAURIZIO CATTELAN, UNTITLED, 1998, project no. 65,
mask, paint, costume, The Museum of Modern Art, New York /
OHNE TITEL, Projekt Nr. 65, Maske, Farbe, Kostüm.
(PHOTOS: THOMAS GREISEL)

chem sie Cattelan mit gehässigen Worten als Clown und Zyniker in einem charakterisierte. Das Fehlen jeglicher Ausstellung von Werken und jeder öffentlichen Diskussion unter den Künstlern hatte die Attacke provoziert. Liu schreibt:

Eine derart zynische und zwiespältige Aktion wie die Karibische Biennale ist nur deprimierend: Man sollte meinen, dass eine Kritik der eigenen Praxis ethische, ja idealistische Qualität hätte. Aber diese Art von Humor war aggressive Performance und Verzweiflungstat in einem, nichts als eine weitere triste Übung in Ironie und Parodie.[3]

Wo die institutionelle Kritik bleibe, mochte man sich fragen. Der Hauptbeweggrund für die Karibische Biennale war, den Künstlern bezahlte Ferien zu verschaffen. Punkt. Diese Tatsache wurde nie beschönigt, sondern offen zugegeben.[4] Die einzige halbwegs «kritische» Äusserung war offensichtlich ein nur schlecht verhüllter Vorwand für die ganze Veranstaltung. Sie verwies auf ein banales und bereits mehr als gründlich seziertes Phänomen: die Übersättigung der internationalen Kunstagenda mit Biennalen und Triennalen (laut letzter Zählung über 40).

Einerseits sind solche Vorwürfe integraler Bestandteil von Cattelans Plan: Sie werden häufig erhoben, sind voll einkalkuliert und lassen sich leicht entkräften, sobald man ihrer Naivität und unzulässigen Vereinfachung etwas auf den Zahn fühlt. Man vergegenwärtige sich nur einmal Cattelans rekordverdächtige Liste seiner «Fluchten» aus traditionellen Ausstellungsräumen. Einige wenige Beispiele: UNA DOMENICA A RIVARA (Ein Sonntag in Rivara, 1992), da wurden aneinander geknüpfte Bettlaken aus einem Galeriefenster gehängt; OBLOMOV FOUNDA-

TION (Oblomow-Stiftung, 1992): Cattelan sammelt von hundert Leuten 10 000 Dollar, die einem Künstler zukommen sollen, der dafür freiwillig für die Dauer eines Jahres auf die Ausstellung seiner Werke verzichten würde, und als die ausgewählten Empfänger die Spende ablehnen, nimmt Cattelan das Geld selbst und flieht – nach New York; LAVORARE È UN BRUTTO MESTIERE (Arbeiten ist ein hässlicher Beruf, 1993): Der Künstler vermietet seinen Ausstellungsraum an der Biennale in Venedig an eine Werbeagentur. Wie konnte nur irgendwer ernsthaft eine «regelkonforme» Biennale erwarten oder eine Form institutioneller Kritik? Welche Werte (kritische Grenzen, Legitimität) liegen denn Lius Enttäuschung und Ablehnung zugrunde?

Trotz seines vernichtenden Urteils könnte Lius Artikel uns dabei helfen, das ewige Gegensatzpaar Clown/Zyniker, das die Rezeption Cattelans bestimmt, endlich zu überwinden. Statt einer «feindlichen Übernahme der Kunstszene von innen», wie Liu einige Zeilen vorher andeutete, gesteht ihr Text zu, dass Cattelan seine Biennale als s t r u k t u r i e r e n d e s I n s t r u m e n t einsetzt. Insofern als Exponenten und Strukturen der Kunstszene dabei halb privat inszeniert werden, könnte man das Ganze als eine Art F e l d s t u d i e betrachten. Wie ein Soziologe schafft und verwendet Cattelan jeweils einen institutionellen oder situationsbedingten Rahmen (in diesem Fall eine Biennale) zu dem Zweck, den Mikrokosmos der Kunstwelt zu beobachten und uns vorzuführen.

Von der Karibischen Biennale bis zu seinem riesenköpfigen Picasso als Themenpark-Maskottchen am Eingang des MoMA oder seinem nicht realisierten, falschen Neonazi-Treffen in Sonsbeek, Niederlande, kann man Cattelans zahllose, provokative Kunst-als-Event-Arbeiten in künstlerischer Nachfolge des soziologischen Pioniers Erving Goffman verstehen. In *The Presentation of Self in Everyday Life* (1959)[5] entwickelte Goffman eine erweiterte Metapher, in der er das Theaterspielen mit dem Spielen sozialer Rollen im Alltag verglich. Im Gespräch nannte der Künstler als einen der entscheidenden soziologischen Faktoren der Karibischen Biennale, dass kein Künstler je «aus der Rolle fiel», obwohl sie alle tausende von Meilen von jeder Galerie entfernt waren.

Dieses Interesse für das durch soziale Strukturen und den Kontext diktierte Verhalten bildet die Hauptquelle für Cattelans Arbeit. Das Alltagsleben selbst wird zum eigentlichen *agent provocateur*.

Dennoch gibt es eine entscheidende Differenz der Motivation zwischen Goffmans und Cattelans «soziologischer» Feldarbeit. Cattelan sagt: «Ich entlehne laufend Elemente – eigentlich nur Brosamen – aus der Alltagswirklichkeit.» Den Kritikern entgeht das Kritische von Cattelans Vorgehensweise, weil seinen Aktionen weder die Suche nach Wahrheit noch eine Behauptung von Legitimität zugrunde liegt. Betrachtet man Cattelans Arbeiten aber als Rahmen für die Brosamen aus der Alltagsrealität – das rückhaltlose Festhalten an den ihm und seinen Mitdarstellern zugeschriebenen Rollen –, so fehlt seinen soziologischen Inszenierungen jegliches urteilende Element. Wie schon Kippenberger, Klein und Koons vor ihm entsagt Cattelan der Rolle des Künstlers als Hüter der Aufklärung und ihrer Ideale – ethische Rationalität, historisches Bewusstsein und Wahrheit. Stattdessen ergibt seine S o z i o l o g i e o h n e W a h r h e i t ein viel brüchigeres Szenario. Anstelle einer oberflächlichen Übung in institutioneller Kritik mit vorgefassten und fixen Interpretationen der Welt verweist Cattelan auf das Fliessende der Werte, welche die alltägliche Selbstinszenierung steuern.

(Übersetzung: Susanne Schmidt)

1) Interview mit Nancy Spector in: Francesco Bonami, Nancy Spector, Barbara Vanderlinden, *Maurizio Cattelan*, Phaidon Press, London 2000, S. 9, 17.
2) Ebenda, S. 17.
3) Jenny Liu, «Trouble in Paradise», in: *Frieze* (London), No. 51, März/April 2000, S. 52–53.
4) Cattelan gesteht bereitwillig ein, dass die Idee der Biennale in bezahlten Ferien für die Teilnehmenden bestand. Vgl. dazu das vorgängig zitierte Interview mit Nancy Spector sowie jenes mit Jens Hoffmann und Massimiliano Gioni, «Blown Away – Blown to Pieces», in: *Material*, Nr. 2, Migros Museum, Zürich 1999. Aber in einer neueren E-Mail-Mitteilung an die Autorin im Zusammenhang mit Lius Aussagen gibt er auch zu, dass es «alles und nichts» gewesen sei und dass «Jenny Liu in gewisser Weise auch Recht habe (und überhaupt nicht Recht habe!), es war nicht ethisch, nicht idealistisch; es war Aggressivität und Ironie, Verzweiflung und Parodie. Und es waren bezahlte Ferien.»
5) Deutsch unter dem Titel *Wir alle spielen Theater: Selbstdarstellung im Alltag* bei Piper, München, erschienen.

Maurizio Cattelan

MAURIZIO CATTELAN, NOVECENTO, 1997, stuffed horse, leather saddlery, rope, pulley, Castello di Rivoli, Museo d'Arte Contemporanea, Turin, 79 x 106 x 27" / ausgestopftes Pferd, Sattel und Zaumzeug, Strick, Flaschenzug. 200 x 270 x 69 cm.

(PHOTO: PELLION)

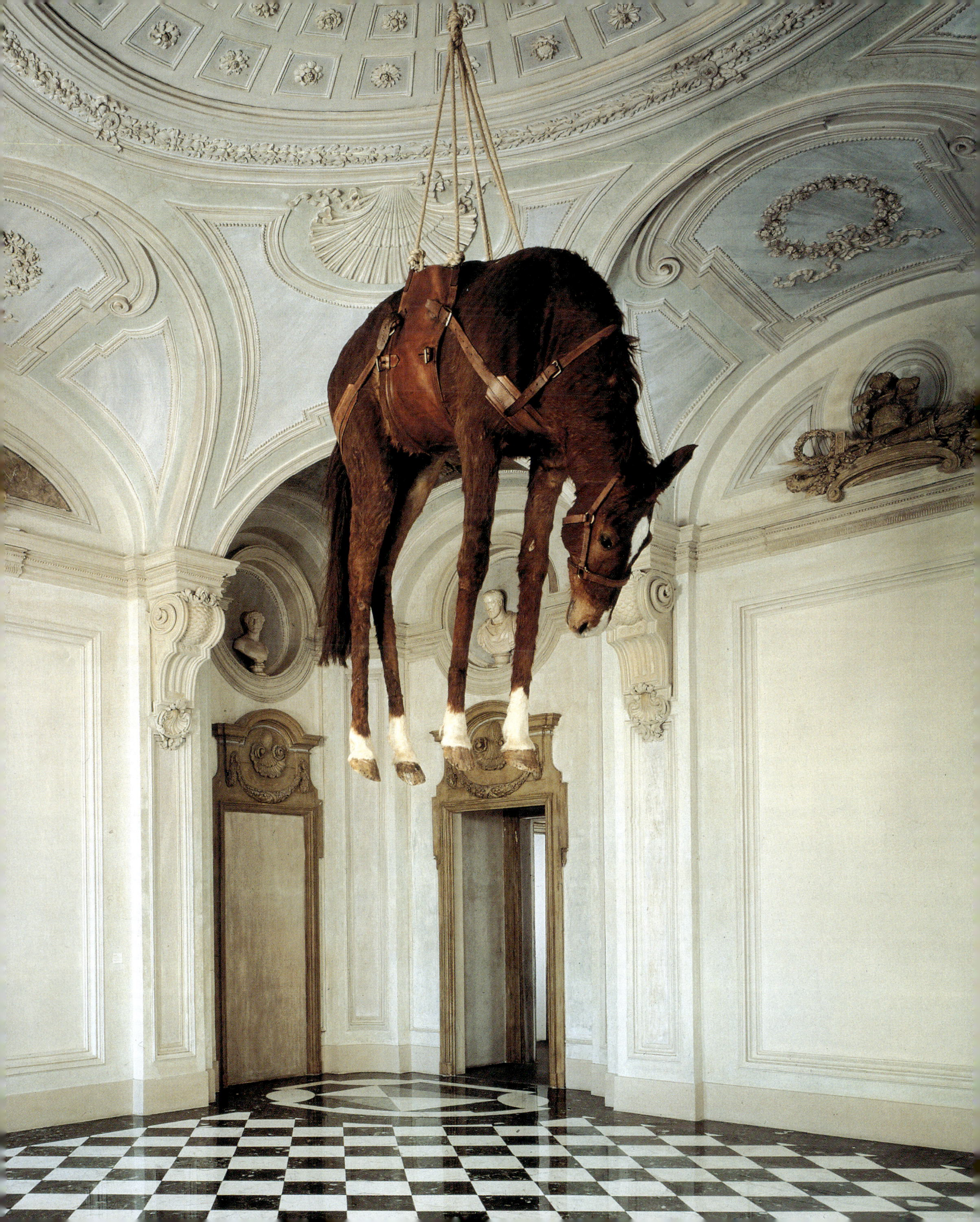

Every Artist Can Be a Man The Silence of Beuys Is Understandable

FRANCESCO BONAMI

I do not want any more esthetic art work, I am making myself a fetish.
                                                                    – Ewald Matare[1]

Stars represent typical ways of behaving, feeling and thinking in contemporary society, ways that have been socially, culturally, historically constructed… Stars are also embodiments of the social categories in which people are placed and through which they have to make sense of their lives, and indeed through which we make our lives—categories of class, gender, ethnicity, religion, sexual orientation, and so on.[2]

Short Frequency

Dir. Ludo Peters, 2000, PG 13, 476 mins.
Short Frequency opens in the fall of 1943, as maverick dive-bomber Joseph Beuys once again risks his life on a death-defying call, but his plane is hit by anti-aircraft gunfire. He succeeds in bringing his plane behind Italian lines only to have the altimeter fail during a sudden and unseasonable snowstorm. His plane can no longer function properly, and it crashes behind the Scrovegni chapel in Padua. A young nurse discovers Joseph Beuys unconscious in the middle of total civilization. She cares for him for about eight days. When he awakens, they make love. An extraordinary solar flare has been lighting up the Padua night sky for weeks. A

German search commando finds Beuys and transports him to a military hospital. After nine months, the nurse gives birth to a boy called Maurizio Cattelan. Then the film jumps ahead—to the same date in 1999, when a similar celestial phenomenon is taking place—to meet the adult Maurizio, an unhappy artist whose father died of rabies after having been bitten by a wild coyote. Maurizio discovers Beuys's old cordless phone (not a cellular phone, just a cordless one) and, presumably due to the quirky solar activity, manages to contact his father in 1943. Maurizio's warning saves Beuys from sex with his mother and from the rabid coyote, but their communication alters other events as well. The film ends with a surreal conversation between four friends: Beuys (Robert Duvall), Janis Kounellis (Richard Dreyfuss), Anselm Kiefer (Maximilian Schell), and Cattelan (John Turturro). Don't bother thinking about *Short Frequency*'s rickety logic. Doing so will only give you less time to enjoy this big hearted, low-tech, and exceptionally rousing yarn. (See Index for venues.)—BB

I adapted this review from an original of the film *Short Frequency* as a pretext for formulating some questions about the idea of destiny in contemporary art and how cutting and pasting different stories, ideas, and works of art could eventually lead to a new kind of individual—and maybe to a new kind of artist and a new race of fetishes.

Icons make history, but what if these icons could, for some kind of "short frequency," be changed?

If Jesus had been hanged instead of crucified, what would have happened to the entire symbolism of Christianity? If Warhol had had short dark hair, what would have happened to the surface of his personality, his diaries, and his semiological impact? If Beuys had not worn a felt hat, a fishing jacket, and a fur coat, what influence would his overwhelming visual personality have had on the arts of his time? If Maurizio Cattelan had a smaller nose, what would have happened to most of his multiple self-portraits, which have made him the last of the contemporary icons, the mask of visual arts? Some art succeeds because of the collective memory produced by the strong feature of an artist. Buster Keaton's art collapsed when sound invaded moviemaking, yet after a period of decline, his image survived and was propelled into a new career in the world of television: While few remember his seminal silent masterpieces, his face remains a work of art. In an unlikely collective amnesia, the art world will always remember Warhol's synthetic face, Beuys's preacher persona, and Cattelan's foolish gaze. Their paintings, their installations, and their sculptural pranks will not save them from oblivion, but their respective bodies will. The moment when the body of an artist becomes the logo of his or her art is the only moment when art gets close to the movie industry. We don't have the story of a boxer, the story of a priest, the story of a cop, the story of a taxi driver. But you have the story of Robert De Niro as a boxer, a priest, a cop or a taxi driver. Cattelan carries on himself all of his iconography: You see him and you can fast-forward his entire production. Likewise, Beuys's figure drags into our minds masses of felt, fat, butter, oaks, and stones. For these artists, their image is superimposed on their objects and their actions. In the case of Warhol his persona was a model for two-dimensional experiences very much related to the art world and to entertainment. Madonna, Jeff Koons, Damien Hirst, and Michael Jackson followed his path. Beuys and Cattelan answer more to a call that comes from spiritual sources. They are very much rooted in the tradi-

FRANCESCO BONAMI is Senior Curator at the Museum of Contemporary Art, Chicago.

*MAURIZIO CATTELAN, UNTITLED (GÉRARD), 1999,
lifesize plastic dummy, clothes, shoes / OHNE TITEL (GÉRARD),
Plastikpuppe, Kleider, Schuhe. (PHOTO: ATTILIO MARANZANO)*

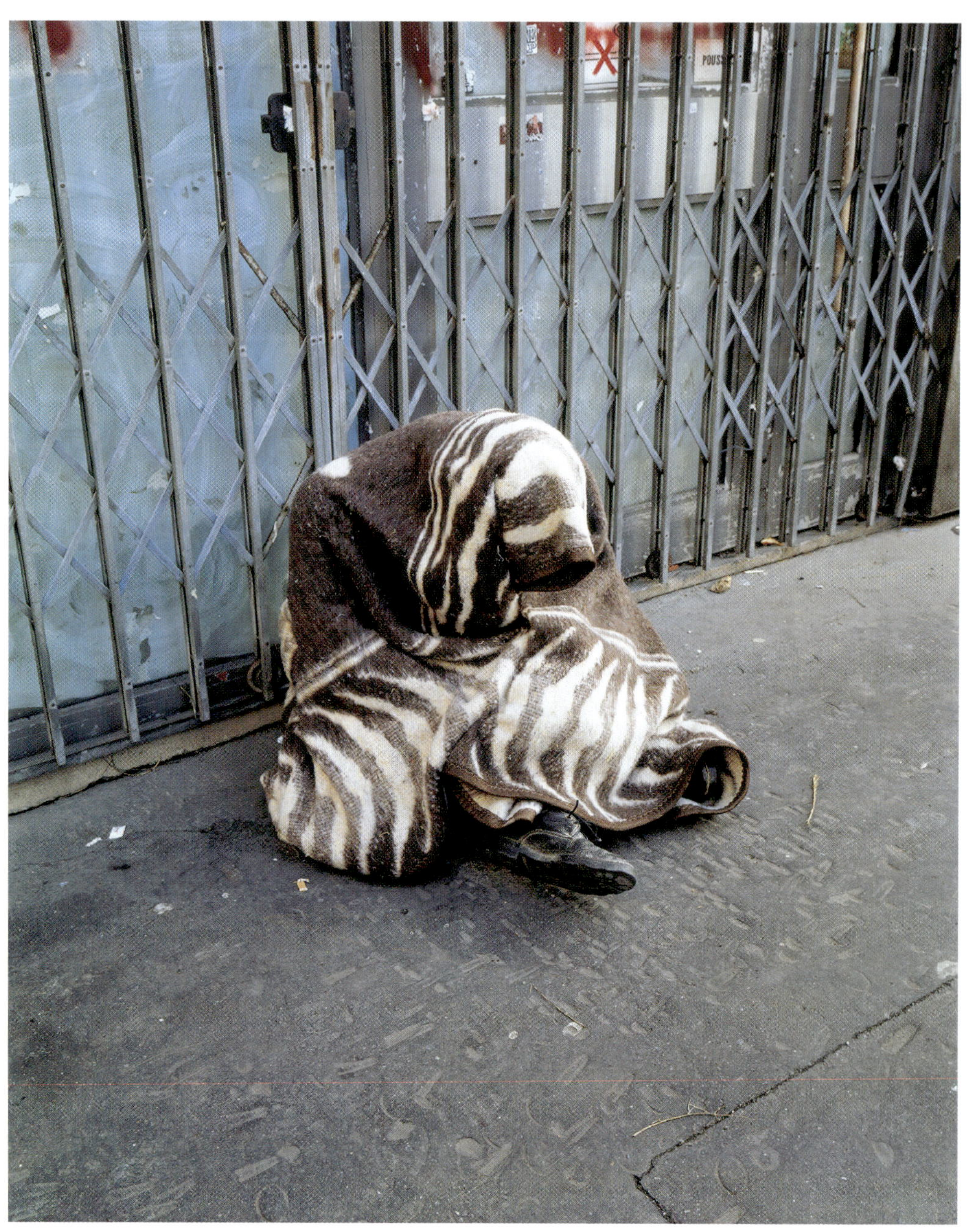

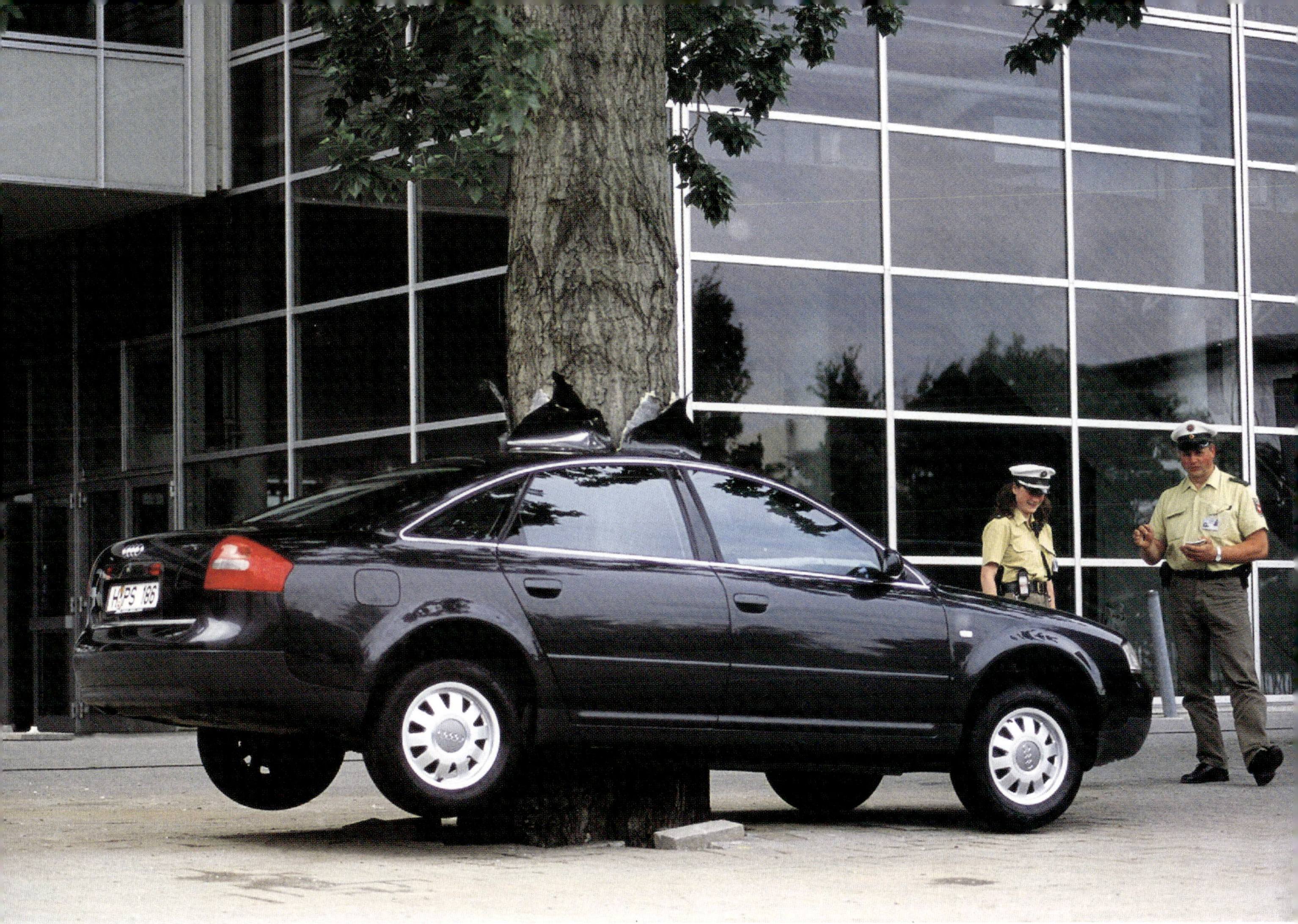

MAURIZIO CATTELAN, UNTITLED, 2000, car installation at the Expo Hannover / OHNE TITEL. (PHOTO: ROMAN MENSING)

tion of European saints and pilgrims. For them, art is a coded language that allows for communication with different species: Their audience is more like St. Francis's birds than Studio 54's paparazzi. Yet never have two artists been more dissimilar from each other—one a shaman and the other a street actor and, like these characters, both sharing a fantastic amount of hypocrisy. They fight, at different levels, the formal narrative of contemporary art, and yet over and over again they are able to create sculptural visions. Their ability is in transforming revolutionary and iconoclastic energy into pure art works, while

avoiding any questions of integrity: *If the birds don't get it we'll talk to dead hares or stuffed dogs.* For different reasons, they belong to the same category (never named before)—"Sculptors of Identification." We identify with Beuys at a cathartic, more abstract level, while with Cattelan, we identify at a sympathetic level: We feel solidarity with the suffering personality. The viewer identifies with the religious aura of Beuys's vitrines, something spiritually and formally perfect that contains all of the energy dispersed in real time. Beuys used the object to create meaning around his hat, his fishing vest, and his coat. If we look at Cattelan's Picasso head (UNTITLED, 1999), we are admiring the contemporary editing of art history and entertainment, a story and history cut and pasted together, to be manifested in a sculpture. Still looking at the goofy Picasso, we also identify with Cattelan as a street actor, nomadic entrepreneur, con artist. By the time we realize that both Beuys and Cattelan stole our money, they are already out of the country, and we are angry but transformed at a spiritual level, enlightened by a successful trick. We know that rabbits cannot be transformed into napkins, but we like to see it happening. Nobody really counted Beuys's oaks and stones, and there is no reason to doubt that there were in fact seven thousand. But who really cared after he declared such a monumental effort? Nobody searched for the woman's body in the Münster lake where Cattelan dumped her one evening. We know that Daniel Buren witnessed the disposal of the body, but at the end of the day who cares about the truth? For the entire day we kept looking for her, happy to indulge in the idea of having incurred another of Cattelan's jokes. We like to be the chosen ones from the audience, looking like a fool when the magician pulls out the dove from our pocket. Beuys was not joking: He was—like his hare—deadly serious. He did not perform tricks but rituals. His animals were transmitters of energy, not entropic tools for entertainment. But Cattelan is allowed to joke about Beuys because people joke about Jesus and Moses. He is allowed to exploit the animal's energy, because the transmitter is the viewer's laugh. What would have happened if Groucho Marx had been one of the apostles? Do we know if jokes were allowed at the Last Supper? Did Beuys ever joke? Maybe he did all the time and Cattelan does not. I think that Beuys was an artist who was desperately trying to be a man, and Cattelan is a man who is desperately trying to be an artist. If Cattelan would explain Arte Povera to a dead squirrel, we would all laugh, of course, but this, in the end, is a matter of historical perspective. Beuys crashed with a plane in Crimea, and Cattelan maybe just crashed with a bicycle in his backyard. Yet looking backwards, we don't really know if Beuys was the revolution, if history was flirting with democracy and freedom but in fact only transformed the subversives into conservative gurus

with feet of clay. Beuys made of his family a piece of art, while Cattelan's family is the reason why he is now an artist. The religious seriousness of Joseph Beuys makes us wonder if he was fooling us. Cattelan makes a fool of himself, and yet he reflects human nature more than anybody else does today.

Beuys dressed himself in 1971 with his felt suit in the action ISOLATION UNIT; Cattelan dressed people like lions and a phallic rabbit. How would he have dressed Beuys? He dressed himself as Beuys with a felt suit, but in order to avoid confrontation, he shrunk the suit and himself. The unit is no longer isolated; he now hangs from a coat hanger. Who takes himself more seriously? Beuys transformed himself into an icon, and Cattelan transforms icons into his own personality, his spirit, his delusions, and his awkwardness. History can be changed, destiny directed. Both Beuys and Cattelan rely on childhood memories, heroic for the former, pathetic for the latter. They use the energy of life, combined with charisma and hypocrisy, faith and deception. Beuys could walk on water while Cattelan follows him, jumping from one stone to the other: Cheating can save lives. The Bible in the hands of one, fairy tales in the hands of the other. The seventies were about dogmatic intervention; now life is about small truths, short lies. If Cattelan would wear a hat, he would look stupid; why didn't Beuys look so? Maybe Jesus was an artist, his crown of thorns a sign of narcissism. So Beuys is a prophet and Cattelan a vicar of a small, isolated parish. If so, his history would be different, funnier, and banal. Today we wish we could call Jesus and Beuys on the telephone, ask them if they ever laugh, ask them if Cattelan were a saint or a fascist, a village fool or a failed monk. The hare didn't really understand painting, but maybe the birds will start laughing at Cattelan's art. The noose, the hat, and the nose—a new symbolism for a new millennium, a new history where parables, speeches, and jokes could have the same function in understanding reality.

1) Albert Schulze Vellinghausen, "Ewald Matare" in: *Prisma* 1/8 (1947), p. 17.
2) Richard Dyer, *Heavenly Bodies: Film Stars and Society* (New York: St. Martin's Press, 1986), p.18.

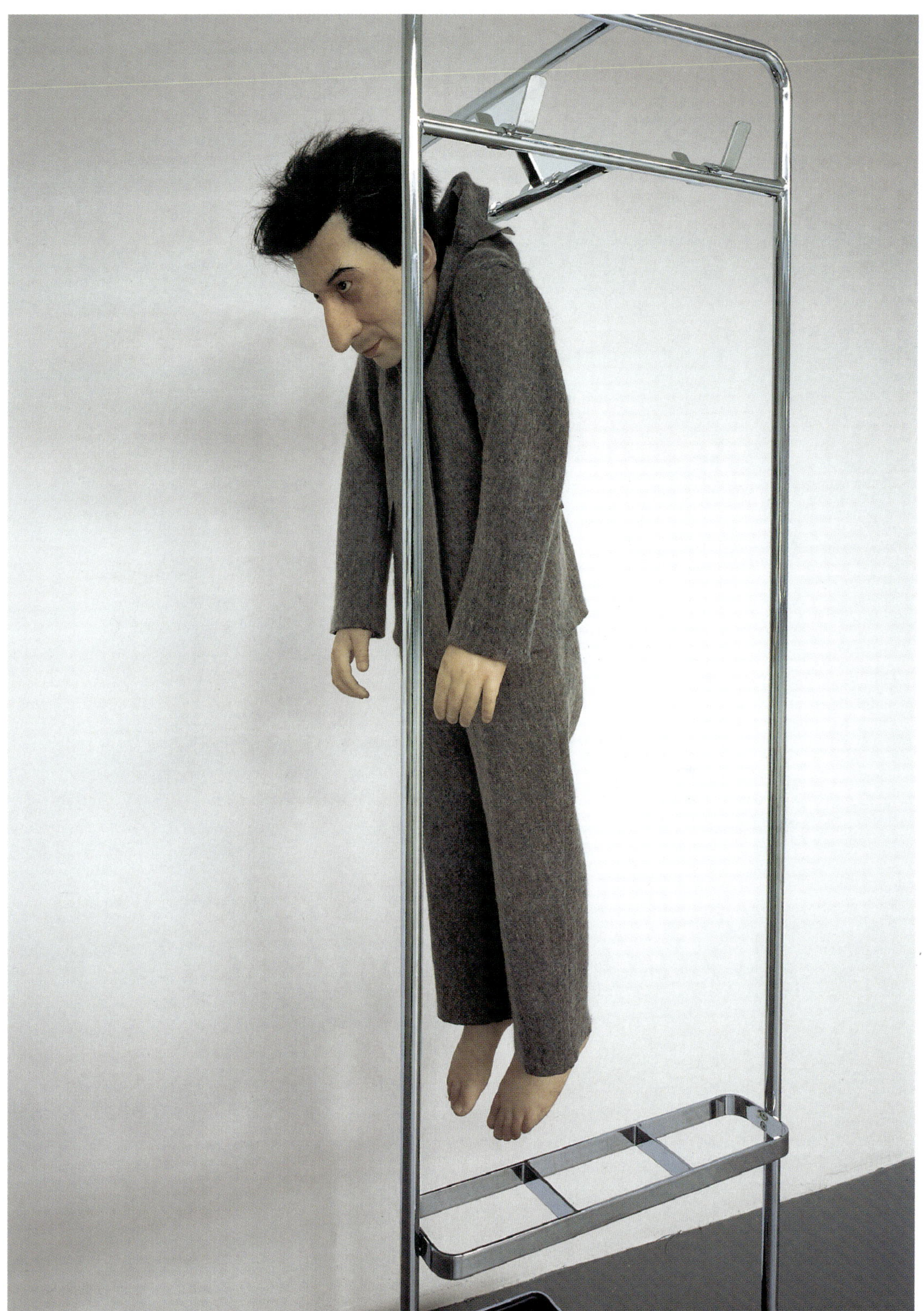

MAURIZIO CATTELAN, LA RIVOLUZIONE SIAMO NOI / WE ARE THE REVOLUTION, 2000,
Migros Museum für Gegenwartskunst, Zürich / DIE REVOLUTION SIND WIR. (PHOTO: ATTILIO MARANZANO)

Jeder Künstler kann Mensch sein

Beuys' Schweigen ist verständlich

FRANCESCO BONAMI

Ästhetische Kunst interessiert mich nicht mehr, ich mache mich selbst zum Fetisch. — Ewald Matare[1]

Stars symbolisieren in unserer Gesellschaft charakteristische Verhaltensweisen, Emotionen und Denkmuster, die gesellschaftlich, kulturell und historisch bedingt sind… Stars verkörpern auch die sozialen Kategorien, unter die Menschen fallen, innerhalb derer wir unserm Leben einen Sinn geben müssen und nach denen wir tatsächlich unser Leben gestalten – Kategorien wie Klasse, Geschlecht, ethnische Zugehörigkeit, Religion, sexuelle Ausrichtung und so weiter.[2]

Short Frequency

Regie: Ludo Peters, 2000, Jugendliche ab 13 Jahren, 476 Minuten.

Short Frequency (Kurzwelle) beginnt im Herbst 1942, als der im Alleingang operierende Stuka-Pilot Joseph Beuys wieder einmal bei einem halsbrecherischen Unternehmen sein Leben risikiert. Seine Maschine wird jedoch beschossen, und er schafft es gerade noch, sich hinter die italienischen Linien zu retten, doch in einem für diese Jahreszeit aussergewöhnlichen Schneesturm fällt der Höhenmesser aus. Seine Maschine ist nicht mehr funktionsfähig und stürzt in Padua hinter der Scrovegni-Kapelle ab. Eine junge Krankenschwester entdeckt den bewusstlosen Beuys inmitten dieser urbanen Umgebung. Acht Tage lang pflegt sie ihn, und als er wieder zu sich kommt, lieben sich die beiden. Ungewöhnliche Sonneneruptionen hatten seit Wochen den Nachthimmel von Padua hell erleuchtet. Ein deutscher

Suchtrupp findet Beuys und transportiert ihn in ein Militärhospital. Nach neun Monaten bringt die Krankenschwester einen Jungen namens Maurizio Cattelan zur Welt. Dann macht der Film einen Sprung ins Jahr 1999, in dem zur selben Zeit ein ähnliches Phänomen am Himmel beobachtet wird. Der erwachsene Maurizio erscheint, ein unglücklicher Künstler, dessen Vater am Biss eines tollwütigen, wilden Kojoten gestorben war. Maurizio entdeckt Beuys' altes, schnurloses Telefon (kein Mobiltelefon, nur eines ohne Kabel), und er kann seinen Vater im Jahr 1943 erreichen, was wahrscheinlich auch den Sonneneruptionen zuzuschreiben ist. Von Maurizio gewarnt, kann Beuys sowohl Maurizios Mutter wie auch dem tollwütigen Kojoten aus dem Weg gehen, aber durch den Anruf werden auch andere Ereignisse beeinflusst. Der Film endet mit einer surrealen Unterhaltung zwischen vier Freunden: Beuys (Robert Duvall), Janis Kounellis (Richard Dreyfuss), Anselm Kiefer (Maximilian Schell) und Cattelan (John Turturro). Die sprunghafte Logik von *Short Frequency* sollte man hinnehmen, sonst verdirbt man sich nur den Spass an dieser grossmütigen, ohne viel technischen Aufwand inszenierten und ungewöhnlich spannenden Geschichte (s. Liste der Spielorte) – BB.

Ich nehme diese kurze Zusammenfassung von *Short Frequency* zum willkommenen Vorwand, um mich mit dem Begriff des Schicksals in der zeitgenössischen Kunst zu befassen und damit, wie durch das Ausschneiden und neu Zusammenfügen verschiedener Geschichten, Gedanken und Kunstwerke ein ganz anderes Individuum, ja vielleicht auch eine ganz andere Art Künstler und ein neues Genre von Fetischen entstehen könnte.

Ikonen machen Geschichte, aber was würde passieren, wenn sich diese Ikonen durch eine besondere Kurzwellentechnik *(short frequency)* verändern liessen?

Hätte man Jesus nicht ans Kreuz geschlagen, sondern gehängt, was wäre aus der christlichen Symbolik geworden? Hätte Warhol kurzes, dunkles Haar gehabt, wie hätte sich das in seinem äusseren Erscheinungsbild, seinen Tagebüchern und seiner semiotischen Wirkung niedergeschlagen? Und hätte Beuys keinen Filzhut, keine Anglerjacke und keinen Pelzmantel getragen, welchen Einfluss hätte seine optisch überwältigende Persönlichkeit dann noch auf die Kunst seiner Zeit gehabt? Wäre Maurizio Cattelans Nase kleiner ausgefallen, wie hätte sich das auf seine seriellen Selbstporträts ausgewirkt, die ihn zur letzten Ikone unserer Zeit, zur Maske der visuellen Künste werden liessen? Manche Kunst behauptet sich, weil sich der Künstler durch eine besonders auffallende Eigenschaft dem kollektiven Gedächtnis eingeprägt hat. Als der Ton die Filmindustrie eroberte, war es erst einmal aus mit Buster Keatons Kunst, doch sein Image war auch nach einer längeren Auszeit noch lebendig und er schaffte es, in der Welt des Fernsehens Fuss zu fassen. Heute erinnern sich nur noch wenige wirklich an seine frühen, stummen Meisterwerke, doch sein Gesicht hat als Kunstwerk überlebt. Selbst bei einer sehr unwahrscheinlichen, allgemeinen Amnesie würde sich die Kunstwelt immer noch an Warhols synthetisches Gesicht erinnern, an Beuys, den Prediger, und an Cattelan mit dem törichten Blick. Nicht ihre Bilder, nicht ihre Installationen und auch nicht ihre bildhauerischen Taten werden sie davor bewahren, in

FRANCESCO BONAMI ist leitender Kurator am Museum of Contemporary Art in Chicago.

Vergessenheit zu geraten, sondern ihre körperliche Erscheinung. Wenn der Körper eines Künstlers zu seinem Markenzeichen wird, berühren sich Kunst und Filmindustrie. Wir sehen nicht die Geschichte eines Boxers, eines Priesters, eines Polizisten, eines Taxifahrers, sondern die Geschichte Robert De Niros als Boxer, als Priester, als Polizist oder Taxifahrer. Cattelan ist eine wandelnde Ikone, man sieht ihn und kann auch schon sein ganzes Werk erahnen. Ähnlich assoziieren wir mit Beuys' Erscheinung Unmengen von Filz, Fett, Butter, Eichen und Steinen. Bei diesen Künstlern überlagert das Image Arbeiten und Aktionen. Im Fall von Warhol diente die von ihm projizierte Person als Vorbild für zweidimensionale, mit der Kunstszene und Unterhaltungsindustrie eng verbundene Erfahrungen. Madonna, Jeff Koons, Damien Hirst und Michael Jackson traten in seine Fussstapfen. Beuys und Cattelan folgen eher dem Ruf spiritueller Quellen. Sie haben ihre Wurzeln in der Tradition der europäischen Heiligen und Pilger. Kunst ist für sie eine kodierte Sprache, dank derer sie mit verschiedenen Lebewesen kommunizieren können, und ihr Publikum bilden eher die Vögel des heiligen Franziskus als die Paparazzi von Studio 54. Doch hat es nie zwei unterschiedlichere Künstler gegeben – der eine ein Schamane, der andere ein Gaukler – und wie diese verfügen sie auch über ein erstaunliches Mass an Scheinheiligkeit. Sie bekämpfen auf verschiedenen Ebenen das formale erzählerische Moment in der modernen Kunst, was sie aber nicht daran hindert, immer wieder neue skulpturale Visionen zu realisieren. Sie sind in der Lage, revolutionäre und ikonoklastische Energie in reine Kunstwerke zu verwandeln und weichen dabei geschickt der Frage nach der Integrität aus: *Wenn die Vögel uns nicht verstehen, sprechen wir mit toten Hasen oder ausgestopften Hunden.* Aus verschiedenen Gründen gehören sie in dieselbe (noch nie erwähnte) Kategorie der «Identifikationsbildhauer». Wir identifizieren uns mit Beuys auf einer kathartischen, eher abstrakten Ebene, mit Cattelan dagegen auf einer gefühlsmässigen; wir empfinden Mitgefühl mit der leidenden Person. Der Betrachter verbindet mit der religiösen Aura von Beuys' Schaukästen etwas Geistiges und formal Vollendetes, das all die in der wirklichen Zeit verstreute Energie enthält. Beuys be-

nutzte Objekte um seinem Hut, seiner Anglerjacke und seinem Mantel Bedeutung zu verleihen. Wenn wir Cattelans Picasso-Kopf betrachten (OHNE TITEL, 1999), bewundern wir den zeitgenössisch adäquaten Umgang mit Kunstgeschichte und Unterhaltung: Eine Geschichte und gleichzeitig die Zeitgeschichte werden zerstückelt und neu zusammengesetzt, um sich in einer Skulptur zu verkörpern. Beim Betrachten des tumben Picasso identifizieren wir uns gleichzeitig mit Cattelan, dem Gaukler, dem fliegenden Händler, dem Schwindler. Und haben wir schliesslich erkannt, dass beide, Beuys wie Cattelan, uns die Taschen geleert haben, sind sie schon über alle Berge, während wir zornig, aber geistig verwandelt, zurückbleiben, erleuchtet durch einen erfolgreichen Trick. Wir wissen, dass Kaninchen sich nicht in Tücher verwandeln lassen, und trotzdem schauen wir gerne dabei zu. Niemand hat Beuys' Eichen und Steine wirklich gezählt, und eigentlich besteht auch kein Grund, daran zu zweifeln, dass es 7000 waren. Aber wen hat das schon interessiert, als er die heroische Tat bekannt gab? Niemand suchte im See von Münster nach der Leiche der Frau, die Cattelan eines Abends dort abgeladen hatte. Wir wissen, dass Daniel Buren bei der Entsorgung dabei war, aber wer zerbricht sich noch den Kopf über die Wahrheit, wenn die Sache gelaufen ist? Den ganzen Tag über haben wir nach ihr Ausschau gehalten, amüsiert bei der Vorstellung, Cattelan wieder einmal auf den Leim gegangen zu sein. Wir lieben es, aus dem Publikum ausgewählt zu werden, und lassen uns gerne zum Narren halten, wenn der Zauberer uns eine Taube aus der Tasche zieht. Beuys machte keine Spässe; er war – wie sein Hase – todernst. Er führte keine Zauberkunststückchen vor, sondern Rituale. Seine Tiere waren Energieleiter, keine vergänglichen Gegenstände der Unterhaltung. Aber Cattelan darf sich über Beuys lustig machen, wie sich die Leute auch über Jesus und Moses lustig machen. Er darf die Energie der Tiere zu seinem Zweck nutzen, weil das Medium den Zuschauer zum Lachen bringt. Was

MAURIZIO CATTELAN, LA NONA ORA / THE NINTH HOUR, 1999, detail, carpet, glass, wax, paint, lifesize figure, Kunsthalle Basel, Switzerland / DIE NEUNTE STUNDE, Teilansicht, Teppich, Glas, Wachs, Farbe, lebensgrosse Figur. (PHOTO: A. MARANZANO)

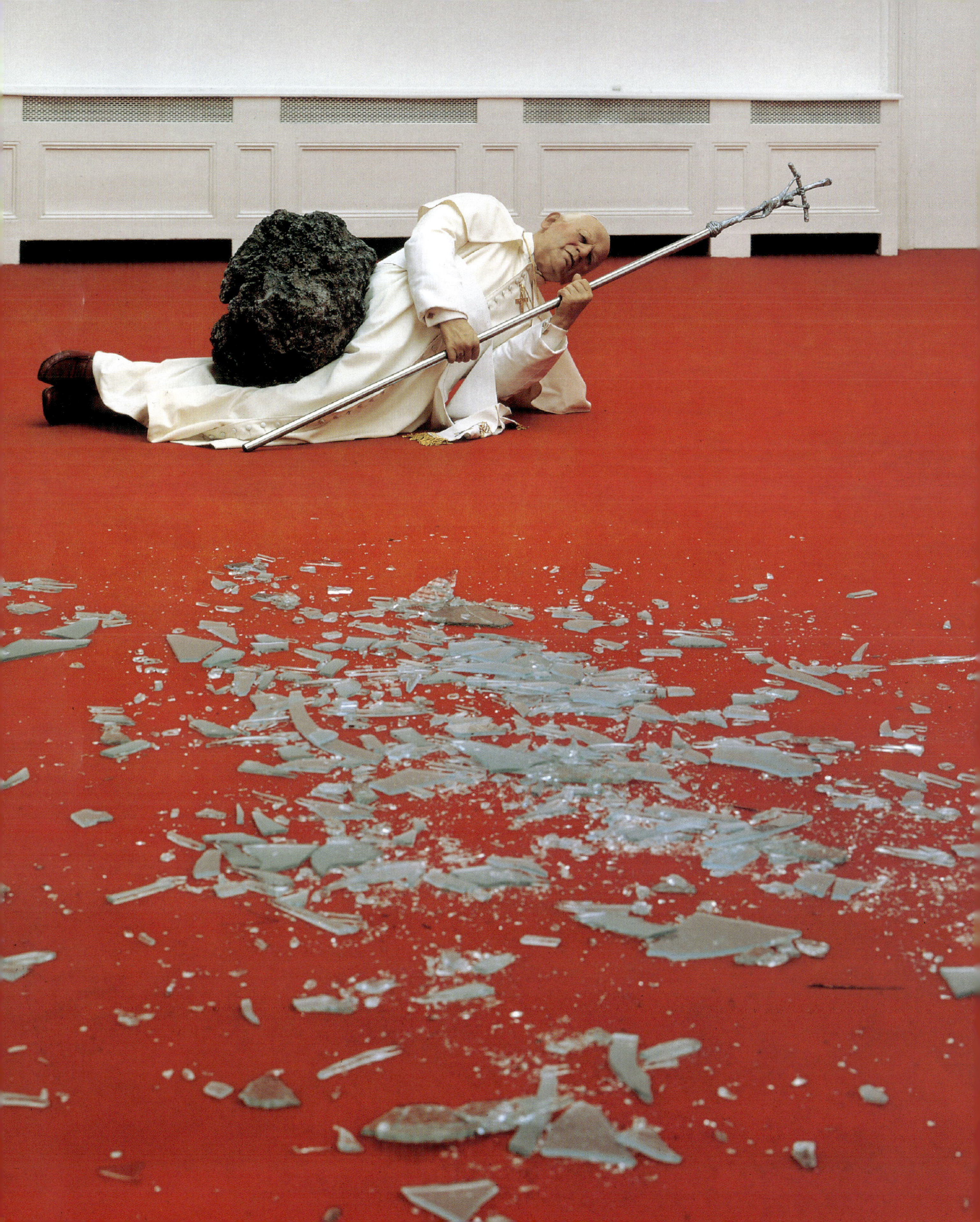

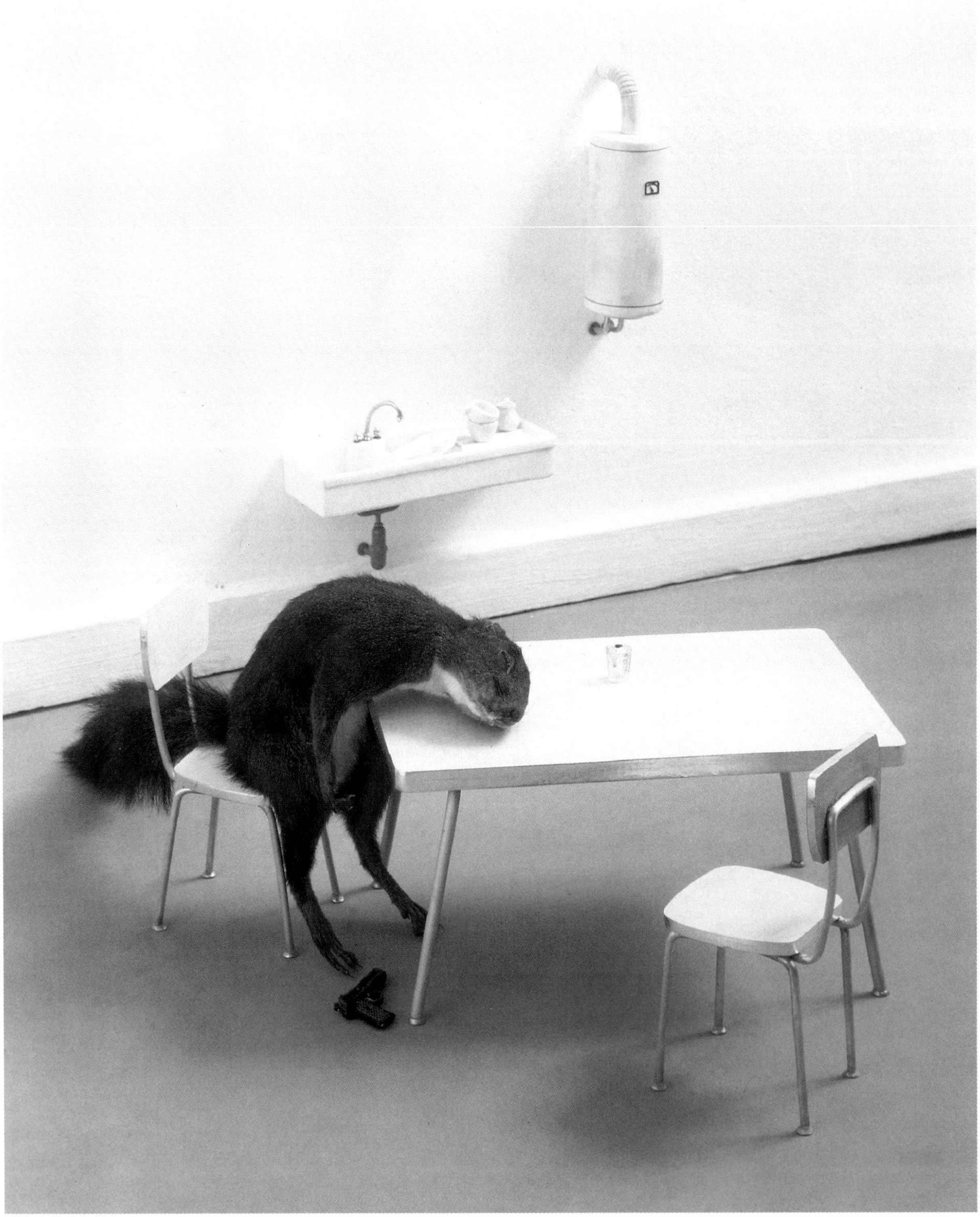

MAURIZIO CATTELAN, BIDIBIDOBIDIBOO, 1996, stuffed squirrel, ceramic, formica, wood, paint, steel, Laure Genillard Gallery, London /

ausgestopftes Eichhörnchen, Keramik, Formica, Holz, Farbe, Stahlrohr.

wäre passiert, wenn Groucho Marx einer der zwölf Apostel gewesen wäre? Wissen wir, ob beim letzten Abendmahl gelacht werden durfte? Hat Beuys jemals einen Witz gemacht? Vielleicht hat er die ganze Zeit über welche gemacht, und Cattelan nie? Ich glaube, Beuys war ein Künstler und versuchte verzweifelt Mensch zu sein, während Cattelan ein Mensch ist, der verzweifelt versucht Künstler zu sein. Würde Cattelan versuchen einem toten Eichhörnchen zu erklären, was Arte Povera ist, würden wir zweifellos lachen, aber letztlich ist es natürlich eine Frage der historischen Perspektive. Beuys stürzte mit seinem Flugzeug auf der Krim ab und Cattelan stürzte vielleicht in einem Hinterhof mit seinem Rad. Rückblickend können wir nicht mehr genau sagen, ob Beuys wirklich die Revolution bedeutete, ob die Geschichte mit Demokratie und Freiheit flirtete, tatsächlich aber nur die Umstürzler in konservative Gurus auf tönernen Füssen verwandelte. Beuys machte aus seiner Familie ein Kunstwerk, während Cattelans Familie der Grund ist, weshalb er überhaupt Kunst macht. Angesichts von Beuys' religiösem Ernst fragen wir uns, ob er uns nicht doch zum Narren hielt. Cattelan macht zwar einen Narren aus sich und sagt doch mehr über die Natur des Menschen aus als jeder andere heutzutage.

Bei seiner Aktion ISOLATIONSZELLE trat Beuys 1971 in seinem Filzanzug auf. Cattelan kostümierte die Leute als Löwen oder phallische Kaninchen. In welches Kostüm hätte er Beuys gesteckt? Er selbst ist als Beuys im Filzanzug aufgetreten, da er aber keinen Ärger bekommen wollte, machte er sich und den Anzug kleiner. Die Zelle ist nicht mehr isoliert und der Anzug hängt am Bügel. Wer nimmt sich wichtiger? Beuys verwandelte sich in eine Ikone, und Cattelan verwandelt Ikonen in seine eigene Person und leiht ihnen seinen Geist, seine Verblendung, sein Ungeschick. Der Lauf der Geschichte lässt sich ändern, das Schicksal lenken. Beide, Beuys und Cattelan, stützen sich auf frühe Erinnerungen, heroische im ersten, jämmerliche im zweiten Fall. Sie setzen die Lebensenergie ein, zusammen mit Charisma und Scheinheiligkeit, Glauben und Täuschung. Beuys vermochte übers Wasser zu wandeln, während ihm Cattelan von Stein zu Stein hüpfend folgt: Mogeln kann lebensrettend sein. Der eine mit der Bibel in

der Hand, der andere mit Sagen und Märchen. In den 70er Jahren waren dogmatische Interventionen angesagt, heute geht es um kleine Einsichten und kurzlebige Lügen. Würde Cattelan einen Hut tragen, sähe er dumm aus. Warum also nicht auch Beuys? Vielleicht war Jesus ein Künstler und seine Dornenkrone ein Zeichen seines Narzissmus. Oder Beuys wäre ein Prophet und Cattelan Pfarrer in einem abgelegenen Dorf. Seine Geschichte wäre eine ganz andere, komischer und gleichzeitig banaler. Wir wünschten uns heute, wir könnten Jesus und Beuys anrufen und sie fragen, ob sie jemals lachten, ob Cattelan eher ein Heiliger oder ein Faschist, ein Dorftrottel oder ein verhinderter Mönch sei. Der Hase hat von Malerei nicht viel verstanden, aber vielleicht werden die Vögel über Cattelans Kunst lachen. Die Schlinge, der Hut und die Nase, eine neue Symbolik für ein neues Jahrtausend, eine neue Geschichte, in der Parabeln, Reden und Spässe vielleicht dieselbe Funktion für das Verstehen der Wirklichkeit haben.

(Übersetzung: Uta Goridis)

1) Albert Schulze Vellinghausen, «Ewald Matare», in: *Prisma*, No. 1/8 (1947), S. 17.
2) Richard Dyer, *Heavenly Bodies: Film Stars and Society*, St. Martin's Press, New York 1986, S. 18.

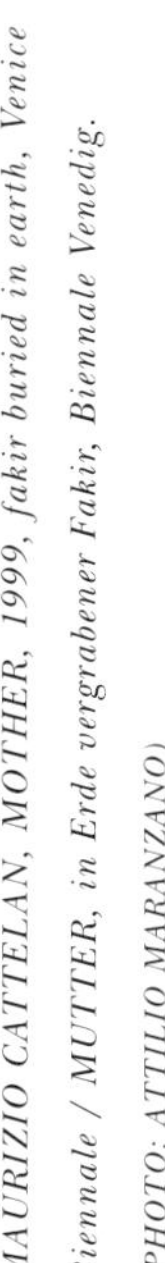
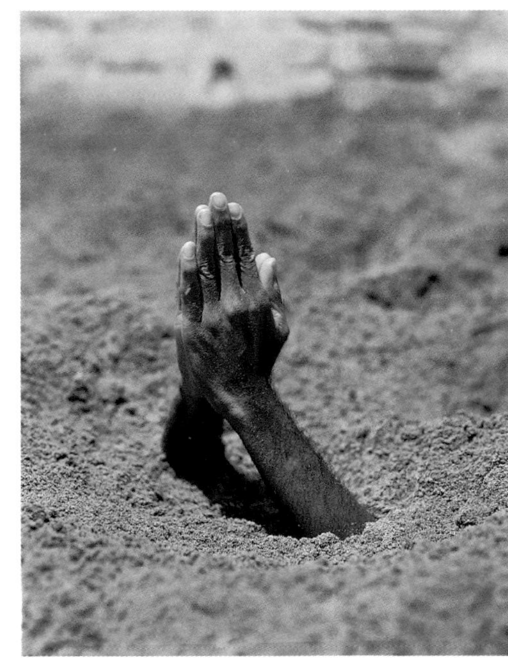

MAURIZIO CATTELAN, MOTHER, 1999, fakir buried in earth, Venice Biennale / MUTTER, in Erde vergrabener Fakir, Biennale Venedig.
(PHOTO: ATTILIO MARANZANO)

Edition for Parkett **Maurizio Cattelan**
Untitled, 2000
Black-and-white photograph, digital print on paper
(Uso Mano), 16¼ x 13″ (image size 12 x 9½″).
Edition of 60, signed and numbered certificate.

Ohne Titel, 2000
Schwarzweiss-Photographie, Digitalprint auf Papier
(Uso Mano), 41,3 x 33 cm (Bildgrösse: 30,5 x 24 cm).
Auflage: 60, signiertes und nummeriertes Zertifikat.

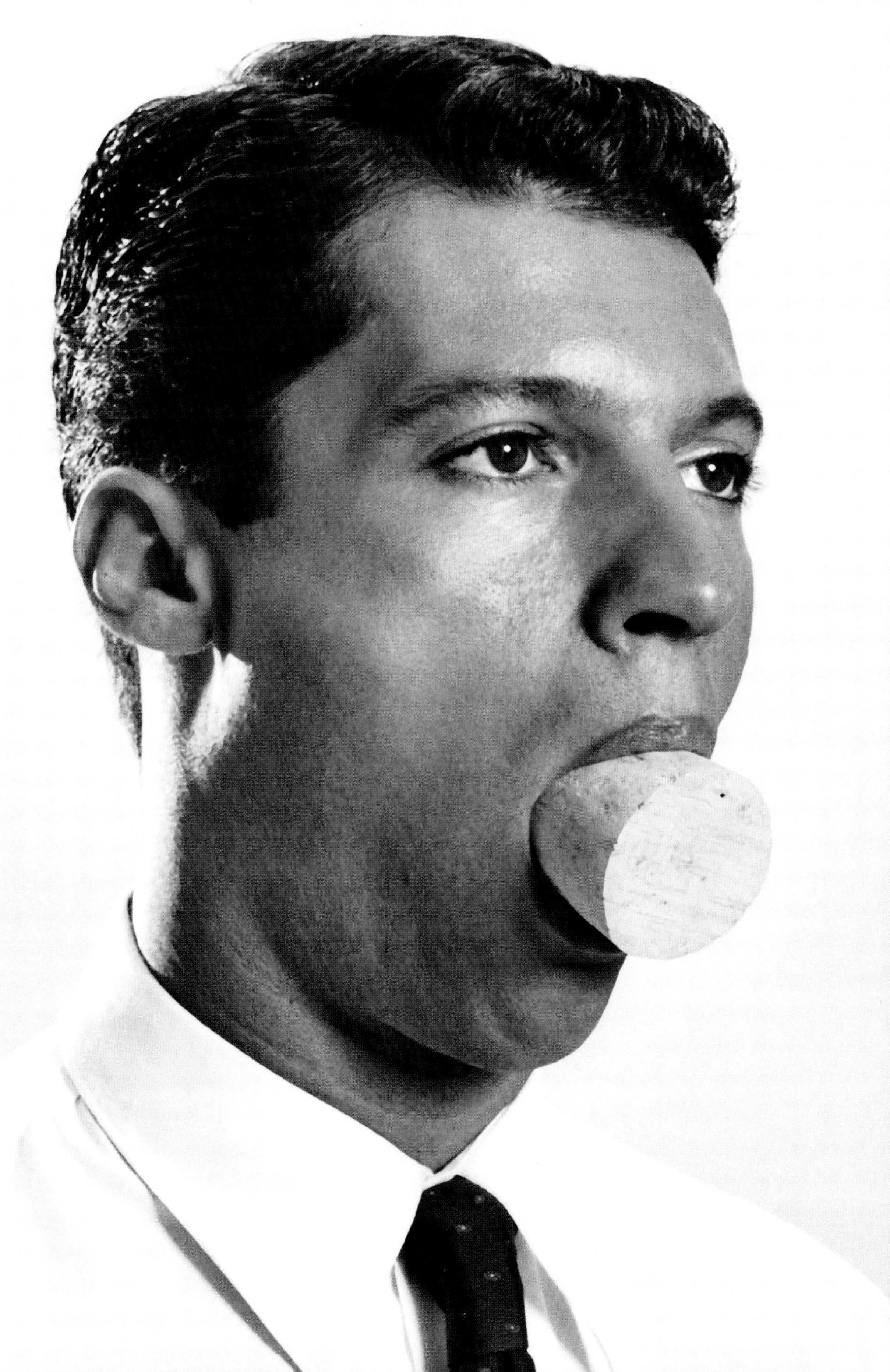

Yayoi Kusama

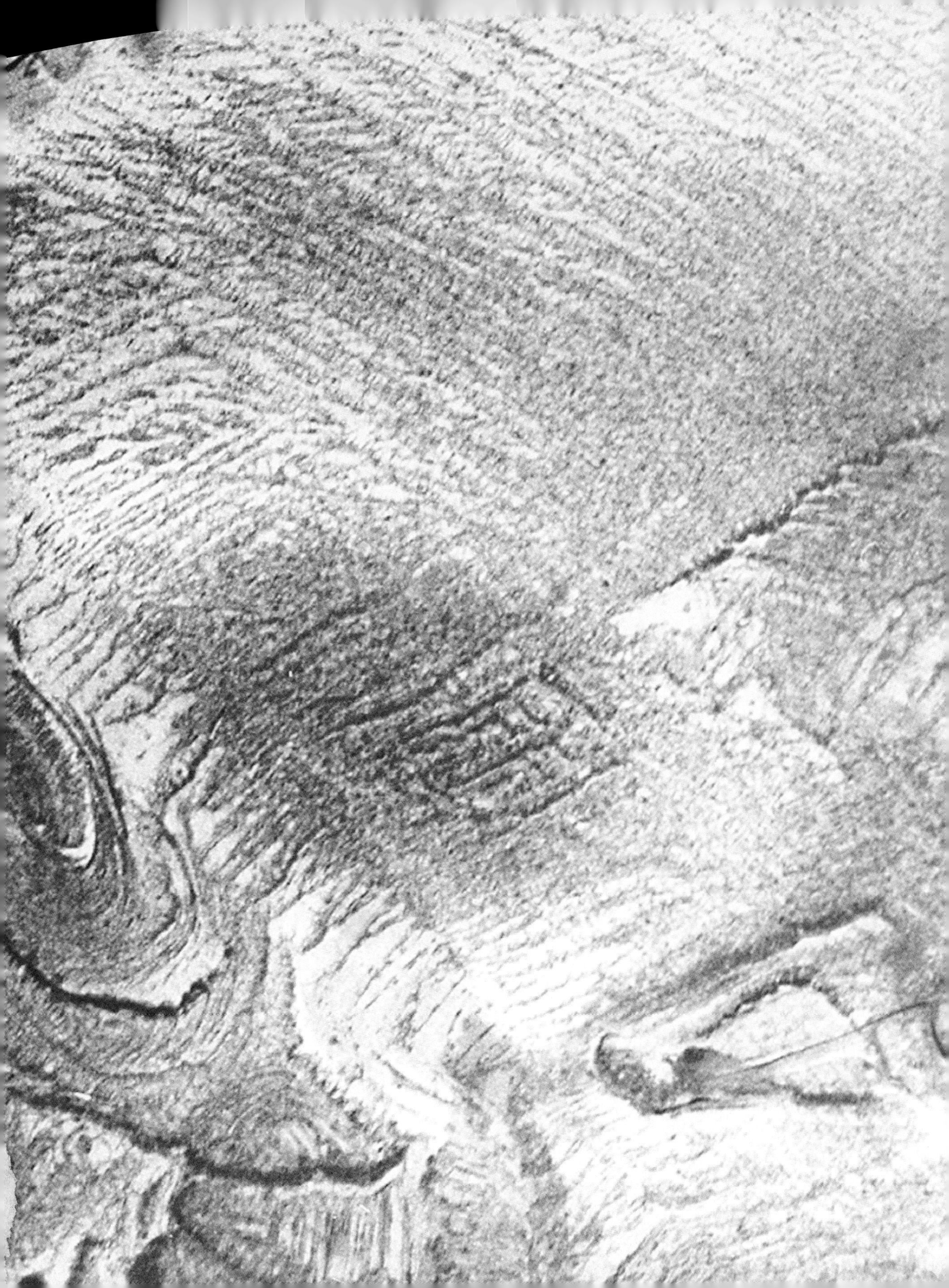

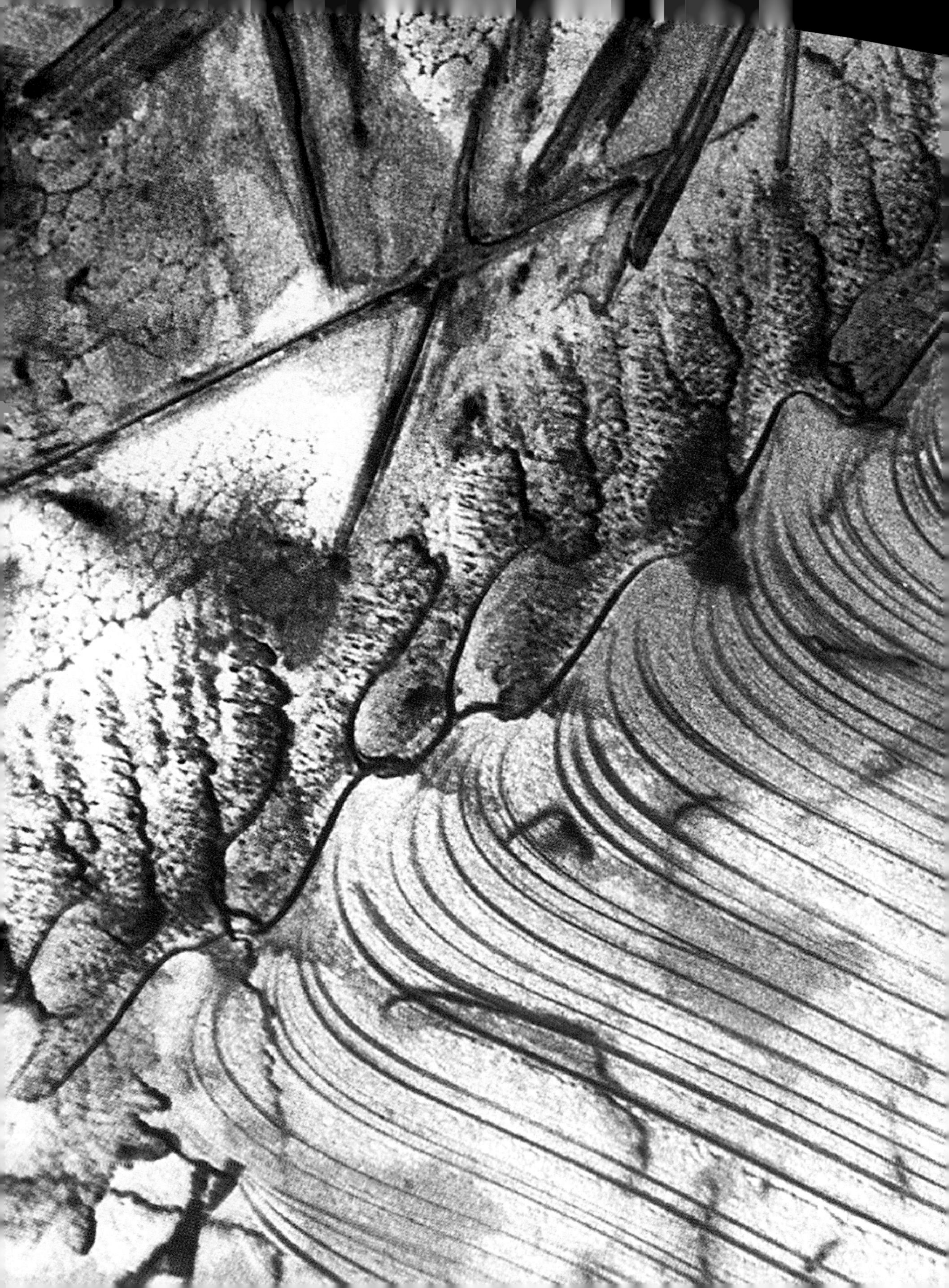

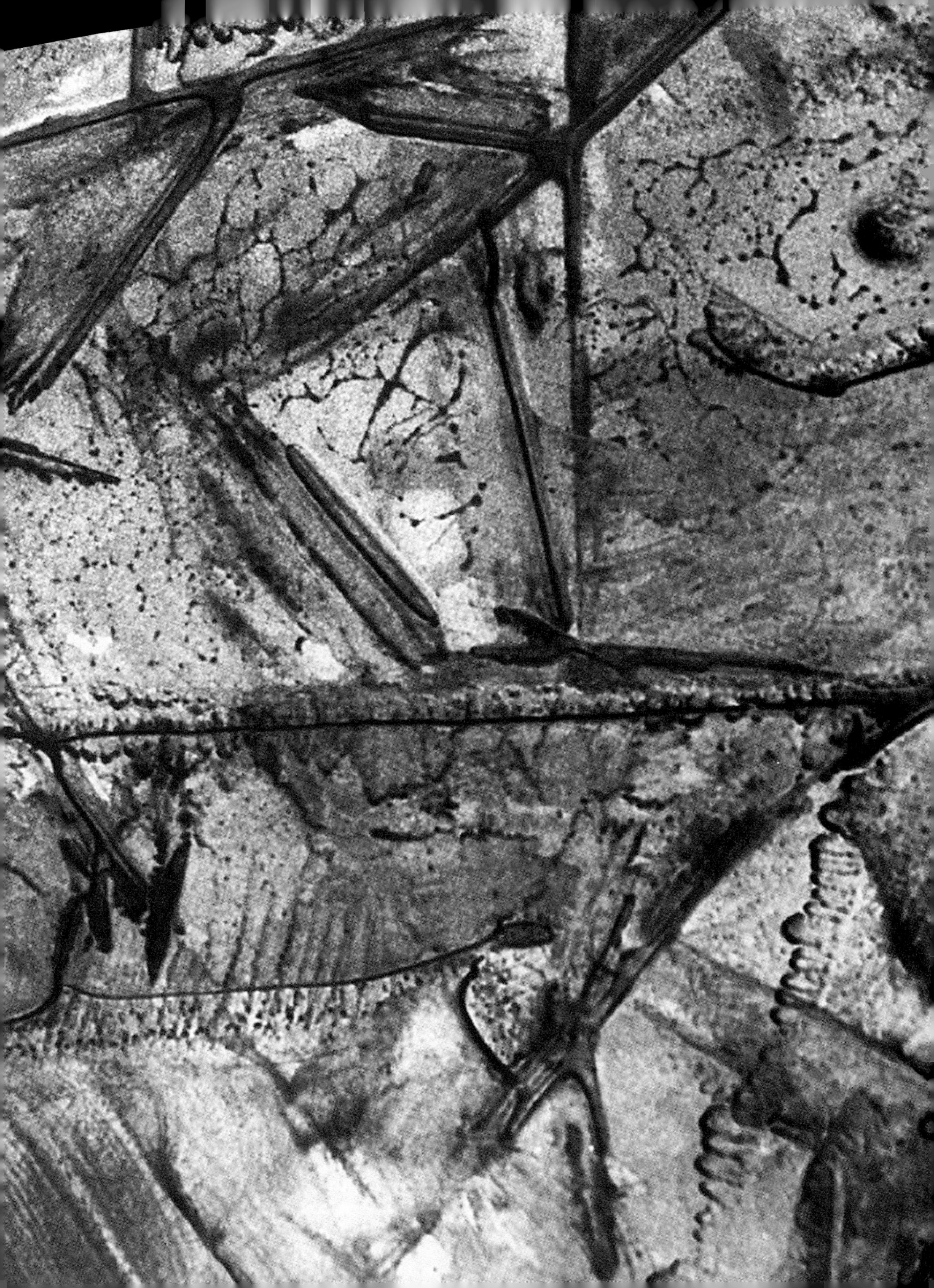

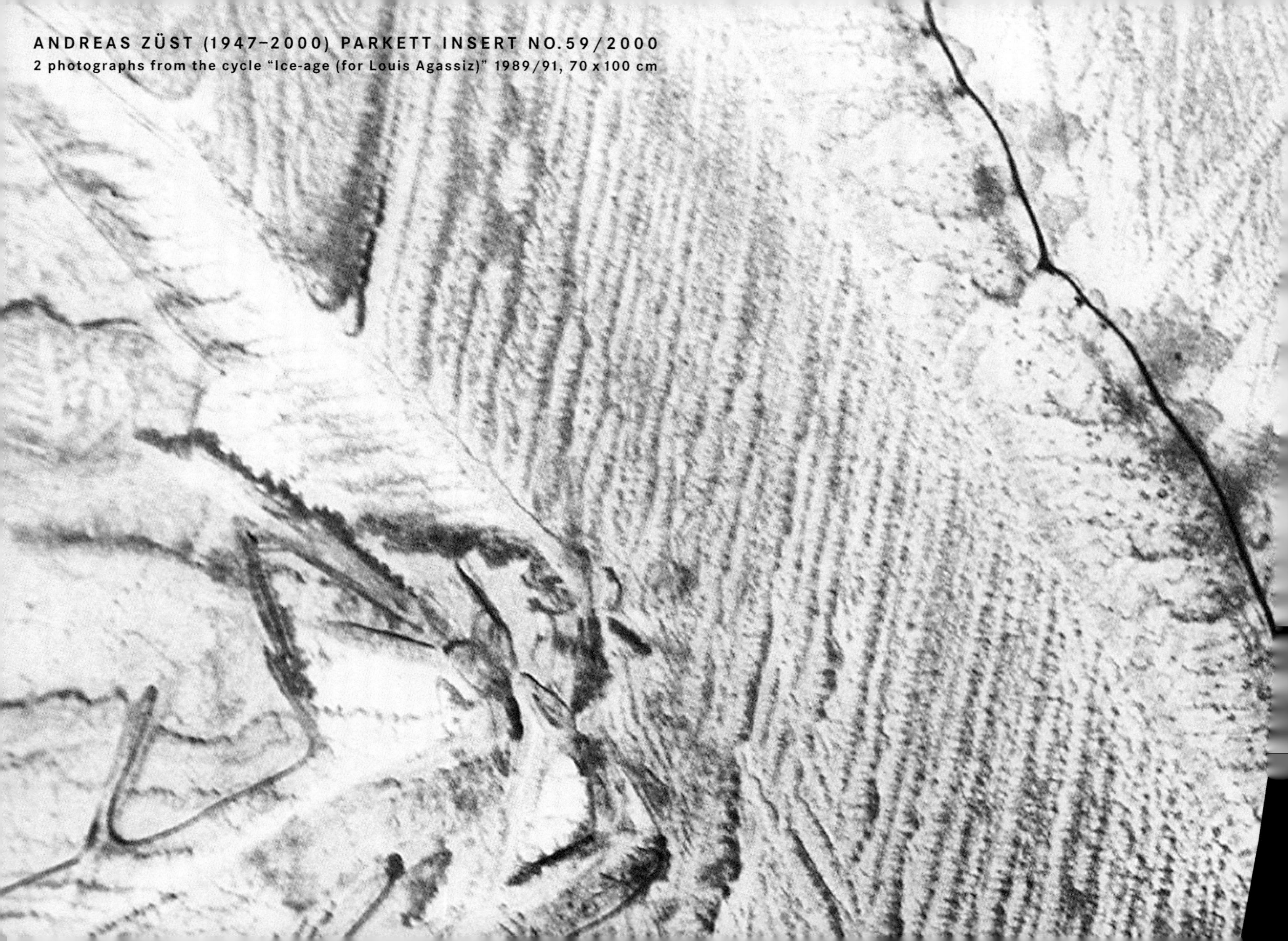

ANDREAS ZÜST (1947–2000) PARKETT INSERT NO.59/2000
2 photographs from the cycle "Ice-age (for Louis Agassiz)" 1989/91, 70 x 100 cm

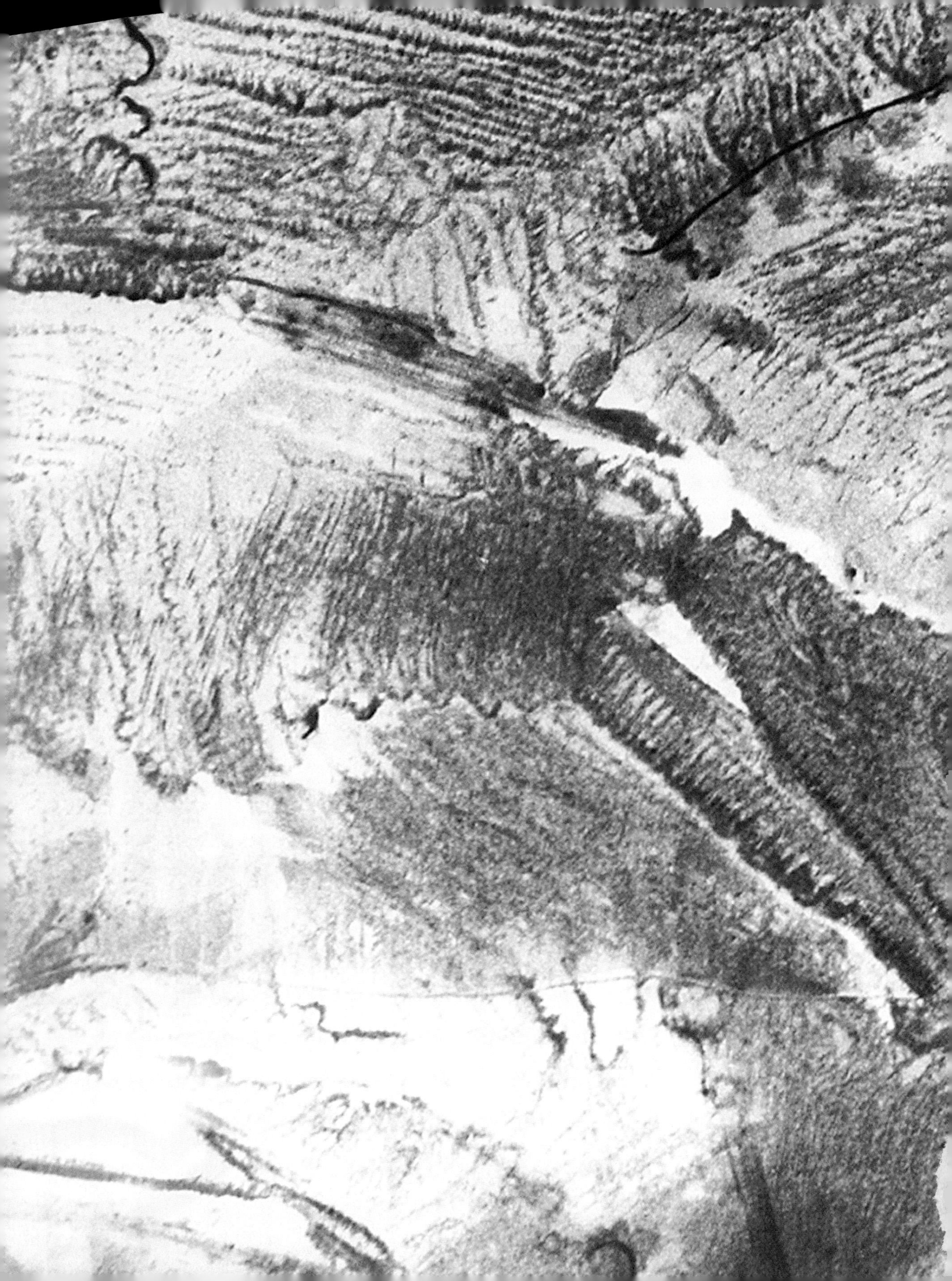

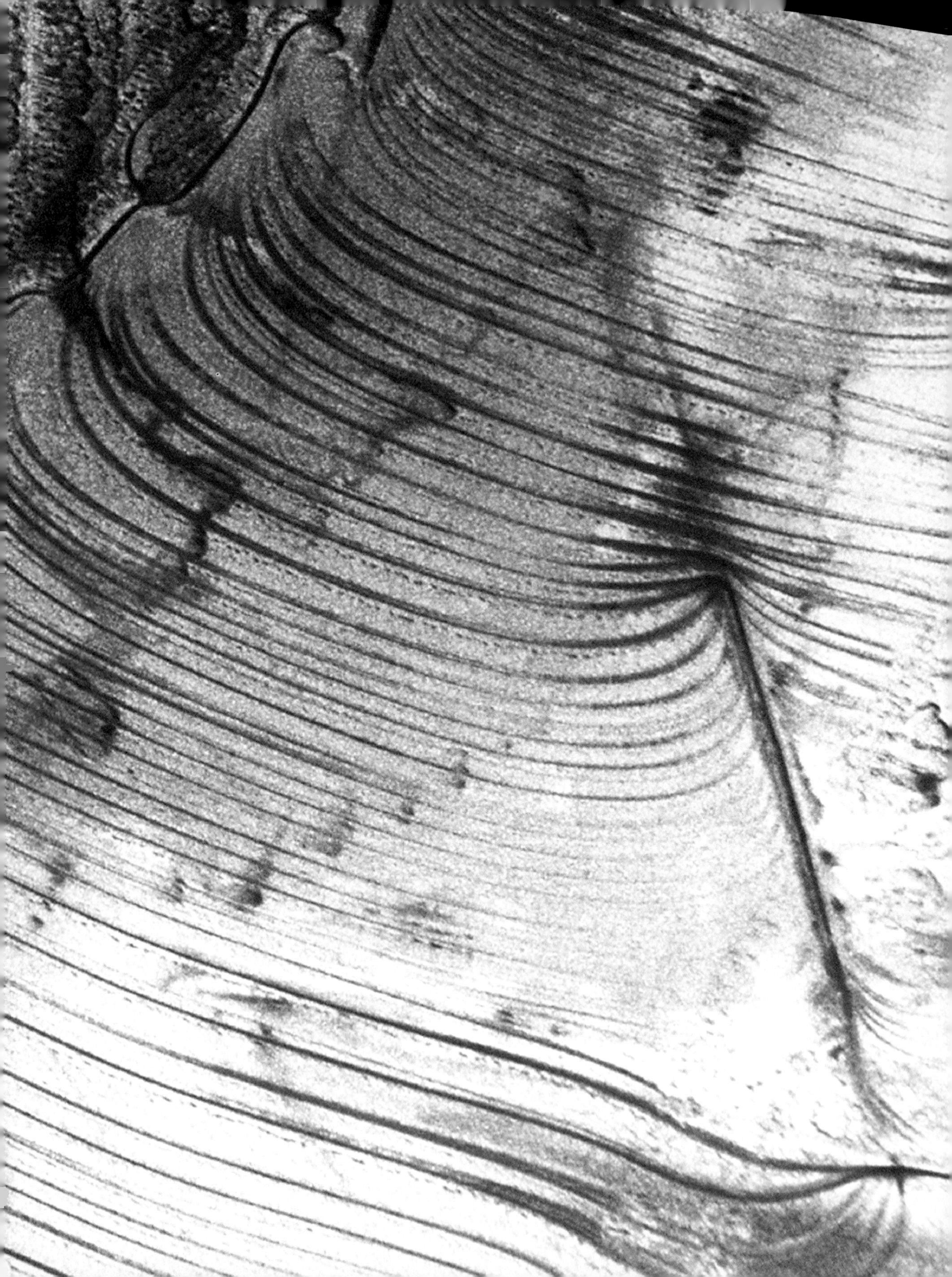

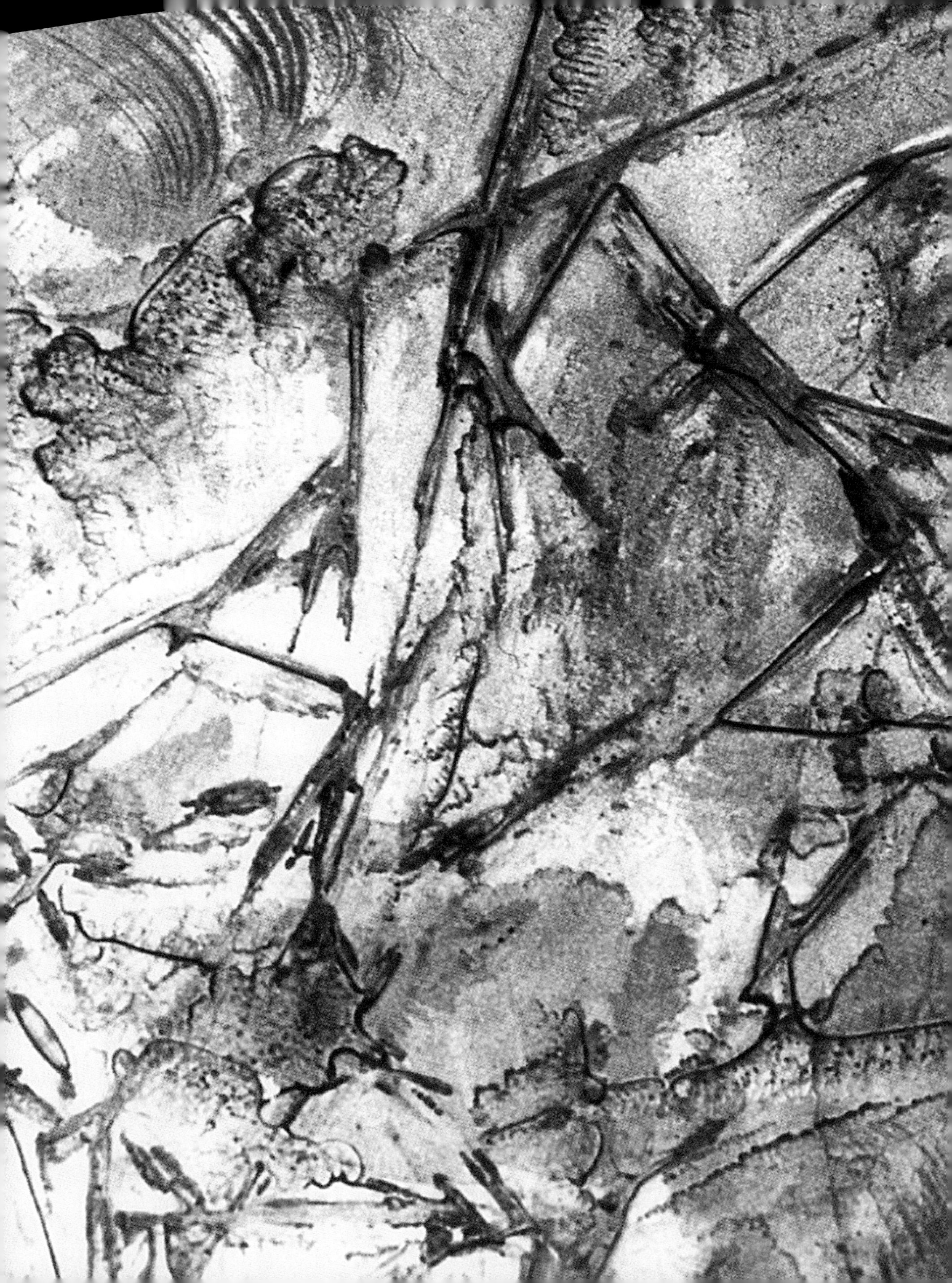

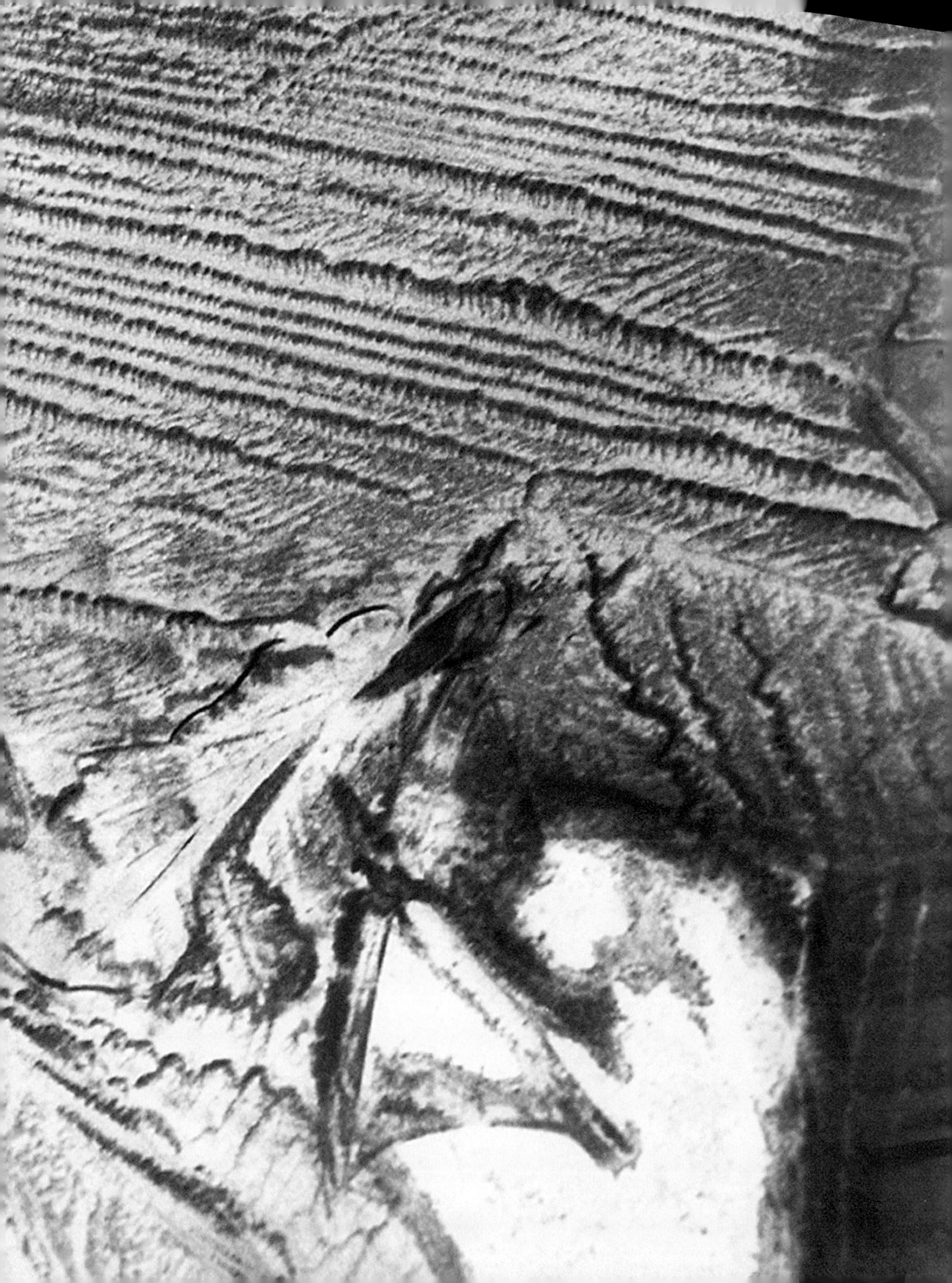

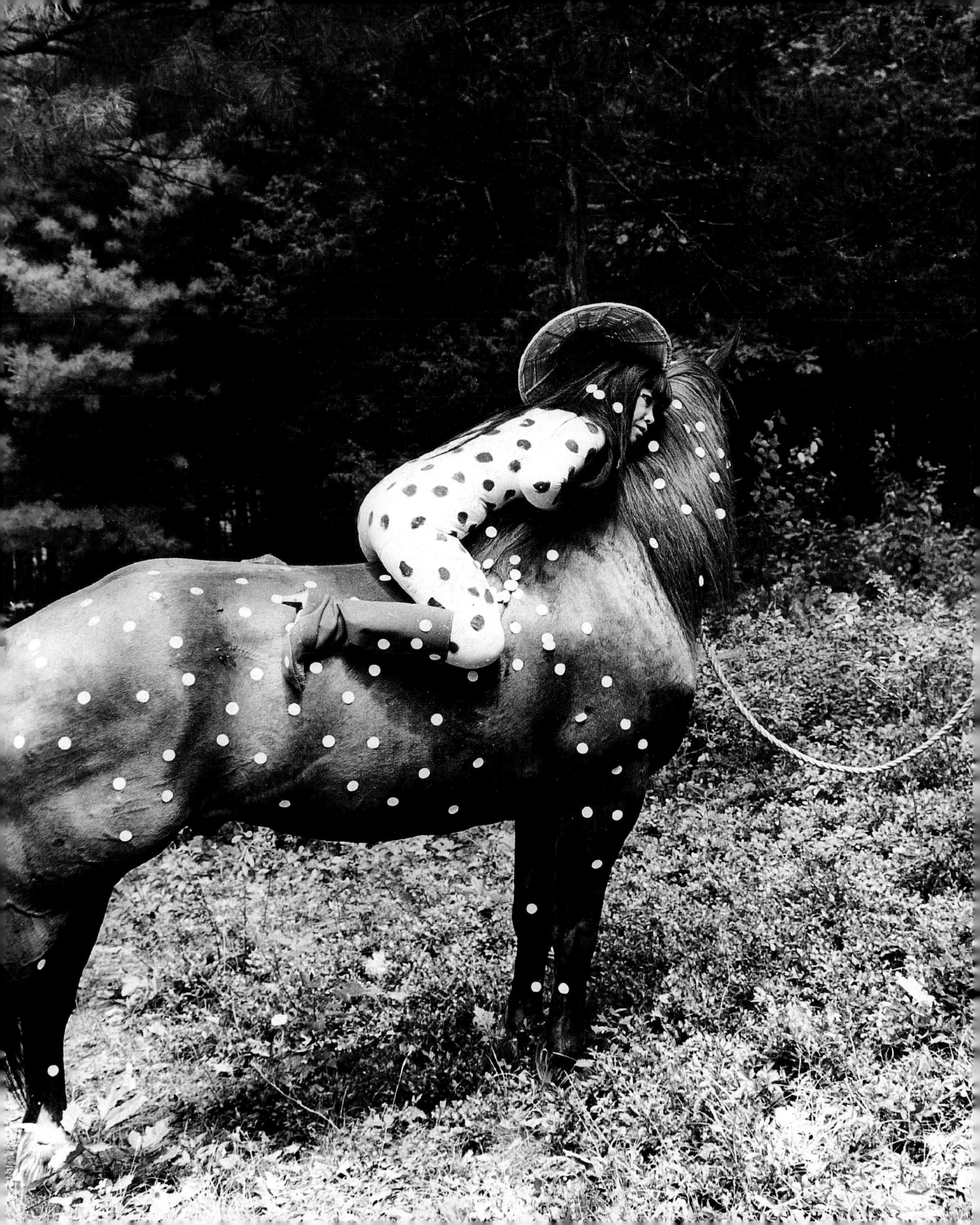

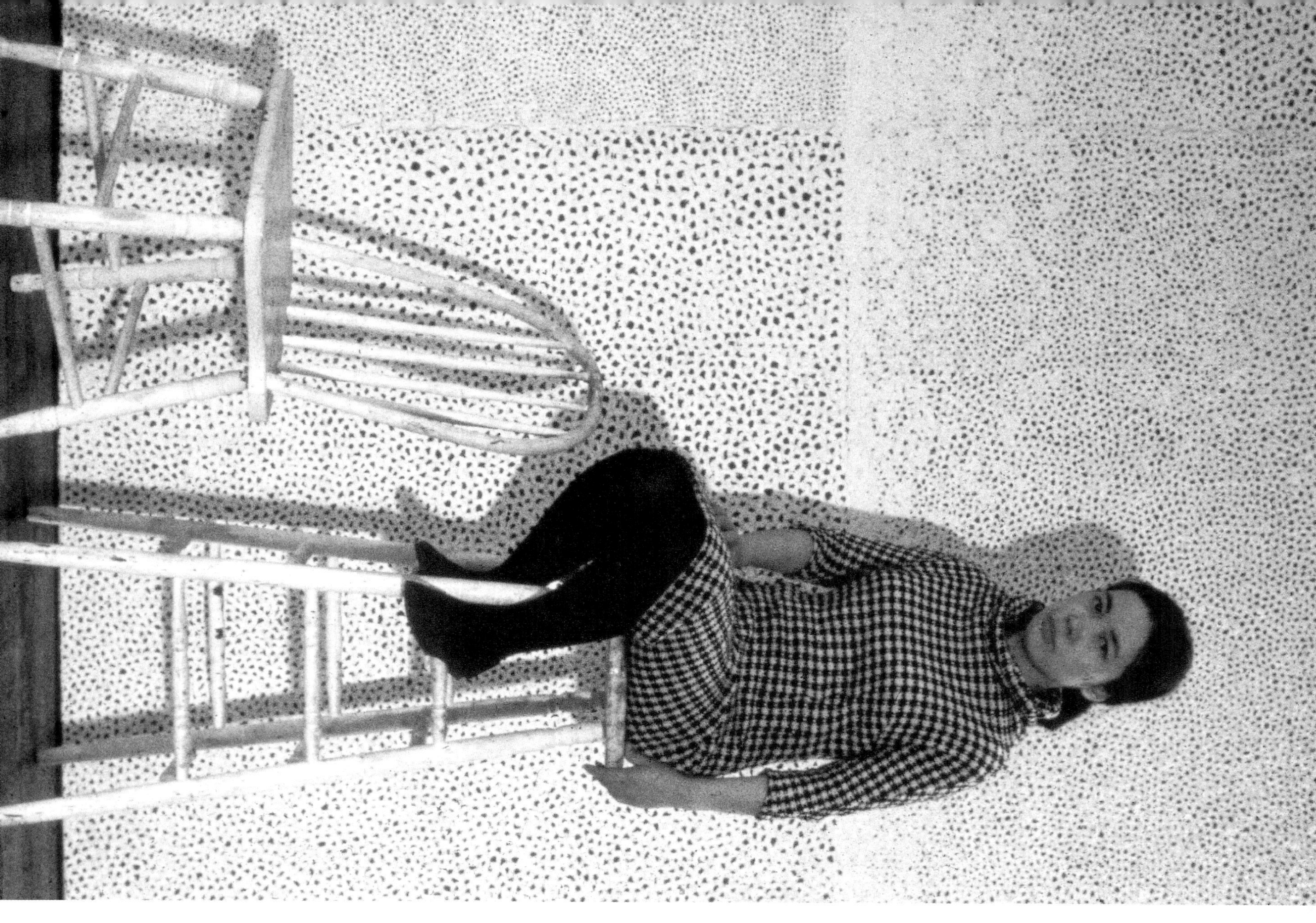

Seite/Page 75: YAYOI KUSAMA, HORSE PLAY, 1967, performance, Woodstock, New York / SPIEL MIT EINEM PFERD.

The artist with INFINITY NET paintings in her New York studio, 1958 / Die Künstlerin in ihrem New Yorker Atelier.

«BETWEEN HEAVEN AND EARTH: This Languid Weight of Life»[1]

URSULA PANHANS-BÜHLER

Es war und ist immer noch eine bedrohliche Sternenlast, unter der das Lebensschiffchen der 1929 geborenen japanischen Künstlerin sich seinen Weg sucht, getrieben von einem nicht geheuren, verheissungsvoll bedrohlichen Wind, der sich in den Segeln ihrer seltsam ungewöhnlichen Werke, diese immer wieder ähnlich und doch anders formend, fängt. In einem kürzlich geführten Interview antwortet Yayoi Kusama auf eine Frage von Akira Tatehata zu ihrer Stellung im und zum Kunstbetrieb: «As you said, I am in my heart an outsider.»[2]

Psychische Aussenseiter sind in der Kunst des zwanzigsten Jahrhunderts nicht nur endemisch. Seit Prinzhorn um Verständnis warb und Dubuffet mit seiner Verteidigung der *art brut* sie rehabilitierte, haben sie spätestens seit Navratil Konjunktur. Die besondere Stellung von Yayoi Kusama jedoch scheint darin zu liegen, dass ihre Beiträge zu den Kunstströmungen ihrer und unserer Zeit so hautnah mit deren Artikulationen sich berühren (die sie im Übrigen nicht nur mitgetragen, sondern teils selbst vorwegnehmend befördert hat), dass man sich des Eindrucks nicht erwehren kann, ihre Kunst spiele kontrapunktisch aus, wovon sich die sozial akzeptierteren Artikulationen seis sublimierend absetzen, seis ironisch distanzieren, seis von einem labilen Diesseits aus hypnotisch angezogen fühlen. In einem kulturellen Rahmen gesehen konfrontieren ihre Werke uns mit einem bedrängend durchschimmernden Revers. Diese dunkle Seite einer prekären aktuellen Selbstbehauptung löst wohl die Faszination aus, die heute Yayoi Kusamas Werk erneut umgibt.

Mit tausenden von Zeichnungen und Aquarellen kommt Yayoi Kusama 1957 mit 28 Jahren nach New York, um hier ihre Fortüne zu machen. 1959 zeigt sie in ihrer ersten Einzelausstellung in der Brata Gallery riesige, die Galeriewände füllende monochrome INFINITY NETS (Unendlichkeitsnetze), das grösste mit einer Seitenlänge von zehn Metern und etwa doppelt so hoch wie die zierliche Künstlerin. Es sind Ölbilder, die in kreisenden Bewegungen um winzige Zentren die Oberfläche weiss in weiss irisierend

URSULA PANHANS-BÜHLER ist Professorin für Kunstgeschichte an der Kunsthochschule Kassel und arbeitet an einer Studie zu Marcel Duchamps WEISSER SCHACHTEL.

in einen unfassbaren Raum verwandeln, eine lautlos pulsierende, magische Zwischenwelt. Serialität, wenngleich mit deutlich subjektiven Spuren des Handanlegens, und Monochromie tragen ihr in der Folgezeit Einladungen zu Ausstellungen im Fahrwasser europäischer Künstlergruppen in Holland, Deutschland und Italien ein. In New York finden die kompositionslosen Netze ohne Anfang und Ende Bewunderung bei Frank Stella und Donald Judd – «my first boyfriend», erklärt sie im Interview mit Tatehata.[3]

Donald Judd hilft ihr bei ihrer nächsten Grenz- und Randüberschreitung, den COMPULSION FURNITURES (Zwanghafte Möbel) oder ACCUMULATIONS, die sie zu einer der Leitfiguren eines neuen Objektverständnisses sowie zur Inkunabel von *Soft Sculpture* aufsteigen lässt und ihr Erfolg in Kreisen der Pop-Art beschert. Für ein Paar muss es eine seltsame Verschiebung intimer Konspiration und Arbeitsteilung gewesen sein, Bettlaken zu zerschneiden um daraus auf einer Nähmaschine Hülsen zu nähen und sie anschliessend zu prallen Phallusprotuberanzen auszustopfen – man könnte auch an erregte Brustwarzen denken, deren übertriebene Grösse dem Erleben des Säuglings nachempfunden ist, oder an Hodensäcke. In überquellender Fülle spriessen diese aus Möbelstücken. Sessel oder Sofa, Tisch oder Kinderwagen, mögliche und unmögliche Haushaltgegenstände in Reichweite werden zu Objekten einer Metamorphose phantasmatischer primordialer Fülle, stalaktitenbewehrte Möbelgrotten, in denen eine kleinasiatische Kybele, behängt mit den ekstatischen Opfergaben ihrer sich selbst verstümmelnden Priester, versinken könnte, die erst eine gnädigere römische Tradition zum Inbild mammaler Fülle mildern sollte.

Mit einem dieser Objekte, einem Ruderboot, verblüfft Yayoi Kusama 1963 die New Yorker Kunstwelt in einer Einzelausstellung in der Galerie von Gertrude Stein. AGGREGATION, ONE THOUSAND BOATS SHOW (Ansammlung, 1000-Boote-Schau), versammelt in der Tat 1000 Boote, ein plastisch veritables, wenngleich schwer beladen mit Protuberanzen, und 999 Photoreproduktionen dieses einzigartigen Bootes, mit denen Wände, Decken und Boden des Ausstellungsraums und einer dunklen Eingangskanüle

tapeziert sind. Kusamas Bootstapete segelt Warhols tapezierten Kuhköpfen um gut zwei Jahre voraus. Das wirkliche Boot und seine Last bringt eine Zweideutigkeit und den ausweglosen Konflikt der Künstlerin zum Vorschein, als sich Yayoi Kusama, nackt vom Rücken gesehen, zwischen Boot und Tapete photographieren lässt. Wie in einer Scherenbewegung läuft die Richtung des Boots und jene seiner Verfertigerin auseinander, unterstrichen von einer über den Bootsrand ragenden Protuberanz.

In mehreren Ausstellungen zeigt Kusama in New York, Mailand und Essen in den folgenden Jahren, wieder ihren Künstlerkollegen voraus, ein Environment, DRIVING IMAGE (Reiztreibendes Bild). Mit den sich ihr aufdrängenden INFINITY NETS überzieht sie Interieurwände, Mobiliar und Schaufensterpuppen, die Netze und zu Punkten reduzierten Gründe nun zweifarbig, jeder Gegenstand poppig bunt in anderen Gegenfarben, der Boden übersät mit trockenen Nudeln, knirschend unter den Tritten der Besucher, auf die Kusama 1964 in New York bei der Vernissage in der Castellane Gallery zwei nudelbefrachtete Hunde loslässt, als wolle deren animalisch aggressives Bellen aus einem selbstvergessen versunkenen Hinübergleiten in eine Auflösung des Unterschieds von Ich und Welt aufschrecken, dem übrigens auch die klaren Konturen der Readymade-Objekte entgegenstanden. Der Drang, Unterschiede einzuschmelzen, trieb auch andere Künstler um. Yves Klein äusserte in dieser Zeit seinen Wunsch, ganz Frankreich mit Yves-Klein-Blau zu überziehen, ein Unterfangen, das wohl schnell an der Lieferfähigkeit seines IKB-Herstellers gescheitert wäre.

1966 waren Betrachter zu einem hexagonalen Spiegelraum, KUSAMA'S PEEP SHOW oder ENDLESS LOVE SHOW, nur optisch zugelassen, durch gesichtsgrosse Öffnungen, um sich augenblicklich im Spiegelraum unendlich vervielfältigt und mit der Fliehkraft der Entfernung entschwinden zu sehen. Der Eindruck wurde durch einen optischen Zeitfaktor dramatisiert. Die Decke war dicht mit verschiedenfarbigen Glühbirnen übersät, die in wechselnd farbigem Rhythmus schockartig aufblinkten. Yayoi Kusama ist die erste, die Spiegelräume inszeniert. Zwei weitere, der Boden übersät mit gepunkteten Phallusprotuberanzen, waren kurz zuvor entstanden.

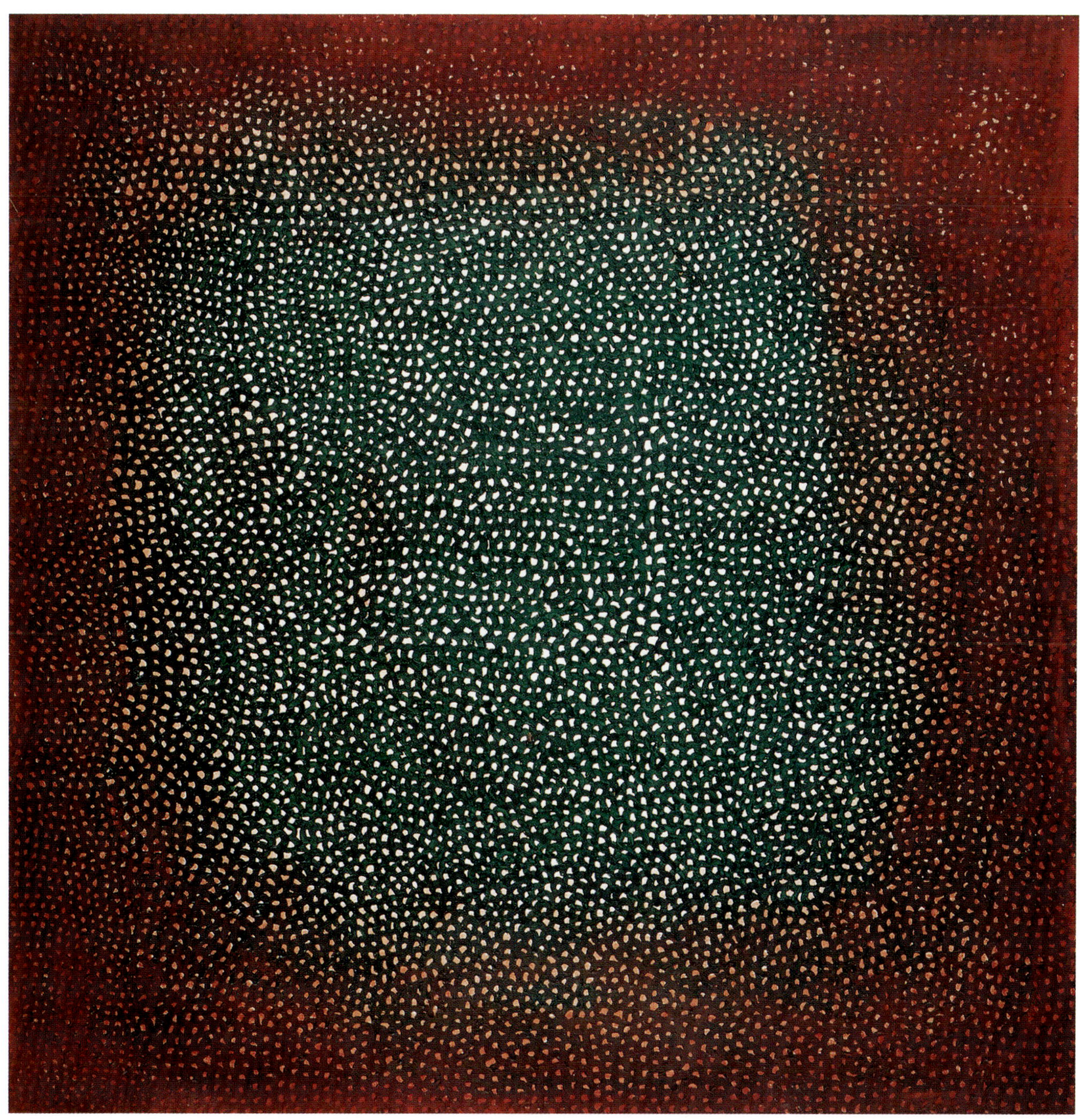

YAYOI KUSAMA, INFINITY NET A, 1965, oil on canvas, 52 x 49½" / UNENDLICHKEITSNETZ A, Öl auf Leinwand, 132 x 126 cm.

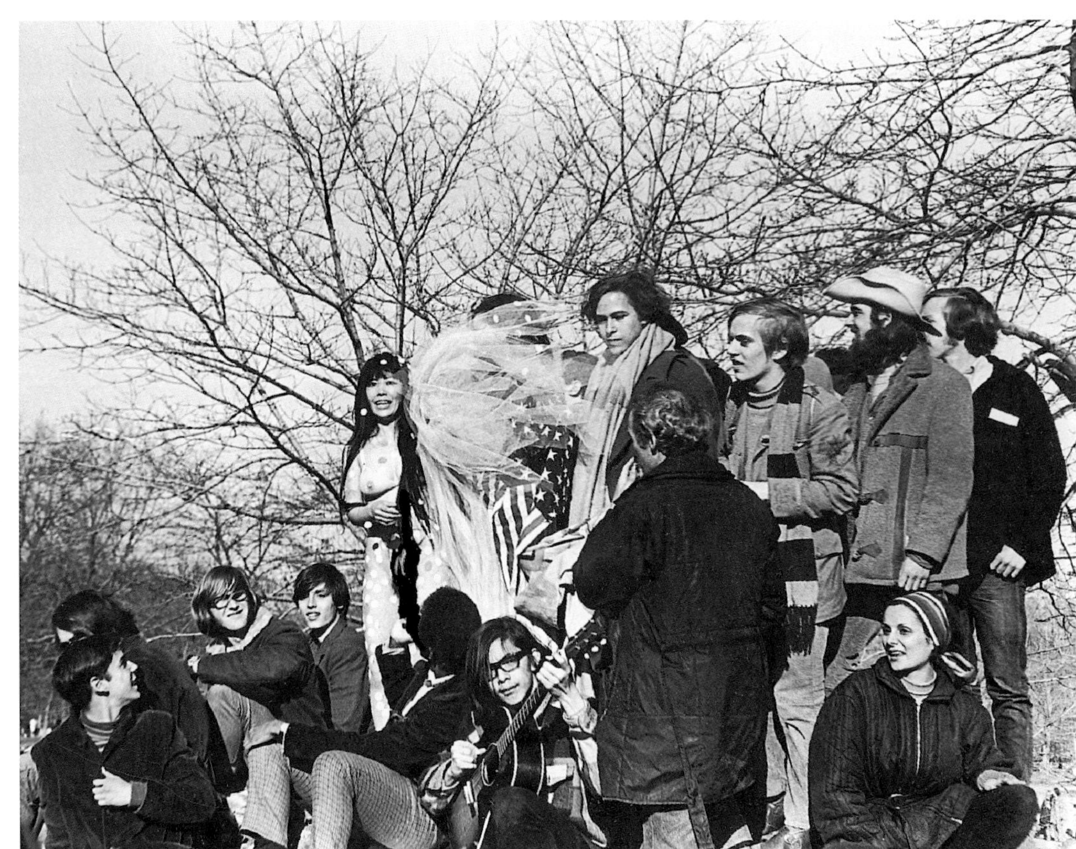

YAYOI KUSAMA, BUST OUT, 1969, performance, Love in festival, Central Park, New York / BRUST RAUS. (PHOTO: STAN GOLDSTEIN)

Ein Feld mit Spiegelbällen, NARCISSUS GARDEN, bescherte ihr eine spektakuläre Pirateriepräsenz auf der Biennale 1966, deren Kunstordnungshüter einschritten, als sie anfing, die einzelnen Bälle für zwei Dollar an Besucher zu verkaufen. Ob bei dem Lichtspektakel des Spiegelraums – sie verteilte im Übrigen *Polka Dots* an Besucher mit der Aufschrift «LOVE FOREVER» und hielt sich selber ein Paar vor die Augen – eine Reminiszenz an Robert Smithson eine Rolle gespielt haben könnte, ist ungewiss. Dieser hatte 1963 zwei Spiegel gegeneinander gekehrt, in der Mitte durch einen Rahmen getrennt, in den gewellte Leuchtstoffröhren eingesetzt waren. Die Reizüberflutung des hektischen An und Aus der Röhren zog dem Betrachter die Sicht auseinander und brachte sie zum Erlöschen. Mit seinem Spiegelkubus überliess wenig später Michelangelo Pistoletto die

Spiegel ihrer eigenen Unendlichkeitsleere – in der Vorstellung des Betrachters: Es gab keinen peependen Blick, man musste mit den beschichteten Rückseiten der Spiegel vorlieb nehmen.

Mit *Polka-Dot*-Performances und -Happenings, Filmen und Modeunternehmungen war Yayoi Kusama in die Sphäre politischer Aktionen der 60er Jahre eingebrochen, die Spektakelwelt einer Medienpräsenz scheint verführerisch auf sie gewirkt zu haben, eine hektische Betriebsamkeit, eine Fortsetzung der Entgrenzung in der Werbung mit nackten Tänzern, Aufforderung und Anleitung zu Publikumsenthüllungen, selbst im Garten des MoMA, eine Befriedung der Welt – in der Zeit des Vietnamkriegs und des Einmarschs der Sowjetunion in Prag – durch ihre Selbstauflösung in der Proklamation alles überschwemmender Liebe. «Obliterate yourself with polka dots (Lös dich in *Polka Dots* auf).» Der Radius wurde grösser und grösser in Presseverlautbarungen, die in unschuldiger Hippie-Manier die führenden Männer der grossen Politik zur Einkehr bewegen wollten, den flachen Sandwich-Reproduktionen ihrer Gesichter aufreizend lebendige nackte Körper unterschoben und in Performances die Politpuppen zum Tanzen brachten. Der Traum von *make love, not war* – die Liebesversprechen in Presseankündigungen werden manisch immer grenzenloser – brach für sie heftiger und plötzlicher zusammen als für viele der 68er Generation, die sich in alle möglichen produktiven und unproduktiven Debatten und Aktivitäten retteten.

Yayoi Kusamas Heimreise nach Japan 1973 sollte zur definitiven Rückkehr werden. In depressiver Grundstimmung beginnt sie zu schreiben: Romane, Novellen, Gedichte, die im japanischen literarischen Untergrund aber auch in der literarischen Öffentlichkeit Beachtung finden. Sie setzt auch ihr plastisches und malerisches Werk fort. Seit 1977 in schützender Obhut einer Tokioter psychiatrischen Klinik, unterhält sie in deren Nähe ein Atelier und eine Wohnung. 1975 eine erste Einzelausstellung in Japan, 1982 «Obsession», eine beachtete Ausstellung in der Fuji Television Gallery, Tokio. Die wachsende Anerkennung ihres Werks in Japan führte dazu, dass ihr 1993 als erster Frau und Einzelperson die Repräsentation ihres Landes an der Biennale in Venedig übertragen wurde. 1998/99 schliesslich tourte eine grosse Retrospektive zu ihrer Zeit in Amerika, «Love Forever – Yayoi Kusama 1958–1968», durch die USA und wurde auch in Japan gezeigt.

Die Titel ihrer Ausstellungen nach 1975, aber auch die Titel vieler Werke wurden zu poetischen Kommentaren, in die eine neue Erfahrung eingeht: «Gate to Hell», «Hat I used to wear when I was alive», «Message of Death from the Hades», «Obsessional Art – Requiem to Life and Death», «Grass Burning Flashes», «Yayoi Kusama's Soaring from the Dark and Bright Swamp», schliesslich «My Solitary Way to Death» und «I Who Commited Suicide» sowie «Beyond my Illusion».[4] Im Interview mit Damien Hirst erklärt sie 1998, «‹Being alone› is the feeling I have when I confront death (‹Alleinsein› ist das Gefühl, das mich angesichts des Todes erfasst).»[5] 1978 hatte

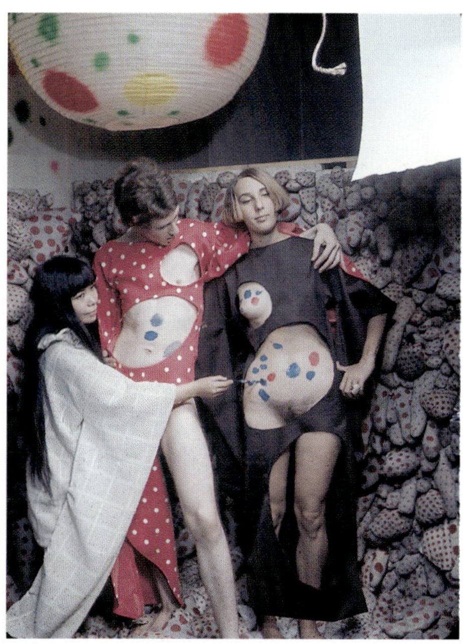

sie eine Autobiographie verfasst, *Manhattan Suicide Addict (Eine Selbstmordsüchtige in Manhattan)*, der 1974 ein «Song of a Manhattan Suicide Addict» vorausgegangen war:

> Swallow antidepressants and it will be gone
> Tear down the gate of hallucinations
> Amidst the agony of flowers,
>   the present never ends
> At the stairs to heaven, my heart expires
>   in tenderness
> Calling from the sky, doubtless, transparent
>   in its shade of blue
> Embraced with the shadow of illusion
> Cumulonimbi arise
> Sounds of tears, shed upon eating the colors
>   of the cotton rose
> I become a stone
> Not in time eternal
> But in the present that transpires.[6]

Sie hat mit ihrer Kunst Halluzinationen kanalisiert, die sie seit ihrer Kindheit bedrängt, überschwemmt und umgarnt haben, aber auch den Sog in Schach gehalten, ihrem Leben ein Ende zu setzen. Vieles in ihrem Werk der letzten zwanzig Jahre ist Wiederholung, Reproduktion oder Paraphrase. Aber es sind auch entscheidende Veränderungen hinzugekommen. In riesigen Bildern erreichen ihre Netzstrukturen und Muster die intuitiv assimilierte Objektivität einer *Histoire Naturelle.* Ihre reliefplastischen grossen Werke, Rahmen, gefüllt mit wilden Entrelacs-Verschlingungen, verblüffend an irisch-northumbrische Buchmalerei unserer Kultur des frühen Mittelalters erinnernd, SLEEPING STAMENS (Schlafende Staubfäden, 1985), oder Rahmen, gefüllt mit irregulären sehnigen Netzen, SHOOTING STARS (1992), wirken, als habe die lange Weisheit einer alten Kultur und nicht ein einzelnes Individuum sie erzeugt. Organische Formen, LEFTOVER SNOW IN THE DREAM (Zurückgebliebener Schnee im Traum, 1982), wirken in ihrer Viszeralität wie präzis geformte organische Empfindungsberichte einer vorsprachlichen Zeit. Neuere serielle Felder mit alten phalloiden Formen, REPETITION (1998), wirken kühl eingeschränkt. Es ist, als ob eine biographisch auferzwungene Rebellion gegen die Logik der Zivilisation in Formen artikuliert würde, die zugleich deren Sehnsüchte und Dramen – und deren Notlüge – als Ausweg enthält. Daher rührt wohl die Verblüffung eines spezifischen Déjà-vu, die Kusamas quasi parallelen Erfindungen zu Strukturen der Natur und der Kulturgeschichte auslösen, und andererseits die – von aussen gesehen – clowneske Note, die in den repetitiven Wucherungen eines einzigen Motivs, des phantasmatischen Phallus liegt.

Anfang der 60er Jahre stiess Yayoi Kusama, so berichtet sie selber, verächtlich gegen eine umgekippte Kiste, die ihr und Donald Judd als Tisch diente, und meinte zu Judd, dies sei sein Stoff. Ob in der Herstellung einer neuen Objektobjektivität in der «minimalistischen» Kunst der 60er Jahre der Versuch einer neuerlichen kulturellen Zähmung des Todes durch «verkleinerndes Nachgeben» steckt, die psychische Annahme der eigenen Sterblichkeit, ein *Noli me tangere* der verlorenen Einheit, zu deren Zeichen die buchstäbliche Abstraktion der Dinge wird, wäre eine

Untersuchung wert. – Yayoi Kusama blieb nur der unabschliessbare Weg aus einer elementaren Verstrickung, die Einsamkeit im Erleben der eigenen Grenze ist zeitlich projektiv hinausgeschoben. *Funny* mögen ihre Skulpturen für uns sein, sie selber spielt dann den unfreiwilligen Clown, der zwischen Spiel und Ernst nicht so leicht die Seiten wechselt. Wem der Himmel samt Sternen auf diese Weise in den Schoss zu fallen droht, dem verwandeln sie sich nicht in leuchtende Taler, wie sie seinerzeit Hans Christian Andersen als leichtere, wenn auch ein wenig zynische Bürde in romantischer Herablassung seiner Märchenfigur philanthropisch ins geschürzte Hemdchen gleiten liess.

1) Zwischen Himmel und Erde: diese träge Last des Lebens, vgl. dazu: Yayoi Kusama, *Manhattan Suicide Addict,* autobiographische Erzählung aus dem Jahr 1978: «I can not give up my existence. Also I can not escape from death. This languid weight of life!» sowie Alexandra Munroe, «Between Heaven and Earth: The Literary Art of Yayoi Kusama» in: *Love Forever: Yayoi Kusama, 1958–68,* Ausstellungskatalog, Los Angeles County Museum of Art, 1998, S. 72. «Between Heaven and Earth» lautete auch der Titel der Einzelausstellung von Yayoi Kusama in der Fuji Television Gallery, Tokio 1991.
2) «Akira Tatehata in Conversation with Yayoi Kusama» in: Laura Hoptman, Akira Tatehata, Udo Kultermann, *Yayoi Kusama,* Phaidon Press, London 2000, S. 11.
3) Ebenda.
4) Deutsch etwa: «Pforte zur Hölle», «Hut, den ich trug, als ich lebte», «Todesbotschaft aus dem Hades», «Besessenheitskunst – Requiem auf Leben und Tod», «Gras versengende Blitze», «Yayoi Kusamas Emporsteigen aus dem dunkel leuchtenden Sumpf», «Mein einsamer Weg in den Tod», «Ich, die Selbstmord beging», «Jenseits meiner Illusion».
5) «Interview with Damien Hirst» in: *Yayoi Kusama: Now,* Robert Miller Gallery, New York 1998, unpaginiert (wieder abgedruckt in: *Yayoi Kusama,* Phaidon Press, London 2000, S. 141).
6) Lied einer Selbstmordsüchtigen in Manhattan: Schluck Antidepressiva und es wird vorbeigehen/Reiss die Pforte der Halluzinationen nieder/Inmitten der Agonie der Blumen endet die Gegenwart nie/Vor den Stufen zum Himmel hört mein Herz vor Zärtlichkeit zu schlagen auf/Vom Himmel herabrufend, zweifelsfrei, durchscheinend in ihrem Blauton/Umhüllt von Schatten der Täuschung/Erheben sich Wolkentürme/Geräusche von Tränen, vergossen über dem Verblassen der Farben der Baumwollrose/Ich werde zu Stein/Nicht in der ewigen Zeit/Aber in der sich ereignenden Gegenwart.

KUSAMA FASHION HAPPENING, 1968, New York / MODEHAPPENING.

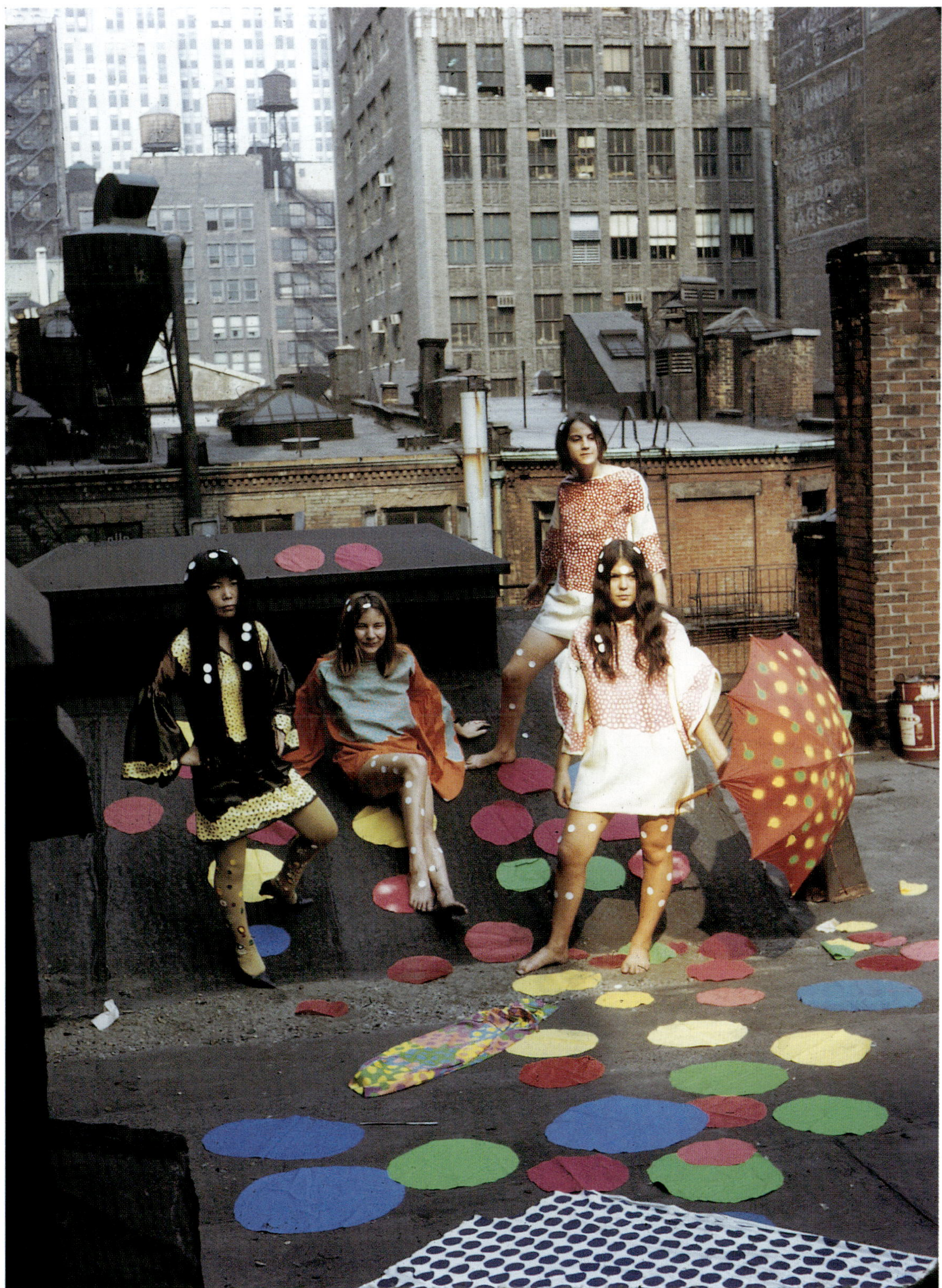

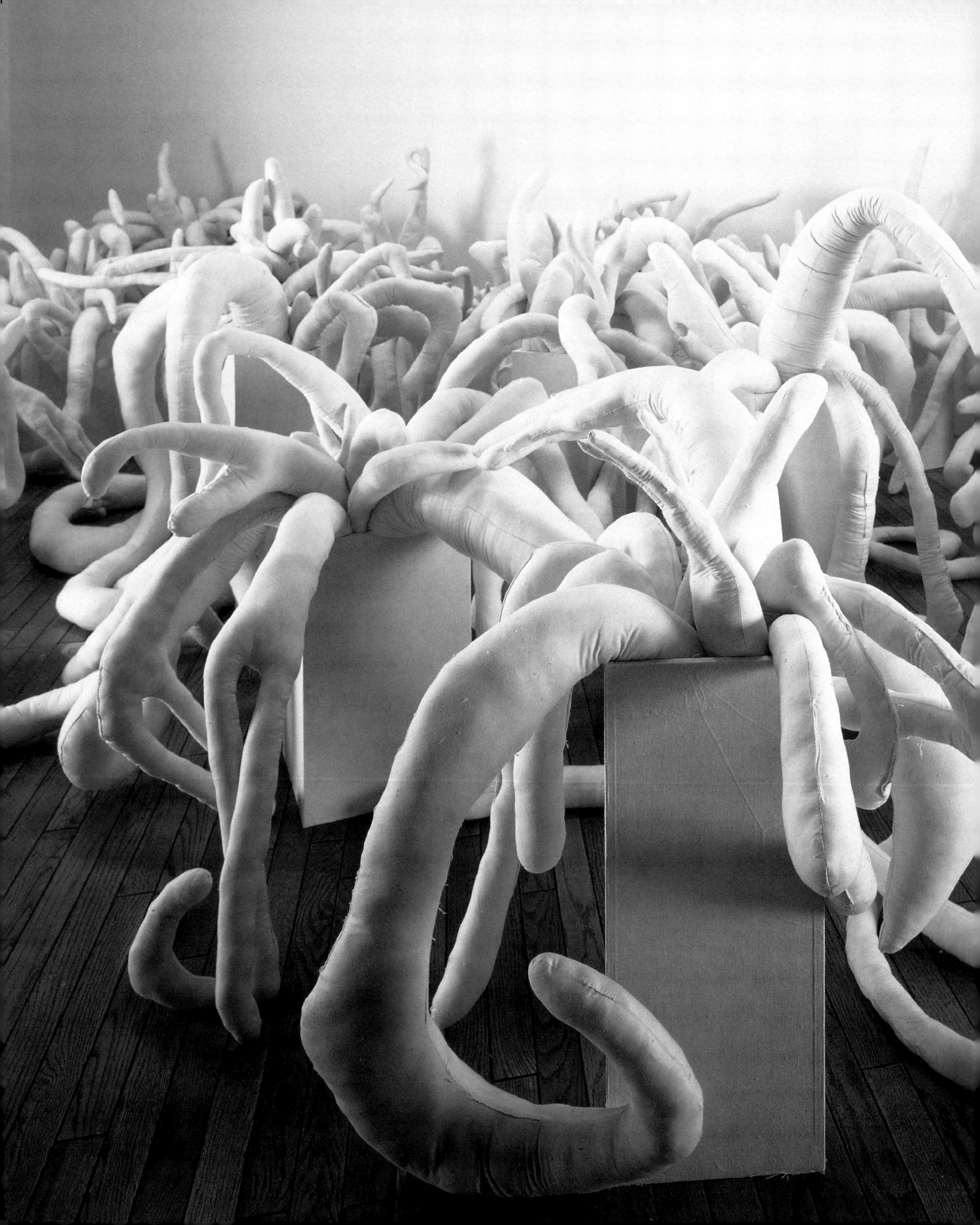

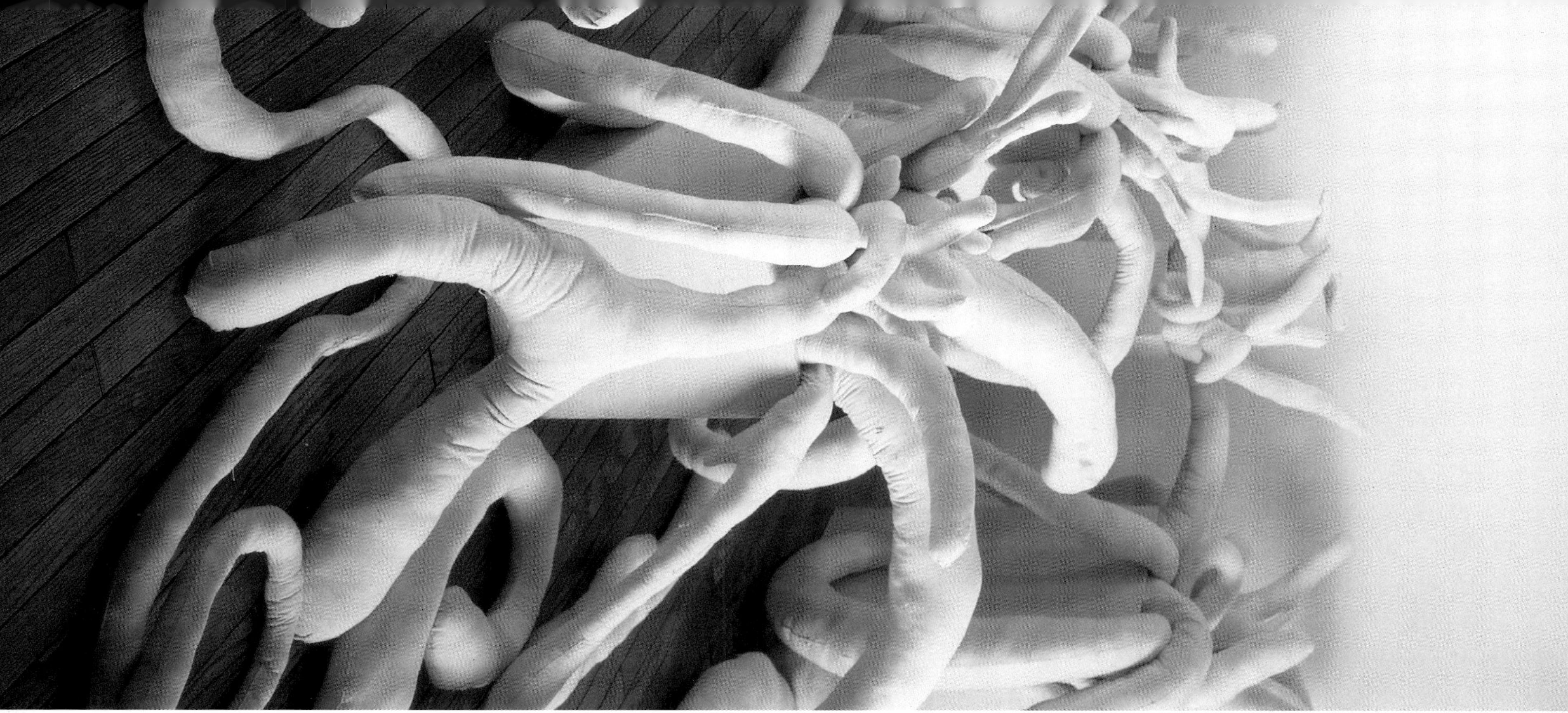

YAYOI KUSAMA, HEAVEN AND EARTH, 1991, mixed media / HIMMEL UND ERDE. (PHOTO: NORIHIRO UENO)

«BETWEEN HEAVEN AND EARTH: This Languid Weight of Life» [1]

URSULA PANHANS-BÜHLER

Menacing are the stars under which the small barque of this Japanese artist has sought to navigate since 1929, driven by an uncanny, auspiciously threatening wind caught in the sails of her strangely unusual works, taking their shape and yet re-forming them. In a recent interview, when Akira Tatehata asked her about her position within and attitude to the art business, Yayoi Kusama simply replied, "As you said, I am in my heart an outsider."[2]

Outsiders were not merely endemic in the art of the 20th century. Ever since Prinzhorn sought to be understood and Dubuffet rehabilitated them with his defence of *art brut*, and certainly at the very latest since Navratil, their currency has been high. Yayoi Kusama's exceptional position, however, seems to be based on the fact that her contributions to art movements then and now run so close to their respective articulations—which she has not just helped carry along, but also anticipated and driven forward—that one cannot help but feel her art operates as a kind of counterpoint, from which socially acceptable forms and articulations maintain a certain distance, be it through sublimation, be it through irony, be it in their hypnotic attraction to a volatile normality. Seen in a cultural context, her works confront us with a flip-side insistently glimmering through. This dark side, matching our own precarious attempts at self-assertion today, may well be the source of the fascination that has once again settled around Yayoi Kusama's work.

In 1957, at the age of 28, with thousands of drawings and watercolors in her case, Yayoi Kusama arrived in New York to make her fortune. In her first solo exhibition, which took place in the Brata Gallery in 1959, she showed her monochrome INFINITY NETS, filling the walls of the gallery, with the largest measuring ten meters from end to end and standing roughly twice as high as the dainty artist. The INFINITY NETS are oil paintings: circular movements around tiny central points turn the white on white, iridescent picture surface into unfathomable space, a silently pulsating, magical in-between world. In the

URSULA PANHANS-BÜHLER is Professor of Art History at the School of Art in Kassel. She is currently working on a study of Marcel Duchamp's WHITE BOX.

time to follow, Kusama's pursuit of monochromatism and seriality—even if it does bear clearly subjective traces of manual activity—brought her invitations to exhibit with European artists' groups in Holland, Germany and Italy. In New York, her compositionless nets without beginning or end were admired by Frank Stella and Donald Judd—"my first boyfriend," as she calls him in an interview with Tatehata.[3]

Donald Judd helped her with her next steps across boundaries and over the edge to her COMPULSION FURNITURES or ACCUMULATIONS, through which she became one of the leading figures in the new perception of objects and in effect one of the first exponents of *Soft Sculpture*, and which made her name in Pop Art circles. For a couple it must have been a strange permutation of the usual intimate conspiracy and division of labor to be cutting up sheets, turning them into giant pods at the sewing machine and finally into plump, stuffed phallic protuberances—or one might think of them as erect nipples exaggerated in the mind of the suckling babe, or of men's scrotums. In teeming plenitude they sprouted out of furniture. Chair or sofa, table or pram, whatever possible and impossible household items were to hand, became the focus of a metamorphosis of phantasmic primordial bounty, stalactite-reinforced furniture grottos which the fabled Cybele from Asia Minor—adorned with the ecstatic sacrificial gifts of her self-mutilating priests—could happily sink into, that same Cybele whom only a milder Roman tradition was to moderate into the epitome of mammary voluptuousness.

In 1963, Yayoi Kusama stunned the New York art world with one of these objects, a rowing boat, in a one-woman show in Gertrude Stein's gallery. AGGREGATION, ONE THOUSAND BOATS SHOW, does indeed consist of 1000 boats: a veritable 3-D boat—albeit heavily laden with protuberances—and 999 photographic reproductions of this remarkable boat, covering the wall, ceiling and floor of the exhibition space and the dark entrance cannula. Kusama's boat-wallpaper set sail a good two years before Warhol's wallpapered cows' heads. The real boat with its burden has about it a certain ambiguity and a photograph of Yayoi Kusama taken during the exhibition and showing her naked from behind, between the

boat and the wallpaper, makes plain the hopeless dilemma facing the artist. In a scissors-movement, the direction of the boat and that of its maker diverge, underscored by a protuberance jutting over the side of the boat.

Over the following years in New York, Milan and Essen—again ahead of her artist colleagues—Kusama showed the environment, DRIVING IMAGE. She returned to the importunate INFINITY NETS and painted them on interior walls, furniture and shop-window mannequins: two-tone nets and grounds reduced to no more than dots, one object as contrasting and brightly colored as the next. The floor was strewn with dried noodles that crunched under the feet of the visitors and, at the opening in the Castellane Gallery in New York in 1964, Kusama set two noodle-covered dogs on the visitors, as though the hounds' aggressive animal barking would jolt the visitors out of their unwittingly oblivious slide into a realm where the distinction between 'I' and the world becomes blurred, which the clear contours of

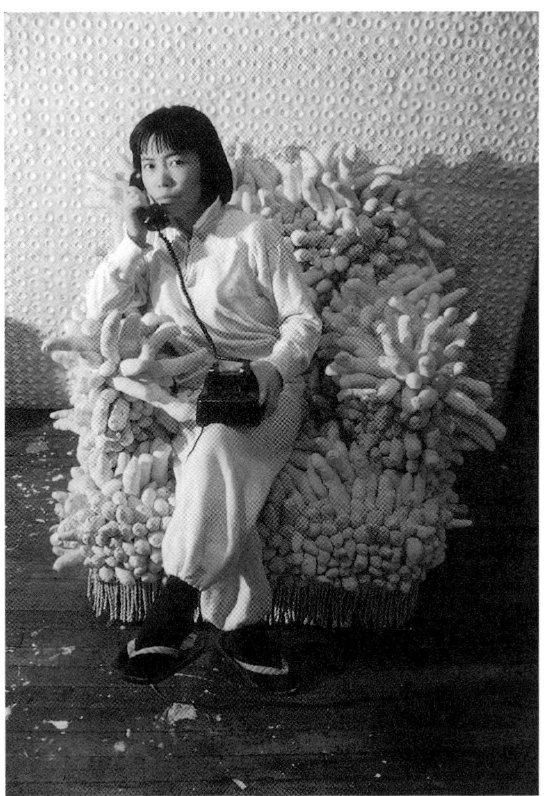

Yayoi Kusama sitting in one of her ACCUMULATION pieces in her New York studio, ca. 1962 / Die Künstlerin in ihrem New Yorker Atelier auf einem ihrer AKKUMULATIONs-Möbel sitzend.

the readymades also militated against. Meanwhile the urge to melt differences away was driving other artists on. This was the time when Yves Klein expressed his desire to cover the whole of France in Yves Klein Blue, an undertaking which would quickly have fallen victim to his IKB producers' limited ability to deliver the goods.

In 1966, viewers were only allowed optical access through face-sized openings to a hexagonal mirror-room, KUSAMA'S PEEP SHOW or ENDLESS LOVE SHOW: in it, for a moment, they saw themselves infinitely multiplied before disappearing again into the centrifugal force of the distance. The effect was dramatized by an optical time factor. The ceiling was thickly covered with bulbs in all different colors emitting shockwaves of changing colored rhythms. Yayoi Kusama was the first to produce mirror-rooms. Prior to KUSAMA'S PEEP SHOW she had already made two others, in which the floor was littered with polka-dotted phallic protuberances. A field with mirror-balls, NARCISSUS GARDEN cast her in a spectacularly piratical role at the Venice Biennale in 1966, until the keepers of cultural order stepped in when she started selling individual balls to visitors for two dollars a piece. It is possible, although not certain, that when Kusama distributed polka dots marked "LOVE FOREVER" to visitors at the light-show in the mirror-room—and held a pair up in front of her own eyes—that a memory of Robert Smithson may have been in the air. In 1963, Smithson had turned two mirrors towards each other, separated in the center by a frame containing wavy neon tubes. The constant exposure to the hectic on and off of the neon tubes distorted the visitors' vision and finally extinguished it altogether. Not long afterwards, Michelangelo Pistoletto, with his mirror-cube, left his mirrors to the void of their own infinity—in the mind of the viewer, that is: there was no peeping glimpse, visitors had to make do with the blank reverse of the mirrors.

With her polka dot Performances and Happenings, her films and her fashion enterprises, Yayoi Kusama broke into the sphere of political Actions in the 1960s. It seems that the world of media spectacles had a seductive effect on her: hectic activity, campaigning with naked dancers for the continued breaking of boundaries, issuing invitations and instructions for laying her audiences bare, even in the garden at MoMA; pacifying the world—at the time of the Vietnam War and when the Soviet Union was marching into Prague—by dissolving herself in a proclamation of a deluge of love. "Obliterate yourself with polka dots." She cast her net ever wider in press announcements in the innocent manner of the hippies, seeking to influence the leading men in

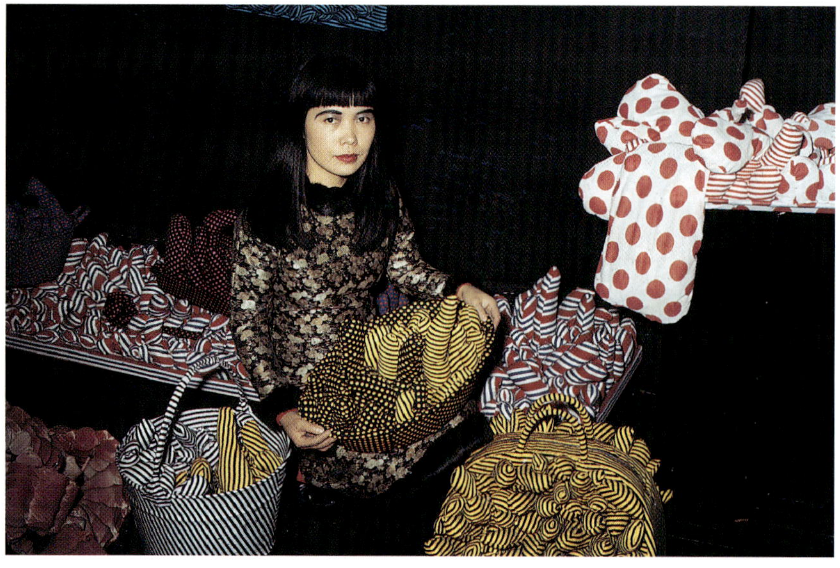

The artist in 1963 with details for
DRIVING IMAGE, 1962–64 /
Die Künstlerin 1963 mit Elementen zu
REIZTREIBENDES BILD.

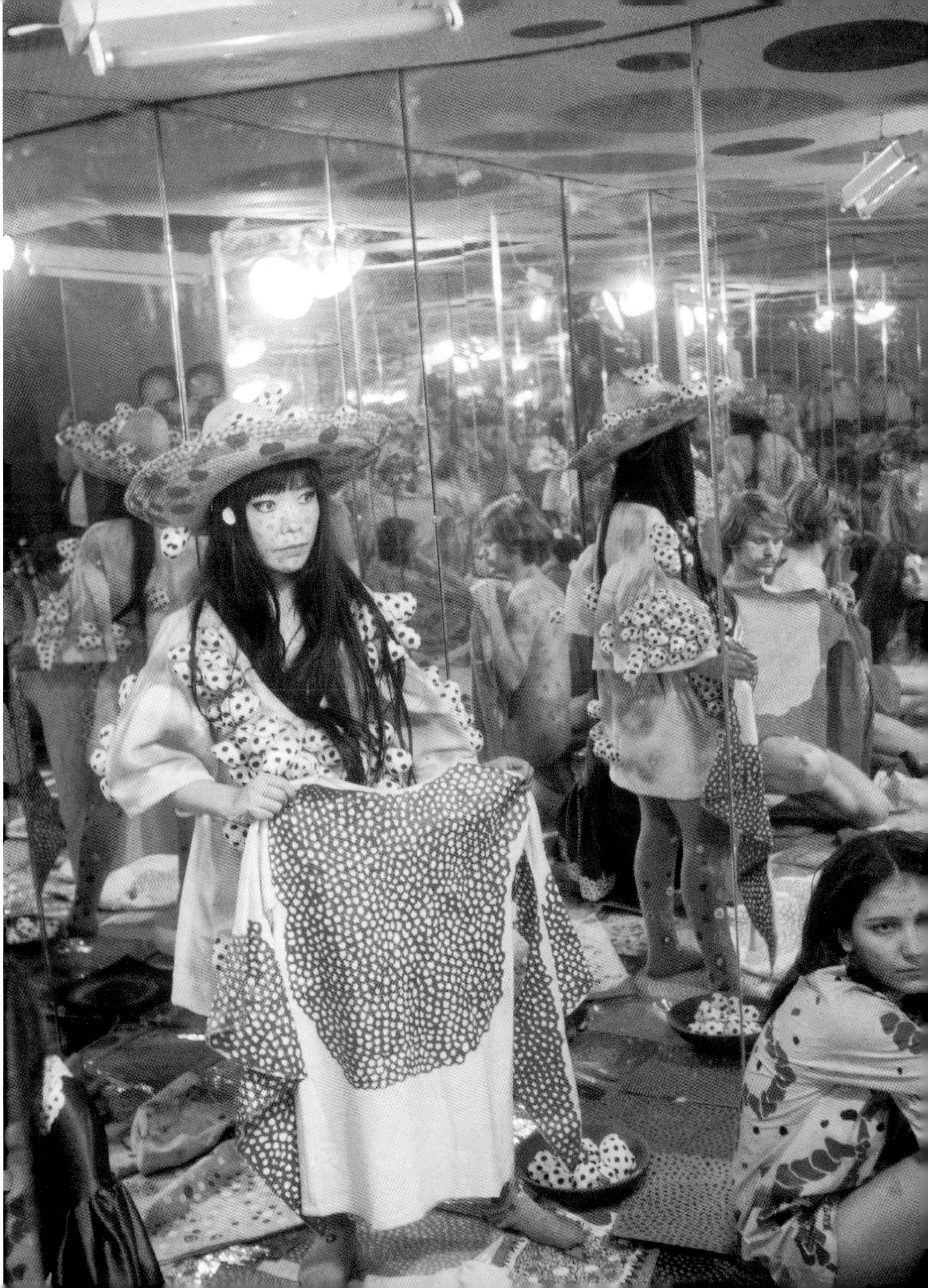

KUSAMA FASHION in INFINITY MIRROR ROOM, ca. 1969 / KUSAMA-MODE in einem UNENDLICHKEITS-SPIEGELSAAL.

power politics to change their ways, with provocatively living, breathing naked bodies supporting flat sandwich-board reproductions of politicians' faces, and making the polit-dolls dance in her performances. The dream of "make love, not war"—the promises of love in her press statements take on manic proportions—collapsed more vehemently and abruptly for Kusama than for many others in the generation of '68 who sought refuge in all kinds of debates and activities both productive and unproductive.

Yayoi Kusama's temporary return to Japan in 1973 has proven to be permanent. Now suffering from an underlying depression, she started to write—novels, novellas, poems—which were met with respect not only in the Japanese literary underground but also in mainstream literary life. She continues to sculpt and to paint. In the care of a psychiatric clinic since 1977, she has a studio and an apartment nearby. 1975 saw her first one-woman show in Japan and 1982 the well-received exhibition "Obsession" in the Fuji Television Gallery, Tokyo. In 1993, her growing reputation led to her becoming both the first woman and the first individual to be entrusted with representing her country at the Venice Biennale. Most recently in 1998/99 "Love Forever—Yayoi Kusama 1958–1968," a major retrospective of her work in the USA, toured through the United States and was also shown in Japan.

The titles of her exhibitions after 1975, as well as the titles of many of her works, are poetic commentaries informed by a new realm of experience: "Gate to Hell," "Hat I used to wear when I was alive," "Message of Death from the Hades," "Obsessional Art—Requiem to Life and Death," "Grass Burning Flashes," "Yayoi Kusama's Soaring from the Dark and Bright Swamp," and lastly "My Solitary Way to Death," "I Who Commited Suicide," and "Beyond my Illusion." In an interview with Damien Hirst in 1998, she explains that "'Being alone' is the feeling I have when I confront death." [4] In 1978 she wrote an autobiography, *Manhattan Suicide Addict*, which had been preceded in 1974 by the "Song of a Manhattan Suicide Addict":

Swallow antidepressants and it will be gone
Tear down the gate of hallucinations
Amidst the agony of flowers,
    the present never ends
At the stairs to heaven, my heart expires
    in tenderness
Calling from the sky, doubtless, transparent
    in its shade of blue
Embraced with the shadow of illusion
Cumulonimbi arise
Sounds of tears, shed upon eating the colors
    of the cotton rose
I become a stone
Not in time eternal
But in the present that transpires.

With her art, Kusama has channeled the hallucinations that have pursued her, overwhelmed her and ensnared her, but with it she has also held in check the lure to end her life. Much in her last twenty years of work could be described as repetition, reproduction or paraphrase. But there have been crucial changes nevertheless. In gigantic pictures, her net structures and patterns have taken on the intuitively assimilated objectivity of a natural history display. Her large reliefs—frames filled with wild interlaced traceries, astonishingly reminiscent of Irish Northumbrian illuminated manuscripts from the early Middle Ages which she has called SLEEPING STAMENS (1985), or frames filled with irregularly sinewy nets, entitled SHOOTING STARS (1992)—seem to have been formed by the long wisdom of an ancient culture rather than by a single individual. Organic forms, LEFTOVER SNOW IN THE DREAM (1982), have a visceral quality that gives them the air of precisely formed organic accounts of emotional states from a pre-verbal era. Newer serial fields with old phalloid forms, REPETITION (1998), exude cool restraint. It is as though a rebellion against the logic of civilization, induced by an individual's particular life history, is being expressed by means of forms that also offer a way out through the longings and dramas—and fibs—of that same civilization. This no doubt accounts on one hand for the baffling sense of a specific déjà-vu generated by Kusama's quasi-parallel world of nature and cultural history, and on the

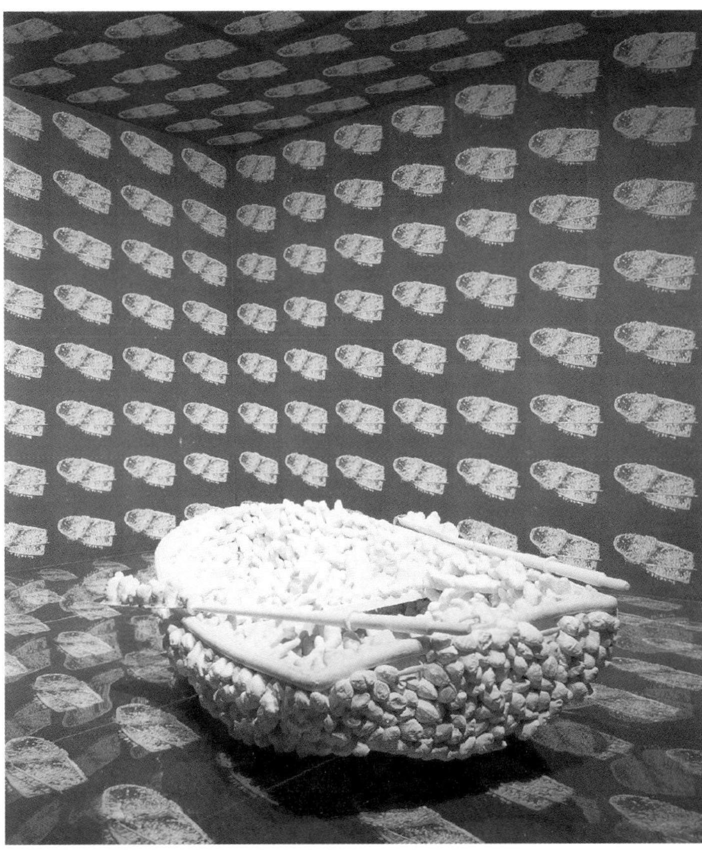

other hand for the—seen from the outside—clownish tone of the repetitive profusion of one single motif, the phantasmic phallus.

As Yayoi Kusama herself has reported, in the early 1960s she once kicked disparagingly against an upturned crate that served her and Donald Judd as a table, and remarked to Judd that this was his material. It would be worth exploring whether the production of a new objecthood in the "minimalist" art of the 1960s was in fact a late cultural taming of death through "reductive submission," the mental acceptance of one's own mortality which comes to be symbolized in the literal abstraction of things.—Yayoi Kusama was left only with the never-ending path out of an elemental entanglement, but she has put off accepting the loneliness of experiencing one's own limits to a later date. Her sculptures may seem "funny" to us, but she herself is playing the reluctant clown, who cannot change so easily from mirth to gravity. When the Heavens and all the stars thus threaten to fall into an individual's lap, they do not also promise to turn into glowing talers for that person like the lighter—if slightly cynical—burden that Hans Christian Andersen, with Romantic condescension, philanthropically showered into the apron of his fairy-tale figure.

(Translation: Fiona Elliott)

1) Yayoi Kusama, *Manhattan Suicide Addict*, an autobiographical story from 1978: "I can not give up my existence. Also I can not escape from death. This languid weight of life!" and Alexandra Munroe, "Between Heaven and Earth: The Literary Art of Yayoi Kusama" in: *Love Forever: Yayoi Kusama, 1958–68*, ex. cat., Los Angeles County Museum of Art, 1998, p.72. "Between Heaven and Earth" was also the title of Kusama's exhibition in the Fuji Television Gallery, Tokyo, 1991.
2) "Akira Tatehata in Conversation with Yayoi Kusama" in: Laura Hoptman, Akira Tatehata, Udo Kultermann, *Yayoi Kusama*, Phaidon Press, London, 2000, p. 11.
3) Ibid.
4) "Interview with Damien Hirst" in: *Yayoi Kusama: Now* (New York: Robert Miller Gallery, 1998), unpaginated; reprinted in: *Yayoi Kusama* (London: Phaidon Press, 2000), p. 141.

Beyond Oedipus: Desiring Production of Yayoi Kusama

MIDORI MATSUI

In spite of her powerful signature style, Yayoi Kusama's artwork never fails to surprise with its fresh intensity that makes one imagine the moment of its genesis. Customarily this intensity refers to the mental illness she has suffered since childhood, and the effects of those psychic forces that Kusama herself does not quite control are referred to as the "creative will." While biographical and chronological explication doubtless secures Kusama's place in art history, what escapes the pathology-related analyses of Kusama's works is precisely the fluidity and richness of her aesthetics. Unfortunately the central characteristics of Kusama's formal execution seem to invite pathological interpretations. A repetition of simple monadic patterns proliferates beyond the boundaries of individual genre, from her early gouaches, INFINITY NETS (1965), and polka dots, to "accumulations" of objects such as classifying labels, macaroni, and flowers. The overwhelming materiality of her accumulated surface unaccompanied by either

MIDORI MATSUI is Associate Professor of American Studies at Tohoku University. She has widely published on contemporary culture and art in Japanese and English. She is also a frequent contributor to *Flash Art*.

rational or structural linking codes suggests an inhuman drive and impersonal mechanicity, and this has been explained in terms of "obsession." While the artist's own comments legitimize this approach, the intense joy of her work, evoked by the sheer force of her productivity, qualitatively differs from explanations based on personal suffering.[1] In fact, it seems that the positive meaning of Kusama's artistic production demands that her repetitive aesthetic be interpreted regardless of her "personality." The impersonal flow of desire that drives her images should be understood not as an effect of her Oedipal lack, but an affirmation of her unlimited energy of life. Numerous scholarly essays offer accounts of Kusama's works in biographical and art-historical contexts; I will venture a rudimentary attempt to explain Kusama's "schizophrenia" as an aesthetic.

Gilles Deleuze and Felix Guattari's theory of "schizophrenia" is useful as a means to unfold Kusama's productivity. As provocatively defined in *Anti-Oedipus* (1972), "schizophrenia" indicates a liberating counter-movement within capitalist culture that resists its functional institutions, or "desiring machines," which turn people into cogs of the repressive social organization.[2] "Schizophrenia" sets

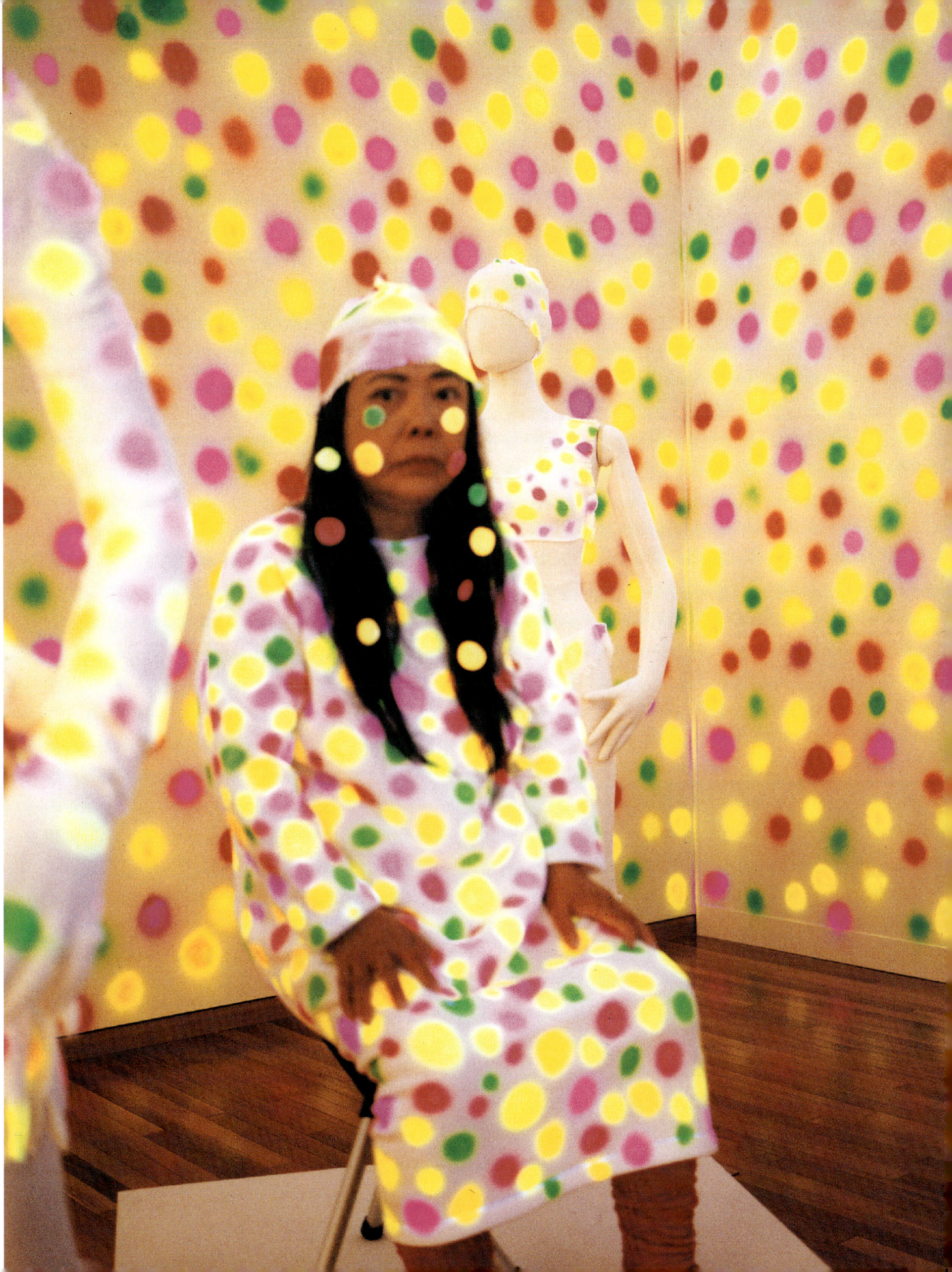

YAYOI KUSAMA, POLKA DOT INSTALLATION AND PERFORMANCE, 1999, collaboration with Issay Miyake, Museum of Contemporary Art, Tokyo.

up a "counter-flow of amorphous, undifferentiated fluids, transforming a part of the libidinal energy that drives human production into the energy of disjunctive inscription," which records the genealogy of desire.[3] Every creation, say Deleuze and Guattari, that radically disperses the dominant patterns of social institutions has this "schizophrenic" character. Creativity, consequently, has nothing to do with the Oedipal triangle, or psychoanalysis. Psychoanalysis is an apparatus for consolidating the repressive social organization, and treats "schizophrenia" as a psychotic phenomena only to reintegrate its subject into the Oedipal unity, blocking the flow of libidinal energy that precedes the social legitimation of the "subject."[4] The subject of schizophrenic production has "no fixed identity," wandering about over the domain of expression, but "always remaining peripheral" to institutional functions, "being defined by the share of product it takes for itself."[5]

A "schizophrenic" is defined as an individualistic creator with his or her own original codes of production, which do not conform to social codes, except in parody; these codes, influenced by desire and delirium, are extremely fluid. Against the repressive Oedipal machine, a "schizophrenic's" production constructs its own machine, a "celibate machine," that forms a new alliance between functional institutions and the expressive domain, "so as to give birth to a new humanity or a glorious organism."[6] Unlike the paranoiac creation of the Oedipal machine that turns every object into a part of its imaginary identity, the celibate machine accumulates molecular elements—"partial objects that enter into indirect syntheses or interactions"—creating "intensities under which a unit of matter always fills space in varying degrees," while its parts are continually referring to an entirely different composition.[7] The schizophrenic "subject" can be seen as a trace of the working of this new machine, which produces intense affects of creative joy and pain: "a celibate misery and glory experienced to the fullest, like a cry suspended between life and death, an intense feeling of transition, states of pure, naked intensity stripped of all shape and form."[8]

Many aspects of Kusama's productivity show affinity with this definition of "schizophrenia": the mechanical distribution of discrete dots in INFINITY NETS that does not suggest an external organizational code or a structural system, but still demonstrates a powerful physical presence. She achieves a

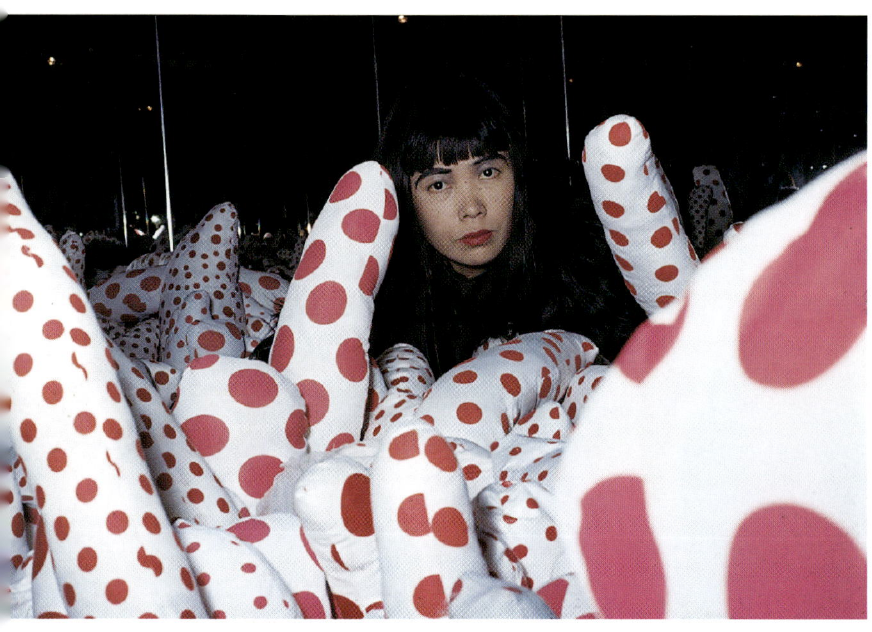

YAYOI KUSAMA, PHALLI'S FIELD, 1964, floor show at Castellane Gallery, New York / PHALLENFELD.

protean transformation of the "polka dot" pattern into the accumulation of banal found objects (airmail stickers, working gloves, sofa springs) and stuffed protruding sculptural units, and maintains stylistic independence from major artistic schools of her time—Abstract Expressionism, Pop, Minimalism, Nouvelle Tendance—while indicating some overlap with their experimental characteristics. More fundamentally, it is Kusama's ability to transmit the intense pain and joy of creation whose relentless process demands her to undergo a state of death in life—"self-obliteration"— in her individual works that confirms her place in Deleuze and Guattari's cosmology.[9] The artist who emerges as a sum of such creative invocations is not the Oedipal daughter sublimating her psychiatric scars through art, but the bold agent of a radical aesthetic.

"Self-Obliteration," the idea Kusama used to justify her performances in the late sixties, reveals the hermetic paradox at the heart of her creation: By covering individual shapes of people and things with polka dots, Kusama erases their subjectivity or identity conferred by institutions and common sense, in order to release them in a flow of vital energy, and envelop them in the realization of "eternity." Kusama's own words reverberate with the Utopian message underlying *Anti-Oedipus's* vision of molecular production: "My performances are a kind of symbolic philosophy with polka dots. A polka dot has the form of the sun, which is a symbol of the energy of the whole world and our living life, and also the form of the moon, which is calm. Round, soft, colorful, senseless, and unknowing. Polka dots can't stay alone; like the communicative life of the people, two or three and more polka dots become movement."[10]

DRIVING IMAGE (1959–64), exhibited between 1964 and 1966 in three cities, brilliantly exemplifies the fluidity and dynamism of Kusama's creation. The first of the three shows, held at the Castellane Gallery in New York, put together ACCUMULATION furniture, arranged like a living room set, phallus-laden dresses, and mannequins covered with dried macaroni, which was also scattered on the floor. Kusama's repetitive aesthetic acquired a dazzling finality in multiplication, whose vertiginous mutual reference mirrored the obliteration of Kusama's "self" in cre-

ation. Just as Deleuze and Guattari maintained that the product of desire is real, not imaginary, the room conveyed the sheer physicality of an internal reality translated into an image.[11]

Unlike the hermetic intensity of its New York counterpart, the last version of DRIVING IMAGE, exhibited at Galerie M.E.Thelen in Essen, in 1966, conveyed an almost light-hearted "estrangement" of the commodity of everyday life, indicating Kusama's link with the "schizophrenic" intensification of material signifiers that characterizes a postmodern experience of reality.[12] In this version, the gallery room was set up as a modern living room with a TV set: female mannequins, three adults and one girl, painted in fluorescent pink and blue, and covered with pink, silver, yellow and green polka dots, posed by the tea table adorned with bottles full of flowers, a tea pot and cups, a dressing table with a large looking-glass, on the macaroni-strewn floor. Painted in pop colors, and incorporating objects linked to female vanity (including a comb, a brush, a handbag, and high-heeled shoes), the installation humorously recreated the glittery surfaces created in postmodern commodity culture. While innocently celebrating a feminine experience, the installation recreated the dizziness of contemporary experience in which consumer "subjectivity" was split between the pain and ecstasy of being lost in the desire for seductive objects.[13]

Kusama's ability to respond to the dual nature of "desiring production"—both personal and social—may have induced Guattari's comments on the ambivalent nature of her creation in his review of her exhibition at Fuji Television Gallery in 1986.[14] The essay itself is a tribute to Kusama's approximation of the great libidinal "celibate machine." Guattari praises Kusama's ability to embody the "germinal state of the world beyond the walls of everydayness." Distinguishing her art from "narcissistic self-supplication" or "autistic reflection," he defies a psychoanalytic approach bound to reduce "the origin of her work to regression or infantile fixation." He also comments that Kusama's work leads her viewers to the discovery of "the potentiality such as possessed by plants, which haunts our subjectivity." This recapitulates his earlier description of the molecular composition operating by the non-humanistic codes that nevertheless possess a unique orientation. Far from being propelled by elementary cathexes or structural patterns, he says, Kusama's art "destroys materials, forms, colors and meanings in order to acquire the vector of creativity far freer than that from which she departed, functioning "like chemistry"; through the process of "undifferentiated and modulated proliferation," Kusama subjects her viewers to the "highly elaborated and differentiated processes," which produce "hyper-complex emotions." Nevertheless, Guattari points out that the "extraordinary apparatuses that subjectively and aesthetically intensify the most contemporary materials" created by Kusama's art are also the ones "through which consumer society secretes its miserable and disenchanted universe." The remark seems to modify the revolutionary optimism of a thesis in *Anti-Oedipus* that "capitalism …produces an awesome schizophrenic accumulation of energy or charge, against which it brings all its vast powers of repression to bear, but which nonetheless continues to act as capitalism's limit."[15]

Guattari ultimately sees Kusama as a great enchantress reborn from the ashes of the Beatnik Generation, who will guide us in the primal as well as unknown future imagination. At the same time, he notices that Kusama's powerful repetitive creation, which transmits the flow of pre-Symbolic imagination, nonetheless renders itself vulnerable to the postmodern exploitation of image for hedonistic seduction. This analysis of her duality reveals a deeply social problematic inscribed in Kusama's "schizophrenic" aesthetic, especially concerning the impeccable material surface created by the even distribution of color and almost stylized flat composition of biomorphic patterns in Kusama's paintings since the late eighties. Nevertheless, it is evident that Kusama presents an exemplary "schizophrenic" desiring production that thwarts the functions of repressive social apparatuses. Above all, embodying the pain of postmodern split, while indicating a possibility of transforming its material fixation, Kusama's art gives the audience, living in the momentary reconfirmation of life through artificial excitation of senses, the model through which to comprehend the profound ambivalence of life and art.

1) Among Kusama's own account of her hallucinations, which reads like poetic transcriptions of her own paintings, the most famous is the childhood memory of seeing red flower patterns everywhere around her and having her first experience of "self-obliteration." Incorporating this, as well as numerous other accounts, into the apt and elaborate analysis of Kusama's stylistic executions, Laura Hoptman's essay treats the sensitive relation between Kusama's psychosis and creativity; see Laura Hoptman, "Yayoi Kusama: A Reckoning" in: *Yayoi Kusama* (London: Phaidon Press, 2000), pp. 34–82. "Kyosei to uchu (Castration and Cosmos)," by Professor Kuni-ichi Ono, on the other hand, treats Kusama's "obsessive repetition of the same" as a "passage to break open the limits of perception" (*Bijutsu Techo*, vol. 40, no. 599, September 1989), p. 119. He praises Kusama's endless repetition of "soft, bright form" as a positive aesthetic that destroys "phallic, well-constructed structures" to fill the world with a cosmic flow, and compares it with Antonin Artaud's metaphorical castration of the rational universe, p. 123.
2) Gilles Deleuze and Felix Guattari, *Anti-Oedipus: Capitalism and Schizophrenia*, transl. by Robert Hurley et. al. (Minneapolis: University of Minnesota Press, 1983), p. 10.
3) Ibid., p. 13.
4) Ibid., p. 13.
5) Ibid., p. 20.
6) Ibid., p. 17.
7) Ibid., pp. 309, 323.
8) Ibid., p. 18.
9) Kusama frequently remarks about how her creation is urged by an impulse, almost indistinguishable from pain, like "the deep, driving compulsion to realize in visible form the repetitive image inside (her)," quoted by Udo Kultermann, "Driving Image, Essen, 1966" in: *Yayoi Kusama* (London: Phaidon, 2000), p. 86. Also in her interview with Akira Tatehata, Kusama explains the paradox of her "self-obliteration" in which she repeats dots, food, and sexual symbols she fears as a rescue from pain, see "Interview: Akira Tatehata in conversation with Yayoi Kusama" in: *Yayoi Kusama*, op. cit., pp. 14, 16.
10) Yayoi Kusama, "Naked Self-Obliteration: Interview with Jud Yalkut, 1968," reprinted in: *Yayoi Kusama*, op. cit., p. 112. Kusama's use of the word "symbolism" must not be confused with the one by Deleuze and Guattari, for whom "symbol" means a sign that mediates unambiguous social communication with one another, whereas she betrays the ambiguity of her "symbolism" by comparing polka dots at once to the sun and the moon.
11) Deleuze and Guattari, op. cit., pp. 6–7.
12) Fredric Jameson, "Postmodernism and Consumer Society" in: *The Anti-Aesthetic*, ed. by Hal Foster (Port Townsend, Washington: Bay Press, 1983), p. 120.
13) Kultermann, "Driving Image, Essen, 1966" in: *Yayoi Kusama*, op. cit., pp. 91–2.
14) Felix Guattari, "Les Riches Affects de Madame Yayoi Kusama" in: *Infinity Explosion* (ex. cat.), Fuji Television Gallery, 1986.
15) Deleuze and Guattari, op. cit., p. 34.

HOMOSEXUAL HAPPENING, 1968, at Kusama's studio, New York / HOMOSEXUELLES HAPPENING. (PHOTO: BILL BARON, NEW YORK)

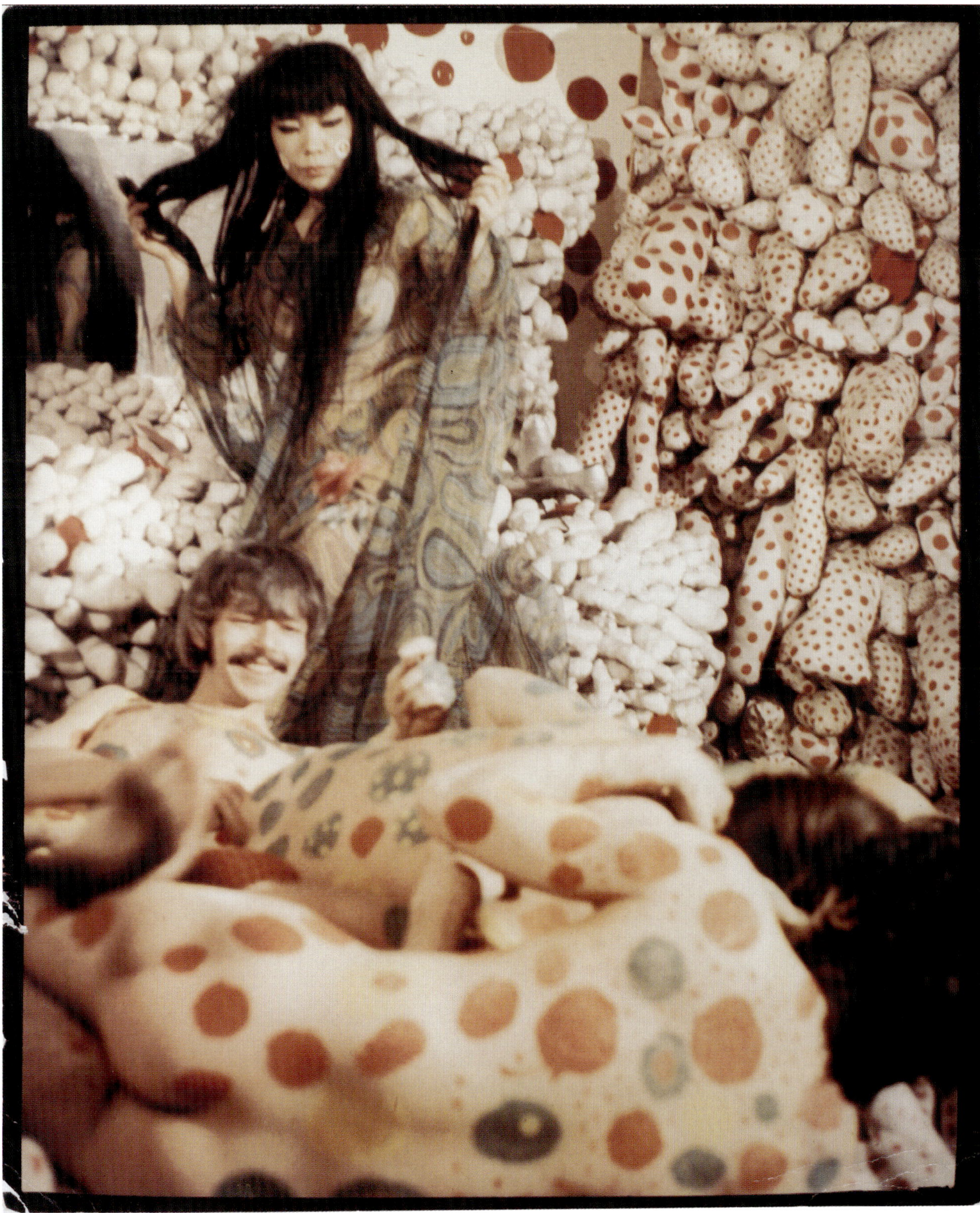

YAYOI KUSAMA, THE GALAXY AQ, 1993, *acrylic on canvas, triptych, 76³/₈ x 51³/₁₆" each panel /*
DIE GALAXIE AQ, Acryl auf Leinwand, Triptychon, jede Tafel 194 x 130 cm.

Jenseits von Ödipus: Yayoi Kusamas Wunschproduktion

MIDORI MATSUI

Trotz ihrer unverkennbaren Handschrift gelingt es Yayoi Kusamas Werk immer wieder aufs Neue, den Betrachter mit einer vitalen Intensität zu überraschen, die ihm quasi den Augenblick der Entstehung vor Augen führt. Gewöhnlich wird diese Intensität mit der Geisteskrankheit in Verbindung gebracht, an der Kusama seit ihrer Kindheit leidet. Die Auswirkungen jener psychischen Kräfte, die sie selbst nicht ganz unter Kontrolle hat, gelten als Ausdruck ihres «schöpferischen Willens». Zweifellos sichert diese biographisch-chronologische Interpretation Kusama einen Platz in der Kunstgeschichte. Doch die überschäumende ästhetische Fülle dieses Werks entzieht sich jeder pathologisch begründeten Analyse. Unglücklicherweise scheint das Hauptmerkmal in Kusamas formalem Zugriff die pathologische Interpreta-

tion geradezu herauszufordern: Sich wiederholende einfache monadische Muster überwuchern die Grenzen des individuellen Genres – von ihren frühen Gouachen, INFINITY NETS (Unendlichkeitsnetze, 1965) und Tupfenmustern bis hin zu «Akkumulationen» von Objekten wie Etiketten, Makkaroni und Blumen. Die überwältigende Materialität ihrer prallen Oberfläche, in der man rationale oder strukturelle Zusammenhänge vergeblich sucht, suggeriert einen beinah unmenschlichen Drang und etwas unpersönlich Mechanisches, was ihr als «Besessenheit» ausgelegt wird. Zwar rechtfertigen die Kommentare der Künstlerin selbst diese Interpretation, doch die intensive Freude, die das Werk dank der schieren Kraft ihrer Produktivität ausstrahlt, setzt es qualitativ ab von jeder Erklärung, die sich auf ihr individuelles Leiden stützt.[1] Tatsächlich legt der positive Inhalt von Kusamas künstlerischer Produktion es nahe, ihre repetitive Ästhetik unabhängig von ihrer «Persönlichkeit» zu beurteilen. Das von der Person losgelöste Dranghafte ihrer Bilder ist nicht als Ausdruck

---

MIDORI MATSUI ist Gastprofessorin für Amerikanistik an der Universität Tohoku. Sie veröffentlichte zahlreiche Schriften in Englisch und Japanisch über zeitgenössische Kultur und Kunst und schreibt regelmässig für *Flash Art*.

eines ödipalen Mangels zu verstehen, sondern vielmehr als Hinweis auf ihre unerschöpfliche Lebensenergie. Zahlreiche wissenschaftliche Aufsätze behandeln Kusamas Werk im biographischen und kunsthistorischen Kontext. Ich möchte wenigstens ansatzweise versuchen die «Schizophrenie» der Künstlerin als ästhetisches Programm zu verstehen.

Hilfreich für das Verständnis von Kusamas Produktivität ist dabei die Theorie der Schizophrenie von Gilles Deleuze und Felix Guattari. In ihrem *Anti-Ödipus* formulierten die Autoren 1972 die provokative These, dass «Schizophrenie» als befreiende Gegenbewegung innerhalb der kapitalistischen Kultur zu verstehen sei und sich deren Produktionsprozessen oder «Wunschmaschinen» widersetze; denn diese machten die Menschen zu Rädchen im Getriebe der gesellschaftlichen «Organmaschine». Dieser setzt der schizophrene «organlose Körper seine glatte, straffe und opake Oberfläche entgegen, den verbundenen, vereinigten und wieder abgeschnittenen Strömen sein undifferenziertes, amorphes Fliessen».[2] Dabei wird ein Teil der libidinösen Energie, die die menschliche Produktion antreibt, in disjunktive Einschreibungsenergie umgewandelt, die die Wunschgenealogie aufzeichnet.[3] Laut Deleuze und Guattari hat jede schöpferische Äusserung, die die herrschenden Muster gesellschaftlicher Institutionen auflöst, diesen «schizophrenen» Charakter. Folglich hat Kreativität nichts mit dem ödipalen Dreieck oder mit Psychoanalyse zu tun. Die Psychoanalyse ist ein Apparat zur Festigung der repressiven Gesellschaftsordnung und behandelt die Schizophrenie als psychotisches Phänomen, um deren Subjekt in die ödipale Einheit zurückzuführen und damit den Strom jener libidinösen Energie zu unterbinden, der der gesellschaftlichen Legitimation des Subjekts vorhergeht.[4] Das Subjekt der schizophrenen Produktion ist «ohne feste Identität»: «Selbst nicht im Zentrum stehend, nicht von der Maschine in Anspruch genommen, am Rande lagernd, ohne feste Identität, immerzu dezentriert, wird es erschlossen aus den Zuständen, die es durchläuft.»[5]

Der oder die Schizophrene wird definiert als individualistische(r) Schöpfer(in) mit ureigenen Produktions-Codes, die – ausser als Parodie – nicht mit den gesellschaftlichen Codes übereinstimmen. Diese von Lust und Delirium geprägten Codes sind äusserst wandelbar. Gegen die repressive ödipale Maschine setzt die schizophrene Produktion ihre eigene, «zölibatäre Maschine», die eine neue Verbindung zwischen Wunschmaschine und organlosem Körper herstellt, «zum Zwecke einer neuen Menschheit oder eines glorreichen Organismus».[6] Im Gegensatz zur paranoiden Kreation der ödipalen Maschine, die jeden Gegenstand zum Teil ihrer eigenen imaginären Identität macht, häuft die zölibatäre Maschine molekulare Elemente an – «Partialobjekte, die indirekte Synthesen oder Interaktionen eingehen» – und erzeugt «Intensitäten, unter denen immer eine Materie den Raum in unterschiedlichen Graden ausfüllt», während ihre Teile unentwegt auf einen ganz anderen Zusammenhang verweisen.[7] Das schizophrene Subjekt kann als Spur des Funktionierens dieser neuen Maschine gelten, welche intensive Gefühle schöpferischer Lust und Qual hervorruft: «zölibatäre Grösse und Elend als höchste Empfindungen, gleich einem Schrei zwischen Leben und Tod, ein Gefühl heftigen Übergangs, Zustände reiner und von jeglicher Formbestimmung entblösster Intensität».[8]

Manches an Kusamas Produktivität erinnert an diese Definition der «Schizophrenie»: die mechanische Verteilung einzelner Tupfen in INFINITY NETS, die weder ein externes noch ein strukturimmanentes Organisationsprinzip erkennen lässt und dennoch eine starke physische Präsenz ausstrahlt. Es gelingt ihr, das Tupfenmuster auf fast proteische Weise in eine Anhäufung banaler Fundobjekte (Luftpostaufkleber, Arbeitshandschuhe, Sofafedern) und prall gefüllter, in den Raum ragender, skulpturartiger Elemente zu verwandeln. Dabei bleibt Kusama stilistisch unabhängig von den grossen künstlerischen Strömungen ihrer Zeit – abstrakter Expressionismus, Pop, Minimalismus, Nouvelle Tendance – und teilt zugleich deren experimentellen Charakter. Letztlich aber ist es Kusamas Fähigkeit, die intensive Lust und Qual ihres gnadenlos konsequenten Schaffensprozesses zu vermitteln – wobei sie sich in jedem Werk einer Art Tod im Leben, einer «Selbstauslöschung» aussetzt –, die ihr einen Platz in der Kosmologie von Deleuze und Guattari sichert.[9] Die Künstlerin, die am Ende aus solch kreativen Beschwörungen hervor-

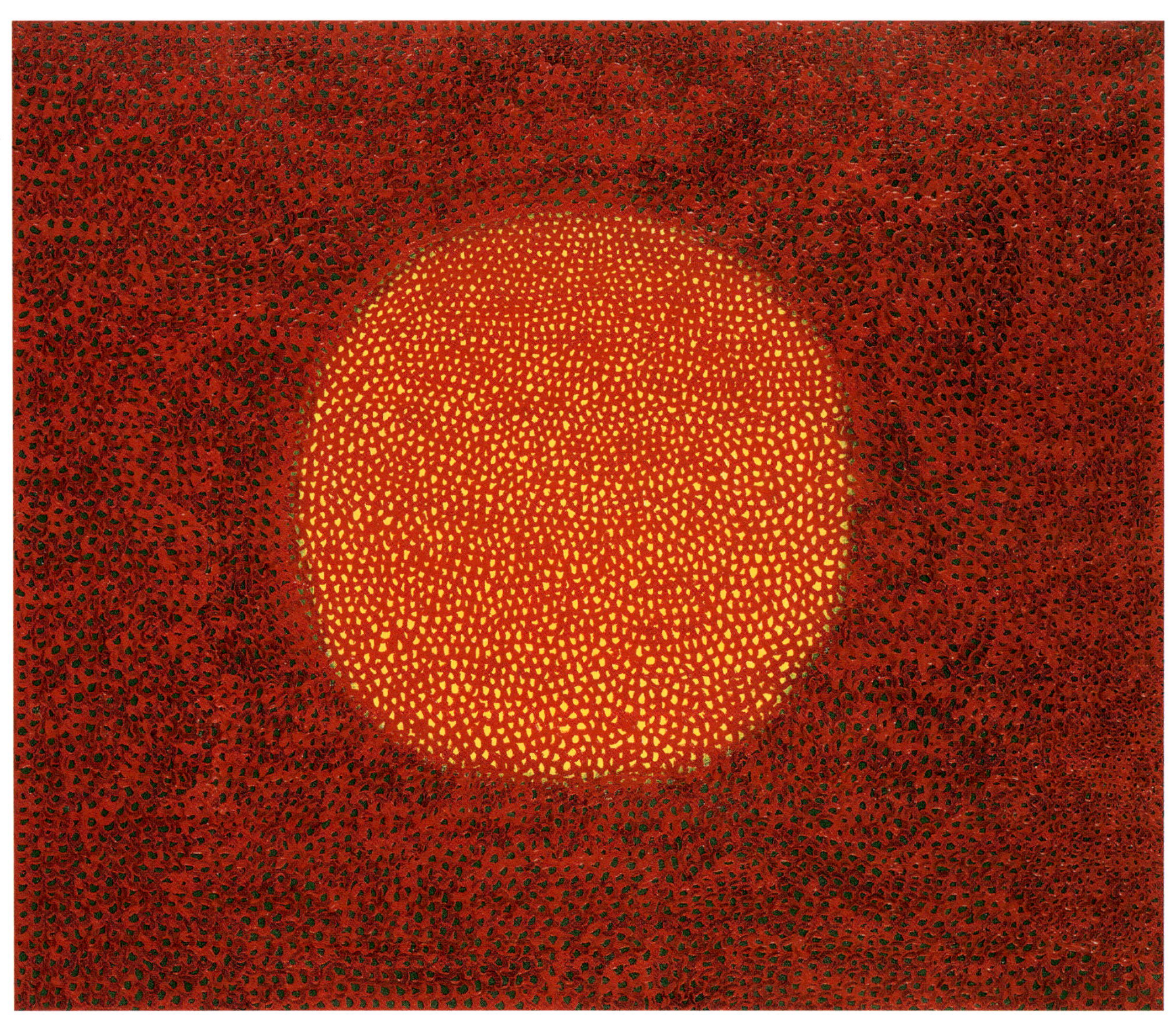

YAYOI KUSAMA, INFINITY NET, 1965,
oil on canvas, 52 x 59⅞" / UNENDLICHKEITSNETZ, Öl auf Leinwand, 132 x 152 cm.

geht, ist nicht die ödipale Tochter, die ihre psychiatrische Versehrtheit durch Kunst sublimiert, sondern kühne Verfechterin einer radikalen Ästhetik.

Die Idee der «Selbstauslöschung», mit der Kusama in den späten 60er Jahren ihre Performances erklärt, verrät das hermetische Paradox, das ihrem Schaffen zugrunde liegt: Indem sie die einzelnen Menschen und Dinge mit Tupfen übersät, löscht Kusama deren auf Institutionen und «gesundem Menschenverstand» basierende Subjektivität oder Identität aus und befreit sie in einem Strom vitaler Energie, auf dass sie die «Ewigkeit» schauen. In Kusamas eigenen Worten klingt jene utopische Botschaft an, die der Schilderung der molekularen Produktion im *Anti-Ödipus* zugrunde liegt: «Meine Performances sind eine Art symbolischer Philosophie in Form von Tupfenmustern. Ein Tupfen hat die Form der Sonne, die ja das Symbol für die Energie der ganzen Welt und unser lebendiges Leben ist, aber auch die Form des Mondes, also der Stille. Rund, weich, farbig, empfindungslos und unwissend. Ein Tupfen kann nicht allein bleiben; wie im kommunikativen Leben der Menschen entsteht Bewegung erst, wenn zwei, drei oder mehr Tupfen zusammenkommen.»[10]

DRIVING IMAGE (1959–64) wurde zwischen 1964 und 1966 in drei Städten gezeigt und ist ein brillantes Beispiel für den Fluss und die Dynamik in Kusamas Schaffen. Die erste der drei Ausstellungen präsentierte eine Ansammlung von Möbeln, die zu einer Art Wohnzimmer arrangiert waren, mit Phallen übersäte Kleider und mit trockenen Makkaroni bedeckte Mannequins, weitere Makkaroni waren über den Boden verteilt. Kusamas repetitive Ästhetik erlangte eine verwirrende Endgültigkeit durch die Multiplikation, in deren Schwindel erregenden wechselseitigen Bezügen sich die Auslöschung von Kusamas Selbst im Schaffensprozess spiegelte. Ganz im Sinn der Aussage von Deleuze und Guattari, dass die Wunschproduktion nicht imaginär, sondern «wesentliche Realität» sei, vermittelte dieser Raum die schiere Körperlichkeit einer ins Bild übersetzten inneren Wirklichkeit.[11]

Im Gegensatz zur hermetischen Intensität der New Yorker Version zeigte sich in der letzten Installation von DRIVING IMAGE (1966, in der Essener Galerie M. E. Thelen) eine fast unbekümmerte «Entfremdung» gegenüber der Warenwelt des täglichen Lebens. Ein Hinweis auf die bei Kusama wirksame und für die postmoderne Realitätserfahrung typische «schizophrene» Intensivierung materieller Bedeutungsträger.[12] Diesmal war aus dem Galerieraum ein modernes Wohnzimmer mit Fernseher geworden: lebensgrosse, fluoreszierend rosa und blau bemalte Puppen, drei Frauen und ein Mädchen, übersät mit rosafarbenen, silbernen, gelben und grünen Punkten, standen um ein Teetischchen, auf dem Flaschen voller Blumen sowie eine Teekanne und Tassen standen. Dann stand da noch ein Toilettentisch mit grossem Spiegel, und der Boden war mit Makkaroni übersät. Mit ihren poppigen Farben und den Symbolen weiblicher Eitelkeit (Kamm, Bürste, Handtasche, Stöckelschuhe) imitierte die Installation augenzwinkernd die glitzernden Oberflächen der postmodernen Warenkultur. Die scheinbar naivlustvolle Wiedergabe einer weiblichen Erlebniswelt führte zugleich den Wahnwitz der zeitgenössischen Konsumerfahrung vor Augen, in der die «Subjektivität» zerrissen ist zwischen Schmerz und Ekstase ihres völligen Aufgehens im Wunsch nach verführerischen Objekten.[13]

Vielleicht hat Kusamas Fähigkeit, auf das Zwiespältige sowohl der individuellen wie der gesellschaftlichen Wunschproduktion zu reagieren, Guattari zu dessen Bemerkungen über die Ambivalenz in ihrem Werk veranlasst.[14] Guattari hebt dabei besonders Kusamas Annäherung an die grosse libidinöse «zölibatäre Maschine» lobend hervor und preist ihre Fähigkeit, dem «ursprünglichen Zustand der Welt jenseits der Mauern der Alltäglichkeit» eine Form zu verleihen. Er sieht ihre Kunst fern von «narzisstischer Selbstbeweihräucherung» oder «autistischer Reflexion» und lehnt eine psychoanalytische Interpretation ab, da sie «den Ursprung ihres Werks auf Regression oder infantile Fixierung» reduziert. Nach seiner Ansicht ermöglicht Kusamas Werk dem Betrachter die Entdeckung eines pflanzenhaften Wachstumspotenzials, das eine Bedrohung unserer Subjektivität darstelle. Er greift damit auf seine frühere Beschreibung der molekularen Ordnung zurück, die nichtmenschlichen Codes unterliegt und dennoch bestimmten eigenen Regeln folgt. Kusamas Kunst gehe keineswegs von elementaren Fixierun-

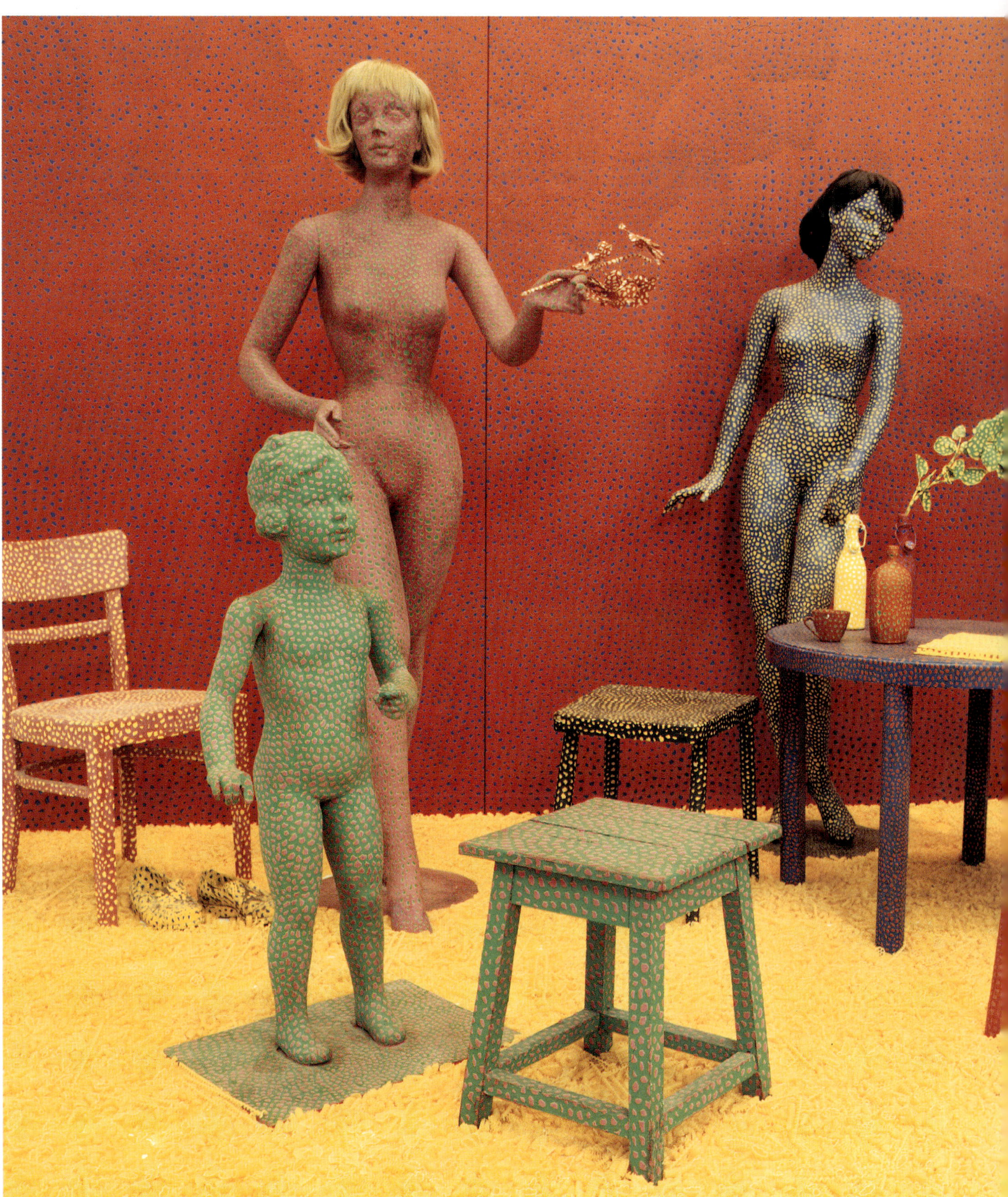

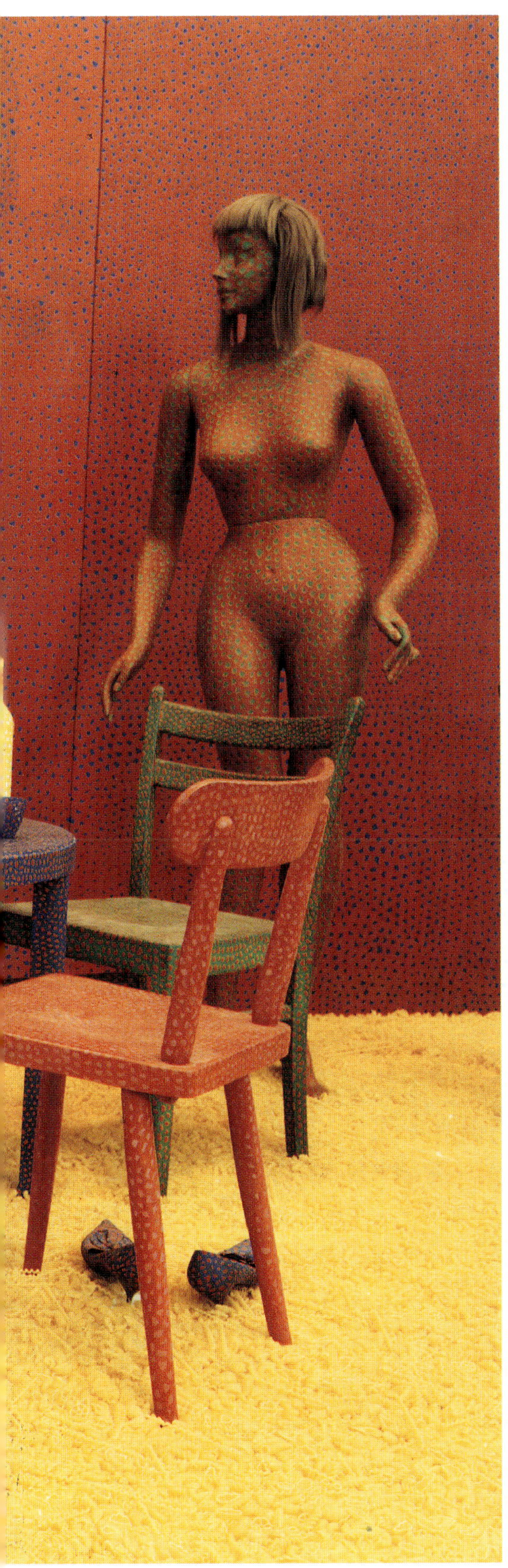

gen oder Ordnungsmustern aus, meint Guattari, sondern zerstöre gerade Materialien, Formen, Farben und Bedeutungen, um grössere kreative Freiheit zu erlangen; in ihren undifferenzierten und modulierenden Wucherungen funktioniere sie wie «ein chemischer Prozess». Kusama setze ihre Betrachter «hochkomplexen und differenzierten Vorgängen» aus, die wiederum «hyperkomplexe Emotionen» hervorriefen. Gleichwohl weist Guattari darauf hin, dass die von Kusama geschaffenen «aussergewöhnlichen Maschinen, die zutiefst zeitgenössische Stoffe subjektiv und ästhetisch intensivieren», dieselben sind, «mithilfe derer die Konsumgesellschaft ihre ebenso erbärmliche wie entzauberte Welt verschleiert». Diese Bemerkung scheint den revolutionären Optimismus der These aus dem *Anti-Ödipus* einzuschränken, «dass der Kapitalismus im Zuge seines Produktionsprozesses eine ungeheure schizophrene Ladung erzeugt, auf der wohl seine Repression lastet, die sich aber unaufhörlich als Grenze des Prozesses reproduziert».[15]

Letztendlich sieht Guattari Kusama als eine grosse Zauberin, die sich wie Phoenix aus der Asche der Beatnik-Generation erhoben hat und uns in die ebenso ursprüngliche wie unbekannte Phantasie der Zukunft führen wird. Zugleich stellt er fest, dass Kusamas kraftvolles repetitives Schaffen, das den Strom einer präsymbolischen Phantasie zum Ausdruck bringe, selbst durchaus anfällig sei gegenüber der postmodernen Ausbeutung des Bildes zum Zweck der hedonistischen Verführung. Diese Analyse ihrer Ambivalenz enthüllt eine zutiefst gesellschaftliche Problematik in Kusamas «schizophrener» Ästhetik. Das betrifft vor allem die perfekte materielle Oberfläche, die in Kusamas Bildern seit den späten 80er Jahren durch die gleichmässige Verteilung der Farbe und die fast stilisiert flache Komposition biomorpher

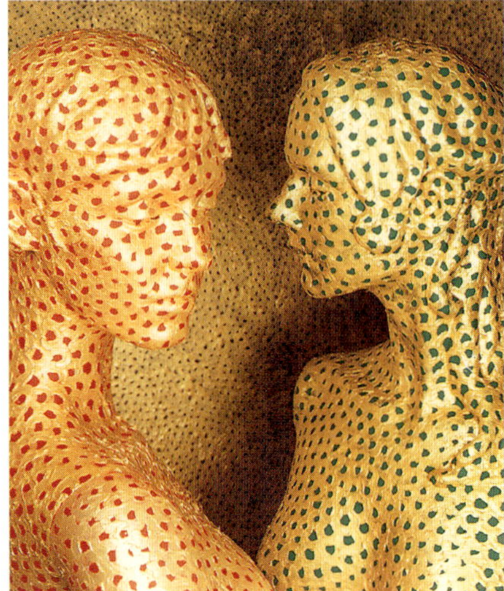

YAYOI KUSAMA, BEYOND MY ILLUSION, 1999,
detail, mixed media installation, dimensions variable /
JENSEITS MEINER ILLUSION.

Muster zustande kommt. Dennoch präsentiert Kusama unbestreitbar eine exemplarische «schizophrene» Wunschproduktion, die den Funktionen repressiver Gesellschaftsmechanismen zuwiderläuft. Vor allem aber verkörpert ihre Kunst den Schmerz der postmodernen Spaltung und zeigt zugleich eine Möglichkeit auf, deren materielle Fixierung aufzulösen: Damit liefert die Künstlerin ihrem Publikum, das in künstlichen Sinnesreizen die flüchtige Bestätigung des Lebens sucht, ein Modell, das uns die tiefe Ambivalenz von Kunst und Leben begreifbar macht.

(Übersetzung: Nansen)

1) Kusamas Schilderungen ihrer Halluzinationen lesen sich wie poetische Übersetzungen ihrer eigenen Bilder. Die bekannteste ist die Erinnerung daran, wie sie in ihrer Kindheit überall um sich herum Muster aus roten Blumen sah und ihre erste «Selbst-Auslöschung» erlebte. Laura Hoptmans Aufsatz berücksichtigt diese und zahlreiche andere Schilderungen in ihrer ebenso ausführlichen wie scharfsichtigen Analyse von Kusamas stilistischen «Selbst-Exekutionen». Ihr Aufsatz behandelt die sensible Beziehung zwischen Kusamas Psychose und Kreativität. Siehe Laura Hoptman: «Yayoi Kusama: A Reckoning» in: *Yayoi Kusama*, Phaidon Press, London 2000, S. 34–82. Kuni-ichi Ono hingegen sieht in seinem Artikel «Kyosei to uchu (Kastration und Kosmos)» Kusamas «obsessive Wiederholung des immer Glei-

chen» als ein «Vorgehen, um diese Grenzen der Wahrnehmung aufzubrechen» in: *Bijutsu Techo*, Bd. 40, Nr. 599, September 1989, S. 119. Er lobt Kusamas endlose Wiederholung der «weichen, strahlenden Form» als positive Ästhetik, die «phallische, durchkonstruierte Strukturen» zerstört, um die Welt mit einem kosmischen Strom zu erfüllen, und vergleicht dieses Vorgehen mit Antonin Artauds metaphorischer Kastration des rationalen Universums. S. 123.

2) Gilles Deleuze und Felix Guattari, *Anti-Ödipus: Kapitalismus und Schizophrenie*, übers. v. Bernd Schwibs, Suhrkamp, Frankfurt am Main 1981, S. 15.

3) Ebenda, S. 20, 21.

4) Ebenda.

5) Ebenda, S. 28.

6) Ebenda, S. 25.

7) Ebenda, S. 398.

8) Ebenda, S. 26.

9) Kusama weist immer wieder darauf hin, dass sie bei ihrer Arbeit einem Impuls folgt, der kaum von Schmerz zu unterscheiden sei, wie «der tiefe, unausweichliche Drang, in der sichtbaren Form das immer wiederkehrende innere Bild zu erkennen». Zitiert nach Udo Kultermann, «Driving Image, Essen 1966» in: *Yayoi Kusama*, Phaidon Press, London, 2000, S. 86. Auch in ihrem Interview mit Akira Tatehata erklärt Kusama das Paradox ihrer «Selbstauslöschung», bei dem sie Punkte, Nahrung und sexuelle Symbole wiederholt, mit denen sie dem Schmerz zu entkommen sucht. Siehe «Interview: Akira Tatehata im Gespräch mit Yayoi Kusama» in: *Yayoi Kusama*, op. cit., S. 14 und 16.

10) Yayoi Kusama, «Naked Self-Obliteration: Interview with Jud Yalkut, 1968», wieder abgedruckt in: *Yayoi Kusama*, op. cit. S. 112. Kusamas Verwendung des Begriffs «Symbolismus» ist nicht zu verwechseln mit jener von Deleuze und Guattari. Letztere verstehen unter «Symbol» ein Zeichen, das eine nicht zweideutige soziale Kommunikation befördert, während Kusama das Zweideutige ihres «Symbolismus» kundtut, wenn sie die Tupfen sowohl mit der Sonne wie mit dem Mond vergleicht.

11) Deleuze und Guattari, op. cit., S. 11.

12) Fredric Jameson, «Postmodernism and Consumer Society» in: *The Anti-Aesthetic*, Hal Foster (Hrsg.), Bay Press, Port Townsend, Washington 1983, S. 120.

13) Udo Kultermann, «Driving Image, Essen, 1966» in: *Yayoi Kusama*, Phaidon Press, London 2000, S. 91–92.

14) Felix Guattari, «Les Riches Affects de Madame Yayoi Kusama» in: *Infinity Explosion*, Ausstellungskatalog, Fuji Television Gallery, 1986.

15) Deleuze und Guattari, op. cit., S. 45.

GRISELDA POLLOCK

Womanliness, therefore, could be assumed and worn as a mask, both to hide the possession of masculinity and to avert the reprisals expected if she was found to possess it—much as a thief will turn out his pockets and ask to be searched to prove that he has not stolen.

– Joan Riviere, 1929[1]

THREE THOUGHTS ON FEMININITY, CREATIVITY AND ELAPSED TIME

The passage from contemporary art criticism to critical art historical analysis of contemporary art pivots, at present, on the continuing status within the former domain of the artist as the referent for the art work versus the function of the artwork as a text to be historically interpreted. As text, this makes art both "always and already" an intertext, part of a disseminated cultural semiotic with both synchronic and diachronic axes. The idea of text also provides access, through the workings of its singular articulation of cultural resources refashioned through individual refractions, with subjectivity that is both transindividual, as a structure, and particular, as the product of this person's history and no other. While clearly it is a matter of considerable importance and historical

record to know what the artist understands and explains her project to be, it is also possible to argue that the work is always more than its own initiating program because the producer is only one, though a very important one term within the over-determined event that is an artistic practice. The artist, moreover, like any other psychically divided, generationally and geographically positioned subject, cannot be entirely known to and by herself. How much more true is this of an artist who feels that she works on the edge: culturally, aesthetically, and psychologically?

Reading the recent literature on Yayoi Kusama, as an art historian, catapults me back into the confusion that surrounded the reception and analysis of Vincent van Gogh, the paradigmatic case of "mad genius" for over a century.[2] With this Dutch painter, the ancient myths about artistic madness collided with emergent psychiatry for which documented artistic biographies became surrogate case studies to produce powerful and persistent popular beliefs in the unmediated self-expressiveness of his work as the testimony of an anguished soul. Even writing this sentence reveals the tangle of ideas enclosed within

GRISELDA POLLOCK is Professor of Social and Critical Histories of Art at University of Leeds and Director of the Graduate Programme (M.A./Ph.D.) in Feminist Theory and the Visual Arts. Recent books include *Generations and Geographies in the Visual Arts* (1996) and *Differencing the Canon: Feminist Desire and the Writing of Art's Histories* (1999), both published by Routledge, London.

the conjunction of art and madness that serve us not at all in dealing with the relations between avant-garde poetics and the culturally created inhospitability to artists who are women and/or outsiders.

We need to keep the critical distance between intense emotional distress, traumatically induced neurotic symptoms, and severer forms of psychological alienation, which sever all links with inter-subjectivity and linguistic communication. Thus the long history of modern artists' interest in "outsider art," art brut, the art of "complete visionaries" as Maurice Tuchman named it in a 1992 exhibition, "Parallel Visions: Modern Artists and Outsider Art" at the Los Angeles County Museum of Art, 1992, circles around uncanny stylistic resemblances and formal coincidences between calculated modern art and spontaneous ahistorical artistic works. There is, however, a categorical difference between the compulsive maker and the artist, however much their practice is energized by some form of psychic distress. The artist is a self-reflexive and socialized presence, not necessarily a complete cause, that opens the artistic practice to its lines of communication with its artistic interlocutors in that necessary game of reference, deference, and difference.

With van Gogh, I wanted to minimize the significance of what I take to have been episodic psychomotor epilepsy and emphasize the need to read the work as the evidence of an ambivalent and discontinuous but calculating engagement with the modern, structured around key thematics of time, memory and consolation. The move is to leave aside whatever personal emotional pain living that life caused the Dutchman before searching through the work for signs of art as the work of a creative subject, a calculating producer of art in the presence of other art. This same move is imperative in order to allow Yayoi Kusama's artistic texts to function historically as the index of an artistic presence shaped by the intense but historically forged dislocated-ness afflicting the tripled alterity of being a Japanese woman artist during the pre-feminist, pre-difference moment of New York in the sixties. There is no lack of related evidence for the paradox of that decade in relation to women and art. We now, belatedly, acknowledge a slew of astonishingly original artists who were women. Yet their positionality—in terms of gender, sexuality, ethnicity, religion, and nationality—could not be fully voiced then even though its pressure determined the very shock and necessity of their inventive and often transgressive artistic tactics that thematized lack of voice, need for presence, and invisibility through race or gender. For me, it was Catherine de Zegher's concept of an elliptical re-traverse of three moments in the twentieth century, in her path-breaking show "Inside the Visible" (1996), that reframed dispersed practices scattered across the thirties, sixties, and nineties as participating in a hitherto invisible dialectic of radical dissidence in which femininity, indelibly linked with other positional differences, constituted a challenge to semiotic as well social authority that was so often ignored or sidelined.[3]

When we review the historical plane of twentieth-century art refocused by this critical feminist lens, it is clear that the situation of the sixties could make the individual as "ill" as that of the twenties, addressed in the paper by Joan Riviere that I invoke as my first epigraph. In 1928, Riviere theorized the anguish of a new, and lonely generation of women intellectuals, catapulted into an inhospitable, phallocentric psycho-symbolic economy as they first entered professions. Anger, silence, and the threat of madness is a thematic we find in the guerrilla tactics waged by the scatological visual profanities of Nancy Spero or her transgender ventriloquism of Artaud's rage in the sixties. Less outraged but as intense are the provocative street performances of Adrian Piper, or the invasive anti-Vietnam photomontages of Martha Rosler. All encode qualities consistently present in the array of practices, happenings, stagings of the self, environments, and personality defining publicity of Kusama in the sixties for which she was reviled by a leading woman critic for her "excess of overexposure." Riviere identifies the relations of mimesis and excess that I see as one logic in the structural habits of Yayoi Kusama's work in the sixties as a pre-feminist artistic *pharmacon:* both symptom and parodic critique, both sign of the poison of and a cure for an impossible situation. Femininity is performed in a variety of guises, performed in the old-fashioned sense, the kimono invoking both an assertion of cultural difference on the streets of New York and an intra-cultural critique of Japanese ideals of femininity; the unclothed body signified both a universalized icon of sexuality and an ethnically specific but artistic nudity.

The insistence, making visible the artist's presence against the depersonalizing screens of laboriously manufactured repetition that runs from inserting herself into her own works and environments, to acting as salesman at the notorious 1966 sideshow to the Venice Biennale, NARCISSUS GARDEN, to the works as happening impresario, AWAKEN THE DEAD (Museum of Modern Art, New York, 1969) underlines the terrible necessity, at the time, visually to embody the artist "in the feminine" in a moment before that possibility could be critically or theoretically articulated as a position from which to speak "in the singular."

Multiplication and repetition of herself as much as of the little phalloi seem intricately linked to a compulsion embedded in the psychosocial context for a Japanese woman artist. Phallocentric cultures are menaced, precisely as in 1928, by the challenge to their homo-social exclusivity and by the outpouring of creativity from the position of the feminine, thereby intesifying their repressive resistance. Against this the Japanese woman artist has to in turn reaffirm her presence through a manic defense by transgressing the deepest taboo of phallocentricism: she not only shows the phallus, which reduces it from its veiled symbolic potency to its facticity as erotic flesh. In its mushrooming, auto-replication, these "little ones" become inverted, a sign of her limitless artistic fertility. Kusama reduces the great invisible signifier of the phallocentric order to its vulnerable thingyness, its soft tumescence, and its replicability. Amidst this aesthetic garden of needle-pierced, stitched up phalloi, the naked body, female and artistic, inserts its singular presence in yet another and still contradictory twist on Paula Modersohn Becker's monumental 1906 Self Portrait's confrontation with the oxymoronic configuration in Western modernism: woman/nude/artist.

I would call "feminine" the moment of rupture and negativity that
conditions the newness of any practice.   – Julia Kristeva, 1974[4)]

I stress, therefore, a social and historical reading of estranged feminine anxiety and its defensive formations as a route into the record of Kusama's work in New York in the sixties. Kusama herself, as well as the critics who engage now with her work, however, emphasize her "mental illness," a term of such extraordinary vagueness in an age of ever increasing precision in the classification of disorders that I feel sure I am falling back into the wonderland of myth. Yet, unlike van Gogh for most of this century, the factor of her mental travail and emotional pain associated with hallucinations and depersonalization has not served to make Kusama's passage into cultural history easier. I think I can identify two reasons: she did not die young and she is a woman. We find ourselves with the current admiration for Yayoi Kusama's sustained practice over four decades in a position not dissimilar from the "rediscovery" of Louise Bourgeois in her advanced years in the early eighties. There are other, disturbing parallels.

Here again we have a critical embrace of a "story" of childhood trauma told by an older woman, in this case French living in New York, who has sustained a long and productive career as an artist despite the intermittence of critical recognition on the international scale that her work now retrospectively demands. I am intrigued by the dependence upon a traumatic "origin" which so often has the effect, in discourse, of infantilizing the woman artist of whom it is told in a manner so at odds with the evidence of a long and productive career constituted as a relentless fight against the disabling effects of threatening psychosis.

In his 1975–76 seminar on the work of James Joyce, a writer whose childhood difficulties should have predisposed him to psychotic disintegration, Jacques Lacan devised the term *sinthôme*, an archaic form of symptom. Instead of reading a symptom as a message that could be deciphered, Lacan invoked a supplementary knotting *sinthôme*, as a trace of *jouissance* that is beyond analysis. Nonetheless, it has some order that enables the subject to live when other factors, such as trauma, disturb the subject's access to the "normal" braiding of the threads of Real, Imaginary (fantasy), and Symbolic (thought) registers. Lacan was intrigued by the hallucinatory experiences of the author as a young person that were refashioned through a manic but creative work on language. Little James became "James Joyce" through self-invention in pressing writing to extremity while producing a text—a weaving of words—that supported this author-name. This led to a pun on *synth-homme*, an artificial self-creation. Could there be a particular structuration of a *synth-femme*? Lacan's theory specifically shifts from hermeneutics of representational content to an analysis of praxis that shimmers on the borderline between hallucinatory "return of the foreclosed real" and a created textuality, or in this case patterning of spatiality.

Might Yayoi Kusama be read as a kind of Joycian figure in that gender/cultural determinacy that draws on the unfathered, the negativity of the feminine in Julia Kristeva's thesis on the historic avant-garde, which the writer "James Joyce" exemplifies? Does not her work take us into and through the hallucinatory spaces of threatened depersonalization, of the subject almost adrift from the signifying chain, a subject at the mercy of the return of the foreclosed real as hallucination, trapping her in a terrifying imaginary of incalculably ubiquitous eyes that never see her (the dots) and the vertiginous mise-en-abîme of infinite dislocating mirrorings in which she can never find her singular, spatialized place? If Joyce could access a pathway through the negativity of the feminine as poetic avant-gardist writing, can the Japanese-woman-artist access that pathway in worlds and culturally specific symbolics for which the feminine is only a negativity at the edge of psychosis? The refusal of the New York art world to grant Kusama her name must have been experienced as a repetition of the very trauma that made her make art.

I totally agree with Kusama's resistance of simplistic art-historical classification of her work as a form of Surrealist automatism. Yet the reference could confirm a kind of surrealist sensibility that articulates a margin or borderline between art and its psychic referents that seems to be traversed, creatively through the Lacanian concept of creativity as *sinthôme*. It might be mere feminist license to link Kusama's experience in New York and her flight to Japan and hospitalization to the experience of Meret Oppenheim at the end of the thirties, whose long cold years of blockage and breakdown after her extraordinary impact in New York in 1936 with the DÉJEUNER EN FOURRURE remind us of the real stresses of being a woman erotically at play in a masculine social and artistic economy.

One critical difficulty of being in and with the work of Kusama is the anxiety induced by the experience of transgressed boundaries made visible as an artistic experience of suffusion, envelopment, and loss of positionality through the INFINITY NETS, the polka dots, the multiplication of tumescent little forms, the mirrored environments, the pulsating effects of vast fields of dotted color. Her artistic world threatens to diffuse all separation, yet this is minimally marked, edged with the uncanniness of the no place that is all, and too much, the trace of an unmastered thus menacing *jouissance*. The project as a whole, monumentalizing the creative energy of a manic and considered defense that snatches up and uses, against the disintegrative threat they pose, the very forms, shapes, and fields of the depersonalizing hallucination that agonizes the artist, could not find a critical space, or a space in the critical discourse of its moments in the sixties to nineties in which this return of the real could be less agonistically handled.

The matrix is a feminine unconscious space of simultaneous co-emergence and co-fading of the I and the stranger that is neither fused nor rejected. Links between several joint part-subjects co-emerging in differentiation in relations without relations, and connections with their hybrid objects, produce/interlace "woman" that is not confined to the contours of the one-body with its inside versus outside polarity, and indicate a sexual difference based on webbing of links and not on essence or negation.

– Bracha Lichtenberg Ettinger, 1995 [5)]

Kusama writes of her distress at analysts she visited in the sixties. They offered no cure and only exacerbated her pain by asking her to speak repeatedly of what her mother had done. The words invited trauma into memories she could not tolerate. The analytical space offered no solace. From the blind spot of Freudian misrecognition of the feminine, they could not provide this woman with what I have named, following Michelle Montrelay, the "relief of signification." Kusama has been forced to invent—artistically as well as through literary texts—structures subordinated to both a semiotic rhythm and a formal, repeatable lexicon, in that they contain and hold outside the invasion of her conscious by "the return of the repressed," the uncanny eruption she calls her hallucinations of the gaze and the infinite inhumanness of the screen—the INFINITY NET. It is a Joycian achievement. And yet, it has been at a cost unimaginable, in terms of suffering.

What would have happened to this woman and this artist had there been an analytic discourse in which her experience of traumatic encounter with the Mother (her real mother's abusive acts being the belated reiteration of an excessive and unmanageable archaic encounter) could have been analytically addressed "in, of and from the feminine," as promised in the theoretical work of Bracha Lichtenberg Ettinger? Lichtenberg Ettinger, as both artist and psychoanalytical theorist, argues that art and sexual difference are closely related since we "enter the function of art by way of the libido and through extensions of the psyche closest to the edges of corpo-reality."[6] She has theorized a possible domain of subjectivity specifically connected with a non-essential yet still psychically differentiating feminine corpo-reality that lies beyond and yet also beside the

YAYOI KUSAMA, THE RETURN TO ETERNITY, 1993,
installation shot from the group show "Art from US," 1993, Land-
mark Hall, Yokohama / DIE RÜCKKEHR IN DIE EWIGKEIT.

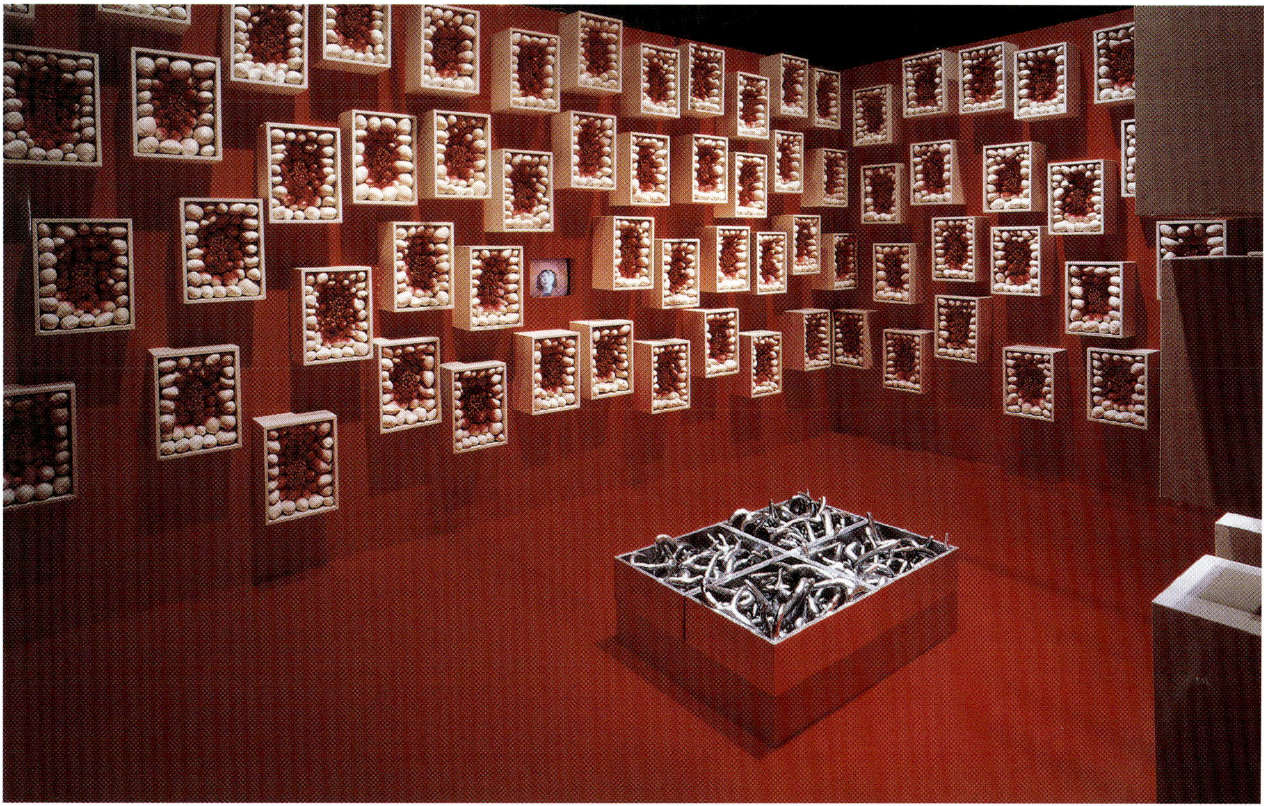

phallocentric order it can shift but not displace, and touches on those elements of a feminine sexual difference that we have not been able to think within existing monistic phallic theories of subjectivity, areas which under this foreclosure (they lack a signifier) by a phallic symbolic can only haunt us as a threatening return of the Real in the form of hallucination. Through her own art work she has theorized a "matrixial gaze" and an aesthetic process she names metamorphosis. "The matrixial *objet a* is a poïetic aesthetic object not in the sense of objects to look at or listen to while the 'influence' flows from the artwork to the spectator, but as objects participating in the act of creating that which will look at us, where activity is not a control but a bringing into being, and where passivity is not subjugation but a donation that allows for an exposure."[7] These precisely address (through a psychoanalytical articulation that works through both Freud on the Uncanny and Lacan's *sinthôme*) the possibility of a supplementary, shifted and specifically aesthetic means of relating the real (trauma), the imaginary, and the symbolic through series, repetitions, and a different relation to time that has specific and not causal relations to signifying the feminine in the spaces of art or meaning.

Kusama's work is not like this. It is a testament to the lack of a means to find such a structure. Like the work of Hanne Darboven, the time taken to make these huge repetitious works inscribes the energy expended in a titanic struggle with pressures that, while they may indeed have their predetermining origin in childhood trauma and abusive experiences, were also aggravated by the xenophobic, by the inhospitality of both American and Japanese culture to this artist for the cheapest of reasons that we must continue to name. Current recognition is belated and cannot erase the gap of time between the chance culture had in the sixties and now. The change, of course, is the result of the way that feminist thought and artistic interventions have deeply altered the dynamics and thematics of contemporary culture. Kusama does not have to acknowledge this, for her artistic practice was the sign of what it was like before such hospitality: but critics should acknowledge what difference feminist thinking and creativity has made.

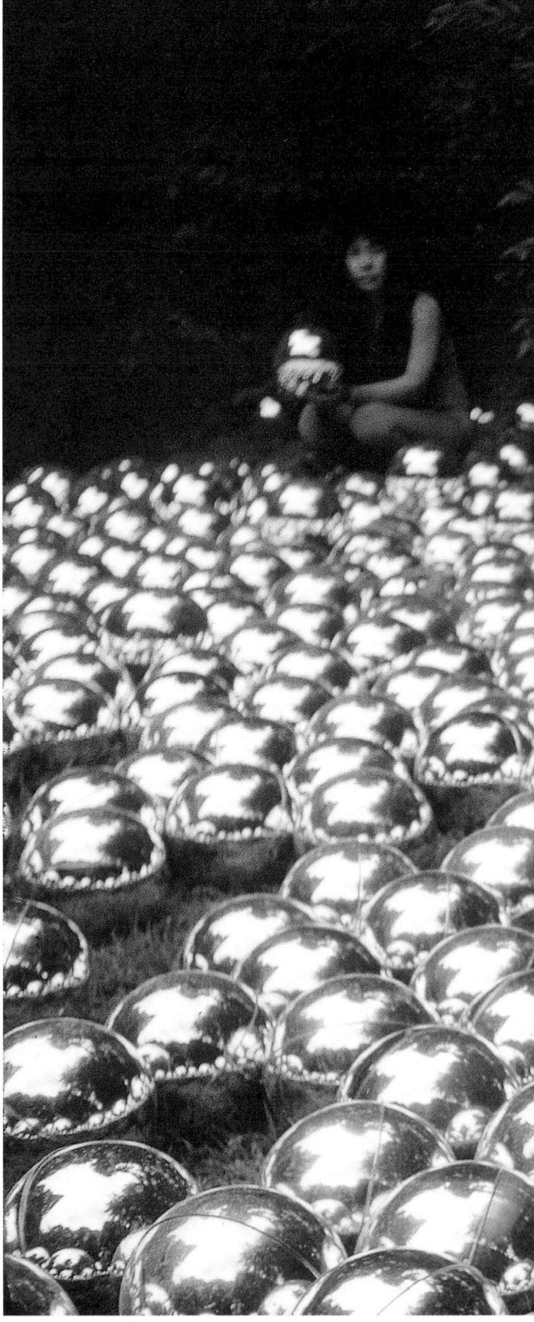

1) Joan Riviere, "Womanliness as Masquerade" in: *International Journal of Psychoanalysis* (vol. 10, 1929) reprinted in: *Formations of Fantasy*, ed. Victor Burgin et al. (London and New York: Methuen, 1986), p. 44.
2) This is over now. Significantly in the catalogue essay for his exhibition, *Parallel Visions: Modern Artists and Outsider Art* (Los Angeles: Los Angeles County Museum of Art, 1992), p. 12, Maurice Tuchman explained the absence of van Gogh from the show when he declared: "His psychological instability was never the basis of his creative expression nor was his influence primarily premised on this instability."

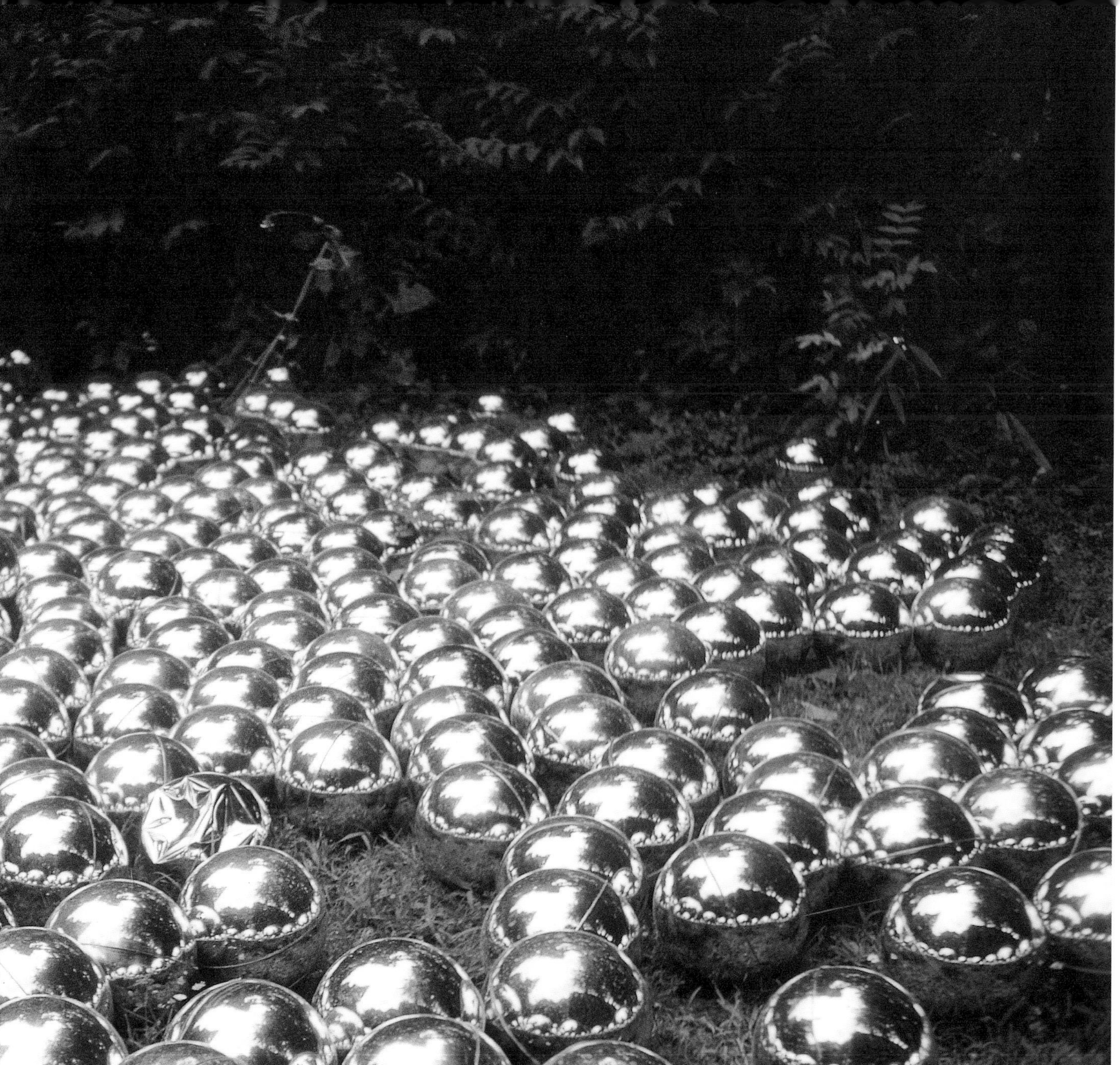

3) Catherine de Zegher, ed., *Inside the Visible: An Elliptical Traverse of Twentieth Century Art in, of and from the Feminine* (Boston: M.I.T. Press, 1996).
4) Julia Kristeva, cited by Anne-Maria Sauzeau-Boetti, "Negative Capability as Practice in Women's Art" in: *Studio International* (vol. 191, no. 979, 1976), p. 24.

5) Bracha Lichtenberg Ettinger, "Metramorphic Borderlinks and Matrixial Borderspace" in: *Rethinking Borders*, ed. by John Welchman (London: MacMillan Press, 1996), p. 125.
6) Bracha Lichtenberg Ettinger, "The With-In-Visible Screen" in: *Inside the Visible*, op.cit., p. 92.
7) Bracha Lichtenberg Ettinger, *The Matrixial Gaze* (Leeds: Feminist Arts and Histories Network Press, 1995), p. 48.

GRISELDA POLLOCK

Weiblichkeit konnte also vorgeschützt und als eine Maske getragen werden – sowohl um den Besitz der Männlichkeit zu verbergen wie auch um die Bestrafung zu vermeiden, wenn der Besitz dieser Männlichkeit bei ihr entdeckt wurde, geradeso wie der Dieb seine Taschen umkehrt und die Durchsuchung verlangt, um zu beweisen, dass er das Gestohlene nicht hat.
– Joan Riviere, 1929 [1]

DREI GEDANKEN ÜBER WEIBLICHKEIT, KREATIVITÄT UND VERLORENE ZEIT

Beim Wandel der zeitgenössischen Kunstkritik zur kritisch kunsthistorischen Analyse zeitgenössischer Kunst hängt zurzeit alles am Gegensatz zwischen dem anhaltenden Status der Künstlerpersönlichkeit als Referentin ihres Werks und der Funktion des Kunstwerks als historisch zu interpretierender Text. Als Text ist Kunst daher «immer und immer schon» intertextuell, das heisst Teil einer allgemein verbreiteten kulturellen Semiotik, die sowohl über eine synchrone wie eine diachrone Achse verfügt. Da damit jeweils eine einzigartige Artikulation kultureller Ressourcen gemeint ist, die dabei durch individuelle Brechung eine neue Form erhalten, und zwar im Rahmen einer Subjektivität, die als Struktur transindividuell und als Ergebnis der Geschichte dieser und

---

GRISELDA POLLOCK unterrichtet Sozialkritische Kunstgeschichte an der Universität von Leeds und leitet das Graduierten-Programm (M.A./Ph.D.) für feministische Theorie und bildende Kunst. Neuere Publikationen: *Generations and Geographies in the Visual Arts* (1996) und *Differencing the Canon: Feminist Desire and the Writing of Art's Histories* (1999), beide Routledge, London.

keiner anderen Person individuell ist, garantiert diese Auffassung der Kunst als Text auch deren Zugänglichkeit. Zu wissen, wie die Künstlerin ihre Arbeit versteht und erklärt, ist natürlich äusserst wichtig und auch historisch von Interesse, doch könnte man auch argumentieren, dass ein Werk immer mehr ist als das Programm, das dahinter steht, denn der Produzent oder die Produzentin ist nur ein, wenn auch ein sehr wichtiger Faktor innerhalb des überdeterminierten Geschehens, das die künstlerische Tätigkeit ausmacht. Wie jedes andere psychisch zerrissene, von Zeit und Ort geprägte Subjekt kann sich auch ein Künstler nie ganz kennen und verstehen. Wie viel mehr muss das auf eine Künstlerin zutreffen, die sich kulturell, ästhetisch und psychologisch als Grenzgängerin erlebt?

Wenn ich als Kunsthistorikerin die jüngsten Veröffentlichungen über Yayoi Kusama lese, muss ich an die Verwirrung um die Rezeption und Analyse von Vincent van Gogh denken, der über ein Jahrhundert lang als Paradebeispiel des «verrückten Genies» herhalten musste. [2] Im Fall dieses niederländischen Malers traf der alte Mythos von der Besessenheit des Künstlers mit einer noch jungen Psychiatrie zusammen, die Künstlerbiographien wie Fallstudien behandelte und so allgemein die hartnäckige Überzeugung entstehen liess, die unmittelbare, sehr persönliche Ausdruckskraft seiner Bilder zeuge von seiner seelischen Not. Allein schon dieser Satz enthüllt die gedankliche Verwirrung in dieser Gleichsetzung von Kunst und Wahnsinn, die uns auch überhaupt nicht weiterhilft, wenn wir die Beziehungen zwischen der poetischen Avantgarde und ihrer kulturell bedingten Ungastlichkeit gegenüber Künstlern untersuchen wollen, die Frauen und/oder Aussenseiter sind.

Dabei darf man die entscheidenden Unterschiede zwischen seelischer Not, traumatisch bedingten neurotischen Symptomen und den schwereren Formen psychischer Erkrankung, bei denen jeder Bezug zur Intersubjektivität und sprachlichen Kommunikation verloren geht, nicht aus dem Blick verlieren. So hat die Begeisterung moderner Künstler für die Kunst von Aussenseitern oder *art brut* – eine Kunst der «totalen Visionäre», wie Maurice Tuchman das Phänomen nannte (in seiner Ausstellung «Parallel Visions: Modern Artists and Outsider Art», Los Angeles 1992) – eine lange Tradition und entzündet sich stets von neuem an den unheimlichen stilistischen Ähnlichkeiten und formalen Übereinstimmungen zwischen bewusst gestalteter moderner Kunst und spontanen ahistorischen künstlerischen Arbeiten. Der triebhaft Schaffende und der Künstler fallen jedoch nicht in die gleiche Kategorie, auch wenn seelische Not für beide eine wichtige Energiequelle ist. Die Künstlerpersönlichkeit ist ein sich selbst reflektierendes, sozialisiertes, wenn auch nicht unbedingt sich selbst genügendes Wesen: daher die Offenheit künstlerischen Tuns für die Auseinandersetzung mit einem künstlerischen Gegenüber, jenes unverzichtbare Spiel mit Referenz, Respekt und Differenz.

Was van Gogh angeht, ging es mir stets darum, seiner Krankheit, die ich für eine episodische psychomotorische Epilepsie halte, weniger Bedeutung beizumessen und stattdessen sein Werk als Ausdruck einer ambivalenten, schubweise auftretenden, aber bewussten Auseinandersetzung mit der Moderne zu verstehen, in der es um Schlüsselthemen wie Zeit, Erinnerung und Trost geht. Vernachlässigen wir die Seelenpein, die das Leben diesem holländischen Künstler bescherte, und durchforsten wir seine Werke nach dem, was sie als Arbeiten eines kreativen Subjekts ausweist, als Werke eines bewussten Kunstproduzenten, der sich mit bestehender Kunst auseinander setzt. Dasselbe ist auch im Fall von Yayoi Kusama angesagt, damit ihre künstlerischen Texte die historische Funktion erfüllen können, auf eine künstlerische Präsenz zu verweisen, die sich durch das tief gehende, aber historisch bedingte Verrückt-Sein auszeichnet, das dem dreifachen Anderssein einer Frau-Japanerin-Künstlerin im vorfeministischen New York der 60er Jahre, bevor alles anders wird, auferlegt ist. Es fehlt nicht an beredten Zeugnissen für die paradoxe Einstellung gegenüber Frauen und Kunst in jenem Jahrzehnt. Verspätet entdecken wir jetzt erstaunlich viele und erstaunlich originelle Künstlerinnen jener Zeit. Doch ihre Position, was das Verhältnis der Geschlechter, Sexualität, ethnische Zugehörigkeit, Religion und Nationalität betrifft, kam damals nicht voll zum Ausdruck; immerhin entstand aus der Not das Schockierende und Überzeugende ihrer neuen, oft bahnbrechenden künstlerischen Strategien, welche die Sprachlosigkeiten, Präsenzbedürfnisse und Unsichtbarkeiten thematisierten, die mit der geschlechtlichen oder ethnischen Zugehörigkeit einhergingen. Ich denke, es war Catherine de Zeghers Konzept einer elliptischen Wiederbegegnung mit drei Zeitabschnitten des zwanzigsten Jahrhunderts, das sie für ihre ganz neue Wege beschreitende Ausstellung «Inside the Visible» (1996) entwickelte, worin ganz verschiedene Strategien aus den 30er, 60er und 90er Jahren als Momente eines bislang unsichtbar gebliebenen, dialektischen und radikalen Widerstandsprozesses gesehen wurden. Und da war es die unauflöslich mit weiteren dissidenten Standpunkten verbundene Weiblichkeit, die eine – oft übergangene oder als nebensächlich beiseite geschobene – Herausforderung der sprach- und gesellschaftspolitischen Autorität darstellte.[3]

Betrachtet man die historische Seite der Kunst im zwanzigsten Jahrhundert durch diese kritische feministische Brille, wird einem klar, dass die Situation in den 60er Jahren das Individuum derart «krank» ma-

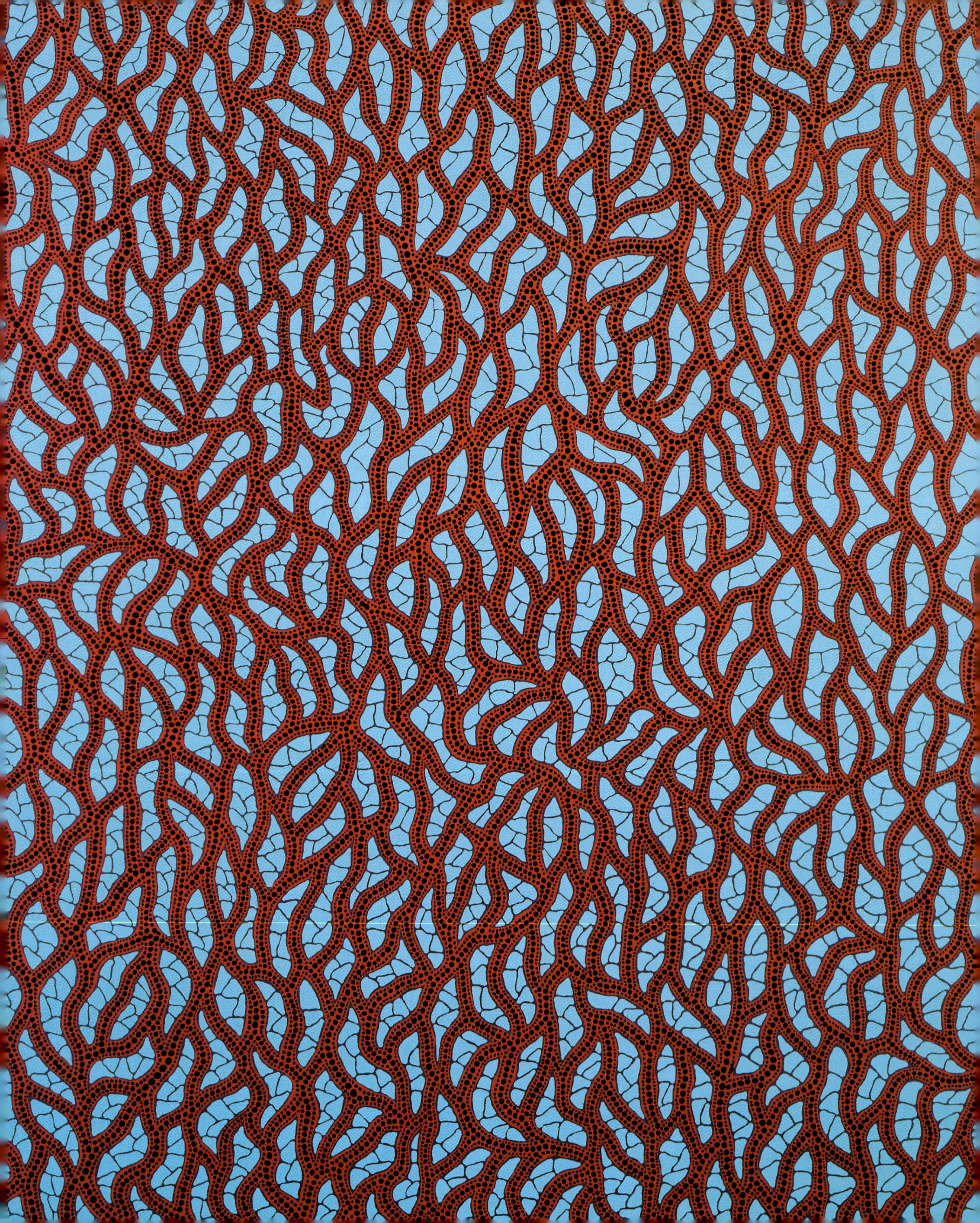

chen konnte, wie es Joan Riviere in ihrem eingangs zitierten Aufsatz aus den 20er Jahren beschreibt. Damals ging Riviere auf die Angst einer neuen, einsamen Generation von weiblichen Intellektuellen ein, die mit der Aufnahme einer Berufstätigkeit in eine feindliche, phallokratisch psycho-symbolische Wirtschaftswelt katapultiert wurden. Wut, Schweigen und drohender Wahnsinn tauchen auch in der Guerilla-Taktik einer Nancy Spero wieder auf, in deren skatologischen Lästerungen oder ihrer die Geschlechtsgrenzen überschreitenden bauchrednerischen Wiedergabe von Artauds Wut in den 60er Jahren. Weniger wutentbrannt, aber genauso intensiv sind Adrian Pipers provozierende Strassenperformances oder Martha Roslers aggressive Photomontagen gegen den Vietnamkrieg. Sie alle enthalten in verschlüsselter Form, was man durchgängig auch in Kusamas Werk der 60er Jahre findet, in diesem breiten Spektrum von Happenings, Selbstinszenierungen, Environments und öffentlichen Auftritten zur persönlichen Abgrenzung, die ihr von Seiten einer bekannten Kritikerin den Vorwurf der «übertriebenen Selbstentblössung» eintrugen. Riviere beschreibt den Zusammenhang zwischen Mimikry und Exzess, von dem ich denke, dass er ein logisches Element in Yayoi Kusamas Werk der 60er Jahre ist, im Sinne eines präfeministischen, künstlerischen Pharmakons: Symptom und parodistische Kritik, Anzeichen der Vergiftung und Gegengift in einem. Weiblichkeit wird in vielen Verkleidungen vorgeführt, auf traditionelle Art und Weise, wobei der Kimono in den Strassen New Yorks auf die kulturelle Differenz verweist und gleichzeitig eine interkulturelle Kritik japanischer Weiblichkeitsideale darstellt. Der unbekleidete Körper ist dabei universelles Symbol der Sexualität, verweist aber auch auf ein kulturspezifisches, künstlerisches Nacktsein.

Der Nachdruck, mit dem die Künstlerin immer wieder vor einem ihre Person auflösenden Hintergrund auftritt, der durch eine mit unendlicher Geduld betriebene Wiederholung zustande kommt – das geht vom Eintauchen der Künstlerin in ihre eigenen Arbeiten und Environments bis zu ihrem Auftreten als Verkäuferin in der berüchtigten Sideshow zur Biennale in Venedig, NARCISSUS GARDEN (Narzissengarten, 1966), und den Arbeiten, in denen sie den Happening-Impresario spielt, AWAKEN THE DEAD (Weckt die Toten, Museum of Modern Art, New York 1989) –, unterstreicht die entsetzliche Notwendigkeit, sich als Künstler «in weiblicher Form» sichtbar zu inszenieren, zu einer Zeit, als diese Position noch nicht kritisch oder theoretisch artikulierbar war als eine, aus der man «im Singular» sprechen konnte.

Die Vervielfachung und Wiederholung sowohl der eigenen Person wie auch der kleinen Phallen scheinen mit dem Zwang zusammenzuhängen, der sich aus dem psychosozialen Kontext einer japanischen weiblichen Künstlerin ergibt. Phallozentrische Kulturen, die sich genau wie in den 20er Jahren von der Explosion weiblicher Kreativität in ihrer homo-sozialen Ausschliesslichkeit bedroht fühlen, verstärkten ihren repressiven Widerstand. Um sich dagegen zu behaupten, baut die Japanerin, Frau und Künstlerin im Gegenzug eine manische Abwehr auf, indem sie das stärkste Tabu des Phallozentrismus bricht. Sie zeigt nicht nur den Phallus, was dessen verborgene symbolische Potenz auf ein Stück erotisches Fleisch reduziert, sondern dadurch, dass sie sie wie Pilze aus dem Boden schiessen und sich selbst vermehren lässt, gibt sie diesen «Kleinen» eine völlig andere Bedeutung: Sie verkehren sich zu Symbolen ihrer eigenen, grenzenlosen künstlerischen Fruchtbarkeit. Kusama macht aus dem grossen unsichtbaren Sinnbild phallozentrischer Macht eine verletzliche Sache, etwas sanft Schwellendes und Reproduzierbares. In diesem ästhetischen Garten aus zusammengenähten, mit Nadeln durchbohrten Phallen behauptet der nackte Körper der Frau und Künstlerin seine singuläre Präsenz durch eine weitere, immer noch widersprüchliche Drehung der Schraube gegenüber Paula Modersohns Aufzeigen der paradoxen Konfiguration in der westlichen Moderne (in ihrem monumentalem Selbstporträt von 1906): Frau/Akt/Künstler.

«Weiblich» würde ich jenen Moment des Bruchs und der Negativität nennen, den jede neuartige Praxis voraussetzt.

– Julia Kristeva, 1974 [4]

Als Annäherung an das in den 60er Jahren in New York entstandene Werk Kusamas bevorzuge ich deshalb eine soziale und historische Interpretation der sich entfremdeten weiblichen Angst und ihrer Abwehrmassnahmen. Kusama selbst und auch die Kritiker, die sich inzwischen mit ihrem Werk beschäftigen, kommen immer wieder auf ihre «Geisteskrankheit» zu sprechen; das ist jedoch ein derart verschwommener Begriff in unserer Zeit der zunehmenden Differenzierung der Klassifikation von Funktionsstörungen, dass ich mich ins Märchenwunderland zurückversetzt fühle, wenn ich ihn nur höre. Doch anders als im Fall von van Gogh hat der Faktor der geistigen und seelischen Not in Verbindung mit Halluzinationen und Persönlichkeitsverlust Kusama das Eingehen in die Kunstgeschichte nicht leichter gemacht. Dafür gibt es zwei Gründe: Sie ist nicht jung gestorben und sie ist eine Frau. Unsere gegenwärtige Bewunderung für Yayoi Kusamas über vier Jahrzehnte lang durchgehaltene künstlerische Tätigkeit erinnert an die «Wiederentdeckung» einer schon betagten Louise Bourgeois in den frühen 80er Jahren. Es gibt aber noch weitere, beunruhigende Parallelen.

Auch damals wurde die «Geschichte» eines Kindheitstraumas kritisch verwertet: der Bericht einer älteren Frau, einer in New York lebenden Französin, die auf eine lange und produktive Karriere als Künstlerin zurückblickte, obwohl sie auf internationaler Ebene nicht immer die kritische Anerkennung fand, die man im Nachhinein ihrem Werk zollen muss. Interessant, dieser Rückgriff auf einen traumatischen «Ursprung», der nur zu oft eine Infantilisierung der Frau und Künstlerin bewirkt, obwohl sich das schlecht mit ihrer langen und produktiven Karriere als Resultat eines unerbittlichen Kampfes gegen die zerstörerische Wirkung der drohenden Psychose vereinbaren lässt.

In seinem Seminar über den Schriftsteller James Joyce (1975–76), dessen schwierige Kindheit einer psychotischen Störung Vorschub zu leisten schien, hat Jacques Lacan die Bezeichnung *sinthôme*, die archaische Form des Symptoms, gebraucht. Statt ein Symptom als entschlüsselbare Botschaft zu lesen, führte Lacan ein zusätzliches komplexes *sinthôme* ein, das sich als Spur der Lust jeder Analyse entzieht. Es bietet dem Subjekt jedoch einen Halt um weiterzuleben, wenn andere Faktoren, etwa ein Trauma, es daran hindern, die Fäden des Realen, Imaginären (Phantasie) und Symbolischen (Denken) «normal»

zu verknüpfen. Lacan war fasziniert von den halluzinatorischen Erfahrungen, die der Autor als Jugendlicher gemacht hatte und die dann durch einen besessenen, aber kreativen Umgang mit der Sprache verarbeitet wurden. Der kleine Joyce wurde *James Joyce* durch Selbsterfindung seiner Person beim Schreiben eines Textes, in welchem er die Sprache bis zum Äussersten strapazierte und ein Wortgewebe schuf, das diesen Autor und Namen hervorbrachte. Das Wortspiel *synth-homme* für die künstliche Selbsterschaffung bot sich an. Könnte es vielleicht auch eine besondere Bildung einer *synth-femme* geben? Lacans Theorie geht von der Hermeneutik des symbolischen Inhalts zur Analyse einer Praxis über, die an der Grenze zwischen der «halluzinatorischen Wiederkehr des ausgeschlossenen Realen» und einer neu erschaffenen Textualität (oder bei Kusama die Auflösung des Räumlichen in Mustern) aufleuchtet.

Könnte Yayoi Kusama als Joyce'sche Gestalt betrachtet werden, in jener Determinierung durch Geschlecht und Kultur, die aus der vaterlosen Negativität des Weiblichen folgt, welche Julia Kristeva in ihrer Arbeit über die historische Avantgarde beschreibt, für die «James Joyce» exemplarisch steht? Führt uns ihr Werk nicht in und durch die halluzinatorischen Räume einer drohenden Auflösung des Subjekts, das beinah aus der Bedeutungskette herausfällt, ein Subjekt, das der Wiederkehr des ausgeschlossenen Realen als Halluzination ausgeliefert ist, gefangen in einer schrecklichen Phantasiewelt mit unzähligen allgegenwärtigen Augen (die Punkte), die es nie wahrnehmen, und im Schwindel erregenden Strudel von tausend, alles durcheinander wirbelnden Spiegelungen, in dem es nie seinen eigenen Platz finden kann? Wenn Joyce seinen Weg durch die Negativität des Weiblichen im avantgardistischen Schreiben fand, kann da die japanische Frau und Künstlerin diesen Weg in Welten und kulturspezifischen Symbolen finden, für die das Weibliche nur ein Negatives am Rande der Psychose bedeutet? Die Weigerung der New Yorker Kunstwelt, Kusamas Bedeutung anzuerkennen, muss für sie eine Wiederholung des Traumas gewesen sein, das sie Künstlerin werden liess.

Ich gehe mit Kusamas Ablehnung einer vereinfachenden kunsthistorischen Klassifizierung ihres

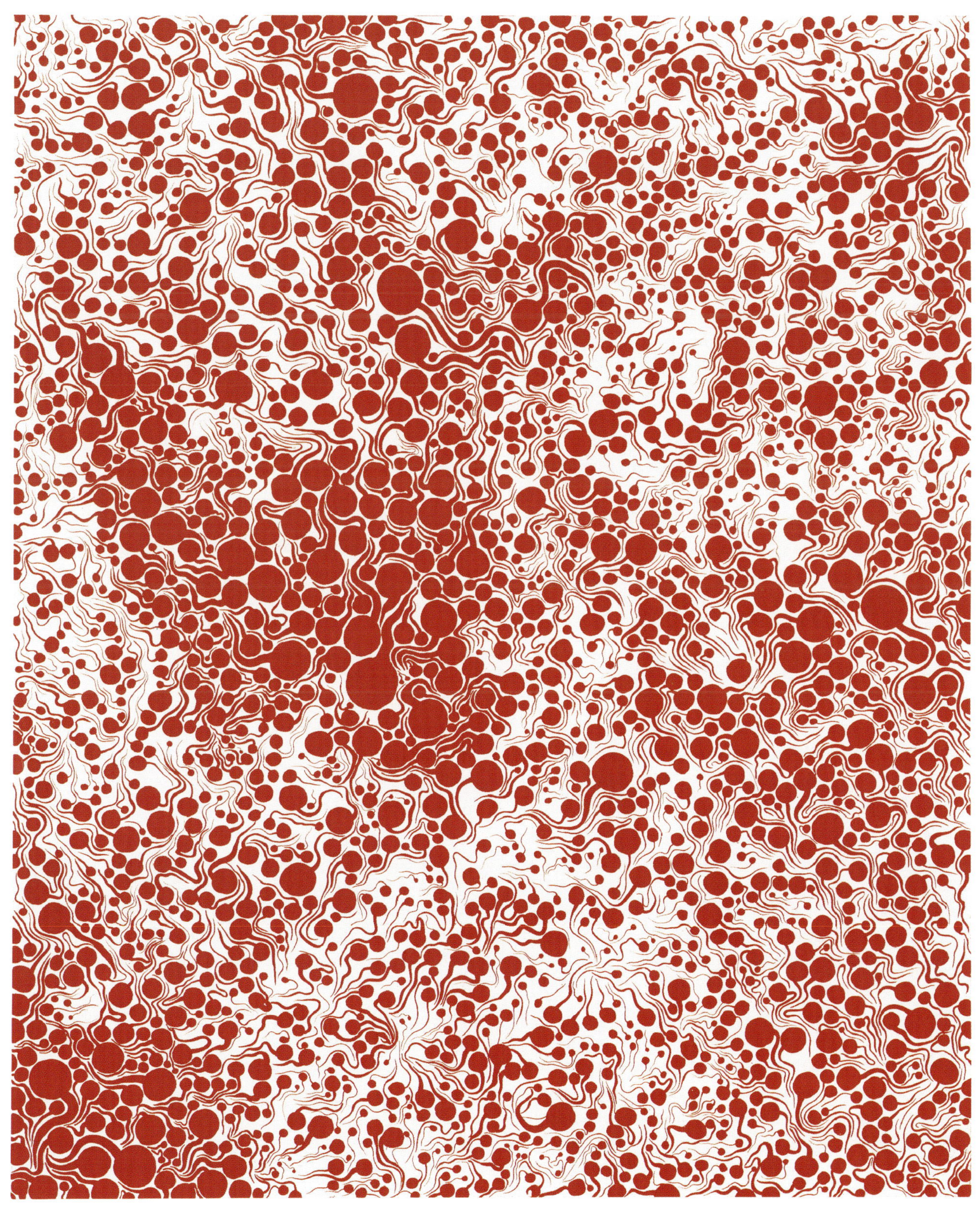

YAYOI KUSAMA, BEYOND THE END OF THE CENTURY, 1987, acrylic on canvas, 63¾ x 51¼" /
JENSEITS DER JAHRHUNDERTWENDE, Acryl auf Leinwand, 162 x 130 cm. (PHOTO: NORIHIRO UENO)

> *Die Matrix ist ein weiblicher unbewusster Ort gleichzeitigen Auftauchens und Verschwindens von Ich und Fremdem, das weder integriert noch ausgeschlossen wird. Verbindungen zwischen mehreren Teilsubjekten, die gemeinsam in beziehungslosen Beziehungen und Verbindungen zu ihren hybriden Objekten auftauchen, ergeben/verweben das «Weibliche», das sich nicht auf die Konturen des einen Körpers mit seiner Innen-Aussen-Polarität beschränkt; sie bezeichnen einen sexuellen Unterschied, der auf der Verflechtung von Verbindungen beruht und nicht auf Essenzialität oder Negation.*

Werkes als Variante des surrealistischen Automatismus völlig einig. Dennoch könnte diese Referenz ein Hinweis auf eine Art surrealistische Sensibilität sein, die eine Nahtstelle oder Grenze zwischen der Kunst und ihren psychischen Entsprechungen markiert, welche das Lacansche Konzept von der Kreativität als *sinthôme* kreativ überschreitet. Vielleicht ist es feministische Willkür, Kusamas New Yorker Erlebnisse, die Flucht nach Japan und ihre Hospitalisierung mit den Erfahrungen Meret Oppenheims Ende der 30er Jahre in Verbindung zu bringen: Deren lange, kalte Jahre der Blockierung und des Zusammenbruchs nach dem überwältigenden Erfolg, den sie 1936 mit ihrem FRÜHSTÜCK IM PELZ in New York errungen hatte, den tatsächlichen Stress in Erinnerung rufen, dem eine Frau ausgesetzt ist, die sich in einem gesellschaftlich und künstlerisch von Männern bestimmten System als erotisches Wesen einbringt.

Eine Schwierigkeit, sich in und mit dem Werk Kusamas zurechtzufinden, hat mit der Angst zu tun, welche das Erlebnis der Grenzüberschreitung auslöst, das als künstlerische Erfahrung von Auflösung, Einhüllung und Standpunktverlust sichtbar wird in den INFINITY NETS (Unendlichkeitsnetze), den Punkten und unzähligen kleinen anschwellenden Formen, in den mehrfach gespiegelten Environments und in der pulsierenden Wirkung nicht enden wollender Farbpunktfelder. Ihre künstlerische Welt droht alle ohnehin kaum noch erkennbaren Unterscheidungen aufzuheben und vermittelt das unheimliche Gefühl eines Nirgendwo, das überall und zu viel ist, Spur einer unbeherrschten und daher bedrohlichen *jouissance*. Das Projekt als Ganzes, das der kreativen Energie einer manischen und durchdachten Abwehr monumentale Dimensionen verleiht – einer Abwehr, die Formen, Konturen und Felder der

entgrenzenden Halluzination aufnimmt und als Mittel gegen die durch diese selbst hervorgerufene, drohende Desintegration einsetzt –, fand von den 60er bis in die 90er Jahre keinen Platz in der Kritik, es kam auch nicht zu einem kritischen Diskurs seiner Momente, in dem diese Wiederkehr des Realen etwas freundlicher behandelt worden wäre.

Kusama beschreibt ihre Verzweiflung über Psychoanalytiker, die sie in den 60er Jahren konsultierte. Sie konnten ihr nicht weiterhelfen, sondern machten alles nur noch schlimmer, indem sie sie aufforderten, immer wieder über ihre Mutter zu sprechen. Die Worte machten traumatische Erfahrungen zu unerträglichen Erinnerungen. Der analytische Raum bot keinen Trost. Mit der Freudschen Blindheit, was das Weibliche betraf, geschlagen, konnten sie dieser Frau nicht anbieten, was ich nach Michelle Montrelay als «Erleichterung durch Sinngebung» bezeichne. Kusama war gezwungen – in ihrer Kunst und mithilfe literarischer Texte – selbst Strukturen zu erfinden, um die drohende Invasion ihres Bewusstseins zu verhindern und aufzuhalten und ihr einen semiotischen Rhythmus und ein formelles, reproduzierbares Lexikon zu verpassen. Diese Invasion durch die «Wiederkehr des Verdrängten», die unheimliche Eruption, die sie als Halluzinationen des Blickes bezeichnet oder als unendliche Unmenschlichkeit der Projektionsfläche – das INFINITY NET. Eine Leistung, vergleichbar mit jener von James Joyce, aber zu einem unvorstellbar hohen Preis persönlichen Leidens.

Was wäre aus dieser Frau und Künstlerin geworden, hätte es einen analytischen Diskurs gegeben, der die traumatische Begegnung mit der «Mutter» (was ihre wirkliche Mutter getan hatte, war nur die späte Wiederholung eines unbewältigten Urerlebnis-

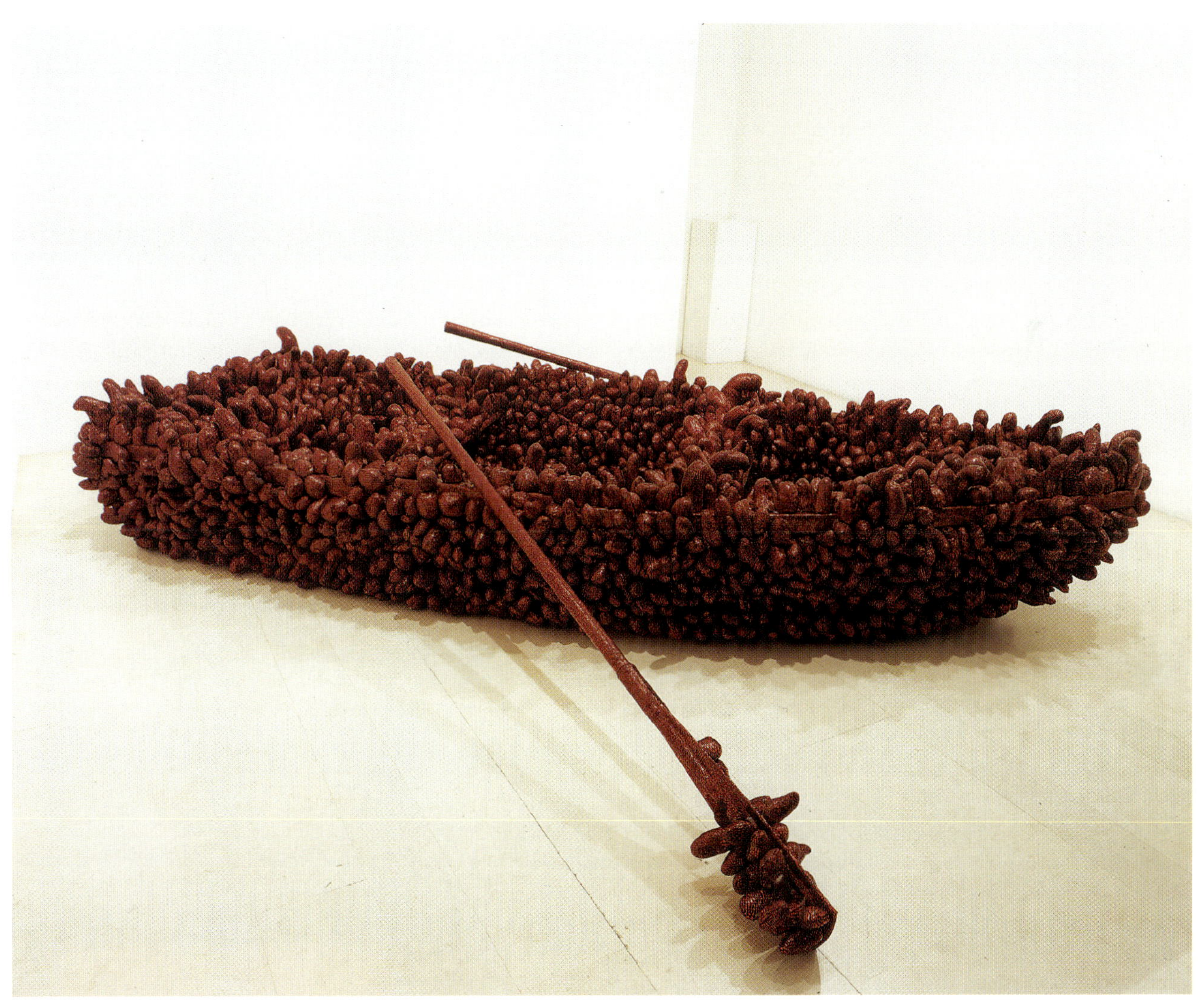

YAYOI KUSAMA, REPETITIVE VISION—PHALLUS BOAT, 2000, installation at Pièce Unique, Paris, March, 2000 /
REPETITIVE VISION – PHALLUS-BOOT.

ses) «in, von und aus dem Weiblichen heraus» analytisch aufgearbeitet hätte, wie es Bracha Lichtenberg Ettinger in ihren theoretischen Arbeiten in Aussicht stellt? Lichtenberg Ettinger, Künstlerin und Psychoanalytikerin, vertritt die These, dass Kunst und sexuelle Differenz eng zusammenhängen, da wir «die Funktion der Kunst über die Libido und eine Erweiterung der Psyche, die bis an die Grenzen des Körpers und seiner Realität geht, erreichen».[6] Sie entwirft einen möglichen subjektiven Bereich einer nicht wesentlichen, aber doch psychisch differenzierenden weiblichen Körperlichkeit, jenseits, aber auch neben der phallokratischen Ordnung, die sich wohl verschieben, aber nicht verdrängen lässt, und sie berührt Elemente einer weiblichen sexuellen Differenz, die wir innerhalb der monistischen, phallischen Subjektivitäts-Theorien nicht denken konnten; Bereiche, die von einer phallischen Symbolik ausgegrenzt bleiben (für die es keine Bezeichnung gab), können uns nur als drohende Wiederkehr des Realen in Form von Halluzinationen verfolgen. In ihrer eigenen Kunst hat sie den Begriff des «Matrix-Blicks» und einen ästhetischen Prozess, den sie Metamorphose nennt, entwickelt. «Das Matrix-*Objekt a* ist ein kreatives, ästhetisches Objekt nicht im Sinn von O b j e k t e n , die man a n s c h a u t oder a n h ö r t , während der ‹Einfluss› vom Kunstwerk zum Betrachter fliesst, sondern von Objekten, die an dem kreativen Akt teilhaben, die uns a n s c h a u e n , wobei Aktivität keine Kontrolle, sondern ein Ins-Leben-Rufen ist und Passivität nicht Unterdrückung bedeutet, sondern ein Geschenk, das die Darbietung ermöglicht.»[7] Dabei geht es (in einer psychoanalytischen Sprache, in der sowohl das «Unheimliche» im Sinne von Freud wie Lacans *sinthôme* anklingt) um ein zusätzliches, verändertes und spezifisch ästhetisches Mittel, um das Reale (Trauma), das Imaginäre und das Symbolische miteinander in Verbindung zu bringen durch Aneinanderreihung, Wiederholungen und ein anderes Verhältnis zur Zeit; ein Mittel, das in besonderer, nicht kausaler Weise mit der Bezeichnung des Weiblichen im Rahmen der Kunst oder der Bedeutung überhaupt zusammenhängt.

Kusamas Werk ist anders. Es zeugt von der Unmöglichkeit eine solche Struktur zu finden. Wie in Hanne Darbovens Werk steht die Zeit, die diese riesi-

gen, repetitiven Arbeiten erfordern, für die Energie in diesem titanischen Kampf gegen Zwänge, die zwar ihren Ursprung in einem Kindheitstrauma und in Missbrauchserfahrungen haben mögen, dann aber noch verstärkt wurden durch die fremdenfeindliche Unfreundlichkeit der amerikanischen wie der japanischen Kultur im Umgang mit dieser Künstlerin, und zwar aus ganz schäbigen Gründen, die wir nicht unter den Tisch fallen lassen dürfen. Die gegenwärtige Anerkennung kommt mit grosser Verspätung und kann die zeitliche Kluft zwischen der Chance, die die Kultur in den 60er Jahren hatte und heute hat, nicht überbrücken. Der Umschwung ist natürlich dem Umstand zu verdanken, dass feministisches Denken und künstlerische Interventionen die Dynamik und Thematik der zeitgenössischen Kultur grundlegend verändert haben. Kusama braucht dem nicht weiter Rechnung zu tragen, denn in ihrem künstlerischen Schaffen drückt sich der Stand der Dinge vor dieser Aufnahmebereitschaft aus. Kritiker hingegen sollten den Einfluss feministischen Denkens und weiblicher Kreativität nicht vernachlässigen.

(Übersetzung: Goridis/Parker)

1) Joan Riviere, «Womanliness as Masquerade», *International Journal of Psychoanalysis*, Bd. 10, 1929. Deutsche Übersetzung: «Weiblichkeit als Maske» in: Joan Riviere, *Ausgewählte Schriften*, Lilli Gast (Hrsg.), Edition Diskord, Tübingen 1996, S. 106.
2) Das ist glücklicherweise vorbei. Bezeichnenderweise erklärte Maurice Tuchman im Katalogtext zu seiner Ausstellung das Fehlen von Vincent van Gogh in der Ausstellung wie folgt: «Seine psychische Labilität bildete zu keiner Zeit die Grundlage seines Schaffens und sein Einfluss beruhte ebenfalls nicht auf dieser Labilität.» In: *Parallel Visions: Modern Artists and Outsider Art*, Los Angeles County Museum of Art, Los Angeles 1992, S. 12.
3) Catherine de Zegher (Hrsg.), *Inside the Visible: An Elliptical Traverse of Twentieth Century Art in, of and from the Feminine*, M.I.T. Press, Boston 1996.
4) Julia Kristeva, zitiert bei Anne-Maria Sauzeau-Boetti, «Negative Capability as Practice in Women's Art» in: *Studio International,* Band 191, Nr. 979, 1976, S. 24.
5) Bracha Lichtenberg Ettinger, «Metamorphic Borderlinks and Matrixial Borderspace» in: John Welchman (Hrsg.), *Rethinking Borders,* MacMillan Press, London 1996, S. 125.
6) Bracha Lichtenberg Ettinger, «The With-In-Visible Screen» in: *Inside the Visible,* op.cit., S. 92.
7) Bracha Lichtenberg Ettinger, *The Matrixial Gaze*, Feminist Arts and Histories Network Press, Leeds 1995, S. 48.

YAYOI KUSAMA WITH PUMPKIN, 1994 / KUSAMA MIT KÜRBIS.

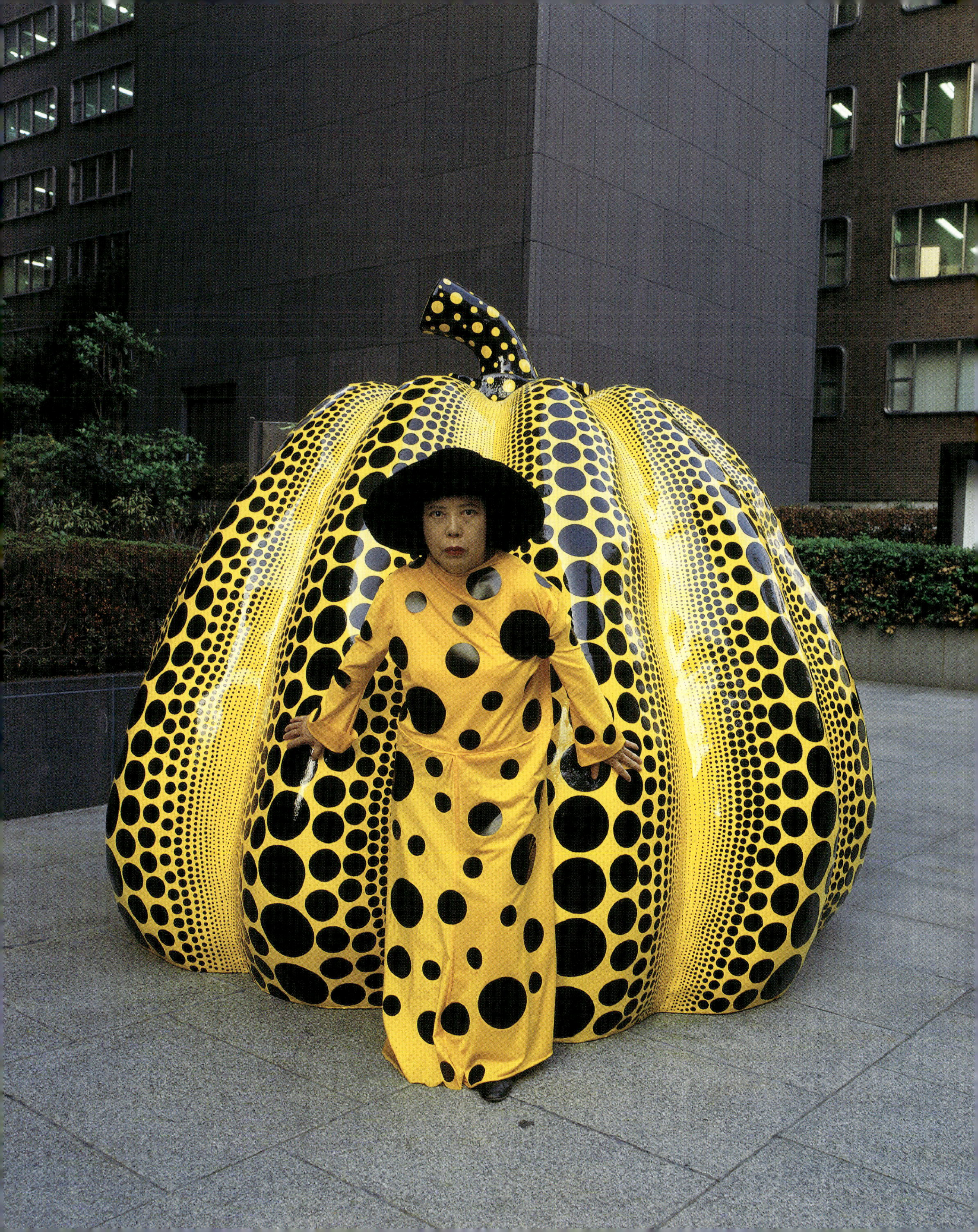

Edition for Parkett Yayoi Kusama
Infinity Nets, 2000
Silkscreen print on mirror, 10 x 8¼".
Edition of 70, signed and numbered on the back.

Unendlichkeitsnetze, 2000
Siebdruck auf Spiegel, 25,5 x 21 cm.
Auflage: 70, auf der Rückseite signiert und
nummeriert.

(PHOTO: MANCIA/BODMER, ZÜRICH)

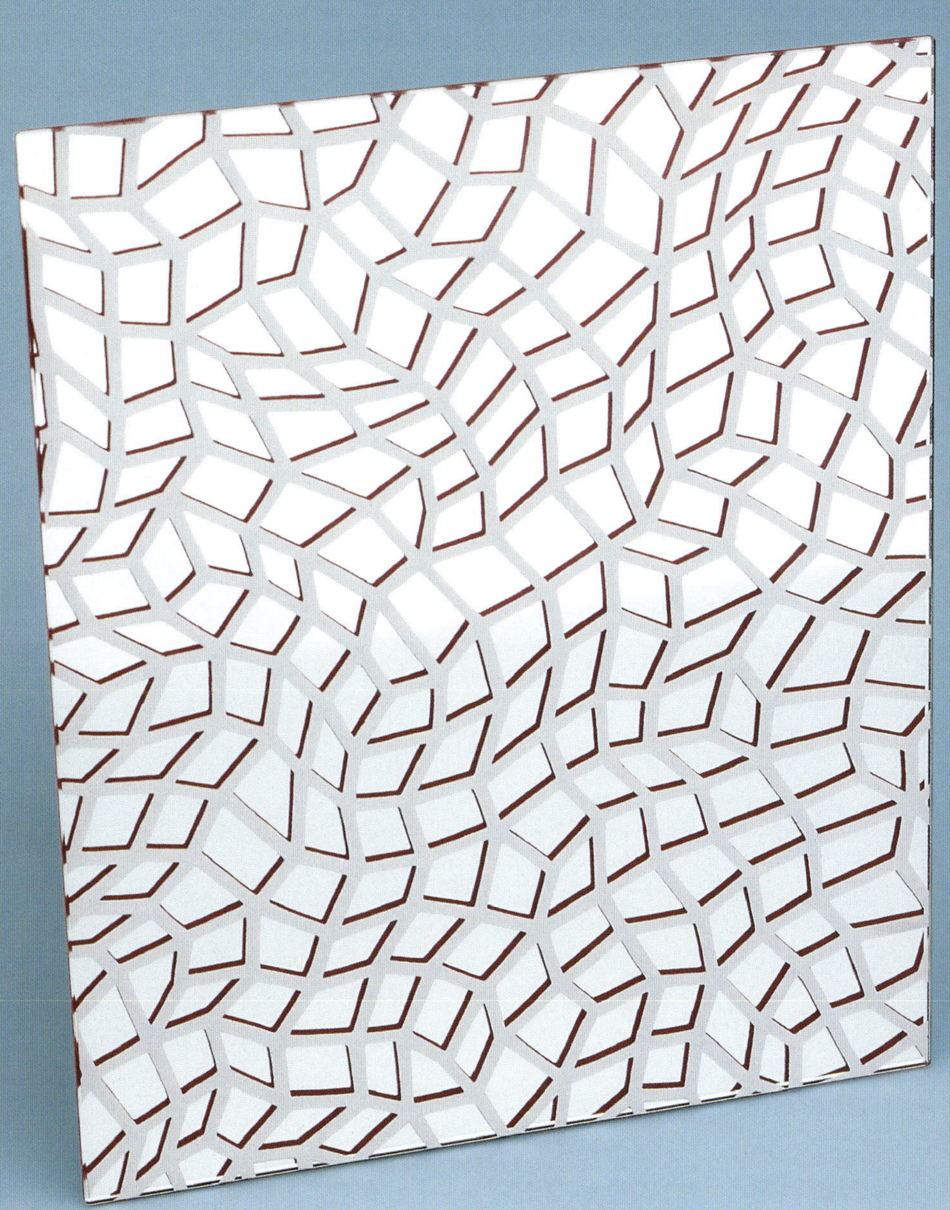

KA RA WAL KER

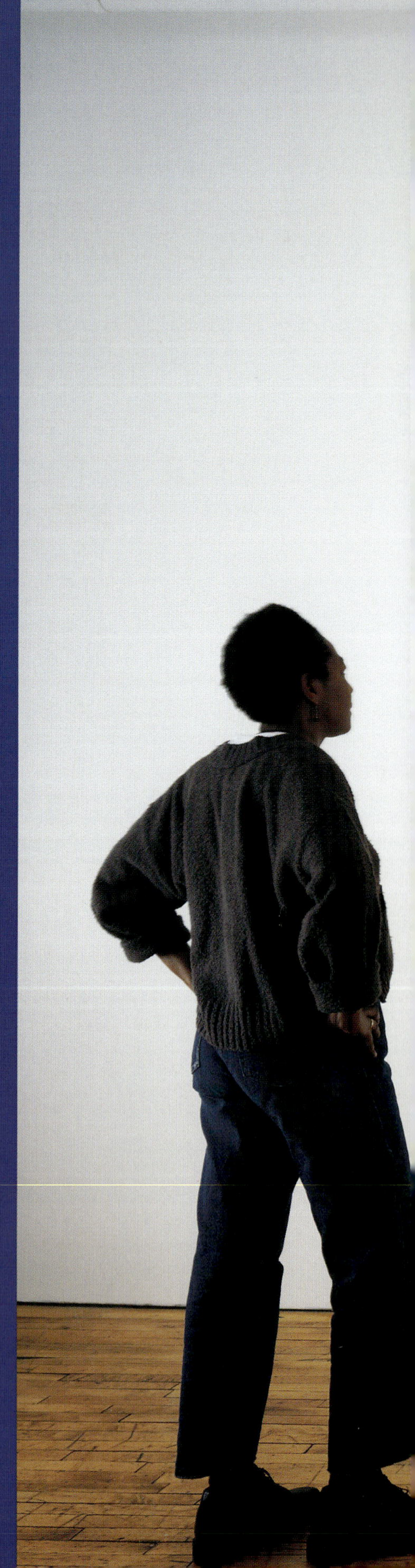

KARA WALKER, LETTER FROM A BLACK GIRL, 1998, text on wall, dimensions variable, installation view at Wooster Gardens, New York / BRIEF EINES SCHWARZEN MÄDCHENS, Text auf Wand, Grösse variabel.

Dear you hypocritical fucking Twerp,

Id just like to thank you for taking hold of the last four years
of my life and raising my hopes for the future. Id like to thank
you for giving me clothes when I needed them and food when I needed it and for fucking my brains out when my brains needed fucking.
I hope that the time we spent in the Quarters with my family sleeping neerby quietly ignoring what you proceeded to do to me- what,
rather I proceeded to do to you- ws worthwhile for you, that you got
the stimulation you so needed, Because now That Im Free of that poison you call Life, that stringy, sour, white strand you called
Sacred and me savior, that peculiar institution we engaged in
because there was no other forseeable alternative, I am LOST.

Before, when there was a before, an upon a time I was a blank space
defined in contrast to your POSITIVE, concrete avowal. now, a blank
space in the void and I have to thank you for forgetting to stick
your neck out for me after I craned my neck so often in your arms.

Dear you duplicitous, idiot,Worm,

NOw that youve forgotten how you like your coffee and why you
raised your pious fist to the sky, and the reason for your stun-
ning African Art collection, and the war we fought together, and
the promises you made and the laws we rewrote, I am left here
alone to recreate My WHOLE HISTORY without benefit of you, my com-
pliment, my enemy, my oppressor, my Love

Should i never be heard from again, follow the Route of my forebears
and quietly,GO, or shall I seek to kill you, burning the last of
the fuel you gave me and expected of me?

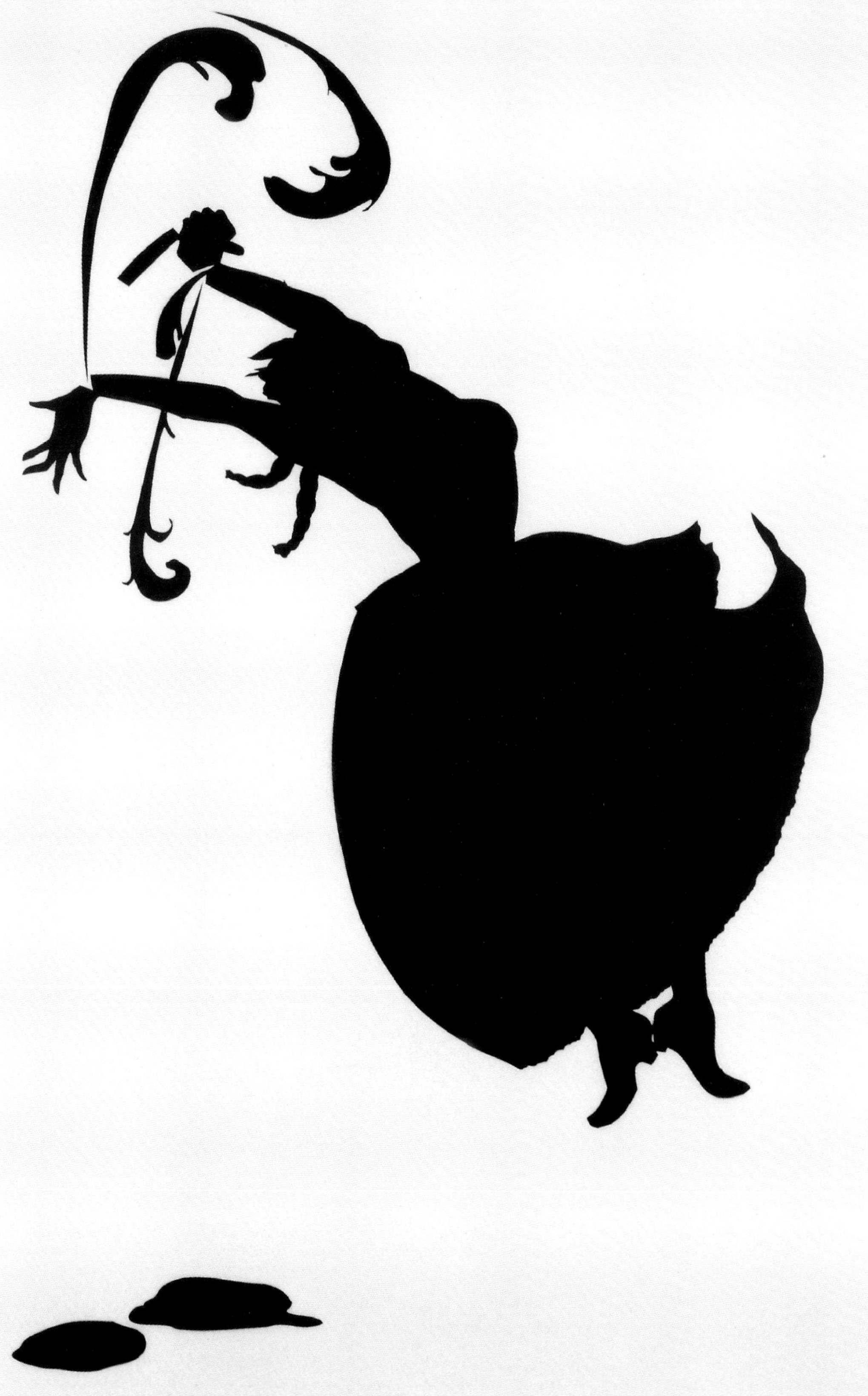

KARA WALKER, CUT, 1998, cut paper and adhesive on wall, 88 x 54" / SCHNITT, an der Wand befestigter Scherenschnitt, 223,5 x 137,2 cm.

GWENDOLYN DUBOIS SHAW

Final Cut

CUT, Kara Walker's 1998 self-portrait, is a life-size silhouette made of black paper glued to a gallery wall showing a young woman sailing through space with her arms thrown back over her head. However, all is not well in this image of airborne ecstasy, for both of her wrists have been cut, nearly severed at the joint by the straight razor that she holds in her left hand. Four sprays of blood erupt from the wounds and gather in two thickened puddles beneath her. This image of grotesque self-mutilation and ambiguous ecstasy speaks of the construction of Walker's artistic persona and her attempts to better understand her own role in history by re-creating it in the present. Based on a photograph of the artist that appeared in *Interview* magazine, CUT is a reaction to the position that Walker, as a contemporary African American woman artist, occupies by virtue of her race, gender, and her social relationships with those members of the art world who would seek to guide, critique, and support her career.

GWENDOLYN DUBOIS SHAW is Assistant Professor of African American Art History at Harvard University.

The pain of constantly performing such an artistic identity may be read in the artist's adaptation of the quartet of unraveling braids found in the photograph. The two tightly bound plaits recall not only the braids of the stereotypical pickaninnies that she is so often accused of exalting in her work, but in their affinity to the hairstyles found on good little black girls, evoke the middleclass assimilationist role that the artist herself has rejected. At the same time they are significant because of her own fetishization within the discourse of both the white and the black art press that has been obsessed with the state of her hair.[1]

In addition to the alterations made to the artist's hair, the couture ensemble by Comme des Garçons comprised of a long skirt, a button-front jacket and an apron worn in the *Interview* photograph, has been re-figured to comment upon Walker's position as the "art world's New Negro."[2] The apron that cast her in the role of a contemporary art slave for the reader/viewers of *Interview* has been altered so that its hem swings up and, in concert with the bottom of the skirt, creates the illusion of a figure trapped beneath the fabric. The profile of a man with his hand upraised can just be made out along the upper line of the silhouette. The trope of the mysterious figure behind the curtains, or in this case beneath the skirts, acting to control an artist has its roots in George Du Maurier's story of the tone-deaf singer Trilby who was hypnotically controlled up until her death by the evil Jewish magician Svengali.[3] In an uncanny way an image of Svengali, in which he holds his baton as if it were a giant needle ready to be run through the entranced Trilby standing before him, is echoed in the profile found within the skirts of CUT.

The same kind of hypnotic power that controls Trilby commands the figure in CUT. Here, Walker's body is out of her own control; she has sliced open her wrists and seems to care little for the damage she has inflicted or its potentially deadly consequences.[4] This action makes an ironic comment about the production of her work being the cause of her own death just as it was for Trilby. She seems to trade the pain of self-mutilation for the pleasure of self-realization: She sacrifices her body for her professional success. "This is the easy way out—my fantasy—in the future I will have a catharsis and go mad… the cause?" wrote Walker in 1997, "No doubt death in the family, death of my career, it never occurs to my fantasy-me that I always maintain a straight face no matter how bad the circumstances… or how good."[5]

This idea of a Svengalian figure acting from behind the scenes to control and guide the career of a young artist, a "fantasy-me" who is on a headlong collision with death, also recalls the relationship of Jean-Michel Basquiat with Andy Warhol.[6] And like the Svengali figure beneath the skirts of the figure in CUT, Warhol was behind Basquiat, both within the artistic world and through their collaborations in the mid-eighties when the two artists worked together on a series of 16 paintings. In one of these works, UNTITLED (1984), Warhol stenciled two Arm & Hammer logos side-by-side on a large rectangular canvas, Basquiat then painted over the logo on the left with the bust of a brown skinned, limbless man with a saxophone clenched between his teeth. Basquiat's image of crippled African American artistic virtuosity resonates with CUT in its construction of the would-be black creator as incapable of controlling the

mode of his/her own artistic production and interpretation. Like the woman in CUT who has nearly severed her own hands, the part of the body after the head that is traditionally symbolic of an artist's creativity, Basquiat's musician is powerless over the mode of his own expression. By asserting a sort of black creative impotence in the face of white power, as symbolized by the Arm & Hammer logos, Basquiat seems to acknowledge that his was an uneven relationship with Warhol.[7] Just as Svengali prepared Trilby for her performances through hypnotic suggestion, Warhol set the figurative stage in their collaborations by priming the canvases upon which Basquiat performed his work.

The menacing power of the activated and upraised arm, like that found in a baking soda icon, lies in the foreknowledge that it will always come down upon the body of its victim, a fact that is no more apparent than in the invitation to the exhibition in which CUT appeared. The image that was chosen by Walker to advertise her show depicts two slave women working in a field under the command of an overseer with an upraised whip that stands between one woman and her unattended child.[8] The overseer literally blocks the slave mother from attending to her physical creation. His gesture, like those of Svengali and the Arm & Hammer, serves to both threaten and control the woman; she may not be his protégé, but he is definitely her master.

Oddly, the question of who is behind Walker's real-life career remains obscure. There is no single figure that might play the Svengali character, no one person preying on her sexual vulnerability and controlling her next direction.[9] Neither is there a famous artist shepherding her through the New York gallery scene, like Warhol did Basquiat. Yet, in the catalogue from her 1997 exhibition at the Renaissance Society at the University of Chicago, Walker writes of the alienation of being an African American artist in the white art world, the feeling of always being under someone else's control: "How do I know that you are motivated and aroused by my presence in your sphere… a spectacle in the round… a blot on your landscape, an embellishment to your high society, a strange new face in a one-horse town, a desirable outsider, a delicious new confection… brought to your kingdom by the conquistadors of consciousness… to be molded and sculpted, cultivated and cuisined, consumed and defecated and consumed again…"[10]) Here the pain of self-performance and of artistic commodification may be read in the description of an artistic body that is feted and then fed upon. Walker recognizes her own status as a consumable item.

Like Basquiat before her, she is the "flavor of the month," a product that is presented to a hungry white art audience waiting to see how good she tastes. Her re-presentation through the popular and the art press alike display her for their consideration in a decidedly Svengalian way. The mere act of being presented in *Interview* magazine for example, the Q & A process, creates her as an object that is available on demand. To return to the photograph, we see the artist following the commands of the art world as she leaps into the air. One can almost hear the command, "Jump! When I say 'jump'!" She responds willingly, with an eager to please grin on her face. And then later, regretting the capitulation to those who would fetishize and control her body, she re-enacts the moment in CUT, under her own control and yet still out of control. For Walker there may be no outside figure that constitutes a Svengalian influence within her career, but rather the entire milieu of the mainstream art world coupled with the artist's own desire for success.

Walker's self-fashioning in CUT is a strategy also witnessed in the early work of the contemporary artist Anselm Kiefer who examined his own artistic identity by interrogating the taboo images of his own cultures' past.[11] In his *Occupations* series from the late sixties Kiefer photographed himself re-enacting the Sieg Heil gesture of the Third Reich (perhaps the most loaded example of the menacing power of the upraised arm) in various locations throughout Europe. As a re-vivified ghost miming an outlawed visual language, Kiefer's lone figure has the peculiar status of existing in two worlds, a phantasm of the past in a nightmarish vision of the present.[12]

Walker's re-vivification of racist imagery operates within the same theater of contestation as Kiefer's work, but the two artists are by no means on equal footing. Walker's oppositional status as an artistic

"'other' of the 'other'" dealing with the weighty subjects of historical domination and exploitation is in stark contrast to Kiefer's status as an ethnic German man dealing with Nazi iconography. She is not allowed the same sort of authority over such negative images: instead she must negotiate with the dominant culture for that ownership. In both artists' work, the act of re-enactment is important in itself, and the role of the artist as provocateur is not to be undervalued, no matter how taboo or painful the materials they present may be. For it is through their pain as artists, as workers in the field of vision, that they are called to wrestle with the legacy of tainted imagery that the non-visual world chooses to ignore, subsume, or reject.

In CUT, Walker attempts to own her fetishized and contested body as it sails across the gallery wall, a mythical blip on the radar screen of the mainstream art world. The artist's wrists are slashed so that the blood spurts out in arcing plumes becoming feathers with pointed tips at their roots, tips that in turn seem to pierce the flesh from which they grow. As she sails through the air, she resembles a fallen angel whose wings have been clipped and then sent plunging rapidly toward the earth. She is the hubris-stained Icarus, whose flight of the artistic soul has been interrupted as the heat of the spotlight, into which she has risen, melts her homemade wings. The figure that presses against her skirts, pushing her forward through the air as if against her will, might well be the ultimate arbiter of her destiny, for only he can see what lies in store. It would seem that there is no possibility of transcendence through visuality, that the pain of invention will all too soon outweigh the pleasure self-expression. The legacy of the past, guided by the example of Kiefer, yet haunted by the ghost of Basquiat and the myth of Trilby, is too much for the artist of the present to overcome. Ultimately there is no alternative but to let the blood pool up in sticky puddles as the body flies, out of control and fixed in place, toward the gallery floor.

1) In an article for the *New York Times Magazine*, European American critic Julia Szabo begins the fetishization of Walker's hair in her first sentences. "In a dimly lighted, subterranean gallery at the Institute of Contemporary Art in Boston, a tall young woman stands near a staircase, contemplating a nine-foot-square sheet

of black paper tacked to the wall," Szabo writes. "Hundreds of long, skinny braids quiver down to her waist, fraying at the tips in Botticelli-brown waves." ("Kara Walker's Shock Art," *New York Times Magazine*, March 23, 1997, p. 49.) In a profile on Walker written for the *San Francisco Examiner*, Venise Wagner thought Walker's braids and height were the significant descriptors of her identity, too. "Her shoulder-length cascade of braids accentuates the elegance of her tall, slim frame," wrote Wagner. ("For this artist, the joke's on all of us," *San Francisco Examiner*, Arts & Ideas section, Sunday, February 16, 1997, C-17.) Her hairstyle of "waist length, auburn braid extensions" also fascinated *International Review of African American Art* editor Juliette Bowles, who felt they were significant enough to mention in her own critique of Walker's work and artistic persona. Bowles claimed that these artificial additions to Walker's hair were a part of the artist's desire to fetishize her own body for the gaze of the white male viewer. ("Extreme Times Call for Extreme Heroes," *IRAAA*, vol. 14, Number 3, p. 7.) Bowles would later explain her comments in direct address to Walker as "a way of raising the question of whether you wore the reddish, straight, almost waist-length, braid extensions because you were adopting part of the costume of your alter egos, 'Missus K. E. B. Walker, Colored' and the 'nigger wench.' Since they wish to be the white slave master's wife, do they also wish to have the white slave mistress's hair?" she queried, conflating the artist with the artistic persona. Bowles then interjected what she termed "a big sister…hair call" by critiquing Walker's braided hairstyle as "tired" and then praising her current "animated" do as more becoming. ("Editor's Response," *IRAAA*, vol. 15, Number 2, p. 50.)

2) James Hannaham, "Pea Ball, Bounce," *Interview*, (November 1998), p. 116.

3) George Du Maurier, *Trilby* (New York: Harper and Brothers, 1894), pp. 457–58: "…with one wave of his hand over her—with one—look of his eye—with a word—Svengali could turn her into the other Trilby, his Trilby—and make her do whatever he liked…you might have run a red hot needle through her and she would not have felt it."

4) Like the visual conflation found in the illustration of the baton with which Svengali conducts Trilby's actions and the red hot needle that he might use to torture her, the razor that the figure in CUT holds alludes to both the blade with which the artist practices her craft and to the classic tool of suicide.

5) Kara Walker, *Kara Walker*, (Chicago: Renaissance Society at the University of Chicago, 1997), unpaginated.

6) In an ironic way, the portrait of the artist for *Interview* magazine, founded by Warhol in 1969 as a film journal, that inspired CUT, constructs Walker as the ghostly inheritor of the Basquiat legacy. Not only do Walker's unkempt braids evoke the clusters of dreads worn by Basquiat, but her costume designed by Comme des Garçons references Basquiat's own turn as a celebrity model for the same fashion house's winter collection in 1985. Given this odd connection and the context, Walker's modeling of Comme des Garçons re-presents her as closer to one of Tama Janowitz's *Slaves of New York* than the temporal escapee from the antebellum South that the style of the clothes would imply.

7) "Recognizing art-world fame to be a male game, one that he could play, working the stereotypical darkey image, playing the trickster, Basquiat understood that he was risking his life—that his journey was all about sacrifice. (…) What must be sacrificed in relation to oneself is that which has no place in whiteness. To be seen by the white art world, to be known, Basquiat had to remake himself, to create from the perspective of the white imagination. He had to become both native and nonnative at the same time—to assume the blackness defined by the white imagination and the blackness that is not unlike whiteness." Bell Hooks, "Altars of Sacrifice: Re-Membering Basquiat," *Art on My Mind: Visual Politics* (New York: New Press, 1995), p. 43.

8) On a speculative note, this image choice may have come about through Walker's anxiety about having to attend to the preservation of her career through the constant increase of her oeuvre, rather than spend her days as a stay-at-home-mom with her daughter who was at the time just over one year old.

9) Her dealer Brent Sikkema, while having no doubt gained through their association, has not acted as an intervening creative force within her production. And her husband Klaus Bürgel, a well-established metalsmith and jewelry designer, is more concerned with maintaining a peak level for his own artistic production than in trying to shape hers.

10) Walker, "MOTIFS and MOTIVAtions: THE HISTORICAL ROMANCE & ME" in: *Kara Walker* (Chicago: Renaissance Society at the University of Chicago, 1997), unpaginated.

11) Andreas Huyssen, "Anselm Kiefer: the Terror of History, the Temptation of Myth" in: *October* no. 48 (Spring 1989), p. 30.

12) According to Huyssen, the images are not entirely negative, but instead are full of irony: The small figure is dwarfed by his surroundings and the jubilant masses of the Nazi period are missing. And yet "are irony and satire really the appropriate mode for dealing with fascist terror?" asks Huyssen in the role of the Devil's advocate. "Doesn't this series of photographs belittle the very real terror which the Sieg Heil gesture conjures up for a historically informed memory?" Ibid., p. 31.

GWENDOLYN DUBOIS SHAW

Letzter Schnitt

CUT (Schnitt), Kara Walkers Selbstporträt aus dem Jahre 1998, ist ein lebensgrosser, an die Wand der Galerie geklebter Scherenschnitt aus schwarzem Papier und zeigt eine junge Frau, die durch den Raum segelt, die Arme über dem Kopf rückwärts ausgestreckt. Es stimmt jedoch einiges nicht in diesem Bild fliegender Ekstase, denn beide Handgelenke sind aufgeschnitten, ja beinahe abgetrennt durch ein scharfes Rasiermesser, das sie in der linken Hand hält. Ein vierfacher Blutstrahl schiesst aus den Wunden und sammelt sich in zwei dicken Pfützen unter ihr. Dieses Bild einer grotesken Selbstverstümmelung und zwiespältigen Ekstase verrät einiges über die Beschaffenheit von Walkers Künstler-Ich und über ihren Versuch, die eigene Rolle innerhalb der Geschichte besser zu verstehen, indem sie sie in der Gegenwart rekonstruiert. CUT geht auf eine in *Interview* veröffentlichte Photographie der Künstlerin zurück[1] und ist eine Reaktion auf die Stellung, die sie als afroamerikanische Frau und Künstlerin innehat aufgrund ihrer Rasse, ihres Geschlechts und ihrer gesellschaftlichen Beziehungen zu jenen Exponenten der Kunstszene, die sie in ihrer Karriere zu leiten, kritisieren und unterstützen suchen.

Die Pein, dauernd eine solche Künstleridentität präsentieren zu müssen, mag man daran ablesen, wie die Künstlerin die vier auf dem Photo sichtbaren, in Auflösung begriffenen Zöpfe umsetzt. Die beiden streng geflochtenen Haarstränge erinnern nicht nur an die Zöpfchen jener stereotypen Negermädchen, deren übertriebene Verwendung man ihr gerne vorwirft, sondern erinnern durch ihre Nähe zu den typischen Frisuren braver kleiner schwarzer Mädchen auch an eine assimilierte Mittelklass-Existenz, eine Rolle, welche die Künstlerin von sich weist. Gleichzeitig haben sie eine Bedeutung im Zusammenhang mit der Fetischisierung, die der Künstlerin in der weissen wie der schwarzen Kunstpresse widerfuhr, in der man sich über ihre Frisur ereiferte.[2]

Aber über die Änderungen an der Frisur hinaus war auch das modische Ensemble von Comme des Garçons, das sie auf dem *Interview*-Photo trug – ein langer Jupe, eine vorn knöpfbare Jacke und eine Schürze –, willkommener Anlass um Walkers Stellung als «neue Negerin der Kunstszene» zu kommentieren.[3] Die Schürze, die sie in den Augen der Leserinnen und Leser von *Interview* in die Rolle einer Sklavin der zeitgenössischen Kunst versetzte, wurde so drapiert, dass ihr Saum nach oben schwingt und im Einklang mit dem unteren Ende des Jupes den Eindruck einer unter dem Stoff gefangenen Figur vermittelt. Am oberen Rand der Silhouette lässt sich gerade noch das Profil eines Mannes mit erhobener Hand ausmachen. Die geheimnisvolle, die Künstlerin kontrollierende Gestalt hinter dem Vorhang oder hier unter dem Rock kennen wir aus George du Mauriers Geschichte von der gehörlosen Sängerin Trilby, die bis zu ihrem Tode unter der hypnotischen Kontrolle des bösen jüdischen Magiers Svengali stand.[4] Im Profil des Rocks von CUT zeichnet sich unheimlicherweise ein Bild von Svengali ab, in dem er seinen Stab wie eine Nadel hält, bereit, sie durch die vor ihm stehende, in Trance versetzte Trilby hindurchzustossen.

Die Figur in CUT steht im Bann derselben hypnotischen Macht, die auch Trilby beherrscht. Walker hat ihren eigenen Körper hier nicht mehr unter

---

GWENDOLYN DUBOIS SHAW ist Assistenzprofessorin für afroamerikanische Kunstgeschichte in Harvard.

Kontrolle; sie hat sich die Handgelenke aufgeschlitzt und scheint sich einen Deut um den damit angerichteten Schaden oder die möglicherweise tödlichen Folgen zu kümmern.[5] Dieses Vorgehen ist ein ironischer Kommentar dazu, dass ihre Kunst zum Tod führen könnte, genau wie bei Trilby. Sie scheint sich das Glück der Selbstverwirklichung gegen den Schmerz der Selbstverstümmelung zu erkaufen: Sie opfert ihren Körper für den beruflichen Erfolg. «Das ist der nahe liegende Ausweg – meine Phantasie – in Zukunft werde ich einmal eine Katharsis erleben und durchdrehen… der Grund?», schrieb Walker 1997: «Sicher ein Todesfall in der Familie, das Ende meiner Karriere, mein Phantasie-Ich bemerkt gar nicht, dass ich immer dieselbe unerschütterliche Miene zur Schau trage, egal wie schlimm die Umstände sein mögen … oder wie gut.»[6]

Die Vorstellung eines Magiers, der hinter den Kulissen agiert und die Karriere eines jungen Künstlers kontrolliert, eines phantasmatischen Ichs, das unweigerlich auf den Tod zutreibt, erinnert auch an die Beziehung zwischen Jean-Michel Basquiat und Andy Warhol.[7] Wie der im Rock verborgene Svengali in CUT stand Warhol hinter Basquiat, und zwar sowohl innerhalb der Kunstszene wie durch ihre Zusammenarbeit Mitte der 80er Jahre, als beide gemeinsam an einer Serie von 16 Bildern arbeiteten. In einem dieser Bilder, UNTITLED (1984), setzte Warhol mithilfe einer Schablone zwei Arm-mit-Hammer-Logos nebeneinander auf eine grosse rechteckige Leinwand und Basquiat übermalte das Logo links mit dem Oberkörper eines dunkelhäutigen, armlosen Mannes, der ein Saxophon zwischen den Zähnen hält. Wie CUT stellt Basquiats Bild einer verstümmelten afroamerikanischen künstlerischen Virtuosität den schwarzen Künstler in seiner Unfähigkeit dar, den eigenen künstlerischen Produktions- und Interpretationsmodus zu kontrollieren. Wie die Frau in CUT, die sich beinah die eigenen Hände abgeschnitten hat (neben dem Kopf traditionell das Symbol künstlerischer Kreativität schlechthin), hat Basquiats Musiker seine Ausdrucksweise nicht im Griff. Indem er gewissermassen eine kreative Impotenz des Schwarzen angesichts der weissen, durch Arm und Hammer symbolisierten Macht ausdrückt, scheint Basquiat einzugestehen, dass sein Verhältnis zu Warhol ein ungleiches war.[8] Genau wie Svengali seine Trilby durch Hypnose für ihren Auftritt präparierte, gab Warhol die figurative Bühne der Collaboration vor, indem er die Leinwände vorbereitete, auf denen Basquiat dann seine Arbeit ausführte.

Das Bedrohliche des kraftvoll erhobenen Armes, dem wir selbst in einem Backpulverlogo begegnen, liegt im Wissen darum, dass er früher oder später auf den Körper seines Opfers aufprallen wird, eine Tatsache, die nirgends deutlicher ist als auf der Einladung zur Ausstellung, in der CUT gezeigt wurde. Das Bild, das Walker für die Ankündigung der Ausstellung gewählt hat, zeigt zwei auf einem Feld arbeitende Sklavinnen und einen Aufseher mit erhobener Peitsche, die zwischen der einen Frau und ihrem unbeaufsichtigten Kind emporragt.[9] Der Aufseher hält die Mutter buchstäblich davon ab, sich um ihren Sprössling zu kümmern. Seine Gebärde dient wie jene Svengalis oder die des hammerbewehrten Arms zugleich der Einschüchterung und der Kontrolle; die Frau mag nicht sein Schützling sein, aber er ist mit Sicherheit ihr Beherrscher.

Es ist merkwürdig, aber wer im richtigen Leben hinter Kara Walkers Karriere steht, bleibt im Dunkeln. Es gibt keine Anwärter für die Rolle Svengalis, keine Person, die ihre sexuelle Verwundbarkeit ausnützen, ihren nächsten Schritt kontrollieren würde.[10] Da ist auch kein berühmter Künstler, der sie durch die Galerienszene New Yorks schleust, wie Warhol das mit Basquiat tat. Und trotzdem schreibt Walker im Katalog zu ihrer Ausstellung in der Renaissance Society 1997 von der Entfremdung, die sie als afroamerikanische Künstlerin in der weissen Kunstwelt erfährt, vom Gefühl, immer von jemand anderem kontrolliert zu werden: «Wie soll ich wissen, ob euch nicht nur meine Gegenwart in eurer Sphäre belebt und erregt… ein Spektakel in der Arena … ein Fleck in eurer Landschaft, eine Dekoration eurer erlesenen Gesellschaft, ein neues Gesicht im Dorf, eine begehrenswerte Aussenseiterin, eine Kostbarkeit …, die die Entdeckungsreisenden des Bewusstseins in euer Königreich mitgebracht haben, die man verändern und formen, kultivieren und mundgerecht zubereiten, sich einverleiben und wieder ausstossen kann, nur um sie erneut zu verzehren …»[11] Hier mag aus der Beschreibung eines

Künstlerleibes, der zuerst gefeiert und dann verzehrt wird, die Pein der Selbstdarstellung und der Verdinglichung der Künstlerexistenz deutlich werden. Walker erkennt ihren Status als Konsumobjekt.

Wie Basquiat vor ihr wird sie zum «Geschmack des Monats», zum Produkt, das man einem hungrigen weissen Kunstpublikum präsentiert, das nur darauf wartet, zu erfahren, wie gut sie ihm schmeckt. Ihre Re-Präsentation durch die populäre und die Kunstpresse stellen sie dem Publikum definitiv nach Art eines Svengali zur Schau. Allein schon die Tatsache, dass sie überhaupt in einer Zeitschrift wie *Interview* vorgestellt wird, sowie die Form des Frage-und-Antwort-Spiels machen sie zu einem Objekt, das auf Abruf zur Verfügung steht. Aber kehren wir zum Photo zurück: Man sieht, wie die Künstlerin auf Befehl der Kunstwelt in die Luft springt. Man kann das Kommando beinah hören: «Spring, wenn ich sage ‹spring›!» Mit einem gewinnenden Lächeln geht sie bereitwillig darauf ein. Später dann, als sie ihre Fügsamkeit gegenüber jenen, die ihren Körper zum Fetisch machen und kontrollieren wollen, bereut, reinszeniert sie den Moment in CUT, nun unter eigener Regie, aber dennoch unkontrollierbar. Im Fall von Kara Walker mag zwar äusserlich keine Gestalt wie Svengali existieren, die einen magischen Einfluss auf ihre Entwicklung ausübt, aber diese Rolle fällt der Mainstream-Kunstszene im Bündnis mit dem eigenen Erfolgswunsch der Künstlerin zu.

Also darf man Walkers Selbststilisierung in CUT auch als Versuch betrachten, mit der Vergangenheit ins Reine zu kommen, indem sie sie in der Gegenwart reinszeniert. Das ist eine Strategie, der man auch im Frühwerk von Anselm Kiefer begegnet, der seine eigene künstlerische Identität einer Prüfung unterzog, indem er die tabuisierten Bilder aus der Vergangenheit seiner eigenen Kultur befragte.[12] In seiner Serie *Besetzungen* aus den späten 60er Jahren photographierte Kiefer sich selbst beim Reinszenieren der im Dritten Reich üblichen Sieg-Heil-Geste (vielleicht das sprechendste Beispiel für das Bedrohungspotenzial des erhobenen Armes) an verschiedenen Orten quer durch Europa. Als reanimiertes Gespenst, das in einer verpönten Gebärdensprache agiert, vermittelt Kiefers einsame Gestalt den merkwürdigen Eindruck in zwei Welten zugleich zu exis-

tieren, ein Phantasma der Vergangenheit in einer albtraumhaften Vision der Gegenwart.[13]

Walkers Wiederbelebung einer rassistischen Bilderwelt spielt in derselben Arena wie Kiefers Arbeit, dennoch sind die Standpunkte der beiden Künstler ganz verschieden. Walkers Widerstandshaltung als künstlerische «Andere» jener «Anderen», die sich mit den übermächtigen Themen historischer Herrschaft und Ausbeutung zu befassen hat, steht in starkem Kontrast zu Kiefers Position eines Deutschen, der sich mit der Bildsprache der Nazis auseinander setzt. Sie verfügt nicht über dieselbe Autorität im Umgang mit diesen negativen Bildern, sondern muss mit der herrschenden Kultur dieses Verfügungsrecht erst aushandeln. In den Arbeiten beider Künstler ist der Akt der Reinszenierung selbst wichtig und die provokative Rolle des Künstlers darf nicht unterschätzt werden, egal wie tabuisiert oder schmerzhaft der Stoff, den sie zur Sprache bringen, auch sein mag. Denn genau durch ihr Leiden als Künstler, als Arbeiter auf dem Gebiet des Sichtbaren, sind sie dazu aufgerufen, den Kampf aufzunehmen mit dem Erbe befleckter Bildwelten, welche eine weniger visuell orientierte Welt lieber ignoriert, vernachlässigt oder von sich weist.

CUT ist Walkers Versuch, von ihrem eigenen, fetischisierten und in Frage gestellten Körper Besitz zu ergreifen, während er über die Wand der Galerie rauscht wie ein imaginärer Leuchtpunkt auf dem Radarschirm der Mainstream-Kunstszene. Aus den geöffneten Pulsadern schiesst das Blut in gekrümmten Strahlen und wird zu Federn mit spitzen Enden. Spitzen, die wiederum das Fleisch scheinen durchbohren zu wollen, aus dem sie gewachsen sind. So durch die Luft segelnd gleicht sie einem gefallenen Engel, dessen Flügel gestutzt und dann in rasendem Fall erdwärts geworfen wurden. Sie ist der durch seine Hybris gestrafte Ikarus, dessen Flug einer Künstlerseele abrupt abbricht, sobald die Hitze des Scheinwerfers, zu dem er sich erhoben hat, die selbst gefertigten Flügel schmilzt. Die Gestalt, die sich an ihren Rock schmiegt und sie wie gegen ihren Willen vorwärts durch die Luft stösst, könnte der letzte Richter über ihr Schicksal sein, denn nur er kann sehen, was vor ihr liegt. Es scheint, dass dem Visuellen die Möglichkeit zur Transzendenz fehlt, dass die Pein des

Schaffens nur allzu bald die Lust am Selbstausdruck überwiegt. Das Erbe der Vergangenheit ist für den Künstler der Gegenwart schlicht nicht zu bewältigen; so ermutigt er sein mag durch Kiefers Beispiel, wird er gleichzeitig heimgesucht vom Geist Basquiats und der Geschichte Trilbys. Letztlich gibt es keine Alternative als das Blut zu klebrigen Pfützen gerinnen zu lassen, während der Körper, an Ort und Stelle fixiert und doch unaufhaltsam, auf den Boden der Galerie zufliegt.

(Übersetzung: Susanne Schmidt)

1) Photographie von Noe DeWitt in: *Interview*, November 1998, S. 115.

2) Die euroamerikanische Kritikerin Julia Szabo leitete die Fetischisierung von Walkers Frisur wie folgt ein: «In einer schwach erleuchteten Soussol-Galerie am Institute of Contemporary Art in Boston steht eine grosse junge Frau neben einer Treppe und betrachtet ein an die Wand geheftetes schwarzes Papier von 275 x 275 cm … Hunderte langer, dünner Zöpfe baumeln bis zur Taille hinunter und fasern an den Enden zu Botticelli-braunen Wellen aus.» («Kara Walker's Shock Art», *New York Times Magazine*, 23. März 1997.) Auch Venise Wagner sah die Zöpfe und die Körpergrösse als entscheidende Faktoren von Walkers Identität: «Ihre schulterlangen Zopfkaskaden unterstreichen die Eleganz ihrer grossen, schlanken Erscheinung.» («For this Artist, the Joke's on All of Us», *San Francisco Examiner*, Sonntag, 16. Februar 1997.) Auch Juliette Bowles, Redaktorin der *International Review of African American Art*, hielt die Haare für wichtig genug, um sie in ihrer Kritik von Walkers Werk und künstlerischer Person zu erwähnen: Sie meinte, dass diese künstliche Ergänzung des Haars dem Wunsch der Künstlerin entspräche, ihren eigenen Körper für den Blick des weissen männlichen Betrachters zu fetischisieren. («Extreme Times Call for Extreme Heroes», *International Review of African American Art*, vol. 14, Nr. 3, S. 7.) Später wandte sich Bowles direkt an Walker und erklärte ihre Kommentare als «eine Art, die Frage aufzubringen, ob du die rötlichen, strengen, beinah taillenlangen Zopfverlängerungen getragen hast, weil du einen Teil des Kostüms deiner Alter Egos übernehmen wolltest, ‹Missus K. E. B. Walker, Colored› und die ‹Negerhure›. Wohl möchten sie die Frau des weissen Sklavenherrn sein, aber möchten sie auch die Frisur der weissen Herrin?», so fragte sie und verwechselte die Künstlerin mit dem Künstler-Ich. Bowles äusserte dann, was sie einen «big sister… hair call» nannte, indem sie Walkers Zopfstil als ausgereizt kritisierte und ihre neue, «lebendige» Frisur als die bessere pries. («Editor's Response», *IRAAA*, vol. 15, Nr. 2, S. 50.)

3) James Hannaham, «Pea Ball, Bounce», in: *Interview*, November 1998, S. 116.

4) «… mit einer Handbewegung – einem Blick – mit einem Wort – konnte Svengali sie in die andere Trilby verwandeln, seine Trilby, und konnte sie tun lassen, was ihm gerade einfiel … man hätte sie mit einer glühenden Nadel stechen können und sie hätte nichts gespürt.» (George Du Maurier, *Trilby*, Harper & Brothers, New York 1894, S. 457–458.)

5) Wie der Stab, mit dem Svengali Trilby manipuliert, im Bild zugleich mit der glühenden Nadel als potenzielles Folterwerkzeug zusammenfällt, verweist auch das Rasiermesser in CUT sowohl auf das Messer als Arbeitsinstrument der Künstlerin wie auf das klassische Mittel zum Selbstmord.

6) Kara Walker, *Kara Walker*, Renaissance Society at the University of Chicago 1997, unpaginiert.

7) Ironischerweise stellt das Porträt in *Interview*, das 1969 von Warhol als Filmzeitschrift ins Leben gerufen wurde, die Künstlerin quasi als geistige Erbin Basquiats dar. Nicht genug, dass ihre ungekämmten Zöpfe an Basquiats Perlenstränge erinnern, auch die Kleidung von Comme des Garçons verweist auf Basquiats Auftritt als Starmodel für die Winterkollektion desselben Modehauses 1985. Betrachtet man diese merkwürdige Verbindung und den Kontext, so macht der Auftritt als Model von Comme des Garçons Kara Walker eher zu einem von Tama Janowitz' *Grossstadtsklaven (Slaves of New York)* als zu einer Entflohenen aus dem alten Süden, wie uns der Stil der Kleidung weismachen will.

8) «Während Basquiat den Ruhm der Kunstwelt als ein Männerspiel durchschaute, bei dem er mitspielen konnte, solange er das stereotype Image des Schwarzen pflegte und den Clown spielte, wusste er genau, dass er sein Leben riskierte und dass er Opfer bringen musste. (…) Man muss das von sich opfern, was im Weisssein keinen Platz hat. Um in der weissen Kunstwelt gesehen und bekannt zu werden, musste Basquiat sich neu erschaffen und zwar aus der Perspektive weisser Vorstellungskraft. Er musste zugleich ursprünglich und nicht wirklich ursprünglich werden um ein Schwarzsein anzunehmen, wie es die weisse Vorstellung definiert, ein Schwarzsein, das dem Weisssein nicht gar so unähnlich ist.» (Bell Hooks, «Altars of Sacrifice: Re-Membering Basquiat», in*: Art on My Mind: Visual Politics*, New Press, New York 1995, S. 43.)

9) Vielleicht hat diese Wahl auch damit zu tun, dass Walker sich Sorgen macht, weil sie, um ihre Karriere nicht zu gefährden, sehr viel arbeitet, statt ihre Tage als Mutter zuhause mit ihrer damals gerade gut ein Jahr alten Tochter zu verbringen.

10) Ihr Galerist, Brent Sikkema, hat zweifellos durch die Verbindung gewonnen, aber er hat sich nie in ihre Arbeit eingemischt. Und ihr Ehemann, Klaus Bürgel, ein etablierter Goldschmied und Schmuckgestalter, ist mehr daran interessiert, künstlerisch sein eigenes hohes Niveau zu halten, als auf ihre Arbeit Einfluss zu nehmen.

11) Kara Walker, «MOTIFS and MOTIVAtions: THE HISTORICAL ROMANCE AND ME», in: *Kara Walker*, op. cit. (vgl. Anm. 6).

12) Andreas Huyssen, «Anselm Kiefer: the Terror of History, the Temptation of Myth», in: *October*, No. 48, Frühjahr 1989, S. 30.

13) Laut Huyssen sind die Bilder nicht nur negativ, sondern stecken voller Ironie: Die kleine Gestalt wirkt in ihrer Umgebung geradezu zwergenhaft und die jubelnden Massen der Nazizeit fehlen ganz. Aber dennoch: «Sind Ironie und Satire wirklich die passenden Mittel in der Auseinandersetzung mit dem faschistischen Terror?», fragt Huyssen quasi als Advocatus Diaboli. «Verniedlicht diese Photoserie nicht den tatsächlichen Schrecken, der für den historisch Unterrichteten mit der Sieg-Heil-Geste verbunden ist?» Ebenda, S. 31.

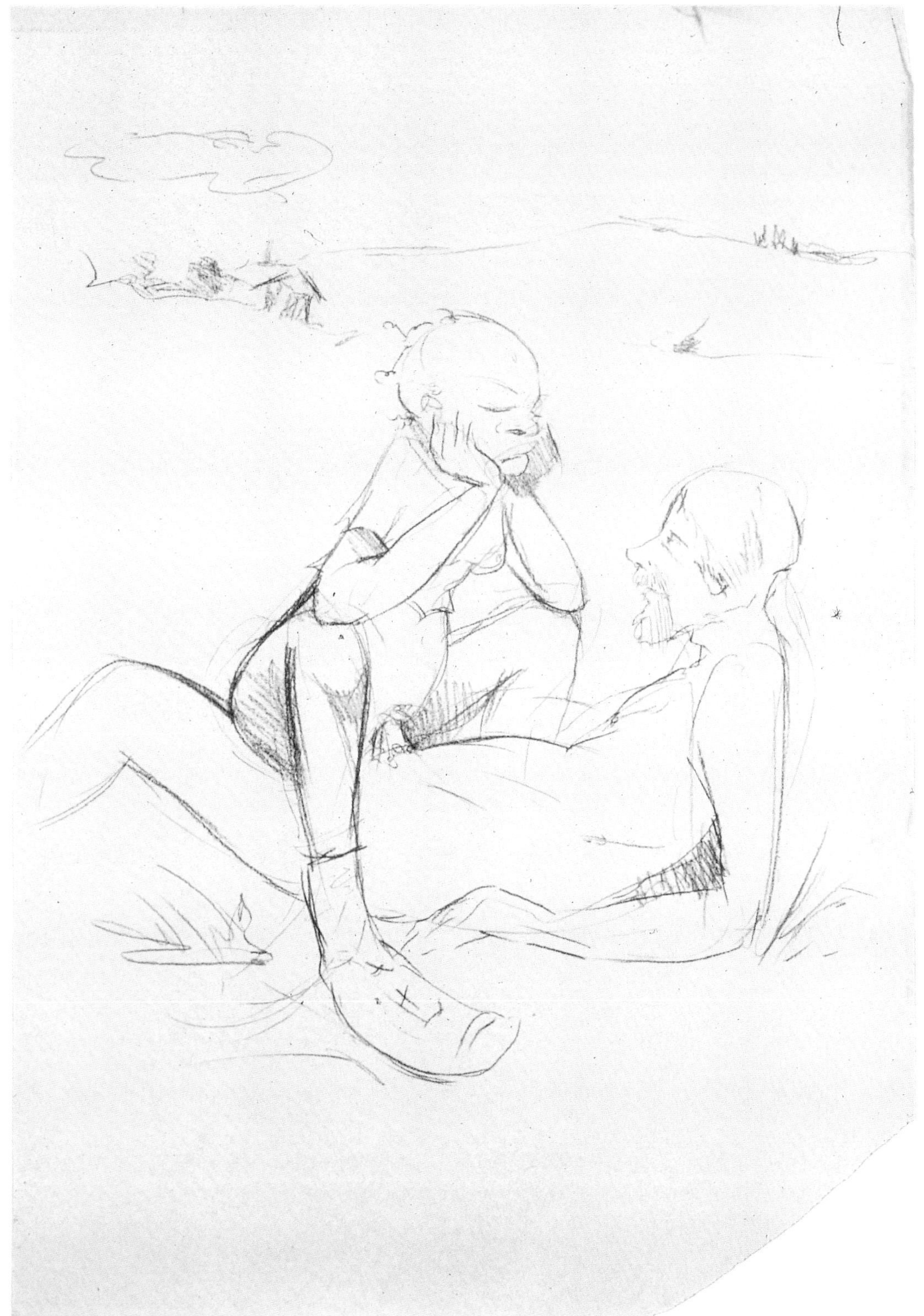

KARA WALKER, UNTITLED, 1995, charcoal on paper, 36 x 24" / OHNE TITEL, Kohle auf Papier, 91,4 x 61 cm.

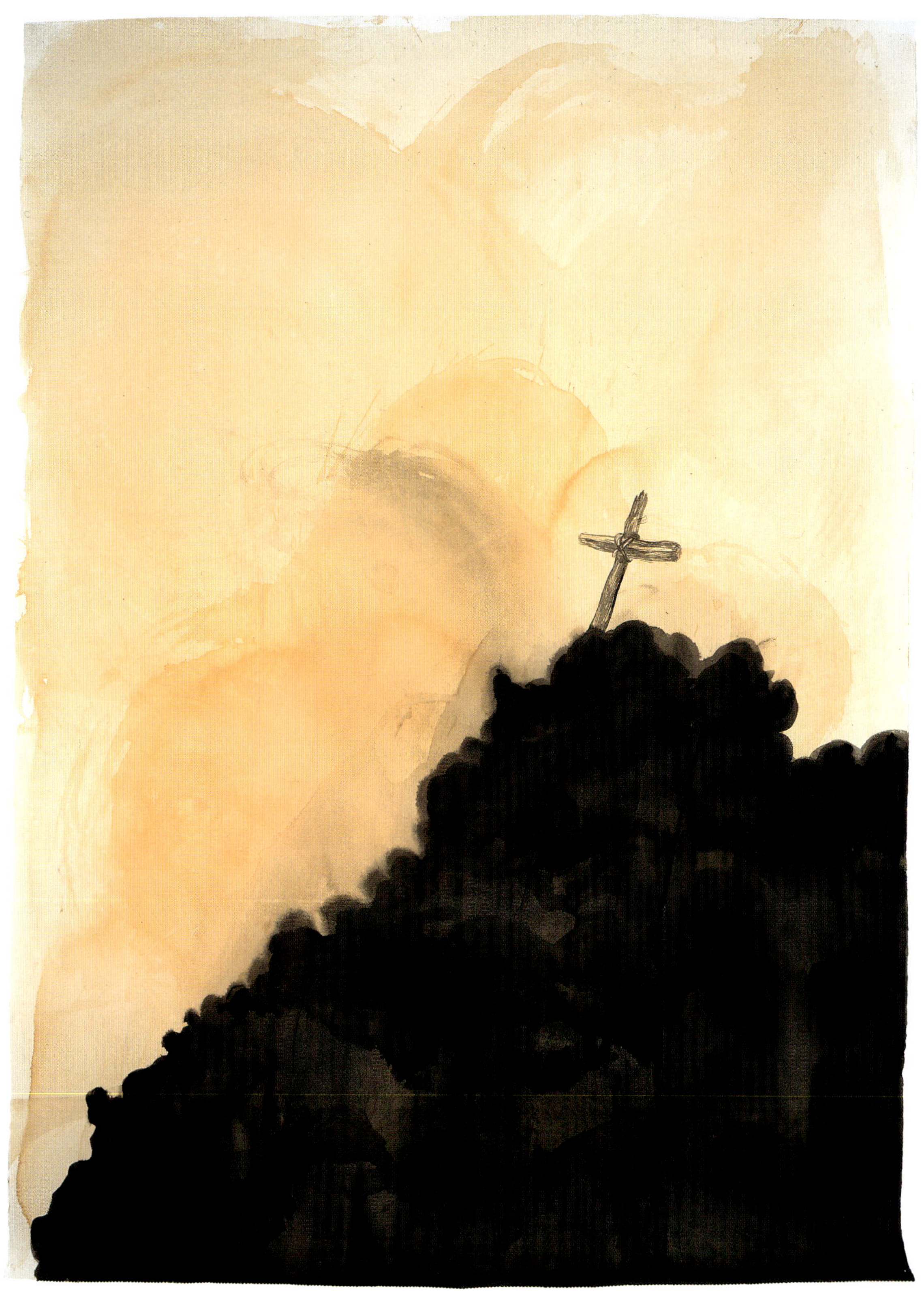

KARA WALKER, NEGRO YOUTH SPEAKS, 1998, coffee and gouache on paper, 75 x 52½" /
DIE NEGERJUGEND SPRICHT, Kaffee und Gouache auf Papier, 190,5 x 133,4 cm.

As American as Apple Pie

ELIZABETH JANUS

When Ralph Ellison was asked how important the search for identity was in American literature, he replied that "it is t h e American theme." Not surprisingly, this quest has special meaning in a country whose mythic reputation as a melting pot of racial, ethnic, and cultural diversity is larger than life. For one's sense of self, tied as it is to a particular place and a common language, also depends upon a shared history. And the relatively recent history of the United States remains something fairly vague in the minds of most of its citizens, embodied in some eighteenth-century revolutionary "tea party" or, more likely, in the civil war that divided north and south over a principle condoning the indentured servitude of a part of its population. For a white Northerner like myself, the South always has seemed closer to history, with visible remnants, both physical and in people's attitudes, of life before "the Surrender," as some Southerners still whisper. At the same time, its forbidden aura as that other, evil place, where slavery was a way of life and racism seems to more overtly rear its ugly head, continues to give a false sense of being comfortably removed from any form of culpability.

Such an over-simplified notion of American history plays right into the hands of Kara Walker, who has lived on both sides of the Mason-Dixon Line. She has understood and uses to poignant effect the fact that a nation's idea of itself often depends upon a reduced, sometimes fictionalized—even distorted—

version of the past in order to feel a deeper sense of belonging. In her art, Walker's own version of the past is played out on an epic scale, in fragmented visual narratives that are told through simple black paper silhouettes using as their backdrop one of America's ugliest or, depending on whom one asks, most glorious periods: the ante-bellum South. She uses this duality to her advantage with characteristic wit and force by ironically twisting a form popular with genteel, nineteenth-century bourgeois Southern "ladies" into glaring indictments of the abhorrent behavior and "garden-variety social dysfunction" attributed to their class.[1]

But if one looks deeper into the history of American art, Walker's craft-inspired method also recalls early colonial painting, particularly that of late seventeenth- and early eighteenth-century anonymous limners, whose styles were rooted in indigenous craft traditions such as sign painting as well as the linear aesthetics of Tudor and Jacobean England, Dutch art and seventeenth- and eighteenth-century English court painting as it was understood on the new continent through prints. More idea than eye bound, these painters presented a reality—usually in the form of a portrait—conceptually, as a concise idea rather than as an empirical expression of three dimensions or through the academic formulae that lead to trompe l'oeil representation. Early canvases by Gilbert Stuart or John Singleton Copley, recognized as two of America's first major artists (the latter an admitted reference for Walker), come directly out of the limner tradition, where gradations of values and tones were eschewed in deference to flat patterns of light and dark.

Walker's own affinity for an elementary, graphic technique makes sense within the context of her

ELIZABETH JANUS is a writer and critic who lives in Geneva.

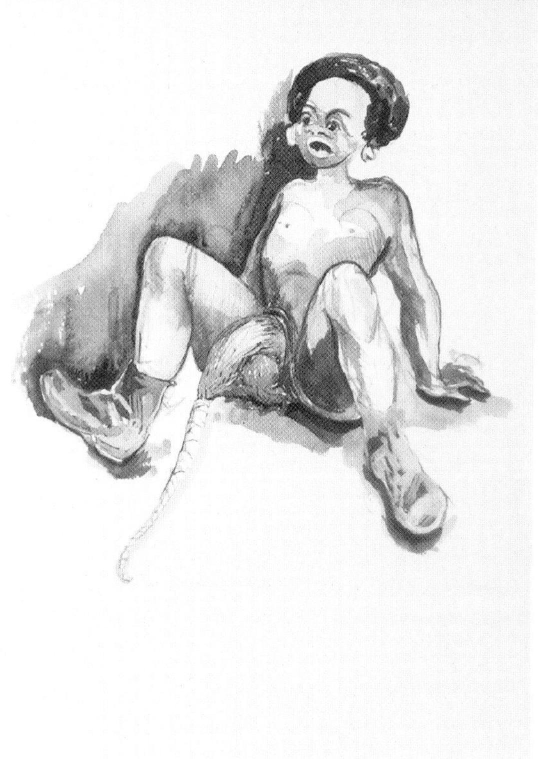

highly charged, content-based work. It belies, however, the artist's accomplishments as a skilled draftswoman, evidenced in both her preparatory sketches and the series of drawings that she has produced since 1995 under the title *Negress Notes*, both of which suggest a hidden interest in the expressionist, even baroque, gesture: a painterly impulse that surfaced in an elaborate, multi-wall installation titled WHY I LIKE WHITE BOYS. AN ILLUSTRATED NOVEL. BY KARA E. WALKER, NEGRESS (2000) shown last spring at the Centre d'Art Contemporain in Geneva. Roughly divided into three narrative sections—INSURRECTION, EMANCIPATION and SALVATION—Walker combined her signature black paper personages with projections of colored lights and shapes that were made by cutting, pasting, and drawing on paper and plastic transparencies, which were then placed on illuminated overhead projectors. The grandest of these, and the exhibition's centerpiece, is a three-wall installation titled INSURRECTION! (OUR TOOLS WERE RUDIMENTARY, YET WE PRESSED ON) (2000), in which one sees an elaborate shadow play set against large areas of red and pools of blue light. In it, an idyll of plantation life is disrupted by episodes of aberrant sexuality (a small group of silhouettes shows a slave girl bending toward her master to perform fellatio, causing the pair to tumble over in

vaudevillian hilarity) and violent revenge (a white man is disemboweled by his kitchen staff in front of three huge blue-lit gothic windows). On the third wall, a woman with a torn rope around her neck carries a basket of fruit-shaped objects resembling dismembered phalluses while behind her The Master thrusts one of these members at a naked black woman leaning against a tree, the whole set under a blood red sky.

What is evident from this latest body of work is that while continuing to use very basic means, Walker has created some of her most theatrical and psychologically riveting art. Cultivating a deep-seated *Sturm und Drang*, she incorporates her sharply delineated figures into broad areas of projected light, color, and curving shadows that give each scene a sweeping sense of unfolding drama. But unlike earlier pieces, where silhouettes appeared isolated on a monochrome background like cameos or the bas-reliefs on Wedgwood porcelain, Walker now makes direct contact with the viewer, whose shadow moves right into the landscape—literally the "nature"—of the installation. Once intertwined with the images of abusers and victims, the spectator is forced into a more immediate recognition of the indifference or repulsion that he/she feels in front of the actions taking place. This passage from passive observation to active involvement, albeit involuntary, with Walker's scenarios represents an evolution in the artist's approach akin to the transition from the quasi-scientific detachment of Neo-Classicism to the privileging of subjective emotions characteristic of Romanticism.

Walker has taken her art to a new level of narrative cohesion using seductive visual effects, but this time without letting us off the hook, content with a furtive look and quick escape. She comes closer than ever to creating a virtual space in which we are unwillingly co-opted as actors in her own version of a passion play. And this play, while rooted in a peculiarly American story, also speaks to a post-colonial Europe that has yet to come to terms with the phantoms in its own closet.

1) Thelma Golden, "Oral Mores: A Postbellum Shadow Play," *Artforum* (September, 1996), p. 93.

ELIZABETH JANUS

So amerikanisch wie «Apple Pie»

Auf die Frage, welche Rolle die Identitätssuche in der amerikanischen Literatur spiele, meinte Ralph Ellison: «Sie ist d a s amerikanische Thema schlechthin.» Es überrascht nicht, dass diese Suche in einem Land besondere Bedeutung erlangt, das als Schmelztiegel der unterschiedlichsten Rassen, Ethnien und Kulturen geradezu legendär ist. Schliesslich ist unser Identitätsgefühl, das sich in Bezug auf einen bestimmten Ort und eine gemeinsame Sprache entwickelt, auch auf eine gemeinsame Geschichte angewiesen. Die relativ junge Geschichte der Vereinigten Staaten ist für die meisten Amerikaner aber nach wie vor eine ziemlich vage Angelegenheit; man sieht vielleicht das Bild einer revolutionären Teegesellschaft des achtzehnten Jahrhunderts vor sich oder denkt – wohl noch eher – an den Bürgerkrieg, den Grundsatzstreit zwischen Nord- und Südstaaten über die Rechtmässigkeit der Sklaverei. Für eine weisse Nordstaatlerin wie mich schien der Süden immer stärker mit Geschichte verbunden zu sein und liess auch im Aussehen und Verhalten der Leute sichtbare Relikte aus der alten Zeit erkennen, der Zeit «vor der Kapitulation», wie sich manche Südstaatler hinter vorgehaltener Hand nach wie vor zuraunen. Zugleich vermittelt die düstere Aura des Südens – die

jenes anderen, üblen Ortes, wo Sklaverei zum Lebensstil gehörte und der Rassismus sein hässliches Gesicht schamloser zeigt als anderswo – die trügerische Sicherheit, weit von alledem entfernt und jeder Schuld enthoben zu sein.

Ein derart simplifizierendes Verständnis der amerikanischen Geschichte ist Wasser auf die Mühle der Kunst von Kara Walker, die selbst auf beiden Seiten der Mason-Dixon-Linie gelebt hat. Sie hat durchschaut, dass das Selbstverständnis einer Nation oft auf einer vereinfachten, manchmal sagenhaften, ja sogar völlig verzerrten Darstellung der Vergangenheit beruht (auf dass das Dazugehören umso überwältigender erlebt werde), und setzt dies zielsicher und höchst wirkungsvoll ein. In ihrer Kunst erhält Walkers eigene Version der Vergangenheit epische Dimensionen und wird in fragmenthaften Bildgeschichten in Form von einfachen, schwarzen Scherenschnitten erzählt, die vor dem Hintergrund von Amerikas übelster oder, je nachdem, wen man fragt, glorreichster Epoche spielen: dem Süden vor dem Bürgerkrieg. In der für sie kennzeichnenden, witzigen und wirkungsvollen Art nützt Walker diese ambivalente Haltung aus, indem sie eine unter wohlerzogenen Bürgerdamen des Südens beliebte Form der Darstellung wählt und zur schonungslosen Entlarvung des abscheulichen Benehmens und der ganz

ELIZABETH JANUS ist Kunstkritikerin und lebt in Genf.

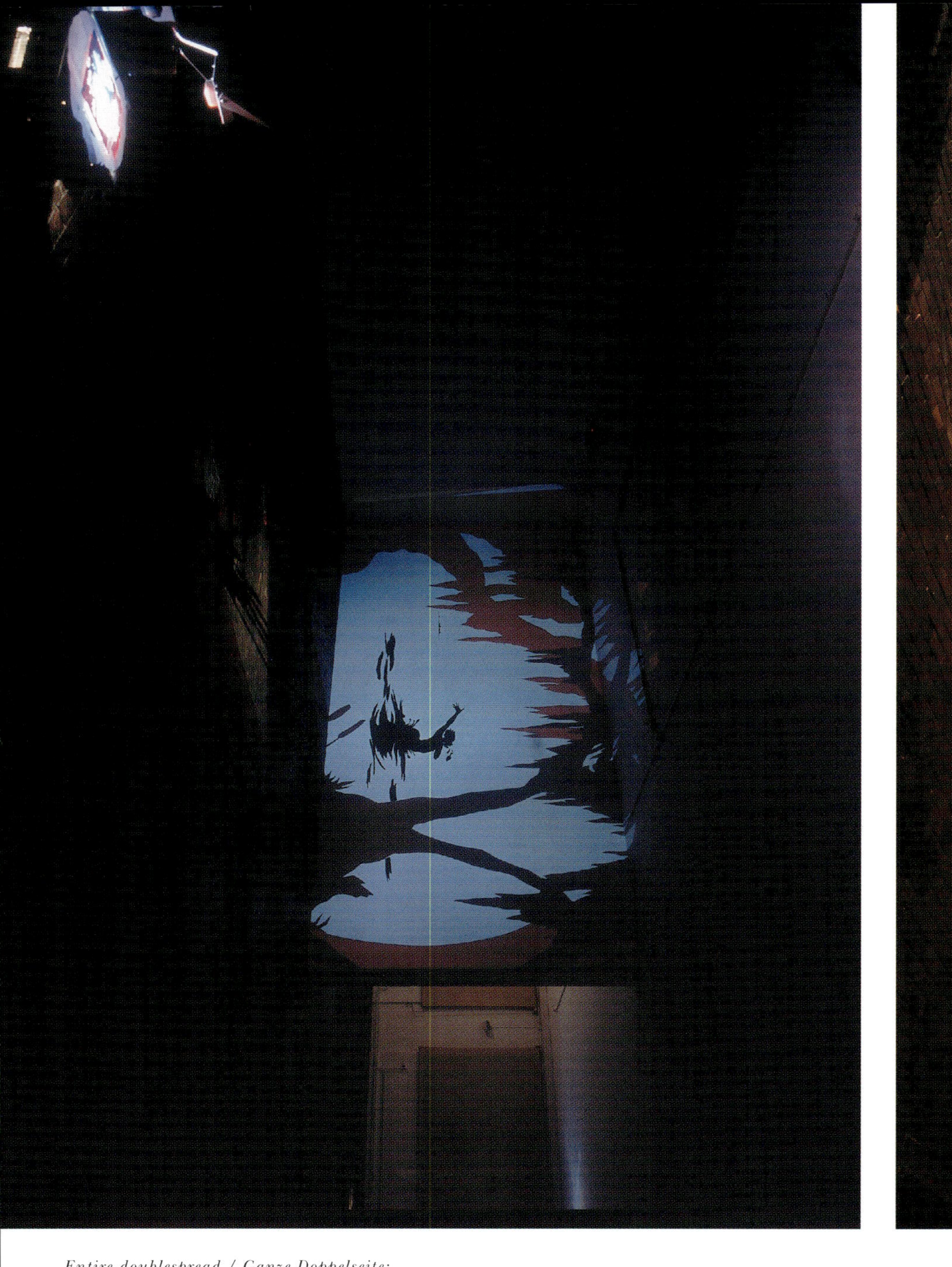

Entire doublespread / Ganze Doppelseite:
WHY I LIKE WHITE BOYS. AN ILLUSTRATED NOVEL. BY KARA E. WALKER, NEGRESS, 2000,
Centre d'Art Contemporain, Geneva / WARUM ICH WEISSE KNABEN LIEBE.
EIN ILLUSTRIERTER ROMAN. VON KARA E. WALKER, NEGERIN.

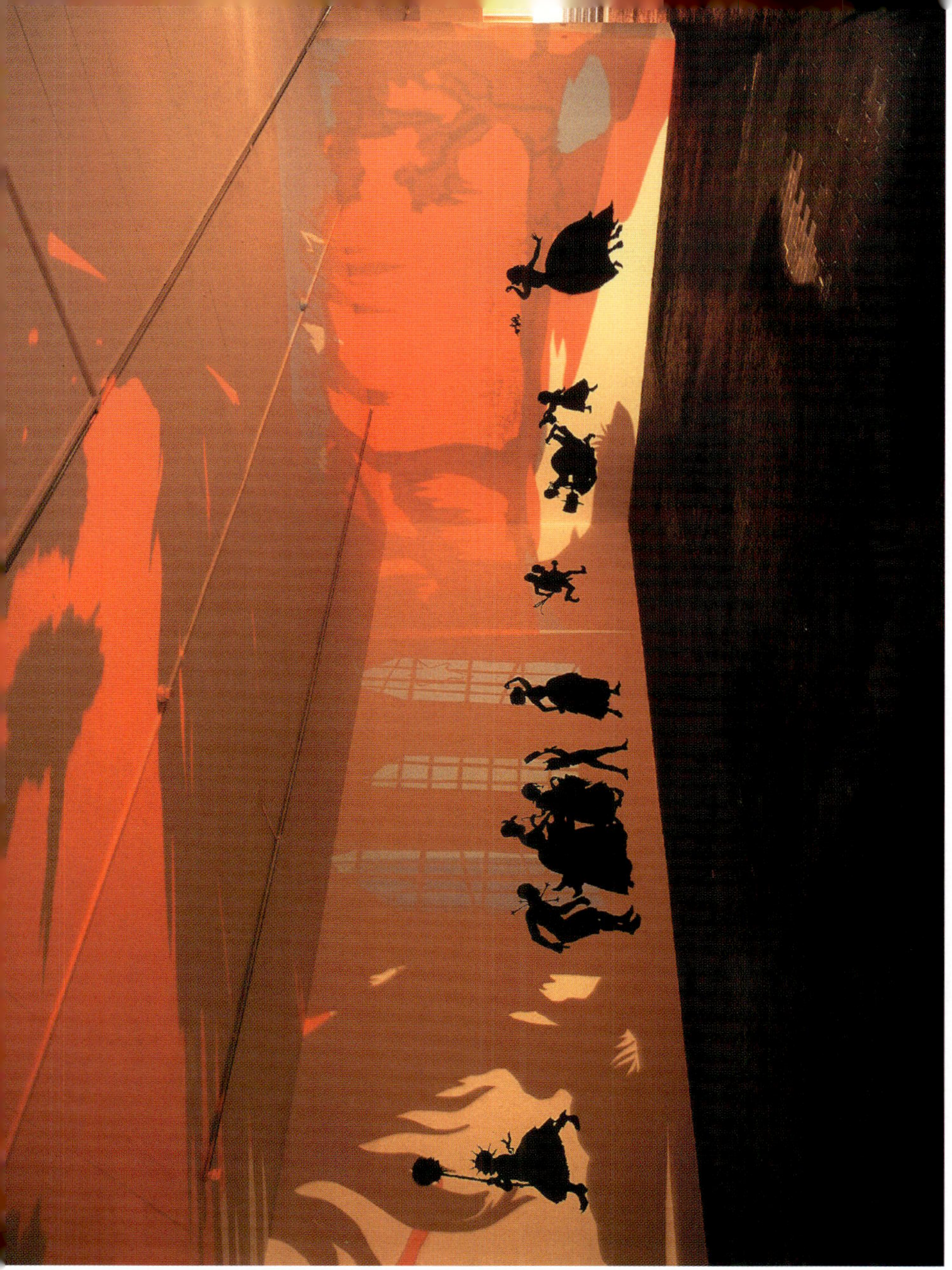

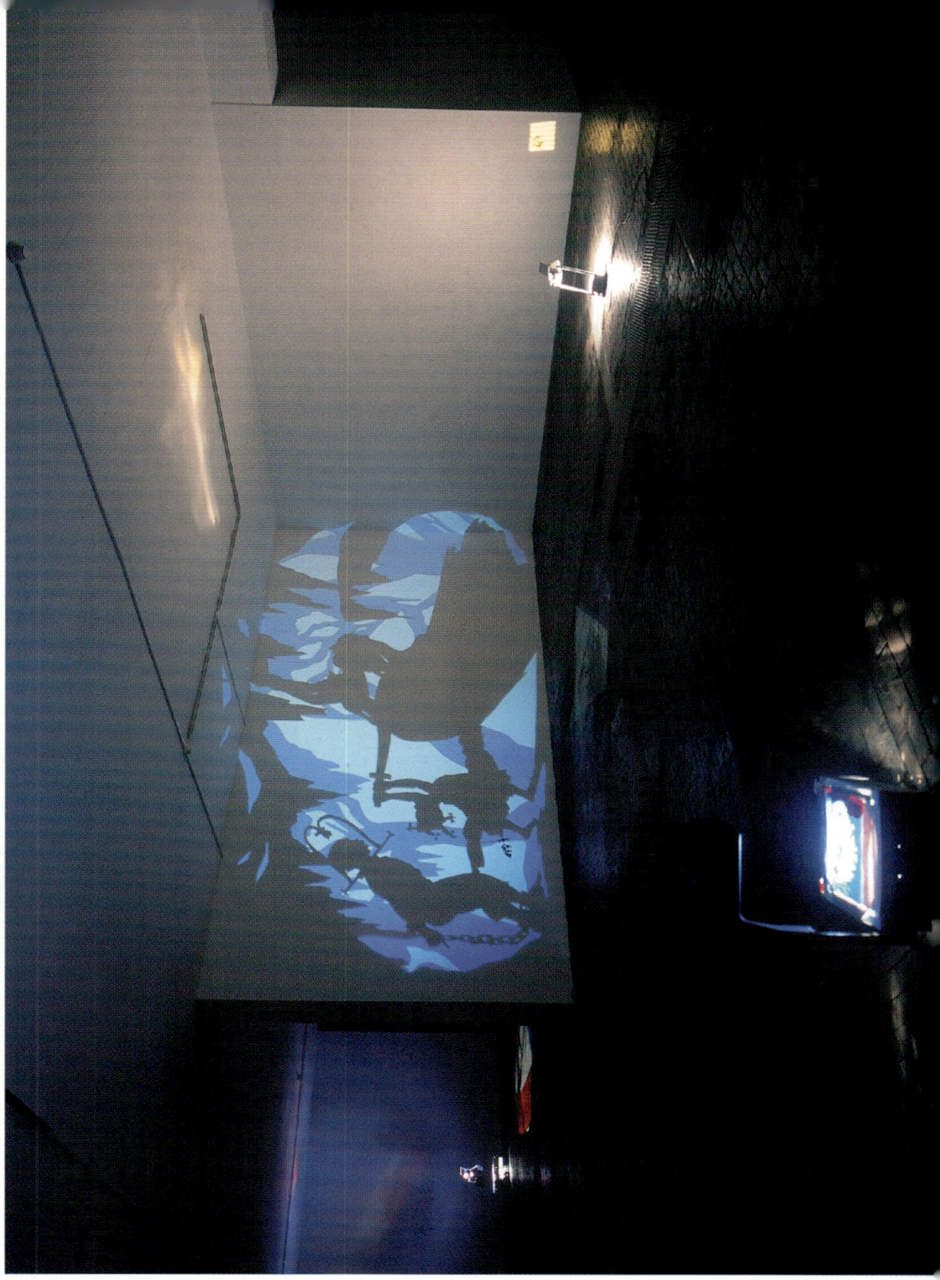

Top / Oben: INSURRECTION! (OUR TOOLS WERE RUDIMENTARY, YET WE PRESSED ON), 2000,
cut paper, adhesive, and overhead projections on 3 walls, Centre d'Art Contemporain, Geneva,
ca. 12 x 21 / 33 / 20½ ft / AUFSTAND! (UNSERE MITTEL WAREN RUDIMENTÄR,
DENNOCH MACHTEN WIR WEITER DRUCK), Scherenschnitte und Hellraumprojektionen
auf 3 Wänden, 3,6 x 6,4 / 10 / 6,3 m.

Bottom / Unten: MISTRESS DEMANDED A SWIFT AND DRAMATIC EMPATHETIC REACTION
WHICH WE OBLIGED HER, 2000, cut paper, adhesive, and projections on 2 walls, ca. 12 x 22 ft each /
DIE HERRIN WÜNSCHTE EINE FLINKE UND DRAMATISCH NACHFÜHLBARE REAKTION, EIN
WUNSCH, DEM WIR NACHKAMEN, Scherenschnitte und Projektionen auf 2 Wänden, je 3,55 x 6,62 m.
(PHOTOS: CENTRE D'ART CONTEMPORAIN, GENEVA)

normalen sozialen Missstände verwendet, die derselben Gesellschaftsschicht zugeschrieben werden.[1]

Vertieft man sich ein bisschen in die amerikanische Kunstgeschichte, so fühlt man sich durch Walkers dem Kunsthandwerk entlehnte Technik auch an die frühe koloniale Malerei erinnert, insbesondere an jene Buchmaler des späten siebzehnten und frühen achtzehnten Jahrhunderts, deren Stil sowohl auf handwerkliche Traditionen der Einheimischen, etwa das Schildermalen, zurückging als auch auf die lineare Ästhetik des jakobäischen und des Tudorstils, die holländische Kunst oder die englische Hofmalerei des siebzehnten und achtzehnten Jahrhunderts, soweit diese in der Neuen Welt in Form von Drucken bekannt waren. Mehr ideell als visuell orientiert stellten diese Maler eine Realität – gewöhnlich ein

Porträt – konzeptuell dar, das heisst, das Bild entsprach eher einer Idee als einer empirisch erfassten Dreidimensionalität beziehungsweise den akademischen Regeln zur Erzeugung der Trompe-l'œil-Wirkung. Die frühen Bilder von Gilbert Stuart oder John Singleton – beide gehören anerkanntermassen zu den ersten bedeutenden Künstlern Amerikas (auf letzteren nimmt Walker ausdrücklich Bezug) – entspringen unmittelbar der Buchmalertradition, wo

KARA WALKER, ALLEGORY, 1996,
watercolor and gouache on paper, 63¾ x 51½" /
ALLEGORIE, Aquarell und Gouache auf Papier, 162 x 130,8 cm.

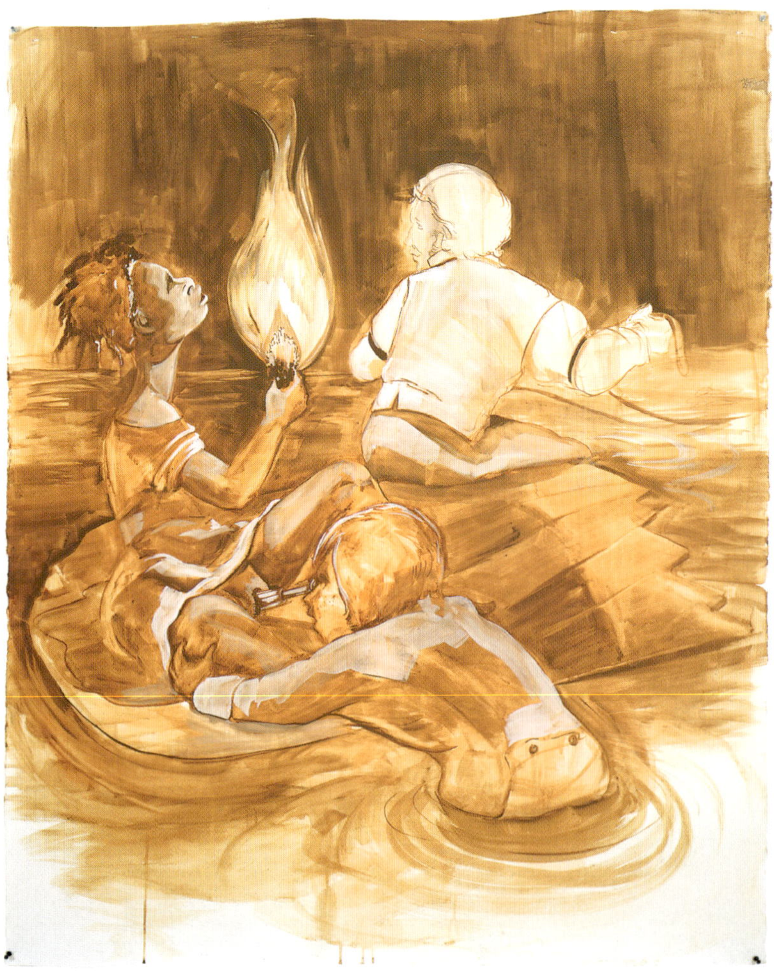

der flache Helldunkelkontrast einer feineren Stufung der Farb- und Tonwerte vorgezogen wurde.

Walkers Wahl einer elementaren, graphischen Technik erscheint sinnvoll im Zusammenhang mit ihren äusserst bedeutungsgeladenen, inhaltsbezogenen Arbeiten. Sie täuscht jedoch über das hohe zeichnerische Können dieser Künstlerin hinweg, das sowohl in ihren vorbereitenden Skizzen wie in den Zeichnungsserien zum Ausdruck kommt, die seit 1995 unter dem Titel *Negress Notes (Notizen einer Negerin)* entstanden sind. Beide zeugen von einem verborgenen Interesse an der expressionistischen, ja barocken Gebärde: einem malerischen Impuls, der in der ausgefeilten, mehrere Wände bedeckenden Installation zutage tritt – WHY I LIKE WHITE BOYS. AN ILLUSTRATED NOVEL. BY KARA E. WALKER, NEGRESS (2000) (Warum ich weisse Knaben liebe. Ein illustrierter Roman. Von Kara E. Walker, Negerin) –, die letzten Frühling im Centre d'Art Contemporain in Genf zu sehen war und drei Teile umfasste: INSURRECTION (Aufstand), EMANCIPATION (Emanzipation) und SALVATION (Erlösung). Walker kombinierte darin ihre typischen schwarzen Papierfiguren mit Projektionen farbiger Lichter und Formen, die durch Schneiden, Kleben und Zeichnen auf Papier und transparente Folien entstanden und dann mit Projektoren auf die Wand projiziert wurden. Das eindrücklichste Beispiel und das Kernstück der Ausstellung bildete die sich über drei Wände erstreckende Installation INSURRECTION! (OUR TOOLS WERE RUDIMENTARY, YET WE PRESSED ON) (2000) / «Aufstand (unsere Mittel waren rudimentär, dennoch machten wir weiter Druck)»: Man sieht ein differenziertes Schattentheater vor grossen Seen roten und blauen Lichts. Idyllische Plantagenszenen werden unterbrochen von Episoden abnormer Sexualität (eine kleine Gruppe von Scherenschnitten zeigt, wie ein Sklavenmädchen sich vor seinem Herrn niederbeugt, um die Fellatio zu vollziehen, was beide in einem schwankhaft ausgelassenen Taumel zu Fall bringt) und Szenen brutaler Rache (vor drei hohen, blau erleuchteten gotischen Fenstern wird ein Weisser von seinem Küchenpersonal kastriert). An der dritten Wand trägt eine Frau mit einem zerrissenen Strick um den Hals einen Korb voll fruchtähnlicher Gegenstände, die an abgeschnittene Phallen erinnern, während

hinter ihr der Herr eines dieser Glieder gegen eine nackte schwarze Frau stösst, die sich an einen Baum lehnt. Das alles unter blutrotem Himmel.

Aus diesen neusten Arbeiten wird eines deutlich, nämlich, dass Kara Walker unter Beibehaltung elementarster technischer Mittel einige ihrer dramatischsten und psychologisch aufwühlendsten Werke geschaffen hat. Einem tief wurzelnden «Sturm und Drang» verpflichtet, setzt sie ihre scharf umrissenen Figuren in weite Projektionsfelder aus Licht, Farbe und gekrümmten Schatten, die den Szenen eine überwältigende Dramatik und Spannung verleihen. Aber anders als in früheren Arbeiten, wo die Scherenschnitte isoliert auf einem monochromen Hintergrund standen – wie Kameen oder die Basreliefs auf Wedgwood-Porzellan –, sucht Walker nun den direkten Kontakt zum Betrachter, dessen Schatten sich geradezu in die Landschaft und damit buchstäblich in die «Natur» der Installation hineinbewegt. Sich selbst inmitten der Bilder von Missetätern und Opfern wiederfindend, muss der Betrachter sich nun seine Gleichgültigkeit oder den Widerwillen, den er angesichts der dargestellten Szenen empfindet, viel unmittelbarer eingestehen. Dieser Übergang von passiver Betrachtung zur aktiven Beteiligung, auch wenn es unfreiwillig geschieht, ist eine Entwicklung in Walkers Arbeit, die mit dem Übergang von der quasi-wissenschaftlichen Neutralität des Neoklassizismus zur Vorliebe für subjektive Empfindungen in der Romantik vergleichbar ist.

Walker verleiht ihrer Kunst eine höhere narrative Qualität, indem sie verführerische visuelle Effekte einsetzt, ohne uns diesmal aber bereits nach einem kurzen verstohlenen Blick wieder entkommen zu lassen. Sie kommt der Schaffung eines virtuellen Raumes, in dem wir wider Willen zu Akteuren in ihrer eigenen Version eines leidenschaftlichen Dramas werden, näher denn je. Und dieses Drama, selbst wenn seine Wurzeln spezifisch amerikanische sind, wendet sich auch an ein postkoloniales Europa, dem die Auseinandersetzung mit den Leichen im eigenen Keller noch bevorsteht.

(Übersetzung: Susanne Schmidt)

1) Vgl. dazu: Thelma Golden, «Oral Mores: A Postbellum Shadow Play», in: *Artforum*, September 1996, S. 93.

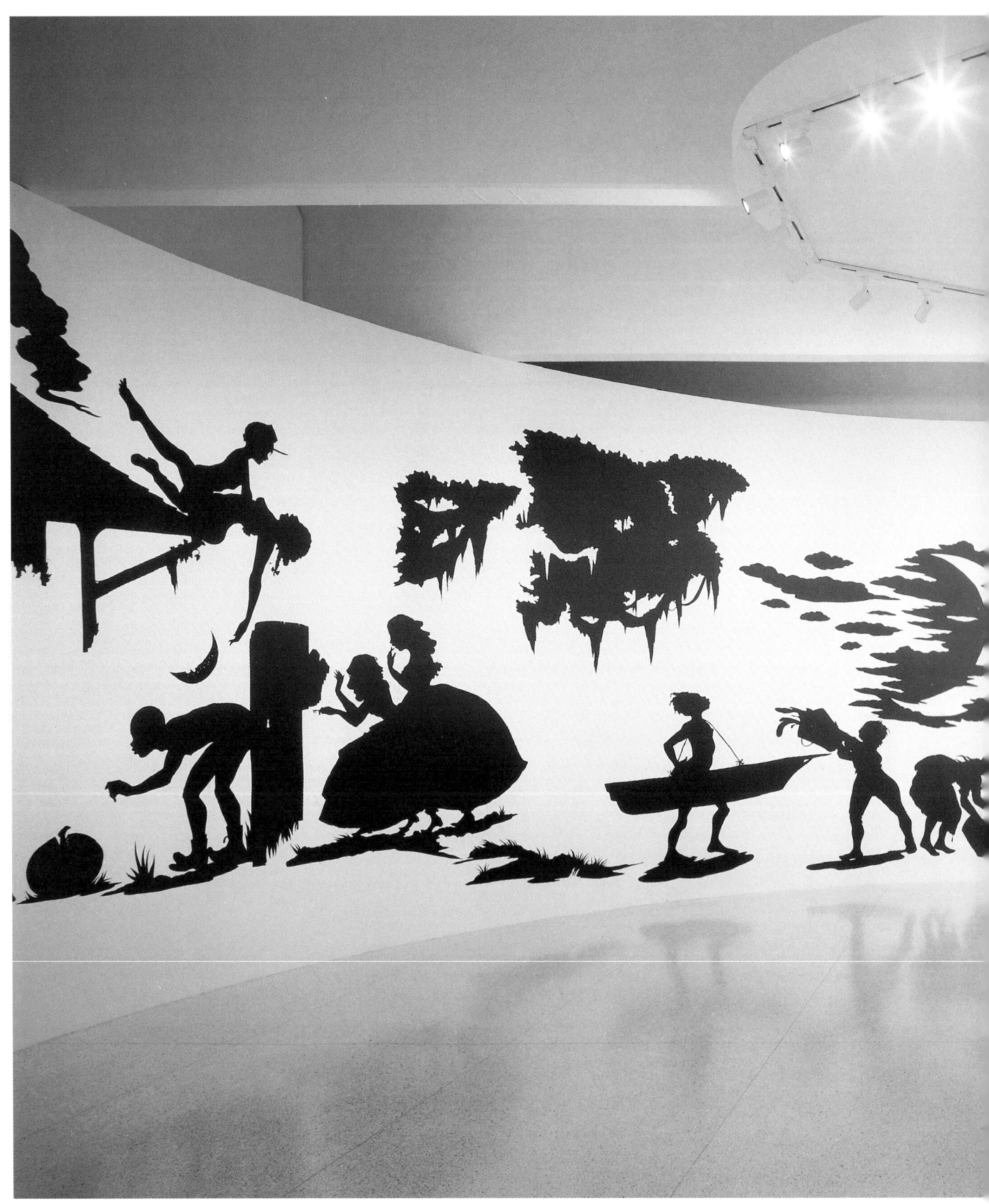

KARA WALKER, SLAVERY! SLAVERY!, 1997, cut paper and adhesive on wall, Walker Art Center, Minneapolis, overall size ca. 12 x 85 ft /

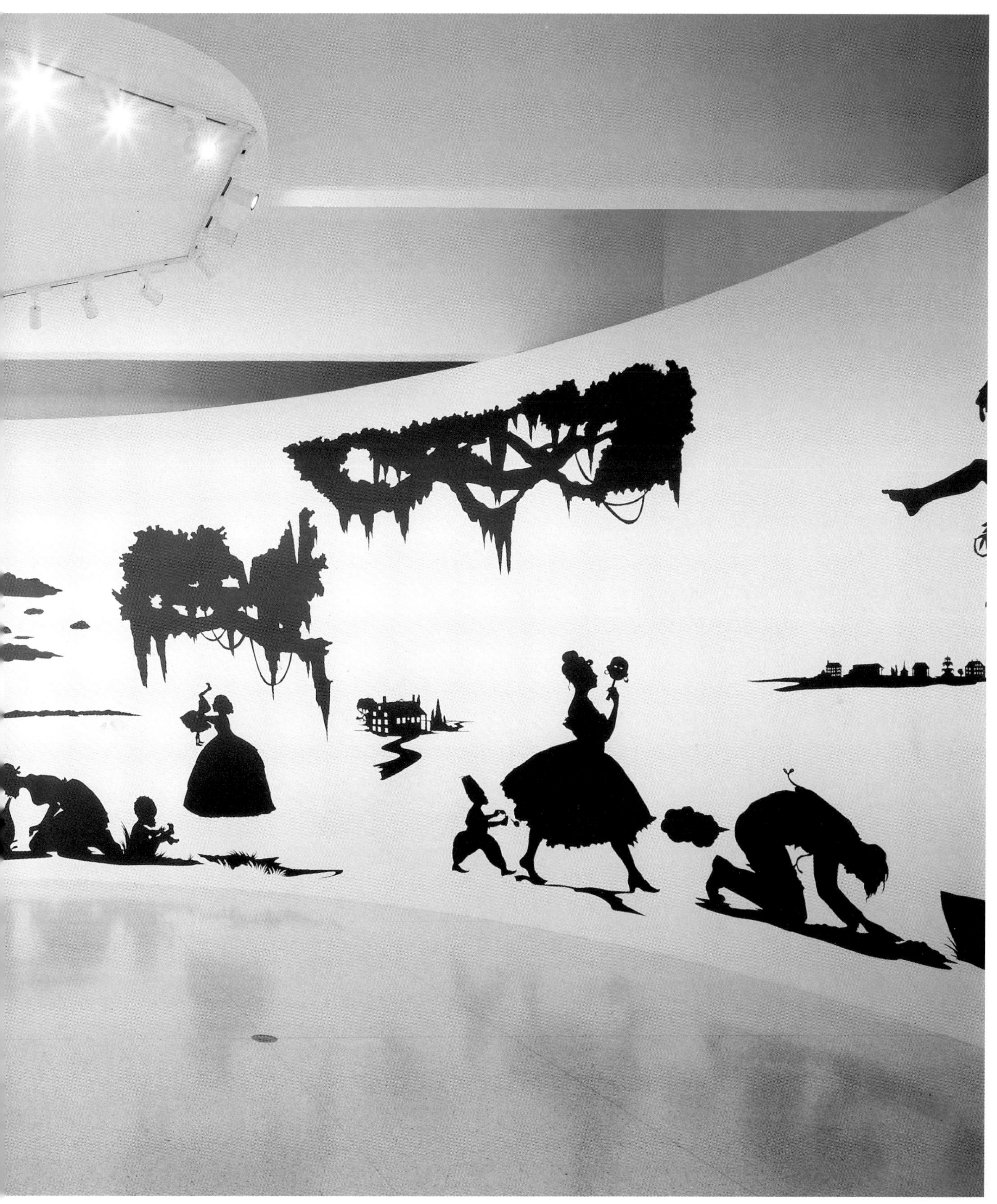

SKLAVEREI! SKLAVEREI!, an die Wand geklebte Scherenschnitte, insgesamt ca. 3,66 x 25,9 m.

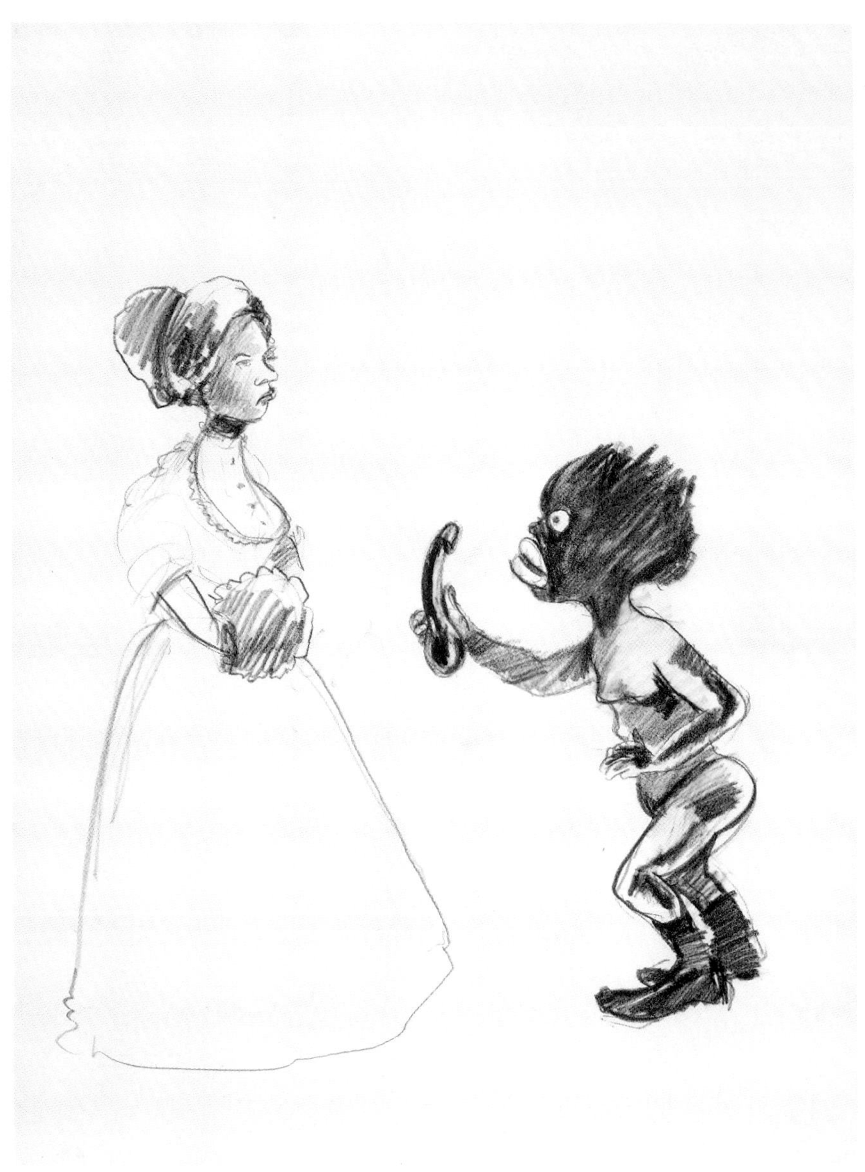

KARA WALKER, UNTITLED, 1995,
charcoal on paper, 24 x 18" / OHNE TITEL, Kohle auf Papier, 61 x 45,7 cm.

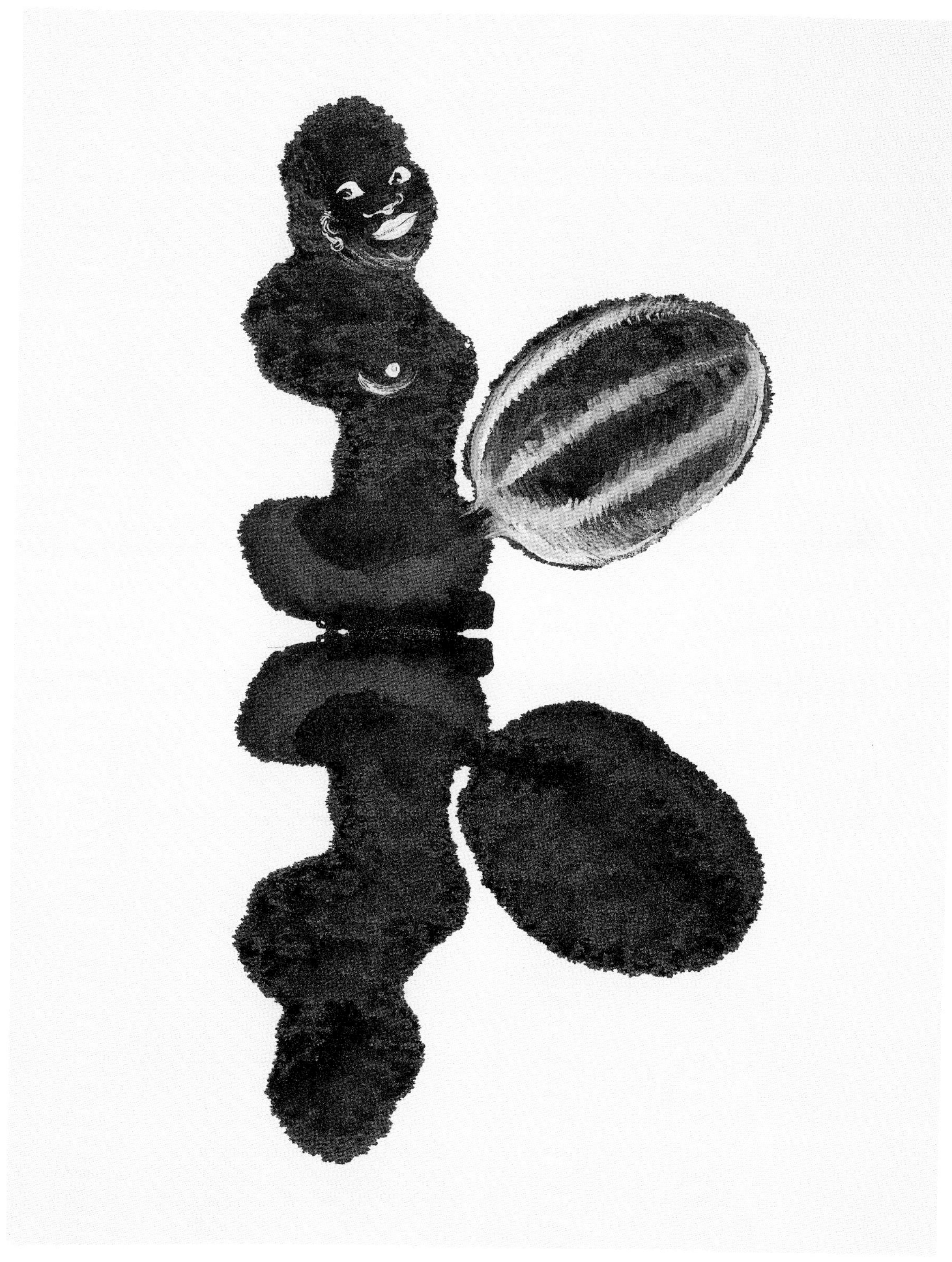

KARA WALKER, UNTITLED, 1995,
ink and gouache on paper, 12 x 8¾" / OHNE TITEL, Tusche und Gouache auf Papier, 30,5 x 22,2 cm.

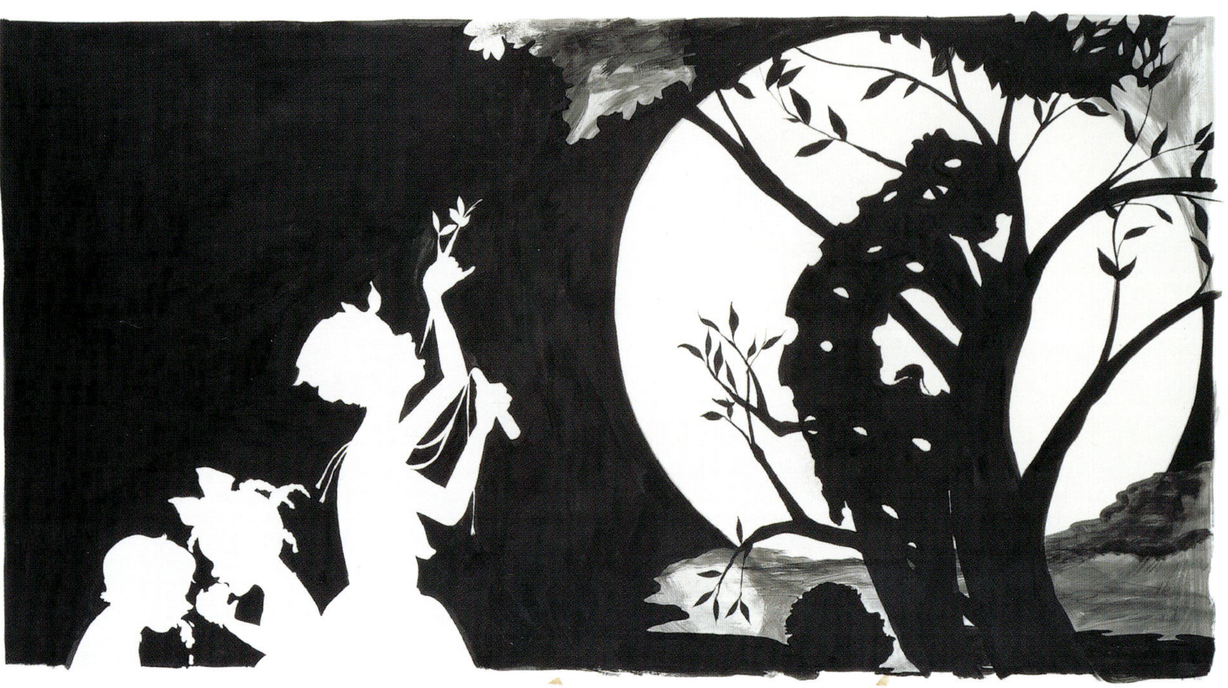

KARA WALKER, UNTITLED, 1998, gouache and pencil on paper, 58 x 101" /
OHNE TITEL, Gouache und Bleistift auf Papier, 147,3 x 256,5 cm.

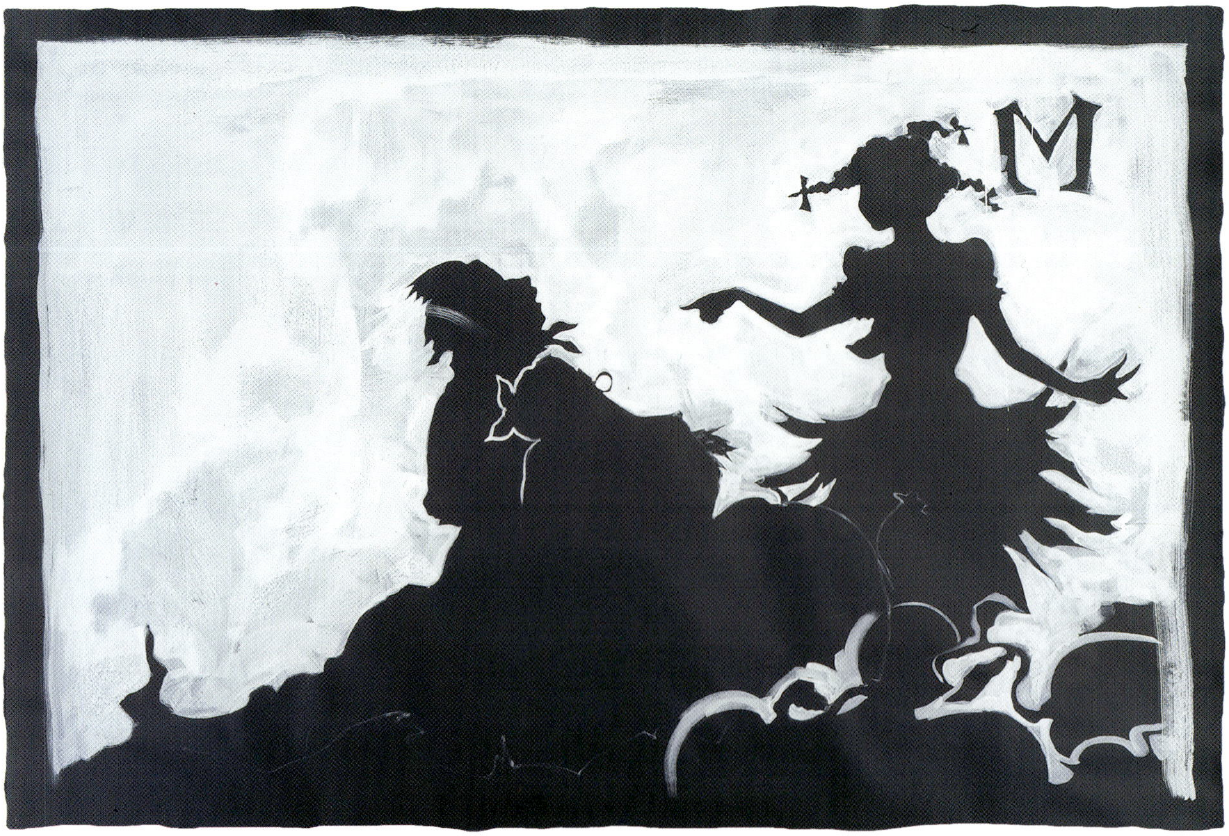

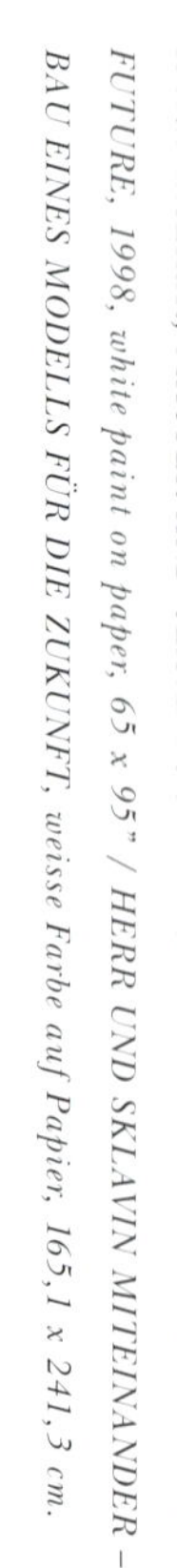

KARA WALKER, MASTER AND SLAVE TOGETHER—BUILDING A MODEL FOR THE
FUTURE, 1998, white paint on paper, 65 x 95" / HERR UND SKLAVIN MITEINANDER–
BAU EINES MODELLS FÜR DIE ZUKUNFT, weisse Farbe auf Papier, 165,1 x 241,3 cm.

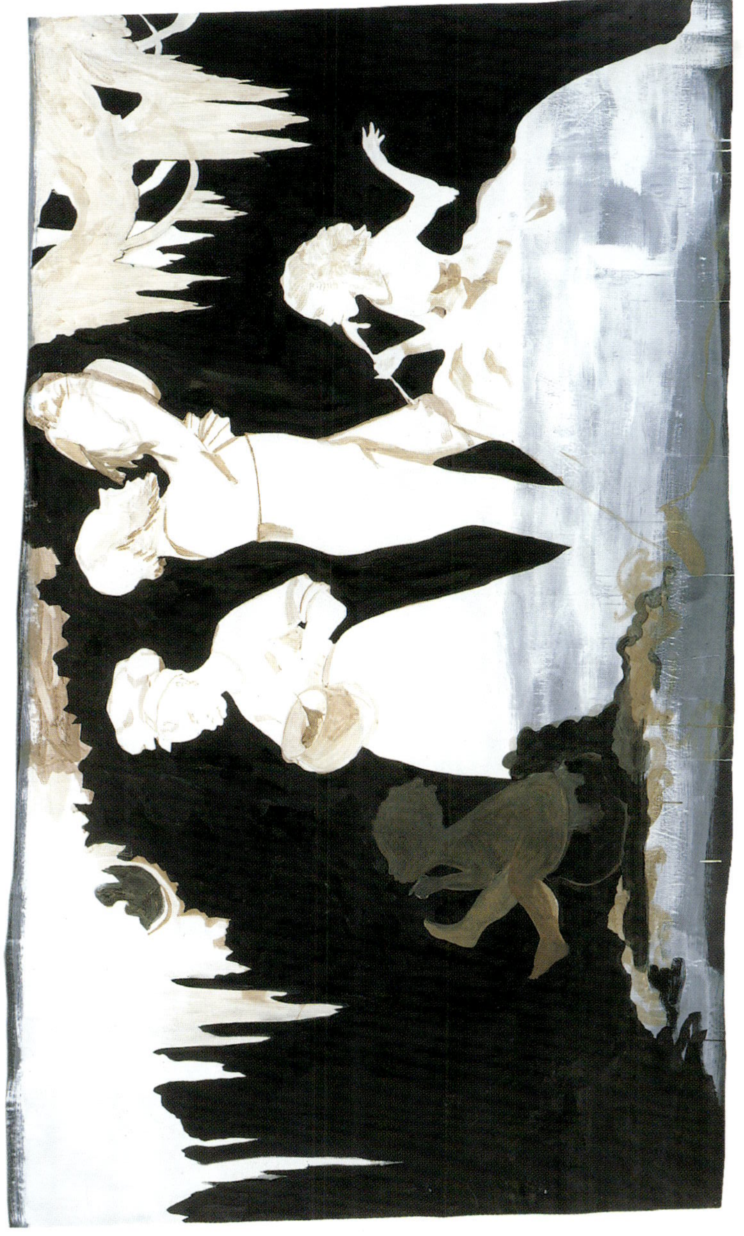

KARA WALKER, A GIVING GESTURE—MONUMENT TO THE NEW SOUTH
(STUDY), 1998, gouache on paper, 66¼ x 106½" / EINE HINGEBUNGSVOLLE HAL-
TUNG – DENKMAL FÜR DEN NEUEN SÜDEN (STUDIE), Gouache auf Papier,
168,3 x 270.5 cm.

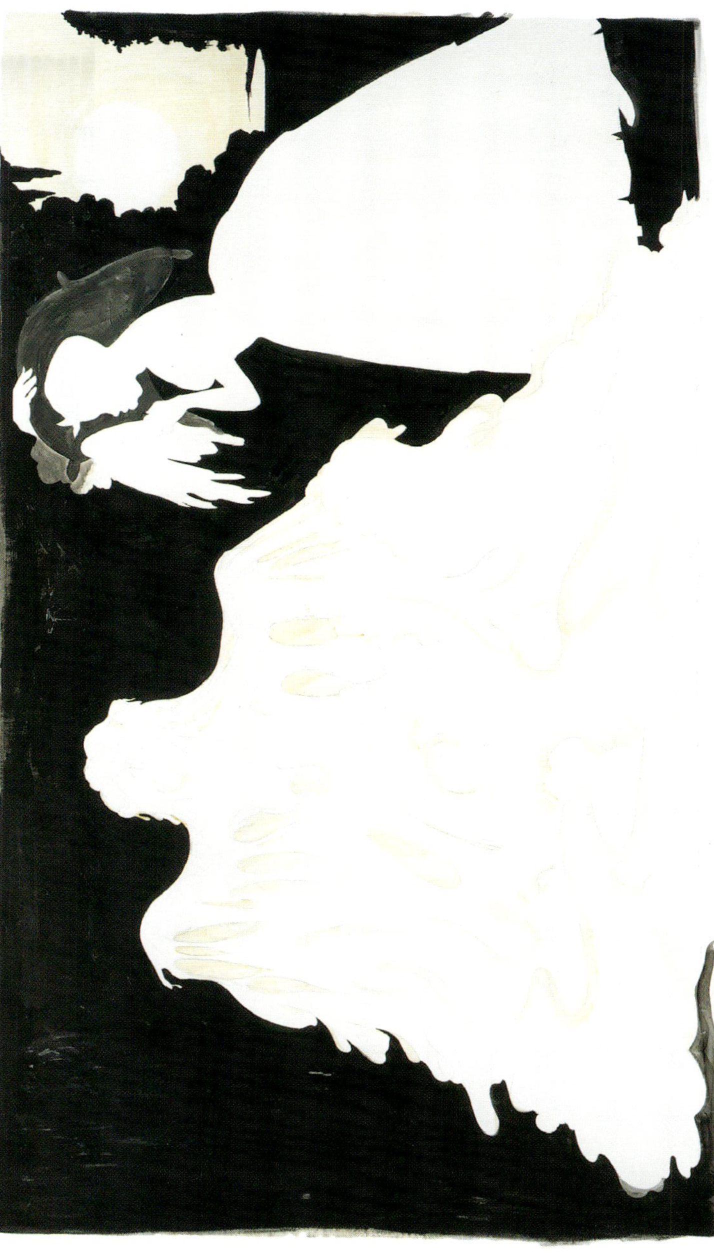

KARA WALKER, ANOTHER FINE MESS, 1998, gouache on paper, 62 x 101" /
NOCH EINE SCHÖNE BESCHERUNG, Gouache auf Papier, 157,5 x 256,5 cm.

Nigger Lover or

HAMZA WALKER

Although race is now readily regarded as a social construct rather than natural or biblical law, eliminating it as a political and psychological reality proves more difficult than say dismantling the Federal Housing Projects on Chicago's South side. When W. E. B. Du Bois speculated that the problem of the twentieth century would be that of race, I wonder if he had any idea that we would leave the century standing on, rather than crossing, the color line. How exactly does race figure into our understanding of a better world? Does the category of race disappear on the horizon of even the most progressive visionary's socio-political landscape? Or to put it in more frank, polemical terms, will there be any black people in utopia?

It depends whose imagination is at work as to whether one finds the idea of utopia with or without race objectionable. On the one hand, black people as I have come to know, love and be one of them, seem to vanish whenever I hear the words "non-racial humanism." And on the other, casting utopia in the present discourse regarding race, particularly that of an abandoned project such as affirmative action, can only register as defensive in the absence of any viable alternatives for change. Skeptical of a humanist vision in which black subjects are unable to see themselves as anything but black and lacking any tangible commitment to dismantling the de facto racial hierarchy, the imagination, when it comes to race, is caught between a rock and a hard place. As if in a machine designed by Willy Wonka cum again as Sun Ra, a black subject, unable to envision subjectivity without race and escape the unsettling terms of the present, is offered two options. He or she can declare themselves a citizen of Saturn or tumble backward into an idiom of race fixed in the past.

HAMZA WALKER is Director of Education at the Renaissance Society at the University of Chicago.

Kara Walker has chosen the latter with a vengeance. Her claims upon the imagination have everything to do with our inability, for better and/or worse, to envision a future without race. The extent to which race and utopia are mutually exclusive becomes apparent the more our imaginations fail at conjuring a world in which skin tone does not immediately correspond to a place within a social hierarchy. This is a noteworthy failure for an imagination praised for having delivered us into a new world order, which for many of us doesn't look so new. Indeed, nothing could be more anachronistic than Walker's decision to revive a medium as historically withered as silhouette portraiture, which is proof that a leap of the imagination is not synonymous with going forward. Instead, Walker's unwieldy imagination is fixated with race in the starkest and most American of terms, black and white, as they were forged in the ante-bellum South, a time not so long ago in a galaxy called here.

Like myself, Walker is a post-civil rights child. I suspect she, too, would have been sent mixed signals, as if the contradictions inherent to notions of a racial utopia could somehow be resolved by watching the television saga *Roots*. In one ear would have been the tepid rhetoric of a color-blind society while in the other, the waning rhetoric of Black Nationalism from its militant to its middle-class varieties. A decade and a half after *Roots*, however, Walker's work cannot help but stand in bold contrast to the relatively anemic dialogue whose signs of exhaustion have taken the

Will There Be Any Black People in Utopia?

form of collective fantasies, ranging from those of an Afrocentric, hopelessly bourgeois order, to the "don't ask, don't tell" fantasy of liberals to the arch conservative fantasy of race being relegated to the private sphere where, like religion, it is something you practice at home. In each instance, the simultaneous maintenance and depoliticization of race reinforces the status quo underscoring our inability to address the real issue, which is that of class. The result has been an overwhelming ambivalence as to h o w, not to mention i f, we shall or even want to overcome the category of race. To say Walker's work assumes such vivid proportion a g a i n s t our better wishes for overcoming race is misleading. Walker's installations situate themselves in the muddled vacancy of the imagination precisely in the absence of any such better wishes. Just as we are unable to imagine a color we haven't seen, or in the case of race, unable to imagine seeing without color, our better wishes for transcending race are inarticulable to our consciousness. Under these circumstances, what might pass as a better wish for a racial utopia is exposed as little more than a mechanism for repressing that which it was meant to transcend. Revealed as such, what lurks below our thoughts of a colorless humanity is a black and white, Manichean realm in which the stereotype thrives.

But when Walker's detractors decry her use of stereotypes, what exactly do they mean by use? Bludgeoning, cannibalization, shitting, and eating are extreme activities, even for mammies, pickaninnies, sambos, belles, dandies, carpetbaggers and the like. Gone is the ubiquitous jiggaboo grin, for Walker's characters have moved on to forms of gratification that involve flesh much more substantial than that of a watermelon. In their animated zeal, Walker's characters proudly declare that they have overcome the taboo in a manner not unlike that of say Jeffrey Dahmer. Lick, suck, devour. Prod, poke, puncture. Shit, fuck, bludgeon. The agents in Walker's freak scene à la de Sade never once acknowledge our presence let alone seek our approval for acts ranging from bestiality to pedophilia, from the sexually explicit to the downright polymorphous perverse. In short, we are an audience for whom her caricatures, frankly my dear Scarlett, don't really give a damn. Independent of any basis in reality, they go about their merry ass licking, cunnilingus craving way as if altogether unobserved and forgotten, which is another way of saying repressed.

Using Walker's artistic hindsight, slavery could just as easily have been dubbed the perverse institution by Sigmund Freud as it was the peculiar institution by Frederick Law Olmsted. Her vision is a skewed triad of race, history and desire, that when it avails itself of a reading, avails itself of one of such surreal and psychological dimensions that it might be better called a diagnosis. This certainly jibes with the work's formal resemblance to a Rorschach test. If Walker's work is about anything, it is about shame or the lack thereof. In fact, the work is shameless three times over, abandoning the historical shame sur-

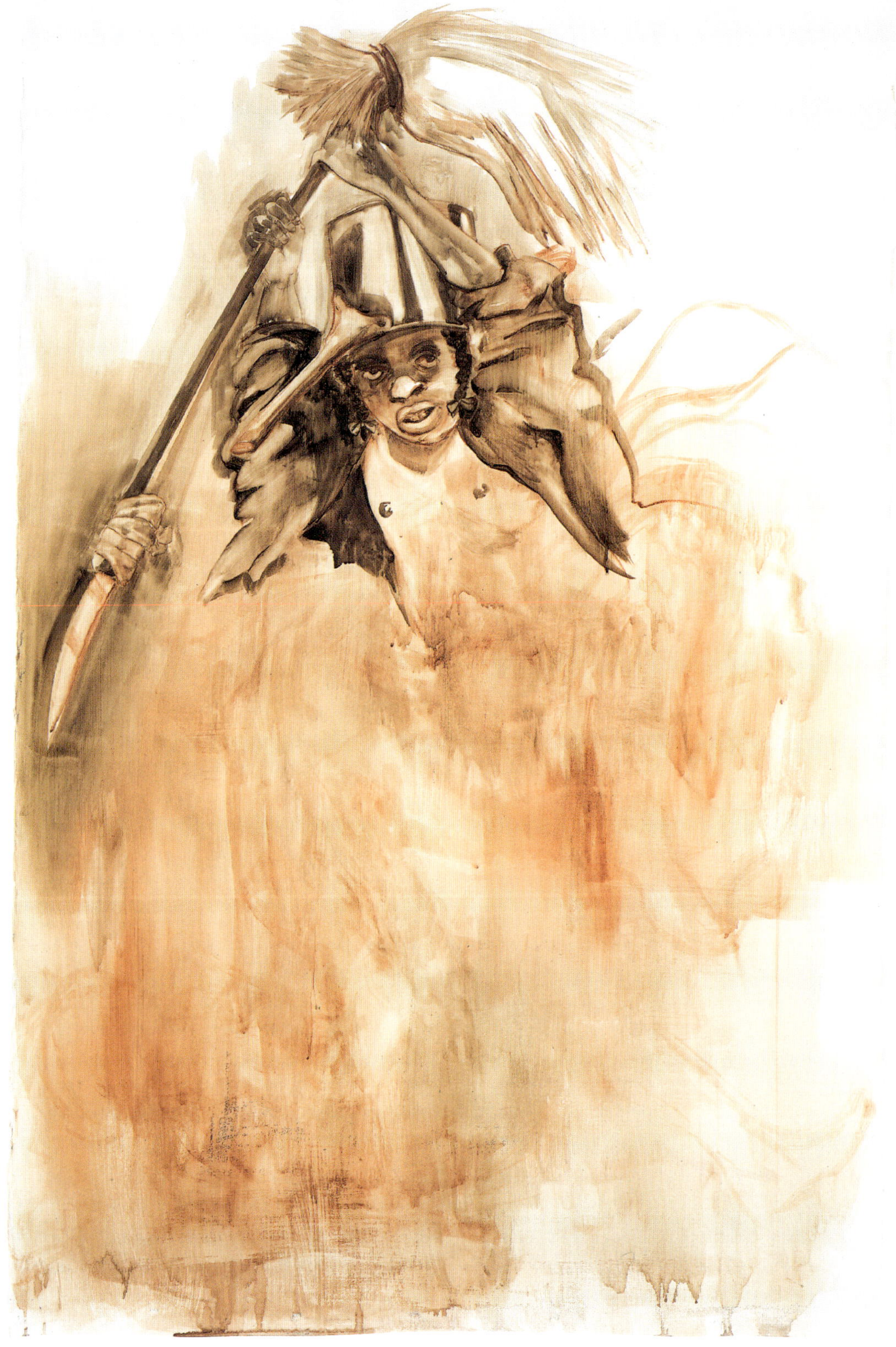

KARA WALKER, INSURRECTION, 1997, gouache on paper, 60 x 42" / AUFSTAND, Gouache auf Papier, 152,4 x 106,7 cm.

KARA WALKER, THE BATTLE OF ATLANTA: BEING THE NARRATIVE OF A NEGRESS IN THE FLAMES OF DESIRE—
A RECONSTRUCTION, 1995, detail, cut paper, adhesive on wall, Nexus Contemporary Art Center Atlanta, Georgia /
DIE SCHLACHT VON ATLANTA: GESCHICHTE EINER NEGERIN IN DEN FLAMMEN DES BEGEHRENS – EINE REKONSTRUKTION,
Teilansicht, an der Wand befestigte Scherenschnitte.

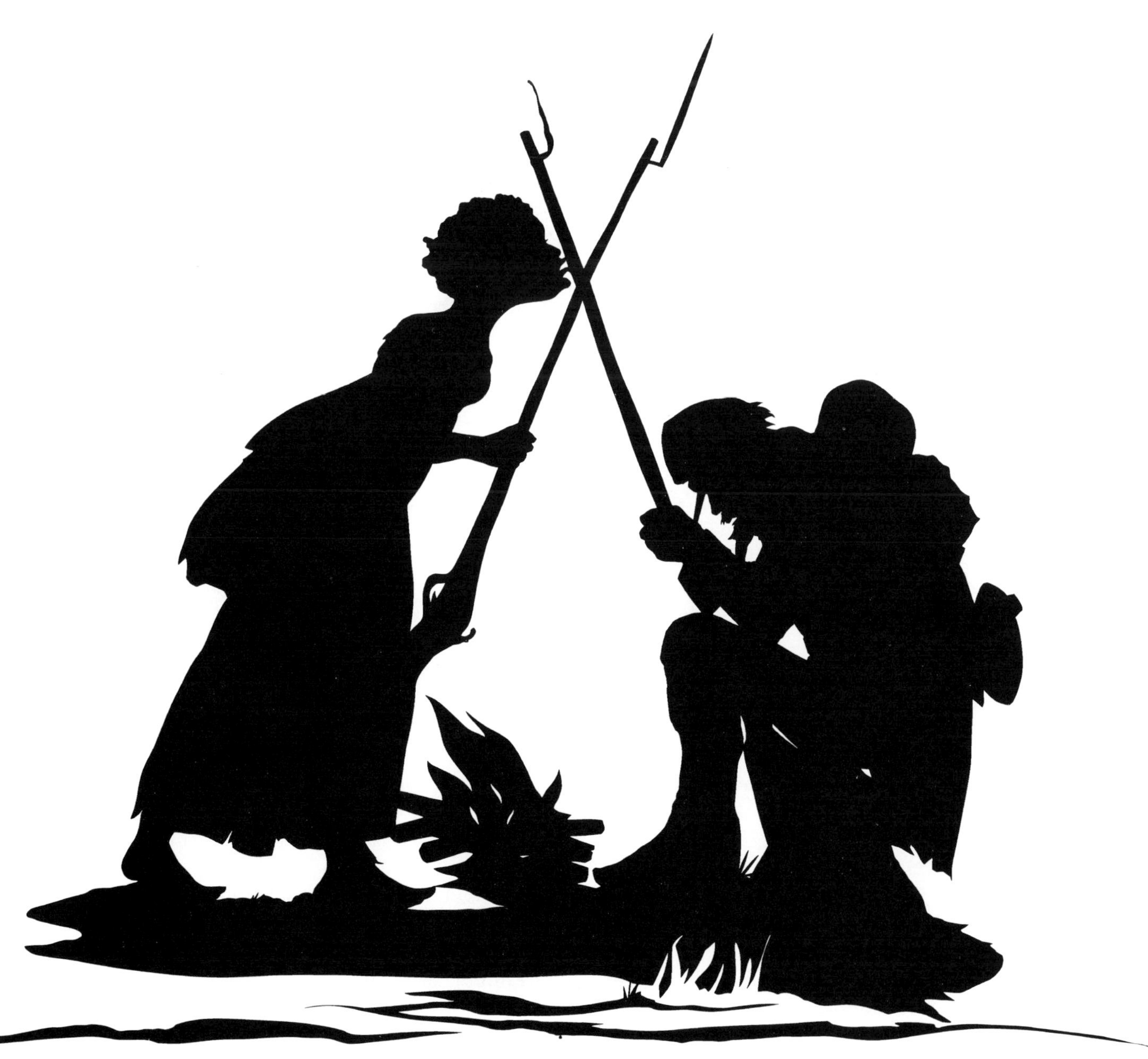

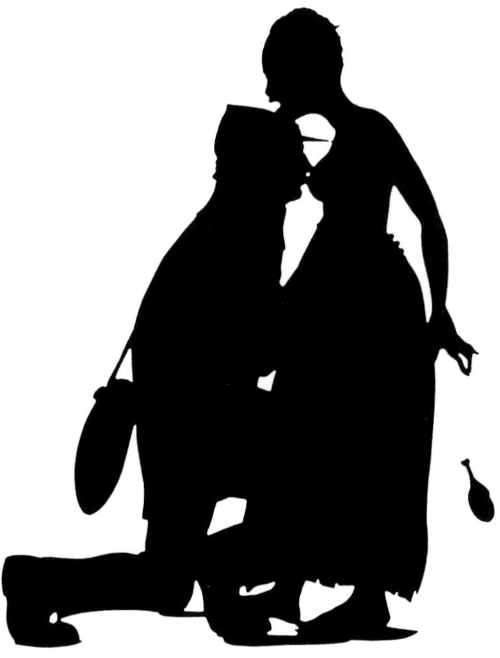

rounding slavery, the social shame surrounding stereotypes, and finally a bodily shame regarding sexual and excretory functions. Walker's characters are all too well aware that to speak of shame is to simultaneously speak of disgust, the overcoming of which is a prerequisite for sexual pleasure. The pursuit of such illicit pleasure under the confines of slavery, however, becomes a rather dubious notion when the economy surrounding slavery is overlapped with that surrounding sex. As Walker's recurring motif of the baby-plopping pickaninny suggests, slavery was a labor force meant to reproduce itself. If sex is theoretically defined as an economy whose poles are reproduction—work or utility—on the one hand, and pleasure—play or surplus—on the other, then slavery would fall into the former category. The tier of breast suckling from THE END OF UNCLE TOM AND THE GRAND ALLEGORICAL TABLEAU OF EVA IN HEAVEN (1995) depicts the transition of sex from reproductive utilitarian ends to an erotic surplus that stands outside the ends of slavery. In short, sexual pleasure becomes the locus of an individual bodily sovereignty, i.e. pleasure as a form of power. But pleasure should not simply be equated with power.

As Michel Foucault would have it, this is "power that lets itself be invaded by the pleasure it is pursuing; and opposite it, power asserting itself in the pleasure of showing off, scandalizing, or resisting. Capture and seduction, confrontation and mutual reinforcement; parents and children, adults and adolescents, educators and students, doctors and patients."[1] And for Walker, this list would include the slave mistress and her conscripted lover. Liberation is not in the form of the plantation rebellion or the runaway slave in search of the Underground Railroad. Instead, it is the naughty tongue of a slave mistress tickling the barrel of a kneeling soldier's rifle, or the chicken drumstick, willfully abandoned in favor of his tender sexual advances.

Needless to say, it is the 250-year history of slavery as it was conducted squarely within our consciousness that makes it possible for Walker to render shameful acts so shamelessly. But Walker's ability to blur the boundaries between forms of shame is the result of race taking on characteristics of the taboo. The more we try to convince ourselves of having overcome race, the more the inarticulable wish for a racial utopia and the Freudian concept of the forbidden wish seem to merge. Race as a category, which the imagination has failed to transcend, becomes a real, yet symbolically charged site of internalized prohibitions. As such race can assume a place in the unconscious alongside prohibitions submerged during childhood, prohibitions that notably involve the mouth, sexual organs, and excretory functions. This would allow Walker the freedom to conjure a Loony Toons ante-bellum where a socially ordained racial hierarchy rather whimsically becomes the mise-en-scène for an infantilized id where lust and avarice are played out as acts of anal sadism and oral aggression. By linking racial stereotypes to infantile, libidinal impulses buried in the unconscious, Walker's vignettes suggest that the construction of stereotypes is part of deeper psychological complexes. Indeed, like the forbidden wish which, albeit for infants, is generated out of situations of anxiety, racism and the inscription of otherness with negative values is a neurosis, a mental projection which Walker has rendered as a psychoanalytic shadow play of blackness without blacks.

Yet in focusing on her use of stereotypes, discussions have obscured the work's larger stakes. Examining the issue of race and its place in the sociopolitical imagination cannot help but double as a critique of the role that African-American history plays in reinforcing rather than resisting the self-congratulatory monologue of liberal democracy's claim to triumph. When it comes to reading African-American history as anything other than a narrative with a beginning, middle, and successful end, doubting Thomases (and let us not forget Clarence) are rare. Read in this manner, African-American history is used as an argument to say that discussions of race, difference and otherness are behind us, as if we had arrived at "the table of humanity" come again as a Benetton ad. If the struggle which African-American history represents is not over, then it is not a question of the extent to which race and utopia are mutually exclusive but the opposite, to what extent race and utopia are inextricably bound.

Although world's apart on their surface, the contrast between Walker's nightmares and Martin Luther King Jr.'s dreams of integration, in which blacks and whites sit as equal partners at the table of humanity, is not as absurd as it would first appear. Walker's work and King's "I Have a Dream" speech are fundamentally about a world in which race and utopia are not mutually exclusive but inextricably linked. It is only through efforts at overcoming categories of difference that we can arrive at profound speculation as to what it means to be human in a broader historical and psychological scope. Whereas King envisioned the efforts of the Civil Rights Movement serving as a catalyst for a one-time social transformation summed up by the expression "We Shall Overcome," Walker's work suggests that race and otherness are libidinally lodged catalysts for perpetual subject transformation. But Walker's decidedly negative critique of subject formation is in no way meant to contradict the aims of social transformation. On the contrary, it is meant to strengthen such objectives by provoking a psychological and visceral vigilance about human nature. "Who Knows What Evil Lurks in the Hearts of Men?" Walker's shadows, no doubt. As it relates to Walker's work and skepticism about overcoming the past and achieving full absolution from the conscious horrors committed by humanity, a most telling passage comes from none other than James Baldwin.

Which of us has overcome his past? And the past of a Negro is blood dripping down through the leaves, gouged out eyeballs, the sex torn from the socket and severed with a knife. But this past is not special to the Negro. The horror is also the past, and the everlasting potential, or temptation, of the human race. If we do not know this, it seems to me, we know nothing about ourselves, nothing about each other; to have accepted this is also to have found a source of strength—source of all our power. But one must first accept this paradox, with joy. [2]

In light of this quote, one could, without reservation, characterize Walker's imagination as joyful. Her work absolves no one from a discussion of race. It is not simply blacks that then bear the onus of speaking up about race, but whites as well, for they are as raced as anyone else. The white wall, the unquestioned arbiter of purity, becomes a stereotype of normalcy against which these discussions play themselves out. If a broader, utopian vision of humanity is in some respect dependent upon categories of difference, constructed and otherwise, then no one

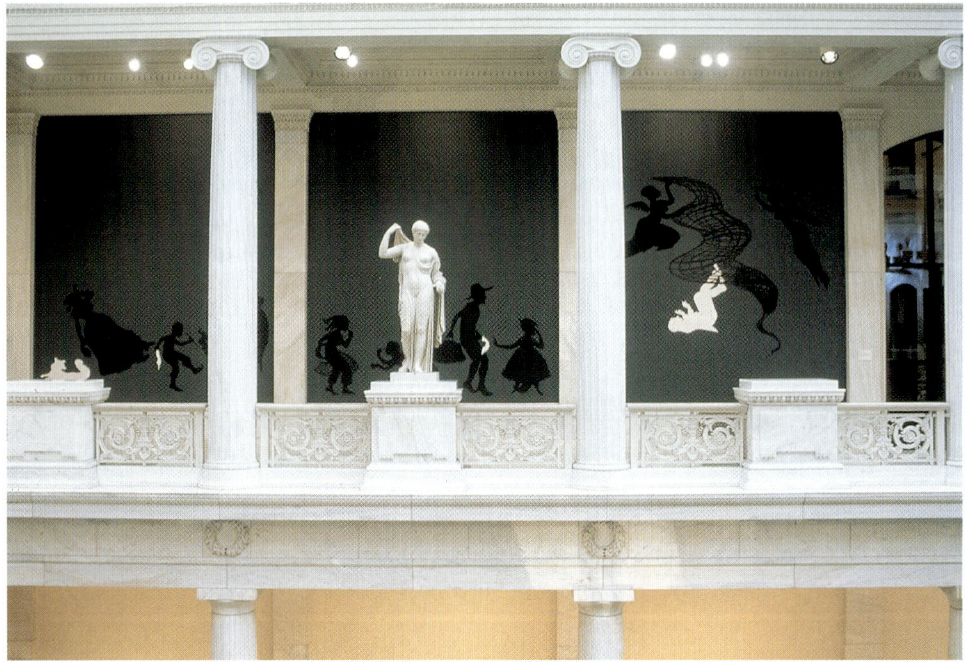

*KARA WALKER, EMANCIPATION APPROXIMATION, 1999, cut paper, adhesive, on wall,
installation details, "1999 Carnegie International," Pittsburgh /
ANNÄHERUNG AN DIE EMANZIPATION, Teilansichten, an der Wand befestigte Scherenschnitte.*

is absolved from a discussion of race. Walker has no choice but to counter the modernist white cube with a radical racial inscription so that white wall, the unquestioned arbiter of purity, is exposed as a stereotype of normalcy against which these discussions have exhausted themselves. Just as the white cube serves as an exalted symbol of clinical objectivity (speaking for all and speaking for no one) Walker's work, in presenting a radically negative critique of humanity, cannot help but alienate its audiences—black, white, Asian, Hispanic, and other. The blank, white wall as it represents the repressive limits of an imagination seeking to transcend race finds its linguistic corollary in "Nigger Lover," an expression featured on a sepia-wash drawing in the shape of a scroll that was included in her 1997 installation at The Renaissance Society.[3] Nigger Lover is in fact the alienated reflection of the words racial utopia. With all of the ambivalence surrounding "lover" and none surrounding "Nigger," the expression is an oxymoron that reinstates the terms of race at their most vulgar, to ask what is or is not being embraced. In this respect, Walker's work shares an affinity with the humor of none other than Richard Pryor, who likewise used the sexually explicit, the psychotic and the vulgar as a means to liberate the presently inescapable terms of race. And like Pryor, t h a t n e g r e s s i s c r a z y !

1) Michel Foucault, *The History of Sexuality: An Introduction*, vol. 1 (Vintage: New York, 1978), p. 45.
2) James Baldwin, *Nobody Knows My Name* (Vintage: New York, 1989), p. 213.
3) This drawing was conspicuously absent from the work's re-installation at The Museum of Contemporary Art, Chicago. It was rumored that black employees of the museum (ironically enough, security guards) demanded that this drawing be removed.

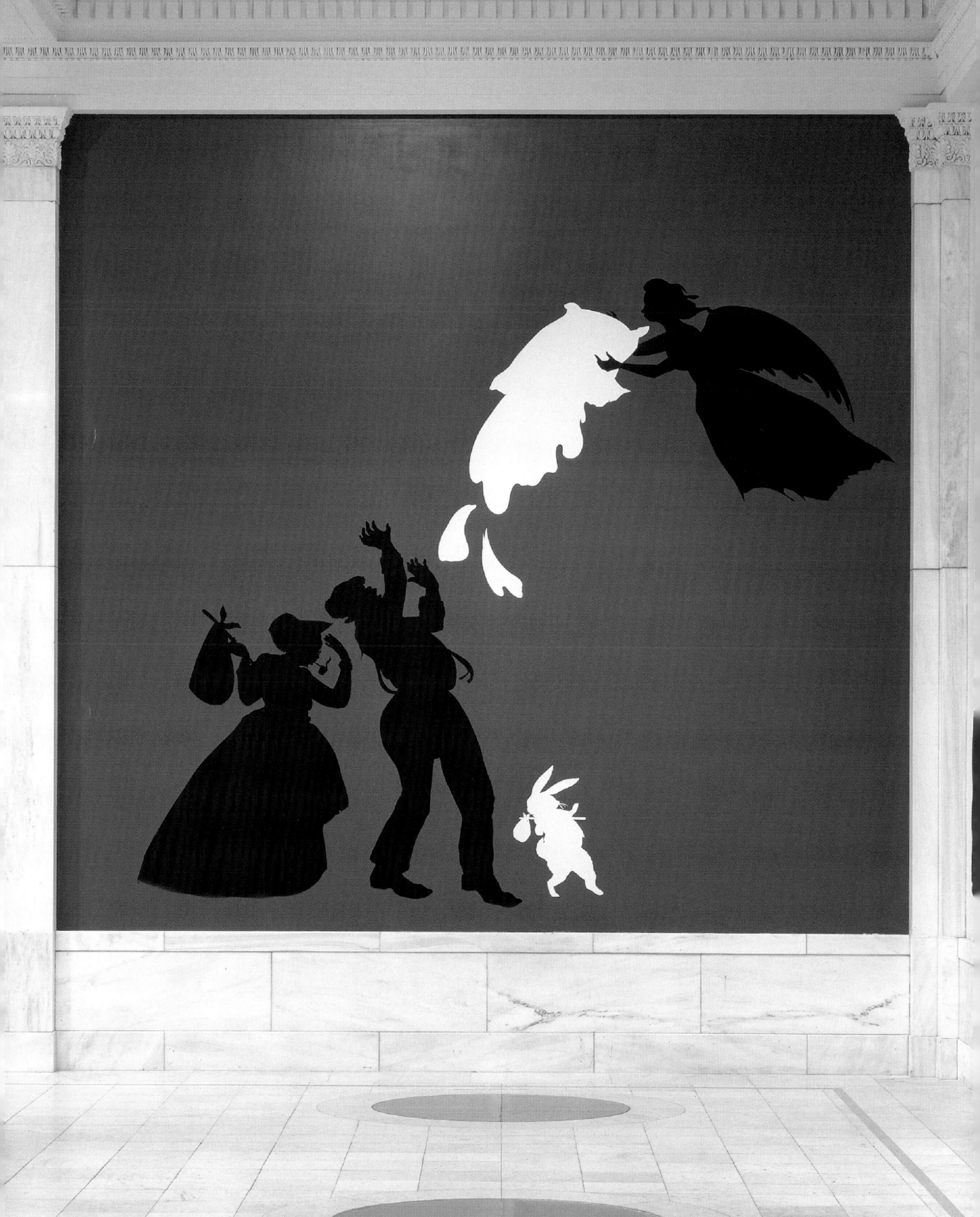

Nigger Lover

HAMZA WALKER

Obwohl Rasse heute allgemein als gesellschaftliches Konstrukt und nicht mehr als natur- oder gottgegeben betrachtet wird, erweist es sich doch als schwieriges Unterfangen, sie als politische und psychologische Realität aus der Welt zu schaffen, schwieriger, als beispielsweise die staatlichen Obdachlosensiedlungen an Chicagos Südufer niederzureissen. Ich frage mich, ob W. E. B. Du Bois,[1] als er mutmasste, dass Rasse das grosse Problem des zwanzigsten Jahrhunderts sein würde, damit rechnete, dass die Grenzen der Hautfarbe auch am Ende des Jahrhunderts noch nicht überwunden sein würden. Welche Rolle spielt die Rassenthematik in unseren Vorstellungen einer besseren Welt? Verschwindet die Kategorie der Rassenzugehörigkeit wenigstens in der fortschrittlichsten Vision der gesellschaftspolitischen Landschaft von der Bildfläche? Oder freier und polemischer gefragt: Wird es in Utopia Schwarze geben?

Ob man den Gedanken an ein Utopia mit oder ohne Rasse fragwürdig findet, hängt davon ab, wessen Phantasie er entspringt. Einerseits scheinen Schwarze, wie ich sie kennen und lieben gelernt habe und von denen ich selbst einer bin, sich in Luft aufzulösen, sobald die Worte «nichtrassistischer Humanismus» fallen. Und andrerseits kann der Entwurf einer Utopie im gegenwärtigen Diskurs zum Thema Rasse, insbesondere nach der Aufgabe der aktiven politischen Selbstbehauptung, nur als defensiv wahrgenommen werden, solange keine realistische Alternative für eine echte Veränderung in Sicht ist. Mit ihrer skeptischen Haltung gegenüber einer humanistischen Sichtweise, in der schwarze Bürger sich ausschliesslich als Schwarze sehen können und in der kein Engagement zum Umsturz der bestehenden Rassenhierarchie zu erkennen ist, steckt unsere Vor-

stellungskraft, was die Rassenfrage angeht, in einer ausweglosen Situation. Wie in einer von Willy Wonka als Reinkarnation von Sun Ra entworfenen Maschine[2] bleiben dem schwarzen Subjekt, das unfähig ist sich eine Zukunft ohne Rasse vorzustellen und den verstörenden Bedingungen der Gegenwart zu entkommen, zwei Möglichkeiten: Er oder sie kann sich entweder als Bürger Saturns deklarieren oder auf eine Ausdrucksform von Rasse zurückgreifen, die der Vergangenheit entstammt.

Kara Walker hat sich rabiat zu Letzterem entschlossen. Ihre Einforderung von Phantasien hat alles zu tun mit der Unfähigkeit, uns überhaupt eine Zukunft ohne Rasse vorzustellen. Wie sehr sich Rasse und Utopie gegenseitig ausschliessen, wird in dem Masse deutlich, wie unsere Vorstellungskraft daran scheitert, eine Welt zu denken, in der die Hautfarbe nicht unweigerlich mit einem bestimmten Platz in der gesellschaftlichen Hierarchie einhergeht. Bemerkenswertes Versagen einer Vorstellungskraft, die immerhin dafür gerühmt wird, dass sie uns in eine neue Weltordnung geführt habe, die allerdings für viele von uns so neu nicht aussieht. Tatsächlich, was gibt es Anachronistischeres als Walkers Rückgriff auf ein derart historisch verstaubtes Darstellungsmittel wie die Porträt-Silhouette, was wiederum zeigt, dass eine neue Idee nicht unbedingt vorwärts gerichtet sein muss. Stattdessen richtet sich Walkers unerbittliche Phantasie auf Rasse im härtesten und im höchsten Grad amerikanischen Sinn, auf das Schwarz und Weiss der amerikanischen Südstaaten vor dem Bürgerkrieg, eine Zeit, die noch gar nicht so lange zurückliegt in der Galaxie namens Hier und Jetzt.

HAMZA WALKER ist «Director of Education» der Renaissance Society der Universität von Chicago.

oder: Wird es in Utopia Schwarze geben?

Genau wie ich ist auch Walker ein Kind aus der Zeit nach der Bürgerrechtsbewegung. Ich vermute, dass auch sie widersprüchlichen Signalen ausgesetzt war, als ob die Widersprüche, die dem Begriff einer Utopie, die Rasse mit einschliesst, anhaften, dadurch gelöst würden, dass man sich im Fernsehen ein Epos wie *Roots* anschaut. Im einen Ohr wird ihr die laue Rhetorik einer farbenblinden Gesellschaft geklungen haben und im anderen die abflauenden schwarznationalistischen Töne von der militanten bis zur Mittelklasse-Variante. Anderthalb Jahrzehnte nach *Roots* jedoch steht Walkers Arbeit in krassem Kontrast zu dem relativ blutleeren Dialog, dessen letztes müdes Aufflackern die Form kollektiver Phantasien angenommen hat, die sich von jener einer afrozentrischen, hoffnungslos bürgerlichen Ordnung über die liberale «Frag nicht, sag nichts»-Phantasie bis zur erzkonservativen Vorstellung erstrecken, dass Rasse etwas Privates sei, was man wie Religion zuhause praktiziert. In jedem Fall festigt das Beharren auf dem Rassebegriff und dessen gleichzeitige Entpolitisierung den Status quo und ist bezeichnend für unsere Unfähigkeit das eigentliche Thema, nämlich das der Klassengesellschaft, anzusprechen. Daraus ergibt sich eine ungeheure Ambivalenz gegenüber der Frage, w i e, gar nicht zu reden von o b überhaupt, wir die Kategorie der Rasse überwinden sollen oder wollen. Zu behaupten, Walkers Arbeit entfalte ihre lebendige Wirkung erst vor dem Hintergrund unseres gesunden Wunsches zur Überwindung der Rassenthematik, ist eine Irreführung. Walkers Installationen beissen sich genau in jenem blinden Fleck unserer Vorstellungskraft fest, der

durch die Abwesenheit dieses gesunden Wunsches entstanden ist. Genauso, wie wir unfähig sind, uns eine Farbe vorzustellen, die wir nie gesehen haben, oder als Zugehöriger einer Rasse, unfähig, ohne Farbe zu sehen, kann unser Bewusstsein auch diesen gesunden Wunsch, den Rassebegriff zu überwinden, nicht formulieren. Unter diesen Umständen erweist sich unser so genannter Wunsch nach einer die Rassenfrage berücksichtigenden Utopie eher als Mechanismus zur Unterdrückung dessen, was er eigentlich überwinden wollte. Demzufolge lauert hinter unseren Vorstellungen einer Menschheit ohne Farben ein schwarzweisser Manichäismus, in dem das Stereotyp prächtige Blüten treibt.

Aber wenn Walkers Gegner ihre Verwendung von Stereotypen kritisieren, was meinen sie genau mit Verwendung? Niederknüppeln, Menschenfressen, Scheissen und Essen sind selbst für Mammies, Pickaninnies, Sambos, Belles, Dandies und weisse Kriegsgewinnler aus dem Norden extreme Tätigkeiten. Auch ist die übliche grinsende Nigger-Grimasse ganz verschwunden, denn das Begehren von Walkers Figuren hat Formen angenommen, die nach ganz anderem Fleisch dürsten als nach dem von Wassermelonen. In ihrem lebhaften Eifer verkünden sie stolz, dass sie alle Tabus überwunden haben, ähnlich wie etwa Jeffrey Dahmer. Lecken, Saugen, Verzehren. Aufstacheln, Stochern, Durchstechen. Scheissen, Ficken, Niederknüppeln. Die Handelnden in Walkers schrägen Szenen à la Sade kümmern sich keinen Deut um unsere Gegenwart, geschweige denn um unsere Billigung ihrer Handlungen, die von Bestialität bis Pädophilie, von schockierend offener

Sexualität bis zur unverblümt polymorphen Perversität reichen. Kurz, wir sind ein Publikum, um das sich ihre Karikaturen, wirklich, meine liebe Scarlett, den Teufel scheren. Ohne jeden Realitätsbezug treiben sie ihr fröhliches Arsch- und Mösenlecken, als wären sie total unbeachtet und vergessen, will sagen verdrängt.

Kara Walkers künstlerischem Rückblick zufolge hätte Freud die Sklaverei mit gleichem Recht pervers nennen können, wie Frederick Law Olmsted[3] sie merkwürdig genannt hat. Walkers Vision ist eine verdrehte Dreifaltigkeit von Rasse, Geschichte und Begehren, die, wenn sie überhaupt eine Interpretation erlaubt, dann eine von solch surrealer und psychologischer Tiefe, dass ihr eher die Bezeichnung Diagnose gebührte. Das passt natürlich zur formalen Ähnlichkeit ihrer Arbeiten mit dem Rorschachtest. Wenn Walkers Werk von etwas handelt, dann von der Scham oder dem Mangel an Scham. In der Tat ist ihr Werk dreifach schamlos, indem es das historische Schamgefühl, das die Sklaverei umgibt, verletzt, aber auch das gesellschaftliche Schamgefühl in Bezug auf das Stereotype und schliesslich die körperliche Scham rund um Sexualität und Körperausscheidungen. Walkers Figuren wissen alle nur zu gut, dass von Scham zu sprechen immer auch heisst von Ekel zu reden, dessen Überwindung wiederum Vorbedingung des sexuellen Genusses ist. Das Verfolgen solch verbotener Freuden im Rahmen der Sklaverei wird jedoch zur dubiosen Angelegenheit, wenn die Machtverhältnisse, die in der Sklaverei spielen, sich mit denen der Sexualität überlagern. Wie Walkers wiederkehrendes Motiv des gebärenden Negermädchens nahe legt, war die Sklaverei als unerschöpfliche Quelle sich selbst reproduzierender Arbeitskräfte gedacht. Definiert man Sexualität als ökonomisches System, dessen Pole Reproduktion – Arbeit oder Nützlichkeit – auf der einen und Lust – Spiel oder Zugabe – auf der andern Seite sind, so gehört die Sklaverei in die erste Kategorie. Die Abfolge des Brustsaugens in THE END OF UNCLE TOM AND THE GRAND ALLEGORICAL TABLEAU OF EVA IN HEAVEN (Das Ende von Onkel Tom und das grosse allegorische Bild von Eva im Himmel, 1995) zeigt den Übergang der Sexualität von utilitaristischen Fortpflanzungszwecken zum erotischen Extra jenseits der Ziele der Sklaverei. Kurz, der sexuelle Genuss steht für die individuelle körperliche Souveränität, das heisst, Genuss ist eine Form von Macht. Aber Genuss sollte nicht einfach mit Macht gleich gesetzt werden. Laut Michel Foucault ist das eine «Macht, die sich von der Lust, der sie nachstellt, überwältigen lässt; und ihr gegenüber (ist) eine Macht, die ihre Bestätigung in der Lust, sich zu zeigen, einen Skandal auszulösen oder Widerstand zu leisten, findet. Erschleichung und Verführung, Konfrontation und gegenseitige Verstärkung: seit dem 19. Jahrhundert haben Eltern und Kinder, Erwachsene und Jugendliche, Erzieher und Schüler, Ärzte und Kranke, der Psychiater mit seiner Hysterischen und seinen Perversen nicht aufgehört, dieses Spiel zu spielen.»[4] Bei Walker würde diese Liste auch die Herrin und den zu Liebesdiensten befohlenen Sklaven enthalten. Die Befreiung findet nicht in der Form des Plantagenaufstandes statt und in Gestalt des entflohenen Sklaven auf der Suche nach dem schützenden Bahntunnel. Nein, es ist die ungezogene Zunge der weissen Herrin, die den Gewehrlauf eines knienden Soldaten leckt, oder das zugunsten sexueller Zärtlichkeiten fallen gelassene Hühnerbein.

Natürlich ist es die in unserem Bewusstsein eingegrabene Schande von 250 Jahren Sklaverei, die es Walker erlaubt schändliche Taten so schamlos wiederzugeben. Aber dass Walker derart die Grenzen zwischen den verschiedenen Arten von Scham verwischen kann, verdankt sie der Tatsache, dass Rasse selbst zum Tabu geworden ist. Je heftiger wir uns einreden, den Rassenbegriff überwunden zu haben, desto mehr scheint sich der unartikulierbare Wunsch nach einer Utopie, in der das Rassenproblem gelöst ist, mit dem Freudschen Begriff des verbotenen Begehrens zu vermischen. Die Rasse als Kategorie, die wir im Denken nicht zu transzendieren vermochten, wird zum realen, aber symbolträchtigen Ort eines verinnerlichten Verbots. Damit kann Rassezugehörigkeit sich im Unterbewussten neben anderen, insbesondere den oralen, sexuellen und analen Verboten der Kindheit festsetzen. Daher steht Walker die Freiheit zu, ein verrücktes Vorbürgerkriegs-Szenario heraufzubeschwören, in der die gesellschaftlich verordnete Rassenhierarchie zur lau-

nigen Inszenierung eines infantilen Es wird, in der
Lust und Geiz sich in Form anal-sadistischer Akte
und oraler Aggressionen austoben. Indem sie Ras-
sensterotype mit infantilen, im Unterbewussten
verborgenen Trieben verknüpfen, deuten Walkers
Vignetten an, dass die Bildung von Stereotypen
einen tieferen psychologischen Grund hat. Und tatsächlich, genau wie das verbotene Begehren, jedenfalls bei Kindern, aus Angstsituationen entsteht, ist
auch der Rassismus und die negative Wertung des
Andersseins eine Neurose, eine Projektion, die Walker als schwarzes psychoanalytisches Schattenspiel
ohne Schwarze wiedergibt.

Aber die Konzentration der Diskussion auf Walkers Verwendung von Stereotypen verstellt den Blick
auf wichtigere Aspekte ihrer Arbeit. Die Über-
prüfung der Rassenthematik und ihrer Bedeutung
für die gesellschaftspolitischen Vorstellungen läuft
notwendig auf eine Kritik an der Rolle der afroamerikanischen Geschichte hinaus, die dem selbst-
zufriedenen Monolog einer liberaldemokratischen
Siegesgewissheit eher noch in die Hände spielt, statt
ihm zu widerstehen. Sobald es darum geht, die afroamerikanische Geschichte nicht in Form einer Erzählung mit Anfang, Mitte und erfolgreichem Ende
zu predigen, so findet sich kaum ein ungläubiger
Thomas (nicht zu vergessen Clarence[5]), der einen
unterstützen würde. So erzählt, wird die afroamerikanische Geschichte zum Beweis für die Behauptung, dass die Diskussionen um Rasse, Verschiedenheit und Anderssein hinter uns liegen, als hätten wir
alle wie in der Benetton-Werbung bereits am Tisch
der Menschheit Platz genommen. Wenn der Kampf,
für den die afroamerikanische Geschichte steht,
noch nicht zu Ende ist, so hat das weniger damit zu
tun, wie sehr sich Rasse und Utopie gegenseitig
ausschliessen, sondern im Gegenteil damit, wie
unauflöslich Rasse und Utopie miteinander verstrickt sind.

Auch wenn oberflächlich betrachtet Welten zwischen ihnen liegen, so ist ein Vergleich von Walkers
Alptraum und Martin Luther Kings Traum von der
Integration, in dem Schwarz und Weiss als gleichbe-
rechtigte Partner am Tisch der Menschheit sitzen,
weniger absurd, als es zunächst scheinen mag.
Walkers Werk und Kings «I Have A Dream»-Rede

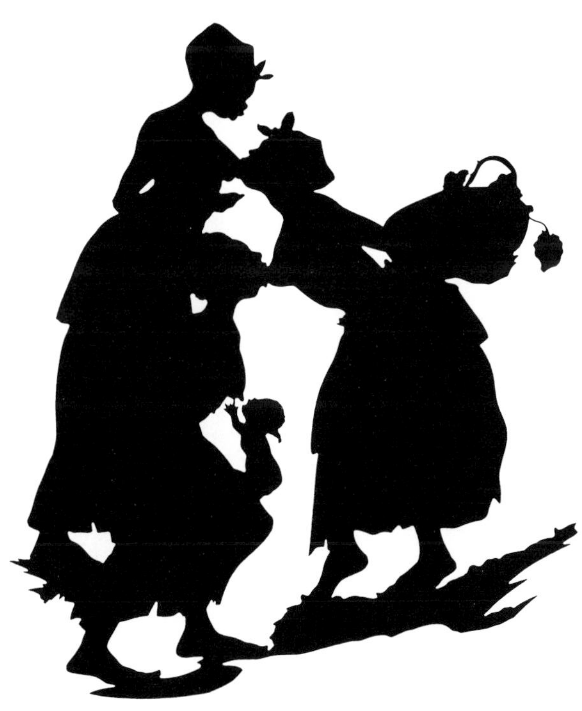

handeln beide von einer Welt, in der Rasse und Utopie einander nicht ausschliessen, sondern untrenn-
bar miteinander verbunden sind. Nur wenn wir uns
darum bemühen, diese Kategorien der Unterscheidung zu überwinden, können wir in einem tieferen,
geschichtlichen und psychologischen Sinn beginnen
zu verstehen, was es heisst, ein Mensch zu sein. King
verstand die Bürgerrechtsbewegung als Katalysator
einer einmaligen gesellschaftlichen Umwälzung, wie
das im Lied «We Shall Overcome (Wir werden sie-
gen)» zum Ausdruck kam. Dagegen legen Walkers
Arbeiten nahe, dass Rasse und Anderssein trieb-
gebundene Katalysatoren für einen andauernden
Wandlungsprozess des Subjekts sind. Aber Walkers

eindeutig negative Bewertung der Subjektwerdung richtet sich nicht gegen das Ziel der gesellschaftlichen Veränderung. Im Gegenteil, sie unterstützt dieses Bestreben, indem sie zu einer psychologischen und instinktiven Wachsamkeit gegenüber der menschlichen Natur aufruft. «Wer weiss, welche Bosheit in menschlichen Herzen schlummert?» Walkers Schattenrisse, so viel ist gewiss. Im Zusammenhang mit der in ihrem Werk zum Ausdruck kommenden Skepsis gegenüber einer erfolgreichen Vergangenheitsbewältigung und der vollständigen Erlösung von den Schandtaten, die Menschen an Menschen verübten, gibt es eine erhellende Passage bei keinem Geringeren als James Baldwin:

Wer von uns hat seine Vergangenheit überwunden? Und die Vergangenheit eines Schwarzen ist Blut, das durchs Laub heruntertropft, aus den Höhlen gestossene Augen, herausgerissene und mit dem Messer abgetrennte Geschlechtsteile. Aber diese Vergangenheit ist nicht dem Schwarzen vorbehalten. Das Erschreckende ist auch die Vergangenheit und die ewig weiter bestehende Möglichkeit oder Versuchung der menschlichen Rasse. Wenn wir das nicht wissen, glaube ich, wissen wir nichts von uns selbst und nichts voneinander; dies akzeptiert zu haben heisst aber auch eine Quelle der Kraft entdeckt zu haben – die Quelle all unserer Macht. Aber zuerst muss man dieses Paradox freudig akzeptieren. [6]

Im Lichte dieses Zitats könnte man Walkers Phantasie vorbehaltlos als eine freudige bezeichnen. Ihre Arbeit erspart niemandem die Diskussion der Rassenfrage. Es sind auch nicht nur die Schwarzen, denen die Last zufällt über Rasse zu sprechen, sondern die Weissen genauso, denn sie sind eine Rasse wie alle anderen auch. Die weisse Wand, als nicht weiter hinterfragtes Kriterium der Reinheit, wird zum Stereotyp der Normalität, auf dessen Hintergrund diese Debatten stattfinden. Wenn eine breitere utopische Vision der Menschheit zum Teil von (konstruierten und anderen) Kategorien der Unterscheidung abhängt, so bleibt niemandem die Diskussion der Rassenfrage erspart. Also hat Walker keine andere Wahl, als dem modernen weissen Kubus eine radikale rassisch bestimmte Inschrift entgegenzusetzen, so dass die weisse Wand als Stereotyp einer Normalität entlarvt wird, auf deren Hintergrund sich diese Diskussion erschöpft hat. So, wie der weisse Kubus

als übersteigertes Symbol einer sterilen Objektivität dient (für alle sprechend und für keinen), kann Walkers Arbeit mit ihrem radikal negativen Menschenbild gar nicht anders, als ihr Publikum zu befremden, egal ob es schwarz, weiss, asiatisch, hispanisch oder sonst was ist. Die blanke weisse Wand, die für die repressiven Grenzen einer Vorstellungskraft steht, die versucht den Rassenbegriff zu transzendieren, findet ihre sprachliche Krönung im Ausdruck «Nigger Lover» in der Sepia-Zeichnung einer Schriftrolle, die mit zur 1997 in der Renaissance Society gezeigten Installation gehörte.[7] In «Nigger Lover» klingt in verzerrter Form der Ausdruck «Rassen-Utopie» an. Es ist – mit der ganzen Ambivalenz, die in «Lover» mitschwingt, und der nicht vorhandenen Ambivalenz in «Nigger» – ein Oxymoron, das die vulgärste Benennung der Rasse wieder aufnimmt, um zu prüfen, was genau hier alles mitspielt. Walker gerät damit in die Nähe des Humors eines Richard Pryor, der ebenfalls das unverblümt Sexuelle, das Psychotische und Vulgäre zur Freisetzung des gegenwärtig unvermeidlichen Rassenbegriffs benutzte. Und genau wie Pryor: d i e s e N e g e r i n i s t v e r r ü c k t !   *(Übersetzung: Susanne Schmidt)*

1) William Edward Burghardt Du Bois, 1868–1963, amerikanischer Bürgerrechtskämpfer, der sich für die Rechte der schwarzen Amerikaner und Afrikaner einsetzte.
2) Willy Wonka ist der Protagonist einer Kinderbuchserie von Roald Dahl, *Charlie and the Chocolate Factory* und *Charlie and the Great Class Elevator*. Wonka ist eine Art verrückter und bösartiger «Candyman», der den Kindern, die alle zu viel Süsses naschen und dafür jedes auf seine Weise büssen müssen, Lektionen erteilt. 1971 entstand auch ein Film mit dem Titel *Charlie and the Chocolate Factory*. Sun Ra war ein bedeutender schwarzer Jazzmusiker (1914–1993), der von sich sagte, er stamme von Saturn und habe grünes Blut. Mit seinem Orchester trat er unter dem Namen Sun Ra & The Arkestra auf.
3) Frederick Law Olmsted, 1822–1903, amerikanischer Landschaftsarchitekt und Chefdesigner des Central Park in New York.
4) Michel Foucault, *Sexualität und Wahrheit, Bd. 1, Der Wille zum Wissen*, Suhrkamp, Frankfurt am Main 1983, S. 61.
5) Anspielung auf Bundesrichter Clarence Thomas, das einzige schwarze Mitglied des amerikanischen Bundesgerichtshofs (1991 von George Bush nominiert).
6) James Baldwin, *Nobody Knows My Name*, Vintage Books, New York 1989, S. 213 (Übers. durch die Red.).
7) Diese Zeichnung fehlte bezeichnenderweise in der späteren Ausstellung im Museum of Contemporary Art in Chicago. Man munkelte, dass schwarze Angestellte des Museums (und zwar ausgerechnet die für die Sicherheit zuständigen Wärter) ihre Entfernung verlangt hatten.

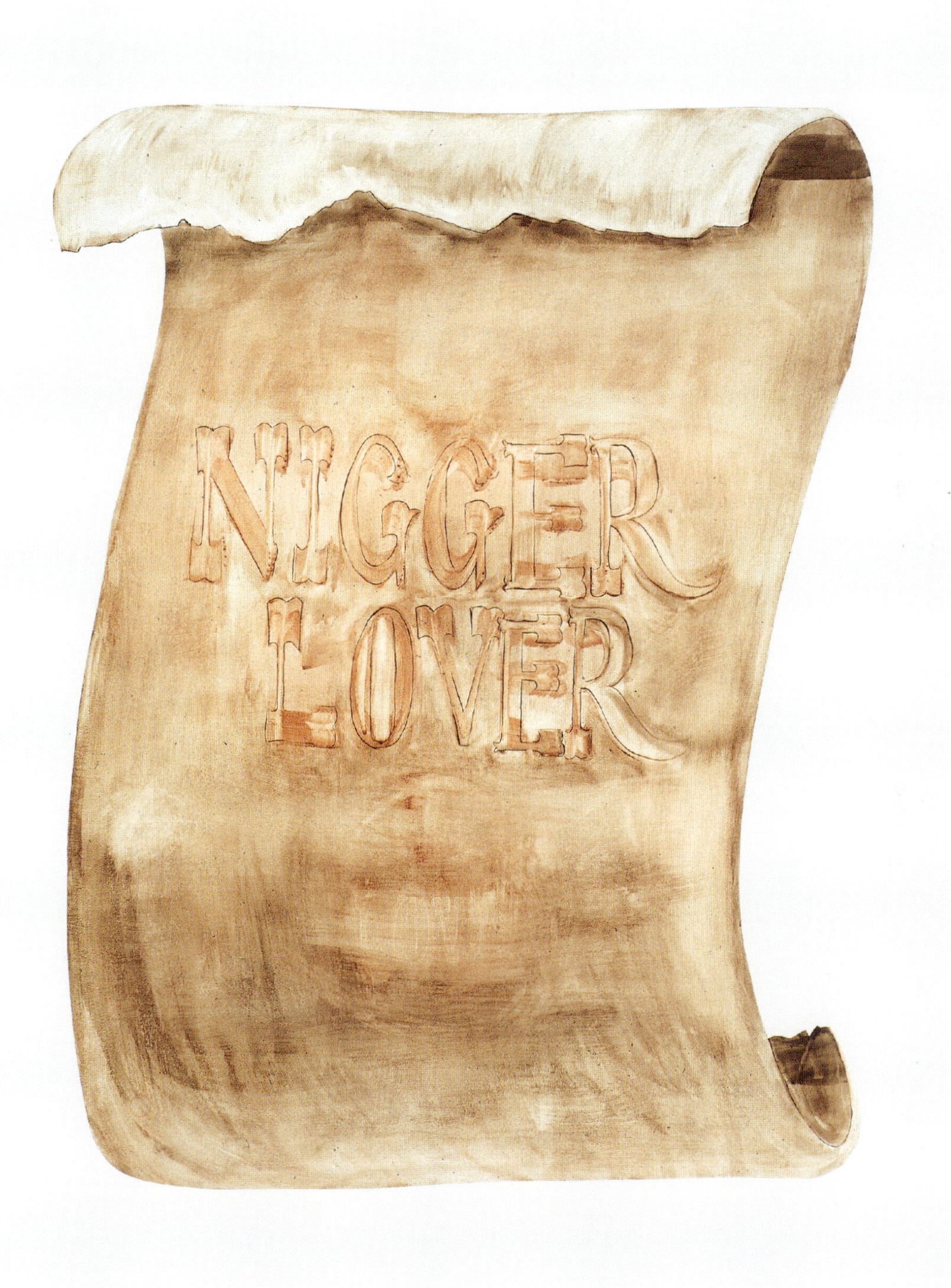

KARA WALKER, PRESENTING NEGRO SCENES UPON MY PASSAGE THROUGH THE SOUTH AND RECONFIGURED FOR THE BENEFIT OF ENLIGHTENED AUDIENCES WHEREVER SUCH MAY BE FOUND BY MYSELF, MISSUS K. E. B. WALKER, COLORED, *detail from the 1997 installation at The Renaissance Society, Chicago /* DARSTELLUNG VON NEGERSZENEN AUF MEINER REISE DURCH DEN SÜDEN, NACHGESTELLT ZUM WOHLE EINES AUFGEKLÄRTEN PUBLIKUMS, WO IMMER EIN SOLCHES VON MIR SELBST, DER FARBIGEN MISSUS K. E. B. WALKER, AUFGESPÜRT WERDEN MAG, *Teil der Installation in der Renaissance Society, Chicago, 1997.*

Edition for Parkett **Kara Walker**
Boo-hoo, 2000
Linocut on Arches Cover White, 40 x 20$^{1}/_{2}$".
Printed by Maurice Sanchez, Derrière L'Etoile Studio,
New York.
Edition of 70, signed and numbered.

Linolschnitt auf Arches Cover White, 101,6 x 52,1 cm.
Gedruckt bei Maurice Sanchez, Derrière L'Etoile
Studio, New York.
Auflage: 70, signiert und nummeriert.

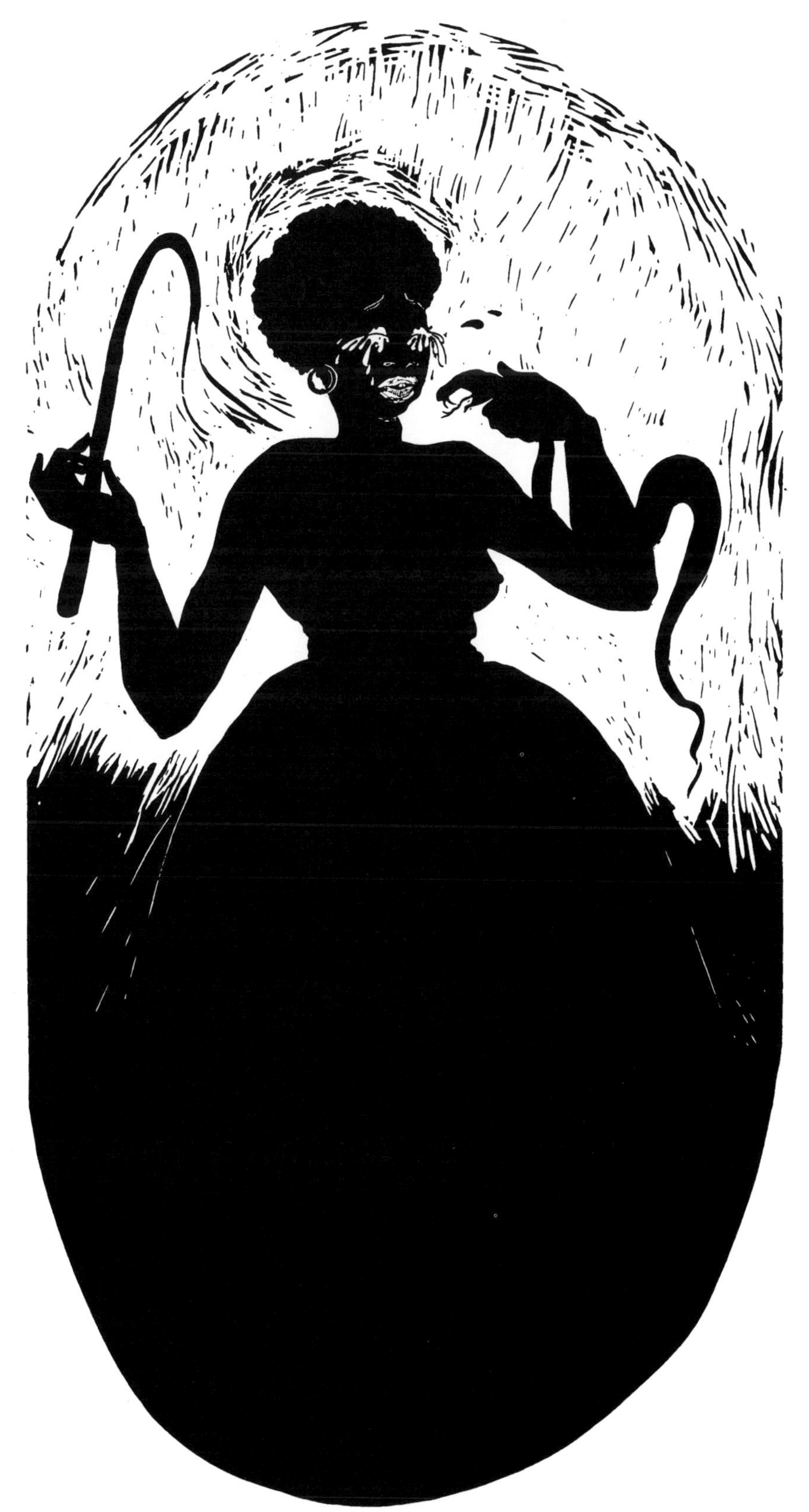

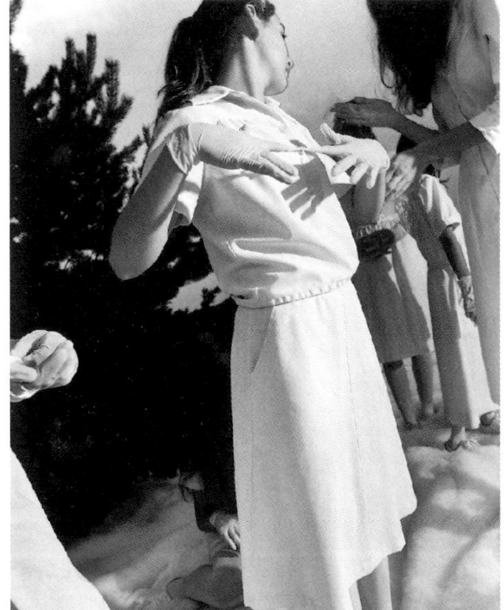

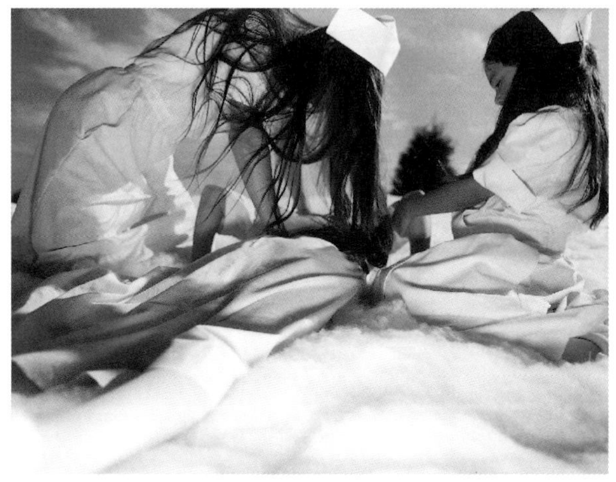

Anna Gaskell's

JAN AVGIKOS

Girl Art

Virginal purity. That's where everything begins in Anna Gaskell's pictures. The first thing you see, the thing you can't take your eyes off, the thing that's right there and real, is the girls in the photographs who are all so peerlessly young, innocent-looking, beautiful and, well, take-your-breath-away kind of naturally gorgeous.

One might argue that all young girls are beautiful, but there's no denying that Gaskell's girls qualify as "model perfect." With that recognition comes association with a legion of other "perfect little girls" that we encounter every day, everywhere we go: the ones who pose professionally for the cameras, the ones who appear in movies and magazines, and ads and art, the ones who are digitized and photo-shopped to be anything we want them to be, the ones who belong to, indeed personify, the visually perfect worlds that teem within commercial image culture—to which, of course, we never truly belong but with which we nevertheless identify.

In addition to dramatic camera angles and lighting, a sense of deliberate artificiality informs Gaskell's imagery. She provokes an association with media-manufactured utopias in the high production values of her photographs. The photographs are flawless. The girls are flawless. "Virginal purity" verges on becoming a veritable thematic vortex; and yet, for all the innocence and perfection, there's

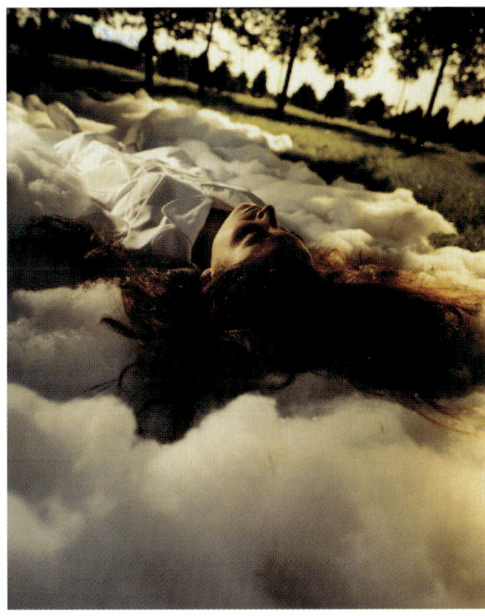

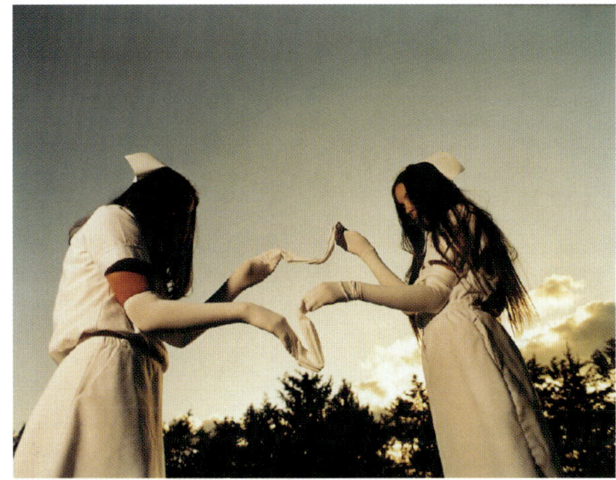

equal emphasis on forms of foul play. Not one, not two, but multiple means of mischief are inventoried by Gaskell from stories she selects and invents from variously sampled fragments, with an eye toward a young heroine who assumes the burden of responsibility for the narrative, or point of view. Stories, such as Lewis Carroll's *Alice in Wonderland*, are radically edited and restructured, linear elements are distilled into clusters of events (drowning, falling down, jumping) and theatrical devices that are repeated within series and overlap from one series to the next. Gaskell, for example, is obsessed with the trappings of innocence—white stockings, Victorian night-gowns, and pinafores which also have their place in the world as fetish gear.

JAN AVGIKOS is an art historian and critic who lives in New York. She is a recipient of the Frank Jewett Mather award from the College Art Association, for distinction in art criticism, and she is a member of the faculty of the School of Visual Art and Columbia University.

The character "Alice" migrates from the *Wonder Series* (1996), where she appears as identical twins, into *Override* (1997), where she merges with a gang of girls, all dressed alike, who are on their own, out in the middle of nowhere and, as it turns out, decidedly up to no good. They push and shove and pull each other's hair, yet despite their unruly behavior, they appear to be highly organized—way more than one would ever expect "real" kids to be. What's real in this instance is the resemblance of Gaskell's images to contemporary fashion photography (where any and all dramatic scenarios "make sense"). What's real is our ability to see these young women as witches, aliens, and warrior princesses (or whatever familiar characters one prefers) at the same time that we see them as unhappy but more or less "regular" little campers, in addition to whomever they might be in real life—model, friend of the family, so and so's daughter. And so it goes, spiraling in complexity. Girls, who are themselves, and lots of other things in addition to that, at the same time that they are not at all what they seem to be. Whether it's "Alice" or "Sally Salt" (another of Gaskell's girl guides into fantasy and the unknown) the same logic applies: This girl is not this girl—which is pretty damn close to "This is not a pipe." What's real, furthermore, is the ever-aggressive presence of the camera, continuously shaping our perception of the girls by means of framing, cropping, hovering, invading, and spying. First

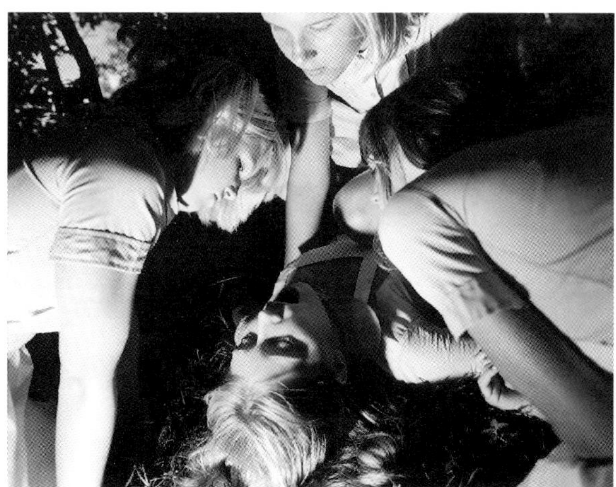

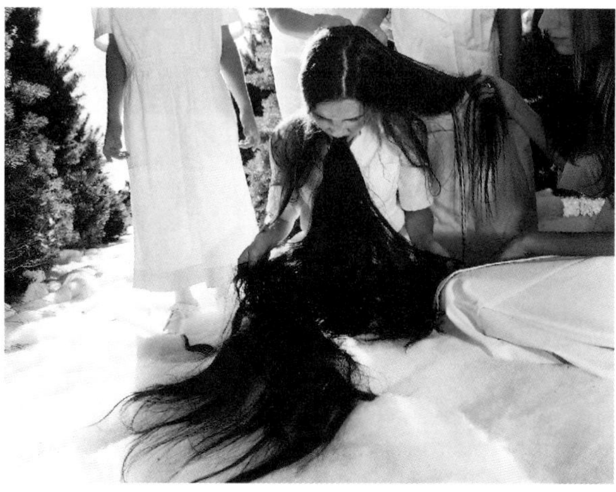

and foremost they are rendered as photographic subjects to be apprehended, captured, and possessed. We never see the girls as themselves but rather, we only see them as a character within a character within a character.

The "pretend evil" Gaskell conjures and its easy interchangeability with everyday life streams straight from the movies and television—*Children of the Corn* and *The Bad Seed* come to mind immediately as potential sources. Both are movies in which children are rendered autonomous, more powerful than adults are, and able to act out against the adult world, perhaps to the point of eliminating it. Whether it's aliens or demon children, or just mean-tempered, bratty little sophisticates one sees in *Override*, or simply beautiful models posing as instructed, the posse of girls dressed up in nurse's uniforms in *By Proxy* (1999) are no less puzzling. They are a somewhat formidable bunch, both in number and in the purposefulness of their ritualistic activities. Are they student nurses? Are they just dressed up to look like nurses? We might not have a clue as to the skeletal narrative of the series, but the girls look as though they know exactly what they're doing—individually and collectively—in the bizarre "natural" setting they inhabit. As a result of their pronounced intent, their so-called "innocence" seems merely to function as a costume accessory.

In contrast to the invincibility that Gaskell's girls project in *Override* and *By Proxy*, their vulnerability is palpable in the highly theatrical series, *Hide* (1998). A splendid, baronial-style mansion is the perfect (albeit visually clichéd) gothic setting for bloody scenes and strange couplings of indeterminate meaning. We peer over a banister and discover "her" lying on top of "the other," both as still as death. There are only two characters, enacted by different pairs of girls (which is to say that no more than two girls appear in the frame at any one time). We spy "her" lying on the floor, looking up under "the other's" nightgown. "She" shows her hand, wet, beside a pool of (could it be?) bloody liquid. "She" holds her hand over the mouth of "the other," perhaps to stifle a scream.

Despite the suggestion of a fictional narrative— the sort that might begin with "It was a dark and stormy night..." or perhaps a social theory of gender and identity, Gaskell never presents clearly plotted characters or story lines, much less specific messages; and yet, there are many recognizable moments in these photographs despite the fact that nothing seems to qualify as personal.

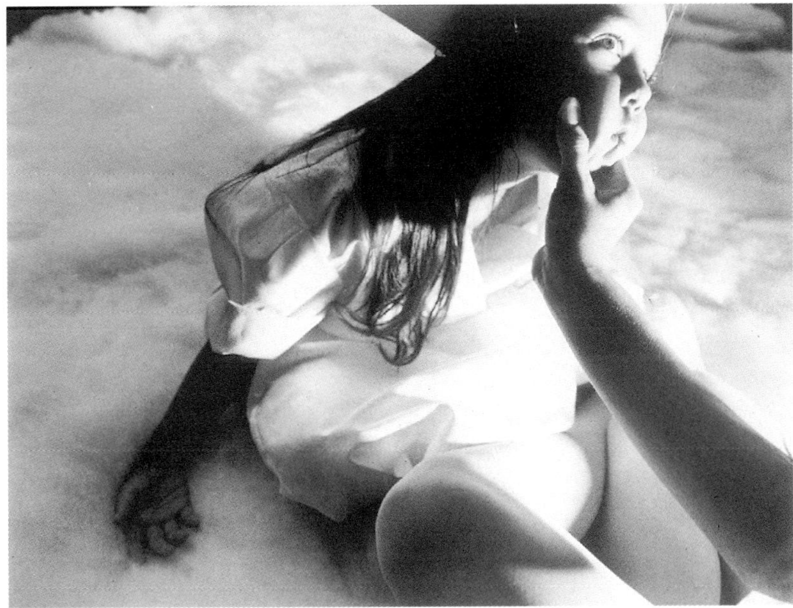

Gaskell's pictures are tightly wound, dramatic vignettes; the elements are culled from art and probably everywhere else, too. We can think about Cindy Sherman and Gregory Crewdson (her teacher at Yale) for openers, but there's also room for random associations with *The X-Files*, low-budget Hollywood thrillers, and feminist theory, all sandwiched together and managed by heavily self-conscious framing and cropping techniques that contribute substantially to the sense of restless tension and a prescribed lack of resolution that is the critical function of her photographs. Intimations of surveillance, the faintest suggestion that the world comes into and goes out of focus in random fashion, lends drama to the sense of misadventure and foreboding that rims the worlds in which we encounter Gaskell's girls.

The artist may set out ostensibly to knit together story fragments that feature girl narrators as a means of instrumentalizing or empowering a female voice, a young woman's voice at that, but do we really ever see the world from the perspective of a young girl, whether she be a heroine or not? Given the intense and exaggerated visual properties of the images, I'm not so sure Gaskell's kind of "girl power" has got much to do, directly or even indirectly, with twelve-year-olds. It's much easier to locate ourselves; after all, these pictures are all about us. We viewers are cast, like it or not, as voyeurs. We're seduced, first, by the virginal beauty of the girls themselves; then, by the quality of the images and the fashionable look they possess; and then, again, by the suggestion of forms of visual pleasure that are mildly freighted with illicit contents.

These pictures are not a paean to the glories of girlhood but rather to adult fantasy. There's low-level eroticism, but nothing more than one would expect, given the subjects and the cultural tendencies we share (and fend off) to eroticize youth. But there's something more, and it concerns the pronounced tendency toward bombast (another cultural standard). To look dangerous as a means to be recognized; to stand out in a crowd as a means of fitting in. To flaunt artistic license and excess as a step toward the achievement of a common visual language. To manufacture a look that is as familiar as it is new, a look that communicates long before the plodding work of slower forms of conventional narrative kick in. It's the look of Gaskell's photographs, rather than the stories that they tell, that is highly theatrical and happily impersonal, and yet photographic tropes of intimacy abound.

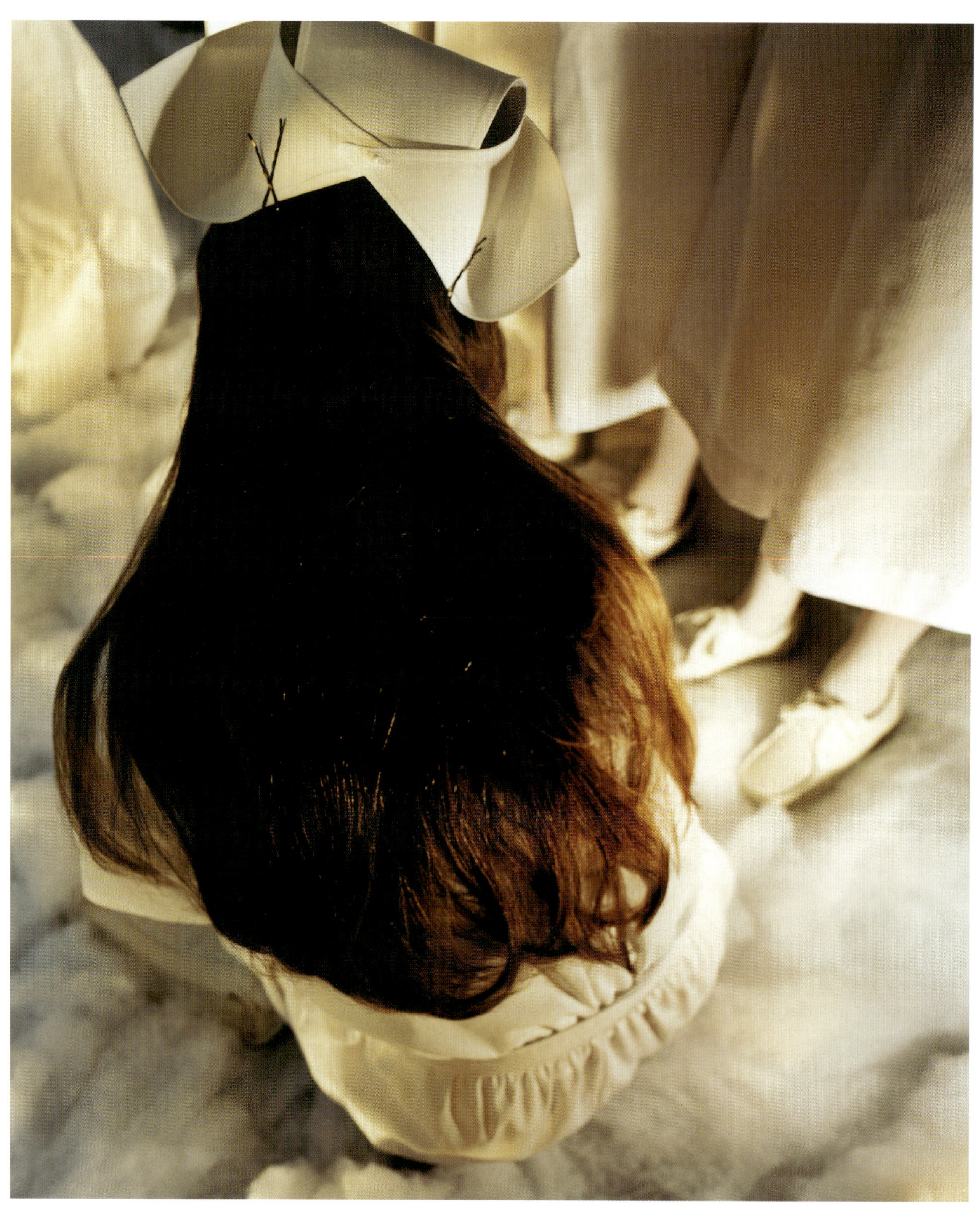

ANNA GASKELL, UNTITLED NO. 59 (BY PROXY), 1999, c-print, 40 x 30" /
OHNE TITEL NR. 59 (STELLVERTRETEND), C-Print, 101,6 x 76,2 cm.

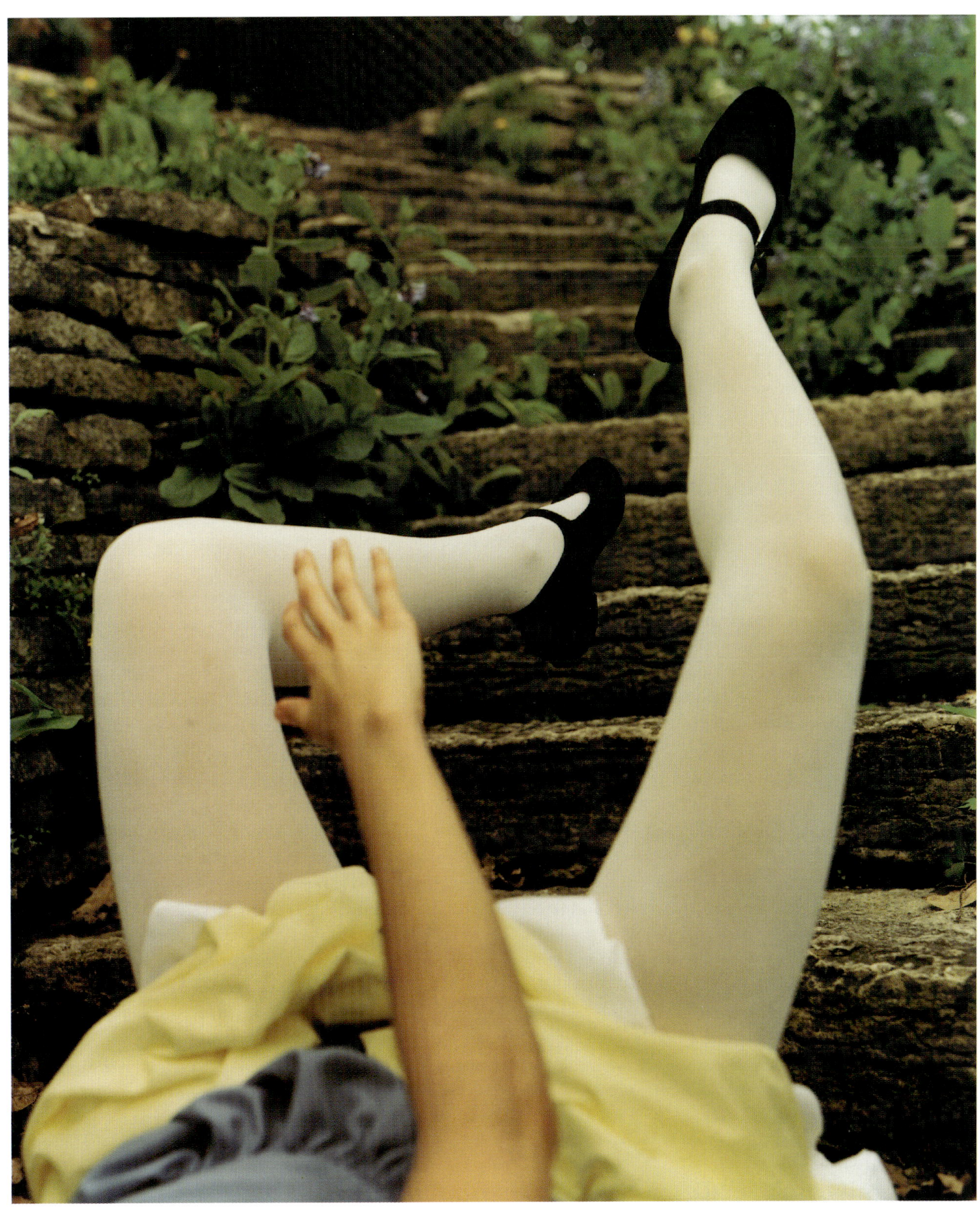

ANNA GASKELL, *UNTITLED NO. 3 (WONDER), 1996, c-print, 60 x 50" /*
OHNE TITEL NR. 3 (STAUNEN), C-Print, 152,4 x 127 cm.

Anna Gaskells
Girlie-Kunst

JAN AVGIKOS

Jungfräuliche Reinheit. Das ist das A und O in Anna Gaskells Bildern. Die jungen Mädchen sind das Erste, was einem ins Auge fällt, wovon man sich einfach nicht losreissen kann, was real ist, was da ist, Mädchen, die so unvergleichlich jung, so unschuldig, so engelhaft schön sind und deren natürlicher Schmelz einem den Atem verschlägt.

Es liesse sich natürlich einwenden, dass alle jungen Mädchen schön sind, aber das ändert nichts an der Tatsache, dass Gaskells Mädchen als «Fleisch gewordene Perfektion» gelten können. Dabei erinnern wir uns sofort an Heerscharen anderer «vollkommener junger Dinger», denen wir jeden Tag an allen Ecken und Enden begegnen: Mädchen, die berufsmässig für Kameras posieren, die in Filmen und Magazinen erscheinen, in der Werbung, in der Kunst; die digitalisiert und mit Photoshop bearbeitet genau so sind, wie wir sie haben wollen, Mädchen, die in die visuell perfekte Bilderwelt der Werbung passen, ja diese verkörpern; eine Welt, zu der wir selbst natürlich nie wirklich gehören, auch wenn wir uns mit ihr identifizieren.

Neben dramatischen Blickwinkeln und effektvoller Beleuchtung zeichnet sich Gaskells Bilderwelt durch eine bewusste Künstlichkeit aus. Der hohe technische Standard ihrer Photographien rückt diese in die Nähe medialer Utopien. Die Bilder sind makellos. Die Mädchen sind makellos. Im Sog der «jungfräulichen Reinheit» scheint sich jedes andere Thema aufzulösen, aber trotz aller Unschuld und

Vollkommenheit haben auch die Verstösse gegen die Regel ihren Platz. Gaskell stellt nicht nur eine oder zwei, sondern gleich eine ganze Auswahl von Möglichkeiten zusammen, wie man Bosheit ausleben kann. Als Vorlage dienen ihr Geschichten, die sie zusammensucht und von unterschiedlichen Fragmenten ausgehend weiterspinnt, immer im Hinblick auf eine junge Heldin, der die Verantwortung für die Handlung oder den darin vertretenen Standpunkt übertragen wird. Geschichten wie Lewis Carrolls *Alice im Wunderland* werden rigoros umgeschrieben und umstrukturiert, aus linearen Elementen wird ein Konglomerat aus Ereignissen (Ertrinken, Stürzen, Hüpfen) und Theatergags, die innerhalb einer Serie wiederholt und in die nächste hinübergezogen werden. Gaskell ist zum Beispiel fasziniert von den Insignien der Unschuld – weissen Strümpfen, viktorianischen Nachthemden und Schürzen –, die auch fester Bestandteil jeder Fetischkult-Ausrüstung sind.

Die Figur der Alice wandert von der *Wonder Series* (1996), in der sie identische Zwillinge verkörpert, zu *Override* (1997), wo sie sich mit einer Gang uniform gekleideter Mädchen zusammentut, die in einem Niemandsland sich selbst überlassen sind, aber, wie sich bald herausstellt, allen möglichen Unfug aushecken. Sie schubsen und stossen einander herum, ziehen sich an den Haaren, erscheinen aber trotz der rüden Umgangsformen straff organisiert – straffer jedenfalls, als wir es «echten» Jugendlichen zutrauen würden. «Real» ist in diesem Kontext vor allem die Ähnlichkeit, die Gaskells Bilder mit moderner Modephotographie aufweisen (bei der jede dramatische Inszenierung «Sinn macht»). Und «real» ist auch unsere Fähigkeit, diese jungen Frauen als Hexen, Ausserirdische, kriegerische Prinzessinnen (oder

JAN AVGIKOS ist Kunsthistorikerin und Kritikerin. Sie erhielt den Frank Jewett Mather Award der College Art Association (für Kunstkritik) und ist Fakultätsmitglied der School of Visual Arts und der Columbia University in New York.

welche vertrauten Figuren man auch immer vorziehen mag) zu betrachten und gleichzeitig als unglückliche, aber ganz «normale» kleine Camperinnen wahrzunehmen, unabhängig davon, was sie im wirklichen Leben auch noch sein könnten – Photomodelle, Kinder aus dem Freundeskreis, Töchter von Bekannten. Und so wird die Sache zunehmend komplexer: junge Mädchen, die sich selbst und noch viel mehr sind, dabei aber auch ganz anders sind, als sie erscheinen. Ob «Alice» oder «Sally Salt» (auch eine von Gaskells Leitfiguren auf dem Weg ins Reich der Phantasie und des Unbekannten), der Mechanismus ist immer derselbe: Dieses Mädchen ist nicht dieses Mädchen – was verdammt nach Magrittes «Dies ist keine Pfeife» klingt. «Real» ist ausserdem die ständig aggressive Gegenwart der Kamera; indem sie den Rahmen, den Ausschnitt, verändert und die Mädchen belauert, bedrängt, bespitzelt, lässt sie uns diese immer wieder anders sehen. In erster Linie werden sie jedoch als photographische Subjekte dargestellt, die es aufzustöbern, festzunageln und zu besitzen gilt. Wir sehen diese Mädchen nie so, wie sie wirklich sind, sondern immer nur als eine Figur in einer Figur in einer Figur.

Das «angeblich Böse», das Gaskell beschwört, seine Austauschbarkeit mit dem, was im Alltag passiert, stammt aus Kino und Fernsehen. Als mögliche Quellen fallen einem *Children of the Corn* (1984) oder *The Bad Seed* (1956) ein. In beiden Filmen werden Kinder mit einer Unabhängigkeit und einer Macht ausgestattet, die jene der Erwachsenen bei weitem übertrifft, so dass sie es mit der Welt der Erwachsenen aufnehmen, ja, sie vielleicht sogar ausschalten können. Ob Ausserirdische oder kleine Teufel oder auch nur gemeine kleine Biester wie in *Override* oder einfach schöne Photomodelle, die auf Kommando bestimmte Posen einnehmen, die Mädchenschar, die in *By Proxy* (1999) in Krankenschwesterntracht auftaucht, ist jedenfalls ziemlich verwirrend. Eine tolle Truppe, allein durch ihre Zahl und die Entschlossenheit, die sie bei ihren Ritualen an den Tag legen. Sind es Krankenschwestern in Ausbildung? Oder sind sie einfach nur als Krankenschwestern kostümiert? Die rudimentäre Erzählung, die der Serie zugrunde liegt, gibt uns kaum einen Hinweis, doch erwecken die Mädchen – als Individuen wie auch als Gruppe – den Eindruck, als wüssten sie genau, was

ANNA GASKELL, UNTITLED NO. 20 (WONDER), 1996,
c-print, 50 x 60" /
OHNE TITEL NR. 20 (STAUNEN),
C-Print, 127 x 152,4 cm.

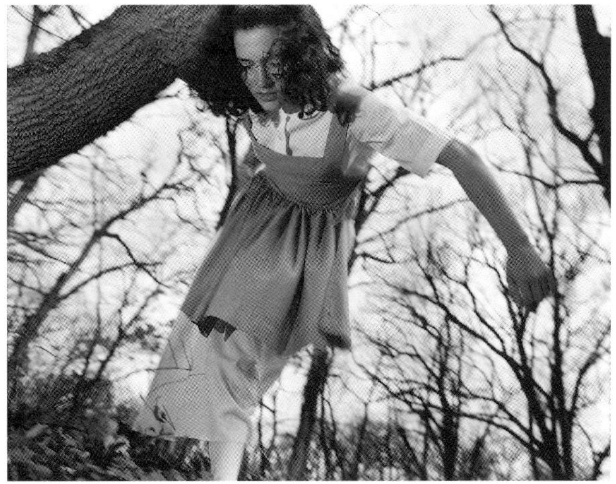

ANNA GASKELL, UNTITLED NO. 49 (SALLY SALT SAYS), 1999,
c-print, 60 x 70" /
OHNE TITEL NR. 49 (SALLY SALT SAGT),
C-Print, 152,4 x 177,8 cm.

sie in dieser merkwürdig «natürlichen» Umgebung verloren haben. Angesichts ihrer Absichten scheint ihre sogenannte «Unschuld» nur die Funktion eines zusätzlichen Accessoires zu erfüllen.

Im Gegensatz zu der Unbesiegbarkeit, die die Gaskell-Girls in *Override* und *By Proxy* an den Tag legen, ist in der hochdramatischen Serie *Hide* (1998) ihre Verletzlichkeit mit Händen zu greifen. Ein feudales Herrenhaus bietet die perfekte (wenn auch optisch klischeehafte) Schauerroman-Kulisse für blutige Szenen und merkwürdige, unklare Paarungen. Wir spähen über ein Geländer und entdecken «sie» auf «der anderen» liegend, beide reglos, beinah wie tot. Es gibt immer nur zwei Charaktere, die von unterschiedlichen Paaren dargestellt werden (das heisst, es tauchen nie mehr als zwei Mädchen gleichzeitig in einem Bild auf). Wir ertappen «sie», auf dem Boden liegend und der «anderen» unters Nachthemd spähend. «Sie» zeigt ihre noch nasse Hand neben einer Blutlache (ist es wirklich Blut?). «Sie» hat «der anderen» die Hand auf den Mund gepresst, vielleicht um einen Schrei zu ersticken.

Trotz der Andeutung einer Geschichte – von der Art, die so anhebt: «Es war eine dunkle, stürmische Nacht...» – oder möglicherweise einer Abhandlung über Gender und Identität, wartet Gaskell nie mit klar umrissenen Charakteren oder Handlungen auf, von spezifischen Botschaften ganz zu schweigen. Trotzdem kommt einem in diesen Bildern vieles bekannt vor, auch wenn nichts wirklich persönlich ist.

Gaskells Bilder sind dicht verwobene, dramatische Vignetten, deren Elemente aus Kunst und wahrscheinlich auch aus anderen Quellen stammen. Nicht nur Cindy Sherman und Gregory Crewdson (ihr Lehrer an der Yale-Universität) kommen in Betracht, auch zufällige Assoziationen mit der TV-Serie *Die X-Akten*, Hollywood-Thrillern mit kleinem Budget oder feministischen Theorien sind zugelassen. Von allem ein bisschen, das Ganze gut gemischt und durch bewusst gewählte Rahmen und Ausschnitte strukturiert, Techniken, die das Gefühl der ruhelosen Spannung verstärken, dann noch ein bewusster Mangel an Tiefenschärfe, der die entscheidende Wirkung ihrer Photographien ausmacht: Das Andeuten einer Überwachung, der wirklich nur ganz leise Hinweis darauf, dass die Welt beliebig ein- und aus-

geblendet werden kann, verleiht dem drohenden Unheil, das an den Rändern der Welten, in denen wir den Gaskell-Girls begegnen, lauert, einen dramatischen Aspekt.

Die Künstlerin verknüpft ostentativ Fragmente zu Geschichten, in denen junge Mädchen als Erzählerinnen auftreten, um so eine weibliche und ausserdem junge Stimme einzusetzen und ihr Gewicht zu verleihen. Aber sehen wir die Welt deshalb aus der Perspektive eines jungen Mädchens, egal ob es sich um eine Heldin handelt oder nicht? Angesichts der extremen, ja übertriebenen Optik der Bilder bin ich mir nicht sicher, ob Gaskells «Girl Power» direkt oder auch nur indirekt etwas mit Zwölfjährigen zu tun hat. Unsere eigene Position zu bestimmen, ist jedenfalls einfacher, denn schliesslich geht es in diesen Bildern um uns. Als Betrachter übernehmen wir *nolens volens* die Rolle des Voyeurs. Zum einen werden wir von der jungfräulichen Schönheit der Mädchen, zum andern von der Qualität der Bilder und ihrer modernen Ästhetik verführt; hinzu kommt die Andeutung von Formen visueller Lust in Verbindung mit einem das Verbotene streifenden Inhalt.

Die Bilder besingen weniger den Liebreiz junger Mädchen als die Phantasie der Erwachsenen. Sie besitzen zwar eine diskrete Erotik, doch nicht mehr, als ihr Thema und der von uns allen geteilte (und zurückgewiesene) Hang, Jugend erotisch zu besetzen, es erwarten lassen. Doch gibt es da noch etwas anderes, was mit einer ausgeprägten Tendenz zum Bombastischen (noch eine Vorgabe unserer Gesellschaft) zu tun hat. Gefährlich dreinschauen, um respektiert zu werden; in der Menge auffallen, um sich seinen Platz zu sichern. Mit künstlerischen Freiheiten und Exzessen prahlen als erster Schritt auf der Suche nach einer gemeinsamen visuellen Sprache. Einen Look kreieren, der ebenso bekannt wie neu ist, einen Look, der etwas kommuniziert, lange bevor der schleppende Mechanismus der langsameren Formen konventioneller Abläufe greifen kann. Es ist vor allem der «Look» von Gaskells Photographien, weniger die Geschichten, die sie erzählen, der hochdramatisch und angenehm unpersönlich wirkt, obwohl die photographischen Tropen der Intimität in diesen Bildern allgegenwärtig sind.

(Übersetzung: Uta Goridis)

176

Back to the Future

ALI SUBOTNICK

You're in your high school gymnasium watching a talent show. You're in your bedroom, with Toto wailing from the stereo as you choreograph a masterpiece for "Dance Fever." It's you and the music and you're the dancing queen, you're the rock star in glitter and spandex. It's *Xanadu* and *Fame*. Jane Fonda aerobics mixed with *The Rocky Horror Picture Show*. You're watching the performance collaborative Fischerspooner.

Headed by charismatic front man Casey Spooner and techno-wizard Warren Fischer, the Fischerspooner cast includes Cindy Greene, Lizzy Yoder, Jordana Toback, Vanessa Walters,

Alyssa Dodson, Mindi McAlister, and Jeremiah Clancy. (Behind stage, a crew of hairdressers, wardrobe stylists, set designers, and make-up artists put the pieces in place.) Clancy is a former groupie who started as a stagehand and recently moved up to the role of on-stage jester. He has performed clumsily along with the others in casual street clothes and he even stripped to his underwear to dance provocatively in a cage.

The Fischerspooner act revives superficial details of the eighties culled from the worlds of fashion, music, and dance without spawning sentimental nostalgia. Instead, the group incorporate these stylistic influences as tools to entertain and provoke an audience accustomed to looking at art from a

safe and controlled distance. They play down the importance of talent and focus on staged failure and the façade of spontaneity.

Sites for Sore Eyes

Occasionally live shows are performed in galleries, but it's rare for a performance art collaborative to stage shows for five nights in a row and draw massive crowds from the art community and beyond. For a recent gallery show in New York, Fischerspooner transformed the white cube into a cave-like

ALI SUBOTNICK is assistant editor for *Parkett* in New York.

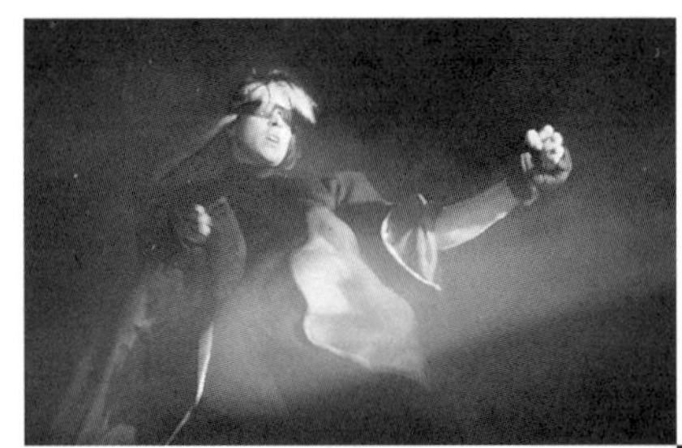

FISCHERSPOONER SHOW NO. 15, March 28 – April 1, 2000,
Gavin Brown's Enterprise, New York, performance views, Casey Spooner.
(PHOTO: YORGO ALEXOPOULOS)

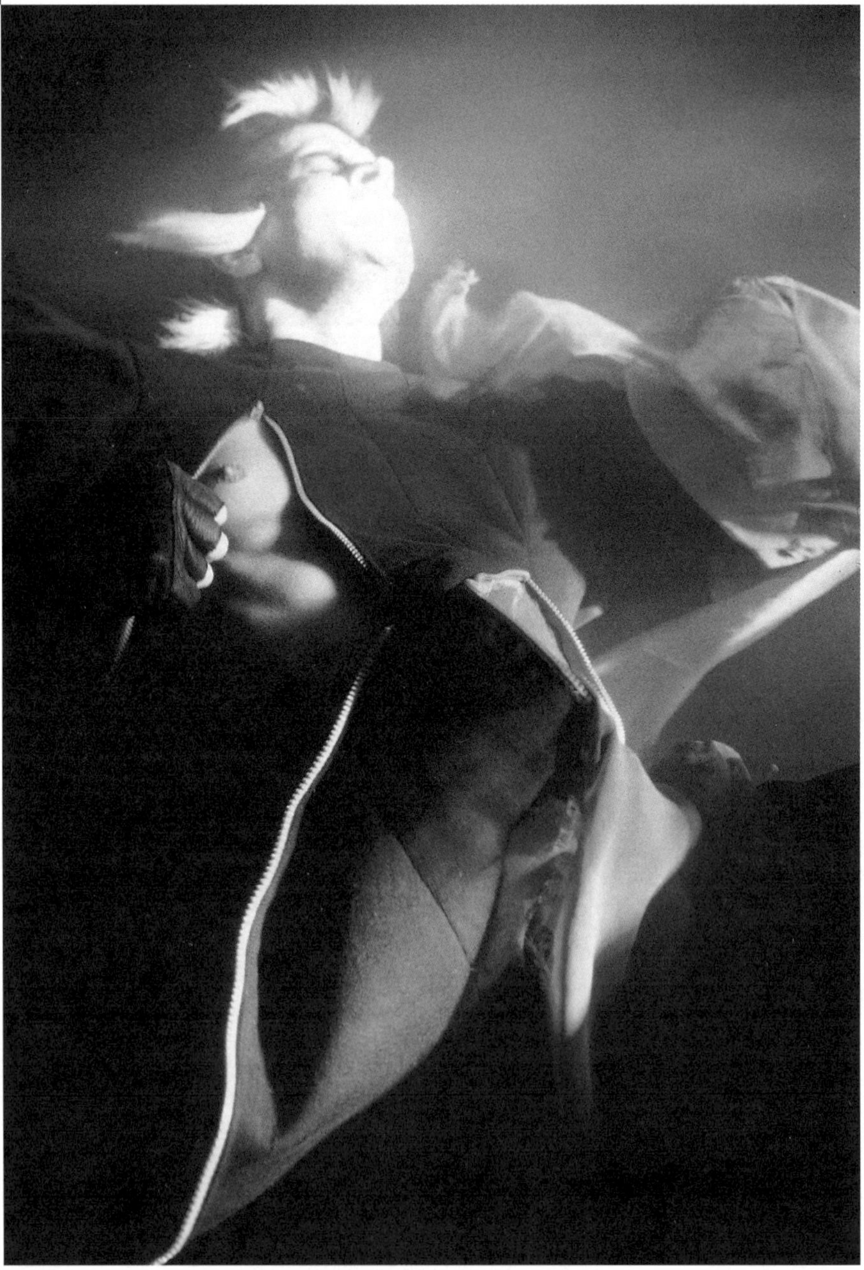

set composed of uneven risers, steel poles, cages, fluorescent lights, and Ernesto Neto-like nylon sacks filled with sand and hanging precariously from the ceiling. Attendees entered the dark space, instructed by a robotic female voice to "Enter. Please Enter." At the end of the set, the inhuman voice returned, telling viewers to exit while listing the performance credits.

There were three different twenty-five-minute sets performed consecutively for three hours each night. The quick in-and-out pace made an impact that longer shows in larger, more public venues are unable to provide. As the nights progressed, the sets grew increasingly plastic and fluid. The performances became instinctual and the entertainers morphed into their roles, concentrating entirely on their veneer. By the end of the week, they achieved total surface. The finale featured a lively, banter-filled set that totally obliterated any distance between the audience and the entertainers. Fischerspooner are at their best when they can play with a handful of viewers and pull them into their world seamlessly.

Rear Window

Fischerspooner lacks the altruism and condescension inherent in most performance art. Instead, they concentrate on style and appearance and how far they can push the audience's tolerance for superficial glamtainment. Watching Fischerspooner perform feels voyeuristic. Their shows lack the façade of a Broadway performance, which is presented through a window with everything laid out for viewers who know that what they are seeing is pure fiction. To watch Fischerspooner though, viewers look through a rearview mirror that offers a glimpse of the past filtered through the present—the rearview mirror reflects what's behind, yet one looks ahead to view it. At times the act seems like it's a dress rehearsal, and it's unclear whether the actors are really ad-libbing and falling on purpose. Is it all an act? Yes, it's an exercise in exposing the ingredients of performance while unraveling those same inherent qualities. The gap between viewer and audience falls away, yet the show is entirely prefabricated.

The device of false starts and onstage costume changes isn't new to performance art. But here it succeeds in humbling the spectacle rather than appearing overly forced. The dancers chat with each other and the crowd between numbers, whining, complaining, and teasing. Spooner confesses: "It's all entertainment. Thanks for coming to watch some contemporary art. Nature—it's all about nature and the body. It's not really a show; it's more of a portrait of a show. It's conceptual art. If we mess up, it's planned." They consistently accuse each other of "pulling focus." When Fischerspooner's audience is conscious of these devices, the performers are able to bring viewers into a space somewhere between art and entertainment. It's a space that blends high and low, private and public, glamour and debasement.

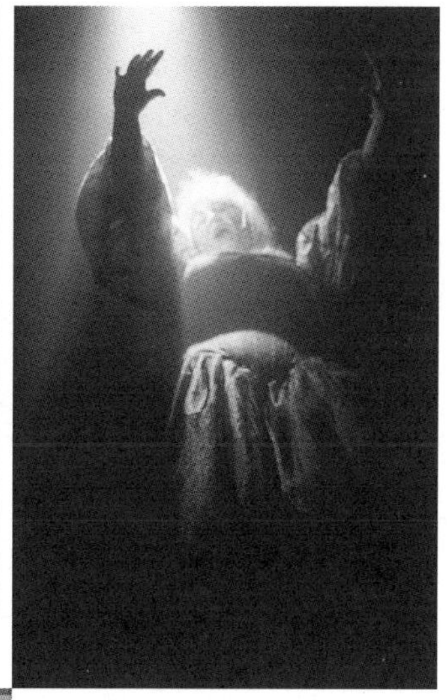

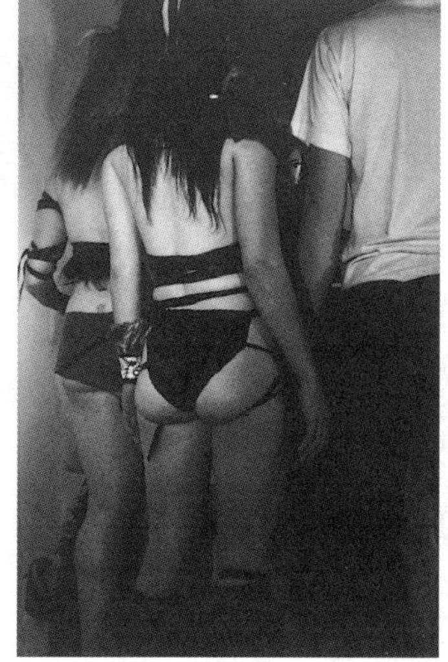

Gotta Dance

Writhing and jumping, the vigorous choreography, by Toback, recalls the styles of Fosse and Madonna, with remnants of aerobics and modern jazz mixed in. The dance routines don't look like they require classical dance training, though four of the dancers are Broadway veterans, but they aren't the sort of moves you'd see at a dance club either. They run in and out of the rooms, up and down the risers, pushing audience-members aside, gyrating in their faces. They swing on poles and crawl on the floor like "Solid Gold" dancers, injecting the crowd with an overwhelming desire to jump onstage and join in.

cious. One night, the dancers wore skirts and dresses decorated with a bird-and-feather-wallpaper design accented with black ruffles and corsets. Spooner donned a rubber monkey suit covered with feathers, and mid-set he slipped on a tuxedo-like suit accented by a Mad Hatter top hat in the same pattern. Another night, the girls exposed more skin, wearing black stretched bikini tops with fishnet stockings. The costumes are designed in a specific, anti-aesthetic guise: *Flashdance*-style torn sweatshirts, leotards in hot pink and Day-Glo blue, mullets, hair extensions and wigs, spiked punk hairdo's and blonde Rapunzel braids, leg warmers, tutus, and leather straps. Their sensibility resembles that of the designer Jeremy Scott, unabashedly embracing the gaudiness of eighties fashion and entertainment without covering up the blemishes. It's so ironic, it's sincere.

The Sound of Music

A classically trained musician, Fischer directs the sound, lighting, and music, which references everything from the Pet Shop Boys, Kraftwerk, and New Order to the Styx, Neil Diamond, and early nineties techno. Robotic beats and a tacky synthesizer bring back the greed-is-good era. "Emerge," one of their signature songs, begins with a rising pulse followed by a stuttering, "Hy. Hy-Hy. Hy-Per. Hypermediocrity." The song continues with quick snippets— "Feels Good. Looks Good. Sounds Good"—followed by a sarcastic "A-ha, that's right." Spooner refers to "Emerge" as their artists' statement. "You don't need to emerge from nothing. You don't need to tear away."

You've Got the Look

The costumes, designed by Peter Soronen, Vilma Maré, and Slava, recall Ziggy Stardust, Duran Duran, Joan Jett, and Boy George. The Fischerspooner look is at once trashy, retro, and preco-

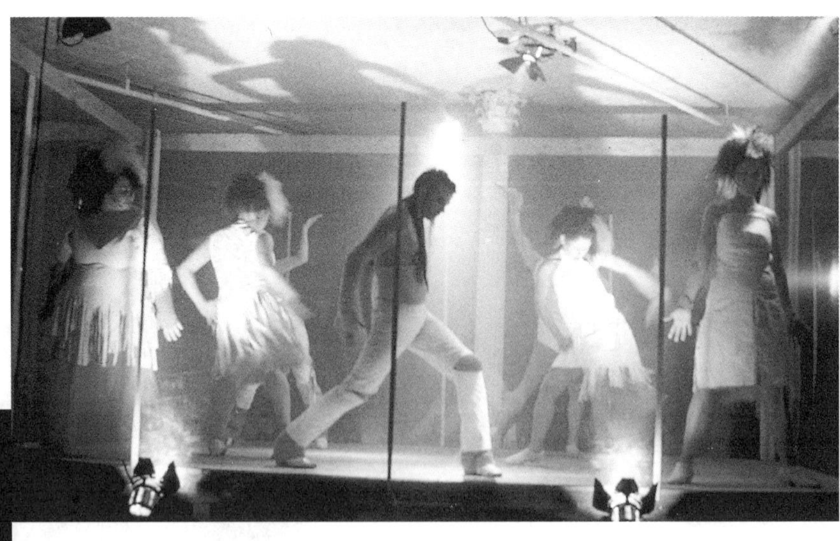

Above / Oben: FISCHERSPOONER SHOW NO. 13, September 15, 1999.
(PHOTO: AARON FODOR)
Left / Links: FISCHERSPOONER SHOW NO. 12, September 10, 1999.
(PHOTO: KELLY McKAIG)

There's no need to fight conformity or get introspective; it's all prescribed anyway. Or, as Spooner puts it, "We're anti-deconstructivism. It's about embracing formula, embracing stereotypes."

Spooner pens the lyrics (except for "The 15th," written by Wire's Colin Newman), which he sings along with Greene and Yoder. However, during performances they shamelessly lip-synch each number. The beat is catchy and the rhythm is attainable by even the most tone-deaf viewers. During one show, a dancer asked Spooner if she could start the next number. "Go ahead, it's not like I'm really singing. We're just lip-synching. It's not about talent," he replied. Milli Vanilli makes a comeback flaunting a Vanilla Ice pretense and Wham! theatrics.

The high point in this gallery show arrived during the number "Horizon," when Spooner appeared on stage dressed in a Michael Jackson-inspired, zippered jumpsuit and black wrap-around sunglasses. Under a beaming spotlight, he danced robotically. Halfway through the number, Clancy assisted him in unzipping the suit. The lights dimmed briefly and returned to reveal a frozen image of Spooner being blasted by a heavy stream of white fog that whipped his scarves and hair behind him. The scene resurrected "Blowaway Man," the classic advertising symbol from Maxell, which depicts a man in a chair being blown away by his sound system. Watching this act is akin to seeing a three-dimensional person transform into a two-dimensional image. Spooner caught in freeze-frame evokes the punkish figures in Patrick Nagel's pop posters from the eighties.

"Turn On," their sexiest piece, starts off:

You're getting warm,
You feel the draw,
It is creepy.
A fever pitch builds slowly,
And spreads,
Tonight.
Winds sweep,
Pull you close,
Through the danger.
I know I've got you where I
Want you,
Tonight.
Pioneer frontier explore
   my heart…

Female voices plead on: "You're getting warmer, warmer, and warmer tonight." The lyrics may be about a sexual encounter—or Lewis and Clark, as Spooner insists—but they also describe the audience's experience:

Red delicious,
Pink and wet,
It's so hot now.
I know I've got you where I
Want you,
Tonight.

Fischerspooner tell their fans, "We have you in the palms of our hands and we're going to tease you and tempt you because we can."

The Future's So Bright

"This is the future," a friend said while watching Fischerspooner perform for his first time. When Andy Warhol took the Velvet Underground on tour for the Exploding Plastic Inevitable shows, society wasn't yet ready for their groundbreaking spectacle. They were up against hippie culture and the peace and love generation. Their hard-edged cynicism wasn't readily embraced on a large scale; they were too underground to break into a wider market. Fischerspooner, however, lack that cynicism. They don't engage a post-modern irony, and their sincere, interdisciplinary approach lends itself to global acceptance. They exaggerate the current climate of increasingly blurred lines between art, fashion, and entertainment. Fischerspooner has emerged at a specific moment in history when a universal acceptance is possible. Their appeal would be just as successful in Milan or Paris, Venice or Kassel, Los Angeles or Detroit. And even though their references are largely culled from American pop culture, they exude so much enthusiasm about it—and so much of the world is familiar with it—that they can be appreciated on a global scale.

Like Pulp and their resurrection of eighties-style pop music, Fischerspooner bring back a time that they were too young to truly experience. They embrace the embarrassing, the tasteless, and the superficial as their medium. Like *American Psycho*—Brett Easton Ellis's detailed portrait of the eighties as a soulless, cutthroat decade in which money, good looks, and ego formed the basis for all value judgments—Fischerspooner resurrects the shallow attitudes that motivated that era's eventual crash. But now, Fischerspooner can incorporate eighties style as part of their act. In the eighties, the art world came closer to entertainment than ever before, while the nineties were a complete backlash and reaction to it. Fischerspooner resurrects the entertainment part and arrives back to the future.

Zurück in die Zukunft

ALI SUBOTNICK

Wir sind in der Schulturnhalle und wohnen einem Talentwettbewerb bei. Wir sind im Schlafzimmer und üben eine tolle Choreographie für «Dance Fever» ein, während Toto aus der Anlage heult. Wir gehen ganz in der Musik auf, wir sind der Tanzstar, der Rockstar im schimmernden Spandexanzug. Ein bisschen *Xanadu* und *Fame*; Jane-Fonda-Aerobics und *The Rocky Horror Picture Show*. Kurz, wir erleben eine Performance von Fischerspooner.

Ausser dem charismatischen Frontman Casey Spooner und dem Techno-Genie Warren Fischer gehören Cindy Greene, Lizzy Yoder, Jordana Toback, Vanessa Walters, Alyssa Dodson, Mindi

ALI SUBOTNICK ist redaktionelle Mitarbeiterin von *Parkett* in New York.

McAlister und Jeremiah Clancy zu der Truppe. (Hinter der Bühne operiert ein Heer von Friseuren, Kostüm-, Bühnen- und Maskenbildnern.) Clancy ist ein Ex-Groupie, der als Bühnenarbeiter angefangen hat und mittlerweile zum Bühnenclown aufgestiegen ist. Zusammen mit den anderen zog er in normaler Strassenkleidung eine hilflose Show ab, zog sich dabei bis auf die Unterhosen aus und tanzte aufreizend in einem Käfig herum.

Die Fischerspooner-Show lässt oberflächliche Details aus Mode, Musik und Tanz der 80er Jahre lebendig werden, ohne jedoch sentimentale Nostalgie aufkommen zu lassen. Vielmehr bedienen sich die Darsteller dieser stilistischen Einflüsse, um ein Publikum zu unterhalten und zu provozieren, das

gewohnt ist Kunst aus sicherem und kontrolliertem Abstand zu betrachten. Sie spielen die Bedeutung von Talent und Begabung bewusst herunter und pflegen stattdessen das inszenierte Versagen, wobei sie sich den Anschein von Spontaneität geben.

Orte für brennende Augen

Auch in Galerien werden gelegentlich Live-Shows aufgeführt, doch gibt es kaum eine Performance-Gruppe, die es schafft, fünf Abende hintereinander aufzutreten und jedes Mal haufenweise Leute in- und ausserhalb der Kunstszene anzulocken. Für einen Galerie-Auftritt in New York verwandelte Fischerspooner den weissen Kubus in eine Art Höhle mit diversen Steigrohren, Stahlstangen, Käfigen, fluoreszierenden Lichtern und sandgefüllten Nylonsäcken, die an Objekte von Ernesto Neto erinnerten und beängstigend von der Decke baumelten. Von einer weiblichen Automatenstimme zum Eintreten aufgefordert – «Enter. Please Enter.» –, betraten die Zuschauer den dunklen Raum. Am Ende der Vorstellung liess sich die synthetische Stimme wieder vernehmen und befahl ihnen, während der abschliessenden Aufzählung aller Mitwirkenden, den Raum zu verlassen.

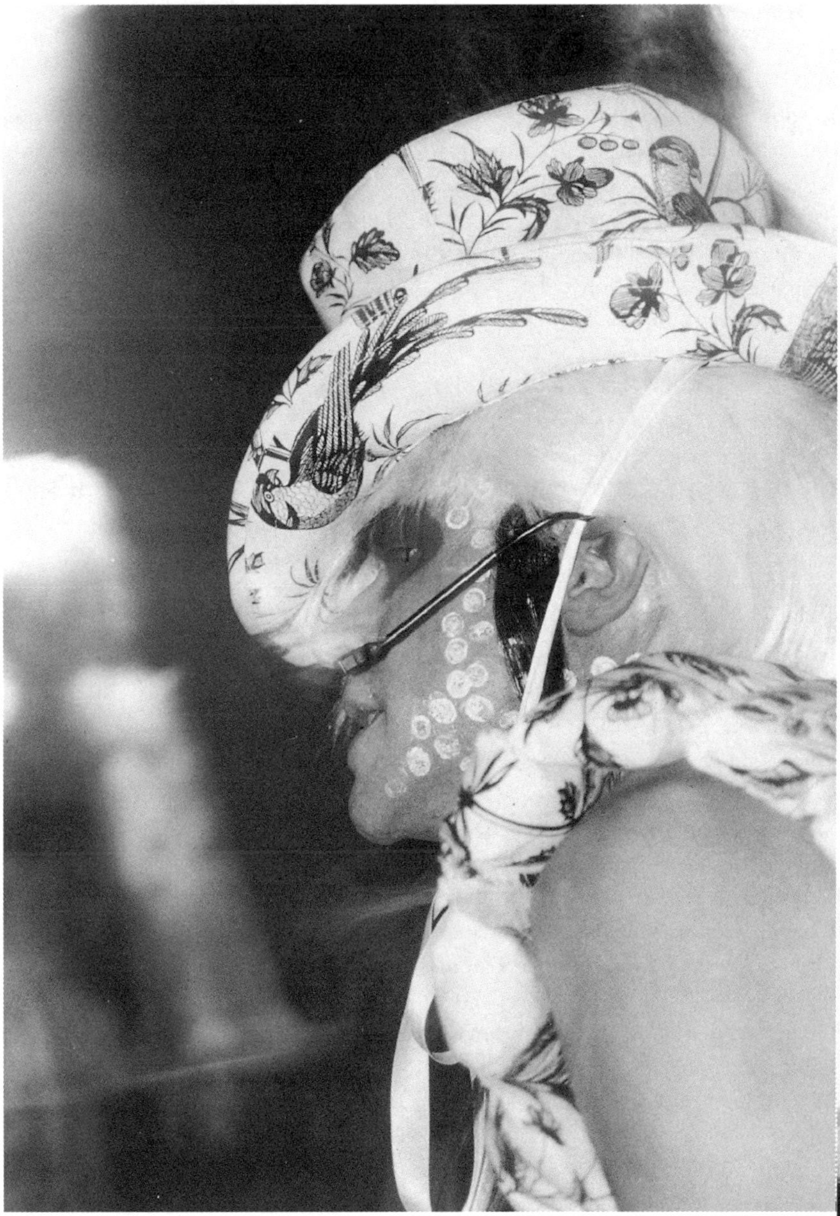

Jede Nacht wurden drei Stunden lang drei verschiedene Stücke von fünfundzwanzig Minuten Länge gespielt. Die schnellen Auf- und Abtritte hatten

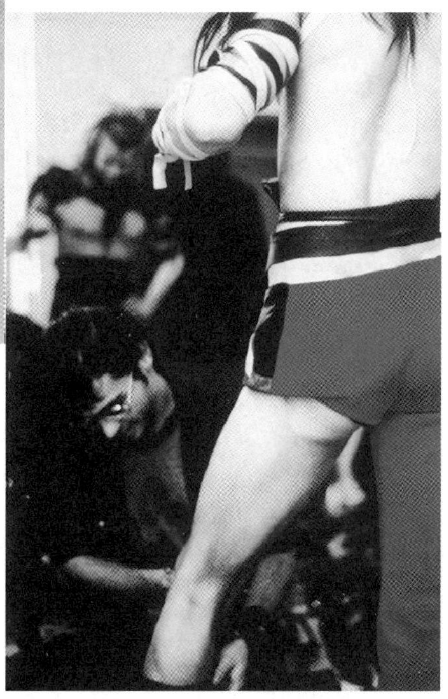

Above / Oben: FISCHERSPOONER SHOW NO. 15, March 28 – April 1, 2000, Gavin Brown's Enterprise, New York. (PHOTO: DOUG HENDERS)
Right / Rechts: FISCHERSPOONER, photoshoot for "Index," December 1999 / Aufnahme für die Zeitschrift «Index». (PHOTO: BEN TISCHER)

eine Wirkung, die von längeren Shows in einem grösseren, öffentlicheren Rahmen nie erreicht wird. Mit jeder Nacht wurde der Vortrag plastischer und fliessender. Die Künstler erreichten einen hohen Grad von Instinktivität und verschmolzen mit ihren Rollen, wobei sie sich ganz auf die Geschliffenheit ihrer Darbietung konzentrierten. Am Ende der Woche hatten sie dann auch absolute Perfektion erreicht. Das Finale bestand aus einer quicklebendigen, ausgelassenen Nummer, in der jede Distanz zwischen Publikum und Akteuren aufgehoben wurde. Fischerspooner laufen zu Hochform auf, wenn sie mit einer Hand voll Zuschauern spielen und sie ganz in ihre Welt einwickeln können.

Der Blick nach hinten

Bei Fischerspooner fehlt die bei Sängern und Schauspielern übliche Mischung aus Anbiederung und Herablassung. Stattdessen konzentrieren sie sich ganz auf Stil und Auftreten und darauf, wie viel oberflächliches Spektakel sie ihrem Publikum zumuten können. Dabei erleben sich die Zuschauer als Voyeure. Diese Aufführungen besitzen nicht die glatte Fassade einer Broadway-Show, die in einem klaren Rahmen stattfindet und für Zuschauer gedacht ist, die genau wissen, dass alles, was sie sehen, pure Fiktion ist. Eine Fischerspooner-Show ist dagegen wie ein Blick in den Rückspiegel, der uns einen Ausschnitt aus der durch die Gegenwart gefilterte Vergangenheit zeigt – der Rückspiegel reflektiert, was

hinter uns liegt, auch wenn wir beim Betrachten nach vorne schauen. Manchmal wirkt die Show wie eine Kostümprobe, und man fragt sich, ob die Schauspieler tatsächlich improvisieren und absichtlich stolpern und hinfallen. Ist wirklich alles inszeniert? Ja, es ist ein Versuch, sichtbar darzustellen, woraus die Kunst der Performance besteht, indem man eben diese spezifischen Eigenschaften durchbuchstabiert. Die Kluft zwischen Zuschauer und Publikum verschwindet, obwohl die Show perfekt einstudiert ist.

Missglückte Anläufe und Kostümwechsel auf offener Bühne sind an sich nichts Neues. Doch hier wirkt der Kunstgriff nicht gewollt, sondern holt die Show tatsächlich vom Sockel der Perfektion herunter. Die Tänzer unterhalten sich zwischen den einzelnen Nummern, plaudern mit dem Publikum, sticheln, jammern, beschweren sich. Spooner gesteht: «Es ist alles Show. Ich möchte mich bei all denen bedanken, die gekommen sind, um sich etwas zeitgenössische Kunst anzuschauen. Natur – im Grunde geht es um die Natur und den Körper. Eigentlich ist es keine Show, eher das Porträt einer Schau. Konzeptkunst. Wenn wir Fehler machen, so ist das geplant.» Die Schauspieler beklagen sich ständig, dass sie von den anderen an die Wand gespielt würden. Sobald das Publikum diese Tricks durchschaut, können die Künstler die Zuschauer in einen Raum irgendwo zwischen Kunst und Unterhaltung versetzen, einen Raum, in dem sich Erhabenes und Niederes, Privates und Öffentliches, Glanz und Elend vermischen.

Tanzfieber

Die Sprünge und Schlängelbewegungen der kraftvollen Choreographie erinnern an den Stil von Fosse oder Madonna, mit ein paar zusätzlichen Aerobic- und Modern-Jazz-Elementen. Die Tanzeinlagen sehen nicht so aus, als erforderten sie ein klassisches Tanztraining, obwohl vier der Tänzer Broadway-Veteranen sind. Die Bewegungen haben aber auch nichts mit dem Tanzstil in Clubs zu schaffen. Die Tänzer rennen rein und raus, klettern Steigrohre rauf und runter, schubsen Zuschauer beiseite, wirbeln unmittelbar vor ihren Gesichtern herum: Sie schwanken auf Stelzen und kriechen wie die Tänzer von Solid Gold auf dem Boden herum, bis die Zuschauer kaum mehr an sich halten können und nur noch den Wunsch haben, auf die Bühne zu springen und mitzumachen.

Der Look stimmt

Die von Peter Soronen, Vilma Maré und Slava entworfenen Kostüme erinnern an Ziggy Stardust, Duran Duran, Joan Jett und Boy George. Der Fischerspooner-Look ist gleichzeitig billig, nostalgisch und altklug. Eines Abends traten die Tänzer in Röcken und Kleidern auf, die wie eine Tapete mit Vögeln und Federn bedruckt waren und dazu noch schwarze Rüschen und Schnürkorsetts aufwiesen. Spooner trug einen mit Federn bedeckten Gummifrack, den er zwischendurch auf der Bühne gegen eine Art Smoking und einen passenden Zylinder im Stil des verrückten Hutmachers (aus Alice im Wunderland) eintauschte. Ein anderes Mal zeigten die nur mit einem schwarzen Stretchbikini und Netzstrümpfen bekleideten Mädchen etwas mehr Haut. Die Kostüme sind gewollt geschmacklos: zerrissene Sweatshirts in *Flashdance*-Manier, Tanztrikots in grellem Pink und fluoreszierendem Blau, Sternchen, Haarteile und Perücken, punkige Igelfrisuren und blonde Rapunzelzöpfe, Wadenwärmer, Tutus und Lederstrapse. Diese Vorlieben erinnern an den Designer Jeremy Scott, der sich schamlos zur effekthascherischen Mode und Unterhaltung der 80er Jahre bekennt ohne ihre Monstrositäten zu kaschieren. Das ist so ironisch, dass es schon wieder aufrichtig ist.

Der Sound ist perfekt

Fischer, ein Musiker mit klassischer Ausbildung, ist zuständig für Sound, Beleuchtung und für eine Musik, die überall Anleihen macht, von den Pet Shop Boys über Kraftwerk und New Order bis zu Styx, Neil Diamond und dem Techno der frühen 90er Jahre. Roboterhafte Beats und schmierige Synthesizerklänge lassen die Ära der geldgeilen 80er Jahre wieder auferstehen. «Emerge», einer der Erkennungssongs, beginnt mit einem anschwellenden Rhythmus, auf den ein gestottertes «Hy. Hy-Hy. Hy-Per. Hypermediocrity» folgt. Nach ein paar kurzen Gesprächsfetzen – «Feels Good. Looks Good. Sounds Good» – hört man ein sarkastisches: «A-ha, that's right.»

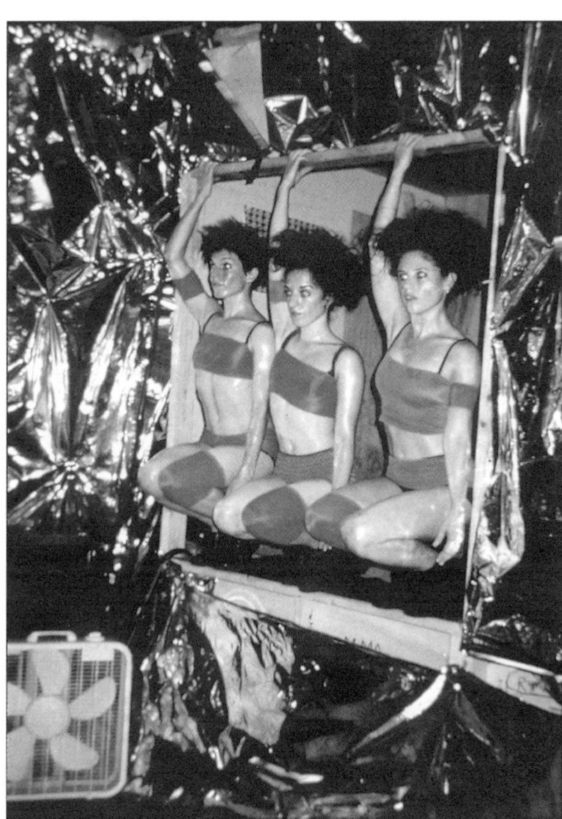

Spooner bezeichnet «Emerge» als künstlerisches Credo der Gruppe. «Man braucht aus nichts herauszukommen. Man muss sich nicht frei schwimmen.» Es ist nicht nötig, sich gegen die Anpassung zu wehren oder zur Besinnung zu kommen. Alles ist sowieso vorherbestimmt oder wie Spooner es formuliert: «Wir sind anti-dekonstruktivistisch. Es geht darum, sich eine Formel zu eigen zu machen, sich die Klischees einzuverleiben.»

Spooner schreibt die Liedtexte (abgesehen von «The 15th», den Colin Newmann von den Wire beigesteuert hat), die er dann zusammen mit Greene und Yoder vorträgt. Während der Auftritte singen sie aber ohne die geringsten Skrupel alles in Playback. Der Takt ist eingängig und der Rhythmus auch für den unmusikalischsten Zuschauer nachvollziehbar. Während einer Show fragte eine Tänzerin Spooner, ob sie mit der nächsten Nummer anfangen dürfe. «Ja, mach nur», meinte der, «ich sing ja nicht wirklich. Es ist nur Playback. Wir müssen nicht unser Talent beweisen.» Milli Vanilli ist wieder da und rauscht mit ihrem falschen Vanille-Eis und viel Theaterdonner über die Bühne.

Der Höhepunkt dieser Galerie-Show war die Nummer «Horizon», als Spooner mit schwarzer Bikerbrille und einem Michael Jackson abgeschauten Overall mit Reissverschluss auf der Bühne erschien und im grellen Scheinwerferlicht roboterhaft tanzte. In der Mitte der Nummer half ihm Clancy, den Reissverschluss zu öffnen. Die Lichter gingen kurz aus, und als es wieder hell wurde, sah man einen erstarrten

Spooner, dem ein kräftiger Nebelschwall entgegenschlug und seine Haare und Schals hinter ihm wirbeln liess. Die Szene liess den «Blowaway Man» lebendig werden, Maxwells klassisches Werbesymbol, das einen Mann auf einem Stuhl zeigt, der vom Sound seiner Anlage weggeblasen wird. Es war, als würde sich eine dreidimensionale Person in ein zweidimensionales Bild verwandeln. Der erstarrte Spooner erinnerte an die Punkgestalten auf Patrick Nagels Pop-Plakaten der 80er Jahre.

«Turn on», das wohl erotischste Stück der Fischspooners, beginnt so:

> You're getting warm
> You feel the draw
> It is creepy
> A fever pitch builds slowly
> And spreads
> Tonight
> Winds sweep
> Pull you close
> Through the danger
> I know I've got you where I
> Want you
> Tonight
> Pioneer frontier explore
>   my heart ... [1]

Flehende weibliche Stimmen fahren fort: «You're getting warmer, warmer, and warmer tonight.» Der Text könnte eine Liebesszene beschreiben – oder Lewis und Clark, wie Spooner behauptet –, aber er könnte genauso gut die Erfahrung des Publikums wiedergeben.

> Red delicious
> Pink and wet
> It's so hot now,
> I know I've got you where I
> Want you,
> Tonight. [2]

Fischerspooner sagen zu ihren Fans: «Wir haben euch in der Hand, und wir werden das auch ausnützen und euch tüchtig einheizen.»

Die Zukunft ist verheissungsvoll

«Das ist die Zukunft», sagte ein Freund, als er Fischerspooner zum ersten Mal sah. Als Andy Warhol für die «Exploding Plastic Inevitable Shows» mit Velvet Underground auf Tournee ging, war die Zeit noch nicht reif für dieses bahnbrechende Spektakel. Sie hatten es mit der Hippiekultur und der Love-and-Peace-Generation zu schaffen. Ihr brutaler Zynismus kam bei den meisten nicht an; sie waren noch zu sehr Untergrundbewegung, um sich einen grösseren Markt erobern zu können. Bei Fischerspooner hingegen fehlt dieser Zynismus. Postmoderne Ironie interessiert sie nicht, und ihr aufrichtiger, interdisziplinärer Umgang mit den Dingen verschafft ihnen allgemeine Akzeptanz. Sie treiben die gegenwärtige Verwischung der Grenzen zwischen Kunst, Mode und Unterhaltung auf die Spitze. Fischerspooner hat die Bühne in genau dem Augenblick betreten, wo diese allgemeine und weltweite Akzeptanz möglich wurde. Die Gruppe wäre in Mailand ebenso erfolgreich wie in Paris, Venedig, Kassel, Los Angeles oder Detroit. Und obwohl sie vor allem aus der amerikanischen Popkultur schöpfen – die ja auch allgemein verbreitet ist –, verströmen sie dabei so viel Begeisterung, dass man sie auf der ganzen Welt versteht.

Wie Pulp mit ihrer Wiederbelebung der Popmusik der 80er Jahre bringen Fischerspooner eine Zeit zurück, die sie nicht wirklich erlebt haben können. Sie begrüssen das Peinliche, Geschmacklose und Oberflächliche als ihr eigentliches Medium. Wie Brett Ellis' *American Psycho* – ein Roman, der die 80er Jahre als seelenloses, blutrünstiges Jahrzehnt schildert, in dem Geld, gutes Aussehen und grenzenloser Egoismus die Grundlage aller Werte bildeten –, thematisiert auch Fischerspooner die oberflächliche Haltung jener Zeit, die schliesslich auch zum Zusammenbruch führte. Aber sie können den Stil der 80er Jahre in ihrem Rollenspiel aufleben lassen. Entertainment war in diesem Jahrzehnt in der Kunst so gross geschrieben wie nie zuvor, während die 90er Jahre als totale Gegenreaktion zu verstehen sind. Fischerspooner lässt das Entertainment wieder auferstehen und katapultiert sich damit zurück in die Zukunft.

(Übersetzung: Goridis/Parker)

1) Allmählich wird dir warm/Du fühlst den Sog/Unheimlich ist das./Langsam steigt das Fieber/Und breitet sich aus/ Heut Nacht./Die Winde brausen/Ziehen dich an sich/Durch die Gefahr hindurch./ Ich weiss, ich hab dich wo ich/Dich will/Heut Nacht./ Grenzkundschafter erkunde mein Herz...
2) Köstliches Rot/Rosa und feucht/So heiss ist es jetzt./Ich weiss ich hab dich, wo ich/Dich will/Heut Nacht.

C U M U L U S

From America

IN EVERY EDITION OF PARKETT, TWO CUMULUS CLOUDS, ONE FROM AMERICA, THE OTHER FROM EUROPE, FLOAT OUT TO AN INTERESTED PUBLIC. THEY CONVEY INDIVIDUAL OPINIONS, ASSESSMENTS, AND MEMORABLE ENCOUNTERS—AS ENTIRELY PERSONAL PRESENTATIONS OF PROFESSIONAL ISSUES.

OUR CONTRIBUTORS TO THIS ISSUE ARE LÁSZLÓ FÖLDÉNYI, ESSAYIST AND CRITIC LIVING IN BUDAPEST, HUNGARY, AND MARGIT ROWELL, CHIEF CURATOR OF DRAWINGS AT THE MOMA NEW YORK SINCE 1994, WHO LEFT THAT POSITION IN APRIL 2000 TO RETURN TO PARIS AND PURSUE INDEPENDENT PROJECTS.

MARGIT ROWELL

At the risk of appearing anachronistic or nostalgic, I will confess that when I chose a museum profession in the late sixties, it was comparable in my eyes to joining a religious order and taking vows, if not of chastity, then probably of poverty, and dedicating my existence to a higher cause. There were no prospects of becoming rich, or a star in the art world firmament. There was nothing in being a museum curator. Nothing, that is to say, except the exhilaration of a life in art.

As a curator, you had the pretext (at once a luxury and a mandate) to spend long hours with artists in their studios. You had the possibility to poke around museum storerooms and also to discover private collections and collectors, activities that were much less common than they are today. If you were lucky (or unlucky and impoverished, so you had no choice), you could also teach, preferably in an art school, like, for example, The School of Visual Arts. There you tried to impart knowledge and values to aspiring young artists, many of whom were more interested in "making it" in the art world than in being exposed to art history; the exercise of going against their grain was a major challenge. All of this, along with research, writing, and developing exhibitions, placed the curator near the heartbeat and pulse of the artistic experience. And the museum exhibition, as the culmination of the curator's efforts, represented an attempt to share this experience, to help the artist's voice to be heard, and the audience to see. In a word, you were extremely privileged; you had time to look, to listen and to think things through. Today, some thirty years later, one might suggest that much has changed.

"Seeing faster" was the title of an essay (by James Gleick) in *The New York Times Magazine* of September 19, 1999. One of many articles published in anticipation of the new millennium, this article dealt with the acceleration of

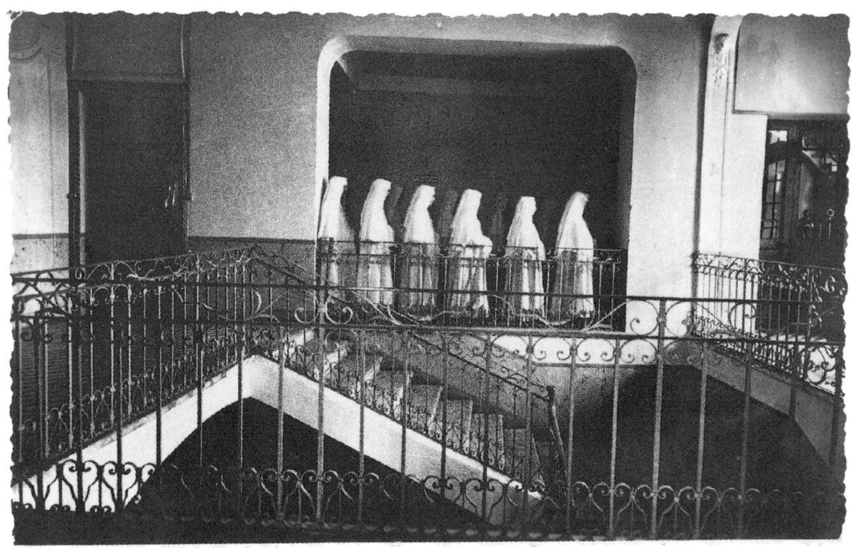

Museum curators... then... / Museumskuratoren... damals...
(POSTCARD: COLLECTION HARVEY TULCENSKY)

modern life. This acceleration is obvious in every aspect of our lives, but never more so than in business (read: making money), which has become the religion, popular culture, and pastime of modern industrial society. As the CEO of a major corporation recently stated: "Business is about reflexive action. If you have to think about a decision, it's already too late." Today the strategies of appropriation and exchange that inform the business world are equally pervasive in the art world. Indeed both spheres appear to be driven by the same ambitions and to share the same values, with analogous means and ends. In the business world, the motivating drive is competition, the modes are reflexive action and acceleration, the criteria are growth potential and performance, and the goal is accumulation of material wealth and public prestige. In the art world, such corporate terms as "acceleration,"

"high-speed innovation," "media-hype," "creative marketing" and "optimum performance" are insidiously replacing earlier notions such as contemplation, discovery and delay. Art, once marginal to the functioning of a society's market economy, has become a cog in the economic wheel.

Traditionally, one difference between business and culture is the coefficient of time: the time it takes to close a deal (ideally a nano-second) versus the time it takes to appreciate a work of art (possibly a lifetime). But it is also the q u a l i t y of time that is very different, and a distinct mindset, devoted to either achieving or exploring, which once again implies a different temporal framework. The current *rapprochement* of these two unlike modes of thinking and acting is indeed a symptom of one of the dysfunctions or dystopias of modern life. For as we are propelled onto the fast track of a pro-

fessional career (whether in the business or the art world), the temporal dimension as we know it may be described as: no past, no future, n o t i m e . This corresponds to a state of denial of the basic medium and substance that defines and informs everything we call life. Lest we forget, time determines the framework, structure and rhythms of all our waking (and sleeping) hours. And the precise ways in which we deal with the past, act in the present, and anticipate the future are what produce the kind of meaning we ultimately give to our lives.

Yet our relationship to time, its existential rhythms as well as its technical instruments of measure, has radically changed over the past few decades. Digital clocks (no dials, no hands), electronic calendars (isolating dates and events), word processors (eliminating preliminary drafts), instant e-mail, voice-mail messages held in

188

abeyance, workdays extending beyond the workplace, meals prepared in microwave ovens or taken on the run, incessant travel and the crossing of time-zones, instant reception of worldwide events, have totally altered traditional notions of time.

Just as temporal distinctions have been transformed or compressed into a momentary present by the information industry, other boundaries have been blurred in our socio-professional lives, such as, for example, the distinctions between the real and the virtual. Although "communication" is one of the words we live by, communication, in this context, is neither real nor immediate, but processed through "fast-forward" or "hold" mechanisms. We rarely see the people we speak to; we rarely hear a human voice. E-mail, and Internet "chats" are common substitutes. People who used to "hang out" in bars and cafes now "hang out" on the web. In the business world, commodities are traded on the Internet at the speed of lightning and (it goes without saying) sight unseen. Ultimately they are abstractions, solely identified by names and numbers. Art too is traded on line, sight unseen, as a name and title (a date also helps). But it is also traded in the real world, sight unseen. We all know of examples where a collector buys a work, stores it in a warehouse, and then puts it up at auction when the market is hot, without it ever gracing his or her walls. In so doing, the artwork is transformed from a physical, sensuous presence, a carrier of existential experience and meaning to an exclusively virtual object of spec-ulation and trade. Concomitantly, the "top lot" at a high-profile auction sale (of an object seen or unseen) is as valuable an investment (and as newsworthy) as the buy-out of the hottest high-tech company. Many artworks and artists have come to exist these days as assets on a spreadsheet. And the collector/buyer is more than ever the media star.

Thus the artwork has left the temple (figuratively speaking) and is more overtly and explicitly identified with the world of commodity trade. Buy when it's low, sell when it's high, invest in more growth are the rules of the day. But once again, this *rapprochement* corresponds to a misunderstanding of the fundamental difference between the "assets" at hand (art, as opposed to commercial goods and services) and

...and now / ...und heute.

(MAGAZINE CLIPPING / ILLUSTRIERTENPHOTO)

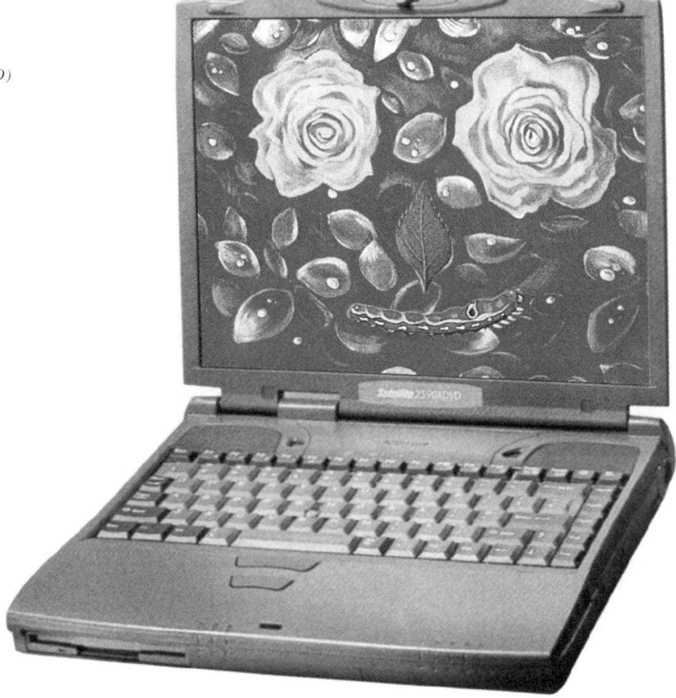

189

the mechanisms of production, communication, appropriation, and exchange germane to each. The commodities market is driven by large groups of like-minded investors who are trained to decipher, follow, and ultimately create marketing trends, the goal being rapid, personal material gain. Widespread agreement based on conventional wisdom is what makes a public offering rise and fall. Art, on the other hand, is traditionally based on a unique vision, singular tastes, and individual response. A literate public does not necessarily like the same books, just as a visually literate viewer does not relate to the same works of visual art. In view of the fact that art (all kinds of art) represents a highly personal statement, a private (but culturally legible) expression of some kind of order and meaning, it proposes a different exchange with each individual, depending on his or her preparation and experience. And the "wealth" of ideas, emotions, and sensations incarnate in the work of art can only be transmitted through isolation from the (economy-driven) mainstream, through exploration and reflection, not acceleration, but delay.

It seems however that, in the business world as in the art world, we are ever more ill equipped to exchange acceleration for delay, the pressures of the fast-forward mode for the threat of being perceived as a non-performer, and eventually a "non-person." The workplace, become a lifestyle, encourages us to trade our inner selves for public personae, private existence for professional performance, with its heady rewards of visibility and celebrity which in today's world are supremely seductive. As a museum curator, I will not talk about money although there is a lot of money in the art world today, and a lot of trade-offs of cultural ideals for material wealth. But these are not on the museum professional's (or the critic's or academic's) priority list. There is less and less time for personal thought or emotion, even communication, as we race to keep up with and respond to the steady stream of (instantly obsolete) data that comes our way. Our minds are held hostage by the words, figures and facts that click and flicker across an omnipresent screen. Our retinas run the risk of becoming fatigued and jaded, our ears of becoming dulled and deafened, our attention spans progressively limited, besieged by information overload, and our memories detached from ourselves, data-based. These time-saving devices and strategies set us up to access the next time-saving strategy; they do not provide us with more time for a meaningful life. Yet if we lose touch with certain realities of life, will we not eventually lose touch with art?

Life, as we recall from an earlier era, contained kinds of personal experience that business ventures or electronic and virtual reality cannot provide: joy and pain, emotions and ideas, expectations and disappointments, memories, intuitions and sensuous pleasures, and private fantasies, insights and desires, to mention only a few. And art, as we also recall, if our memory has not altogether abandoned us, was not about public performance or celebrity, but about private investigation and experiment, not about the power of authority but about mysterious forces of persuasion, not about material gain or social status, but about self-discovery and spiritual growth.

Has art changed, or have we changed? The focus and pace of our lives have certainly shifted and quickened. But time-saving is not life-enhancing; and seeing faster is not necessarily seeing better. We can only hope that there will always be art and artists (and indeed some art-world professionals) to remind us to refocus and slow down. And yet one is obliged to ask the question: in the new millennium, what kind of time or space will remain for life? And, by the same token, in our digitally-clocked existences, what kind of time or place will be reserved for art?

Auf die Gefahr hin, unzeitgemäss oder nostalgisch zu erscheinen, gebe ich zu, dass meine Entscheidung für einen Museumsberuf in den späten 60er Jahren mir damals durchaus mit dem Eintritt in einen religiösen Orden vergleichbar erschien. Wenn auch nicht Keuschheit, so gelobten wir doch Armut und versprachen unser Leben einem höheren Zweck zu widmen. Damals bestand keinerlei Aussicht, reich oder gar ein Stern am Kunsthimmel zu werden. Museumskuratorin zu sein bedeutete gar nichts. Nichts, ausser dem erhebenden Gefühl, für die Kunst zu leben.

Als Kurator hatte man immerhin einen Vorwand um stundenlang mit Künstlern in deren Ateliers zusammenzusitzen – Vergnügen und Auftrag waren eins. Man hatte die Möglichkeit in Magazinen von Museen herumzustöbern und auch private Sammlungen und Sammler zu entdecken, Dinge, die damals noch viel weniger üblich waren als heute. Wenn man Glück hatte (oder das Pech arm zu sein und daher gar keine Wahl), konnte man unterrichten, am liebsten an einer Kunstschule, etwa der School of Visual Arts. Dort versuchte man sein Wissen und seine Wertvorstellungen mit jungen ehrgeizigen Künstlern zu teilen, von denen die meisten mehr darauf aus waren, den Sprung in die Kunstszene zu schaffen als sich mit Kunstgeschichte zu beschäftigen; sich gegen sie, ihrem eigentlichen Interesse zum Trotz zu behaupten, war eine echte Herausforderung. All das, zusammen mit der wissenschaftlichen Arbeit, dem Schreiben und dem Vorbereiten von Ausstellungen, liess einen Kurator hautnah an der künstlerischen Erfahrung teilhaben. Und die Ausstellung im Museum, Glanzpunkt in der Arbeit jedes Kurators, stellte den Versuch dar, diese Erfahrung mitzuerleben, dazu beizutragen, dass die Stimme des Künstlers gehört würde und dass das Publikum etwas zu sehen bekäme. Mit einem Wort, man war äusserst privilegiert; man hatte Zeit hinzusehen, zuzuhören und über alles nachzudenken. Heute, rund dreissig Jahre später, sieht das ganz anders aus.

«Schneller sehen» lautete der Titel eines Essays (von James Gleick) im *New York Times Magazine* vom 19. September 1999. Es war einer jener zahlreichen Artikel, die im Hinblick auf das neue Millennium erschienen, und sein Thema war die Beschleunigung des modernen Lebens. Diese Beschleunigung manifestiert sich offensichtlich in allen Lebensbereichen, aber nirgends deutlicher als im Geschäftsleben (sprich: Geld Scheffeln), das in der modernen Industriegesellschaft zu Religion, Volkssport und Zeitvertreib in einem avanciert ist. Wie meinte doch der Geschäftsführer einer grösseren Firma kürzlich: «Beim Geschäftemachen geht es um Reflexhandlungen. Wenn man über eine Entscheidung nachdenken muss, ist es bereits zu spät.» Dieselben Strategien des Aneignens und Austauschens, die heute die Geschäftswelt prägen, bestimmen auch die Kunstszene. Tatsächlich scheinen in beiden Sphären bei analogen Mitteln und Zielen dieselben Ambitionen und Werte wirksam zu sein. In der Geschäftswelt heisst der Antrieb Wettbewerb, die Mittel Reflex und Beschleunigung, die Kriterien Wachstumspotenzial und Geschäftserfolg, und das Ziel ist die Anhäufung von Reichtum und öffentlichem Ansehen. In der Kunstwelt verdrängen Termini aus dem Wirtschaftsleben wie «Akzeleration», «schnelle Innovation», «Medienstrategie», «kreatives Marketing» und «optimale Performance» nach und nach ältere Begriffe wie Kontemplation, Entdeckung, Verweilen. Die Kunst, einst unbedeutend für das Funktionieren der Marktwirtschaft, ist zu einem Rad in ihrem Getriebe geworden.

Im Zeitfaktor lag traditionell ein wichtiger Unterschied zwischen Wirtschaft und Kultur: die Zeit, die es braucht, um ein Geschäft abzuschliessen (im Idealfall eine Nanosekunde), gegenüber der Zeit, die es braucht, um ein Kunstwerk zu würdigen (möglicherweise ein Leben lang). Aber auch die Qualität der Zeit ist eine ganz andere und die geistige Einstellung, die entweder auf Erfolg oder auf Erforschung aus ist, was wiederum verschiedene zeitliche Rahmenbedingungen erfordert. Die Annäherung, die diese beiden grundverschiedenen Denk- und Handlungsweisen zurzeit erfahren, ist tatsächlich Symptom einer Entgleisung oder Fehlentwicklung des modernen Lebens. Denn sobald wir in die schnelle Schiene der professionellen Karriere gestossen werden (egal, ob in der Geschäfts- oder der Kunstwelt), lässt sich die zeitliche Dimension, wie wir sie kennen, wie folgt beschreiben: keine Vergangenheit, keine Zukunft, keine Zeit. Das entspricht einer Leugnung des ursprünglichen Mediums und der Grundsubstanz, die alles, was wir Leben nennen, definiert und prägt. Wir dürfen nicht vergessen, dass die Zeit den Hintergrund, die Struktur und den Rhythmus unseres Wachens und Schlafens bestimmt. Und die Art, wie wir mit der Vergangenheit umgehen, in der Gegenwart handeln und die Zukunft vorwegnehmen, ermöglicht überhaupt erst, dass wir unserem Leben so etwas wie Sinn verleihen.

Aber unser Verhältnis zur Zeit hat sich in den letzten Jahrzehnten dramatisch verändert, sowohl im Hinblick auf existenzielle Rhythmen wie, was die Zeitmessung angeht. Digitale Uhren (ohne Zifferblatt und Zeiger), elektronische Kalender (die Daten und Ereignisse isoliert präsentieren), elektronische Textverarbeitung (das Ende der Weiterexistenz aller vorläufigen Fassungen und Entwürfe), die im Handumdrehen zu empfangende E-Mail, auf Abruf bereite, gesprochene Botschaften, Arbeitstage, die sich über den Arbeitsort hinaus erstrecken, Mahlzeiten aus der Mikrowelle oder unterwegs eingenommen, das unablässige Reisen und Überqueren von Zeitzonen und die unverzügliche Rezeption aller Ereignisse weltweit haben unser traditionelles Zeitverständnis völlig verändert.

Genau wie die zeitlichen Differenzierungen, die durch die Mediengesellschaft verändert und zu einer einzigen momentanen Gegenwart komprimiert wurden, sind auch andere Grenzen unseres sozialen und beruflichen Lebens verwischt worden, so zum Beispiel die Unterscheidung zwischen dem Realen und dem Virtuellen. Obwohl «Kommunikation» etwas bezeichnet, was wir zum Leben brauchen, ist Kommunikation in diesem Kontext weder real noch unmittelbar, sondern erfolgt mittels «Schnell vorwärts»- oder «Stopp»-Tasten. Selten sehen wir die Leute, mit denen wir sprechen; selten ist es eine menschliche Stimme, die wir hören. Stattdessen unterhält man sich per E-Mail oder Internet-Chat. Leute, die früher in Bars und Cafés herumlungerten, lungern jetzt im Netz herum. Waren werden im Internet blitz- und lichtgeschwind und (selbstverständlich) unbesehn gehandelt. Es sind abstrakte Einheiten, lediglich durch Namen und Zahlen identifizierbar. Auch Kunst wird online gehandelt, unbesehen, als Name und Titel (auch ein Datum ist gut). Aber sie wird auch in der wirklichen Welt unbesehen gehandelt. Wir alle kennen Fälle von Sammlern, die ein Werk kaufen, es in einem Lagerhaus verschwinden lassen und wieder auf den Markt bringen, wenn der Zeitpunkt günstig ist, ohne dass es je die eigenen Wände geziert hätte. Dadurch wird das Kunstwerk von einer physischen, sinnlichen Gegenwart, einem Medium existenzieller Erfahrung und Bedeutung zum rein virtuellen Spekulations- und Handelsobjekt.

Gleichzeitig stellt das (sichtbare oder unsichtbare) Hauptlos einer bedeutenden Kunstauktion eine genauso lohnende Investition dar wie die Aktienmehrheit der höchstdotierten Hightech-Firma (und ist auch genauso schlagzeilenträchtig). Viele Kunstwerke und Künstler schlagen heute auf der Gewinnseite zu Buche. Und der Sammler oder Käufer wird je länger je mehr zum Medienstar.

Das Kunstwerk hat also buchstäblich den Tempel verlassen und wird nun ganz offen und ausdrücklich als Handelsware betrachtet. Kaufen, wenns billig ist, verkaufen, wenns teuer ist, und wachstumsorientiert investieren, so lautet die Parole. Aber diese Angleichung läuft auf ein Missverständnis der grundlegenden Verschiedenheit der vorliegenden Werte (Kunst im Gegensatz zu Waren und Dienstleistungen) und der zugehörigen Mechanismen von Produktion, Kommunikation, Aneignung und Austausch hinaus. Der Konsumgütermarkt wird von grossen Gruppen ähnlich denkender Investoren gesteuert, die darin geübt sind, Trends zu erkennen, ihnen zu folgen oder auch selbst welche zu schaffen, um möglichst schnell einen persönlichen materiellen Gewinn zu erzielen. Weitgehende Übereinstimmung aufgrund konventioneller Weisheiten bewirkt das Steigen und Fallen der Aktien. Kunst dagegen stützt sich traditionell auf die Vision von Einzelnen, auf den Geschmack, der aus der Reihe tanzt, und auf individuelle Reaktionen. Ein belesenes Publikum liebt nicht unbedingt dieselben Bücher, genauso wie visuell gebildete Betrachter sich nicht von denselben Werken der bildenden Kunst angesprochen fühlen. Da Kunst (in all ihren Spielarten) immer eine sehr persönliche Aussage darstellt und privater (aber kulturell lesbarer) Ausdruck einer bestimmten Ordnung und Bedeutung ist, ist der Austausch mit jedem Betrachter und jeder Betrachterin immer wieder anders, je nach Vorbereitung und Erfahrung des jeweiligen Individuums. Und der im Kunstwerk enthaltene Reichtum der Gedanken, Gefühle und Empfindungen kann sich nur abseits vom (marktorientierten) Mainstream entfalten, durch Untersuchung und Reflexion, nicht durch Beeilung, sondern im Verweilen.

Es scheint jedoch, dass wir sowohl in der Geschäftswelt wie in der Kunstszene je länger, je weniger dazu imstande sind, die Eile mit Weile zu vertauschen, den Zwang zum beschleunigten Vorlauf mit der Gefahr als Niete zu gelten und damit über kurz oder lang als ein Niemand. Der Arbeitsplatz, der zur Lebensform geworden ist, hält uns dazu an, unser inneres Selbst gegen eine öffentliche Person einzutauschen, unser Privatleben gegen den beruflichen Erfolg und die lockende Belohnung des Gesehen- und Berühmtwerdens, was in der heutigen Welt im höchsten Grade verführerisch ist. Als Museumskuratorin werde ich nicht von Geld sprechen, obwohl in der Kunstszene heute eine Menge Geld in Umlauf ist und der Ausverkauf kultureller Ideale gegen materiellen Reichtum in vollem Gange. Aber das hat nicht erste Priorität für jemanden, der in einem Museum (oder als Kritiker oder Wissenschaftler) tätig ist. Es bleibt immer weniger Zeit für persönliche Gedanken oder Gefühle, ja sogar für die Kommunikation beim Versuch, im stetigen Strom der uns überflutenden (und im Handumdrehen veralteten) Daten nicht den Überblick zu verlieren. Wir sind nichts als Geiseln der Worte,

Zahlen und Fakten, die über den allgegenwärtigen Bildschirm ticken und flackern. Unserer Netzhaut droht Ermüdung und Überreizung, unseren Ohren Schwerhörigkeit und Taubheit. Die Spanne unserer Aufmerksamkeit wird immer kürzer inmitten dieser Informationsüberfülle, und unser Gedächtnis haben wir auf Datenträger ausgelagert. Diese zeitsparenden Mittel und Strategien bereiten jedoch nur den nächsten zeitsparenden Schritt vor; sie verschaffen uns nicht mehr Zeit für ein sinnvolleres Leben. Wenn wir aber den Kontakt zur Lebenswirklichkeit verlieren, verlieren wir damit über kurz oder lang nicht auch den Kontakt zur Kunst?

Das Leben, wie wir es von früher kennen, war mit persönlichen Erfahrungen verbunden, die ein Finanzabenteuer oder die elektronische und virtuelle Realität nicht vermitteln können: Freude und Schmerz, Gefühle und Gedanken, Erwartungen und Enttäuschungen, Erinnerungen, Einfälle und sinnliche Freuden, heimliche Phantasien, Einsichten und Wünsche, um nur einige wenige zu nennen. Und in der Kunst ging es, wenn die Erinne-

rung uns noch nicht vollends trügt, früher nicht um Öffentlichkeit und Berühmtheit, sondern um stille Untersuchungen und Versuche, nicht um die Macht der Autorität, sondern um geheimnisvolle Überzeugungskräfte, nicht um materiellen Gewinn oder sozialen Status, sondern um Selbstfindung und geistiges Wachstum.

Hat sich die Kunst verändert oder sind wir anders geworden? Die Ausrichtung und das Tempo unseres Lebens hat sich gewiss verlagert und beschleunigt. Aber Zeit sparen bedeutet kein intensiveres Leben; und schneller sehen heisst nicht unbedingt besser sehen. Wir können nur hoffen, dass es immer Kunst und Künstler geben wird (und auch einige beruflich mit Kunst sich Befassende), die uns daran erinnern, unsere Sehgewohnheiten zu überprüfen und uns mehr Zeit zu nehmen. Dennoch muss die Frage gestellt werden: Welche Art von Zeit und Raum wird dem Leben im neuen Jahrtausend bleiben? Und desgleichen: Welche Art von Zeit und Ort wird in unserer digital bemessenen Existenz für die Kunst bleiben?

(Übersetzung: Susanne Schmidt)

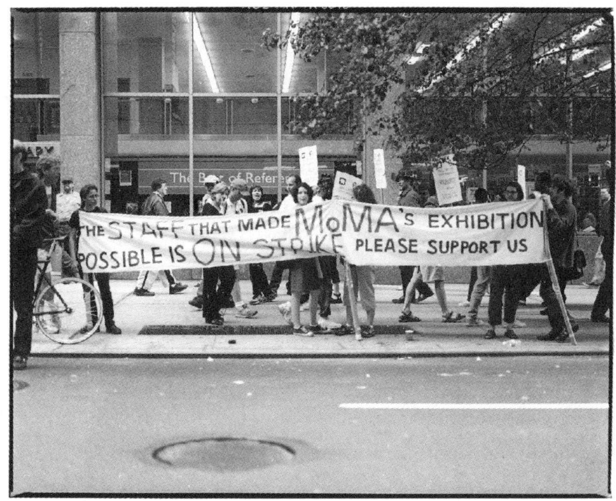

MoMA staff on strike, New York, June 2000 / Streikende Belegschaft des Museum of Modern Art in New York. (PHOTO: JENNIFER McCABE)

CUMULUS

IN JEDER AUSGABE VON PARKETT PEILT EINE CUMULUS-WOLKE AUS AMERIKA UND EINE AUS EUROPA DIE INTERESSIERTEN KUNSTFREUNDE AN. SIE TRÄGT PERSÖNLICHE RÜCKBLICKE, BEURTEILUNGEN UND DENK- WÜRDIGE BEGEGNUNGEN MIT SICH – ALS JEWEILS GANZ EIGENE DAR- STELLUNG EINER BERUFSMÄSSIGEN AUSEINANDERSETZUNG.

IN DIESEM HEFT ÄUSSERN SICH LÁSZLÓ F. FÖLDÉNYI, KUNSTKRITIKER UND ESSAYIST AUS BUDAPEST, SOWIE MARGIT ROWELL, VON 1994 BIS APRIL 2000 LEI- TENDE KURATORIN FÜR ZEICHNUNGEN AM MUSEUM OF MODERN ART, NEW YORK, JETZT FREIE KURATORIN IN PARIS.

LÁSZLÓ F. FÖLDÉNYI

DIE SCHWIERIGKEIT DES DIALOGS

Nach Ansicht der alten Griechen können zwei Menschen nicht denselben Traum träumen. Die Erfahrung lehrt jedoch, dass Gruppen von Menschen sehr wohl ähnlichen Träumen nachhängen können. Zumindest in Mitteleuropa, wo Träume folglich mehr Wirkung zeitigen als sonstwo auf dem Kontinent. Es gibt hier Gruppen, die ausschliesslich von ihrer eigenen Grösse träumen; andere wiederum nur von ihrem Betrogensein; manche werden durch ihre Träume in ihrem Gekränktsein und Selbstmitleid bestärkt; wieder andere träumen davon, dass der Westen sie als gleichwertige Partner behandelt; manche träumen, ihr Leben sei genauso normal wie das aller anderen in Europa; und es gibt auch solche, die vom Träumen träumen und sich dabei in einer Welt aus Nebel einschliessen. Aber was die einzelnen Gruppen auch immer träumen, eines haben sie alle gemeinsam: Der Traum und die Träumerei spielen in dieser Gegend eine nicht weniger wichtige Rolle als im Westen die nüchterne Wachsamkeit, der Realitätssinn und der Pragmatismus. Das gilt für die Welt der Politik genauso wie für die anderen Bereiche der gesellschaftlichen Öffentlichkeit. Und natürlich auch für die Kunst, die sich in Mitteleuropa seit Generationen so zur westeuropäischen Moderne verhält wie das Unterbewusste zum Bewusstsein: Mal wirkt sie anre gend, mal bremsend, Mal läuft sie ihr entgegen, mal bleibt sie auf fatale Weise zurück. Doch nur in den seltensten Fällen vermag sie ein harmonisches Verhältnis mit ihr einzugehen.

1989 schien ein historischer Augenblick zu sein, in dem Mitteleuropa aufzuwachen schien. Es schien, als würde diese Gegend nicht mehr dem Zwang unterliegen, sich in Träumen auszuleben. Der Westen nahm die Befreiung der hiesigen Völker euphorisch auf, und es schien, als würde die verhängnisvolle Teilung Europas ein Ende nehmen. Die Euphorie hatte ihren Grund zum Teil darin, dass Mitteleuropa für den Westen damals eine Art Modellcharakter besass: Es schien, als könne hier von Grund auf, gleichsam aus dem Nichts die ideale Demokratie errichtet werden, ohne ihre westlichen Schattenseiten. Und parallel dazu wuchs im Westen auch die Neugierde, ob die fast ein halbes Jahrhundert hermetisch abgeschlossene, mitteleuropäische Kunst vielleicht noch über verborgene Reserven verfüge, die – wie schon einmal, zu Beginn des Jahrhunderts – befruchtend auf die westliche Kunst wirken könnten.

Ausstellungen, welche die klassische Avantgarde beziehungsweise die zeitgenössische Kunst Mitteleuropas zum Thema hatten, gingen durch ganz Europa. Die wichtigsten waren: «Europe Unknown» (Polen 1990); «Reduktivismus: Polen, Tschechoslowakei, Ungarn 1950–1980» (Wien 1992); «La coesistenza dell'arte» (Biennale in Venedig, 1993); «Europa, Europa» (Bonn 1994); «Aspekte/Positionen: 50 Jahre Kunst aus Mitteleuropa» (Wien 1999); «After the Wall: Art and Culture in Post-Communist Europe» (Stockholm 2000). Die Kuratoren, vor allem Lóránd Hegyi, der Direktor des Museums Moderner Kunst Stiftung Ludwig Wien, hatten sich zum Ziel gesetzt, die jahrhundertealte Bruchstelle zu beseitigen. Es galt vor allem, dem westlichen Publikum die Kunst einer Region vorzustellen, die sich im Lauf eines halben Jahrhunderts weiter von Westeuropa entfernt hatte als Japan oder Korea. Es galt, einen unbekannten, weissen Fleck nachträglich auszufüllen. Die Ausstellungen brachten jedoch ungeahnte Deutungsschwierigkeiten mit sich.

Die Vertreter der polnischen, tschechischen oder ungarischen klassischen Avantgarde vor dem Zweiten Weltkrieg sind auch heute weltweit bekannt. Nach 1948 entbehrte das künstlerische Leben in diesen Ländern jeder Öffentlichkeit (mit Ausnahme des sozialistischen Realismus, der jedoch nirgends eine restlose Hegemonie erringen konnte). In Ost- und Mitteleuropa schufen die bedeutenden Künstler über ein halbes Jahrhundert für die sogenannte «zweite Öffentlichkeit», deren Spielregeln, Gesetze und Institutionen sich radikal von denen der «ersten Öffentlichkeit» im Westen unterschieden. Gemäss der Logik des Kalten Krieges tangierte sich das Kunstschaffen beider Seiten kaum, und wenn doch, so blieb die Wirkung selbst dann noch einseitig. Die Kunst Westeuropas war vor allem westlich, die Mitteleuropas vor allem östlich. Als sich nach 1989 die Möglichkeit ergab miteinander in Dialog zu treten, zeigte sich bald, mit wie abweichenden Bedeutungen ein anderer Kontext scheinbar ähnliche Ausdrucksformen der Kunst belasten kann. Bis heute haben der Westen und der Osten keine gemeinsame Sprache gefunden, die weder westlich noch östlich, sondern europäisch wäre.

Die erwähnten Ausstellungen fördern das Verständnis und dienen der Selbsterkenntnis, die Voraussetzung für jeden Dialog ist. Sie führen nicht nur der westlichen Öffentlichkeit vor, was sich auf der anderen Seite getan hat, sondern machen auch die mitteleuropäischen Künstler selbst darauf aufmerksam, dass die Kunst Mitteleuropas spezifische Wurzeln hat, die sich nicht in westlichen Boden verpflanzen lassen ohne Schaden zu nehmen. Denn die mitteleuropäischen Kunstrichtungen haben, auch wenn sie durch noch so viele Fäden mit der westlichen verknüpft sind, und wenn noch so viele formale Ähnlichkeiten bestehen, auch spezifische Kriterien, deren Verständnis einer geschichtlichen Psychoanalyse gleichkommt.

Welche Kriterien sind dies? Als Erstes fällt auf, wie sehr die Werke der mitteleuropäischen Künstler im Vergleich zu ihren westlichen Kollegen mit «Gehalt» beladen sind. Das ergibt sich zum Teil aus der Abgeschlossenheit sowie aus jenem jahrhundertealten Zwang, dass in Mitteleuropa mangels demokratisch organisierter, politischer Institutionen meist den Künstlern die Aufgabe zufiel, Dinge aufzudecken, zu beleuchten, den Weg zu weisen. Diese «Bürde» kommt nicht nur in den Themen der Kunst und ihrem übermässig «literarischen» Charakter zum Ausdruck, sondern auch im Umgang mit den Materialien, bei dem der selbstzweckhafte, ästhetische Genuss des Materials merklich hinter der metaphorischen Bedeutung zurücktritt (Magdalena Abakanowicz). Zweitens wird die Kunst, wenn sie in die «zweite Öffentlichkeit» abgedrängt wird, unvermeidlich zu einer Kunst von wenigen Auserwählten – eine Art Ersatzreligion (das gilt sogar für den stark mitteleuropäisch verwurzelten Hermann Nitsch). Was im Westen in den letzten Jahrzehnten zunehmend kitschverdächtig wurde (zum Beispiel Pathos), ist in Mitteleuropa Quelle existenzieller Erfahrungen. Deshalb ist die Kunst auch nicht eine Institution unter vielen, geregelt durch den freien Markt, sondern eine «heilige» Tätigkeit, die es sogar wert ist, sein Leben dafür zu opfern. Das verleiht dem Werk der bedeutendsten mitteleuropäischen Vertreter der Body-Art – Tibor Hajas, Marina Abramovic – einen Unterton, der sie von den Vertretern der westeuropäischen Body-Art unterscheidet. Zugleich hat – als drittes Kriterium – nicht nur die Kunst einen anderen «Stellenwert» als im Westen, sondern auch die Politik. Als Folge der historischen Benachteiligung ist die Politik in Mitteleuropa nach wie vor von existenziellem Gewicht, weshalb politische Anspielungen hier – anders, als in der westlichen Kunst – nicht bremsend, sondern inspirierend wirken. Deshalb kann die politisch engagierte Kunst (Braco Dimitrijevic) authentisch bleiben. Das verleiht etwa der Kunst eines Milan Knizak eine Färbung, die man bei westeuropäischen oder amerikanischen Vertretern der Fluxusbewegung vergeblich sucht.

Die Liste der Unterscheidungsmerkmale liesse sich fortsetzen. Was auffällt, ist, dass wenn es zu einem Dialog zwischen der mitteleuropäischen und der westlichen Kunst kommt, beide Seiten zwar die gleiche Sprache sprechen, einander aber dennoch kaum verstehen können. Die Ungarn Vilmos Huszár oder László Moholy-Nagy liessen, nachdem sie nach Westeuropa ausgewandert waren, einen Grossteil ihres Werkes aus ihrer vorkonstruktivistischen Zeit hinter sich. Lajos Kassák hingegen, der in Ungarn blieb, verknüpfte seinen eigenen konstruktivistischen Stil mit einer Farben- und Formenwelt, die seine Werke viel persönlicher, zuweilen fast schon empfindsam werden liess. Er blieb «mitteleuropäischer» als seine Meister. Und in der nächsten Generation öffnete Imre Bak, der bis heute konsequenteste Vertreter des ungarischen Konstruktivismus, seine Kunst dem Einfluss archaischer, aussereuropäischer Kulturen, während er sich zugleich glänzend der auch im Westen verständlichen, konstruktivistischen Tradition bediente. Seine Werke wirken zugleich archaisch (zum Teil auch wegen seiner Sensibilität für Transzendenz) und modern. Baks Werk ist im Westen zwar verständlich, aber ausserhalb seines Kontexts dennoch nur schwer zu rezipieren. Und dasselbe lässt sich über das Werk aller bedeutenden, zeitgenössischen Künstler Mitteleuropas sagen, unabhängig davon, ob sie international etabliert oder nur wenigen bekannt sind: Die Werke von Roman Opalka, Günter Brus, Julia Kneifer, Tadeusz Kantor, Akos Birkás oder Stanislav Kolibal haben alle auch Schichten, die erst im mitteleuropäischen Kontext wirklich verständlich sind.

Sollte man den Werken die Schuld geben, dass sie von wenigen Ausnahmen abgesehen nicht in den Kreislauf der Weltkunst gelangt sind? Wohl kaum. Viel eher schon jener verhängnisvollen Teilung, die die Identität Europas selbst in Frage stellte. Wegen der Teilung in der Zeit des Kalten Kriegs konnten Konflikte auf dem Gebiet der Kunst zwischen West- und Mitteleuropa nicht offen (und gesund) ausgetragen werden, wie das zwischen den Vereinigten Staaten und Westeuropa der Fall war. Zudem erlebt Europa als Folge der nach der Euphorie von 1989 eingetretenen Ernüchterung eine neuerliche Teilung. Nunmehr verläuft die Trennlinie nicht mehr zwischen zwei politischen Systemen, sondern zwischen den Erfolgreichen und den Aussenseitern. Und so verwundert es nicht, dass heute immer mehr Künstler in Mitteleuropa vor allem den Anschluss suchen, mit anderen Worten im künstlerischen Reigen der Erfolgreichen mittun möchten. Wenn es sein muss, sogar auf Kosten des gewaltsamen Ausbruchs aus dem eigenen Medium und Kontext. Ihre Ungeduld ist verständlich: Die jahrzehntelange Isolation führte zu Atemnot. Der künstlerische, auch durch Institutionen abgestützte Markterfolg ist für viele schon jetzt gesichert. Doch das Vergessen des komplexen Hintergrundes der mitteleuropäischen Kunst – neuer, drohender Alptraum! – ist ein viel zu hoher Preis dafür.

(Aus dem Ungarischen von Akos Doma)

LÁSZLÓ F. FÖLDÉNYI

THE DIFFICULTY OF DIALOGUE

The ancient Greeks claimed that two individuals cannot dream the same dream, but we have learned from experience that groups of people can most certainly dwell on similar dreams. At least in Central Europe, where dreams have a greater capacity for mobilizing emotions than elsewhere on the continent. Here, there are some who dream exclusively of their own greatness; others of having been cheated; still others find reinforcement in dreams for their sense of injury and self-pity; some dream of being treated as equal partners by the West; some dream that their lives are just as normal as everyone else's in Europe, and then there are those who dream of dreaming and wall themselves up in a fortress of fog. But no matter what these groups dream about, they all have one thing in common: Dreams and dreaminess play as much of a determining role in this part of the world as down-to-earth wakefulness, a sense of reality, and pragmatism do in the West. This applies not only to the world of politics but to all fields of public life. And, of course, to art as well. For generations art in Central Europe has been related to Western Modernism in much the same way as the unconscious is related to the conscious: sometimes it is stimulating, sometimes obstructive, at other times contradictory, and occasionally disastrously behind the times. Only on the rarest of occasions does it manage to establish a harmonious relationship with the West.

1989 was supposedly a historic moment; Central Europe seemed to be waking up, ready to shake the habit of vicarious fulfillment through dreams. The West responded euphorically to the liberation of peoples on this side of the invisible barrier and it looked as if the fateful division of Europe would become history. The euphoria was due partly to the fact that Central Europe was something of a model for the West, a testing ground where ideal, unadulterated democracies could be created from scratch. And then Westerners also wondered whether close to fifty years of hermetically isolated Central European art might not possess hidden reserves that could enrich Western art— much like the events at the turn of the last century.

Exhibitions on the classical avant-garde or contemporary art of Central Europe swept across Europe, notably: "Europe Unknown" (Poland, 1990), "Reduktivismus: Polen, Tschechoslowakei, Ungarn 1950–1980" (Vienna, 1992), "La coesistenza dell'arte" (Venice Biennale, 1993), "Europa, Europa" (Bonn, 1994), "Aspekte/Positionen: 50 Jahre Kunst aus Mitteleuropa" (Vienna, 1999), and "After the Wall: Art and Culture in Post-Communist Europe" (Stockholm, 2000). The curators, Lóránd Hegyi, director of the Museum Moderner Kunst Stiftung Ludwig Wien, in particular, had set themselves the goal of bridging the centuries-old gap. It was time to show the public in the West the art of a region that had drifted farther away from Western Europe than Japan or Korea. It was time to explore an unknown patch of white. Instead, these exhibitions found themselves faced with unforeseen difficulties of interpretation.

The exponents of the classical avant-garde from Poland, Czechoslovakia, or Hungary prior to the Second World War are also internationally renowned today. After 1948, artistic life in these countries had no public profile whatsoever (with the exception of Socialist Realism, though it was unable to achieve complete hegemony). Im-

197

portant artists in the Balkans and Central Europe spent fifty years working for what might be called a "secondary public" whose rules, laws and institutions were radically different from those of the "primary public" in the West. Given the logic of the Cold War, the two sets of practitioners rarely made contact, and if they did, the influence was always uni-lateral. Art of Western Europe was primarily W e s t - e r n , the art of Central Europe was primarily E a s t e r n . When the possibility of dialogue arose in 1989, the onus of divergent meanings in divergent contexts, despite seemingly similar artistic idioms, soon became unmistakably evident. To date, East and West have yet to find a common language that is neither Eastern nor Western, but rather European.

The exhibitions listed above aimed at fostering understanding. They sought insight, which is a prerequisite of dialogue. They not only showed a Western public what has been happening on the other side; they also demonstrated that Central European art has a rootedness which prevents it from being transplanted to the soil of the West without suffering injury. For, no matter how many feelers it has in the West and no matter how great the formal common ground, Central European directions in art still have distinctive criteria whose comprehension requires nothing short of historical psychoanalysis.

What are these criteria? The first thing one notices is how heavily the works of Central European artists are loaded with "content" in comparison to those of their colleagues in the West. This is due in part to isolation but also to the fact that, for centuries, artists have borne the burden of pointing the way, of lighting the path, for want of

democratically organized, political institutions. This "burden" is manifest not only in the subject matter of their art and its excessively "literary" character but also in the use of materials chosen less for the delight in their (non-utilitarian) aesthetic than for their metaphorical impact (Magdalena Abakanowicz). Moreover, art that is sidelined inevitably becomes art for the few, for the elect—a kind of ersatz religion (which even applies to Hermann Nitsch with his strong roots in Central Europe). Those things increasingly suspected of being kitsch in the West (pathos, for instance) are a spring of existential experience in Central Europe. For this reason art is not one institution among many, governed by the free market, but rather a "sacred" activity that is even worth dying for. This lends a frisson to the work of the most important Central European exponents of body art—Tibor Hajas and Marina Abramovic—which clearly sets them off against their counterparts in the West. And thirdly, the status not only of art but also of politics is entirely different from that in the West. Due to the historical disadvantage, politics in Central Europe still have an existential significance for which reason political allusions—in contrast to the West—are not a hindrance but rather an inspiration. In consequence, politically oriented art (Braco Dimitrijevic) retains it authenticity, and the work of such an artist as Milan Knizak acquires a coloring that one seeks in vain among West European or American representatives of the Fluxus movement.

The list of differences could go on. At issue here, however, is the realization that when a dialogue does takes place between Central European and Western art, the two sides are hard put

to understand each other although they speak the same language. The Hungarians Vilmos Huszár or László Moholy-Nagy left the greater part of their pre-Constructivist work behind when they emigrated to Western Europe, while Lajos Kassák, who remained in Hungary, linked his own Constructivist style with a world of colors and forms that gave his works a personal and at times almost sensitive touch. He remained more "Central European" than his masters. And in the generation that followed, Imre Bak, the most uncompromising of all representatives of Hungarian Constructivism, opened his work to archaic, non-European cultures while brilliantly exploiting a Constructivist tradition that was intelligible in the West as well. His works seem both archaic (partially due to their sensitivity to transcendence) and modern. Bak's oeuvre is no doubt understandable in the West but difficult nonetheless, when removed from its context. And the same may be said of all of the important contemporary artists in Central Europe regardless of whether they are internationally established or lesser known figures: The works of Roman Opalka, Günter Brus, Julia Kneifer, Tadeusz Kantor, Akos Birkás or Stanislav Kolibal also have subtexts that are really only understandable in the Central European framework.

Should these works be blamed for not having flowed for the most part into the circulatory system of world art? Hardly. The problem lies rather in that fateful division which has undermined the very identity of Europe itself. The Cold War deprived art in Western and Central Europe of the opportunity to engage in open and healthy argument, unlike the exchange between the

United States and Western Europe. In addition, as disenchantment supplants the euphoria of 1989, Europe is once again faced with division. The dividing line no longer runs between two political systems but rather between those who are thriving and those who are not. It is no wonder that more and more artists in Central Europe want to join the ranks of their successful peers, even at the expense of violently breaking with their own cultural context. One can appreciate the impatience: Decades of isolation have led to shortness of breath. And there are many who have already begun to enjoy the advantages of the artistic market and the security of institutional success. But disregard of the complex background of Central European art demands a price that may be too high: another nightmare threatens.

(Translation: Catherine Schelbert)

BALKON

Die Jetzt-Idee:
Stickerei

MICHELLE NICOL

Das moderne Kunstwerk gewinnt Dauerhaftigkeit, weil es sich dem jeweiligen Zeitgeschmack widersetzt. Und aus diesem Grund wurde die Technik Stickerei zur Jetzt-Idee der aktuellen Kunst: Weil das Unverhoffte sich gerade dort niederlässt, wo man es am wenigsten erwartet. Stickerei ist anachronistische und arbeitsintensive Handarbeit mit Nadel und Faden. Von der Kunst des zwanzigsten Jahrhun-

MICHELLE NICOL ist Kunstkritikerin und freie Kuratorin. Sie lebt in Zürich.

derts wurde diese Technik verachtet, weil sie hausfraulich und kunsthandwerklich konnotiert ist. Der Kreuzstich sei nichts als Kitsch und Tand. Im suburbanen Alltag mache er die häuslichen Dinge zwar generell etwas schöner, etwas erträglicher. Mehr nicht.

Um es vorwegzunehmen, folgende Künstler arbeiten heute mit der Technik Stickerei: **Cosima von Bonin.** Sie stickt zum Beispiel ein minimales Wappen mit Baumwolle auf Samt, näht Herrentaschentücher zusammen, oder klebt eine Yves-Saint-Laurent-Einkaufstüte auf ein Stück rot-weiss kariertes Tuch. Diesen fraulichen Operationen setzt sie sich selber als das Klischee einer vermännlichten Künstlerpersona gegenüber (sie trägt massgeschneiderte Herrenanzüge). **Tracey Emin.** Für ihr Zelt EVERYONE I HAVE EVER SLEPT WITH 1963–1995 bestickte sie das Innere der Skulptur mit den Namen aller Menschen, mit denen sie jemals

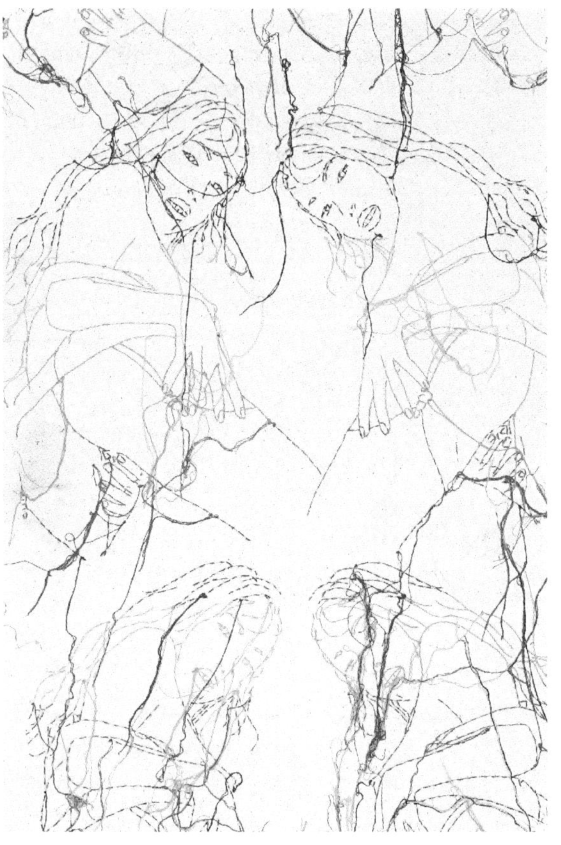

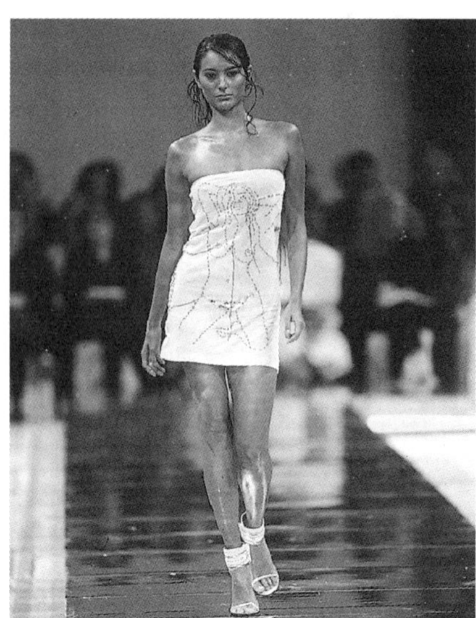

GHADA AMER, UNTITLED (DÉGRADÉ), 1999, detail, embroidery, gel medium on canvas, 42 x 26" / OHNE TITEL (VERKOMMEN), Stickerei und Gel auf Leinwand, 106,7 x 66 cm.

Summer 2000 designer dress by Chloé / Modellkleid aus der Sommerkollektion 2000 von Chloé. (PHOTO: DAN LECCA)

geschlafen hat. Sie bestickt Kissen und Bettdecken mit ihrem eigenen Namen und nähte einst zusammen mit **Sarah Lucas** einen Anzug, der mit Vögeln bestickt war und den sie Tippi Hedren nannten. **Klat.** Die Künstlergruppe aus Genf, die sich in ihrer Arbeit als autonomer Minikosmos reflektiert, bestickte kürzlich einen Vorhang mit einem Totenkopf als Referenz an die im Kunstkontext modisch gewordene Biker-und-Goth-Kultur. **Mai-Thu Perret.** Ihr Wandbehang DEATH VALLEY 69 (2000) setzt ein Zeichen für die nostalgische Sehnsucht nach Teenagekultur. **Vidya Gastaldon & Jean-Michel Wicker.** Diese französischen Künstler erforschen psychische Landschaften und stellen das Kindliche und Heimische stilistisch ins Zentrum ihrer Forschungsarbeit.

Sie machen Pompons, stricken, applizieren und sticken. Für eine Ausstellung bei Robert Prime 1999 produzierten sie einen «Ashram», ein kleines Zentrum zur Übung geistiger Konzentration bestehend aus handgefertigten Kissen, Gruppen gestrickter Reifen, organisch geformten Tüten. Manche Kissen waren bestickt: mit einem Schmetterling, mit einem Schaf. Gastaldon & Wicker gebrauchen das Medium der Stickerei, weil es eine romantische Vorstellung von Natur und Heim evoziert. Der ästhetische Charme dieser Arbeiten wird auch «Euro-Chic» genannt. **Michael Raedecker.** Er malt minimalistische helle Landschaften und Interiors, die er mit dem Einsatz von Fäden und Stickerei emotionalisiert und ambivalisiert. Ohne jedoch den

coolen kinematischen Swing zu verlieren. **Kim Bennett.** Die junge Amerikanerin gebraucht das Medium Stickerei als phantastisches und ausuferndes Erzählmedium.

Und jetzt zwei Strategien aus dem vestiär orientierten Feld: **Bless.** Sie fabrizierten für den Sommer 2000 die Kollektion «merchandising fanitems». Diese funktioniert zweifach. Erstens wurden Hosen, Pullover und Schals obsessiv und von Hand mit dem Schriftzug «Bless» bestickt und kennzeichnen den Träger als Bless-Fan. Zweitens präsentierten sie ein Video, in welchem ihre Freunde in Bless-Fan-Outfits Modeschauen anderer Designer besuchen und fröhlich in die Kamera winken. Bless bekennt sich damit selbst als Fan der Kleidermode und deren System der Wellenbewegung. **Susan Ciancolo.** Ihre Run-9-Kollektion beinhaltet kleine handgemachte Tiere, die entweder mit Klett an den Kleidern befestigt werden oder direkt auf den Stoff gestickt sind. Man muss wissen, dass Ciancolos Kleider Anti-Produkte sind. In ihrer Unbestimmtheit, Nicht-Logik und Unfertigkeit mit traditionellen Kleidungsstücken nicht vergleichbar, sind ihre Stücke und Installationen als textile Recherchen im Feld der Volkskultur zu verstehen. Apropos Mode: richtige Mode. Das französische Modehaus Chloé hat sich für seine Sommerkollektion 2000 im Feld der Kunst umgeschaut und ebenfalls die Stickerei entdeckt. Jeans und Kleider wurden mit sinnlichen Frauenkörpern bestickt. Der Künstlerin **Ghada Amer,** die sich mittels Stickerei mit der Ambivalenz der weiblichen Repräsentation befasst, kamen diese Motive bekannt vor. Die Klage gegen Chloé läuft.

Die Jetzt-Stickerei hat nichts zu tun mit einer Annäherung von Kunst und Kunsthandwerk. Nichts mit der Bauhaus-Idee, die im Sinne eines künstlerischen Totalkonzeptes Kunst und Leben zusammenführen wollte. Die Vormacher der neuen Stickerei heissen zum Beispiel **Mike Kelley.** Auch wenn er selbst wohl nie einen Kreuzstich ausgeführt hat. Mitte der 80er Jahre begann Kelley mit kunsthandwerklichen Materialien zu arbeiten. Mit gefundenen Stofftieren, mit Bannern, mit Teppichen. Dieses Spiel mit weiblichen Tropen war aber kein kritischer Akt gegen geschlechtsspezifische Konditionierung. Das wäre zu einfach. Es ging um die Frage, wie diese anti-minimalistischen Dinge als soziale Signifikanten funktionierten. Warum selbst gebastelte Stofftiere, die eigentlich hässlich sind, vom Publikum als «süss» wahrgenommen werden. Und warum sie, kaum dem privaten Bereich entrissen, im Kunstkontext wiederum als Trash klassifiziert werden. (Stellen Sie sich vor, Ihre vierjährige Cousine schenkt Ihnen eine absonderlich zusammengeflickte und bestickte Puppe. Sie denken «niedlich» und nicht «trashig», auch wenn das Objekt wie ein kleines Monster aus-

sieht.) Kelleys Kunsthandwerk-Appropriation war eine ästhetische Übung gegen das anonyme konzeptuelle Kunstwerk und für die Anerkennung einer bestimmten Materialität. **Rosemarie Trockel** ist die zweite Vormacherin. Auch wenn sie ihre gestrickten Bilder mit dem Wollsiegel auf dem Computer entwerfen und von Maschinen stricken liess. Es gab immer die Referenzen von Logokultur, Marketingstrategien und eben: «etwas Schönes für die Familie machen». Sie gebrauchte bewusst ärmliche Zutaten und peinliche Techniken und befragte damit die Lesekonvention eines bestimmten Genres. (Übrigens: Der Titel der Kunstbuchreihe, in welcher Sie diesen Text lesen, wurde ebenfalls in Handarbeit gestickt!) Aber was ist anders an dieser kunstimmanenten Stickerei, wie sie heute virulent ist? Sie ist nicht-heroisch, populistisch, volksnah und funktioniert weniger auf der Ebene von Verführung als auf Sympathie. Einem gestickten Bild kann man einfach nicht böse sein. So stellt der Kreuzstich sofort eine Beziehung zum Betrachter, zur Betrachterin her und befragt gleichzeitig seine, ihre Akzeptanz, indem er unspektakulär Grenzen und Möglichkeiten des Genres

Stickerei befragt. Die aktuelle Stickerei ist manchmal nahe an der vestiären Mode angesiedelt. Aber das ist ihr egal, denn sie ist ganz und gar selbstbewusst. Weil die Stickerei eine neo-popistische Attitüde einnimmt und das Potenzial zur Massendistribution in sich trägt – jeder würde ein besticktes Tracey-Emin-Kissen zu Hause auf sein Sofa legen, weil es dekorativ ist, und jede könnte ein gesticktes Tierkleid von Susan Ciancolo tragen, weil sie damit einfach besser aussieht –, wird sie im besten Falle temporäre autonome Zonen bilden. Nach Hakim Bey eine Art von Aufstand, der nicht zur direkten Konfrontation führt. Wie die Operation einer Guerilla, die ein Gebiet befreit und sich dann auflöst, um sich irgendwo, irgendwann zu re-formieren. So gesehen könnte sich die Jetzt-Stickerei ziemlich subversiv auswirken. Darauf freue ich mich. Und hier noch ein kleines Bonmot, das die Esszimmerstühle von Filmemacher John Waters betrifft. Wie mir berichtet wurde, liess er diese zentralen Möbelstücke in Gobelintechnik mit Veduten jener Baltimore-Gebäude besticken, die ihn beeindruckt und geprägt haben: die Schule, das Gefängnis und so weiter.

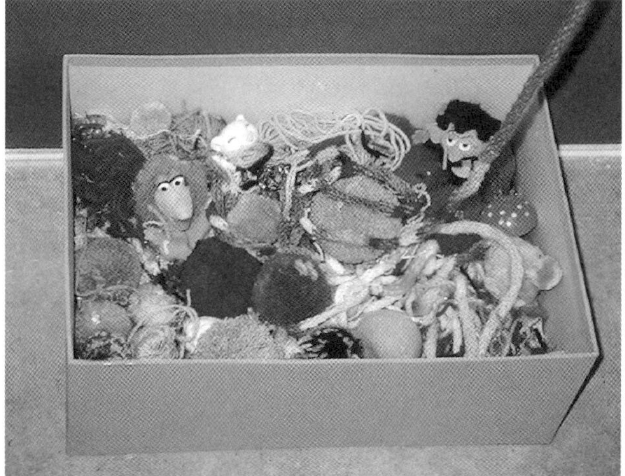

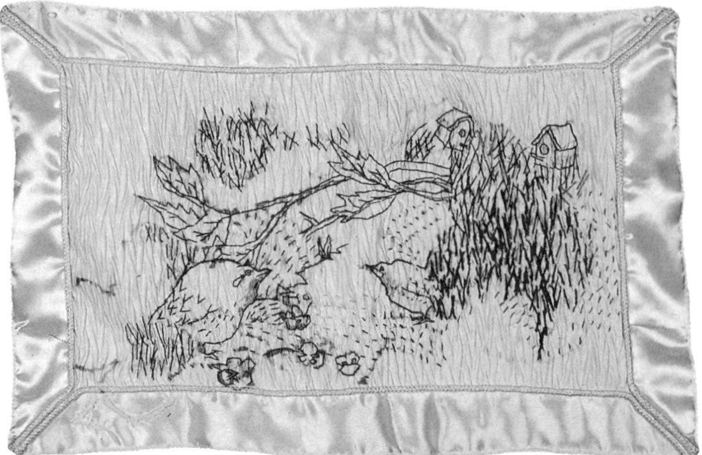

KIM BENNETT, SATIN AND BLUSH, 1999,
polyester, embroidery, 12½ x 19" /
SATIN UND ROSA HAUCH, Polyester, Stickerei,
31,8 x 48,3 cm.

The Now Idea:
Embroidery

MICHELLE NICOL

The modern work of art acquires permanence because it contests the prevailing rules of taste. That may explain why embroidery has become the Now Idea of current art. The unanticipated invariably settles down in the most unlikely places. Embroidery is an anachronism; it is a labor-intensive manual effort with needle and thread. Art of the twentieth century spurned the technique because it connotes housewifery, domesticity, and arts-and-crafts. The cross-stitch is kitsch incarnate. Perhaps it makes the domestic drudgery of suburban life a little more bearable, a little prettier, but that's about it.

MICHELLE NICOL is an art critic and freelance curator who lives in Zurich, Switzerland.

This said, the following artists currently busy themselves with the technique of embroidery. **Cosima von Bonin.** She embroiders a minimal coat of arms in cotton on velvet, sews mens' handkerchiefs together, or pastes an Yves Saint Laurent shopping bag on a red-and-white, checkered fabric, then pits herself against these womanly operations by adopting the cliché of a mannish artistic persona and wearing tailor-made mens' suits. **Tracey Emin.** On the inside of her tent sculpture, EVERYONE I HAVE EVER SLEPT WITH 1963–1995, she embroidered the names of all the people she had ever slept with. She stitches her own name on pillows and blankets and once made a suit with **Sarah Lucas,** on which they embroidered birds and which they named Tipi Hedren. **Klat.** These artists from Geneva, whose work is a commentary on their group as an autonomous miniature cosmos, recently embroidered a death's head onto a curtain in reference to art's currently fashionable embrace of biker and goth culture. **Mai-Thu Perret.** Her wall hanging DEATH VALLEY 69 (2000) addresses the nostalgic longing for the life and times of teen-age abandon. **Vidya Gastaldon & Jean-Michel Wicker.** The mental landscapes of these French artists present a stylistic take on things child-like and homey. They make pompoms, knit, appliqué, and embroider. For a show at

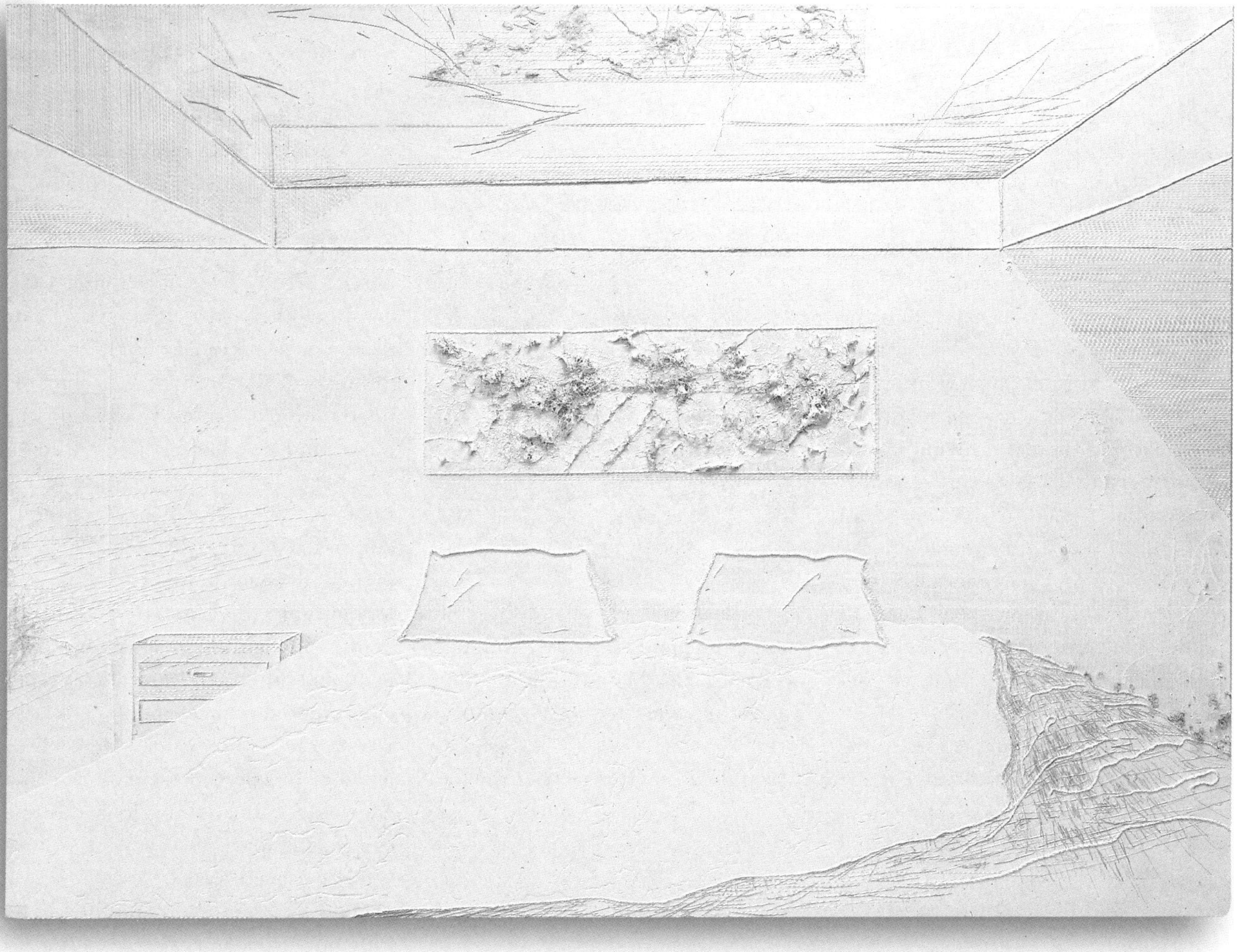

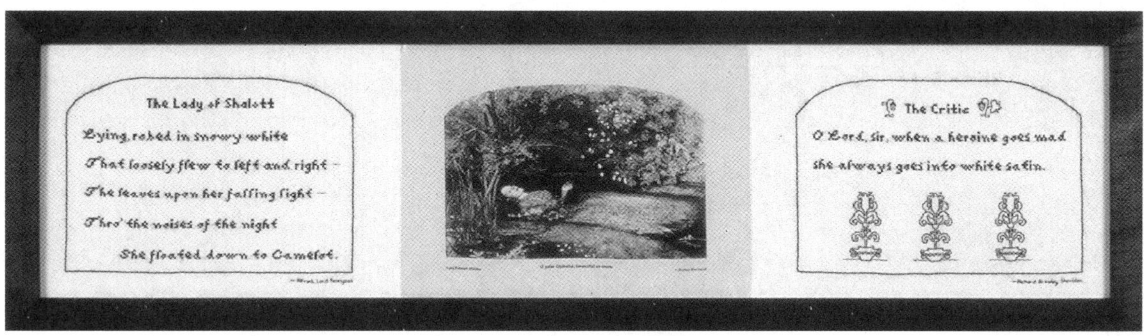

MICHAEL RAEDECKER, EXTRACT, 1999, acrylic and thread on linen, 60 x 80" / EXTRAKT, Acryl und Garn auf Leinen, 152,5 x 203 cm. (PHOTO: THE APPROACH GALLERY, LONDON)

ELAINE REICHEK, SAMPLER (THE LADY OF SHALOTT), 1999, transfer print and embroidery on linen, 11 x 38¼" / STICKTUCH (THE LADY OF SHALOTT), Abreibedruck und Stickerei auf Leinen, 28 x 97,2 cm.

Robert Prime in 1999, they produced an "Ashram," a small center for training sessions in spiritual concentration, consisting of handmade cushions, knitted tires, and organically shaped bags. Some cushions had embroidery, like a butterfly or a sheep. Gastaldon & Wicker. They use the medium of embroidery because it evokes romantic notions of nature and home. The aesthetic charm of such works has also been labeled "euro-chic." **Michael Raedecker.** He paints bright minimalist landscapes and interiors, lending them an emotional and ambivalent aura through the use of thread and embroidery, but without surrendering their cool, cinematic swing. **Kim Bennett.** Young and American, she uses the medium to tell fantastic and fantastically elaborate stories.

And now two strategies from the vestiary oriented arena. **Bless.** For the summer 2000 season, they produced

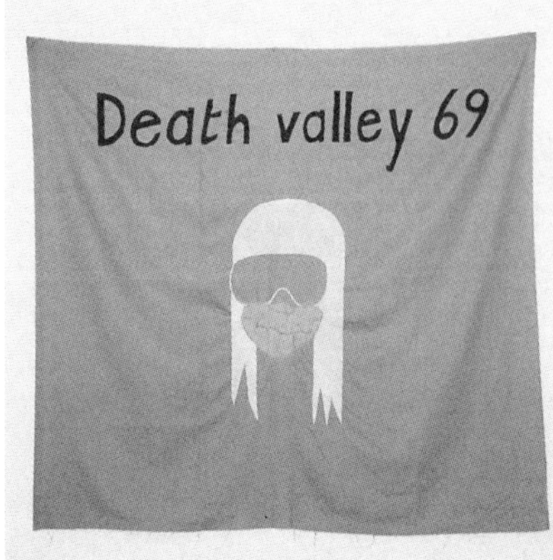

MAI-THU PERRET,
DEATH VALLEY 69, 2000.

the collection "merchandising fanitems." The "fanitems" are profiled in two ways. First, the lettering of "Bless" is obsessively embroidered by hand on slacks, sweaters, and scarves. Secondly, a video shows their friends at the fashion shows of other designers. We see

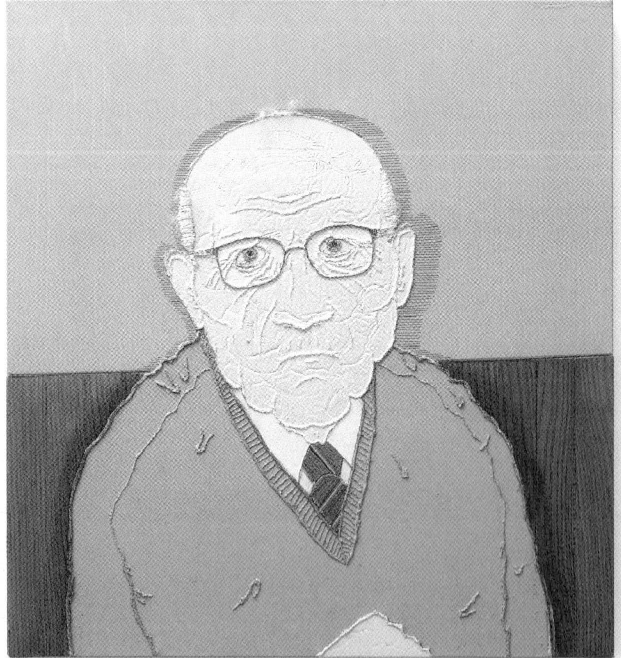

MICHAEL RAEDECKER, TRONIE X, 2000, acrylic, veneer and thread on canvas, 26 x 24" / Acryl, Furnierholz und Garn auf Leinwand, 66 x 61 cm. (PHOTO: THE APPROACH GALLERY, LONDON)

them decked out in Bless fan outfits and cheerfully waving into the camera. Bless professes a delight in fashions and its undulations. **Susan Ciancolo.** Her Run-9 collection offers little handmade animals that are either attached to the garment with velcro or embroidered directly onto the fabric. Ciancolo's clothes are, nota bene, antiproducts. Undefined, unlogical, and unfinished, they cannot be compared to traditional wearing apparel; the pieces and installations use textiles as a vehicle for ethnological research. Speaking of fashions—real fashions: For its summer 2000 collection, the French fashion house Chloé took a look around the art scene and discovered—you guessed it—embroidery. Jeans and other items sported sensually embroidered women's bodies. To artist **Ghada Amer,** who explores the ambivalence of female representation in her embroidery, the motifs looked suspiciously familiar. The lawsuit against Chloé has been filed.

Now Embroidery has nothing to do with a rapprochement between fine art and arts-and-crafts, nor with the Bauhaus idea of blending art and life into a great, comprehensive artistic whole. **Mike Kelley** might be named as a prototypical Now Embroiderer even though he probably never made a cross-stitch in his life. In the mid-eighties, Kelley began working with arts-and-crafts materials. With found stuffed animals, banners and rugs. But his deployment of female tropes did not take a critical jab at gender-specific conditioning. That would be too simple. The question was how these anti-minimalist things function as social signifiers. Why basically ugly, homemade stuffed animals are still perceived as "cute" and why they are classified as trash the

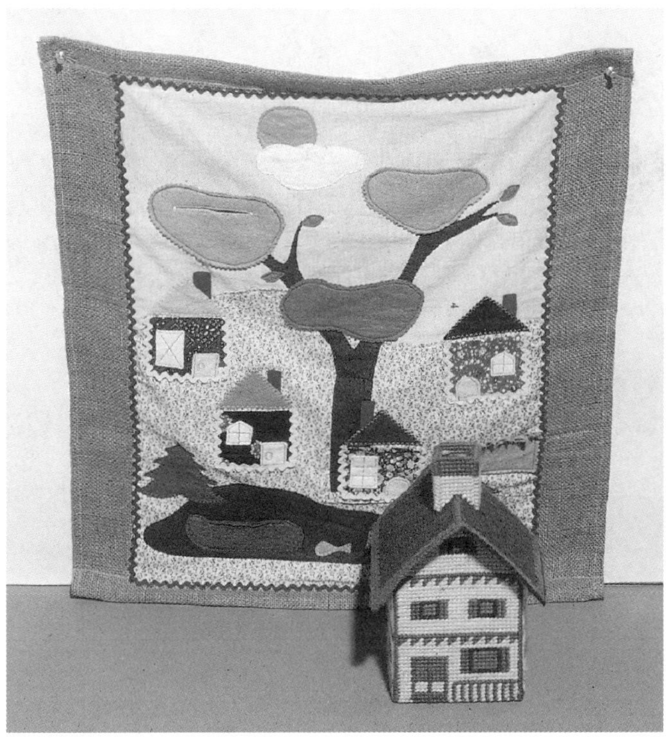

minute they are snatched away from their private life in the home and placed in the art context. (Let's say your four-year-old cousin gives you a bizarrely patched and embroidered doll. Your mind registers "cute" and not "trash" even if the thing looks like a monster en miniature.) Kelley's arts-and-crafts appropriation was an aesthetic enterprise in opposition to the anonymous, conceptual work of art and in favor of the appreciation of a certain materiality.

Rosemarie Trockel is the second prototypical Now Embroiderer. It matters not that she used the computer to design her wool-logo knitted pictures and had them made on a knitting machine. Her frame of reference consistently targets the logo mentality, marketing strategies, and, of course, the business of "making something beautiful for the family." She intentionally uses beggarly ingredients and embarassing techniques, thereby undermining the conventional reading of a

certain genre. (Incidentally, the title of the series in which you are now reading this article was also embroidered by hand! In 1984.)

But what makes today's art-immanent embroidery different? It is anti-heroic, populist and popular, and seems to work more on the level of sympathy than seduction. You simply can't get incensed about an embroidered picture. The cross-stitch establishes an instant rapport with the viewer and simultaneously rattles his/her acceptance by questioning the unspectacular limits and potential of the genre of embroidery. Current embroidery is sometimes very close to clothing. But it doesn't care, it is perfectly confident and self-assured. Besides, embroidery will at best produce temporary autonomous zones because it takes a neo-Pop approach and intrinsically entails the potential of mass distribution—anybody would put an embroidered Tracey Emin cushion on the couch at home because it's decorative and anybody would wear one of Susan Ciancolo's animal dresses because it inevitably makes the wearer look good. According to Hakim Bey, it's the kind of revolt that does not lead to direct confrontation. Like a guerilla operation: Once an area has been liberated, the group disbands only to reunite again somewhere else. Seen in this light, Now Embroidery could prove to have pretty subversive consequences. I'm looking forward to the fray. And, in conclusion, a little gem regarding filmmaker John Waters' dining room chairs. I'm told he had these vital pieces of furniture embroidered in Gobelin pics of the buildings in Baltimore that played a seminal role in his life: the school, the jail, etc.

(Translation: Catherine Schelbert)

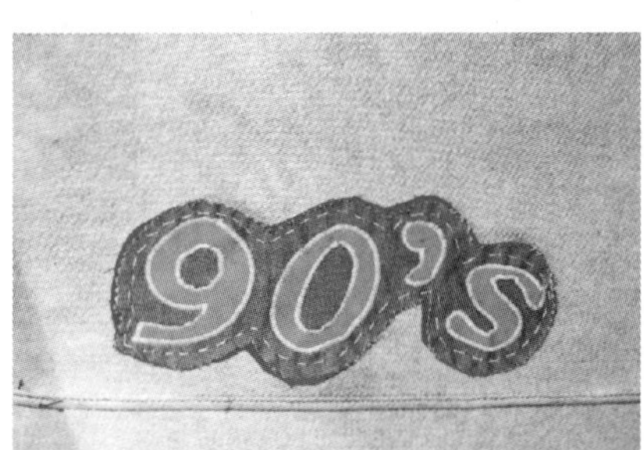

KLAT, 90'S, 1999.

RONI HORN
MARIKO MORI
BEAT STREULI
SCHORR, GUNNARSSON, GOROVOY, LEWIS
SPECTOR, BRYSON, NAKAZAWA, NICHOLS
GOODEVE, STALS, DANTO, AMANO, SMITH
INSERT: **MATTHEW RITCHIE**
VINCENT KATZ: **ALEX KATZ**
HORST BREDEKAMP: **STEPHAN VON HUENE**
PAUL D. MILLER: **SHIRIN NESHAT**
LES INFOS:
OKWUI ENWEZOR & WILLIAM KENTRIDGE
CUMULUS: VALÉRIA PICCOLI, MARIA LIND

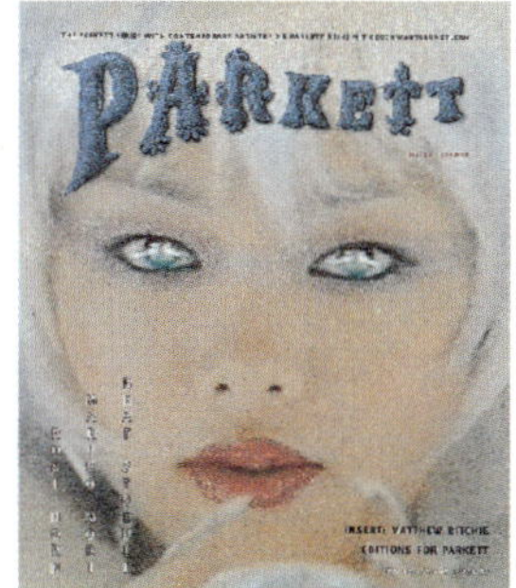

No. 54 - ISBN 3-907582-04-7

TRACEY MOFFATT
ELIZABETH PEYTON
WOLFGANG TILLMANS
MARTIN, LAJER-BURCHARTH, RIMANELLI
PILGRIM, URSPRUNG, LIEBMANN, MATSUI
WAKEFIELD, BUDNEY, NESBITT, ZIEGLER
INSERT: **DAVID SHRIGLEY**
CATHERINE BERNARD: **JOHAN GRIMONPREZ**
BERNARD MARCADÉ: **ROBERT GOBER**
LES INFOS DE L'ENFER: VALERIA LIEBERMANN
CUMULUS: BLESSING, AUPETITALLOT
BALKON: STEINER/MAGNAGUAGNO

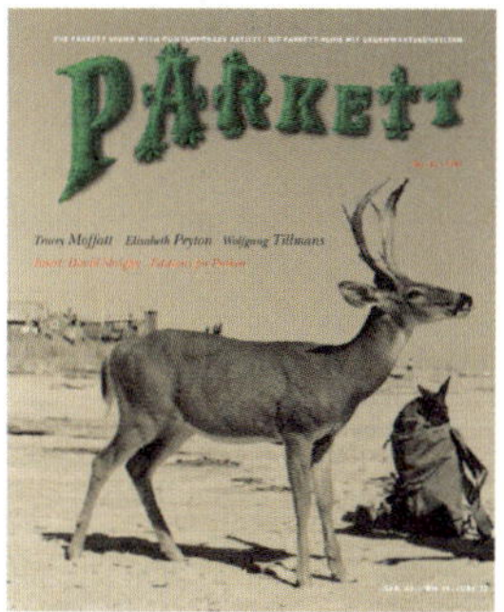

No. 53 - ISBN 3-907582-03-9

KAREN KILIMNIK
MALCOLM MORLEY
UGO RONDINONE
SCHORR, BÜRGI, JUNCOSA, MORLEY,
EBENSZTEJN, BONAMI, VERWOERT, HOPTMAN,
INSERT: **THOMAS BAYRLE**
ED WHITE: **JEAN MICHEL OTHONIEL**
NEVILLE WAKEFIELD: **RICHARD SERRA**
GILDA WILLIAMS: **GILLIAN WEARING**
ROBERT GRESKOVIC: **MERCE CUNNINGHAM**
CUMULUS: WALKER, KURZMEYER
BALKON: CECILIA VICUÑA

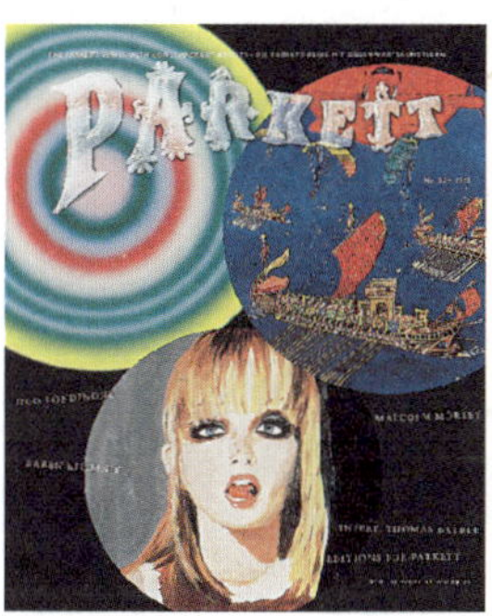

No. 52 - ISBN 3-907582-02-0

JOHN M ARMLEDER, JEFF KOONS
JEAN-LUC MYLAYNE
THOMAS STRUTH, SUE WILLIAMS
DI PIETRANTONIO, BOVIER, MUNIZ,
SEWARD, LOERS, NICHOLS GOODEVE,
COOKE, DION, ARNAUDET, MYLAYNE,
CURIGER, LINGWOOD, OKUTSU, BRYSON,
SCHJELDAHL, NESBIT, DANNATT, CAMHI
INSERTS: **TOBA KHEDOORI, TACITA DEAN**
ONFRAY: **HYACINTHE RIGAUD**, NICOL: **SAM SAMORE**
MURPHY, VAN DER WALLE, STEINER,
KURT W. FORSTER: **FRANK GEHRY**
CUMULUS: COLEMAN, BIRNBAUM

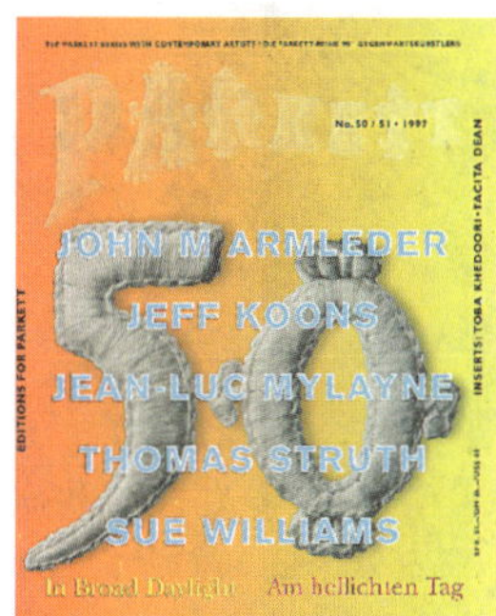

50/51 - ISBN 3-907582-00-4

LAURIE ANDERSON
DOUGLAS GORDON
JEFF WALL
FLOOD, BEZZOLA, FERGUSON
GILLICK/GORDON, BRYSON, PONTBRIAND
SCHORR, ANDERSON, BURCKHARDT, BUDNEY
INSERT: **SILVIA BÄCHLI**
COLIN DE LAND: **JOHN WATERS**
ROBERT STORR: **SEYDOU KEITA**
DANIELA SALVIONI: **CLEGG & GUTTMANN**
CUMULUS: KITTELMANN, MEYER

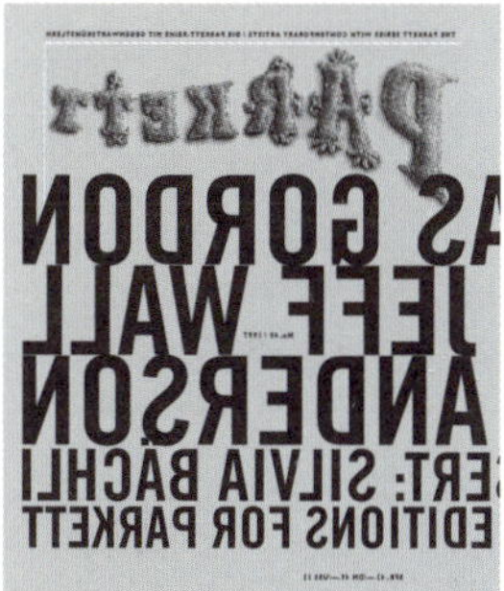

No. 49 - ISBN 3-907509-99-4

GARY HUME
GABRIEL OROZCO
PIPILOTTI RIST
BOVIER, MUIR, FOGLE, BONAMI
DE ZEGHER, SPECTOR, URSPRUNG
BABIAS, COLOMBO, ANDERSON
INSERT: **RUDY BURCKHARDT**
VINCENT KATZ: **RUDY BURCKHARDT**
VAN DER WALLE: **CHARLES LONG
& STEREOLAB**
FAYE HIRSCH: **BRUCE CONNER**
CHRISTOPH DOSWALD: **IAN ANÜLL**
CUMULUS: LEGGAT, SCHNEIDER

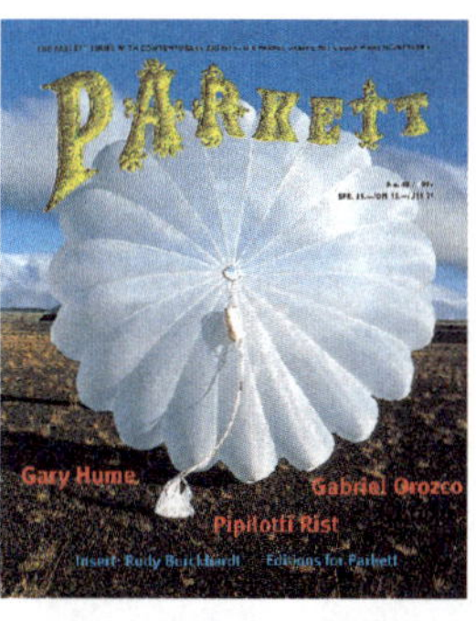

No. 48 - ISBN 3-907509-98-6

TONY OURSLER
RAYMOND PETTIBON
THOMAS SCHÜTTE
COOKE, RICHARD, NERI,
LEWIS, GROYS, ALS, RUGOFF,
GOODEVE, SEARLE, MARI, REUST,
WAKEFIELD, LOOCK, JANUS
INSERT: **ZOE LEONARD & CHERYL DUNYE**
JURI STEINER: **EMMA KUNZ**
MAX WECHSLER: **CHRISTOPH RÜTIMANN**
SUSAN MORGAN: **DIANE ARBUS**
CUMULUS: PRINCENTHAL, BOVIER/CHERIX

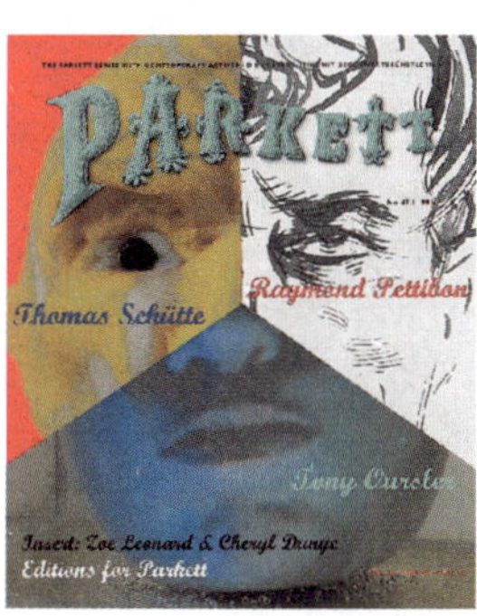

No. 47 - ISBN 3-907509-97-8

RICHARD ARTSCHWAGER
CADY NOLAND
HIROSHI SUGIMOTO
DEITCHER, SCHAFFNER, FORSTER, MUNIZ
ARMSTRONG, RELYEA, BOGDAN, GOODEVE
NICKAS, BRYSON, RUGOFF, DENSON
INSERT: **JOHN M ARMLEDER**
ROLAND WÄSPE: **ERWIN WURM**
DANIEL BIRNBAUM: **ÖYVIND FAHLSTRÖM**
LES INFOS DU PARADIS: ROBERT FLECK
CUMULUS: MILLER, VETTESE
BALKON: MARTIN HELLER

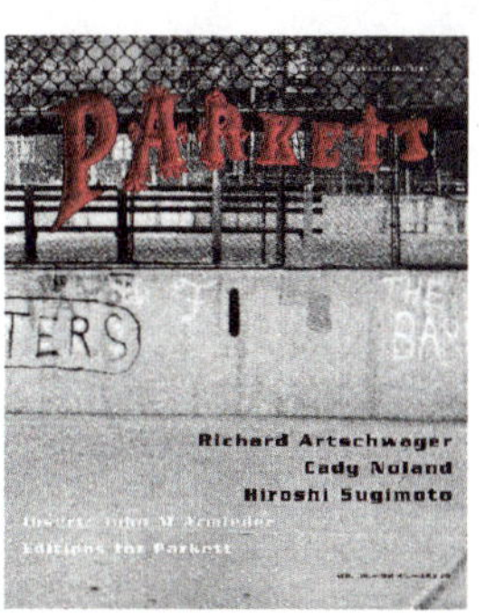

No. 46 - ISBN 3-907509-96-X

MATTHEW BARNEY
SARAH LUCAS
ROMAN SIGNER
BRYSON, ONFRAY, SEWARD, GOODEVE,
SALTZ, VAN ADRICHEM, SCHORR, FREEDMAN,
JOUANNAIS, BITTERLI, DOSWALD,
VIEWING, WECHSLER, DELAND
INSERT: **ELLIOTT PUCKETTE**
HEIDI GILPIN: **WILLIAM FORSYTHE**
ROBYN McKENZIE: **GEOFF LOWE**
MICHAEL TARANTINO: **CHANTAL AKERMAN**
CUMULUS: McEVILLEY, WAKEFIELD

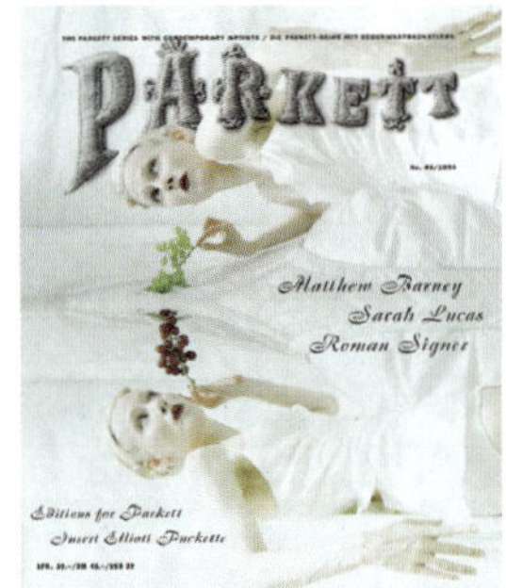

No. 45 - ISBN 3-907509-95-1

VIJA CELMINS
ANDREAS GURSKY
RIRKRIT TIRAVANIJA
PRINCENTHAL, LEWIS, SILVERTHORNE
SHIFF, CRIQUI, BURCKHARDT, WAKEFIELD
SCHORR, MELO, GILLICK, FLOOD, STEINER
INSERT: **HANS DANUSER**
LES INFOS: LIAM GILLICK & DOUGLAS GORDON
LYNNE COOKE, DAVID DEITCHER
DANIEL KURJAKOVIC: **MARIE JOSÉ BURKI**
NAN GOLDIN: **PETER HUJAR**
NOEMI SMOLIK: **ANDREAS SLOMINSKI**
JASON SIMON: **MARK DION**
LUK LAMBRECHT: **MARK LUYTEN**

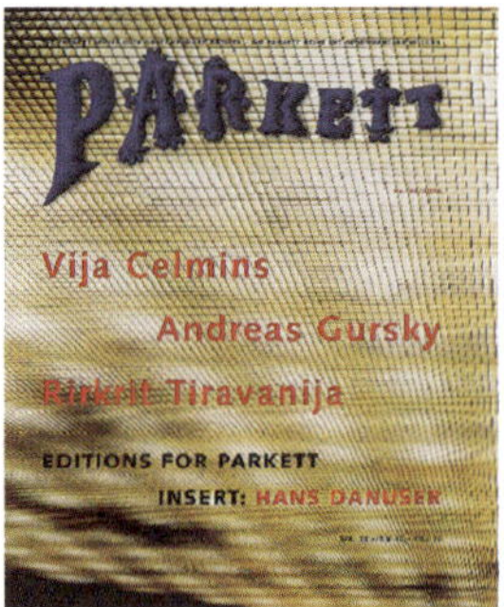

No. 44 - ISBN 3-907509-94-3

JUAN MUÑOZ
SUSAN ROTHENBERG
LYNNE COOKE, ALEXANDRE MELO
JAMES LINGWOOD, GAVIN BRYARS
ROBERT CREELEY, INGRID SCHAFFNER
JEAN-CHRISTOPHE AMMANN
MARK STEVENS, JOAN SIMON
INSERT: **ROBERT SMITHSON**
NEVILLE WAKEFIELD
MICHELLE NICOL: **CARSTEN HÖLLER**
HANS-ULRICH OBRIST: **FABRICE HYBERT**

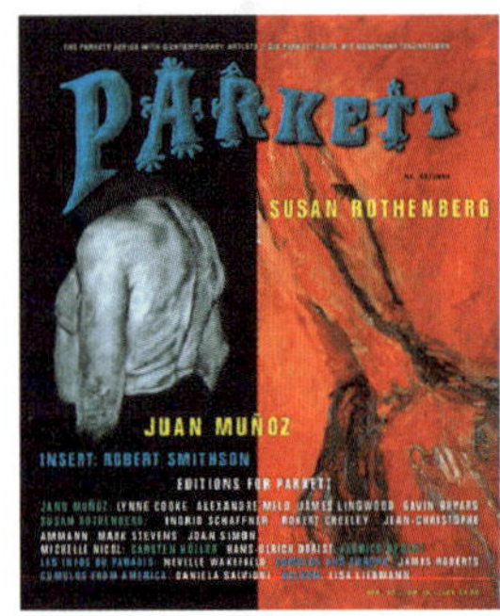

No. 43 - ISBN 3-907509-93-5

LAWRENCE WEINER
RACHEL WHITEREAD
BROOKS ADAMS, FRANCES RICHARD
DIETER SCHWARZ, DANIELA SALVIONI
ED LEFFINGWELL, LANE RELYEA
NEVILLE WAKEFIELD, RUDOLF SCHMITZ
TREVOR FAIRBROTHER, SIMON WATNEY
INSERT: **NAN GOLDIN**
VINCE LEO: **ROBERT FRANK**
CLAUDE RITSCHARD: **MARKUS RAETZ**

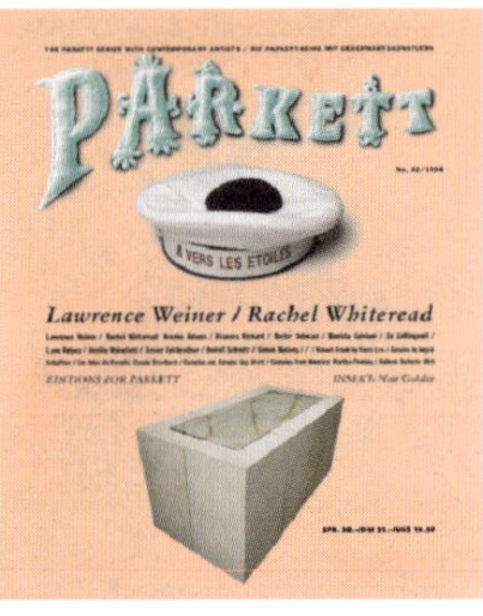

No. 42 - ISBN 3-907509-92-7

FRANCESCO CLEMENTE
GÜNTHER FÖRG
PETER FISCHLI/DAVID WEISS
DAMIEN HIRST
JENNY HOLZER
REBECCA HORN
SIGMAR POLKE
HOLLAND COTTER, BORIS GROYS
MAX WECHSLER, DAVID RIMANELLI
JOAN SIMON, GORDON BURN
GILBERT LASCAULT, WERNER SPIES
BICE CURIGER, JEFF PERRONE
G. ROGER DENSON, VIK MUNIZ
DAVE HICKEY

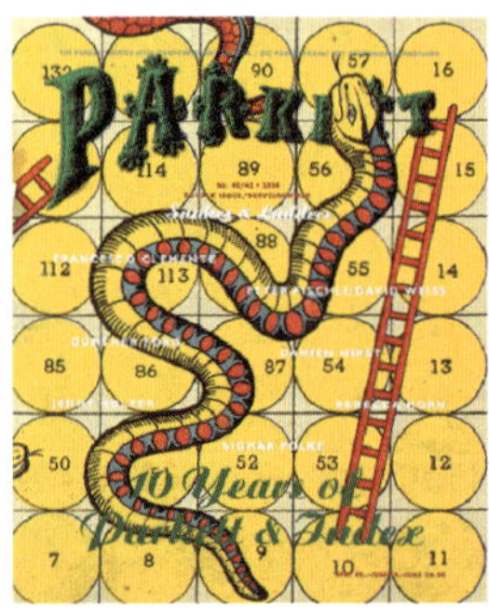

40/41 - ISBN 3-907509-90-0

FELIX GONZALEZ-TORRES
WOLFGANG LAIB
NANCY SPECTOR, SIMON WATNEY,
SUSAN TALLMAN, DIDIER SEMIN,
CLARE FARROW, JEAN-MARC AVRILLA,
THOMAS McEVILLEY
CLAUDE GINTZ: **GABRIEL OROZCO**
WALTER GRASSKAMP: **AXEL KASSEBÖHMER**
NEVILLE WAKEFIELD: **MATTHEW BARNEY**
INSERT: **RONI HORN**
LES INFOS DU PARADIS: **BURT BARR**
CUMULUS: **MEYER VAISMAN**

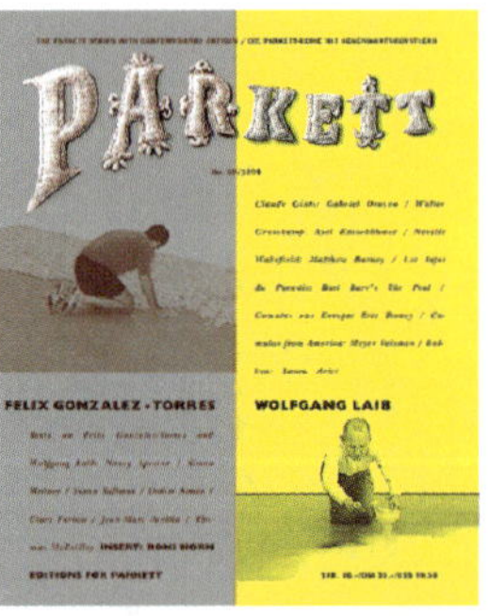

No. 39 - ISBN 3-907509-89-7

CHARLES RAY
FRANZ WEST
KLAUS KERTESS, CHRISTOPHER KNIGHT
PETER SCHJELDAHL, ROBERT STORR
JAN AVGIKOS, AXEL HUBER
MARTIN PRINZHORN, ELISABETH
SCHLEBRÜGGE, HARALD SZEEMANN,
DENYS ZACHAROPOULOS
INSERT: **PIPILOTTI RIST**
JEAN BAUDRILLARD
HANS RUDOLF REUST: **LUC TUYMANS**
PARKETT INQUIRY:
CHERCHEZ LA FEMME PEINTRE !

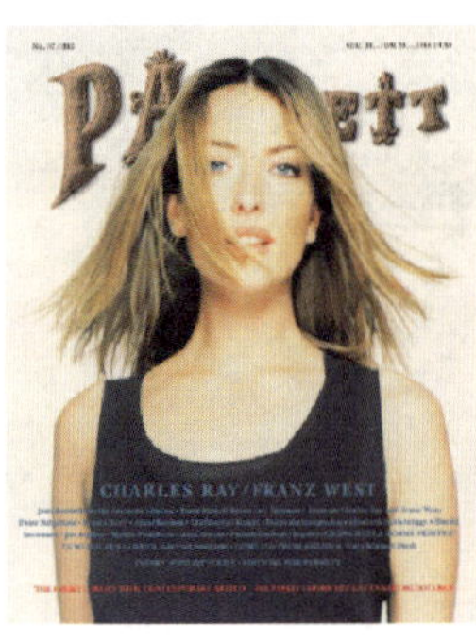

No. 37 - ISBN 3-907509-87-0

STEPHAN BALKENHOL
SOPHIE CALLE
NEAL BENEZRA, VIK MUNIZ, MAX KATZ
JEAN-CHRISTOPHE AMMANN
LUC SANTE, JOSEPH GRIGELY
PATRICK FREY, ROBERT BECK
INSERT: **RICHMOND BURTON**
URSULA PANHANS-BÜHLER: **EVA HESSE**
DOUGLAS BLAU: **JON KESSLER**
KIRBY GOOKIN: **LIZ LARNER**
LÁSZLÓ FÖLDÉNYI:
RUDOLF SCHWARZKOGLER

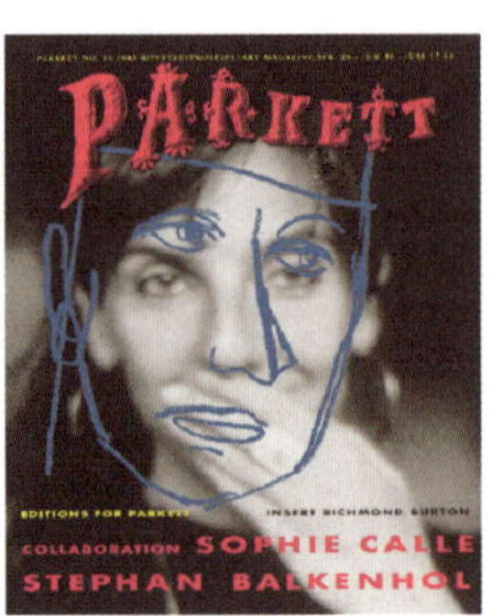

No. 36 - ISBN 3-907509-86-2

The PARKETT Series is created in collaboration with artists, who contribute an original work available exclusively to the subscribers in the form of a signed limited SPECIAL EDITION. The available works are also reproduced in each PARKETT issue.

Each SPECIAL EDITION is available by order from any one of our offices in New York or Zurich. Just fill in the details below and send this card to the office nearest you. Once your order has been processed, you will be issued with an invoice and your personal edition number. Upon receipt of payment, you will receive the SPECIAL EDITION. (Please note that supply is subject to availability. PARKETT does not assume responsibility for any delays in production of SPECIAL EDITIONS. Postage is not included.)

☐ As a subscriber to PARKETT, I would like to order the following Special Edition(s), signed and numbered by the artist.

PARKETT No.	ARTIST		NAME:
PARKETT No.	ARTIST		ADDRESS:
PARKETT No.	ARTIST		CITY:
PARKETT No.	ARTIST		STATE/ZIP:
PARKETT No.	ARTIST		COUNTRY:
PARKETT No.	ARTIST		PHONE:

☐ I have indicated my way of payment on the reverse side of this form.

Send this form to the PARKETT office nearest you:

PARKETT PUBLISHERS 155 AV. OF THE AMERICAS NEW YORK, NY 10013 PHONE (212) 673-2660 FAX (212) 271-0704

PARKETT VERLAG QUELLENSTRASSE 27 CH-8031 ZÜRICH TELEFON +41-1-271 81 40 FAX +41-1-272 43 01

PARKETT VERLAG TANNENWALDALLEE 17 D-61348 BAD HOMBURG FAX 06172-937 444 www.parkettart.com

---

PARKETT · KÜNSTLEREDITIONEN FÜR PARKETT-ABONNENTEN · 59

Die PARKETT-Buchreihe entsteht in Zusammenarbeit mit Künstlern, die eigens für die Abonnenten einen Originalbeitrag in Form einer limitierten und signierten EDITION gestalten. Diese Editionen sind auch in der Zeitschrift abgebildet und können mit dieser Bestellkarte in jedem unserer Büros in Zürich, Frankfurt oder New York bestellt werden. Sie erhalten dann Ihre persönliche Editionsnummer und eine Rechnung. Sobald wir Ihre Zahlung erhalten haben, schicken wir Ihnen Ihre Edition(en). (Lieferung nur solange vorrätig. PARKETT übernimmt keine Verantwortung für allfällige Verzögerungen bei der Herstellung der Vorzugsausgaben. Versandkosten zuzüglich.)

☐ Ich bin PARKETT-Abonnent(in) und bestelle folgende EDITION(EN), numeriert und vom Künstler signiert:

PARKETT Nr.	KÜNSTLER/IN		NAME:
PARKETT Nr.	KÜNSTLER/IN		STRASSE:
PARKETT Nr.	KÜNSTLER/IN		PLZ/STADT:
PARKETT Nr.	KÜNSTLER/IN		LAND:
PARKETT Nr.	KÜNSTLER/IN		TEL.:

☐ Meine Zahlungsweise habe ich auf der Rückseite angegeben.

Senden Sie die Bestellkarte an das PARKETT-Büro in Ihrer Nähe:

PARKETT VERLAG QUELLENSTRASSE 27 CH-8031 ZÜRICH TELEFON +41-1-271 81 40 FAX +41-1-272 43 01

PARKETT VERLAG TANNENWALDALLEE 17 D-61348 BAD HOMBURG FAX 06172-937 444 www.parkettart.com

PARKETT PUBLISHERS 155 AV. OF THE AMERICAS NEW YORK, NY 10013 PHONE (212) 673-2660 FAX (212) 271-0704

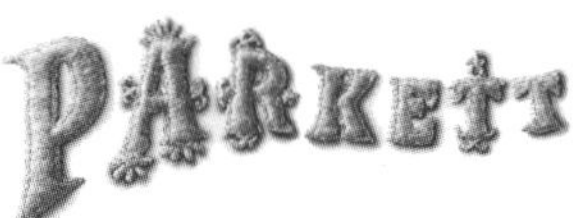

SUBSCRIBE, COMPLETE OR SEND A GIFT SUBSCRIPTION TO THE BEST BOOK SERIES ON CONTEMPORARY ARTISTS

I subscribe to the PARKETT series, starting with issue no. _______
- ☐ for 1 year (3 issues) at US$ 80 (USA/Canada), SFr. 118.– (Europe), SFr. 140.– (Rest of the world).
- ☐ for 2 years (6 issues) at US$ 145 (USA/Canada), SFr. 215.– (Europe), SFr. 265.– (Rest of the world).
- ☐ for 1 year (3 issues) at a 20% student discount (US$ 65 for USA/Canada, SFr. 95.– for Europe). A copy of my student ID is enclosed.

Send a gift subscription in my name, starting with issue no. _______
- ☐ for 1 year (3 issues) at US$ 80 (USA/Canada), SFr. 118.– (Europe), SFr. 140.– (Rest of the world).
- ☐ for 2 years (6 issues) at US$ 145 (USA/Canada), SFr. 215.– (Europe), SFr. 265.– (Rest of the world). A gift card in my name will be sent to the recipient.

Postage included. All prices subject to change.

- ☐ I wish to complete my PARKETT collection and order the following issue no(s):

  ____
  at SFr. 43.– each (up to no 43: SFr. 30.–; no. 44–48: SFr. 39.–), postage not included. Within the USA & Canada $ 32 (up to no. 43: $ 22.50; no. 44–48: $ 29), add postage: $ 5 (USA), $ 10 (Canada). (Sold out: No. 1–10, 13, 16, 19, 27, 29–31, 35)

- ☐ I wish to order the catalog raisonné of all PARKETT Artists' Editions from 1984–98 (60 pages, 120 color ill., published for the show at the Ludwig Museum, Cologne), for SFr. 15.– (USA: $ 12), excl. postage.

- ☐ I wish to order _______ copies of the new set of 101 postcards featuring PARKETT Artists' Editions for SFr. 48.– (USA: $ 32) per set, excl. postage.

NAME: _______________________

ADDRESS: _______________________

CITY: _______________________

STATE/ZIP: _______________________

COUNTRY: _______________________

TEL.: _______________ FAX: _______________

GIFT RECIPIENT: _______________________

ADDRESS: _______________________

CITY: _______________________

STATE/ZIP: _______________________

COUNTRY: _______________________

- ☐ Charge my Visa Card ☐ Mastercard ☐ AMEX

Card No. | | | | | | | | | | | | | | | | Expiration date _______

- ☐ Payment enclosed (US check or money order) ☐ Bill me

DATE _______________________

SIGNATURE _______________________

Send this form to the PARKETT office nearest you:

PARKETT PUBLISHERS 155 AV. OF THE AMERICAS NEW YORK, NY 10013 PHONE (212) 673-2660 FAX (212) 271-0704

PARKETT VERLAG QUELLENSTRASSE 27 CH-8031 ZÜRICH TELEFON +41-1-271 81 40 FAX +41-1-272 43 01

PARKETT VERLAG TANNENWALDALLEE 17 D-61348 BAD HOMBURG FAX 06172-937 444 www.parkettart.com

---

59

ABONNIEREN, VERVOLLSTÄNDIGEN ODER VERSCHENKEN SIE DIE UMFASSENDSTE BUCHREIHE ÜBER GEGENWARTSKÜNSTLER

Ich abonniere die PARKETT-Reihe ab Nr. _______
- ☐ für 1 Jahr (3 Ausgaben) zu: DM 130.– (BRD), SFr. 108.– (Schweiz), SFr. 118.– (übriges Europa).
- ☐ für 2 Jahre (6 Ausgaben) zu: DM 238.– (BRD), SFr. 190.– (Schweiz), SFr. 215.– (übriges Europa).
- ☐ für 1 Jahr (3 Ausgaben) mit 20% Studentenermässigung (BRD: DM 104.–/Schweiz: SFr. 87.–/Europa: SFr. 95.–). Eine Kopie meines Studentenausweises lege ich bei.

Ich verschenke ein PARKETT-Abonnement ab Nr. _______
- ☐ für 1 Jahr (3 Ausgaben) zu: DM 130.– (BRD), SFr. 108.– (Schweiz), SFr. 118.– (übriges Europa).
- ☐ für 2 Jahre (6 Ausgaben) zu: DM 238.– (BRD), SFr. 190.– (Schweiz), SFr. 215.– (übriges Europa). Das Geschenk-Abo mit einer Geschenkkarte wird in meinem Namen versandt.

Preise einschliesslich Versandkosten. Preisänderungen vorbehalten.

- ☐ Ich möchte meine PARKETT-Sammlung vervollständigen und bestelle die folgende(n) noch erhältliche(n) Ausgabe(n) Nr. _______________________
  zu je DM 49.–/SFr. 43.– (bis Nr. 43: DM 35.–/SFr. 30.–; Nr. 44–48: DM 45.–/SFr. 39.–, zzgl. Versandkosten (vergriffen: Nr. 1–10, 13, 16, 19, 27, 29–31, 35)

- ☐ Ich bestelle das Werkverzeichnis der PARKETT-Künstlereditionen von 1984–98 (60 S., 120 Farbabb., erschienen zur Ausstellung im Museum Ludwig, Köln) für DM 18.–/SFr. 15.– zzgl. Versandkosten.

- ☐ Ich bestelle _______ Ex. des neuen Postkarten-Sets mit 101 PARKETT-Künstlereditionen zum Preis von DM 55.–/SFr. 48.– pro Set, zzgl. Versandkosten.

NAME: _______________________

STRASSE: _______________________

PLZ/STADT: _______________________

LAND: _______________________

TEL.: _______________ FAX: _______________

BESCHENKTE(R): _______________________

STRASSE: _______________________

PLZ/STADT: _______________________

LAND: _______________________

- ☐ Ich zahle mit Visa ☐ Eurocard/Mastercard ☐ AMEX

Karten Nr. | | | | | | | | | | | | | | | | Gültig bis _______

- ☐ Mein Scheck über SFr./DM _______________________ liegt bei.

- ☐ Bitte senden Sie mir eine Rechnung.

DATUM _______________________

UNTERSCHRIFT _______________________

Senden Sie die Bestellkarte an das PARKETT-Büro in Ihrer Nähe:

PARKETT VERLAG QUELLENSTRASSE 27 CH-8031 ZÜRICH TELEFON +41-1-271 81 40 FAX +41-1-272 43 01

PARKETT VERLAG TANNENWALDALLEE 17 D-61348 BAD HOMBURG FAX 06172-937 444 www.parkettart.com

PARKETT PUBLISHERS 155 AV. OF THE AMERICAS NEW YORK, NY 10013 PHONE (212) 673-2660 FAX (212) 271-0704

ILYA KABAKOV
RICHARD PRINCE
BORIS GROYS, ROBERT STORR
JAN THORN-PRIKKER
CLAUDIA JOLLES, EDMUND WHITE
SUSAN TALLMAN, DANIELA
SALVIONI, KATHY ACKER
INSERT: **TATSUO MIYAJIMA**
GUDRUN INBODEN: **ASTA GRÖTING**
LYNNE COOKE: **GARY HILL**
PATRICK McGRATH: **STEPHEN ELLIS**

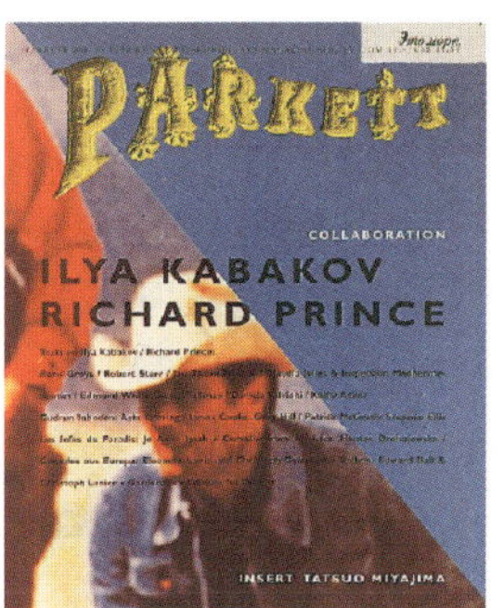

No. 34 - ISBN 3-907509-84-6

PARKETT

WOOL

TROCKEL

33

No. 33 - ISBN 3-907509-83-3

ROSEMARIE TROCKEL
CHRISTOPHER WOOL
VERONIQUE BACCHETTA,
BARRETT WATTEN,
ANNE WAGNER, JIM LEWIS,
GREIL MARCUS, JEFF PERRONE,
DIEDRICH DIEDERICHSEN
INSERT: **ADRIAN SCHIESS**
MARINA WARNER: **PENIS PLENTY**
G. ROGER DENSON:
DENNIS OPPENHEIM
CAMIEL VAN WINKEL

IMI KNOEBEL
SHERRIE LEVINE
RUDOLF BUMILLER
RAINER CRONE/DAVID MOOS
LISA LIEBMANN, DANIELA SALVIONI
ERICH FRANZ, HOWARD SINGERMANN
INSERT: **DAMIEN HIRST**
SHEENA WAGSTAFF: **VIJA CELMINS**
JIM LEWIS: **LARRY CLARK**
LIAM GILLICK: **BETHAN HUWS**
THOMAS KELLEIN: **WALTER DE MARIA**

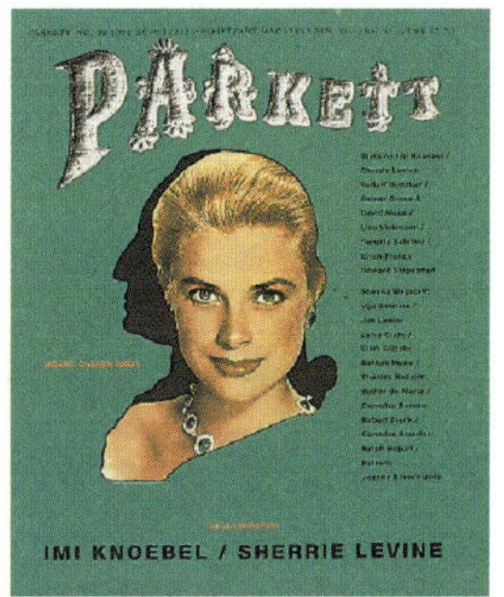

No. 32 - ISBN 3-907509-82-X

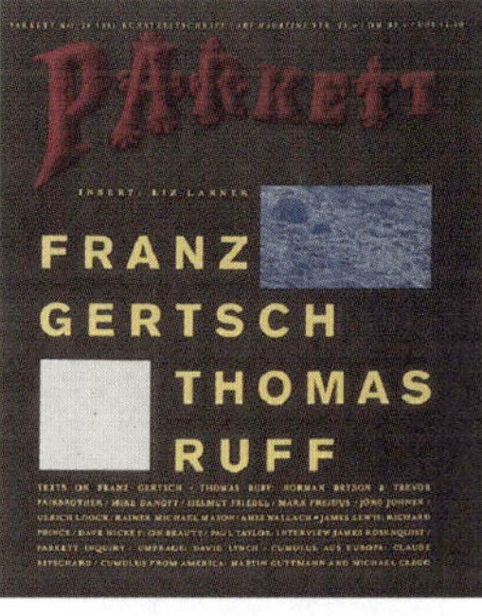

No. 28 - ISBN 3-907509-78-1

FRANZ GERTSCH
THOMAS RUFF
HELMUT FRIEDEL, ULRICH LOOCK
I. MICHAEL DANOFF, AMEI WALLACH
RAINER MICHAEL MASON
MARC FREIDUS, JÖRG JOHNEN
TREVOR FAIRBROTHER/NORMAN BRYSON
INSERT: **LIZ LARNER**
JAMES LEWIS: **RICHARD PRINCE**
DAVID HICKEY:
THE INVISIBLE DRAGON/
DER UNSICHTBARE DRACHEN
PAUL TAYLOR: **JAMES ROSENQUIST**

ALIGHIERO E BOETTI
JEAN-CHRISTOPHE AMMANN
GIOVAN BATTISTA SALERNO
RAINER CRONE & DAVID MOOS
FRIEDEMANN MALSCH
JEAN-PIERRE BORDAZ
ALAIN CUEFF
INSERT: **CINDY SHERMAN**
SHEENA WAGSTAFF:
SOPHIE CALLE
HERBERT LACHMEYER/
BRIGITTE FELDERER: **FRANZ WEST**
JUTTA KOETHER: **MIKE KELLEY**

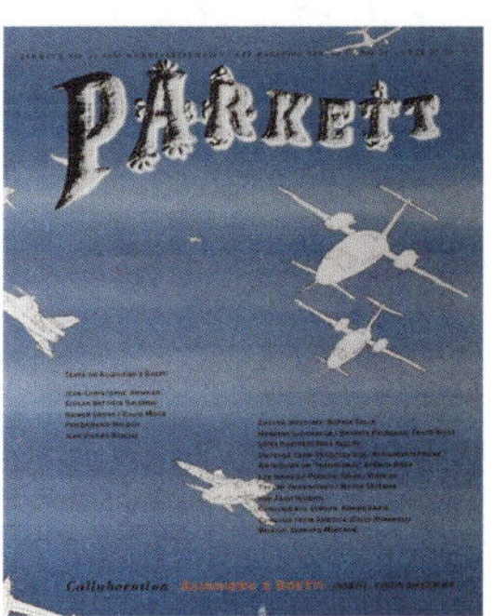

No. 24 - ISBN 3-907509-74-9

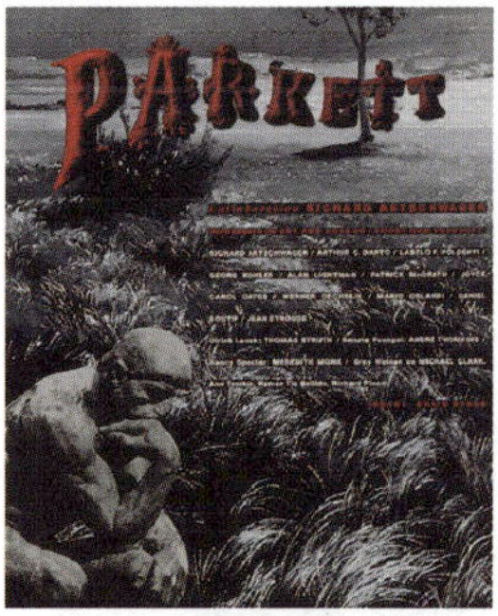

No. 23 - ISBN 3-907509-73-0

RICHARD ARTSCHWAGER
ARTHUR C. DANTO, GEORG KOHLER,
MARIO A. ORLANDO, JOYCE
CAROL OATES, WERNER OECHSLIN,
ALAN LIGHTMAN, PATRICK
McGRATH, DANIEL SOUTIF,
LASZLO F. FÖLDENYI, JEAN STROUSE
INSERT: **DAVID BYRNE**
RENATE PUVOGEL: **ANDRÉ THOMKINS**
ULRICH LOOCK: **THOMAS STRUTH**
NANCY SPECTOR: **MEREDITH MONK**

ALEX KATZ
JOHN RUSSELL, BROOKS ADAMS,
DAVID RIMANELLI, FRANCESCO
CLEMENTE, MICHAEL KRÜGER,
RICHARD FLOOD, PATRICK FREY,
CARL STIGLIANO, BICE CURIGER,
GLENN O'BRIEN
INSERT: **WILLIAM WEGMAN**
LISA LIEBMAN: **ROBERT GOBER**
JACQUELINE BURCKHARDT:
GIULIO ROMANO

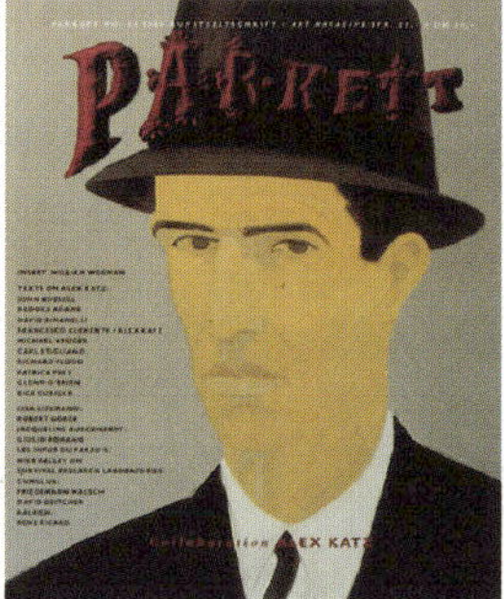

No. 21 - ISBN 3-907509-71-4

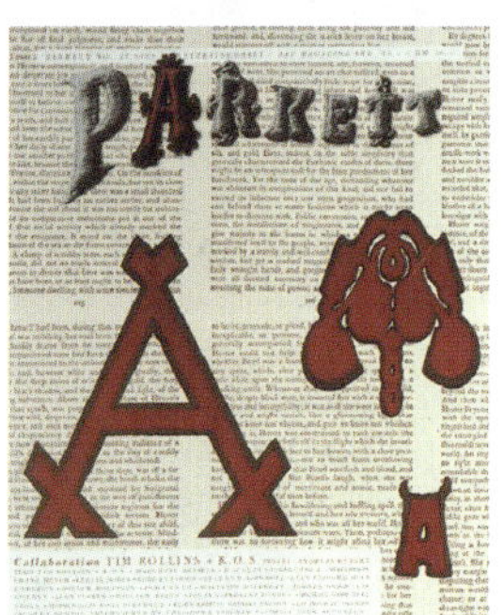

No. 20 - ISBN 3-907509-70-6

TIM ROLLINS + K.O.S.
MARSHALL BERMAN
TREVOR FAIRBROTHER
STATEMENTS, DIALOGUE 5
INSERT: **ANDREAS GURSKY**
MICHAEL NASH: **BILL VIOLA**
STEPHEN ELLIS: **ROSS BLECKNER**
KLAUS KERTESS: **TRISHA BROWN**

EDWARD RUSCHA
DAVE HICKEY, DENNIS HOPPER
ALAIN CUEFF, JOHN MILLER
CHRISTOPHER KNIGHT
INSERT: **BOYD WEBB**
JAN THORN-PRIKKER: **WOLS**
LYNNE COOKE: **TONY CRAGG**
BROOKE ADAMS: **JULIAN SCHNABEL**
DER KÜNSTLER ALS EXEM-
PLARISCH LEIDENDER?
EINE UMFRAGE / THE ARTIST AS A
MODEL SUFFERER? AN INQUIRY

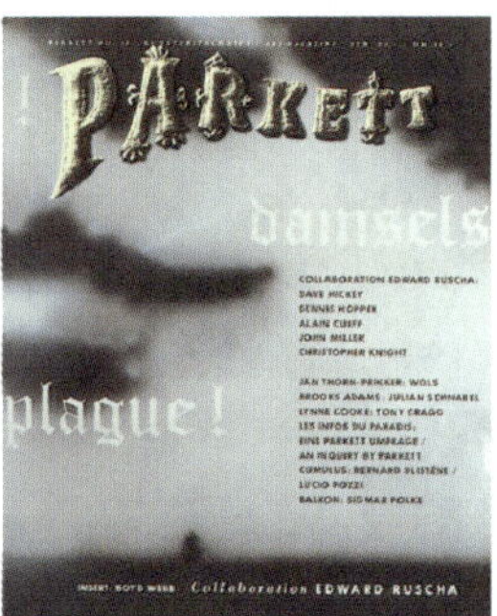

No. 18 - ISBN 3-907509-68-4

MARIO MERZ
MARLIS GRÜTERICH, JEANNE
SILVERTHORNE, DEMOSTHENES
DAVVETAS, HARALD SZEEMANN,
DENYS ZACHAROPOULOS
INSERT: **GENERAL IDEA**
MAX KOZLOFF: **GILLES PERESS**
FRIEDEMANN MALSCH:
GEORG HEROLD
BRUNELLA ANTOMARINI:
FRANCESCA WOODMAN

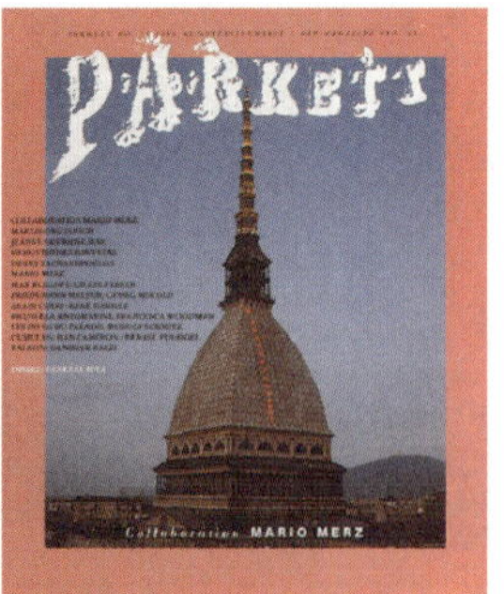

No. 15 - ISBN 3-907509-65-X

GILBERT & GEORGE
DUNCAN FALLOWELL, MARIO
CODOGNATO, JEREMY COOPER,
DEMOSTHENES DAVVETAS,
WOLF JAHN
INSERT: **ROSEMARIE TROCKEL**
ROBERT STORR: **NANCY SPERO**
HAIM STEINBACH: **MANIFESTO**
JÖRG ZUTTER: **THOMAS HUBER**

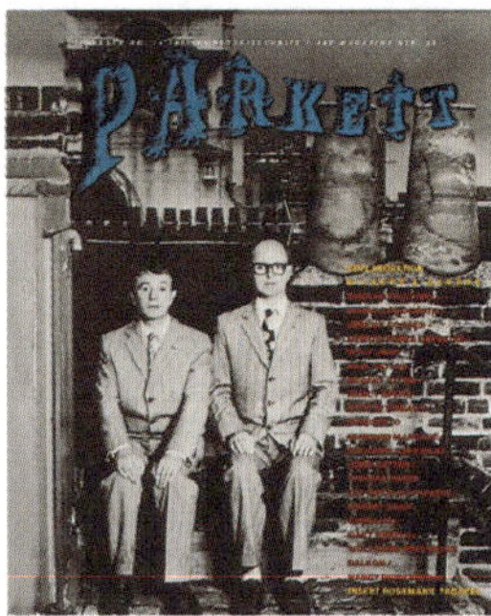

No. 14 - ISBN 3-907509-64-1

GEORG BASELITZ
REMO GUIDIERI, DIETER
KOEPPLIN, ERIC DARRAGON,
RAINER MICHAEL MASON, FRANZ
MEYER, JOHN CALDWELL
INSERT: **BARBARA KRUGER**
GRAY WATSON: **DEREK JARMAN**
CAROL SQUIERS:
PHOTO OPPORTUNITY
ROSETTA BROOKS:
TROY BRAUNTUCH

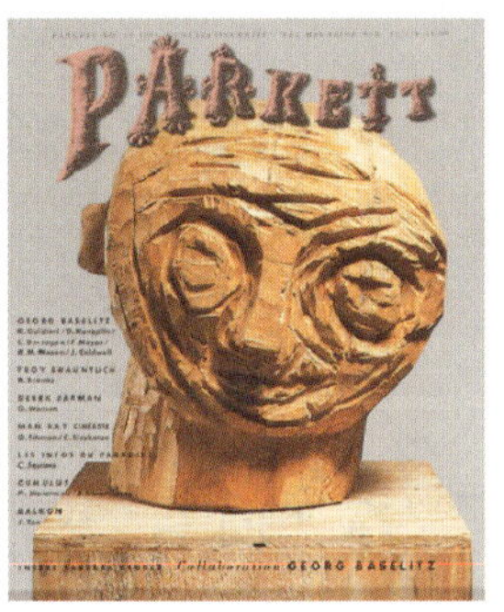

No. 11 - ISBN 3-907509-61-7

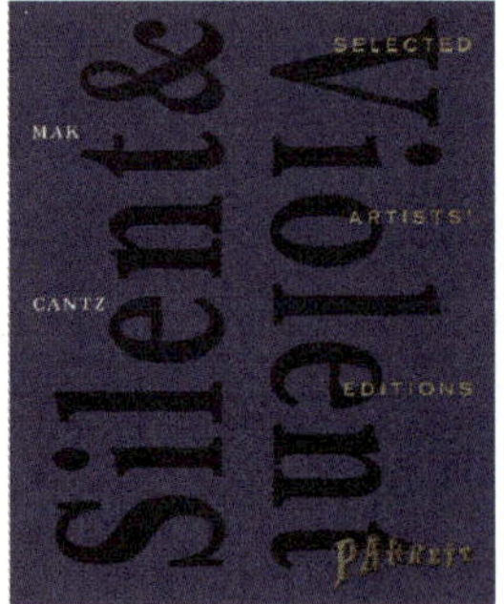

SILENT & VIOLENT
CATALOG RAISONNÉ OF ALL PARKETT ARTISTS' EDITIONS
from No. 1–44, 183 pages, 144 in color
text by Susan Tallmann, short biographies of all artists

WERKVERZEICHNIS ALLER PARKETT-KÜNSTLER-EDITIONEN
von Nr. 1–44, 183 Seiten, davon 144 in Farbe
Text von Susan Tallmann, Kurzbiographien der Künstler

sFr. 49.– / $ 39

ISBN 3-89322-796-3 (engl.), ISBN 3-89322-787-3 (dt.)

NEW PARKETT-POSTCARD SET
featuring 101 artists' editions made for Parkett

DAS NEUE PARKETT-POSTKARTEN-SET
mit 101 Editionen, die von Künstlern für
Parkett geschaffen wurden.

sFr. 48.– / $ 32

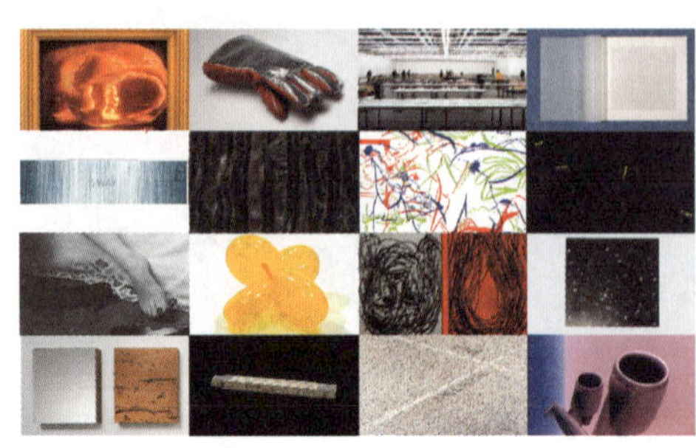

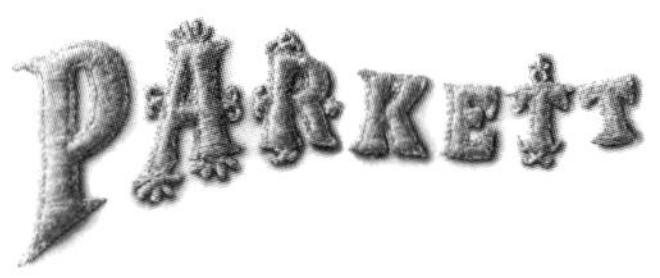

Doug Aitken, vol. 57
Laurie Anderson, vol. 49
John Armleder, vol. 50/51
Richard Artschwager, vol. 23, vol. 46
John Baldessari, vol. 29
Stephan Balkenhol, vol. 36
Matthew Barney, vol. 45
Georg Baselitz, vol. 11
Vanessa Beecroft, vol. 56
Ross Bleckner, vol. 38
Alighiero e Boetti, vol. 24
Christian Boltanski, vol. 22
Louise Bourgeois, vol. 27
Sophie Calle, vol. 36
Maurizio Cattelan, vol. 59
Vija Celmins, vol. 44
Francesco Clemente, vol. 9 & 40/41
Chuck Close, vol. 60
Enzo Cucchi, vol. 1
Martin Disler, vol. 3
Marlene Dumas, vol. 38
Eric Fischl, vol. 5
Peter Fischli/David Weiss, vol.17, 40/41
Sylvie Fleury, vol. 58
Günther Förg, vol. 26 & 40/41
Katharina Fritsch, vol. 25
Franz Gertsch, vol. 28
Gilbert & George, vol. 14
Robert Gober, vol. 27
Nan Goldin, vol. 57
Felix Gonzalez-Torres, vol. 39
Douglas Gordon, vol. 49
Andreas Gursky, vol. 44
David Hammons, vol. 31
Thomas Hirschhorn, vol. 57
Damien Hirst, vol. 40/41
Jenny Holzer, vol. 40/41
Rebecca Horn, vol. 13 & 40/41
Roni Horn, vol. 54

Gary Hume, vol. 48
Ilya Kabakov, vol. 34
Alex Katz, vol. 21
Mike Kelley, vol. 31
Ellsworth Kelly, vol. 56
Karen Kilimnik, vol. 52
Martin Kippenberger, vol. 19
Imi Knoebel, vol. 32
Jeff Koons, vol. 19, 50/51
Jannis Kounellis, vol. 6
Yayoi Kusama, vol. 59
Wolfgang Laib, vol. 39
Sherrie Levine, vol. 32
Sarah Lucas, vol. 45
Brice Marden, vol. 7
Mario Merz, vol. 15
Tracey Moffatt, vol. 53
Mariko Mori, vol. 54
Malcolm Morley, vol. 52
Juan Muñoz, vol. 43
Jean-Luc Mylayne, vol. 50/51
Bruce Nauman, vol. 10
Cady Noland, vol. 46
Meret Oppenheim, vol. 4
Gabriel Orozco, vol. 48
Tony Oursler, vol. 47
Jorge Pardo, vol. 56
Raymond Pettibon, vol. 47
Elizabeth Peyton, vol. 53
Sigmar Polke, vol. 2, 30 & 40/41
Richard Prince, vol. 34
Markus Raetz, vol. 8
Charles Ray, vol. 37
Jason Rhoades, vol. 58
Gerhard Richter, vol. 35
Pipilotti Rist, vol. 48
Tim Rollins & K.O.S., vol. 20
Ugo Rondinone, vol. 52
James Rosenquist, vol. 58

Susan Rothenberg, vol. 43
Thomas Ruff, vol. 28
Edward Ruscha, vol. 18 & 55
Thomas Schütte, vol. 47
Cindy Sherman, vol. 29
Roman Signer, vol. 45
Andreas Slominski, vol. 55
Beat Streuli, vol. 54
Thomas Struth, vol. 50/51
Hiroshi Sugimoto, vol. 46
Philip Taaffe, vol. 26
Sam Taylor-Wood, vol. 55
Diana Thater, vol. 60
Wolfgang Tillmans, vol. 53
Rirkrit Tiravanija, vol. 44
Rosemarie Trockel, vol. 33
James Turrell, vol. 25
Luc Tuymans, vol. 60
Kara Walker, vol. 59
Jeff Wall, vol. 22 & 49
Andy Warhol, vol. 12
Lawrence Weiner, vol. 42
Franz West, vol. 37
Rachel Whiteread, vol. 42
Sue Williams, vol 50/51
Robert Wilson, vol. 16
Christopher Wool, vol. 33

vol.	Collaboration			vol.	Collaboration			vol.	Collaboration		
60	Chuck Close			44	Vija Celmins	m		20	Tim Rollins + K.O.S.	m	
	Diana Thater				Andreas Gursky	m		19	Martin Kippenberger		
	Luc Tuymans				Rirkrit Tiravanija	m	e		Jeff Koons		
59	Maurizio Cattelan	m	e	43	Juan Muñoz	m	e	18	Ed Ruscha	m	
	Yayoi Kusama	m	e		Susan Rothenberg	m	e	17	Fischli/Weiss		
	Kara Walker	m	e	42	Lawrence Weiner	m	e	16	Robert Wilson		
58	Sylvie Fleury	m	e		Rachel Whiteread	m		15	Mario Merz	m	e
	Jason Rhoades	m	e	40/41	Francesco Clemente	m	e	14	Gilbert & George	m	
	James Rosenquist	m	e		Fischli/Weiss	m		13	Rebecca Horn		
57	Doug Aitken	m	e		Günther Förg	m		12	Andy Warhol		
	Nan Goldin	m			Damien Hirst	m		11	Georg Baselitz	m	
	Thomas Hirschhorn	m			Jenny Holzer	m		10	Bruce Nauman		
56	Vanessa Beecroft	m			Rebecca Horn	m		9	Francesco Clemente		
	Ellsworth Kelly	m			Sigmar Polke	m	e	8	Markus Raetz		
	Jorge Pardo	m	e	39	Felix Gonzalez-Torres	m		7	Brice Marden		
55	Edward Ruscha	m			Wolfgang Laib	m	e	6	Jannis Kounellis		
	Andreas Slominski	m	e	38	Ross Bleckner	m		5	Eric Fischl		
	Sam Taylor-Wood	m			Marlene Dumas	m		4	Meret Oppenheim		
54	Roni Horn	m	e	37	Charles Ray	m		3	Martin Disler		
	Mariko Mori	m			Franz West	m	e	2	Sigmar Polke		
	Beat Streuli	m	e	36	Stephan Balkenhol	m	e	1	Enzo Cucchi		
53	Tracey Moffatt	m		36	Sophie Calle	m					
	Elizabeth Peyton	m		35	Gerhard Richter						
	Wolfgang Tillmans	m		34	Ilya Kabakov	m					
52	Karen Kilimnik	m	e		Richard Prince	m	e				
	Malcolm Morley	m	e	33	Rosemarie Trockel	m					
	Ugo Rondinone	m	e		Christopher Wool	m					
50/51	John Armleder	m	e	32	Imi Knoebel						
	Jeff Koons	m	e		Sherrie Levine						
	Jean-Luc Mylayne	m		31	David Hammons						
	Thomas Struth	m			Mike Kelley						
	Sue Williams	m	e	30	Sigmar Polke						
49	Laurie Anderson	m	e	29	John Baldessari						
	Douglas Gordon	m			Cindy Sherman						
	Jeff Wall	m		28	Franz Gertsch	m	e				
48	Gary Hume	m			Thomas Ruff	m	e				
	Gabriel Orozco	m		27	Louise Bourgeois						
	Pipilotti Rist	m			Robert Gober						
47	Tony Oursler	m		26	Günther Förg	m					
	Raymond Pettibon	m			Philip Taaffe	m					
	Thomas Schütte	m	e	25	Katharina Fritsch	m	e				
46	Richard Artschwager	m			James Turrell	m	e				
	Cady Noland	m		24	Alighiero e Boetti	m	e				
	Hiroshi Sugimoto	m		23	Richard Artschwager	m					
45	Matthew Barney	m		22	Christian Boltanski	m					
	Sarah Lucas	m			Jeff Wall	m					
	Roman Signer	m	e	21	Alex Katz	m	e				

m = available monograph / erhältliche Monographie, e = available edition / erhältliche Edition
Delivery subject to availability at time of order / Lieferung solange Vorrat

Each volume of PARKETT is created in collaboration with artists, who contribute an original work specially made for the readers of PARKETT. The works are available in a signed and numbered Special Edition. Prices are subject to change. Postage is not included.

EDITIONS FOR PARKETT

Jeder PARKETT-Band entsteht in Collaboration mit Künstlern, die eigens für die Leser von PARKETT Originalbeiträge gestalten. Diese Vorzugsausgaben sind als nummerierte und signierte Editionen erhältlich. Preisänderungen vorbehalten. Versandkosten und MwSt. (Schweiz) nicht inbegriffen.

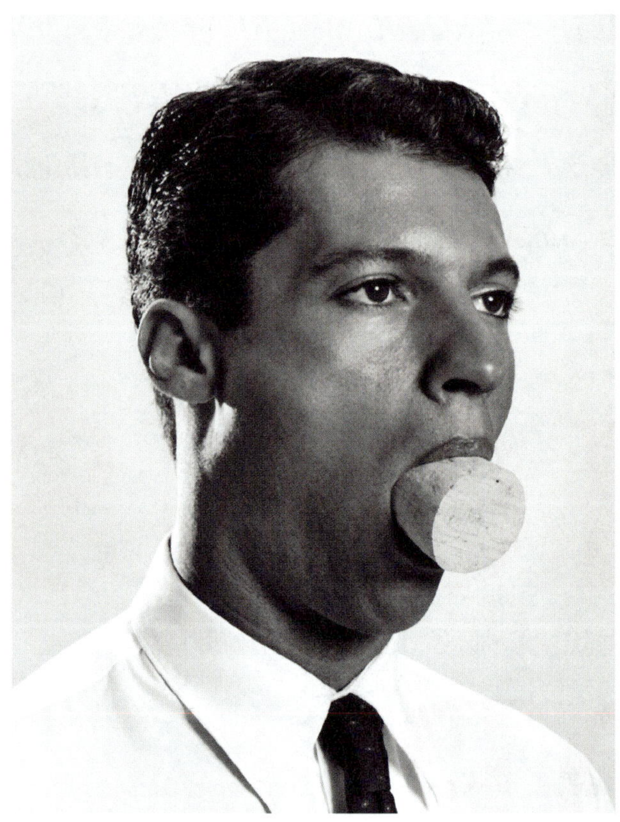

PARKETT 59

MAURIZIO CATTELAN

UNTITLED, 2000
Black-and-white photograph, digital print on paper (Uso Mano),
16¼ x 13" (image size 12 x 9½").
Edition of 60, signed and numbered certificate, **$ 800 / € 860**

OHNE TITEL, 2000
Schwarzweiss-Photographie, Digitalprint auf Papier (Uso Mano),
41,3 x 33 cm (Bildgrösse: 30,5 x 24 cm).
Auflage: 60, signiertes und nummeriertes Zertifikat, **sFr. 1350.–**

PARKETT 59

YAYOI KUSAMA

INFINITY NETS, 2000
Silkscreen print on mirror, 10 x 8¼".
Edition of 70, signed and numbered on the back,
$ 850 / € 890

UNENDLICHKEITSNETZE, 2000
Siebdruck auf Spiegel, 25,5 x 21 cm.
Auflage: 70, auf der Rückseite signiert und nummeriert,
sFr. 1400.–

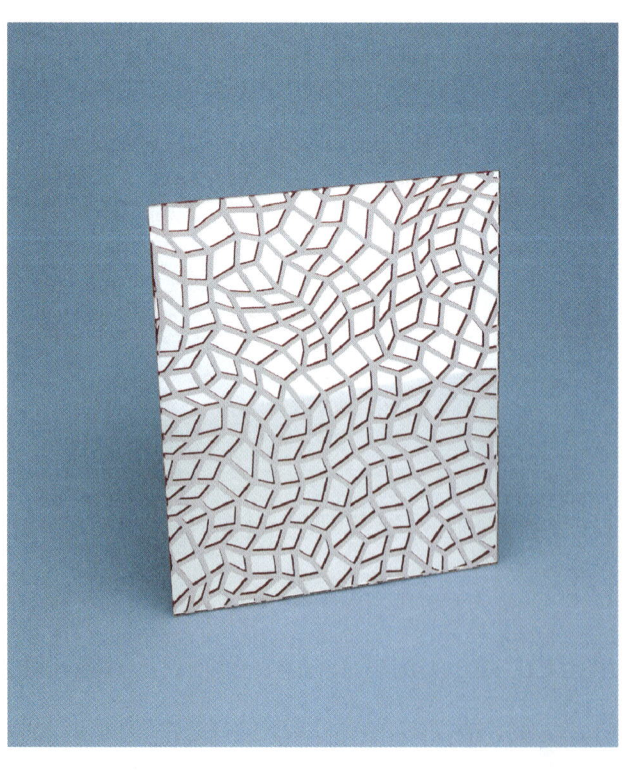

PARKETT 59

KARA WALKER
BOO-HOO, 2000

Linocut on Arches Cover White, 40 x 20½".

Printed by Maurice Sanchez, Derrière L'Etoile Studio, New York.

Edition of 70, signed and numbered, **$ 900 / € 950**

Linolschnitt auf Arches Cover White, 101,6 x 52,1 cm.

Gedruckt bei Maurice Sanchez, Derrière L'Etoile Studio, New York.

Auflage: 70, signiert und nummeriert, **sFr. 1500.–**

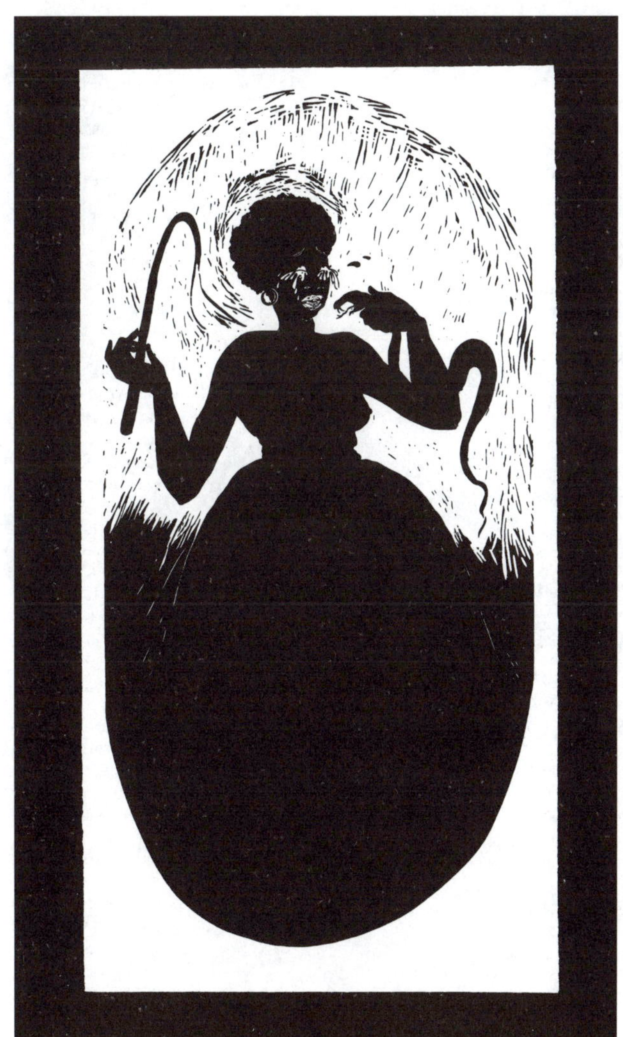

<h1 align="center">P A R K E T T   I N   B O O K S H O P S   (Selection)</h1>

NORTH & SOUTH AMERICA, ASIA, AUSTRALIA
DISTRIBUTOR / VERTRIEB
D.A.P. (DISTRIBUTED ART PUBLISHERS)
155 AVENUE OF THE AMERICAS, 2ND FLOOR,
NEW YORK, NY 10013

USA
AUSTIN, TX
BOOK PEOPLE
603 N. LAMAR
BERKELEY, CA
BERKELEY ART MUSEUM
2625 DURANT AVENUE
CODY'S BOOKS
2454 TELEGRAPHE AVENUE
BEVERLY HILLS, CA
RIZZOLI
9501 WILSHIRE BOULEVARD
BOSTON, MA
INSTITUTE OF CONTEMPORARY ART
955 BOYLSTON STREET
TRIDENT BOOKSELLERS
338 NEWBURY STREET
BUFFALO, NY
TALKING LEAVES
3158 MAIN STREET
CAMBRIDGE, MA
MIT PRESS BOOKSTORE
292 MAIN STREET
CHICAGO, IL
ART INSTITUTE OF CHICAGO
104 S. MICHIGAN
MUSEUM OF CONTEMPORARY ART
220 EAST CHICAGO AVENUE
QUIMBY'S
1854 W. NORTH AVENUE
SMART MUSEUM OF ART
5550 S. GREENWOOD AVENUE
CINCINNATI, OH
CONTEMPORARY ARTS CENTER
115 E. 5TH STREET
COLUMBUS, OH
COLUMBUS MUSEUM OF ART
372 COMMONS MALL
WEXNER CENTER BOOKSTORE
30 W. 15TH STREET
CORAL GABLES, FL
BOOKS & BOOKS
296 ARAGON ROAD
HOUSTON, TX
BRAZOS BOOKSTORE
2421 BISSONNET
CONTEMPORARY ARTS MUSEUM
5216 MONTROSE BOULEVARD
MENIL COLLECTION
1520 SUL ROSS
HUNTINGTON, WV
HUNTINGTON MUSEUM OF ART
2033 MCCOY ROAD
LOS ANGELES, CA
BOOKSOUP
8818 SUNSET BOULEVARD
MUSEUM OF CONTEMPORARY ART
250, S. GRAND
UCLA / ARMAND HAMMER MUSEUM OF ART
10899 WILSHIRE BOULEVARD

MIAMI, FL
BOOKS & BOOKS
296 ARAGON AVENUE, CORAL GABLES
MUSEUM OF CONTEMPORARY ART
770 N.E. 125TH STREET NORTH MIAMI
MINNEAPOLIS, MN
THE WALKER ART CENTER BOOKSTORE
VINELAND PLACE
NEW YORK, NY
GUGGENHEIM DOWNTOWN MUSEUM
575 BROADWAY
MUSEUM OF MODERN ART
11 W. 53RD STREET
NEW MUSEUM OF CONTEMPORARY ART
583 BROADWAY
RIZZOLI
454 WEST BROADWAY
SAINT MARK'S BOOKSTORE
31 3RD AVENUE
OAKLAND, CA
DIESEL, A BOOKSTORE
5433 COLLEGE AVENUE
OAK PARK, MI
BOOK BEAT LTD.
26010 GREENFIELD
OMAHA, NE
JOSLYN ART MUSEUM
2200 DODGE STREET
PHILADELPHIA, PA
AVRIL 50
3406 SANSOM STREET
WATERSTONE BOOKSELLERS
2191 HORNIG ROAD
PITTSBURGH, PA
CARNEGIE INSTITUTE
4400 FORBES AVENUE
PORTLAND, OR
POWELL'S BOOKS
7 NW 9TH STREET
PROVIDENCE, NY
ACCIDENT OR DESIGN
128 N. MAIN STREET
RHODE ISLAND SCHOOL OF DESIGN
2 COLLEGE STREET, 1765
SAN ANTONIO, TX
SLOAN / HALL SAN ANTONIO
5930 BROADWAY
SAN FRANCISCO, CA
A CLEAN WELL LIGHTED PLACE
601 VAN NESS AVENUE
CITY LIGHTS BOOKSHOP
261 COLUMBUS AVENUE
SAN FRANCISCO MUSEUM OF MODERN ART,
MUSEUMBOOKS
151 3RD STREET, 1ST FLOOR
ST. LOUIS, MO
LEFT BANK BOOKS
399 NORTH EUCLID
SANTA MONICA, CA
ARCANA
1229 3RD STREET PROMENADE
HENNESSEY & INGALLS BOOKS
1254 3RD STREET PROMENADE
ST. PAUL, MN
HUNGRY MIND BOOKSTORE
1648 GRAND AVENUE
SEATTLE, WA
UNIVERSITY BOOKSTORE
4326 UNIVERSITY WAY

WASHINGTON D.C.
NATIONAL GALLERY OF ART
6TH STREET & CONSTITUTION AVENUE, NW

CANADA / KANADA
CALGARY
TREPANIER BAER GALLERY
105 999 8TH STREET SW
MONTREAL
ARTEXTE
3575 STREET LAURENT
OLIVIERI LIBRAIRIE BOOKSTORE
185 STREET CATHERINE WEST
TORONTO
ART GALLERY OF ONTARIO
317 DUNDAS STREET WEST
ART METROPOLE
788 KING STREET WEST
DAVID MIRVISH BOOKS ON ART
596 MARKHAM STREET
VANCOUVER
VANCOUVER ART GALLERY
750 HORNBY STREET

AUSTRALIA / AUSTRALIEN
DARLINGHURST
EAST SYDNEY BOOKSTORE
THE DOME, THE ELAN BUILDING
1 KINGS CROSS ROAD
SYDNEY
MUSEUM OF CONTEMPORARY ART
140 GEORGE STREET, CIRCULAR QUAY NORTH
GLEE BOOKS
191 GLEBE POINT ROAD, GLEBE

NEW ZEALAND / NEUSEELAND
AUCKLAND
PROPAGANDA
2 CARR ROAD, MT ROSKILL

ASIA / ASIEN
JAPAN
TOKYO
AOYAMA BOOK CENTRE, SHIBUYA-KU
COSMOS AOYAMA GARDEN FLOOR B2F
5-53-97, JINGUMAE
ART & BOOKS
2-1-13-307
TAKANAWA, MINATO-KU
WATARI MUSEUM OF CONTEMPORARY ART,
ON SUNDAYS BOOKSHOP
376 JINGUMAE SHIBUYA-KU

SINGAPORE / SINGAPUR
PAGE ONE BOOKSTORE
20 KAKI BUKIT VIEW TECHPARK

GREAT BRITAIN / GROSSBRITANNIEN
DISTRIBUTOR / VERTRIEB
CENTRAL BOOKS
99, WALLIS ROAD
LONDON E9 5LN
BRISTOL
ARNOLFINI BOOKSHOP
16 NARROW QUAY
LONDON
BORDERS BOOKSHOP
120 CHARING CROSS ROAD

BORDERS BOOKSHOP
203–207 OXFORD STREET
CAMDEN ARTS CENTRE
ARKWRIGHT ROAD
HAYWARD GALLERY
SOUTH BANK
IAN SHIPLEY BOOKSHOP
70 CHARING CROSS ROAD
INSTITUTE OF CONTEMPORARY ARTS
12 CARLTON HOUSE TERRACE
THE MALL
SERPENTINE GALLERY
KENSINGTON GARDENS
TATE MODERN
BANKSIDE
ZWEMMER LTD. ART BOOKS
24 LITCHFIELD STREET

IRELAND / IRLAND
DUBLIN
DOUGLAS HYDE GALLERY
TRINITY COLLEGE

GERMANY / DEUTSCHLAND
DISTRIBUTOR / VERTRIEB
GVA VERLAGSSERVICE GÖTTINGEN
ANNA-VANDENHOECK-RING 36
D-37081 GÖTTINGEN
BERLIN
BÜCHERBOGEN AM SAVIGNYPLATZ
STADTBAHNBOGEN 593
GALERIE 2000 KUNSTBUCHHANDLUNG
KNESEBECKSTRASSE 56/58
WALTHER KÖNIG BUCHHANDLUNG, MUSEUM FÜR
GEGENWARTSKUNST
INVALIDENSTRASSE 50–51 IM HAMBURGER BAHNHOF
BREMEN
KUNST UND BUCH, AM NEUEN MUSEUM
WESERBURG, TEERHOF 20
BREMERHAVEN
KABINETT FÜR AKTUELLE KUNST
KARLSBURG 4
DÜSSELDORF
LITERATUR BEI RUDOLF MÖLLER
NEUSTRASSE 38
WALTHER KÖNIG BUCHHANDLUNG
HEINRICH-HEINE-ALLEE 15
FRANKFURT
KUNSTHALLE SCHIRN, KUNST-BUCH
RÖMERBERG 7
PETER NAACHER BUCHHANDLUNG
ZIEGELHÜTTENWEG 27–31
SCHUMANN & COBET BUCHHANDLUNG
BÖRSENSTRASSE 2–4
WALTHER KÖNIG BUCHHANDLUNG
DOMSTRASSE 6
HAMBURG
HELMUT VON DER HÖH BUCHHANDLUNG
GROSSE BLEICHEN 21
SAUTTER + LACKMANN BUCHHANDLUNG
ADMIRALITÄTSTRASSE 71/72
HANNOVER
MERZ KUNSTBUCHHANDLUNG
KURT-SCHWITTERS-PLATZ
KARLSRUHE
HANS MENDE BUCHHANDLUNG
KARLSTRASSE 76
KÖLN
SCHADEN.COM BUCHHANDEL
BURGMAUER 10
WALTHER KÖNIG BUCHHANDLUNG
EHRENSTRASSE 4
MÜNCHEN
HANS GOLTZ BUCHHANDLUNG
FÜR BILDENDE KUNST
TÜRKENSTRASSE 54
ILKA KÖNIG BUCHHANDLUNG
MAXIMILIANSTRASSE 35

L. WERNER BUCHHANDLUNG
TÜRKENSTRASSE 30
NÜRNBERG
HUGENDUBEL BUCHHANDLUNG
LUDWIGSPLATZ 1
STUTTGART
GALERIE VALENTIEN
KÖNIGSBAU
LIMACHER BUCHHANDLUNG
KÖNIGSTRASSE 28 / KÖNIGSBAU
WIESBADEN
OTTO HARRASSOWITZ BUCHHANDLUNG
TAUNUSSTRASSE 5

SPAIN / SPANIEN
BARCELONA
1+1 LLIBRES D'ART-ART BOOKS
PASSEIG DE SANT JOAN, 108
LAIETANA DE LLIBRETERIA
PAU CLARIS 85
MADRID
MUSEO NACIONAL REINA SOFIA
C/ SANTA ISABEL, 52

FRANCE / FRANKREICH
PARIS
COLETTE
213, RUE SAINT-HONORÉ
CENTRE POMPIDOU, FLAMMARION 4
26, RUE JACOB
GALERIE NATIONALE DU JEU DE PAUME
1, PLACE DE LA CONCORDE
LIBRAIRIE DU MUSÉE D'ART MODERNE
9, RUE GASTON DE SAINT-PAUL

ITALY / ITALIEN
MILANO
A&M BOOKSTORE
30, VIA TADINO
ROMA
GALLERIA NAZIONALE D'ARTE MODERNA
131, VIA DELLE BELLE ARTI
GALLERIA PRIMO PIANO
203, VIA PANISPERNA

NORWAY / NORWEGEN
OSLO
THE NATIONAL MUSEUM OF CONTEMPORARY ART
BANKPLASSEN 4 / SKATTEFOG

PORTUGAL
LISBOA
MODULO CENTRO DIFUSOR DE ARTE
CALÇADA DOS MESTRES 34 A–B
PORTO
MODULO CENTRO DIFUSOR DE ARTE
AV. BOAVISTA 854

SWEDEN / SCHWEDEN
STOCKHOLM
KULTURHUSET KONSTIG
MEDIA & KONSTBOKHANDEL
SERGELS TORG 3
MODERNA MUSEET
SKEPPSHOLMEN

TURKEY / TÜRKEI
ISTANBUL
ROBINSON CRUSOE BOOKS PUSULA PRODUCTIONS
389 ISTIKAL CADDESI BEYOGLU

**NETHERLANDS, BELGIUM
AND LUXEMBURG**
DISTRIBUTOR / VERTRIEB
IDEA BOOKS
NIEUWE HERENGRACHT 11
NL-1011 RK AMSTERDAM

NETHERLANDS / NIEDERLANDE
AMSTERDAM
ART BOOK
VAN BAERLESTRAAT 126

ATHENAEUM NIEUWSCENTRUM
SPUI 14–16
ROBERT PREMSELA BOOKSHOP
VAN BAERLESTRAAT 78
GRONINGEN
SCHOLTENS / WRISTERS BOOKSHOP
FULDENSTRAAT 20
ROTTERDAM
DONNER BOOKSHOP
LIJNBAAN 150

BELGIUM / BELGIEN
ANTWERPEN
F.N.A.C.
GROENPLAATS
BRUXELLES
TROPISMES LIBRAIRIES
GALERIE DES PRINCES 11
GENT
COPYRIGHT BOOKSHOP
JACOBIJNENSTRAAT 8

LUXEMBOURG / LUXEMBURG
LUXEMBOURG
CASINO LUXEMBOURG
41, RUE NOTRE-DAME

SWITZERLAND / SCHWEIZ
DISTRIBUTOR / VERTRIEB
B+I BUCH + INFORMATION
OBERFELDERSTRASSE 35
CH-8910 AFFOLTERN A. A.
BASEL
FONDATION BEYELER
BASELSTRASSE 77, RIEHEN
GALERIE STAMPA
SPALENBERG 2
JÄGGI BUCHHANDLUNG
FREIE STRASSE 32
KUNSTHALLE BASEL
KLOSTERGASSE 5
BERN
HANS HUBER AG BUCHHANDLUNG
MARKTGASSE 59
STAUFFACHER BUCHHANDLUNG
IM KUNSTMUSEUM
HODLERSTRASSE 12
LUZERN
RÄBER BÜCHER AG
FRANKENSTRASSE 7-9
GENÈVE
LIBRAIRIE PAYOT
5, RUE DE CHANTEPOULET
MENDRISIO
GABRIELE CAPELLI LIBRERIA ARCHITETTURA
4, VIA NOBILI BOSIA
ST. GALLEN
RÖSSLITOR BÜCHER
WEBERGASSE 5
ZÜRICH
CALLIGRAMME BUCHHANDLUNG
HÄRINGSTRASSE 4
HOWEG BUCHHANDLUNG
WAFFENPLATZ 1
KRAUTHAMMER BUCHHANDLUNG
OBERE ZÄUNE 24
KUNSTGRIFF BUCHHANDLUNG
LIMMATSTRASSE 270
KUNSTHAUS ZÜRICH
HEIMPLATZ 1
KUNSTKIOSK
LIMMATQUAI 31
ORELL FÜSSLI BUCHHANDLUNG
FÜSSLISTRASSE 4
SCALO BOOKS & LOOKS
WEINBERGSTRASSE 22 A
SEC 52 BUCHHANDLUNG
JOSEFSTRASSE 52

ZÜRICH

ACP	Klingenstrasse 42	MARTIN NOËL – on the road	**7.9.–21.10.2000**
VIVIANE EHRLI	8005 Zürich	RENKO – Recent paintings	**26.10.–23.12.2000**
	Tel. 01 271 61 61	SERENA AMREIN – Drawings FL 2000	**18.11.–23.12.2000**
ARS FUTURA	Bleicherweg 45	OLAF BREUNING – Ugly Yelp Installation	**23.9.–11.11.2000**
	8002 Zürich	MARTIN PARR – Think of England	**24.11. bis Mitte JAN.**
	Tel. 01 201 88 10		
BOB VON ORSOUW	Limmatstrasse 270	PAUL GRAHAM	**26.8.–30.9.2000**
	8005 Zürich		
	Tel. 01 273 11 00		
BOB GYSIN	Ausstellungsstrasse 24	CHRISTOPH SCHREIBER –	
	8005 Zürich	THOMAS GALLER	**8.9.–21.10.2000**
	Tel. 01 278 40 60	STEPHEN CRAIG	**27.10.–2.12.2000**
MAI 36 GALERIE	Rämistrasse 37	PAUL THEK	**25.8.–30.9.2000**
	8001 Zürich	STEPHAN BALKENHOL	**6.10.–26.11.2000**
	Tel. 01 261 68 80		
MARK MÜLLER	Gessnerallee 36	KATHARINA GROSSE – Nonnenbilder	
	8001 Zürich	im Guestroom: MARTIN BOYCE, JIM LAMBIE,	
	Tel. 01 211 81 55	TOBY PATERSON, MARY REDMOND,	
		EVA ROTHSCHILD, CATHY WILKES curated by	
		The Modern Institute, Glasgow and	
		Frédéric Dedelley	**24.8.–14.10.2000**
		BEAT ZODERER – Neue Arbeiten	
		im Guestroom: SURPRISE	**21.10.–16.12.2000**
		ART Cologne 2000 – KünstlerInnen der Galerie	
		ART Cologne 2000 – Förderkoje –	
		RETO BOLLER, Bilder	**5.11.–12.11.2000**
SEMINA RERUM	Cäcilienstrasse 3	MICHEL GRILLET	**25.8.–7.10.2000**
IRÈNE PREISWERK	8032 Zürich	ERIK STEFFENSEN	**13.10.–17.11.2000**
	Tel. 01 251 26 39	SILVIA GERTSCH / XERXES ACH	**25.11.–13.1.2001**

E X H I B I T I O N S

GALERIE SCHEDLER	Josefstrasse 53	STEPHEN BARKER – nightswimming	
	8005 Zürich	CHRISTOPH WACHTER – 94 etchings	**bis 30.9.2000**
	Tel. 01 440 61 20	ATTILA RICHARD LUKACS – works on paper	**7.10.–4.11.2000**
		WALTER PFEIFFER – photography	**10.11.–30.12.2000**

ANNEMARIE VERNA	Neptunstrasse 45	REE MORTON (1936–1977)	**12.9.–4.11.2000**
	8032 Zürich	ROBERT WILSON	**9.11. bis JAN. 2001**
	Tel. 01 262 38 20		

JAMILEH WEBER	Waldmannstrasse 6	ROBERT RAUSCHENBERG	**SEPT./OKT. 2000**
	8001 Zürich	GEORG BASELITZ	**NOV./DEZ. 2000**
	Tel. 01 252 10 66		

BRIGITTE WEISS	Müllerstrasse 67	SHIRLEY JAFFE	**23.8.–21.10.2000**
	8004 Zürich	art forum berlin 2000, Halle/Stand 22a/24	**26.9.–1.10.2000**
	Tel. 01 241 83 35	CHRISTINA ZURFLUH	**27.10.–23.12.2000**

BERN

GALERIE FRIEDRICH	Lorrainestrasse 19	MARIO SALA	**8.9.–14.10.2000**
	3013 Bern	SUZAN FRECON	**20.10.–24.11.2000**
	Tel. 031 331 33 30		

GENÈVE

DANIEL VARENNE	8, rue Toepffer	PAINTINGS AND DRAWINGS	
	1206 Genève	19TH AND 20TH CENTURY	
	Tel. 022 789 16 75		

ST. GALLEN

WILMA LOCK	Schmiedgasse 15	OPEN – BERNHARD FRIZE, JÜRGEN PARTENHEIMER	
	9001 St. Gallen	FRANZ E. WALTHER, ERWIN WURM,	
	Tel. 071 222 62 52	KELLY WOOD	**7.10.–9.12.2000**

ZUG

KUNSTHAUS ZUG	Dorfstrasse 27	Projekt Sammlung (3)	
	6300 Zug	MOZES – Die Künstler-Gruppe «Russia»	
	Tel. 041 725 33 44	und Pavel Pepperstein	**bis 5. NOV. 2000**
		HOMMAGE À JOSEF HERZOG	**bis 14. JAN. 2000**

Galerie Emmanuel Perrotin

30, rue Louise Weiss 75013 Paris T: 33 (0)1 42 16 79 79 F: 33 (0)1 42 16 79 74
E-mail : perrotin@wanadoo.fr   Web : www.galerieperrotin.com

Lilian Bourgeat, Maurizio Cattelan, Eric Duyckaerts, Bernard Frize, Noritoshi Hirakawa,
Wendy Jacob, Henrik Plenge Jakobsen & Jes Brinch, Jean-Pierre Khazem, Kolkoz, Guy Limone,
Mariko Mori, Takashi Murakami, Terry Richardson, Christophe Touzot, Kenji Yanobe, ...

Setembre : Kenji Yanobe
Septembre Maria Marshall
Octobre : FIAC
Novembre : Art cologne
Novembre : Paris Photo
Novembre : Nicole Tran Ba Vang
Janvier : Takashi Murakami
Mars : Jeff Burton
Mai : Paul Morisson
Juin : Paula Pivi

Maurizio Cattelan

VICTORIA MIRO GALLERY

representing:

YAYOI KUSAMA

&

DOUG AITKEN

CECILY BROWN

ANNE CHU

THOMAS DEMAND

PETER DOIG

INKA ESSENHIGH

IAN HAMILTON FINLAY

ANDREAS GURSKY

ALEX HARTLEY

CHANTAL JOFFE

ISAAC JULIEN

UDOMSAK KRISANAMIS

ABIGAIL LANE

BRAD LOCHORE

ROBIN LOWE

DAWN MELLOR

TRACEY MOFFATT

CHRIS OFILI

HADRIAN PIGOTT

ADRIANA VAREJÃO

STEPHEN WILLATS

FRANCESCA WOODMAN

Please note that the gallery at 21 Cork Street will close on 29 September 2000

All enquiries should be addressed to the new gallery from 2 October 2000

16 Wharf Road London N1. Tel: 020 7336 8109 fax: 020 7251 5596

OTA FINE ARTS

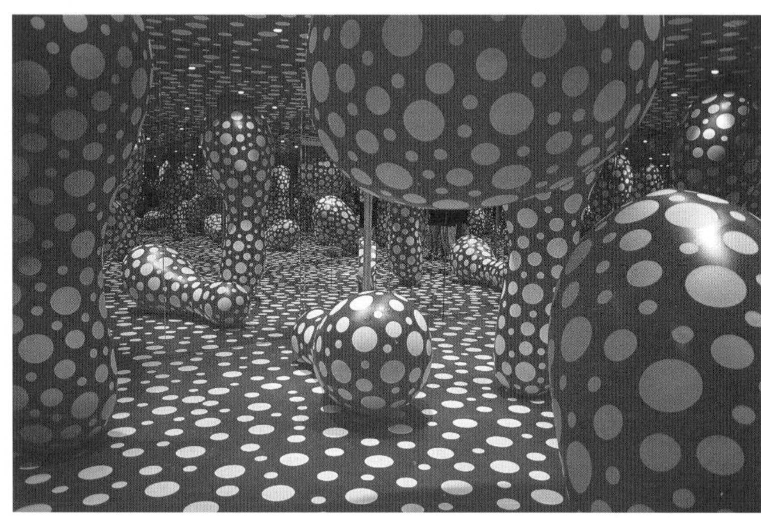

Yayoi Kusama

Le Consortium, Dijon
October 20 - January 20, 2001
www.leconsortium.com

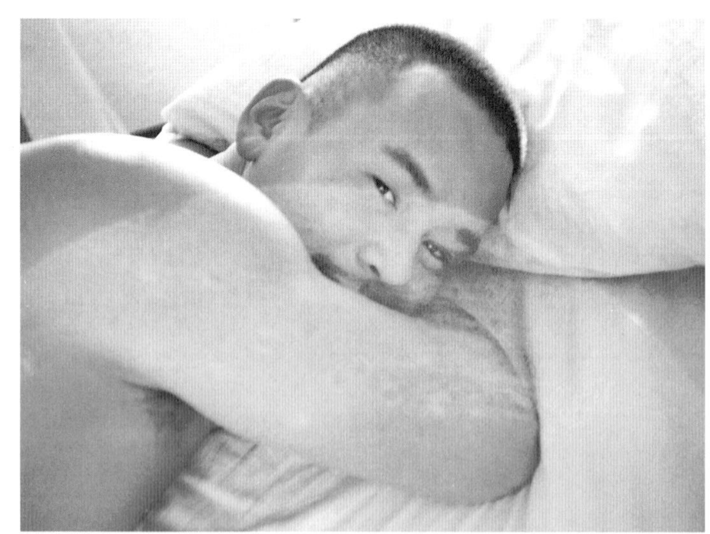

Akira the Hustler
October 27 - November 18
Ota Fine Arts, Tokyo

2-8-11 Ebisunishi Shibuyaku Tokyo 1500021 JAPAN
Tel: 03-3780-0911   Fax: 03-3780-0450

RACHEL BERWICK

SEPTEMBER 9 – OCTOBER 14

ARTURO HERRERA

OCTOBER 21 – NOVEMBER 25

KARA WALKER

IS REPRESENTED BY

BRENT SIKKEMA

530 WEST 22ND STREET NEW YORK NY 10011 TEL 212.929.2262

FAX 212.929.2340 EMAIL BSIKKEMA@VERIOMAIL.COM

RACHEL BERWICK · MITCH EPSTEIN · JEFF GAUNTT

JAN HENLE · ARTURO HERRERA · JAMES HYDE · MERLIN JAMES · JOSIAH McELHENY

VIK MUNIZ · CAROL RHODES · AMY SILLMAN · KARA WALKER

MEG WEBSTER

SEPTEMBER – OCTOBER

CARL ANDRE

OCTOBER – NOVEMBER

ZOE LEONARD

OCTOBER – NOVEMBER

SOL LeWITT

DECEMBER

ADRIAN PIPER

DECEMBER

PAULA COOPER GALLERY
521/534 WEST 21ST STREET NEW YORK NY 10011
TEL 212.255.1105 FAX 212.255.5156

14 SEPTEMBER – 2 DECEMBER 2000

Opening Thursday, 14 September, 6 to 9 pm

Robert Ryman

Paintings from the sixties

Xavier Hufkens

Sint-Jorisstraat 6–8 rue Saint-Georges

Brussel 1050 Bruxelles

TEL. 32 (0)2 639 67 30 – FAX 32 (0)2 639 67 38

info@xavierhufkens.com
http://www.xavierhufkens.com

Open Tuesday to Saturday, noon to 6 pm

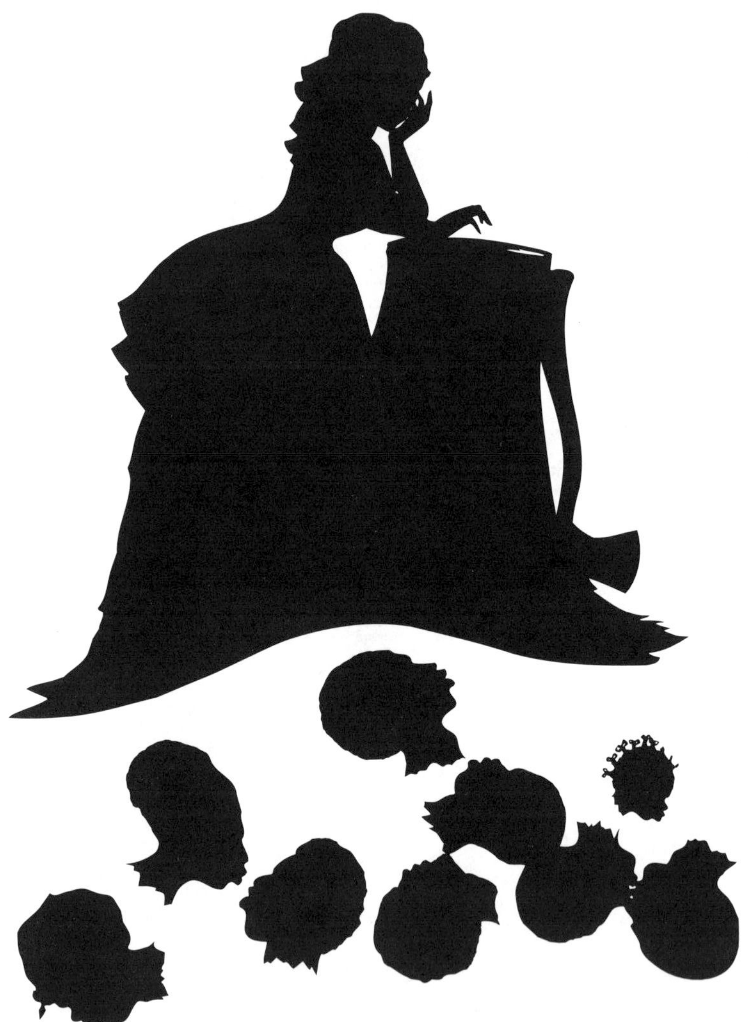

KARA WALKER

EMANCIPATION APPROXIMATION

From *Emancipation Approximation,* 2000.
Portfolio of 26 silkscreen prints, 44 x 34 inches each, edition of 20. Plus 5 individual prints in an edition of 25.

Jenkins Sikkema Editions
530 West 22nd Street New York, NY 10011 p. 212.929.2262 f. 212.929.2340 email bsikkema@veriomail.com

Also editions by Arturo Herrera, Josiah McElheny, Glenn Ligon, Vik Muniz

GIUSEPPE PENONE

RINEKE DIJKSTRA

SEPTEMBER 12 – OCTOBER 28

MARIAN GOODMAN GALLERY

24 WEST 57TH STREET   NEW YORK, NY 10019   TEL 212 977-7160

FAX 212 581-5187   GOODMAN@MARIANGOODMAN.COM

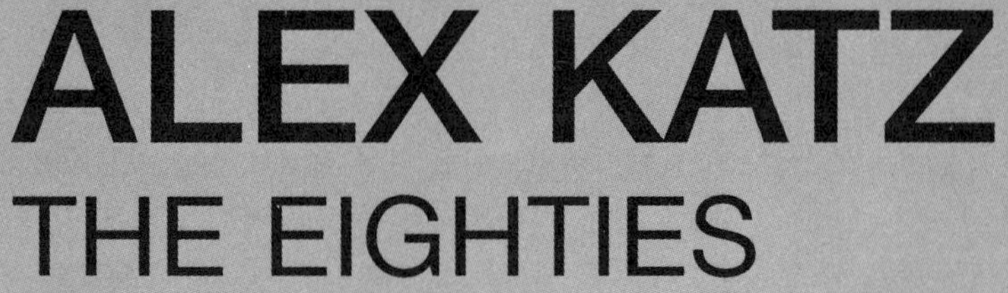

ALEX KATZ
THE EIGHTIES

CATALOGUE

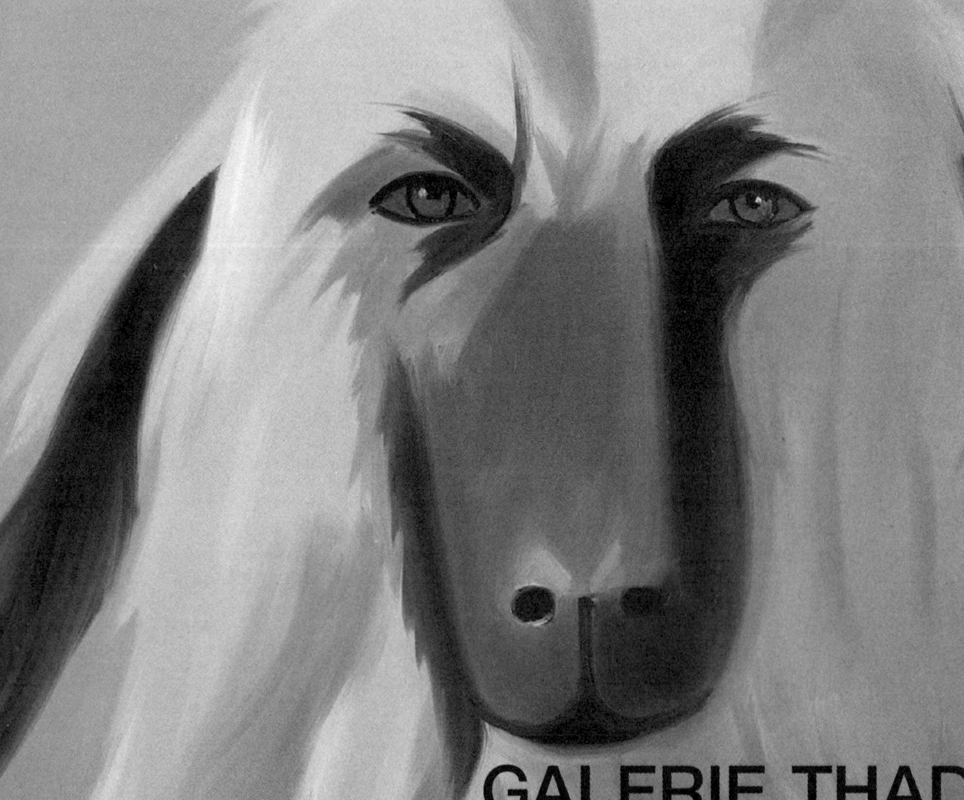

GALERIE THADDAEUS ROPAC
SALZBURG

Tel. +43 662 881 393 · www.ropac.net

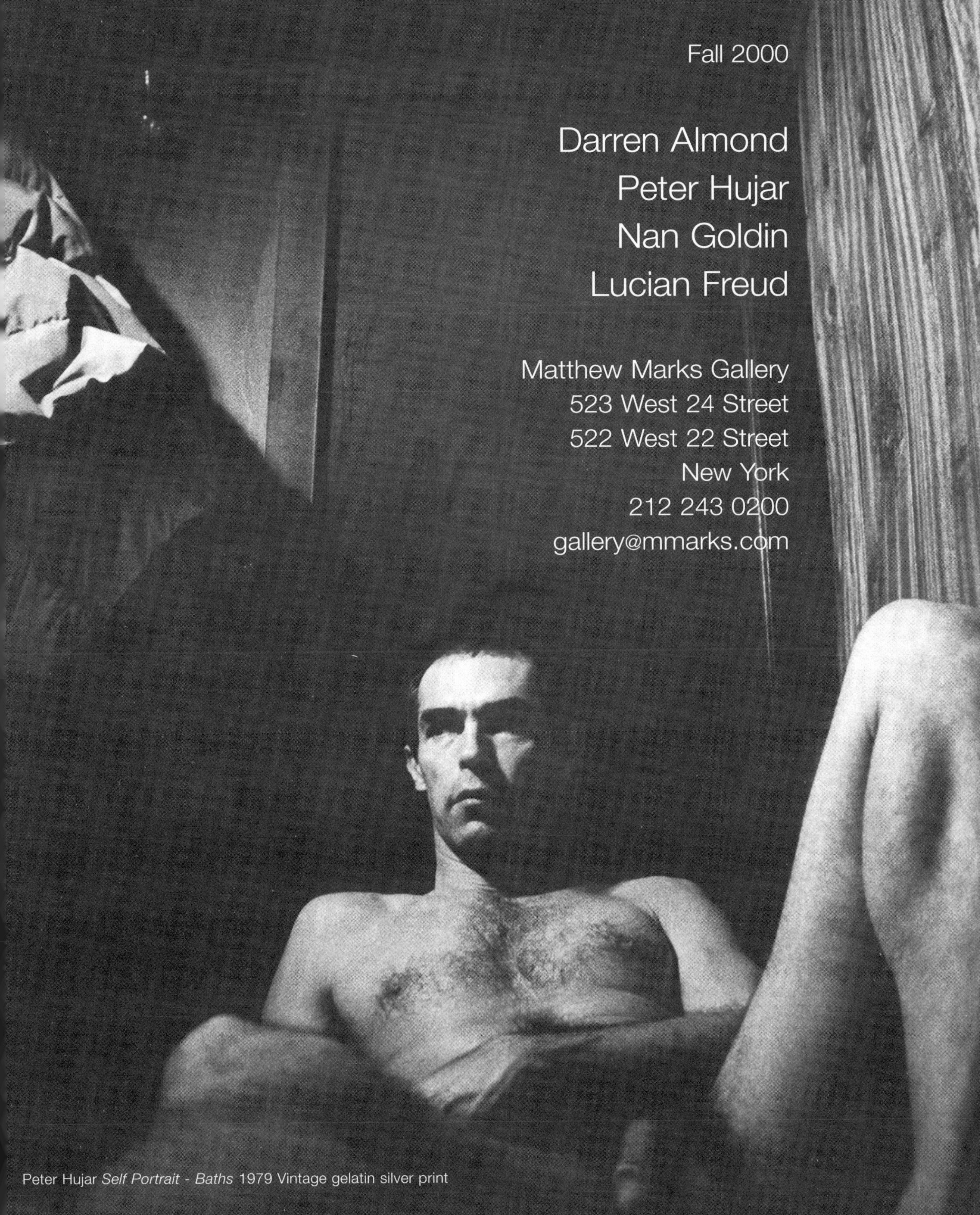

Peter Hujar *Self Portrait - Baths* 1979 Vintage gelatin silver print

MAI 36 GALERIE

VITO ACCONCI
FRANZ ACKERMANN
IAN ANÜLL
JOHN BALDESSARI
STEPHAN BALKENHOL
TROY BRAUNTUCH
ANKE DOBERAUER
PIA FRIES
ANDREAS GURSKY
LES LEVINE
RITA MCBRIDE
HARALD F. MÜLLER
MATT MULLICAN
MANFRED PERNICE
CHRISTOPH RÜTIMANN
THOMAS RUFF
JÖRG SASSE
PAUL THEK
LAWRENCE WEINER
RÉMY ZAUGG

PAUL THEK

August 25 – September 30, 2000

STEPHAN BALKENHOL

October 6 – November 26, 2000

art forum berlin Hall 22a Booth 24
September 27 – October 1, 2000

Rämistrasse 37, CH-8001 Zürich, Tel. 01 261 68 80, Fax 261 68 81

JEAN-MARC BUSTAMENTE

OCTOBER-NOVEMBER 2000

HELMUT DORNER

DECEMBER-JANUARY 2001

ABIGAIL LANE

FEBRUARY-MARCH 2001

vera munro

GALERIE VERA MUNRO

HEILWIGSTRASSE 64

20249 HAMBURG

TELEFON 040 - 47 47 46

TELEFAX 040 - 47 25 50

INTERNET WWW.VERAMUNRO.DE

E-MAIL GALLERY@VERAMUNRO.DE

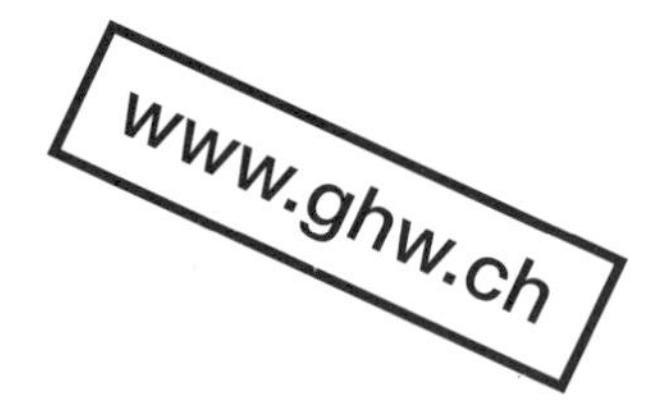

26. AUGUST BIS 21. OKTOBER 2000

PALERMO

LOUISE BOURGEOIS · DAN GRAHAM · PAUL MCCARTHY · JOHN MCCRACKEN · MARY HEILMANN
THE ESTATE OF EVA HESSE · RICHARD JACKSON · ON KAWARA · RACHEL KHEDOORI · RAYMOND PETTIBON
JASON RHOADES · PIPILOTTI RIST · ROMAN SIGNER · DIANA THATER

GALERIE HAUSER & WIRTH
Limmatstrasse 270, 8005 Zürich / Tel: +41 1 446 80 50, Fax: +41 1 446 80 55 / www.ghw.ch / Öffnungszeiten: Di- Fr 12 - 18, Sa 11 - 16 Uhr

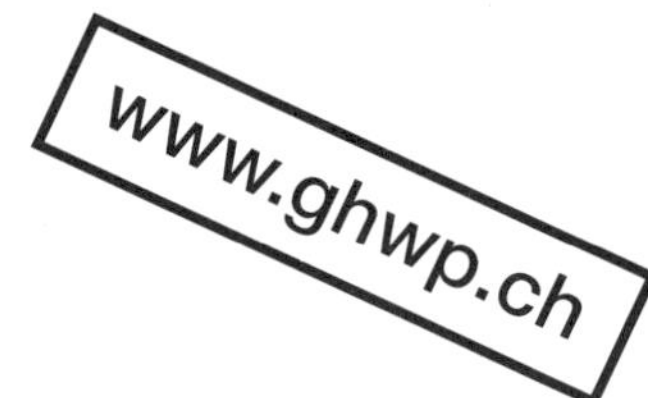

26. AUGUST BIS 21. OKTOBER 2000

URS FREI

DOUG AITKEN · EMMANUELLE ANTILLE · ANGELA BULLOCH · MARIA EICHHORN · URS FISCHER · PETER FISCHLI / DAVID WEISS
SYLVIE FLEURY · URS FREI · LIAM GILLICK · DOUGLAS GORDON · CANDIDA HÖFER · KAREN KILIMNIK · GERWALD ROCKENSCHAUB
UGO RONDINONE · DIETER ROTH · JEAN-FRÉDÉRIC SCHNYDER · BEAT STREULI · FRANZ WEST · SUE WILLIAMS

GALERIE HAUSER & WIRTH & PRESENHUBER
Limmatstrasse 270, 8005 Zürich / Tel: +41 1 446 80 60, Fax: +41 1 446 80 65 / www.ghwp.ch / Öffnungszeiten: Di- Fr 12 - 18, Sa 11 - 16 Uhr

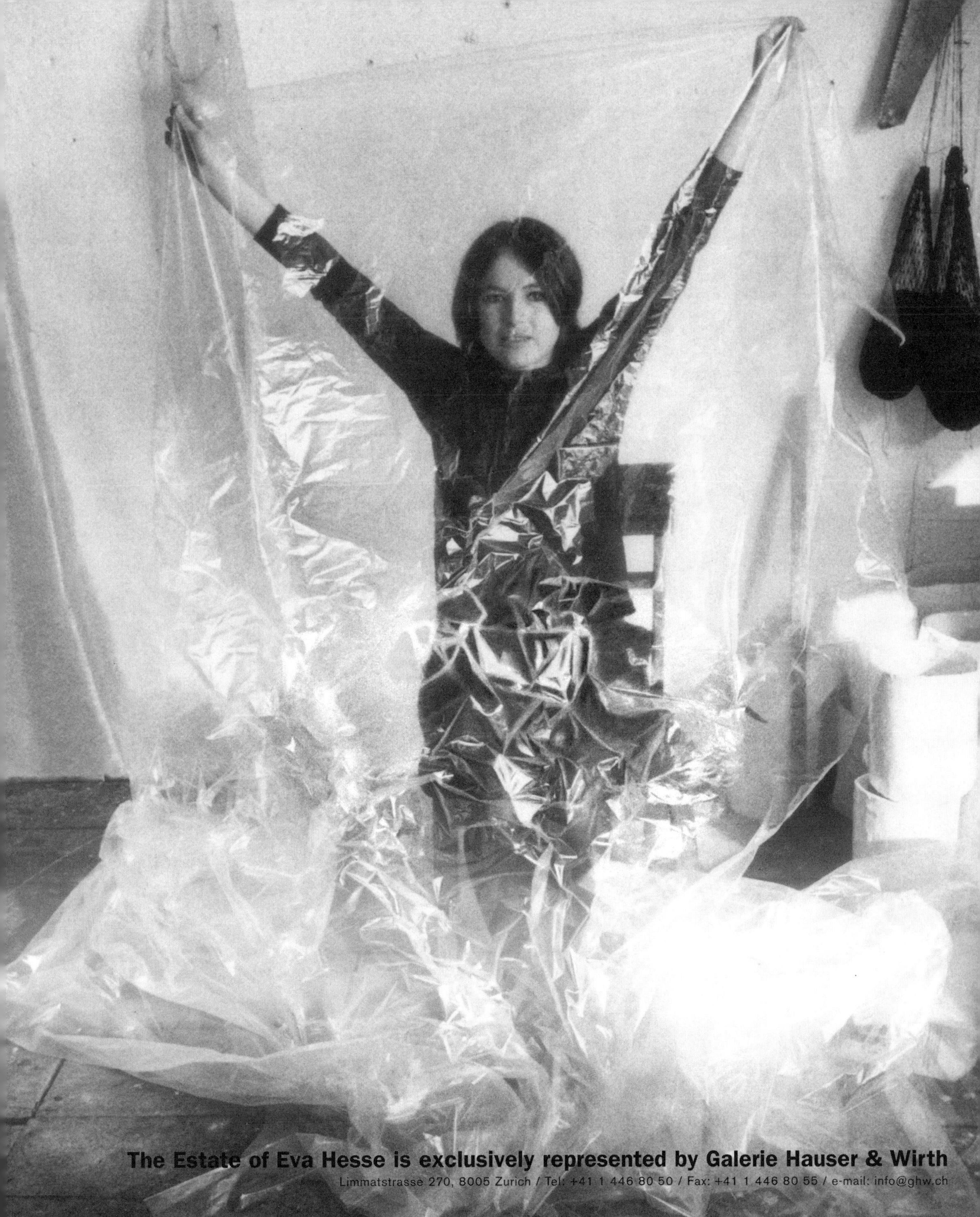

The Estate of Eva Hesse is exclusively represented by Galerie Hauser & Wirth

Limmatstrasse 270, 8005 Zurich / Tel: +41 1 446 80 50 / Fax: +41 1 446 80 55 / e-mail: info@ghw.ch

GALERIA ■ HELGA DE ALVEAR

DR. FOURQUET 12, 28012 MADRID.TEL:(34) 91 468 05 06   FAX:(34) 91 467 51 34
e-mail: dealvear@w3art.es   www.artnet.com/dealvear.html

September 20 - November 11

JOSÉ MALDONADO

November 16 – January 13

AXEL HÜTTE

January 18 – March 2

JEFF WALL

March 8 – April 21

GERHARD MERZ

May 18 – June 30

JOHN HILLIARD

September 26 - October 1

ART FORUM BERLIN

November 5 - 12

ART COLOGNE

karyn lovegrove gallery

Ingrid Calame: Drawings
9 September–30 September

Ingrid Calame: Paintings
7 October–11 November

Floyd Claypool
17 November–23 December

Karyn Lovegrove Gallery
6150 Wilshire Boulevard #8
Los Angeles CA 90048 USA
Telephone: 323 525 1755
Facsimile: 323 525 1245
Email: lovegrovek@aol.com
karynlovegrovegallery.com

GALERIE 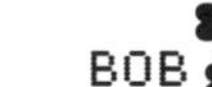 BOB GYSIN

WWW.BG-GALERIE.CH

AUSSTELLUNGSSTRASSE 24, 8005 ZÜRICH
T 01 278 40 60—F 01 278 40 50—INFO@BG-GALERIE.CH

Christoph Schreiber—Thomas Galler
8. September–21. Oktober—Eröffnung 7. September 2000—18–21 Uhr

VORTRAG ‹KUNST UND NEUE MEDIEN›—
DONNERSTAG, 28. SEPTEMBER, 19 UHR—PROF. DR. H.P. SCHWARZ,
REKTOR HOCHSCHULE FÜR GESTALTUNG UND KUNST

Stephen Craig
27. Oktober–2. Dezember—Eröffnung 26. Oktober 2000—18–21 Uhr

DI–FR 12–18—SA 11–16

GOTTFRIED HELNWEIN

THE FIRST AMERICAN PAINTINGS

SEPTEMBER – NOVEMBER, 2000

MODERNISM 685 MARKET STREET SAN FRANCISCO
CALIFORNIA 94105 415/541-0461 FAX: 415/541-0425

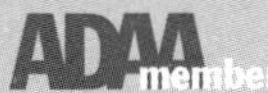

GALERIE MEERT RIHOUX

CARLA ACCARDI

ROBERT ADAMS

JOHN BALDESSARI

ROBERT BARRY

ENRICO CASTELLANI

HANNE DARBOVEN

MARIA ANNA DEWES

PAUL DRISSEN

SYLVIE EYBERG

ISA GENZKEN

JEF GEYS

MIMMO JODICE

PETER JOSEPH

DONALD JUDD

BRANDT JUNCEAU

LOUISE LAWLER

SOL LEWITT

KEN LUM

ROBERT MANGOLD

LILIANA MORO

FRED SANDBACK

THOMAS STRUTH

RICHARD TUTTLE

MICHAEL VENEZIA

IAN WALLACE

JEFF WALL

21 SEPT - 26 NOV

RUE DU CANAL 13
1000 BRUXELLES
VAARTSTRAAT 13
1000 BRUSSEL
TEL 02/219 14 22
FAX 02/219 37 21
greta.meert@skynet.be

ILYA KABAKOV PAVEL PEPPERSTEIN

how to meet an angel

3 oct - 28 oct

GREG COLSON TOM FRIEDMAN TOLAND
GRINNELL TIM HAWKINSON TOM SACHS

hand-Made in U.S.A.

2 nov - 2 dec

SPROVIERI   27 heddon street london w1 t +44 20 7494 9797

GEORG KARGL

Elke Krystufek
Muntean/Rosenblum
Gerwald Rockenschaub
Inés Lombardi
Herbert Hinteregger
Gabi Trinkaus
Matt Mullican
Mark Dion
Chuck Close
John Waters

Thomas Locher
Christian Philipp Müller
Elizabeth Peyton
Raymond Pettibon
Rudolf Stingel
Peter Fend
Paul de Reus
Lisa Ruyter
Julia Scher

SCHLEIFMÜHLGASSE 5 WIEN 1040
TEL 5854199 FAX 58541999

Peter Halley, born 1953 in New York, lives and works in New York; seven recent paintings will be on show from September 15th to November 10th at **Galleria Massimo Minini** Via Apollonio,68 25128 Brescia Italy tel.030.383034; fax 030.392446; e-mail: galleriaminini@numerica.it www.artnet.com/minini.html
Ettore Spalletti, born 1940 in Cappelle sul Tavo, lives and works in Pescara; we will present a one-man-show of the artist at FIAC, Paris, (24-30 October).
Ryan Mendoza, born 1971 in New York, lives and works in Naples and München. He will show seven new paintings in our gallery from November 16th 2000 to January 2001.

09-10-11/2000

GALERIEN IN DÜSSELDORF

Art Galerie Leuchter+Peltzer A. Fürst Zum 80. Geburtstag **/** ARAG Kunstpreis **Menikheim, Louis / K. Geldmacher** Lichtobjekte

bis 10.9.00 / 14.9.-7.10.00 / 21.10.-3.12.00 / Ratingerstr. 23 / 40213 Düsseldorf/ Tel. +49 (0)211 32 97 91 Fax 13 20 91 / art-leuchter@t-online.de / Mo.-Fr. 9-18.30, Sa. 11-14

Galerie Beck & Eggeling Vom Wesen des Menschen **u. a. Giacometti, Abakanowicz /** Werke des Impressionismus und Postimpressionismus

25.8.-29.10.00 /10.11.-7.1.01/ Bilker Straße 5 / 40213 Düsseldorf / Tel. + 49 (0)211 49 15 890 Fax 49 15 899 / Beck-Eggeling@t-online.de / www.dobefineart.com / Di.-Fr. 11-19, Sa.10-16

Galerie Bugdahn und Kaimer E. Chell Vanishing Point **/ Abigail O´Brien** Extreme Unction–The Ophelia Room

25.8.-7.10.00 / 27.10.-23.12.00 / Mühlengasse 3 40213 Düsseldorf / Tel. + 49 (0)211 32 91 40 Fax 32 91 47 / bugdahn.kaimer@t-online.de / www.artnet.com / Di.-Fr. 10-13+14-18, Sa. 11-14

Galerie Karin Fesel A. Wachter Realistische Malerei

14.10.-17.11.00 / Prinz-Georg-Str. 47 / 40477 Düsseldorf / Tel. + 49 (0)211 46 02 01 Fax 48 05 30 Mobil 0173 29 76 708 / Di-Fr. 12-18 u.n.V. Schwarze Str. 144 / 47665 Sonsbeck

Konrad Fischer Galerie GmbH Y. Takeoka Neue Arbeiten **S. Nieweg** Landschaft **/ R. Long J. Lambie**

26.8.-7.10.00 / 14.10.-25.11.00 / Platanenstr. 7 / 40233 Düsseldorf / Tel. +49 (0)211 68 59 08 Fax 68 97 80 / Konradfischergalerie@mail.isis.de / Di.-Fr. 11-18, Sa. 11-13

Galerie M.+R. Fricke Düsseldorf-Berlin V. Pfeiffer Neue Bilder **/** Artists and Photographs   Saltoarte   SMS (Shit must Stop)

25.8.-14.10.00 / 20.10.-2.12 / Poststr. 3 40213 Düsseldorf / Tel. +49 (0)211 32 32 34 Fax 32 95 69 / MandRFricke@compuserve.com / Di.-Fr. 11-19, Sa. 12-16 u. n. V.

Galerie Wolfgang Gmyrek R. Fischer Fotoarbeiten 1997-2000 **/** 20 Jahre Galerie Wolfgang Gmyrek Jubiläumsausstellung

25.8.-11.11.00 / 25.11.-22.12.00 / Mühlengasse 5 PLZ 40213 / Tel. + 49 (0)211 32 77 70 Fax 13 39 93 / Di.-Fr. 11-18, Sa. 11-14 u. n. V.

Galerie Cora Hölzl S. Kandić Malerei **/ B. Kowanz** Lichtobjekte

25.8.-14.10.00 / 20.10.-2.12. / Citadellstr. 11 40213 Düsseldorf / Tel. +49 (0)211 32 64 12 Fax 13 12 35 / cora.hoelzl@t-online.de / Di.-Fr. 11-18.30, Sa. 12-16 u. n. V.

Galerie Gaby Kraushaar Fotografie **Mayer, Schmitz, Muller, Sommerfeldt / Bachhuber, Grossarth, Hinsberg, Newman, Prangenberg**

25.8.-15.10.00 / 20.10.-20.12.00 / Orangeriestr. 6 / 40213 Düsseldorf / Tel. + 49 (0)211 13 16 66 Fax 13 16 66 / Mi.-Fr. 13-19, Sa. 12-15

Galerie Hans Mayer GmbH B. Willikens

Sept. / Grabbeplatz 2 / 40213 Düsseldorf / Tel. + 49 (0)211 13 21 35 Fax 13 29 48 / Mo.-Fr. 9.30-18, Sa. 10-14 / Kaistr. 10 PLZ 40221 n.V.

Galerie Ute Parduhn C. Bruch Zeichnungen und Objekte **/** BIS DAHIN..., 20 Jahre Galerie Ute Parduhn

25.8.-29.9.00 / 27.10.-31.1.01 / Kaiserwerther Markt 6a / 40489 Düsseldorf / Tel. +49 (0)211 40 06 55 Fax 40 67 0 / Mi.-Fr. 14-18 u. n. V.

Galerie Clara Maria Sels GmbH D. Michals Fotografie

bis Okt. / Poststr. 3 / 40213 Düsseldorf / Tel. +49 (0)211 32 80 20 Fax 32 80 26 / cmsels@mail.isis.de / Di.-Fr. 14-19, Sa. 11-15

Galerie Christa Schübbe M. Prem Fotoprojekt **/** Gruppe Spur **Sturm, Zimmer, Prem / A. Schmidt** Rhein

25.8.-25.9.00 / 6.10.-10.11.00 / 21.11.-6.1.01/ Hasseler Str. 85 / 40822 Mettmann / Tel. +49 (0)2104 5 33 48 Fax 5 15 80 / Di.-Fr. 15-18 + Neubrückstr. 6 / Tel. +49 (0)211 32 89 85 / Mi.-Do. 14-18.30

Sies+Höke Galerie C. Mollura Installation **/** Art Forum Berlin **/ T. Matelli** Installation **/** Art Cologne

25.8.-23.9.00 / 27.9-1.10.00 / 28.10.-2.12.00 / 5.-12.11.00 / Poststr. 7 / 40213 Düsseldorf / Tel. +49 (0)211 13 56 67 Fax 13 56 68 / sies-hoeke@t-online.de / Di.-Fr. 12-18.30, Sa. 12-14.30

Galerie Hans Strelow H. Münch / E. Schumacher

15.9.-21.10.00 / 27.10.-23.12.00 / Luegplatz 3 / 40545 Düsseldorf / Tel. +49 (0)211 55 55 03 Fax 57 63 08 / Di.-Fr. 10-18.30, Sa. 10-13.30

Galerie Thomas Taubert D. Evers

25.8.-20.10.00 / Mühlengasse 3 / 40213 Düsseldorf / Tel. +49 (0)211 46 28 49 Fax 48 49 491 / galerie@taubert.net www.taubert.net / Di.-Fr. 10-18, Sa. 12-16 u. n. V.

Galerie Peter Tedden Malerei **Barnickel, Fandler, Lehmann, Lucas, Pfeiffer, Pohl de Rozende / K. Lampert**

25.8.-30.9.00 / Okt.-Nov. / Bilker Str. 6 / 40213 Düsseldorf / Tel. +49 (0)211 13 35 28 Fax 13 35 28 / Di.-Fr. 13-19, Sa. 10-16

Galerie Vömel GmbH P. Picasso Graphiken und Keramiken **/ H. Tisdall** Gouachen und Ölbilder

25.8-31.10.00 / Nov.-Dez. / Orangeriestr. 6 / 40213 Düsseldorf / Tel. +49 (0)211 32 74 22 Fax 13 52 67 / Dorothee.Vömel@t-omline.de www.galerie-vömel.de / Mo.-Fr. 10-18, Sa.10-13

S C A L O

Louise Bourgeois
The Insomnia Drawings

Insomnia has been a longtime-companion of Louise Bourgeois' night hours. Between November 1994 and June 1995, she has committed to paper whatever thoughts, memories, and images surfaced during her long sleepless nights. The resulting 220 drawings are the quintessence of all the impulses, sources, and motifs inspiring her work. *The Insomnia Drawings* show the artist's mind at work: drawings and sketches alternate with poems and aphorisms in both French and English, interspersed with laundry lists reminiscent of the hustle-bustle of everyday life. The series is a unique mirror of an extraordinary woman's life and work: beautiful, disquieting, passionate, inquiring, and imbued with a quirky sense of humor.

L'art/ou est/la vie,/toi et vous/inspire/unafraid: Art/est le/contraire/du acting
La nuit/à quoi penses-tu/pendant la nuit
Water is the/opposite of continuity/water can be the best but it can be worse//M is for mother/in the water/it is subject/to change/or even to reversal.
Louise Bourgeois

As soon as the artist agreed to entrust *The Insomnia Drawings* to the Daros Collection, Zurich, it was clear that this extraordinary work should be presented as a book. The result is a handsome slipcased two-volume publication. The first volume contains facsimiles of both the recto and verso of the 220 drawings. The second volume provides the reader with valuable background information on this complex and exhilaratingly beautiful work of art. Marie-Louise Bernadac, a leading Bourgeois scholar, places *The Insomnia Drawings* in the context of Bourgeois' oeuvre, providing biographical references for many notes, and pointing out the leitmotifs of Bourgeois' imaginary universe. In a lucid and beautifully written essay, Elisabeth Bronfen traces the nocturnal mysteries of insomnia and places this work of art in a larger cultural context. Furthermore, the second volume offers annotated transcriptions of all texts and notes. *She presents herself as a lady-in-waiting, silent and patient, with the night promising to save her from the array of desires such as love, faith, faithlessness, tenacity, ambition, while her sleeplessness prevents any salvation from her psychic distress. If in these drawings and texts the night is metaphorically conceived of as an expanse of water that might engulf her, while sleep would restore her, insomnia is what prevents any voyage into inundation. (...) Because her insomnia brings states of ambivalence to the fore, she keeps returning to question of being suspended between two emotions—between plenitude and lack, proximity and absence, agreement and contradiction.—Elisabeth Bronfen*

This landmark publication is a must for everyone wanting to take part in the imaginative journeys of one of today's most important artists.
Should you wish more information about this extraordinary book, which will be published in a deluxe, limited, and standard edition, please send an e-mail to: publishers@scalo.com!
Please include your full address, and we will send you a brochure with detailed information.

BLIND SPOT

ISSUE FIFTEEN $14

UTA BARTH

ELLEN BROOKS

TIM DAVIS

ANDY GOLDSWORTHY

LAURENT MILLET

JOYCE CAROL OATES

RICHARD PRINCE

MARK STEINMETZ

CATHERINE WAGNER

SUBSCRIPTIONS • EDITIONS FOR SALE • ARTIST REPRESENTATION
BLIND SPOT 210 Eleventh Avenue New York, NY 10001 Tel 212 633 1317 Fax 212 627 9364 www.blindspot.com

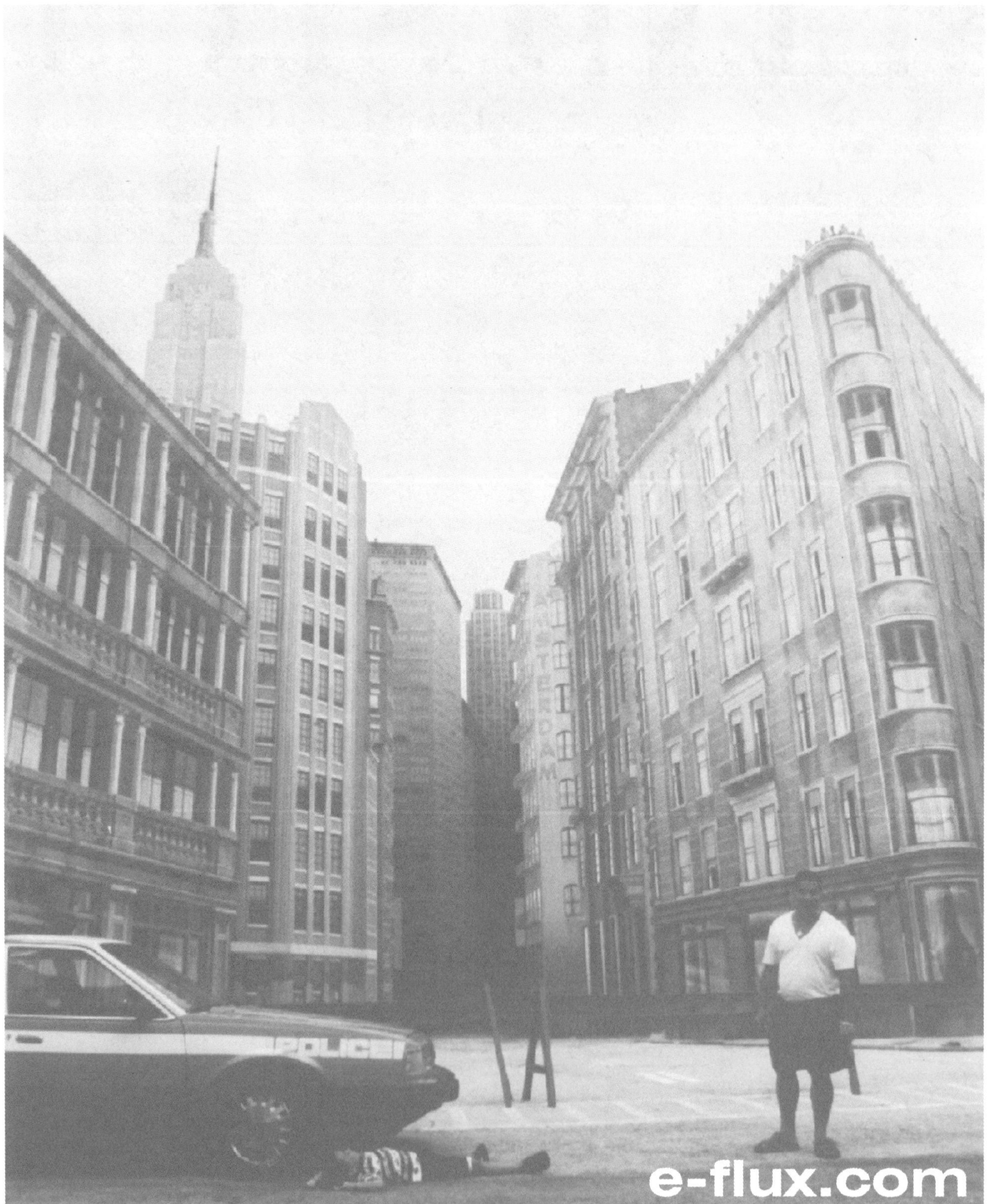
POLICE
e-flux.com

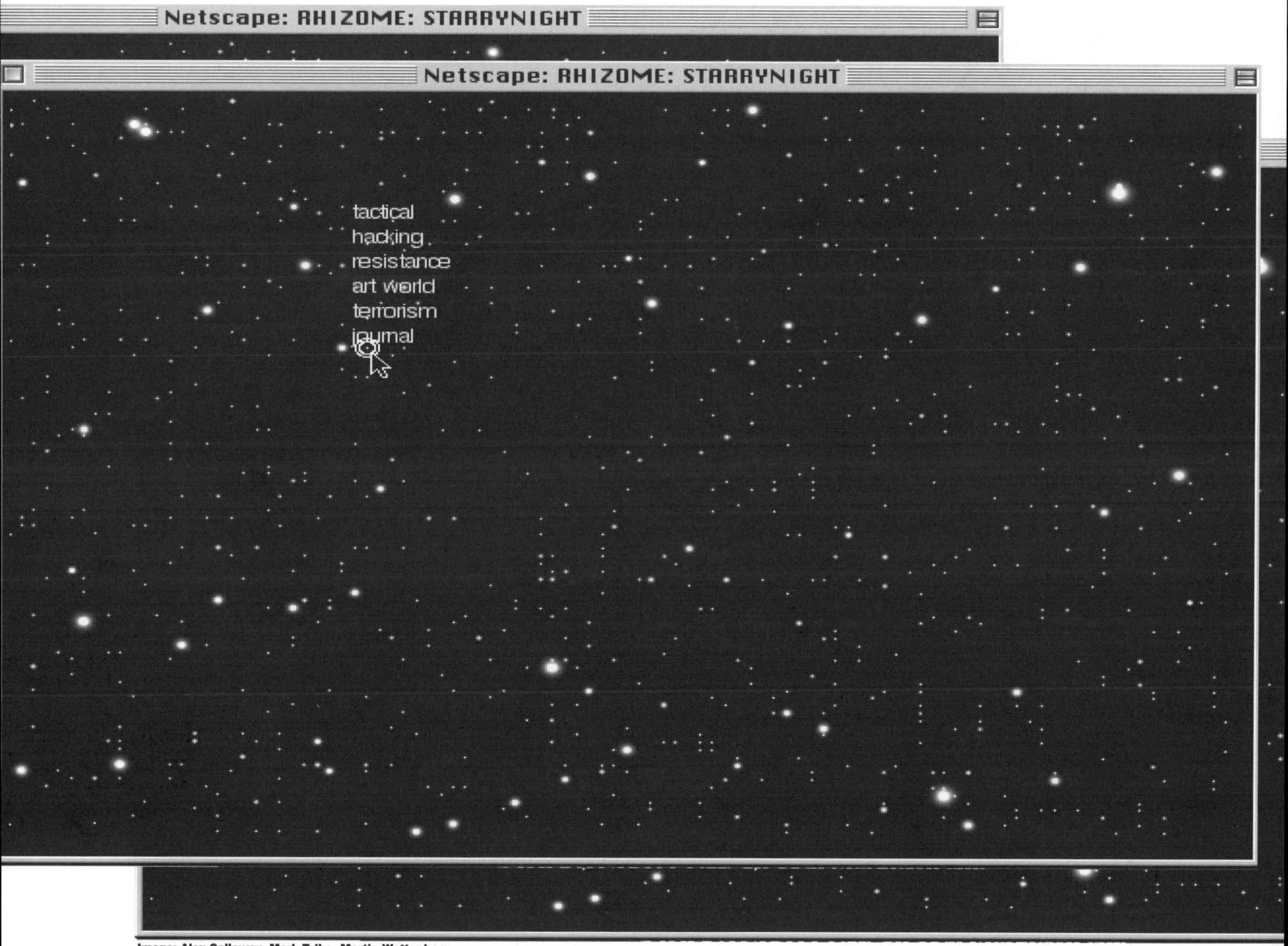

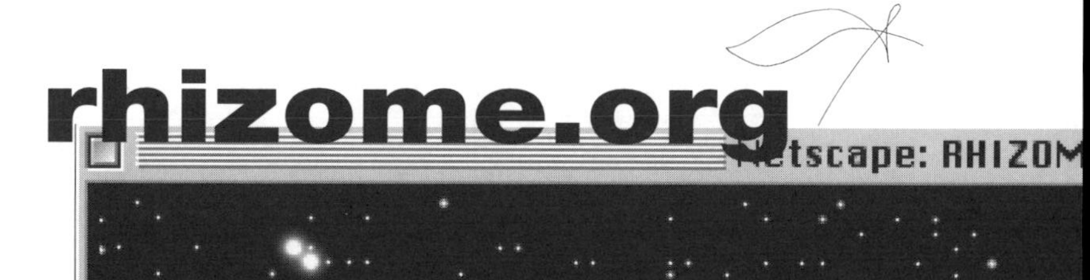

Image: Alex Galloway, Mark Tribe, Martin Wattenberg
Design: Munro Galloway

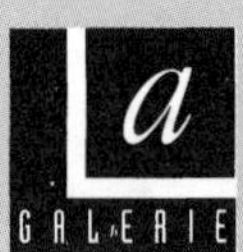

L.A. Galerie – Lothar Albrecht

Domstrasse 6, D-60311 Frankfurt, Telefon: (49) 69 - 28 86 87, Fax: (49) 69 - 28 09 12

Representing:

ART FAIRS:

OLIVER BOBERG Feb. – Mar. 2001	NAOYA HATAKEYAMA	ART BASEL
BERNARD FAUCON	KARY KWOK	ART COLOGNE
ROBERT F. HAMMERSTIEL	EDGAR LISSEL	THE ARMORY SHOW, NY
JOHN HILLIARD	KEN LUM Nov. 2000 – Jan. 2001	
TRACEY MOFFATT Sept. – Oct. 2000	MABEL PALACIN	
LUKAS EINSELE	HIROSHI SUNAIRI	
JOAN FONTCUBERTA	JAVIER VALLHONRAT	

S c h e d l e r

Aktiengesellschaft

Galerie Schedler
Josefstrasse 53
CH 8005 Zürich
T +41 1 440 61 20
F +41 1 440 61 21

Tuesday to Friday 12 - 6 p.m.
Saturday 11 a.m. - 4 p.m.

Galerie und Edition Schedler
Dorfstrasse 56
CH 8532 Warth
T +41 52 747 19 46
F +41 52 747 19 48

Saturday 2 - 5 p.m.
Sunday 11 a.m. - 5 p.m. and by appointment

mail @ schedler.ch
www.schedler.ch
Member of
Association of Swiss Galleries AGS

Galerie Schedler Zurich

Stephen Barker, nightswimming
Christoph Wachter, 94 etchings
until 30 September 2000

Attila Richard Lukacs, works on paper
7 October to 4 November 2000

Walter Pfeiffer, photography
10 November to 30 December 2000

Galerie Schedler Warth

Rolf Zurfluh, Kinderbildnisse
until 24 September 2000 (catalogue available)

Joseph Beuys, 50 multiples from a private collection
29 October 2000 to 25 March 2001

Representing: Stephen Barker, Fredi Bissegger, Jean Crotti, Jan Czerwinski, Allen Frame, Max Grüter, Dieter Hall, Christoph Hänsli, Attila Richard Lukacs, Margaret Morgan, Andrea Muheim, Richard Müller, Hironori Murai, Walter Pfeiffer, Eliane Rutishauser, Monika Rutishauser, Stefan Saner, Christoph Schneeberger, Philipp Späti, Pierre Sutter, Christoph Wachter, Rodney White, Alfred Wirz, Hans Witschi, Uwe Wittwer

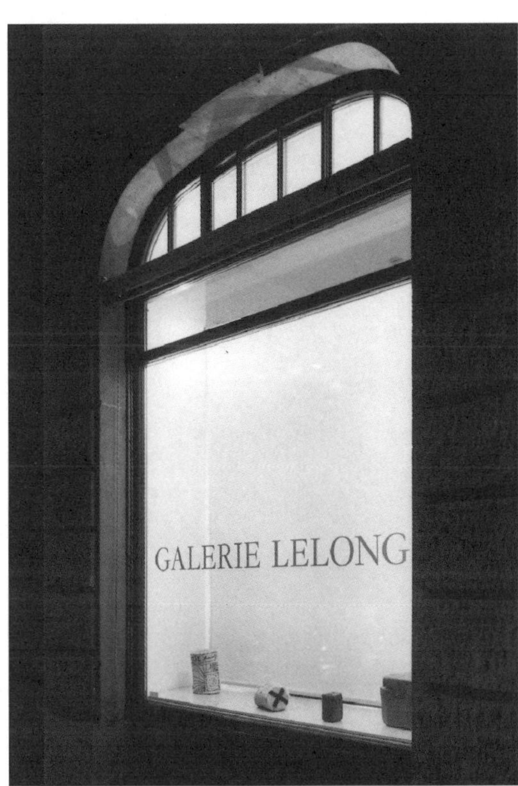

OKTOBER – DEZEMBER

DAN FLAVIN

GALERIE TRABANT

A - 1040   WIEN   SCHLEIFMÜHLGASSE 13   TEL / FAX   0043 1 587 52 65

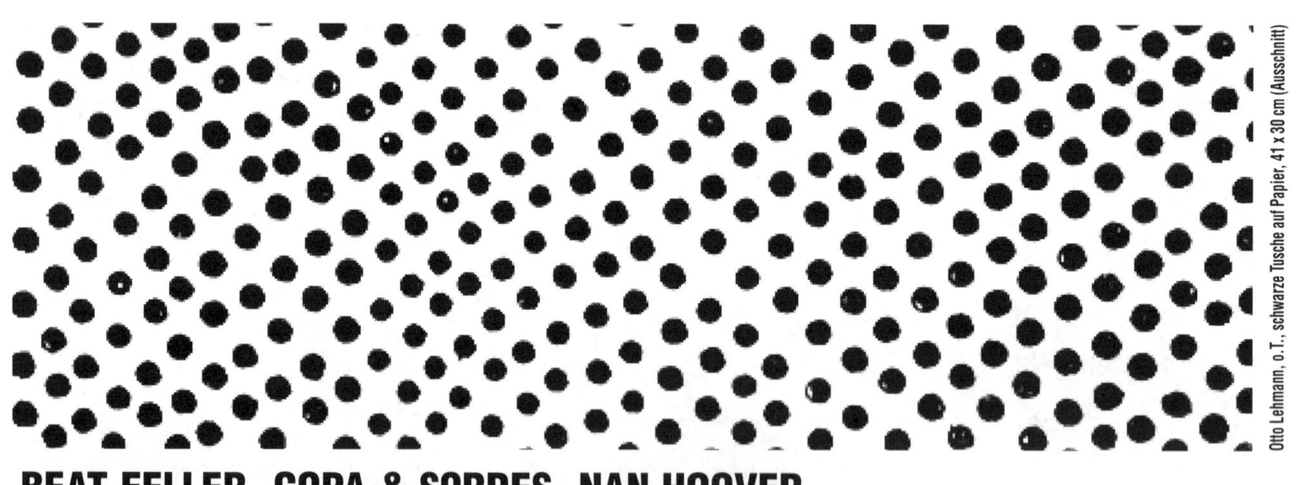
Otto Lehmann, o.T., schwarze Tusche auf Papier, 41 x 30 cm (Ausschnitt)

BEAT FELLER. COPA & SORDES. NAN HOOVER.
INNOCENTE. THOMAS KOHL. OTTO LEHMANN.
PLUMCAKE.   HOWARD SMITH.   JÜRG ZAHND.   23.08.-30.09.2000

MARIANNE WEREFKIN   07.10.-09.11.2000

GALERIE PATRIK FRÖHLICH

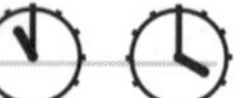
Mittwoch bis Freitag   Samstag

DIENERSTRASSE 21, 8004 ZÜRICH, FON+FAX: ++41 1 242 89 00, email:patrikfroehlich@access.ch, www.artnet.com/pfroehlich.html

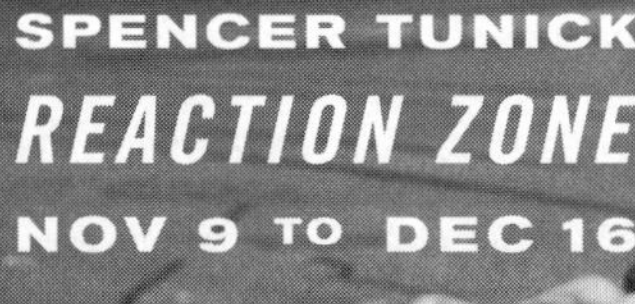

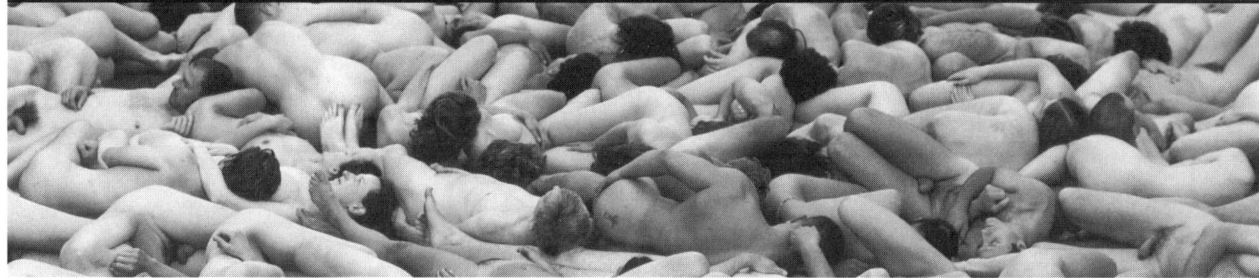

529 WEST 20TH ST NY 10011   TEL: 212-645-1100   FAX: 212-645-0198   W: I-20.COM   TUE-SUN 11-6

gallery bob van orsouw   limmatstrasse 270   8005 zurich
phone +41-1-273 11 00   fax +41-1-273 11 02   mail@bobvanorsouw.ch

august 26 until september 30, 2000 **paul graham**

art forum berlin, september 27 until october 1, 2000

INK•TREE

Bibliophile Books & Editions
Contemporary Art

JOHN BALDESSARI / LAWRENCE WEINER (COLLABORATION)

SOL LEWITT / SACHIKO CHO (COLLABORATION)

JENNY HOLZER • JANINE ANTONI • ADRIAN SCHIESS

in preparation:

CHRISTOPHER WOOL • WOLFGANG LAIB

Seestrasse 21 · CH-8700 Küsnacht · T +41 1 910 71 76 · F +41 1 910 67 90 · e-mail: inktree@access.ch · www.inktree.ch

---

nk@ed

presents

"RANAKPUR"

a portfolio of 6 etchings by

CLAUDIO MOSER

for further information please contact

www.nk-ed.com

Contemporary Art and Technology Biennial
September 2–October 31, 2000
Seoul, Korea

media_city seoul 2000

media_city seoul is an international biennial event—on view in museums and public venues throughout Seoul—that presents and explores the convergence of technology and the contemporary arts. The theme for the inaugural biennial, **city: between 0 and 1**, interprets the ways in which the digital revolution is transcending physical boundaries of space and time.

www.mediaseoul.org

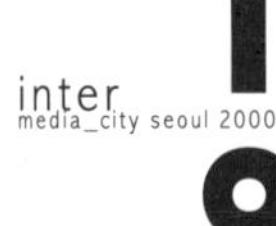

Artists:
Including Vito Acconci, Pil Yun Ahn, Chantal Akerman, Laurie Anderson, Matthew Barney, Christian Boltanski, Cleaning Project, Stan Douglas, Dominique Gonzalez-Foerster and Ole Scheeren, Douglas Gordon, Dan Graham, Zaha Hadid, Bernd Halbherr, Gary Hill, Myungseop Hong, Michel Jaffrennou, Kichul Kim, Sooja Kim, Alexander Kluge, Rem Koolhaas, Bul Lee, Junmok Lee, Steve McQueen, Bruce Nauman, Tony Oursler, Nam June Paik, Paul Pfeiffer, Rosemarie Trockel, Jane and Louise Wilson, Bill Viola, Pipilotti Rist, Danny Rozin, Il Gon Song, SUPARTIST, Tamas Waliczky and Hyunjung Yu.

General/Artistic Director:
Misook Song, Art Historian and Critic

Curators:
Barbara London, The Museum of Modern Art, New York; Jeremy Millar, The Photographers' Gallery, London; Hans Ulrich Obrist, Le Musée d'Art Moderne de la Ville de Paris; Byoung Hak Ryu, Independent Curator; Shin Eui Park, Art Historian and Critic; and, Chang Ik Jang, Magic I Entertainment Co. Ltd.

Organizers:
media_city seoul 2000 Organizing Committee

Sponsors:
Seoul Metropolitan Government
Seoul Industry Promotion Foundation

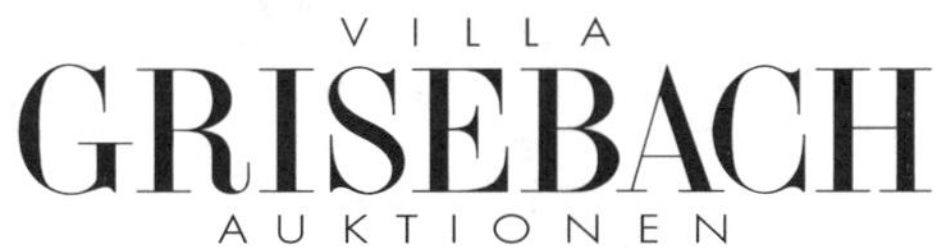

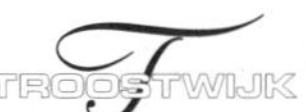

SECESSION

A–1010 Wien, Friedrichstraße 12, Telefon 43–1–587 53 07
Telefax 43–1–587 53 07–34, www.secession.at

AA BRONSON 5. 10. – 26. 11. 2000

DOUG AITKEN 18. 10. – 23. 11. 2000

WALTER OBHOLZER 7. 12. 2000 – 21. 1. 2001
RÓZA EL-HASSAN 7. 12. 2000 – 21. 1. 2001

M S

Mondriaan Stichting
(Mondriaan Foundation)

For more information
please contact
the Mondriaan Foundation in Amsterdam and
ask for our brochure:
Phone +31-20-6762032
Fax +31-20-6762036
E-mail mondriaan@mondriaan
foundation.nl

The Mondriaan Foundation is
a Dutch cultural organisation, which provides
cultural funding for special activities
related to visual arts, design and museums.
The Mondriaan Foundation supports
projects which are of exceptional quality, as
well as projects which promote the standing of
Dutch art, design and museums abroad.
The Mondriaan Foundation is also
responsible for the organisation of the Dutch
contribution to the Venice Biennial.

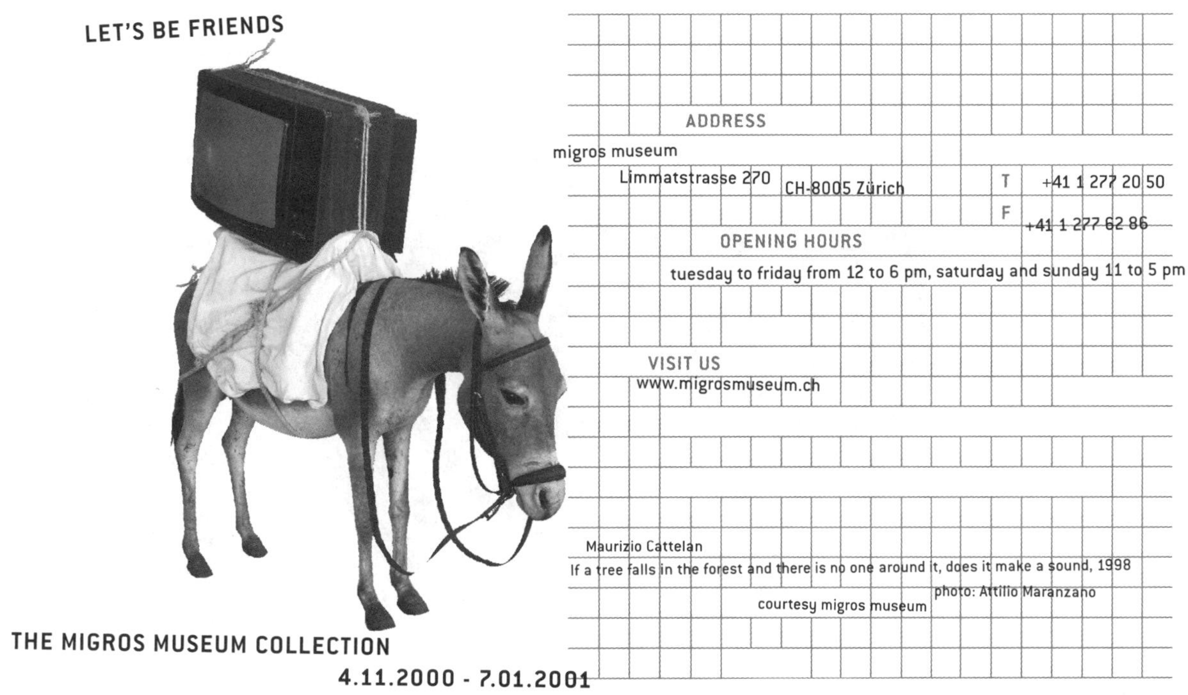

LET'S BE FRIENDS

ADDRESS
migros museum
Limmatstrasse 270   CH-8005 Zürich   T   +41 1 277 20 50
                                       F   +41 1 277 62 86
OPENING HOURS
tuesday to friday from 12 to 6 pm, saturday and sunday 11 to 5 pm

VISIT US
www.migrosmuseum.ch

Maurizio Cattelan
If a tree falls in the forest and there is no one around it, does it make a sound, 1998
                                          photo: Attilio Maranzano
                    courtesy migros museum

THE MIGROS MUSEUM COLLECTION
4.11.2000 - 7.01.2001

Jan van Eyck Akademie

Fine art | Design | Theory

The Jan van Eyck Akademie is an international post graduate centre for fine art, design and theory. Each department offers a programme directed towards both the individual work of participants and the possibility of linking it with other participants' work. The possibility to encounter practitioners from different areas, the wide variety of workshops, and the media and documentation centre create a unique set of conditions for a research-linked production.

The wealth of languages and of cultural backgrounds at the academy shapes the practice of translation as the modus operandi of the fine art department, focused on the performance of language in the digitized public space. Participants are expected to have an openness towards possibilities of an active presence in the fluid pattern of society. Translating such openness into an experimental post graduate research is not seen as a matter of working in more than one discipline, context or culture, but rather of letting the experience of thinking in one area and specific context play a role in another one.

Future fine art participants beginning a two year working period on 1 January 2001, are invited to apply.
For further information on the fine art, design or theory programme, or to request an application form, please contact Leon Westenberg, Jan van Eyck Akademie, Academieplein 1, 6211 KM Maastricht, Netherlands, www.janvaneyck.nl, t +31 (0)43 3503737, f +31 (0)43 3503799, e info@janvaneyck.nl

---

September 2 - October 15, 2000
Open: Wed - Sun 10 - 17
Tuesday 10 - 19

Michel François

Projektraum
Sous la terre, il y a le ciel
Curated by
Evelyne Jouanno

Marco Brambilla

Kunsthalle Bern
Helvetiaplatz 1
CH-3005 Bern
Phone +41 31. 351 00 31
Fax   +41 31. 352 53 85
E-mail: kunsthalle@bluewin.ch
www.kunsthallebern.ch

Eröffnung

Kunstmuseum
Liechtenstein
12. November
2000

Städtle 32 FL-9490 Vaduz
www.kunstmuseum.li

KUNSTMUSEUM
LIECHTENSTEIN

Symposium

Kunsthäuser
Architektur versus Kunst
Kunst versus Museum

Ein Symposium zum Spannungsverhältnis von
Gegenwartskunst – Museum – Museumsarchitektur – Gesellschaft
veranstaltet von Kunsthaus Bregenz und Kunstmuseum Liechtenstein

Information und Anmeldung
Kunsthaus Bregenz
Eva Thole
Telefon: (+43-5574) 485 94-13
Fax: (+43-5574) 485 94-8
Mail: eva.thole@vlr.gv.at
Web: www.kunsthaus-bregenz.at

Bregenz | Vaduz
16. bis 18. November 2000

DIE NEUEN MUSEEN
SIND AUS UNKENNTNIS, VERWIRRUNG
ODER IN DER GLÜCKLICHEN EUPHORIE
VON UNSCHULDIGEN ODER IRREN
ENTSTANDEN.

Rémy Zaugg

SUBSCRIBE TO A SMALL MUSEUM AND A LARGE LIBRARY WITH CONTEMPORARY ARTISTS.

ABONNIEREN SIE EIN KLEINES MUSEUM UND EINE GROSSE BIBLIOTHEK MIT GEGENWARTSKÜNSTLERN.

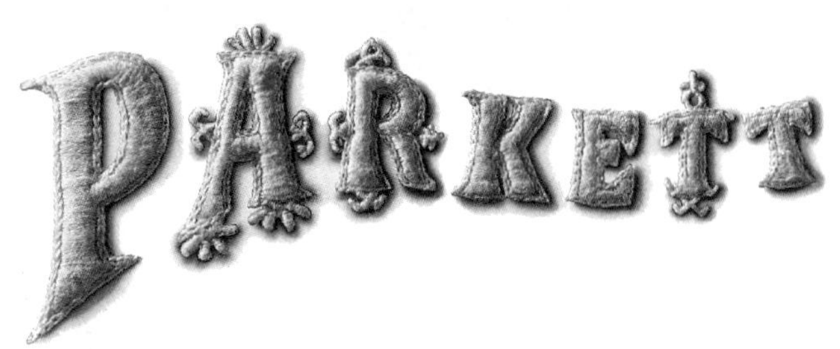

THE PARKETT SERIES WITH CONTEMPORARY ARTISTS

DIE PARKETT-REIHE MIT GEGENWARTSKÜNSTLERN

Please use the order form enclosed in this issue and send it to the following address: Bitte benützen Sie die Bestellkarte, die in diesem Band beiliegt, und schicken Sie diese an folgende Adresse:

PARKETT, Quellenstrasse 27, CH-8031 Zürich, Tel. +41-1-271 81 40, Fax +41-1-272 43 01

PARKETT, 155 Avenue of the Americas, 2nd floor New York, NY 10013
phone (212) 673 2660, fax (212) 271 0704

www.parkettart.com

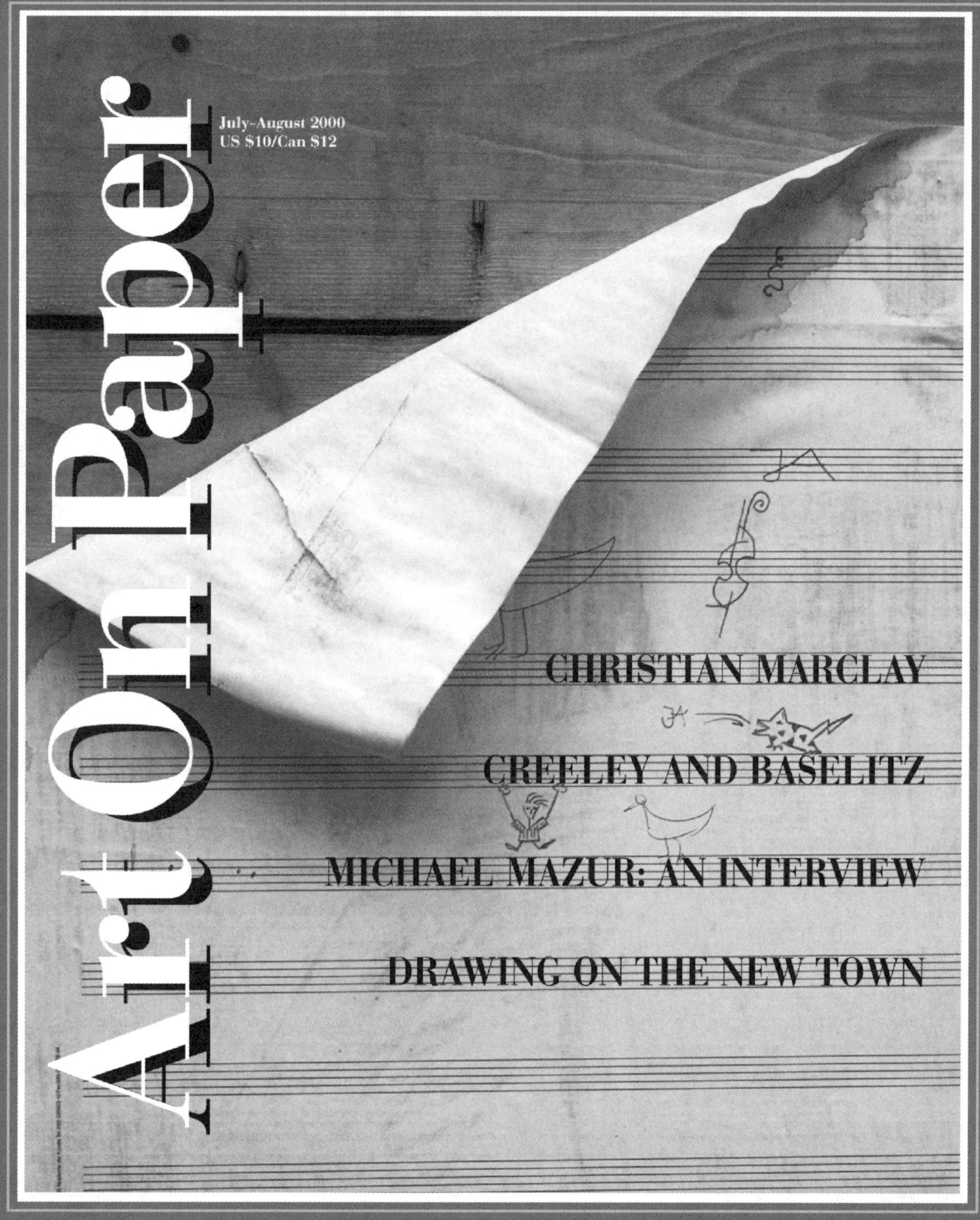

The International Art Magazine Dedicated to
Prints, Drawings, and Photography

www.artonpaper.com

For Subscriptions & Information: Call 1 800 685 9777 or Fax 212 988 6107

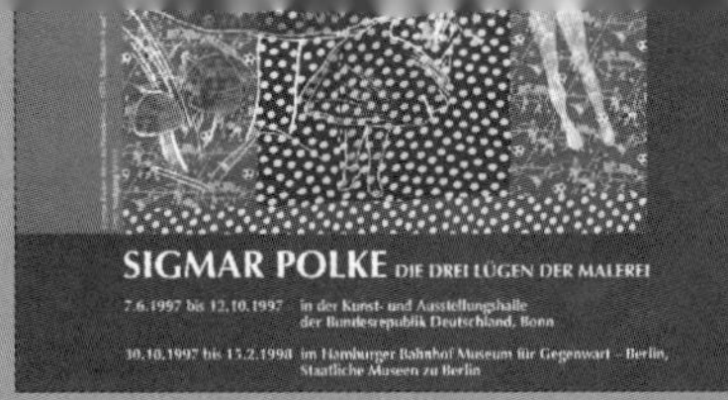

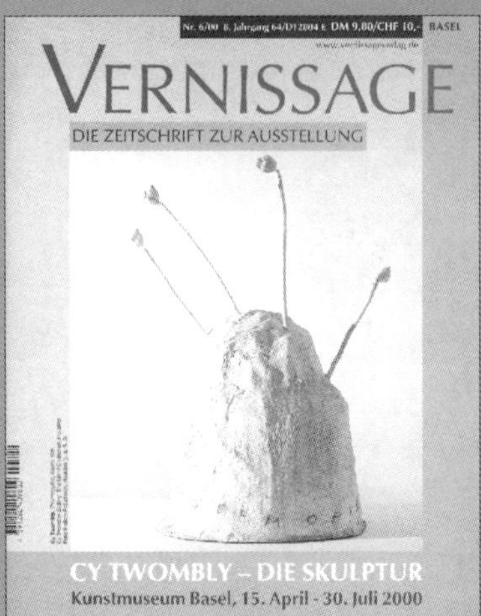

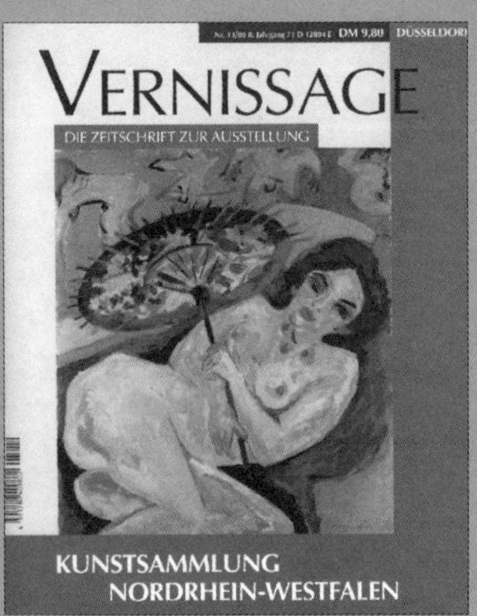

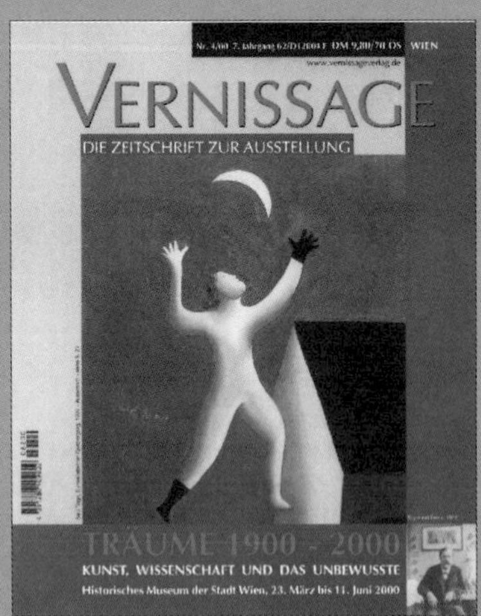

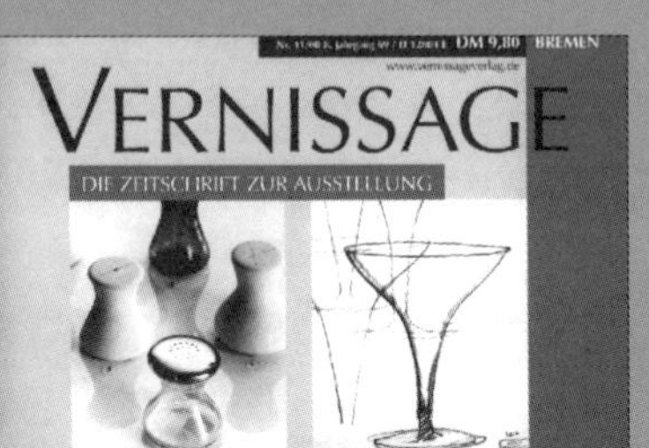

VERNISSAGE
DIE ZEITSCHRIFT ZUR AUSSTELLUNG

...es folgen:

- **Pablo Picasso**

  Das Lithographische Werk,
  Eröffnung des Graphikmuseums
  Pablo Picasso, Münster

- **Joseph Beuys**

  Pflanze, Tier, Mensch
  Städtische Galerie
  Villingen-Schwenningen

- **Die Klassische Moderne:**

  Eine Kunstreise durch die Schweiz

- **Horst Janssen**

  Eröffnung des Horst-Janssen-
  Museum Oldenburg

[www.vernissageverlag.de]

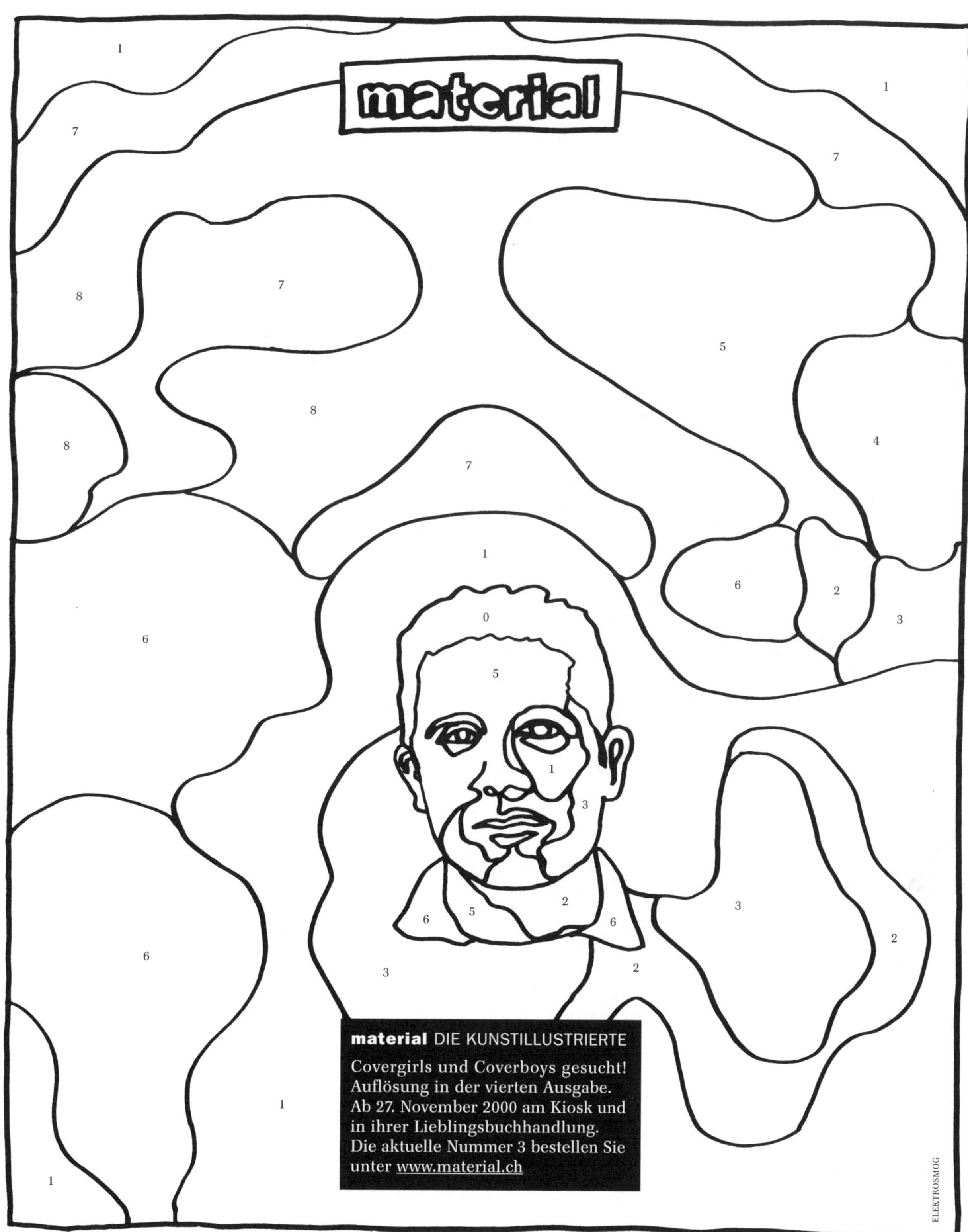

material

material DIE KUNSTILLUSTRIERTE
Covergirls und Coverboys gesucht!
Auflösung in der vierten Ausgabe.
Ab 27. November 2000 am Kiosk und
in ihrer Lieblingsbuchhandlung.
Die aktuelle Nummer 3 bestellen Sie
unter www.material.ch

ELEKTROSMOG

Zürichsee
Druckereien AG

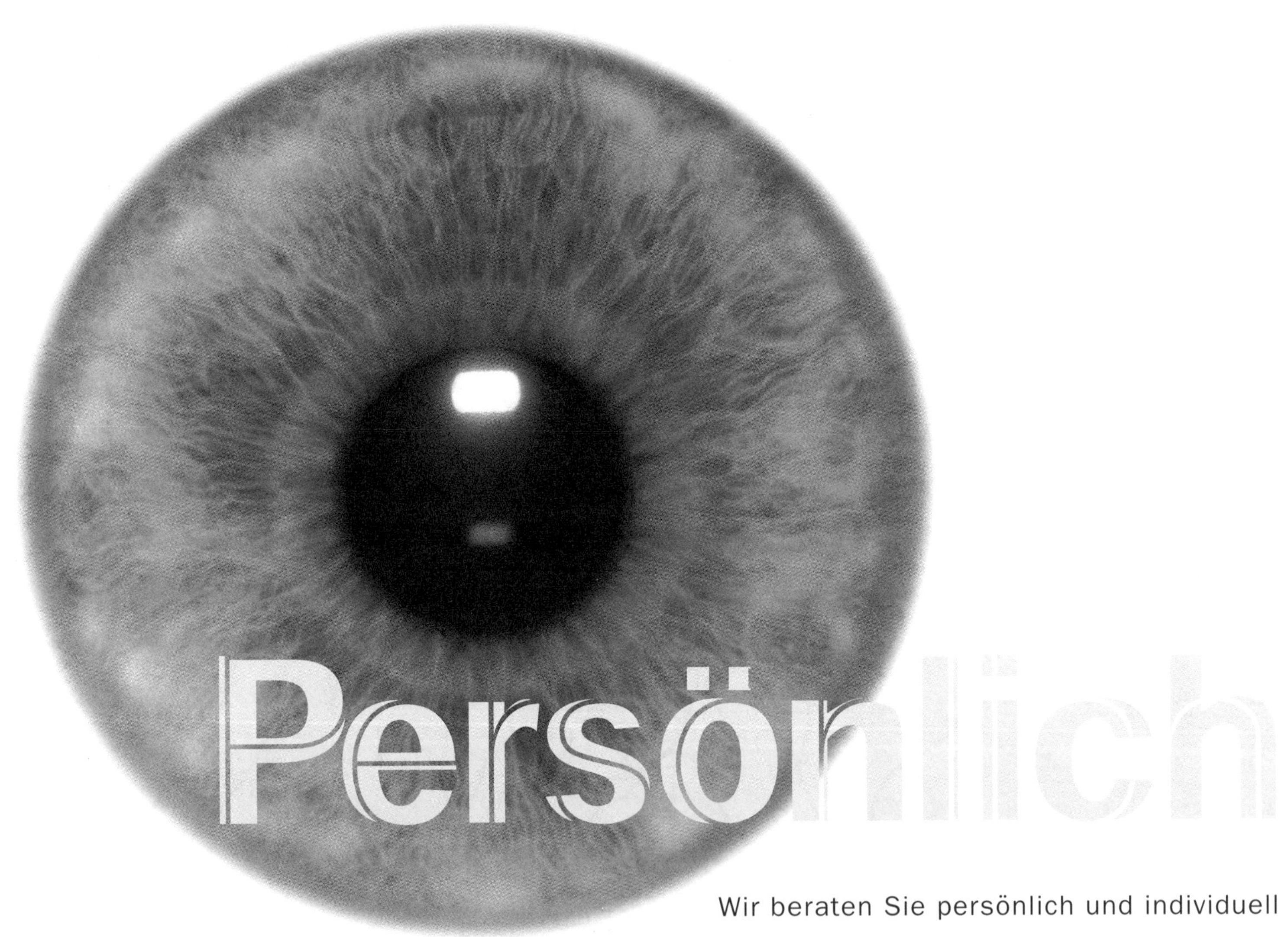

Persönlich
Wir beraten Sie persönlich und individuell

Zürichsee Druckereien AG • Seestrasse 86 • Postfach • 8712 Stäfa • Telefon 01 928 53 03 • Telefax 01 928 53 10 • Internet http://www.zsd.ch

Kunsttransporte in alle Erdteile

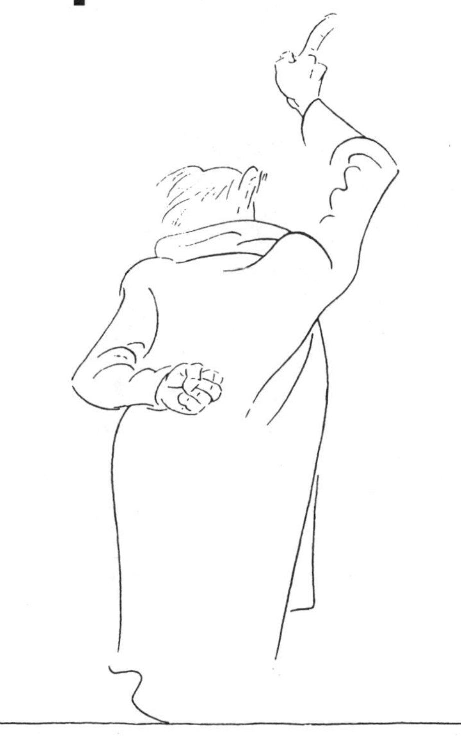

«In den Kunsttransporten, wer nicht das Beste hat, hat nichts»
(frei nach Olaf Gulbransson)

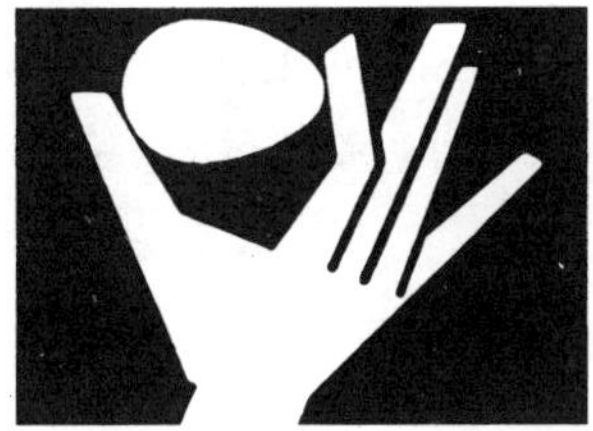

**MÖBEL-
TRANSPORT
______________ AG**

**für
sorgfältige
Transporte**

Gaswerkareal	Genuastrasse 14
8010 Zürich	4142 Münchenstein-Basel
Tel. 01 733 51 11	Tel. 061 331 88 55
Fax 01 730 88 80	Fax 061 331 80 47

E-Mail: moebel@moebel-transport-ag.com
http://www.moebel-transport-ag.com
Filialen in Chiasso und Frankfurt Flughafen.

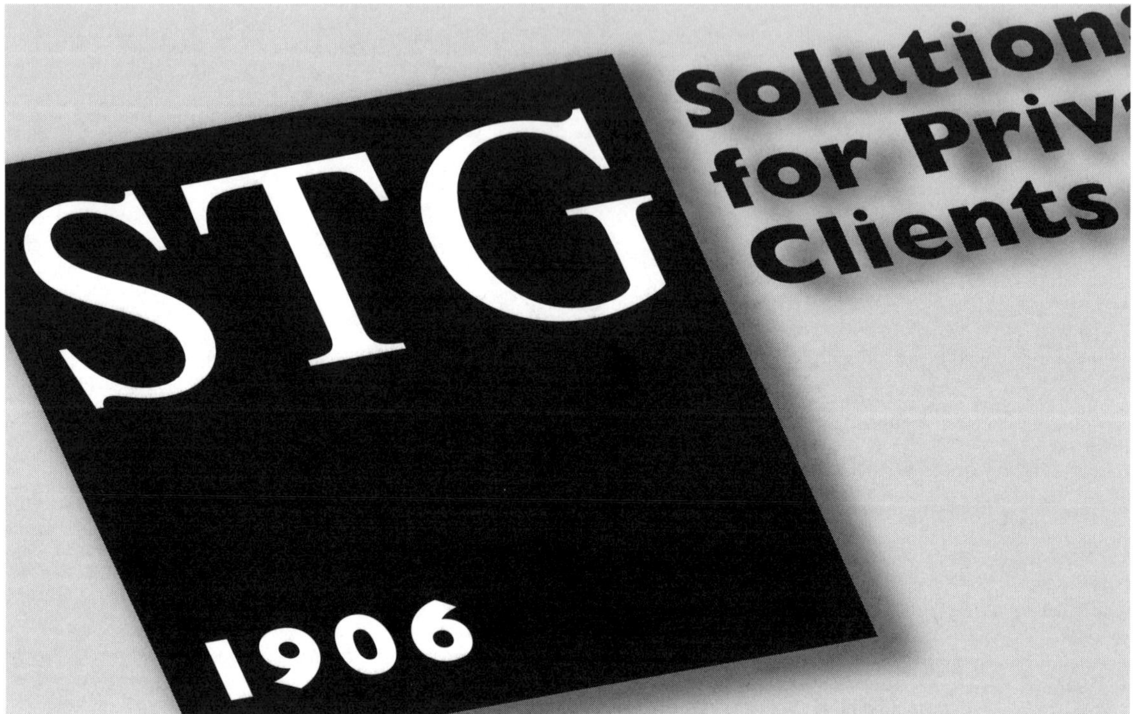

STG
1906
Solutions
for Priv...
Clients

Art|32|Basel |13–18|June|2001
The Art Fair

Art 32 Basel, P.O. Box, CH-4021 Basel
Tel. +41 61 686 20 20, Fax +41 61 686 26 86, E-Mail: Info@ArtBasel.com, www.ArtBasel.com
Messe Basel.

sponsored by ✣ UBS

Adelantado, Valencia
Carmen Calvo, Marta Perez Bravo,
Santiago Ydañez
Air de Paris, Paris
Stéphane Dafflon
Andreu, Santiago
Gonzalo Cienfuegos
Anton Weller, Paris
Laura Lamiel
Applicat-Prazan, Paris
Atlan
Ariel, Paris
Yasse Tabuchi
Arlogos, Paris
Sophie Ristelhueber
Arndt & Partner, Berlin
Sophie Calle
Art & Public, Geneva
Wang Du
Art Attitude Hervé Bize, Nancy
Peter Rösel
Art: Concept, Paris
Richard Fauguet
Art of this Century, New-York
Manolo Valdès
Artiaco, Napoli
Perino & Vele, Bianco & Valente
Astuni, Fano
Aldo Mondino
Boghici, Rio
Antonio Dias
B&D Art Studio, Milano
Micha Klein
Baronian, Brussels
Eric Poitevin
Barquet, New-York
José Bédia
Bärtschi, Geneva
Jan Fabre
Baudoin Lebon, Paris
Robert Mapplethorpe
BCA-Boukamel,
London
Rainer Fetting
Beaubourg, Vence
Charles Matton
BF-15, Monterrey
Los Lichis
Borzo, Hertogenbosch
Geer Van Velde
Bouche, Paris
Charles Maussion
Franck Bordas, Paris
Gilles Aillaud
Hervé Bordas, Venezia
Zoran Music
Carré & Cie, Paris
Maurice Estève
Carzaniga + Ueker, Basel
Catherine Gfeller
Cats, Brussels
Jean Dubuffet
Cent 8, Paris
Gloria Friedmann
Charim Klocker, Wien
Milica Tomic
Chave, Vence
Eugène Gabritschevsky
Chez Valentin, Paris
Mathieu Mercier
Chinese Contemporary, London,
Yue Minjun
Chobot, Wien
Henri Michaux
Ci-Gong, Tae Gu
Lee Kang-So
Claude Bernard, Paris
Armando Morales
Clot, Bramsen & Georges,
Paris
Antonio Saura
Contini, Venezia
Graham Sutherland
Continua, San Gemignano

Loris Cecchini, Serse
Crane Kalman, London
Hans Hofmann
CRG Gallery, New-York
Russell Crotty
Crousel, Paris
Collection Yoon Ja &
Paul Devautour
Zelda Cheatle, London
Helen Chadwick
Damasquine & Aeroplastics,
Brussels
Annie Sprinkle
De Pauw, Brussels
Carla Arocha
Denise René, Paris
Jesus Rafael Soto
Di Meo, Paris
Piero Pizzi Cannella
Dina Vierny, Paris
Robert Couturier
Dorfmann, Paris
Patrick Raynaud
Durand Le Gaillard, Paris
Pascal Bernier
El Museo, Bogota
Paloma Navares
Entwistle, London
Anton Henning
Éric Dupont, Paris
Didier Mencoboni
Fagglonnato, London
Thomas Schütte
Ferranti, Roma
Domenico Bianchi
Fanal, Basel
Aurélie Nemours
Farber La Serre, Trêts
Jean-Marc Spaans,
Yves Oppenheim
Ferran Cano, Barcelona
Pep Guerrero
Forum, New-York
Odd Nerdrum
Fournier, Paris
Stéphane Bordarier
Frank, Paris
Lisa Ruyter,
Ariane Lopez-Huici
Galerie de France, Paris
Eugène Leroy
Gam, Monaco
René Magritte
Gan, Tokyo
Tokihiro Sato
Gana Art, Séoul
Lee Ufan
Gandy, Praha
Elke Krystufek
Gmurzynska, Köln
Alexander Rodtschenko
Marian Goodman, Paris
Daniel Buren
Gutharc, Paris
Delphine Kreuter
Hoss, Paris
Pablo Gargallo
Hachmeister, Munster
Mark Tobey
Haime, New-York
Adam Straus
Haas, Berlin
Jean Fautrier
Hecey, Luxemburg
Fabrice Hybert
Herold, Paris
Zao Wou-Ki
Max Hetzler, Berlin
Yves Oppenheim
Hilger, Wien
Alain Balzac,
Gunter Damisch,
Anselm Glück,
Nikolaus Moser

Holtmann, *Koln*
Heinz Mack, Arnulf Rainer
Hue-Williams, London
Susan Derges
Hufkens, Brussels
John Chamberlain
Hussenot, Paris
Chen Zhen
I-20, New-York
Marina Kappos,
Peter Sarkisian,
Spencer Tunick
Innocenti, Montecatini
Luigi Ontani
Issert, St-Paul de Vence
François Morellet
Item, Paris
Jean-Michel Alberola
Jousse, Paris
Serge Comte
Jacobson, London
Jules Olitsky
Janssen, Brussels
Yan Pei-Ming
Jeanne Bucher, Paris
Fermin Aguayo
JGM, Paris
Tom Wesselmann
Jordan, Paris
Sylvie Fanchon
Jour Agnès B, Paris
Jonas Mekas
Kinge, Paris
Victor Brauner
Keitelman, Brussels
Nam June Paik
Krinzinger, Wien
Wim Delvoye,
Natacha Lesueur,
Erwin Wurm
Linard, La Garde Adhemar
Erik Dietman
La Citta, Verona
Jacob Hashimoto
Lacourière-Frélaut, Paris
Olivier Debré
Lahumière, Paris
Jean Legros
Lambert, Paris
Bertrand Lavier
Lanzenberg, Brussels
Michael Irmer
Larock Granoff, Paris
Jean Messagier
Ledune, Brussels
Olivier Mosset
Lelong, Paris
Ernest Pignon Ernest
Lisson, London
Jason Martin
Lowenstein, Buenos Aires
Eduardo Hoffmann
Luhring Augustine,
New-York, *Tunga*
Menocal, Mexico
Arturo Cuenca, Sandra Ramos,
Agustin Bejarano
Galerie 1900-2000, Paris
Ben
Marco Noire, Torino
Zwelethu Mthethwa
Marlborough, London
Stephen Conroy
Martin, Madrid
Daniel Blaufuks
Xawery Wolski
Masoero, Torino
Carol Rama
Meier, San Francisco
Donald Judd
Mennour, Paris
Peter Beard
Metta, Madrid
Eduardo Arroyo

Meyer, Paris
Man Ray
Milleventi, Milano
Christiano Pintaldi
Minini, Brescia
Ettore Spalletti
Moderne Silkeborg,
Silkeborg
Carl-Henning Pedersen
Mogabgab, Beyrouth
Charles Belle
Montenay- Giroux, Paris
Denis Laget
Victoria Miro, London
Tracey Moffat
De Noirmont, Paris
Pierre & Gilles
Nelson, Paris
Robert Filliou
De Osma, Madrid
Joaquin Torres-Garcia
Obadia, Paris
Albert Oelhen
OMR, Mexico
Maruch Santiz Gomez,
Marina Nuñez,
Cisco Jimenez,
Oniris, Rennes
Jean-Pierre Pincemin
Pariente, Paris
Barbara & Michael Leisgen
Pauli, Lausanne
Jaume Plensa
Pailhas, Marseille
Dan Graham et Jeff Wall
Palix, Paris
Orlan, Pablo Reinoso
Papillon-Fiat, Paris
Gunter Brus
Parkett, Zurich
Jeff Koons
Pasnic, Paris
Michel Haas
Paviot, Paris
Anna & Bernhard Blume
Perrotin, Paris
Eric Duyckaerts &
Jean-Pierre Khazem
Persano, Torino
Per Barclay
Peyroulet & Cie, Paris
Roy Arden
Photo & co, Torino
Karen Knorr
Pièce Unique, Paris
Sophia Vari
Pieters, Knokke le Zoute
Niki de Saint Phalle
Pixi, Paris
Serge Poliakoff
Polaris, Paris
Stéphane Couturier
Praz Delavallade, Paris
Jim Shaw
Projektraum, Wien
Edgar Honetschlager
Punto, Valencia
Maribel Domenech,
Francisca Mompo
Putman Editions, Paris
Georg Baselitz
Le Reverbère, Lyon
Dirk Braeckman
Raab, Berlin
Daniel Spoerri
Rabouan Moussion, Paris
Jean Degottex,
Oleg Kulik
Rachlin Lemarié, Paris
Robert Combas
Rein, Paris
Grazia Toderi
Ropac, Paris
Gilbert & George

Le Sous Sol, Paris
François Curlet
Samuel, Paris
Gérard Fromanger
Sapone, Nice
Alberto Burri
Scheibler, Koln
Alessandro Twombly
Schultz, Berlin
Markus Lüpertz
Seroussi, Paris
Martial Raysse
Seydoux, Paris
Pierre Buraglio
Sfeir-Semler, Hamburg
Katharina Grosse,
Herbert Hamak
Sheehan, New-York
Andy Warhol
Sollertis, Toulouse
François Morellet
Solomon, New-York
Nam June Paik
Sparta, Chagny
Mario Merz
Spencer Brownstone, New-York
James Rielly
Gian Enzo Sperone, Roma
Julian Schnabel
Sperone Westwater, New-York
Richard Tuttle
E&K Thoman, Innsbruck
Franz West
Tanit, Munich
Julia Mangold,
Ed Ruscha
Tega, Milano
Julio Larraz
Templon, Paris
François Rouan
Tendances, Paris
Georg Grosz
The Box Associati, Torino
Nicus Luca
Tornabuoni, Firenze
Lucio Fontana
Trigano, Paris
Hans Hartung
Turetsky, Geneva
Pierrette Bloch,
Aliska Lahusen
Aline Vidal, Paris
Herman De Vries
De Villepoix, Paris
Jean-Luc Moulène
G.P. & N. Vallois, Paris
Gilles Barbier
Varfok, Budapest
Laszlo Feher
Vedovi, Brussels
Ju Ming
Velge & Noirhomme,
Brussels
Hervé Charles
Veranneman, Kruishoutem
Fernando Botero
Vidal-Saint Phalle, Paris
Max Neumann
Vivita, Firenze
Francis Picabia
Woolworth, Paris
William Mac Kendree
Xippas, Paris
Vik Muniz, Valérie Belin
Zabriskie, New-York
Man Ray
Zannettacci, Geneva
Jacques Monory
Zonca & Zonca, Milano
Piero Dorazio
Zürcher, Paris
Michel Huelin
Zwirner & Wirth, New-York
Francis Picabia

FIAC 2000

25 - 30 October

200 ONE-PERSON EXHIBITIONS FOR FIAC 2000

Pavillon du Parc

Paris expo

Porte de Versailles

OIP — Reed Exhibition Companies, Delivering Business Contacts

Reed-OIP
11 rue du Colonel-Pierre-Avia
BP 571 - 75726 Paris Cedex 15

Tel: (33) (0) 1 41 90 47 80
Fax: (33) (0) 1 41 90 47 89

Email: fiac@reed-oip.fr
Site Internet: www.fiac-paris.com

For your hotel reservation call the Bureau
des Salons de Paris: tel: 33 (0) 1 43 48 42 19
or fax: 33 (0) 1 43 48 45 20

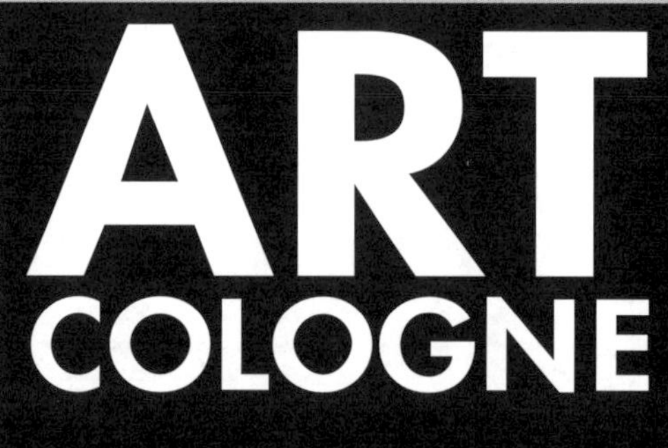

34. Internationale Messe
für Moderne Kunst

ART
COLOGNE

Internationaler
Kunstmarkt

5.–12. November 2000

Informationen:
KölnMesse GmbH
Postfach 21 07 60, 50532 Köln
Telefon: 02 21/8 21-0
Fax: 02 21/8 21-37 34
Internet: www.artcologne.de

KölnMesse

Kunst

2000

Zürich

International Contemporary Art Fair

24–27 November

ABB Hall 550

Zurich-Oerlikon

Phone +41 1 381 00 52

www.kunstzuerich.ch

Combined Ticket for city art museums

of Zurich and Winterthur

Tourist Service

Phone +41 1 215 40 00

Open Gallery Weekend

24–26 November

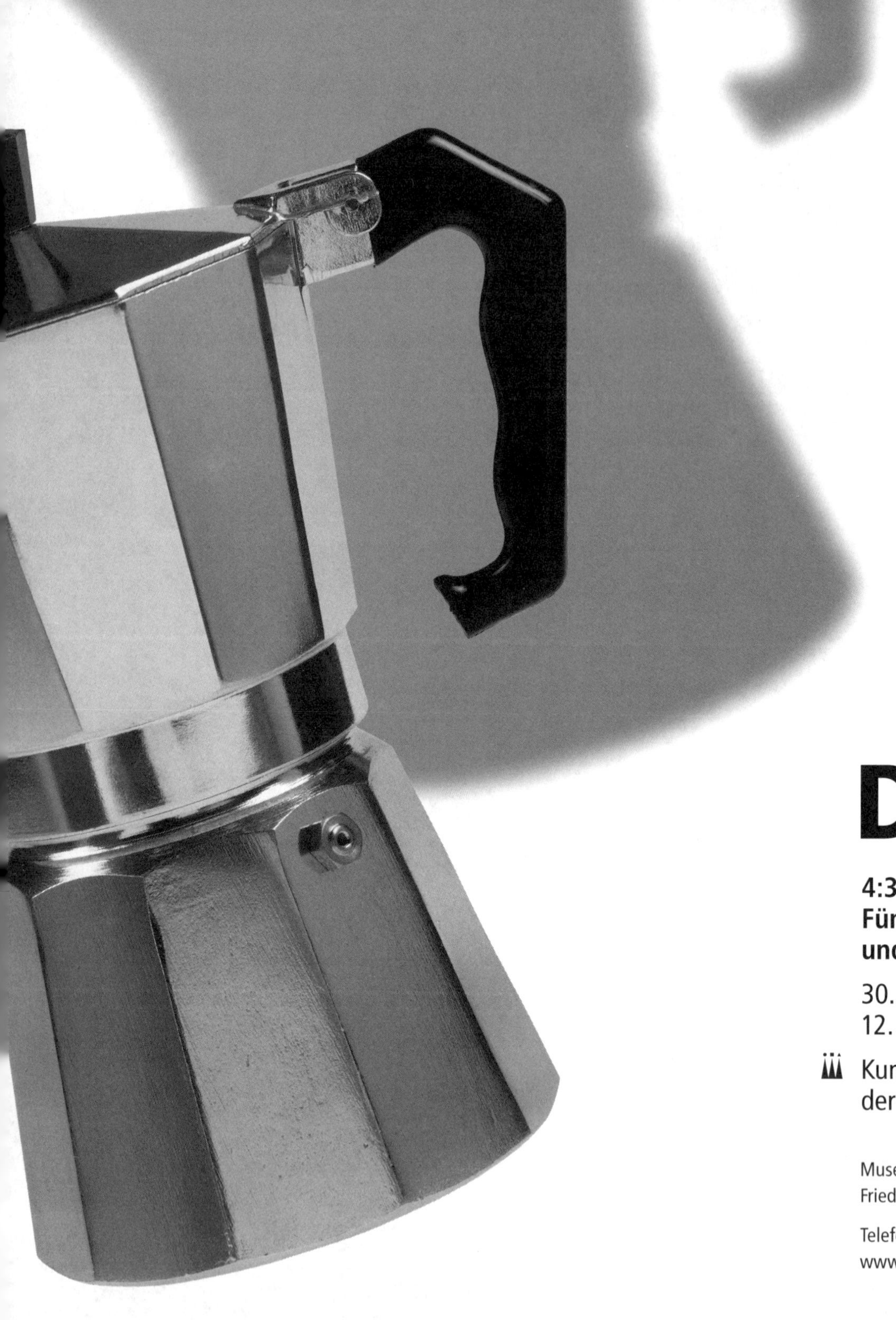

Design

4:3
Fünfzig Jahre italienisches
und deutsches Design

30. Juni bis
12. November 2000

Kunst- und Ausstellungshalle
der Bundesrepublik Deutschland

Museumsmeile Bonn
Friedrich-Ebert-Allee 4

Telefon 0228/9171-200
www.bundeskunsthalle.de

Rúa Ramón del Valle Inclán s/n
15704 Santiago de Compostela
Tel.: +34 981 546 619
Fax: +34 981 546 605
cgac@xunta.es
www.cgac.org

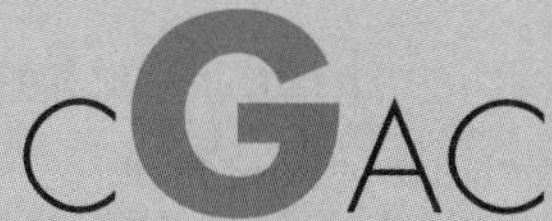

CENTRO GALEGO DE ARTE CONTEMPORÁNEA

Exhibition Programme
September - December 2000

Rebecca Horn
Closing September 10

Interferences: Inflight Lounge
Closing September 17

Georges Rousse
September 12 - November 19

José Antonio Hernández-Díez
September 19 - November 19

Transfer
September 22 - November 12

French and Italian Artists in ARCO
Foundation and CGAC Collections
November 24 - January 7

Mondophrenetic
November 24 - January 7

Sarah Dobai
November 24 - January 14

Florence Paradise
November 24 - January 14

Marine Hugonnier
November 24 - January 14

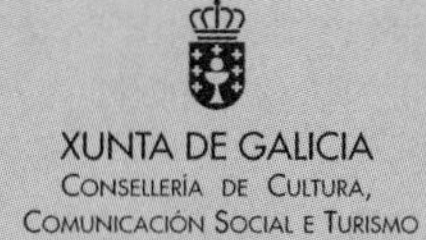

Luis Camnitzer
Lygia Clark
Juan Downey
Alberto Greco
David Lamelas
Lea Lublin
Ana Mendieta
Cildo Meireles
Marta Minujín
Hélio Oiticica

Publikation

15. Sept. – 22. Dez. 2000

vivências / Lebenserfahrung

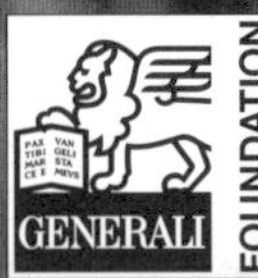

Generali Foundation
Wiedner Hauptstrasse 15
1040 Wien

Telefon (+43 1) 504 98 80
Telefax (+43 1) 504 98 83
found.office@generali.at

www.gfound.or.at

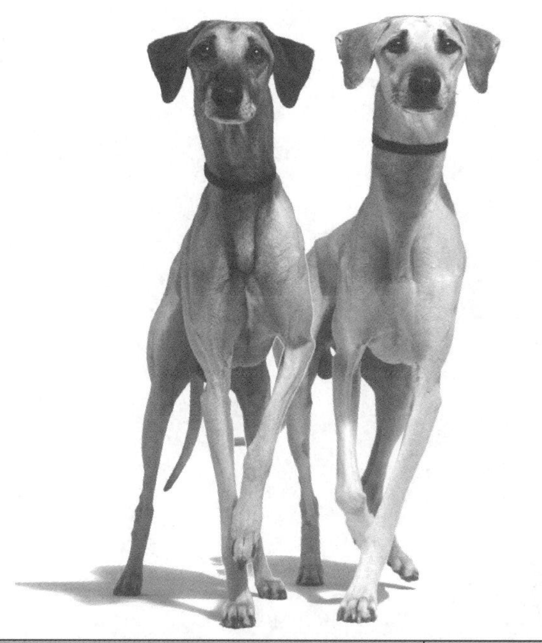

AUSSENDIENST

PHASE 1
weiterhin zu sehen

PHASE 2
23.09.-29.10.2000
In Kooperation mit Interface

PHASE 3
SOMMER 2001

Bogomir Ecker
Tita Giese
Ronald Jones
Manfred Pernice
Christoph Schäfer
Roman Signer
Thomas Stricker

abgeschlossen:
Fiona Tan

Angela Bulloch
Peter Dittmer
Ulrike & David Gabriel
Liam Gillick &
Jeppe A. Andersen
Knowbotic Research
Silvia Kolbowski
Katya Sander
Julia Scher
"Sound aka Space" mit
Thomas Brinkmann
Chicks on Speed &
Pablo Alonso
Felix Kubin
Carsten Nicolai aka noto
Daniel Pflumm/EMD
Scanner
Miki Yui/Felix Hahn
Kuratiert von Nina Möntmann

Monika Bonvicini
Ania Corcilius
Maria Eichhorn
Alicia Framis
Swetlana Heger &
Plamen Dejanov
Hans van Houwelingen
Stefan Kern
Aernout Mik
Olaf Nicolai
Jorge Pardo
"Plastik im Freien"
Andreas Slominski
Serge Spitzer
Berend Strik &
Matthijs Bouw
Rirkrit Tiravanija

KUNSTPROJEKTE IN ÖFFENTLICHEN RÄUMEN HAMBURGS

EINE KOOPERATION VON KULTURBEHÖRDE UND KUNSTVEREIN IN HAMBURG

AUSSENDIENST / Klosterwall 23 / 20095 Hamburg

Fon +49.40.303 932 20 / Fax +49.40.325 261 13 / e-mail: aussendienst@iphh.de / www.aussendienst.hamburg.de
Kuratiert von Stephan Schmidt-Wulffen und Achim Könneke

opening new space:
January 2001
C.so di P.ta Nuova 38 I-20121 Milano
in collaboration with
Gian Enzo Sperone New York

GALLERIA CARDI
P.zza S.Erasmo, 3 I-20121 Milano
Tel. + 39 02 29003235   Fax + 39 02 29003382
cardi.galleria@all.it   www.galleriacardi.com

donald **BAECHLER**

alighiero **BOETTI**

greg **BOGIN**

maurizio **CANNAVACCIUOLO**

francesco **CLEMENTE**

greg **COLSON**

wim **DELVOYE**

nicola **DE MARIA**

graham **GILLMORE**

peter **HALLEY**

guillermo **KUITCA**

milan **KUNC**

richard **LONG**

malcom **MORLEY**

vik **MUNIZ**

mimmo **PALADINO**

jennifer **REEVES**

tom **SACHS**

julian **SCHNABEL**

gianni **STEFANON**

richard **TUTTLE**

not **VITAL**

andy **WARHOL**

william **WEGMAN**

jan **WORST**

SEPTEMBER | OCTOBER
TONY FEHER | **WOLFGANG LAIB**

ANTHONY MEIER FINE ARTS
3007 jackson street san francisco ca 94115
415.351.1400 | www.anthonymeierfinearts.com

SEAN KELLY GALLERY

43 MERCER STREET
NEW YORK NY 10013
TELEPHONE 212 343-2405
FAX 212 343-2604
www.skny.com

Pia Stadtbäumer

SEPTEMBER - OCTOBER 2000

Joseph Kosuth

OCTOBER - NOVEMBER 2000

Callum Innes

DECEMBER - JANUARY 2001

THOMAS AMMANN FINE ART AG ZURICH

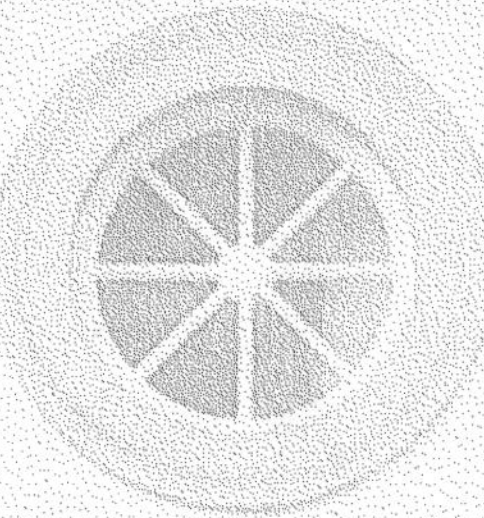

IMPRESSIONIST & 20TH CENTURY MASTERS

SELECTED WORKS BY MAJOR ARTISTS

BACON
BALTHUS
BEUYS
BRAQUE
CALDER
CHAGALL
ERNST
GIACOMETTI
KANDINSKY
KIRCHNER
KLEE
DE KOONING
LEGER
LICHTENSTEIN
MARDEN
MATISSE
MIRO
PICASSO
RYMAN
ROTHKO
TAAFFE
TWOMBLY
WARHOL

RESTELBERGSTRASSE 97   CH-8044 ZÜRICH   TEL. (411) 360 51 60   FAX (411) 360 51 61

www.ammann-fineart.ch

robert rauschenberg

september – october 2000

georg baselitz

november – december 2000

galerie jamileh weber

waldmannstrasse 6

ch – 8001 zürich

telefon 01 252 10 66

telefax 01 252 11 32

email: jamilehweber@access.ch

www.jamilehweber.ch